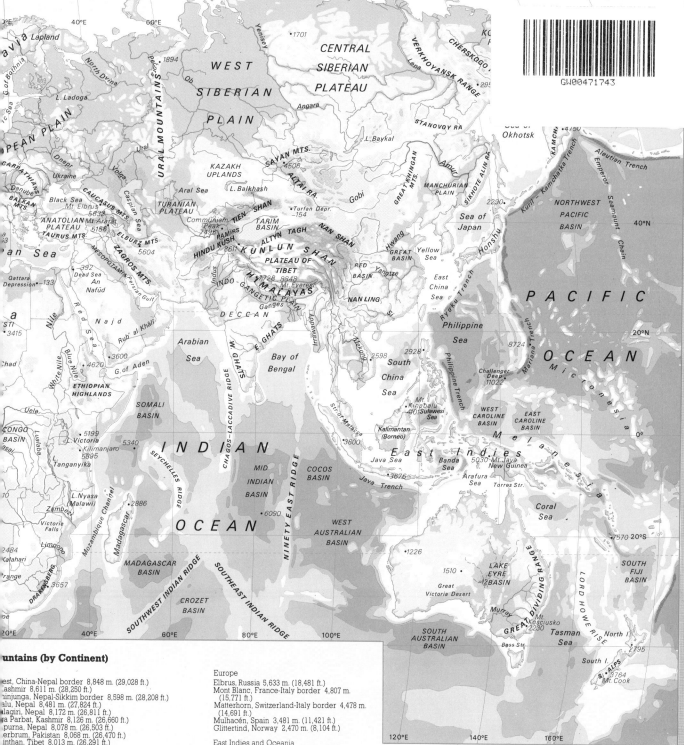

## ...untains (by Continent)

...est, China-Nepal border 8,848 m. (29,028 ft.)
...ashmir 8,611 m. (28,250 ft.)
...hinjunga, Nepal-Sikkim border 8,598 m. (28,208 ft.)
...alu, Nepal 8,481 m. (27,824 ft.)
...lagiri, Nepal 8,172 m. (26,811 ft.)
...a Parbat, Kashmir 8,126 m. (26,660 ft.)
...purna, Nepal 8,078 m. (26,503 ft.)
...erbrum, Pakistan 8,068 m. (26,470 ft.)
...sinthan, Tibet 8,013 m. (26,291 ft.)
...agh Ata, China 7,723 m. (25,338 ft.)
...munism Peak, Tajikistan 7,495 m. (24,590 ft.)
...ama, Japan 3,776 m. (12,388 ft.)

...merica
...cagua, Argentina 6,960 m. (22,835 ft.)
...del Salado, Argentina-Chile border 6,863 m. (22,516 ft.)
...caran, Peru 6,768 m. (22,205 ft.)
...ni, Bolivia 6,462 m. (21,201 ft.)
...ou, Bolivia 6,360 m. (20,867 ft.)
...borazo, Ecuador 6,267 m. (20,561 ft.)
...taxi, Ecuador 5,897 m. (19,347 ft.)

...merica
...nley, USA 6,194 m. (20,320 ft.)
...a, Canada 6,050 m. (19,850 ft.)
...ney, USA 4,418 m. (14,494 ft.)
...t, USA 4,398 m. (14,431 ft.)

...a
...anjaro, Tanzania 5,895 m. (19,340 ft.)
...enzori, Uganda-Zaire border 5,174 m. (16,794 ft.)
...Dashen, Ethiopia 4,620 m. (15,157 ft.)
...Toubkal, Morocco 4,167 m. (13,671 ft.)
...eroon Mountain, Cameroon 4,070 m. (13,353 ft.)
...a Ntlenyana, Lesotho 3,482 m. (11,425 ft.)

### Europe
Elbrus, Russia 5,633 m. (18,481 ft.)
Mont Blanc, France-Italy border 4,807 m. (15,771 ft.)
Matterhorn, Switzerland-Italy border 4,478 m. (14,691 ft.)
Mulhacén, Spain 3,481 m. (11,421 ft.)
Glittertind, Norway 2,470 m. (8,104 ft.)

### East Indies and Oceania
Puncak Jaya, Indonesia 5,030 m. (16,503 ft.)
Kinabalu, Malaysia 4,101 m. (13,455 ft.)
Cook, New Zealand 3,764 m. (12,349 ft.)
Kosciusko, Australia 2,228 m. (7,310 ft.)

### Antarctica
Vinson Massif 5,139 m. (16,860 ft.)
Erebus 3,743 m. (12,280 ft.)

## Rivers (approximate lengths)

Nile, Africa 6,400 k. (4,000 miles)
Amazon, S. America 6,280 km. (3,900 miles)
Mississippi-Missouri, N. America 6,100 km. (3,800 miles)
Yangtze, Asia 5,500 km. (3,400 miles)
Ob-Irtysh, Asia 5,150 km. (3,200 miles)
Congo (Zaire), Africa 4,700 km. (2,900 miles)
Huang He (Yellow River) 4,700 km. (2,900 miles)
Amur, Asia 4,410 km. (2,740 miles)
Lena, Asia 4,350 km. (2,700 miles)
Mekong, Asia 4,200 km. (2,600 miles)
Niger, Africa 4,200 km. (2,600 miles)
Yenisei, Asia 3,860 km. (2,400 miles)
Mackenzie, N. America 1,800 km. (1,100 miles)

## Lakes and Inland Seas

Caspian Sea (salt), Asia 420,000 sq. km. (162,000 sq. miles)
Lake Superior, N. America 82,000 sq. km. (32,000 sq. miles)
Lake Victoria, Africa 70,000 sq. km. (27,000 sq. miles)
Aral Sea (salt), Asia 64,000 sq. km. (25,000 sq. miles)
Lake Huron, N. America 60,000 sq. km. (23,000 sq. miles)
Lake Michigan, N. America 58,000 sq. km. (22,000 sq. miles)
Lake Tanganyika, Africa 33,000 sq. km. (13,000 sq. miles)
Lake Baikal, Asia 32,000 sq. km. (12,300 sq. miles)
Great Bear Lake, N. America 31,000 sq. km. (11,900 sq. miles)
Great Slave Lake, N. America 29,000 sq. km. (11,000 sq. miles)
Lake Malawi (Lake Nyasa), Africa 29,000 sq. km. (11,000 sq. miles)
Lake Erie, N. America 26,000 sq. km. (10,000 sq. miles)
Lake Winnipeg, N. America 24,000 sq. km. (9,000 sq. miles)
Lake Chad, Africa 21,000 sq. km. (8,000 sq. miles)
Lake Ontario, N. America 20,000 sq. km. (7,700 sq. miles)
Lake Ladoga, Europe 18,000 sq. km. (7,000 sq. miles)
Lake Balkhash, Asia 17,000 sq. km. (6,500 sq. miles)
Lake Maracaibo, S. America 16,000 sq. km. (6,000 sq. miles)
Lake Onega, Europe 9,800 sq. km. (3,800 sq. miles)
Lake Turkana (salt), Africa 9,100 sq. km. (3,500 sq. miles)
Lake Eyre (salt), Australia 8,800 sq. km. (3,400 sq. miles)
Lake Titicaca, S. America 8,300 sq. km. (3,200 sq. miles)
Lake Nicaragua, C. America 8,000 sq. km. (3,100 sq. miles)

**OXFORD**
**ILLUSTRATED**
**ENCYCLOPEDIA**

## Volume 1
# THE PHYSICAL WORLD

# OXFORD
## ILLUSTRATED
### ENCYCLOPEDIA

## Volume 1

# THE PHYSICAL WORLD

*Volume Editor*
Sir Vivian Fuchs

*Revised edition*

OXFORD
OXFORD UNIVERSITY PRESS
NEW YORK   MELBOURNE
1993

Oxford University Press, Walton Street, Oxford OX2 6DP
Oxford New York Toronto
Delhi Bombay Calcutta Madras Karachi
Kuala Lumpur Singapore Hong Kong Tokyo
Nairobi Dar es Salaam Cape Town
Melbourne Auckland Madrid
and associated companies in
Berlin Ibadan

Oxford is a trade mark of Oxford University Press

First edition 1985
Revised edition 1993
First published as a Set 1993

British Library Cataloguing in Publication Data
Data available

Library of Congress Cataloging in Publication Data
Data available
ISBN 0–19–869217–X (Volume 1)
ISBN 0–19–869223–4 (set)

Data-capture by Alliance, Pondicherry, India
Typeset by Oxuniprint, Oxford
Printed in Hong Kong

# General Preface

The *Oxford Illustrated Encyclopedia* is designed to be useful and to give pleasure to readers throughout the world. Particular care has been taken to ensure that it is not limited to one country or to one civilization, and that its many thousands of entries can be understood by any interested person who has no previous detailed knowledge of the subject.

Each volume has a clearly defined theme made plain in its title: no previous knowledge is required, there is no jargon, and references to other volumes are avoided. Nevertheless, taken together, the eight thematic volumes (and the Index and Ready Reference volume which completes the series) provide a complete and reliable survey of human knowledge and achievement. Within each independent volume, the material is arranged in a large number of relatively brief articles in A–Z sequence, varying in length from fifty to one thousand words. This means that each volume is simple to consult, as valuable information is not buried in long and wide-ranging articles. Cross-references are provided whenever they will be helpful to the reader.

The team allocated to each volume is headed by a volume editor eminent in the field. Over four hundred scholars and teachers drawn from around the globe have contributed a total of 2.4 million words to the Encyclopedia. They have worked closely with a team of editors at Oxford whose job it was to ensure that the coverage and content of each entry form part of a coherent whole. Specially commissioned artwork, diagrams, maps, and photographs convey information to supplement the text and add a lively and colourful dimension to the subject portrayed.

Since publication of the first of its volumes in the mid-1980s, the *Oxford Illustrated Encyclopedia* has built up a reputation for usefulness throughout the world. The number of languages into which it has been translated continues to grow. In compiling the volumes, the editors have recognized the new internationalism of its readers who seek to understand the different cultural, political, technological, religious, and commercial factors which together shape the world view of nations. Their aim has been to present a balanced picture of the forces that influence peoples in all corners of the globe.

I am grateful alike to the volume editors, contributors, consultants, editors, and illustrators whose common aim has been to provide, within the space available, an Encyclopedia that will enrich the reader's understanding of today's world.

HARRY JUDGE

# CONTRIBUTORS

Dr Humphry Bowen

Dr P. A. Bull

Peter Clare

Dr Alexandra Clayton

Angela Colling

J. E. P. Cooper

Dr A. F. Cuthbertson

Pamela Mayo Dale

Dr Basil Gomez

Jane Gregory

Bridget Hadaway

Sandy Harrison

Dr D. P. John

Allan Clive Jones

Dr Barbara A. Kennedy

Ian A. Lavender

Dr Gaynor Leggate

W. H. S. MacKeith

Sue Mayhew

Dr Richard Moody

Dr W. D. Phillips

Dr Susan Pirie

Stephen Pople

Dr W. G. Richards

Christopher Riches

Denis Riley

J. D. Rolls

Dr H. M. Rosenberg

Dr P. R. Scott

S. J. Shuttleworth

Dr R. J. Towse

B. Wilcock

Emma Morgan Williams

Dr J. B. Wright

John W. Wright

# Foreword

Life as we know it on our planet must of necessity obey the natural laws which govern both the Earth and the Universe. Through the ages human understanding of the physical world and the behaviour of matter have been expanding—in recent years at an increasingly rapid pace. Thus each generation produces advances in knowledge, developing new concepts which need to be tested by new methods and technologies. These in turn must often be quantified in new terms. Every question answered raises another question. How many of us know what neutrinos or the chaos theory are, or even heteroatoms and black-body radiation? New names come to our attention, or familiar ones appear in an unfamiliar context: who was Lise Meitner and what was Andrey Sakharov's contribution to science?

This volume draws upon the work of scientists and explorers, both past and present, who have specialized in the study of the physical world, many of whom have devoted their working lives to unravelling its complexities. All aspects of our physical environment are covered in this Encyclopedia—geography, climate, geomorphology, soils, and minerals among them—while for the students of pure science there are many entries on the composition of matter, on physics, chemical elements, compounds, processes, and on the structures and techniques of mathematics. Biographical entries on scientists and explorers explain the contributions they have made to their fields, and place them in a historical and human context.

The editors have, where appropriate, presented the entries with an interdisciplinary emphasis, for advances in one field can greatly contribute to our understanding of another. Thus the reader who looks up one subject can be helped to extend his or her knowledge of related fields without the need to search through a number of specialist reference books. For example, physical geography is as much concerned with the form and structure of the Earth's land masses as with the waters that flow around them and the atmosphere that envelopes them. Explorers have made, and continue to make their contribution, but physical geography is a composite subject that is constantly being enlarged by more specialist sciences, such as geology, physics, chemistry, oceanography, and meteorology. As these sciences have advanced, our knowledge of our planet and the way in which all matter behaves has expanded beyond our ancestors' imagination, to encompass, for example, the discovery of new dimensions in the structure of the atom and the implications of 'holes' in the ozone layer. Photographs, maps, and diagrams have been carefully selected and drawn to help the reader towards a visual understanding of complex subjects which are often difficult to convey in words alone.

Yet the world remains full of mysteries to engage the imagination, ranging from our understanding of the structure of matter to the movement of continents and the influence of the polar ice-sheet on world climate. Here we have tried to provide accurate and up-to-date information about the physical world that may inform and stimulate the general reader as well as the student. We have tried also to present it in a form that is attractive and readily comprehensible, avoiding terminology bewildering to the non-specialist. I hope that this volume will bring many hours of pleasure and satisfaction to all those fortunate enough to have a copy in their home or place of work.

VIVIAN FUCHS

# A User's Guide

ALPHABETICAL ARRANGEMENT  The entries are arranged in strict A–Z order of their headwords up to the first comma (thus **Baffin, William** comes before **Baffin Island**), and after a comma the alphabetical order begins again (thus **wave, atmospheric** precedes **wave, electromagnetic**). Names beginning with 'Mac' or 'Mc' are placed as though all were spelt 'Mac' (**McKinley, Mount** appears before **Maclaurin, Colin**). Names beginning with 'St' are placed as though spelt 'Saint' (**Saint Elias Mountains** comes after **Sahara** but before **Sakhalin Island**).

HEADWORDS  Entries are usually placed under the keyword in the title (the surname, for instance, in a group of names). In cases where there is no obvious keyword, an entry appears under the word that most users are likely to look up first (thus **electromagnetic radiation** and **radiation, thermal** feature as apparent inconsistencies). In cases of geographical names with alternative forms, that most commonly used in the English-speaking world has been adopted (**Finland** rather than Suomi, for example) except in instances where a local form has gained international currency (thus **Huang He** for Yellow River and **Tonga** for Friendly Islands). The entry heading appears in the singular unless the plural form is the more common usage.

ALTERNATIVE NAMES  Where alternatives are in frequent use, a single-line cross-reference guides the reader to that which heads the entry. This applies also to scientific and specialist terms—for example, **acetic acid** *ethanoic acid, and **craton** *shield (in geology).

CROSS-REFERENCES  An asterisk (*) in front of a word denotes a cross-reference and indicates the headword of the other entry to which attention is being drawn. Cross-references in the text appear only in places where reference is likely to amplify or increase understanding of the entry you are reading. They are not given automatically in all cases where a separate entry can be found, so if you come across a name or a term about which you would like to know more, it is worth looking for an entry in its alphabetical place even if no cross-reference is marked. The cross-references can also be used as an index might be: if, for instance, you seek information on the San Andreas Fault and know what it is but have forgotten its name, you will find a reference to the relevant entry in both **earthquake** and **fault, geological**.

WEIGHTS AND MEASURES  Both metric measures and their American equivalents are given throughout, and in the scientific entries SI units are used. A full list of abbreviations is given in the table under SI units on p. 302. Large measures (such as the lengths of rivers) are generally rounded off, partly for the sake of simplicity and occasionally to reflect differences of opinion as to a precise measurement.

TERMINOLOGY  Technical and professional terms that do not appear in standard dictionaries are defined and, where necessary, explained. In the descriptions of climatic temperature the following words have particular meanings: 'extremely cold' (below −10 °C, or 14 °F), 'very cold' (−10–0 °C, or 14–32 °F), 'cold', 'cool', 'mild', 'warm', 'very warm', 'hot' (each denoting an additional 5 °C or 9 °F, rise in temperature), and 'very hot' (over 30 °C, or 86 °F). Similarly, in describing annual precipitation, 'arid' means light rain or snow (less than 500 mm, or 20 inches), 'moderate' means wet (500–1,500 mm, or 20–60 inches), and 'heavy' means very wet (over 1,500 mm, or 60 inches).

ILLUSTRATIONS  Pictures and diagrams almost invariably occur on the same page as the entries to which they relate or on a facing page, and where this is not the case the position of a diagrammatic illustration is indicated in the text. The picture captions supplement the information given in the text and indicate in bold type the title of the relevant entry.

RELATIONSHIP TO OTHER VOLUMES  This survey of the physical world is part of a series, the *Oxford Illustrated Encyclopedia*, comprising eight thematic volumes and an Index and Ready Reference volume:

1 *The Physical World*
2 *The Natural World*
3 *World History: from earliest times to 1800*
4 *World History: from 1800 to the present day*
5 *The Arts*
6 *Invention and Technology*
7 *Peoples and Cultures*
8 *The Universe*
9 *Index and Ready Reference*

The volume is self-contained, having no cross-references to any of its companions, and is therefore entirely usable on its own. Some aspects of certain topics are, however, the subjects of other volumes. The histories of regions and countries will be found in Volumes 3 and 4, for example, and their human or social geography in Volume 7. Similarly, applications of many of the scientific topics described here will be covered in Volume 6. Such items appearing in more than one volume will be linked by a general index in Volume 9.

# A

**Abelian group** (in mathematics), a group that, in addition to satisfying the conditions necessary for a mathematical group, is commutative (see *commutativity). For example, the set of *real numbers under the operation of multiplication forms an Abelian group, as do *vectors under addition. Abelian groups are named after the Norwegian mathematician, Niels Henrik Abel (1802–29). When only 19, Abel proved the impossibility, in general, of solving all equations of the fifth degree or above by means of a formula similar to the familiar one for quadratic equations. It was a problem that had been studied since the 16th century. Abel also published articles on applied mathematics and on elliptic functions.

**abrasion** (in geomorphology), the scouring action that occurs when rock particles rub together. It is caused by rock debris embedded in bases of glaciers, bedloads of rivers, and sand and shingle carried by wind or waves.

**absolute zero**, the lowest temperature theoretically possible (equivalent to −273.15 °C). According to the *kinetic theory, the temperature of a substance is a measure of the average energy which its molecules possess because of their motion. The lower the temperature, the lower the energy of each molecule, and the less vigorously it moves. According to this simple theory, absolute zero is the temperature at which molecules would have no energy, and molecular motion would cease. However, according to *quantum theory, atoms and molecules still have some energy, the *zero-point energy, at absolute zero. It is not possible to reach absolute zero experimentally, though substances have been cooled to within a few millionths of a degree of it. Temperatures measured from absolute zero are called absolute temperatures and are expressed in *kelvins (symbol K). An increase in temperature of 1 K is equal to an increase of 1 °C; 273.15 K equals 0 °C.

**abyssal plain**, a flat or very gently sloping area of the ocean basin floor, reaching to depths of between 2,200 and 5,500 m (7,200 and 18,000 feet). Abyssal plains lie generally between the foot of a *continental rise and a *mid-oceanic ridge. They result from the blanketing of an originally uneven surface of *oceanic crust by fine-grained sediments, mainly clay and silt. Much of this sediment is deposited from *turbidity currents which have been channelled from the continental margins along submarine canyons down into deeper water. The remainder (of the sediment) comprises chiefly dust (clay particles) blown out to sea from land, and the remains of small marine plants and animals (*plankton), which have sunk from the surface. Where planktonic remains predominate among the sediments of the deep sea, they are sometimes called *oozes. Abyssal plains are less common in the Pacific than in other major ocean basins, because sediments from turbidity currents are trapped in the submarine trenches which border the Pacific.

**acceleration**, the rate of change of *velocity with time. It is a *vector quantity with magnitude and direction. It has the symbol $a$ and in the *SI system is measured in units of

Fine ooze blankets the **abyssal plain** at 5,340 m (17,520 feet) off the Iberian Peninsula. Mounds, tracks, and hollows reveal the activities of marine organisms; tube-worms, about 2.5 cm (1 inch) high, can be seen protruding above the surface, and in the foreground are the radiating feeding tracks of a buried mud-feeder.

$m/s^2$. If $v$ is the velocity vector then $dv/dt$, the *derivative with respect to time, is the acceleration. When the movement is in a straight line then $v$ and $dv/dt$ can be treated as *scalars, but when the object is travelling along a curved path there will be two acceleration components, one along the tangent to the curve at the point and the other along the normal to the curve. In uniform circular motion the velocity is constant along the tangent, and so the acceleration is only towards the centre of the circle; it is called the centripetal acceleration. It has a numerical value of (tangential speed)$^2$/radius of curvature. The concept may be applied to motion along any curve. Angular acceleration is the rate of change of angular velocity with time.

Acceleration due to gravity is the downward acceleration of an object which is falling freely under the influence of gravity. Denoted by the symbol $g$, its value near the Earth's surface is 9.8 $m/s^2$, meaning that a freely falling object will gain an extra 9.8 m/s of downward speed every second. The acceleration due to gravity has the same value for all objects; in the absence of air resistance, a light object falls with precisely the same downward acceleration as a massive one. A massive object experiences a greater gravitational pull, but this is exactly offset by its greater resistance to acceleration. The measured value of $g$ varies slightly from one point to another around the Earth, though by no more than 1 per cent at most. It is least at the Equator, partly because of the effect of the rotation of the Earth, and partly because the distance from the Earth's centre is greatest here and the gravitational pull is fractionally reduced as a result. Above the Earth's surface, the value of $g$ decreases with increasing height. At 25,000 km (15,500 miles) above the Earth, its value is less than 1 $m/s^2$.

**acetic acid**   *ethanoic acid.

**acetone**   *propanone.

**acetylene**   *ethyne.

**acid**, any chemical compound of a class, the members of which commonly have a sour taste, and are mostly poisonous and corrosive. Those acids that derive from mineral sources (mineral acids) are almost always stronger than acids derived from organic sources (carboxylic acids). Corrosive acids such as nitric acid and sulphuric acid are mineral acids; weaker acids such as citric acid, found in citrus fruits, and formic acid, found in some insects, are carboxylic acids. Acids are soluble in water; strong acids dissociate entirely to become good *electrolytes, while weak acids only partially dissociate. Acidic solutions react readily with metals to form salts and hydrogen, and with *bases to form salts and water, a reaction in which the acid is neutralized. A solution is acidic if its *hydrogen ion concentration is less than 7 on the pH scale: it will turn litmus red. Two theories have been proposed to explain the properties of acids. According to the Brønsted–Lowry theory an acid is a compound that donates protons, in the form of hydrogen ions, $H^+$, which can be accepted by particles with a *lone pair of electrons. In the Lewis theory, however, acids are considered as electron-pair acceptors, accepting an electron pair from a base in order to form a bond.

**acid anhydride**, an organic compound formed in a condensation reaction (see *chemical reaction) between two molecules of a *carboxylic acid. The general formula is $RCO-O-OCR'$, where R and R′ represent *alkyl or *aryl groups. Acid anhydrides react with water to re-form the carboxylic acids from which they were created. They are unpleasant-smelling liquids and are used to manufacture esters and synthetic polymers (such as polyesters).

**acid–base titration**, a controlled *neutralization reaction in which an acid is added to a base, or vice versa. Typically, a known quantity of acid is placed in a flask, and an *indicator is added. *Alkali is then added from a burette, so that the volume of alkali that has been let out at any time may be read off. As the alkali is added, neutralization proceeds and the pH of the solution rises. When neutralization is complete, the end-point of the titration is indicated by the change in colour of the indicator. Acid–base titrations can be put to several uses. For example, if the concentration of the acid is unknown, it can be determined by titration against alkali of known concentration. Or if, in the preparation of a *salt, it is desired to ensure that complete neutralization occurs, this can be done by carrying out a titration and stopping as soon as the end-point is reached. The solution will then contain neither excess alkali nor acid, but only the salt and water.

**acid rain**, rain with dissolved gaseous oxides of sulphur and nitrogen from burnt fossil fuels. Most rain is slightly acidic due to a small amount of dissolved carbon dioxide from the atmosphere, when it has a *pH of about 5.5. Acid rain has a pH of between 5–2.2 and has corrosive effects on most metals, limestone, and paper. It may fall many hundreds of miles from its source, by which time it is a dilute solution of nitric and sulphuric acids. The rain is lethal to water life and damages forests and the soil. It also corrodes buildings and may to be hazardous to human health.

**actinide**, any metallic element of a series in the *periodic table with atomic numbers from 89 (actinium) to 103 (lawrencium). The first four members of the series, actinium to uranium, occur naturally. All the actinides generally resemble each other and the lanthanides. They form a range of *ionic compounds, such as sulphates, nitrates, and chlorides, in which the metal shows a valency of 3 but higher valencies are found, for example, thorium (4) and uranium

(4, 5, and 6). The actinides are radioactive, and those with atomic numbers greater than 92, the *transuranic elements, are formed by bombardment of heavy nuclei. Uranium and plutonium have fissionable nuclides which have been widely used for producing nuclear energy, but the actinides occurring later in the series are very unstable, and several have been produced only in tiny quantities.

**action and reaction** (in physics), terms used in discussion of the application of a *force to an object. The force itself is the 'action'. As described by the third of *Newton's laws of motion, for every action there is an equal and opposite 'reaction'. This reaction is a force which is always in opposite direction to the original force. Thus, if we try to push a heavy object—for example, a car—then a reverse force arises which pushes us backwards, and this can be felt: our feet tend to slip. All rockets use this principle; burning gases are ejected with tremendous force from the rear end of the rocket and as a consequence there is a reaction that propels it forwards.

**activation energy**, the difference in energy between the reactants and the *transition state in a chemical reaction. As the reactant molecules approach, bonds are broken, and there is an increase in energy, even though some new bonds start to form. The increase in energy continues until a maximum, the transition state, is reached, after which energy is given out as product molecules form (or the reactants are re-formed). If the reactant molecules have enough energy to reach the transition state, they will react to form products.

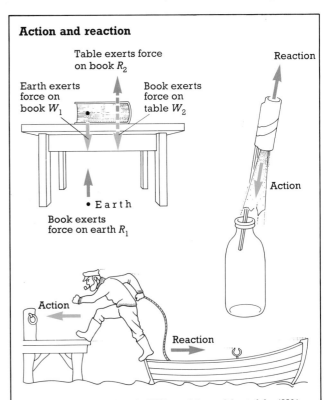

**Action and reaction**

Table exerts force on book $R_2$

Earth exerts force on book $W_1$

Book exerts force on table $W_2$

Reaction

• Earth

Book exerts force on earth $R_1$

Action

Action

Reaction

The weight of the book ($W_1$) and that of the table ($W_2$) — the actions — are exactly balanced by an equal and opposite reaction ($R_1$ and $R_2$ respectively), giving the static situation shown.

The example of the rocket is explained in the text.

The action of the man stepping forward produces a backward force on the boat.

The energy required to do so is called the activation energy, and it varies from one reaction to another, as does the amount of energy that is liberated or absorbed.

**active layer** (in geomorphology), the temporarily thawed surface of *permafrost, or permanently frozen ground. It thaws in summer and may become boggy (as in Alaska and northern Canada), impeding the construction of buildings, roads, and pipelines.

**activity series**, a series of elements or compounds listed in order of their reactivity with respect to a particular type of reaction. For example, the halogens can act as *oxidizing agents. Their reactivity in this capacity can be summarized in the following activity series, the strongest oxidizing agent being listed first: fluorine, chlorine, bromine, iodine, and astatine. The *electrochemical series is another example of an activity series.

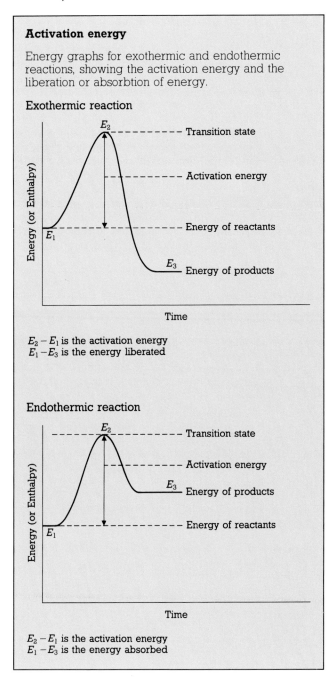

**Activation energy**

Energy graphs for exothermic and endothermic reactions, showing the activation energy and the liberation or absorbtion of energy.

Exothermic reaction

$E_2 - E_1$ is the activation energy
$E_1 - E_3$ is the energy liberated

Endothermic reaction

$E_2 - E_1$ is the activation energy
$E_1 - E_3$ is the energy absorbed

**addition reaction**   *chemical reaction.

**adiabatic change**, any physical change occurring when no heat either enters or leaves the system in which it occurs. Experiments on a material contained in a vacuum flask, for example, would be under adiabatic conditions because the inside of the flask is well insulated. When air rises it expands adiabatically as atmospheric pressure falls. This causes its temperature to decrease, the rate of fall being given by a *lapse rate. In contrast, an *isothermal change is one in which there is no change in temperature.

**Adirondack Mountains**, a group of mountains composed of igneous rock in the north-east of the USA. Separated from the Appalachian Mountains by Lake Champlain to the east and the Mohawk valley to the south, they are among the oldest bodies of uplifted granite in the world. The highest point is Mount Marcy at 1,629 m (5,344 feet). Ancient glaciers have left rugged gorges, lakes, and waterfalls; the region with its forests is one of great scenic beauty.

**adobe**, a sun-dried mixture of *silt and *clay used to make reddish-brown bricks. The mixture was deposited under water in what are now flat desert basins, where it lies in thick sheets. It has been used extensively in South America, the south-western USA, and Africa.

**Adriatic Sea**, an arm of the Mediterranean Sea, extending for some 760 km (470 miles) up the eastern side of Italy, north-west from the Strait of Otranto to the Gulf of Venice. The distance from the Italian coast to the coast of the Balkan Peninsula varies from 73 km (45 miles) at the Strait to about 220 km (136 miles) at the widest point. It is a shallow sea in the main, but 1,250 m (4,100 feet) at its deepest; the Po and other rivers constantly deposit silt on its floor, and the former coastal town of Adria from which it takes its name is now inland. The eastern, Dalmatian, coast is jagged and fringed with offshore islands, while the Italian shore has some fine, sandy beaches. In summer the climate is warm and the breezes gentle; but the *bora winds cause cold winters.

**advection**, the horizontal transport of heat or cold, either in the atmosphere by the large-scale movement of air or in the oceans by currents of seawater. In both cases a major example is the transport of cold masses from the polar regions to lower latitudes. Vertical transport is more localized and is known as *convection.

**Aegean Sea**, an arm of the eastern Mediterranean Sea, extending northward from Crete for nearly 640 km (400 miles) between Greece and Turkey. It is linked by the Dardanelles, the Sea of Marmara, and the Bosporus to the Black Sea, to which it was once joined. Lying at a junction of crustal *plates, its southern islands are volcanic and its bed is subject to occasional earth tremors; in the north there are rich reserves of oil. The islands are generally grouped in archipelagos: the Cyclades, and the northern and southern Sporades. They are mainly extensions of the two land masses, the Balkan Peninsula and Asia Minor, whose coasts are deeply indented by the sea.

**Aeolian Islands**   *Lipari Islands.

**aeon**, a term that is normally used to denote a division of geological time made up of several *eras: the *Phanerozoic

Once compressed and trimmed to size in the buildings at the rear, **adobe** bricks are laid out to dry in the sun at a factory in the Bolivian Andes.

Aeon, for example. There is a move to use 'aeon' as the name of a unit of measurement: equivalent to $10^9$ years.

**aerosol**, a dispersion of finely divided solid or liquid particles in a gas (see *colloid). Aerosols can be natural, such as fog, or manufactured, such as smoke. The term also applies to a device (containing a liquid and propellant gas under pressure) for producing a fine aerosol spray. *Chlorofluorocarbons (CFCs) were at one time the most widespread aerosol propellants; however, these have been banned in many countries, owing to their adverse environmental effects. Accumulation of chloro-fluorocarbons in the upper atmosphere, where they are exposed to ultraviolet light, causes *ozone depletion.

**Afghanistan**, a mountainous, land-locked country of central Asia, bounded on the west by Iran, on the south and east by Pakistan, and on the north by Turkmenistan, Uzbekistan, and Tajikistan. Its eastern region is dominated by the vast range of the Hindu Kush, and most of the country is high plateau. In winter much of it is under snow; but in spring grass appears, soon to be scorched dry and swept by the dust storms of summer. Only where there are wells and streams is sheep-raising and agriculture possible, although fruit and nut trees do well on the lower mountain slopes. There is coal in the centre of the country, oil in the west, and iron, copper, and lead in the north. It also has considerable deposits of lapis lazuli.

**Africa**, the second largest continent, extending south from the Mediterranean Sea and bounded by the Atlantic and Indian oceans and the Red Sea. The Equator passes through the middle of Africa, so that all but the very north and south are tropical, although regional differences in climate and landscape are vast. The cultivable north-west coastal plains rise up to the High Atlas Mountains, which, southward, fall more gently to the plateau of the Sahara. Most of northern Africa is desert, the only significant waterway being the Nile; on its southern and western fringes there are deposits of copper, uranium, iron, and oil. The west, watered by the Niger and other rivers, is rich in tropical forests, though in many coastal regions there is only swamp. The swampy land continues south to the mouth of the Congo River and beyond; inland, however, the ground rises first to savannahs and then to hilly, wooded plateaux in the centre of the continent. Here are some of the largest copper deposits in the world, and also of gold, diamonds, uranium, cobalt, and other minerals. Eastern Africa is a region of great lakes, mountains, and high plateaux. It is split from north to south by the Great Rift Valley and offers spectacular scenery, as well as a mild, almost temperate climate. The coastal plains are narrow but well watered. South of the Zambezi River are more highlands, with trees and tall grass, giving way in the south-west to the Kalahari Desert. Then the land rises again, to the temperate *veld with its winter frosts and summer storms. This good farming country is very rich in minerals—notably gold, diamonds, uranium, and coal. To the south-east is the igneous rock of the Drakensberg Mountains. The long curve of the southernmost coastal plain is ideal for fruit and plantation crops, being watered in winter by light rainfall brought by the westerly winds of the South Atlantic Ocean.

**Agassiz, (Jean) Louis (Rodolphe)** (1807–73), Swiss-born geologist and palaeontologist who in 1840 introduced the idea of the *Ice Age, a period when glaciers and ice-sheets covered most of the northern hemisphere. The concept not only caused an enormous popular sensation but also provided a vital key to the scientific study of much of the Earth's landscape. In 1846 he moved to the USA, where he dominated palaeontology and geology until his death. His *Contributions to the Natural History of the US* (four volumes, 1857–62) firmly rejected the views of *Lyell and Darwin's theory of natural selection.

**agate**, a form of *chalcedony, a variety of quartz, formed in the steam cavities found in the lavas of volcanic rock. It is always striped or banded due to impurities of iron and manganese, the shape of the bands depending on that of the cavity. The colour varies too, onyx (white or grey) and cornelian

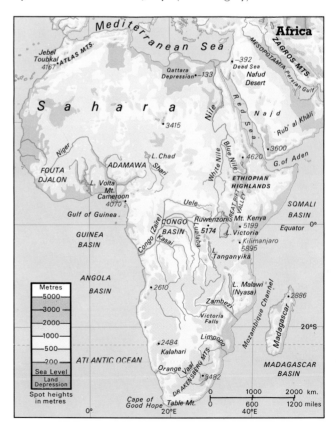

(red) being among those prized as semiprecious stones. The best agates come from Brazil and Uruguay.

**agglomerate** (in geology), a deposit, produced by a volcano, that consists of a mixture of volcanic fragments and ash. Agglomerates are usually deposited as part of a volcanic cone, but may also be found in the necks of volcanoes. They generally show a roughly layered structure. 'Volcanic breccia' is an equivalent term. Agglomerates are classed as pyroclastic deposits.

**aggradation** (in geomorphology), a process which occurs whenever rivers, glaciers, winds, or waves deposit the sediment they carry. The deposits raise the surface and may steepen the local slope of the ground. Much of the High Plains of the USA results from aggradation by rivers draining eastwards from the Rocky Mountains.

**Agulhas, Cape**, the southernmost tip of the African continent, its name (derived from the Portuguese for 'needles') describing the sharp-edged reefs and sunken rocks extending from the shore. It defines the boundary between the Atlantic and Indian Oceans and marks the northern end of the Agulhas Plateau, a major submarine ridge. It also lends its name to the Agulhas Current, a warm surface current that is part of the westerly-moving South Equatorial Current. Off-shore the Agulhas Banks provide good fishing grounds.

**air**, a general term for the gases that make up the *atmosphere. On average, it is 78 per cent nitrogen, 21 per cent oxygen, and 1 per cent argon, with traces of carbon dioxide, the other *noble gases, and hydrogen. In addition there are small variable amounts of other gases such as sulphur dioxide and ozone. Its precise composition at any given time and place depends not only on altitude but also on temperature, humidity, and pollution. Invisible, odourless, and tasteless

The mineral **agate**, a form of fibrous quartz, is characterized by convoluted fine colour-banding, displayed in this sample.

but life-supporting, it always contains *water vapour drawn from water on the Earth's surface. Having weight, it is held to the Earth by gravitation, generally below a height of 80 km (50 miles).

**air mass**, a vast, relatively homogeneous body of air which, at any particular atmospheric level, is distinguished by physical characteristics such as humidity, temperature, and *lapse rate. These properties are acquired when a mass of air stagnates over a particular part of the Earth's surface for at least several days. This happens in the large *anticyclones of the subtropical and polar regions throughout the year and in those which form over the cold continental land surfaces of North America and Eurasia in winter. The slow-moving surface layers of air gradually acquire the relatively uniform temperature and humidity characteristics of the underlying surfaces, which may be deserts, the polar regions, or tropical seas. There are two principal types of air mass: cold (polar) ones originating in high latitudes and warm (tropical) ones from low latitudes. Both can be subdivided into continental (cP, cT) or maritime (mP, mT), depending on their source areas. As they move away from these areas their temperatures may be modified by warmer or cooler conditions on the Earth's surface and their humidity by gain or loss of moisture. These changes affect the stability of the air, as does any vertical motion.

**air pollution**, pollution caused by the release into the atmosphere of gases, or finely dispersed solid or liquid particles, at rates too great to dissipate or to be incorporated into the land or water. Natural causes of air pollution include dust storms, forest or grass fires, and volcanic activity. Air pollution caused by humans comes from a variety of sources. Motor car fuel emission is responsible for major urban air pollution, in particular smog (smoke plus fog), and lead pollution arising from the addition of tetraethyl lead to petrol (see *antiknock). Another major source of air pollution is the burning of *fossil fuels in power-stations. Pesticides have been discovered in Antarctica, where they have never been used, indicating that the atmosphere can carry pollutants over large distances. Atmospheric pollution with radioactive contaminants is a continual threat as long as nuclear power plants are used to provide electricity.

Efforts are being made to reduce air pollution from some sources. Air pollution from volatile hydrocarbons may be reduced by the development of solvent-free paints. Devices such as the catalytic converter (see *catalyst) are used to reduce carbon monoxide and hydrocarbon levels in motor car exhaust emissions, and the use of lead-free petrol is mandatory in some countries and strongly encouraged in others. Low pollution methods for burning fossil fuels plus the shift to less polluting forms of power generation—*wind and *solar power, for example—can be used to reduce air pollution significantly. (See also *greenhouse effect, *acid rain.)

**air resistance**, the *frictional force felt by any object moving through air. This force acts to slow the motion of the object. The size of the force depends on how fast the object is moving: the faster the motion, the greater the air resistance. A falling object accelerates downwards due to the force of gravity, and as it speeds up the air resistance increases. The object continues to speed up until the air resistance matches this downward force: once this point has been reached the object keeps falling at the same speed, the terminal velocity. Air resistance is bigger for objects which present a larger surface to the air. For example, a sheet of paper held horizontal and then dropped will experience more air resistance —and so will fall with a lower terminal velocity— than an identical sheet of paper that has been crumpled into a ball. Parachutes work because their large area means that the air resistance on them is high, and the parachutist does not have to accelerate for very long until terminal velocity is reached. This means that the terminal velocity is low, and the parachutist can fall safely.

**alabaster**, a fine-grained, banded variety of the mineral *gypsum. White or pale reddish-brown in colour, it is formed by direct precipitation from salt-rich waters, often from hot volcanic springs. The alabaster of the ancient world, called 'oriental alabaster' or onyx marble, occurs both in spring deposits and in cave formations.

**Alaska**, largest state of the USA, comprising the great peninsula in the north-west of North America. It is a vast, cold land of mountains (many of them volcanic), forests, lakes, glaciers, and rivers. In the far north, within the Arctic Circle, the Brooks Range stretches westward from Canada to the sea. In the centre, the valley of the Yukon River is under snow and ice for most of the year. In the south, the Alaska Range, with Mount McKinley and other snow-capped peaks, rings the southern coast, where the climate is relatively mild, although here frequent earthquakes and associated *tsunami make settlement dangerous. Oil, coal, copper, and gold have been found in great quantities; there

The wild, unspoilt landscape of the Denali National Park in south central **Alaska** in early summer. It provides a sanctuary for animals and plants adapted to one of the harshest of Earth's habitats.

are many other minerals too. The forests hold plentiful supplies of soft timber, much of it accessible, while the rivers and seas are well stocked with fish.

**Albania**, a small country on the Adriatic coast of the *Balkan Peninsula, with Montenegro, Kosovo, and Macedonia to its north and east, and Greece to its south. Its coastal plain is marshy in the north but mostly fertile. Inland are rugged mountains, forested hills, and fast-flowing rivers. It also has the shores of three large lakes within its frontiers. In winter the *bora blows cold from the north and in summer the *sirocco blows Saharan dust over the crops. Rainfall is generally moderate. The country's mineral wealth includes coal and oil, copper, chromite, nickel, and iron.

**albedo**, the percentage of incident radiation reflected by a surface without heating the receiving surface. In the case of *solar radiation reflected by the Earth and its atmosphere, the albedo is approximately 36 per cent, which means that 36 per cent of the Sun's energy is reflected directly back into space. The albedo of both forest vegetation and urban sprawl is about 18 per cent. Grassland has an albedo of 25 per cent, desert sand 40 per cent, sea water 50 per cent, and fresh snow a maximum of 85 per cent.

**Alberta**, the most westerly of the Canadian prairie provinces, bordering British Columbia and the Rocky Mountains. The province extends into the foothills and ranges of the Rocky Mountains and is a broken plateau of mainly *Mesozoic sedimentary and volcanic rocks sloping from west down to east. Three mountain passes give access to the western coast of Canada. The area is rich in resources, notably oil—such as in the Athabasca tar sands in the north of the province—as well as low-grade coal and natural gas.

'The Alchemist', painted in the 19th century by Joseph Wright, typifies the popular image of the mystery and intrigue that surrounded **alchemy**.

The southern quarter is virtually treeless, and on these prairie lands wheat is the predominant crop.

**alchemy**, the art of transmuting metals. The study of alchemy, based on the concept of the possible transmutation of all matter, grew to be far wider in scope than the familiar attempts to turn base metals into gold. It attracted such medieval scholars as Roger *Bacon and Albertus Magnus, and was patronized by princes and emperors. The influential Swiss writer Paraclesus (16th century) was primarily concerned with its medical application to his search for a chemical therapy for disease; his followers developed specialized chemical medicines and sought a universal elixir which they dreamed would prolong life and restore youth. Alchemy made a considerable, if largely accidental, contribution to chemistry; many leading scientists, including Isaac *Newton, retained an interest in transmutation. The rise of mechanical philosophy in the 17th century gradually undermined alchemy and other forms of the occult, and later alchemists chose to emphasize its mystical aspects in esoteric movements such as that of the Rosicrucians.

**alcohol** (or alkanol), any of a large group of organic compounds containing one or more hydroxyl (−OH) groups bonded to an *alkyl group. If the alkyl group is denoted by R, the formula of an alcohol is ROH. The simplest members of the group are *methanol ($CH_3OH$) and *ethanol ($C_2H_5OH$). Alcohols containing a small number of carbon atoms are readily soluble in water: for example, all alcoholic drinks are solutions of ethanol in water. When the hydroxyl group is bonded to a benzene ring the compounds are called *phenols.

**aldehyde**, any of a group of organic compounds with a general formula RCHO in which a carbon atom forms a double bond with an oxygen atom and is also bonded to a hydrogen atom and another group denoted by R, which can be a second hydrogen atom, an *alkyl group, or an *aryl group. Aldehydes undergo addition and condensation reactions, and are rapidly oxidized to form carboxylic acids, unlike the related group of compounds, the *ketones. Short-chain aldehydes, such as methanal (or formaldehyde, HCHO), and ethanal (or acetaldehyde, $CH_3CHO$), are unpleasant-smelling liquids widely used in the chemical industry, while aromatic aldehydes frequently have pleasant smells and are used as flavourings and perfumes; benzaldehyde ($C_6H_5CHO$), for example, smells of bitter almonds.

**Aleutian Islands**, an archipelago of about seventy islands in US possession, stretching along the south of the Bering Sea from Alaska for 1,900 km (nearly 1,200 miles) towards the Kamchatka Peninsula in the North Pacific. The islands are volcanic, being near the northern edge of the Pacific plate. Heavy rainfall and fog prevail. The islands are covered with grasses, sedge, and plants.

**alfisol**, a type of soil with a grey, brown, or red upper *horizon, containing little organic matter and overlying a zone of clay accumulation. This clayey horizon is generally rich in exchangeable *bases, such as calcium and magnesium compounds. This, with the fact that they are usually moist for all but a small part of the year, makes these soils relatively good for agriculture. Alfisols are found in areas with humid and subhumid climates, particularly in central North America, southern Europe, and south-east Australia.

**algebra**, a branch of mathematics which developed as an extension of arithmetic by using symbols in place of numbers. Thus the statement that the area of a rectangle is $a \times b$, where $a$ and $b$ represent the lengths of adjacent sides, is an algebraic statement. It is true for all rectangles. The great utility of algebra lies in its potential for economically relating algebraic quantities (such as $a$ and $b$ above). Equations can be constructed and manipulated to yield new relationships, unsuspected consequences, or unique numerical solutions to problems. For example, the equation $ax^2 + bx + c = 0$, where $a$, $b$ and $c$ are arbitrary constants and $x$ is an unknown variable, can be shown by manipulation to allow, at most, two solutions for $x$. If $a$, $b$ and $c$ are given values (for example, respectively 1, −5 and 6), manipulation of the equation shows that $x$ takes the values 2 and 3. The entities and *operations of algebra have expanded from those derived from arithmetic to include many that have no arithmetical counterpart, for example, *irrational numbers, *imaginary numbers, *matrices, *integration, convolution, and so on. As the gap between algebra and arithmetic widened in the 19th century, mathematicians increasingly viewed the rules and definitions of algebra as arbitrary. Alternative algebras were developed (for example, Boolean algebra, a symbolic *logic). Thus the study of abstract algebraic systems grew. These systems are *sets of elements with one or more operations. The real numbers, with the operations of addition and multiplication, are merely one example of one kind of system. The word algebra comes from the Arabic *al-jabr*, which refers to the transposition of terms in an equation.

**Algeria**, a country extending from the North African coast southward across a large part of the Sahara, its narrow coastal strip being bounded by Morocco on the west and Tunisia on the east. The coast has an equable Mediterranean climate well suited to agriculture. Inland the ground rises until it is mountainous, though here also the valleys are fertile. Plains and plateaux provide grazing, while many of the mountain slopes are forested. South is the desert—dry and with temperatures over 35 °C (95 °F)—and further south-east are more mountains with desolate plateaux and volcanic cones and craters. But the desert yields oil and natural gas, particularly in the area of the Great Eastern Erg or 'sand-sea'. In the hills on the Tunisian border and elsewhere, iron, zinc, lead, and phosphates are found.

**Algonquin Provincial Park**, a national park which lies on the southern edge of the Canadian Shield in Ontario, between Georgian Bay and the Ottawa River. Its area of 7,653 km² (2,955 sq. mi.) includes more than 1,200 lakes, the largest of which is Lake Opeongo. It is a hilly area and forms the watershed between the Ottawa River and streams feeding into Georgian Bay. The lakes and streams are full of lake trout, bass, pickerel, and muskellunge.

**algorithm**, a procedure or set of instructions for carrying out a mathematical or symbolic operation in a finite number of steps. For example, an algorithm for dividing a whole number by a fraction might be: invert the fraction; multiply the number by that which is now the numerator; divide the result by the denominator. Computer programming involves designing such procedures, since computing is the automation and execution of algorithms. Humans apparently follow algorithms when they do straightforward calculations; but whether intellectual and creative thinking is algorithmic is controversial. Similarly, whether computers will ever think for themselves is a controversial issue. These questions, and others, are the province of artificial intelligence. The word algorithm originates from the name of an Arab mathematician, al-Kuwarizmi (*c.*830) who wrote an extensive account of the Hindu system of numerals and numeration, from which current systems are derived.

**alicyclic compound**, any of a class of organic compounds similar to *aliphatic compounds except that they are cyclic, that is, they contain one or more rings of carbon atoms that are not *benzene rings (with a benzene ring the compound would be classed as *aromatic). For example, the cycloalkanes have the general formula $C_nH_{2n}$, where $n$ is a whole number, and, like the *alkanes, possess only single bonds between carbon atoms. Thus, cyclohexane, $C_6H_{12}$, consists of a hexagonal ring of carbon atoms which can adopt either the chair or boat *conformation. In general, alicyclic compounds exhibit chemical properties similar to those of their non-cyclic counterparts. Thus, cycloalkenes, which contain a double bond between two carbon atoms, undergo addition reactions (see *chemical reaction), like the *alkenes.

**al-Idrisi** (*c.*1100–60), Arabian geographer in the service of Roger of Sicily. He collected descriptions of Africa, Asia, and Europe from his own travels and from Arabic works.

His *Book of Roger* (1145) is the best account of the geography of the world as it was known at that time.

**aliphatic compound**, any of a class of organic compounds that do not possess a ring of carbon atoms; thus they complement *aromatic and *alicyclic compounds. They are either straight-chain compounds where the carbon atoms are joined in one continuous line; or branched-chain compounds where the line of carbon atoms has one or more branches coming off it. Aliphatic compounds can be further classified as *saturated or *unsaturated. Saturated compounds contain only single bonds: for example, the *alkanes contain carbon–hydrogen bonds and carbon–carbon single bonds. Unsaturated compounds, in contrast, contain at least one multiple bond: for example, *aldehydes contain a carbon–oxygen double bond.

**alkali**, any chemical compound of a class that form caustic solutions, and include the hydroxides of the Group I and Group II metals of the *periodic table. They turn litmus paper blue and have a *hydrogen ion concentration of more than 7 on the pH scale. They have a soapy feel, and neutralize acids forming salt, water and heat.

**alkali metal**, any of the elements found in Group I of the *periodic table: lithium, sodium, potassium, rubidium, caesium, and francium. They are soft, reactive metals and are stored in oil for safety. They react readily with water and non-metals, and explosively with acids; their reactivity increases from lithium to francium. Their atoms contain one valence electron, and they form ionic compounds in which the metal has a valency of 1; almost all their compounds are soluble in water. They are called the alkali metals because of the alkalinity of their hydroxides.

**alkaline earth metal**, any of the elements found in Group II of the *periodic table: magnesium, calcium, strontium, barium, and radium. They are reactive metals, although less so than the alkali metals; their reactivity increases as the elements become heavier, and barium is stored in oil for safety. They react readily with non-metals and acids, forming ionic compounds in which the metal has

Soda ash (sodium carbonate) is an **alkali** which, although manufactured by the chemical industry, does occur naturally. This is the world's largest underground soda-ash mine at Green River, Wyoming, USA.

a valency of 2. Beryllium appears at the top of Group II but is not usually included among the alkaline earth metals as it differs quite markedly from other members of the group.

**alkali soil**, a type of soil found in low-lying depressions in steppe or desert areas where evaporation greatly exceeds precipitation. Weathered material, brought in by intermittently flowing streams in times of flood, accumulates in these areas. As the floodwater evaporates, dissolved mineral salts such as sodium and calcium carbonates crystallize out. As a result of poor drainage and intense evaporation, these salts are carried up through the profile by capillary action and redeposited at or near the soil surface. This process is known as *salinization. The two main types of alkali soils are known as *solonchaks and *solonetz.

**alkane**, any of a series of *saturated aliphatic hydrocarbons having the general formula $C_nH_{2n+2}$, where $n$ is a whole number. They contain only single bonds between carbon atoms. Chemically they are fairly unreactive; hence they can be used as solvents. The reactions they undergo are mostly substitution reactions (see *chemical reaction), in which hydrogen atoms are replaced by other atoms. For example, they undergo a *photochemical reaction with halogens, to form *halocarbons. In the process known as cracking, long-chain alkanes that occur in oil are broken down into smaller alkanes and industrially useful alkenes by being passed over a heated catalyst.

**alkanol**    *alcohol.

**alkene**, any of a series of *unsaturated aliphatic hydrocarbons containing a double bond and having the general formula $C_nH_{2n}$, where $n$ is a whole number. This double bond is the part of the molecule where most reactions occur. These reactions are generally addition reactions (see *chemical reaction), in which one or more atoms are added to each carbon of the double bond, converting it to a single bond. For example, they react with hydrogen, in the presence of a catalyst, to form the corresponding alkanes. Simple alkenes, such as *ethene, $C_2H_4$, and propene, $C_3H_6$, are widely used in the synthesis of polymers and other organic compounds.

**alkyl group**, a group of atoms derived from an *alkane by the removal of one hydrogen atom. Thus the general formula is $C_nH_{2n+1}$, where $n$ is a whole number. When alkyl groups bond to *functional groups, they give rise to the corresponding alkyl derivatives.

**alkyne**, any of a series of *unsaturated aliphatic hydrocarbons containing a triple bond and having the general formula $C_nH_{2n-2}$, where $n$ is a whole number. Alkyl groups themselves are reactive intermediates with lifetimes less than one second. They are unsaturated compounds, all containing a triple bond between two carbon atoms. As with the *alkenes, the multiple bond is the part of the molecule where most reactions occur. These reactions are generally addition reactions (see *chemical reaction). For example, in the presence of a catalyst, alkynes react with hydrogen to form the corresponding alkenes. *Ethyne, $C_2H_2$, is the simplest alkyne and has many industrial applications.

**Allegheny Mountains**, ranges of old Hercynian *fold mountains forming the western section of the *Appalachian system in eastern North America. They run parallel to the Blue Ridge for over 800 km (500 miles) from Pennsylvania

A huge **alluvial fan** dumped at the mouth of a steep side-valley in the Karakoram range in Kashmir. The outer margin of the fan is undergoing rapid erosion by the main-valley river in the foreground.

in the north to Tennessee in the south. With a mean elevation of some 900 m (3,000 feet), they have been much reduced by erosion. A steep eastern escarpment is a natural impediment to most crossings, and there are few passes. They are well timbered; and their sedimentary rock contains iron and huge deposits of coal, especially in the north.

**allotrope**, any of several different forms of an element which share the same state (solid, liquid, or gas) but differ in some way in their physical properties. Because allotropes are chemically identical they react to give identical chemical compounds. For example, carbon has two allotropes, graphite and diamond, the physical properties of which are different. However, both chemically combine with oxygen to give carbon dioxide.

**alluvial fan**, a cone-shaped deposit of cobbles, sand, gravel, silt, and clay, built up by rivers where the slope of the bed is sharply reduced and the speed of flow decreases. Alluvial fans are akin to arcuate *deltas, but are built on land rather than underwater and have much steeper slopes. Most fans occur at junctions between mountains and plains, where the flow of steep upland rivers carrying coarse debris is checked by the change in gradient and the rivers are forced to deposit much of their load. The sediment wedge that is built up has a convex outer edge and forms half a cone, with its apex at the point where the river emerges from the uplands. The process of building a fan is complicated, because the river channel shifts from one place to another across the surface, as deposition changes the slope. Fan-making flows usually occur as sudden floods, which may contain so much debris that they are *mudflows. Fans are common in arid and semi-arid areas. Some provide fertile soil for agriculture and they are usually reliable sources of *groundwater, but they are treacherous places to build on.

**alluvium**, material deposited by rivers in their channels or over surrounding *floodplains. Strictly speaking, debris of any size carried by rivers can be described as alluvium, but nowadays it is common to apply the term only to deposits of very fine particles: silt and clay. All rivers deposit some alluvium, but really large ones such as the Mississippi and the Ganges have built immense plains and deltas from silt and clay and continue to add thin layers of new alluvium in every flood. Such alluvial areas are very fertile. Some, as in the lower Nile valley, have supported intensive farming for thousands of years.

**al-Masudi** (d. 957 in Cairo), Arab historian and traveller. Born in Baghdad, more than twenty books have been attributed to him, but his major work (now lost) was *The History of Time* in thirty volumes. In this he attempted to combine an encyclopedic history of the world with a large-scale survey of scientific geography. He later used this material in his most famous book, *The Meadows of Gold and the Mines of Gems*, half of which is devoted to the life of the Prophet Muḥammad and the other half to a social, economic, religious, cultural, and political survey of the Islamic and the non-Islamic world of his day.

**alpha particle**, the nucleus of a helium atom. Alpha particles are stable particles and consist of two protons and two neutrons. They are often emitted when a radioactive nucleus decays. Rays of alpha particles are called alpha radiation. Alpha radiation does not have great penetrating power and can be stopped by a sheet of paper, but intense ionization occurs along its track. Thus alpha radiation is a form of *ionizing radiation.

**Alps**, high ranges of young Tertiary *fold mountains stretching in a crescent from south-east France, through Switzerland and Italy, and into Austria, a distance of nearly 970 km (600 miles). Their structure is complex. During the Mid-Tertiary mountain-building period, some ten million years ago, *nappes were thrown up in series to lie on top of each other in an intricate pattern. Denudation has since worn away less resistant rock, leaving a series of crystalline peaks. Their great height is due to an upward earth move-

**Aluminium** ingots waiting to be shipped. Note the silvery white reflective surface of the metal; aluminium is used to form reflective coatings on telescope mirrors and in the making of 'silver' paper.

ment which took place before the latest ice age, leaving them above the invading ice sheets. Glaciers cut out the valleys, blocking some with debris, so that the Swiss and Italian lakes were formed. The highest mountains, including Mont Blanc, are in the western ranges; but even the Austrian Alps stand at over 3,500 m (11,500 feet). Above 1,830 m (6,000 feet) snow lies for six months of the year, and on the high peaks all year round. In winter it is quite warm in the sun and the crisp dry air, but when the sun sets the temperature falls suddenly. Cold air fills the sheltered valleys facing south, making them colder than the slopes above. The main through valley, the Brenner Pass, connecting Italy with Austria, lies towards the east.

**alternating current**   *electric current.

**alternative energy**   *energy resources.

**alum** (potassium aluminium sulphate, $KAl(SO_4)_2 \cdot 12H_2O$), a white crystalline compound used in the dyeing industry as a *mordant, in water purification, in dressing leather, sizing paper, in waterproofing fabrics, in fireproofing, and in medicine as a styptic and astringent. It is manufactured by treating bauxite with sulphuric acid and then potassium sulphate. The name alum also refers to a general type of double sulphate salt.

**alumina** (aluminium oxide, $Al_2O_3$), a white solid that is virtually insoluble in water. It is an *amphoteric compound and reacts with both acids and bases. It occurs naturally as anhydrous aluminium oxide in the mineral *corundum, or is obtained from *bauxite, which is an impure hydrated form of the oxide, by heating to 90 °C. The properties of the compound make it a versatile material and its applications are widespread. It is used as a catalyst in petrochemical processes, as an absorbent in chromatography, and, as bauxite, as the commercial source of aluminium. As it is a very hard ceramic material it is used as an abrasive and as an electrical insulator. Alumina ceramic fibres are used for high-temperature thermal insulation and as reinforcements in

composites. Many naturally occurring gemstones are composed of aluminium oxide crystals coloured by impurities. Artificial gemstones can be manufactured from alumina for various applications: for example, sapphire crystals are used as insulating substrates in electronics, while artificial rubies have applications in lasers. Alumina is also an important constituent of many pottery and porcelain compositions.

**aluminium** (US, aluminum: symbol Al, at. no. 13, r.a.m. 26.98), a silver metallic element in Group III of the *periodic table. It is a reactive metal, but often appears inert, as it is protected in air by a thin film of aluminium oxide. When the film is removed, aluminium reacts with water, non-metals, acids, and alkalis, giving compounds in which it has valency 3. It is the most abundant metal in the Earth's crust and is obtained commercially from *bauxite by *electrolysis. Aluminium has a low density, and is widely employed in the construction of ships and aircraft; it is also used for building, cooking utensils, and kitchen foil.

**aluminium oxide**   *alumina.

**amalgam** (in chemistry), an alloy of *mercury. Many metals dissolve in mercury to form amalgams, which may be liquid or solid. For example, amalgams of silver, with or without some copper or zinc, are used as fillings for teeth.

**Amazon**, the greatest river complex in the world, measuring 6,280 km (3,900 miles) from the source of its main headstream, high in the Andes, South America, to its mouth on the east coast of Brazil. For the last 650 km (400 miles) it is tidal and a large area of the Atlantic Ocean is stained muddy red by the silt it carries. Many of its tributaries are longer than any European river, and it drains an area of 6 million km² (2.5 million sq. mi.), more than twice the catchment area of the Nile, the only river that exceeds the Amazon in length. After leaving the waterfalls and gorges of its upper reaches, it enters the vast, tropical Amazon Basin, a lowland which stretches eastward from Peru, between the Guiana Highlands in the north and the Mato Grosso plateau in the south. This includes the largest area of rain forest in the world. So dense is the vegetation that sunlight rarely penetrates below the twisted, coiled plant-growth near the forest floor. The major throughways are the river, its tributaries, and innumerable lakes, which are often flooded either by melted snow from the Andes or by tropical rains. Flooded areas can be 320 km (200 miles) across. Although the climate today is hot and very wet, it was much colder and drier at other times during the Pleistocene Epoch, when there was grassland and even sand dunes in place of today's forest.

**amber**, a fossilized resin that has been formed from the gum exuded from conifers. It occurs in irregular masses in estuarine deposits that in geological terms are relatively young. It is found notably south of the Baltic. Insects are occasionally embedded in it. Brittle and easily broken, it is light in weight and warm to the touch. In colour it is typically orange or yellow, but ranges from white to darkish brown, and may be transparent or cloudy. Amber can be carved and polished.

**amethyst**, a form of *quartz found in *igneous rock, notably in Brazil and Uruguay, and prized as a semi-precious gem. Transparent and violet to purple in colour, it must not be confused with the rarer oriental amethyst which is a variety of corundum.

**amine**, an organic compound derived from ammonia, $NH_3$, by replacement of one or more hydrogen atoms by an *alkyl or *aryl group. If these groups are represented by R, R′, and R″, a primary amine has the general formula $RNH_2$, a secondary amine RR′NH, and a tertiary amine RR′R″N. Like ammonia, amines are *bases; they dissociate in water (some very weakly) and react with acids to give salts and with acid anhydrides to form amides. Simple amines have a characteristic fishy smell. Amines have many uses, for example, as insecticides, dyestuffs (the best known being aniline), pharmaceuticals, and rust-inhibitors.

**ammonia** (nitrogen trihydride, $NH_3$), a colourless, pungent gas, and very soluble in water, giving an *alkaline solution. It is manufactured on a large scale by the Haber process, in which nitrogen and hydrogen are mixed at high temperature and pressure in the presence of an iron catalyst. It is converted into ammonium compounds, which are important fertilizers; is oxidized to make nitric acid ($HNO_3$) and explosives; and is used in cleaning materials. Easily liquefied by cooling or compression, it is also used in refrigeration and air conditioning.

**ampere** (symbol A), the *SI unit of electric current. It is named after the French physicist André Marie *Ampère. A current is a flow of *electric charge, usually in the form of electrons. A current of 1 A is equivalent to a flow of about $10^{19}$ electrons per second. The ampere is defined in terms of the magnetic force it produces: a current of 1 A flowing in each of two infinitely long, straight, narrow wires $1\mu$ apart in a vacuum produces a force between the two wires of $2 \times 10^{-7}$ newton per metre length.

**Ampère, André Marie** (1775–1836), French physicist and mathematician who made important discoveries concerning the magnetic effect of an *electric current. He demonstrated that a current-carrying coil behaves similarly to a bar magnet, that iron placed in such a coil becomes magnetized, and that there is a magnetic force between two nearby current-carrying conductors. The unit of current, the ampere, is named after him. His name is also given to a law used for calculating the strength of the magnetic field produced by a current.

**amphiboles** (from Greek, 'ambiguous'), a common group of minerals found mainly in *igneous and *metamorphic

A winged insect, 40 million years old, perfectly preserved in **amber** found in the Baltic region.

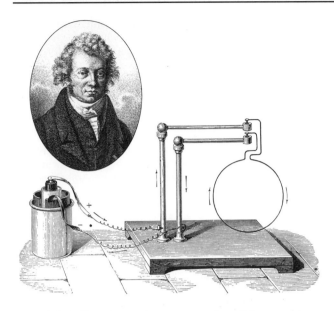

André Marie **Ampère** and a reconstruction of his apparatus for investigating the magnetic behaviour of a current-carrying wire loop. The loop is suspended in small cups of mercury so that it can pivot freely without breaking the electrical contact between the ends of the wire and the battery.

The Norwegian Roald **Amundsen** achieved more 'firsts' as an explorer than any other man of his generation.

rocks. They are characterized by a double chain structure of linked silicate tetrahedra. Iron, calcium, sodium, magnesium, aluminium, and other elements may be present: *hornblende, a common rock-forming mineral, is the commonest member of the group. Certain amphiboles occur in fibrous form, and belong to the *asbestos group.

**amphoteric compound**, a compound, usually an oxide or hydroxide, that can behave as both an *acid and *base. The elements whose oxides can show amphoteric character are the metals towards the right-hand side of the *periodic table. For example, zinc oxide, ZnO, is amphoteric. It acts as a base by dissolving in aqueous acids to give solutions of zinc salts, and it acts as an acid by dissolving in aqueous alkali to form solutions of the zincate-ion, $Zn(OH)_4^{2-}$.

**amplitude** (in physics), a quantity which varies periodically, the maximum departure from a mean or base value. In the case of a vibration or oscillation it is half the total extent of the motion. Of waves, it is the greatest distance by which a wave departs from its mean position. The greater the energy of the wave, the larger is its amplitude.

**Amu Darya**, a great river of central Asia, known to the West in classical times as the Oxus. It flows for 1,415 km (879 miles) from the confluence of the Pyandzh and Vakhsh Rivers, and 2,540 km (1,578 miles) from the furthest headstreams in the Pamirs, to its delta on the Aral Sea. The flow is largely dependent on melt water from snow and ice in the upper basin, the discharge increasing from March to May. Navigation is difficult but there is great potential for hydroelectric power.

**Amundsen, Roald** (1872–1928), Norwegian explorer who in 1911 was the first to reach the South Pole, ahead of Robert *Scott. In an earlier voyage (1903–6) he had also been the first to complete the long-sought *North-West Passage from the Atlantic to the Pacific, locating the northern

magnetic pole on the way. He was lost when flying from Bergen to Spitsbergen to take part in the search for Umberto Nobile's airship *Italia* in 1928.

**Amur**, a river forming part of the boundary between Siberia and China. It is formed by the confluence of the rivers Shilka and Argun 2,824 km (1,755 miles) from its wide, bell-shaped estuary, 48 km (30 miles) long, which enters the Sea of Okhotsk. The river basin is fed by summer and autumn monsoon rains, with floods from May to October. These can raise the water level in the upper Amur to 14 m (45 feet) above normal, while the lower Amur has low banks and overflows into extensive marsh. Much of the river is navigable, but little of its hydroelectric potential has been developed.

**anabatic wind**, a light up-slope flow of air which occurs during daytime in valleys in hilly and mountainous areas. It results from the greater intensity of *insolation received by sunward-facing valley sides as compared with shaded valley sides and floors. The air warmed by contact with the sunlit ground expands, rises, and is replaced by cooler air from elsewhere in the valley. At any given altitude, air in the valley not warmed by contact with the ground remains cooler, and therefore denser, than the rising air and sinks to replace it. (See also *katabatic wind.)

**analysis** (in chemistry), the determination of the composition of a substance. This can be carried out by physical means: for example, the melting-point of an unknown substance can be measured, and a suggestion made as to its identity by comparison with a table of melting-points. An important branch is *spectroscopy. Substances absorb and emit characteristic wavelengths of light in all regions of the visible spectrum. For example, salts of certain metals impart characteristic colours to a flame, and a flame test can be carried out to determine the presence of these metals. Analysis can also be carried out by chemical means, both qualitative and quantitative. Qualitative analysis establishes only the presence or absence of substances; it cannot determine their quantities or concentrations. This is the objective of quantitative analysis, which can be carried out in many ways. In gravimetric analysis, a precipitate is formed and is then weighed; and knowledge of its mass allows the original concentration to be determined. In volumetric analysis, a *titration is carried out: the substance of unknown concentration is titrated against a substance of known concentration, which reacts specifically with it. By measuring the quantity required for complete reaction, the unknown concentration can be determined. Analysis has many practical applications, not least in forensic science.

In mathematics, analysis involves the study of infinite processes. These processes may proceed either by indefinite accretion (as when terms are added in an infinite *series) or by indefinite diminution (as when the separation of two points on a continuous line is allowed to contract indefinitely). Thus analysis encompasses the mathematics of *calculus, continuity, limits, series, and related topics. For centuries mathematicians solved analytic problems by appeal to intuition, to *geometry, or to empirical knowledge (calculus is usually still taught in this way). However, such methods lead to *paradoxes. In the 19th century, Augustin-Louis *Cauchy, Karl Weierstrass, Richard Dedekind, Georg *Cantor and others made analysis (and calculus) rigorous by basing it on the concept of number alone. Their work is known as the arithmetization of analysis. In complex analysis the main entities are *complex numbers, whereas functional analysis, a 20th-century abstraction, explores spaces whose 'points' are not numbers but functions themselves.

**Anatolia**   *Turkey.

**Andalusia**, the southernmost region of Spain, with coasts on the Atlantic Ocean, the Strait of Gibraltar, and the Mediterranean Sea. Its interior was formed by the gradual collapse of land between the ancient crystalline block of the Sierra Morena and the folded coastal mountains, so that the Guadalquivir River now flows between the desolate ridges and narrow valley of the Sierra Morena, which borders Portugal in the north and the Sierra Nevada and other ranges in the south.

**Andes**, the great mountain system of South America extending over 6,400 km (4,000 miles) along its length. It forms the backbone of the continent, running parallel to the Pacific coast from Tierra del Fuego in Argentina in the south through Chile, Bolivia, Peru, and Ecuador to the Caribbean coasts of Colombia and Venezuela in the north. Its summits include Aconcagua, 6,960 m (22,835 feet), the highest mountain in South America, and such other well-known peaks as Illimani, Chimborazo, and Cotopaxi. The range was formed largely by folding and faulting in the Cretaceous and Tertiary periods and is still rising. There are volcanic formations in several places along its length, and earthquakes are a frequent occurrence. The snowline descends from 5,300 m (17,500 feet) at 15° S. in the western cordilleras to 800 m (2,500 feet) in southern Patagonia, where glaciers occur. Many important non-ferrous metals such as copper, silver, tin, and antimony are found in the Andes; oil is also found.

**andesite**, fine-grained volcanic rock of intermediate composition (that is, with up to 60 per cent silica) containing *plagioclase feldspar, with *biotite, *hornblende, or *pyroxene. Andesites are grey or grey-black in colour. Chemically more or less equivalent to *diorites, they occur as *dykes and *sills, and also as extrusive rocks at the surface.

The central **Andes** near Cuzco, Peru. Several peaks have radiating arêtes formed by massive erosion.

**Andorra**, a small co-principality in the heart of the Pyrenees, between France and Spain. It has a landscape of valleys at around 900 m (3,000 feet) which rise to peaks at 2,900 m (9,600 feet). Bisected by the Valira River, it contains three distinct natural regions: the valleys of the north and east Valira, and that of the Gran Valira. The attractive mountain scenery is snow-covered for several months of the year.

**andosol**, dark-coloured soil which forms on certain types of volcanic deposits, including ashes and basic lava. In humid conditions these materials weather rapidly into clay-rich soils which are initially extremely fertile and often support luxuriant plant growth. The soils therefore tend to be rich in organic matter, but their natural fertility is rapidly destroyed under cultivation unless care is taken to replace the nutrients removed by crops. Important areas of andosols occur in New Zealand, Japan, Hawaii, and the north-west United States.

**Angel Falls**, at 979 m (3,212 feet), the highest uninterrupted waterfall in the world. The falls are in south-east Venezuela, on a tributary of the Caroní River, which runs down from the Guiana Highlands.

**angle** (in geometry), the point where two lines intersect, or the line where two planes intersect. If a line is pivoted at one end and rotated about the pivot, its initial and final positions intersect to create an angle whose size can be expressed as a fraction of a full turn. Angles are commonly measured in degrees (symbol °) or radians. A degree is 1/360 of a full turn. A quarter turn, or right angle, is 90°. In science and mathematics, radian measure is widely used because it simplifies certain calculations and derivations. A *radian is the angle subtended at the centre of a circle by a part of the circumference whose length equals the circle's radius. A radian is about 57.3°. Angles are classified by means of their relation to a right angle. They are acute if less than one right angle, obtuse if between one and two right angles, and reflex if larger than two right angles. An angle between curved lines is defined as the angle between the *tangents at the point of intersection.

**angle of dip**   *dip.

**angles of incidence and reflection**   *reflection and *refraction.

**Angola**, a country of south-central Africa bounded by the Atlantic on the west, Zaïre and Zambia on the north and east, and Namibia on the south. Most of the country lies on a high plateau; but there is a coastal plain which, starting near the mouth of the Congo River, is broad and fertile until, southward, it becomes drier and narrower as it approaches the Namib desert. The vast plateau is a region of *savannah, watered by rivers that flow outwards from highlands near the centre and usually have swamps along their valleys. Power generated from the rivers provides most of the country's electricity. The country has some reserves of iron, copper, manganese, and oil.

**angström** (symbol Å), a *unit of length equal to $10^{-10}$ m (one ten-thousand millionth of a metre). Named after the Swedish physicist Anders Jonas Ångström (1814–74), the unit is used to measure lengths on an atomic scale. For example, the radius of an argon atom is 1.92 Å. In the *SI system, the nanometre ($10^{-9}$ metre) is preferred.

**Anguilla**, a tropical island country, one of the Leeward Island group of the Caribbean Islands. Flat and scrub-covered, its area is only 91 km² (35 sq. mi.) of coral formation with fine, sandy beaches, but it is flanked by many islets. The climate is dry and warm, and fresh water is scarce. Salt deposits are the main natural resources, and fish and lobster are the island's chief export.

**angular momentum**, a measure of the effect of *momentum in a rotating system. It is a *vector and a conserved quantity. It is defined as the *moment of inertia of the body about the axis of rotation, multiplied by the angular velocity (the rate of change of angle with time). Since angular momentum is conserved, a reduction in the moment of inertia leads to an increase in angular velocity. The stability of spinning tops and gyroscopes illustrates the conservation of angular momentum.

**angular velocity** (symbol ω), the rate at which an object rotates. It is normally measured in *radians per second. A complete revolution (360°) is equal to $2\pi$ radians—so an object rotating at, for example, 5 revolutions per second would have an angular velocity of $10\pi$ (31.4) radians per second.

**anhydrite** (anhydrous calcium sulphate, $CaSO_4$), an *evaporite mineral, white in colour with a pearly or vitreous lustre. It occurs in sedimentary rocks, commonly with its hydrated form, gypsum, and halite (rock salt), in various places. It is used as a fertilizer, in the manufacture of plaster, and as a raw material for making sulphuric acid.

**anhydrous compound**, a compound containing no water. The term is frequently applied to inorganic salts. For example, anhydrous calcium chloride, $CaCl_2$, contains only the elements calcium and chlorine; on exposure to atmospheric moisture, the compound becomes hydrated, its formula now being $CaCl_2 \cdot 2H_2O$. This capacity to absorb moisture means that anhydrous compounds can be used as *drying agents. If the hydrated compound is heated, the water is given off and the anhydrous compound is re-formed.

**anion**, a negatively charged ion, so called because it is attracted by the anode, or positive electrode, in *electrolysis. Anions are formed from neutral atoms or molecules by gain of electrons. For example, fluorine, which has seven electrons in its *valence shell, gains one more to form the fluoride ion, $F^-$, which has a complete valence shell of eight electrons.

**Annapurna**, in north-central Nepal, one of the great mountains of the Himalayas. Of its four snow-covered peaks, two are among the highest in the world. Annapurna I, in the west, rises to 8,078 m (26,503 feet) while Annapurna II, in the east, rises to 7,938 m (26,041 feet). The great ridge of Annapurna is 48 km (30 miles) long and stretches between the basins of the Kali Gandak and the Marsyandi Rivers.

**annihilation of matter**, a phenomenon which occurs when an *elementary particle interacts with its corresponding antiparticle (*antimatter). Their combined mass is converted into electromagnetic radiation in accordance with the Einstein formula $E = mc^2$, where $E$ represents the energy released, $m$ the combined mass, and $c$ the speed of light in a vacuum.

**anode**, a positive electrode in a device such as an electro-chemical cell or thermionic valve. In *electrolysis anions lose electrons at the anode.

**Antarctica**, a continent surrounding the South Pole and lying almost wholly to the south of latitude 66° 33′ S., the Antarctic Circle, within which the Sun neither rises at mid-winter nor sets at midsummer. The average temperature at the South Pole is −50 °C (−58 °F), and an extremely thick ice-cap covers the continent, forming a vast plateau which rises to over 2,700 m (9,000 feet). Strong winds often blow from the centre of this ice-cap; it is usually too cold to snow, and such snow as does fall takes hundreds of years to turn to ice. The ice grows and moves so slowly that parts of the ice-cap are millions of years old. Changes in the cold temperatures often cause strong downslope winds, and intense local blizzards are frequent. In several of the coastal regions there are mountain ranges through which glaciers flow. Where they emerge into the frozen sea the *Ross and other great ice-shelves make the continent on the map seem larger than it really is. In other places, where the rocky shore is exposed, little patches of summer moss and lichen can be seen. Antarctica is uninhabited but territorial claims have been made by many countries. An international treaty at present prohibits mining operations on the large deposits of coal and other minerals.

**Antarctic Ocean**  *Southern Ocean.

**anthracite**, a hard, shiny black metamorphic rock of the *coal family which is clean to handle and burns very hot, with a short flame and little or no smoke. It is an organic sed-imentary rock that has been subjected to heat and pressure. Most anthracites were formed in the *Carboniferous Period. They are found most notably in huge deposits in eastern Pennsylvania, USA.

**anticline**, a geological *fold structure that has the form of an arch. This form is the result of compressional forces act-ing in a horizontal plane on stratified rocks. The older rocks are normally in the core of the fold, the younger rocks occu-pying the outer positions. An anticline is the opposite of a *syncline. A special type of anticline in which the beds dip outwards in all directions is called a *dome.

**anticyclone**, a system of light and outwardly rotating winds, occurring in areas of high atmospheric pressure and subsiding air. Anticyclones are associated with settled weather conditions and, in general, move more slowly and persist for longer periods than do barometric *lows. Owing to the Earth's rotation, the circulation is clockwise in the northern hemisphere and anticlockwise in the southern. Cold anticyclones, such as the *Siberian High which forms over the Asian continent in winter, are shallow features con-fined to the lower 3 km (10,000 feet) of the atmosphere. In the western Atlantic Ocean they commonly develop when cold polar air pushes south behind a *front, and are gener-ally short-lived. Warm anticyclones, such as the *subtropical highs, are deeper and more persistent features; and short-lived extensions of them often form over such mid-latitude regions of the northern hemisphere as the western Atlantic. When warm anticyclones are stationary for several days or weeks and impede the movement of depressions, which are forced to travel round them, they are known as blocking anticyclones. Blocking anticyclones thus bring spells of warm and settled weather.

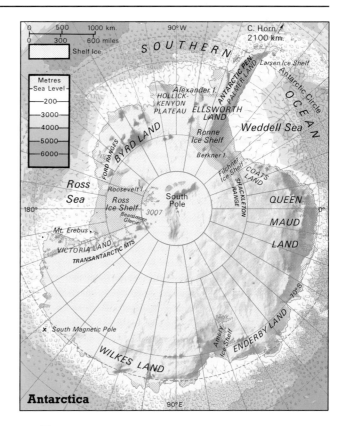

Antarctica

**antifreeze**, now almost always an approximately equal mixture of ethylene glycol ($CH_2OH \cdot CH_2OH$) and de-ionized water to which rust inhibitors are added. Such for-mulations are used extensively to protect *cooling systems such as car radiators, which rely on circulating water. Antifreezes give freeze protection down to −40 °C and boil at about 116 °C.

**Antigua**, a tropical island in the Leeward Island group of the *Caribbean Islands. It comprises 280 km² (108 sq. mi.) of fairly bare scrubland. Formed of volcanic rock in the south-west and coral in the north and east, it is moderately hilly, rising to 405 m (1,329 feet). The coastline is indented. The climate is dry and warm, although there are occasional hur-ricanes in summer. Water is scarce. Sugar cane and cotton are the main crops. Together with Barbuda and Redonda, it forms an independent state.

**antiknock**, a substance added to fuel to prevent it from premature combustion and thereby improve performance. Knock is a term describing the characteristic noise in inter-nal-combustion engines when uncontrolled combustion occurs. In petrol engines this may happen when the 'end gas', the last part of the mixture to burn, becomes over-heated and undergoes spontaneous combustion: shock waves strike the cylinder head and walls. Tetraethyl lead and 1,2-dibromoethane are used as an antiknock in petrol. However, lead compounds from car exhausts cause *air pol-lution and are a health hazard. In the last decades of the 20th century various attempts have been made to cope with the problem of lead emissions, including fitting filters to exhausts (see *catalyst) and banning lead additives in petrol.

**Antilles**  *Caribbean Islands.

**antimatter**, matter composed of antiparticles. For each *elementary particle there is a corresponding antiparticle which has the same properties as the particle itself but with the opposite electric charge (if it is charged) and the opposite *spin and magnetic moment. If a particle meets its antiparticle they *annihilate one another and their combined mass is converted into electromagnetic radiation. For example, the positron is the antiparticle to the electron and they can combine to form two or three *photons. Because there is a preponderance of matter in the universe, antimatter particles are very short-lived as they are rapidly annihilated by particles of matter.

**antimony** (symbol Sb, at. no. 51, r.a.m. 121.75), a silvery *metalloid in Group V of the *periodic table. Reacting with non-metals and some metals rather slowly, it forms compounds in which it shows valencies 3 and 5. It is alloyed with lead to give increased strength, and is added to germanium and indium in the production of semiconductors.

**antinode**, the position between the *nodes in a wave system where the *amplitude of oscillation is a maximum. In a *standing wave the position of the antinodes does not move and so they can be detected as the points at which the disturbance is greatest.

**antioxidant**, a general term to describe compounds that prevent reaction of a substance with *oxygen from the air. Antioxidants are important food preservatives, and are used in the formulation of paints and plastics and to prevent the formation of gum in the petrol for car engines.

**antiparticle** *antimatter.

**antipodes**, any two places on the Earth's surface that are diametrically opposite one another, so that a straight line joining them passes through the centre of the Earth. Their latitudes will be equal and opposite and their longitudes will add up to 180°. Midnight at one place will occur simultaneously with midday at the other, and summer at one place will occur during winter at the other. Although the UK and New Zealand are often referred to as antipodes they are not really so, the UK not being far enough south.

**Antipodes Islands**, an outlying island group of New Zealand in the South Pacific Ocean, lying 3° of latitude further south than the southern tip of New Zealand, comprising a central island and several islets.

**apatite**, a widely distributed calcium phosphate mineral that contains chlorine or fluorine and sometimes both. Crystalline in form, it is translucent, usually sea-green or yellowish green, but can be found in several other colours. It occurs in minor quantities in many types of *igneous rock. Commercially it is used in phosphatic fertilizers.

**Apennines**, a mountain range 1,350 km (840 miles) long running the entire length of the Italian peninsula. The central division of the Apennines contains the highest mountains, including Monte Corno at 2,914 m (9,560 feet). Numerous rivers, providing hydroelectric power, fall steeply down the eastern slope to the Adriatic Sea and more gently to the western Tyrrhenian Sea. The Apennines contain crater lakes, mineral springs, and volcanic hills. Near Naples is a region subject to earthquakes where the active volcano Vesuvius is located. There is a variety of minerals, and in the north-west Apennines are the quarries of the renowned Carrara marble.

Italian quarrymen working monumental blocks of white marble in the Carrara quarries in the north-western part of the **Apennines**. From this area, stone was taken for many of Michelangelo's most famous sculptures.

**Appalachian Mountains**, a wide belt of mountains stretching for 2,600 km (1,600 miles) down the eastern side of North America, from Newfoundland to Alabama. The northern section includes the White and the Green Mountains; then, south of the Hudson River, are the Catskills and the long ranges of the Allegheny Mountains; and finally, in the southern section, the Blue Ridge, the Black, and the Great Smoky Mountains. Together they form a massive barrier between the centre of the continent and its eastern coastal plains. Much older than the Rocky Mountains, they were formed by the *folding of Hercynian sedimentary rocks and have been greatly worn down by erosion. Their summits tend to be rounded and their slopes gradual, though rugged in the east. No peaks are high enough to be in perpetual snow. Much of the land is forested, with pine, cedar, spruce, birch, ash, and maple, especially in the north. Much is too hilly for cultivation; but the valleys are broad and well rivered, and the Great Valley, which runs for most of the system's length, is very fertile. There are enormous supplies of coal, the Pennsylvania coalfields being the largest in the world; iron, oil, and natural gas are also abundant. Many of the rivers are large enough to be significant sources of hydroelectricity.

**Appleton layer**, a very strongly ionized region in the upper part of the *ionosphere which reflects short *radio waves back to Earth. Its presence, at heights of 200 to over 400 km (125 to 250 miles), was established by the British physicist Edward Appleton (1892–1965) and enables radio transmission to take place at night, after the electron concentration in lower layers has fallen away owing to the absence of sunlight.

**aquamarine**, a transparent and usually greenish-blue variety of the mineral *beryl. Yellow ('golden beryl'), pink ('morganite'), and green (*emerald) varieties of beryl also occur. It is found in cavities in granite and pegmatite in

A crystal of **aquamarine**. Its name is derived from the Latin *aqua marina* (sea water) because of its colour.

the Ural Mountains and in Brazil, Sri Lanka, Madagascar, and the USA.

**aqua regia**, a mixture of three volumes of concentrated hydrochloric acid (HCl) to one volume of concentrated nitric acid ($HNO_3$). It is a very strong *oxidizing agent: for example, it will oxidize and thus dissolve gold, a reaction which none of the common acids can perform individually.

**aquiclude**, a layer of rock that is unable to yield water. Aquicludes may be impermeable or they may be porous but unable to release water in any appreciable quantity. Clay, for example, may have a *porosity of 40 per cent but because of its fine grain size, its *permeability is very low and water cannot be transmitted through it.

**aquifer**, a water-bearing stratum. Aquifers are commonly sandstones or limestones. Water is stored within the rock because of its *porosity and is transmitted through it because of its *permeability. The water can be released in springs or tapped in wells. In the USA, the Dakota Sandstone provides an extensive aquifer; another substantial aquifer underlies Long Island. In the London Basin the main aquifer is *chalk.

**Arabia**, the great peninsula of south-west Asia which rises steeply above the Red Sea and slopes eastward to the Gulf. Bounded on the north by Jordan and Iraq, its larger part is occupied by Saudi Arabia, though several other countries form its southern and eastern edges. This tilted plateau of old hard rock, with its limestone and sandstone covering, is swept by hot, dry winds under a burning sun. The result is desert, with numerous dunes and intersecting wadis but no perennial streams. From the Nafud Desert in the north to the Rub' al-Khali (a vast area of sand) in the south, there are only occasional oases. The coastal regions are somewhat different. A south-west monsoon brings light rainfall in summer to the mountainous south. Here, and especially in Yemen, the valleys and hillsides are protected from the sun by rising mists, and mocha coffee can be grown. In the Wadi Hadhramaut region, trees of the genus *Boswellia* and *Commiphora* grow, which yield the aromatic gum resins frankincense and myrrh. On the Gulf of Oman there are more mountains, where the air is moist; and in hilly Fujairah, one of the United Arab Emirates, tobacco is an important crop. The island-strewn coast of the Gulf holds enormous deposits of natural gas and oil, both on shore and off shore.

**Arafura Sea**, between Australia and east Indonesia, a westward extension of the Pacific Ocean and the Coral Sea, to which it is linked by the hazardous Torres Strait between New Guinea and the Cape York Peninsula of Australia. It is a shallow sea, with a mean depth of only 197 m (646 feet). It has a tropical monsoon climate.

**Arago, (Dominique) François (Jean)** (1786–1853), French physicist whose researches did much to establish (1838) the wave nature of light, according to which light should be retarded as it passes from a rarer to a denser medium. He was the first to discover that *polarized light is twisted by certain types of crystal, and with Augustin *Fresnel, he proposed laws describing the behaviour of polarized light. Arago also discovered the principle of the production of magnetism by the rotation of a non-magnetic conductor. An active republican and liberal reformer, he became a goverment minister in 1848.

**aragonite** (or mother-of-pearl), a calcium carbonate ($CaCO_3$) mineral. It can show attractive lustrous crystals of pointed shape. It tends to change into calcite, a more stable form of calcium carbonate, and it is therefore found only in younger deposits, as at Fort Collins, Colorado, USA. Another source of supply is from the shells of certain molluscs, of which it forms the lining. Delicate but very brittle, and white and grey in colour, it is widely used for ornament.

**Aral Sea**, in west-central Asia, the world's fourth largest lake. Slightly saline, it was once part of a large sea which also contained the Caspian Sea to its west, but it is now surrounded by the deserts of Kazakhstan and Uzbekistan. Very shallow—less than 70 m (220 feet)—and much islanded, it presents hazards to navigation during the nine months in the year when it is free of ice. It is fed by two major rivers, the Amu and Syr, but loses much water during summer by evaporation. Diversion of waters for massive irrigation projects led to a one-third reduction in area between 1960 and 1990 and has now cut inflow to the lake to almost nothing.

**Ararat**, a volcanic massif with two peaks some 11 km (7 miles) apart: Great and Little Ararat, the former rising to 5,165 m (16,945 feet). It lies generally isolated on the Armenian plateau in present-day eastern Turkey, a region of low rainfall; the snowline is high, the upper slopes containing fields of hard, granular snow. Good pasture covers the middle slopes, except on the northern face of Great Ararat, where a glacier falls from the foot of a great chasm that runs into the heart of the mountain. According to tradition, Noah's Ark came to rest on Ararat at the end of the Flood.

**Arbuckle Mountains**, in southern Oklahoma, USA, a range of low, rolling hills rising 200 m (700 feet) above the surrounding plains. They are a remnant of mountains formed in the Precambrian Era and have interesting geological formations that result from the different erosional rates of a variety of rock types.

**arch** (in geomorphology), a natural opening through a rock mass. Most commonly an arch is formed by marine erosion through a narrow headland.

**Archaean Aeon** (from the Greek, 'beginning'), the earlier of the two geological aeons into which the *Precambrian Era is customarily divided. (The other is the *Proterozoic.) It represents the period of time from the formation of the Earth (about 4,600 million years ago) to 2,500 million years ago. The earliest known rocks, from western Greenland, are about 3,800 million years old. Certain metamorphosed sediments (as at Barberton, Transvaal, South Africa) exhibit evidence of primitive life some 3,500 million years ago.

**Arches National Park**, eastern Utah, USA, an area of spectacular scenery overlooking the gorge of the Colorado River. It is renowned for its rock formations: water, frost, and wind have combined to shape and cut tall towers, pinnacles, windows, and arches out of the sandstone.

**Archimedes** (c.287–212 BC), Greek mathematician and inventor. Although best known as a brilliant mathematician and the founder of the sciences of statics and hydrostatics, he was also an ingenious engineer who applied his talents to a wide range of practical problems. When the Romans besieged his native Syracuse in 213 BC, he invented a range of ballistic weapons that considerably delayed the capture of the city. Archimedes also developed in detail the principle of the lever and of the multiple pulley. However, inventions such as the Archimedean screw (a screw mechanism used to raise water from lower levels) may have been wrongly ascribed to him. His principle, which states that a body immersed displaces a weight of fluid equal to its own apparent loss of weight, is applied to calculations of density, and in studies of flotation.

Arctic

**archipelagic apron**, layers of volcanic rock that create a fanshaped slope around groups of ancient or recent islands, mostly found in the central and southern Pacific oceans.

**archipelago**, a group of islands scattered over an area of sea and separated from one another only by narrow straits or channels. Formerly applied to an area of water containing numerous small islands, the term has gradually come to mean the islands themselves. Archipelagos are typical of relatively enclosed, shallow seas such as the Aegean, the original archipelago or 'great sea'.

**Arctic Ocean**, the expanse of sea and ice north of latitude 66° 33′ N., the Arctic Circle, within which the sun neither rises at midwinter nor sets at midsummer. With a diameter of 5,300 km (3,300 miles) and with the North Pole at its centre, it lies between the Pacific and the Atlantic oceans and between the coasts of North America, Asia, and Europe. The greatest depth is 5,440 m (17,850 feet). The surrounding *continental shelf is wide, however, and supports numerous islands; it is rich in oil and gas. Winter storms tear the ice apart to form linear areas of open water known as leads, and push it together to form ridges as much as 80 m (244 feet) thick. Only some of the ice melts each summer, and the result of the *floes continually rafting upon one another, or forming ridges, is a hummocking of 'multi-year' ice. The general surface current system consists of a flow from the Bering Straits across to the Greenland Sea (the Transpolar Current), to the west of which is a clockwise gyre (the Beaufort Gyre). The warm *North Atlantic Drift flows in through the Norwegian Sea.

**arenaceous rock** (or arenite), a sandy *sedimentary rock composed of eroded fragments of pre-existing rocks. The individual particles are of about the same size as sand grains: from 0.05 to 2 mm (0.002 to 0.08 inches) is the usual definition. They thus include grits and siltstones as well as sandstones. Rocks of this type can be of marine, fresh-water, terrestrial, or glacial origin. Quartz sandstone is the most common type, and the terms 'arenite' and 'sandstone' are often used interchangeably. Special types of arenaceous rocks include *greywackes, *greensands, and *arkoses.

**arête**, a knife-edged ridge formed in glaciated mountains when two *cirque glaciers cut backwards towards one another from either side of a divide. The ridge is formed in bare rock which is attacked by frost. The frost action breaks off chunks and fragments which slide and roll down into the cirques, forming screes or slopes of loose rock below the arête.

**Argand, Jean Robert** (1768–1822), Swiss mathematician who was renowned for his development of a diagram representing *complex numbers geometrically, in the form $a + bi$, in which $a$ and $b$ are real numbers and $i$ is the square root of $-1$, one axis represents the pure, imaginary numbers (those consisting of the $bi$ portion only); the second represents the real numbers ($a$ values only). This allows the complex numbers to be plotted as points in the field defined by the two axes.

**Argentina**, the second largest country of South America, occupying nearly the whole of the south-east of the continent, from the Andes to the Atlantic Ocean and from tropical Bolivia to the Southern Ocean, the latter being a distance of nearly 3,700 km (2,300 miles). In the west the

The Bietschhorn (3,934 m, 12,907 feet) in Switzerland is a typical glaciated peak, pyramidal in shape with radiating knife-edge **arêtes** formed where cirques have met back to back.

*cordillera, some of it volcanic, contains deposits of many minerals, copper, zinc, tungsten, and mica among them. The foothills are wooded, except in the south, and shelter valleys with vineyards and orchards. In the extreme north is the Gran Chaco, an area of subtropical forest and swamp, from which run tributaries of the Paraná. The Chaco yields hardwoods, and its southern part opens into land suitable for plantation crops. Southward, in the centre of the country, lie the *pampas—a vast region of high plains which supports some of the best agricultural and livestock farming in the world. Further south is Patagonia, a series of cold, infertile plateaux which are suitable only for sheep grazing. This, however, is a region rich in coal and oil, both of which are also found on the coastal plain and elsewhere.

**argentite** (silver sulphide, $Ag_2S$), the main ore of silver, often found together with other silver minerals. It is soft, very dense, and has an opaque, bright lustre. Argentite is formed at high temperatures, deep underground in veins. There are deposits in many places, and sizeable ones in Nevada and Colorado, USA, and in Peru.

**argillaceous rock** (or argillite), a clayey *sedimentary rock of fine-grained sediments composed of particles that are less than 0.0625 mm (0.002 inches) in size. Mudstones, clays, shales, marls, and silts are all examples. Most argillaceous rocks contain material of two types: clay minerals and rock flour, the latter consisting of very fine particles of quartz, feldspar, and other rock-forming minerals. The great majority of argillaceous rocks have been deposited in water, whether in the sea, in estuaries, or in lakes. There are

The Argentine Chaco has its eastern boundary with the Paraguay and Paraná Rivers. During the humid summer season, vast tracts of the Chaco become flooded with water. The Chaco area of **Argentina** covers over 256,000 km² (99,000 sq. mi.).

also terrestrial deposits in this category, such as *loess and clays of glacial origin.

**argon** (symbol Ar, at. no. 18, r.a.m. 39.95), a colourless gas which forms nearly 1 per cent of the atmosphere. It is one of the *noble gases and forms no chemical compounds. Commercially it is used as an inert atmosphere in filament lamps, being obtained by the fractional distillation of air. Most argon has arisen from the decay of radioactive potassium-40.

**aridisol**, a type of soil which forms in semi-desert or desert areas, where water is only available for plant growth during limited periods. Under such conditions vegetation is restricted to ephemeral grasses or drought-resistant shrubs, so these soils contain little organic matter. Soluble salts such as calcium carbonate and gypsum often accumulate as distinct *horizons, which are sometimes cemented to form *hardpans. Some aridisols, known as argids, also have a clay-rich horizon. As clay accumulation is generally produced by *leaching, such horizons are thought to be a relic of moister conditions in the past.

**arkose**, a category of *arenaceous rock, a *sandstone that is usually reddish in colour and made up chiefly of quartz and feldspar. It is formed typically by the disintegration of granites or similar rocks.

**Armenia**, a region south of the Caucasus in Asia Minor, comprising the republic of Armenia but also parts of eastern Turkey and northern Iran. Its northern part is very mountainous, containing high plateau-basins of which the largest is the vast Lake Sevan, while its Turkish part contains Mount Ararat and the sources of the Euphrates and Tigris Rivers. The summits, snow-covered for most of the year, embrace many extinct craters; and huge red, grey, and black boulders litter the region, which is subject to earthquakes. Copper, zinc, and aluminium are mined. The slopes are wooded or grassy, suitable for pasture, while in the valleys cotton, fruit-trees, grain, and vines are cultivated.

**Arnhem Land**, an area in the north-east of Northern Territory, Australia, extending from Van Diemen Gulf east and south-east to the Gulf of Carpentaria. Named after the Dutch vessel which originally explored the coast (1623), it now primarily refers to the large Aboriginal reserve in the area. The flat and indented coasts of mangrove swamp gradually rise inland to a low mountain range. In recent decades bauxite and uranium mining have become important in the region.

**aromatic compound**, any of a group of organic compounds that contain in their molecule the *benzene ring or a ring with similar characteristics. Strictly, an aromatic compound is defined as one which has ($4n + 2$) electrons shared over its ring, where $n$ is an integer, and aromaticity refers to the structural and chemical properties common to these compounds. It is the distribution of electrons in the aromatic ring that determines the type of chemical reactions they undergo. Reagents with high electron density (*nucleophiles) are repelled and thus do not react. On the other hand, reagents with regions of high positive charge (*electrophiles) are attracted by the aromatic ring. Most reactions of aromatic compounds are electrophilic substitutions in which the electrophilic reagent displaces another electrophile, normally the hydrogen ion, $H^+$, from the molecule.

Examples of aromatic compounds include benzene, $C_6H_6$; thiophen, $C_4H_4S$; and benzole, $B_3N_3H_6$. An example of an electrophile is the nitronium ion, $NO_2^+$. This reacts with benzene, displacing a hydrogen ion and forming nitrobenzene, $C_6H_5NO_2$.

**aromaticity** *aromatic compounds.

**Arrhenius, Svante August** (1859–1927), Swedish chemist who investigated the conduction of electricity in solutions and in 1887 proposed his theory of electrolytic *dissociation, which laid the foundations for the study of electrochemistry. He also studied the rates of chemical reactions and derived an equation giving the relationship between the rate and the temperature of a reaction. In 1903 he was awarded the Nobel Prize for Chemistry.

**arroyo** (also called wash, dry wash, or coulee, Arabic wadi, French oued), originally the bed of an ephemeral stream; a gully or flat-floored, steep-sided valley common in semi-arid regions such as south-western USA, Australia, and northern Africa. Arroyos form in areas where the general slope of the ground is gentle and where there are deposits of fine-grained sediment. The streams which cut the arroyos usually flow only after thunderstorms or when snow is melting, and they frequently exhibit *braiding across the valley floors. Many arroyos caused by poor land management have been formed since the 19th century, destroying grazing land and causing flooding and *aggradation in larger river valleys.

**arsenic** (symbol As, at. no. 33, r.a.m. 74.92), a *metalloid in Group V of the *periodic table; its most stable *allotrope is grey. It reacts with concentrated acids, non-metals, and some metals, forming compounds in which it shows valencies 3 and 5. Many of its compounds are highly poisonous and have been used as insecticides, wood preservatives, poison baits, and weedkillers. It is also used in alloys, particularly lead shot, and in germanium semiconductors.

**artesian spring**, a discharge of water under pressure from an *aquifer. The aquifer is a water-bearing stratum that is confined between impermeable strata above and below it. Provided that the difference in height between its highest and lowest parts is large enough, the water in the lower parts may rise to the surface under pressure: water entering the upper part of the aquifer forces water from lower down through any fissures that may exist in the overlying layer of impermeable rock. The world's largest system of this kind is the Great Artesian Basin of eastern Australia. Artesian springs are named from the famous Artois Basin in France.

**aryl group**, a group of atoms derived from an *aromatic compound by the removal of one hydrogen atom from the aromatic ring. The simplest aromatic compound is benzene, $C_6H_6$, and the simplest aryl group is therefore the phenyl group, $C_6H_5-$. When aryl groups bond to *functional groups, they give rise to the corresponding aryl compounds. For instance, if the functional group is a halogen atom, the resulting compound is an aryl halide, of which chlorobenzene, $C_6H_5Cl$, is an example.

**asbestos**, the general name for a fibrous variety of *amphiboles and several other silicate minerals. They generally have either a double chain of linked silicate tetrahedra or a layered structure. Asbestos minerals occur in metamorphic

Mangrove swamps and shallow lagoons fringe the **Arnhem Land** coastline in Australia's Northern Territory.

and basic *igneous rocks. Different varieties are found in Canada, South Africa, Cyprus, and elsewhere. Their fibres are long enough to be separated and then felted and woven into layers or sheets which are excellent insulators and do not ignite. It is the non-flammable nature of asbestos fibre that gives it its industrial importance. Applications include brake linings, *building materials, electrical equipment, and thermal *insulation materials. Asbestos fabrics are used for *fire-fighting suits, safety apparel, and fire curtains. Since the early 1970s there has been growing concern about the effect of short asbestos fibres on human health. The short fibres are thought to cause asbestosis, a lung disorder leading to progressively greater breathing difficulties plus concomitant heart strain, and mesothelioma, a rapidly fatal form of lung cancer. This has led to a limitation in its use and to elaborate procedures for its safe removal from public buildings.

**ash, volcanic**, tiny, unconsolidated fragments of lava emitted from volcanoes. The ejection of ash is usually caused by an obstruction in the vent or inner wall of the crater. Huge quantities enter the atmosphere at the time of eruptions, sometimes in a *nuée ardente. Suspended in the air as dust it can be carried round the globe by high-level winds. After precipitation, soil resulting from its decomposition

becomes extremely fertile, and as a result, settlements grow around volcanoes in spite of dangers. Among the most important volcanic soil regions of the world are large parts of the Mediterranean Basin, Japan, the Cordillera of North America, the Pacific coast of North and South America, the Andes mountain ranges, and the Pampas regions of Argentina.

**Asia**, the world's largest continent, occupying a third of its land surface. Set in the Northern Hemisphere, it stretches from the Arctic to the Equator and from the Ural Mountains to the Pacific Ocean. A peninsula, Asia Minor, extends from the Caspian to the Mediterranean Sea. Part of Asia also consists of hundreds of islands, ranging in size from Borneo to mere rocks. The extreme north is mainly tundra, supporting only mosses and lichens, and south of this is the vast expanse of Siberia. Then the land begins to rise, to the plateau of Kazakhstan in the west, to the forested Sayan Mountains north of Mongolia, and up the valleys of the tributaries of the Lena River in the east. Much of Asia is high, and its central mountain ranges are the highest in the world. Their melting snows entering rivers such as the Indus, the

Ganges, the Mekong, and the Yangtze provide water and sediment for great areas in the Indian subcontinent to the south and in China to the south-east and east. Monsoon rains, alluvial lowlands, and swampy deltas make these regions rich in natural vegetation. In the north-east of the continent is the part of Russia known as Yakutsk, with its own ranges and rivers and the cold, mountainous Kamchatka Peninsula pointing southward to Japan. The Japanese islands, together with those of the Philippines and Indonesia in the hot, wet tropics, ring the eastern part of the continent. They have many volcanoes, and earthquakes are frequent, for they are on the very edge of the Eurasian *plate. Over 8,000 km (5,000 miles) to the west, the semi-arid plateau of Asia Minor is equally close to plate boundaries. South of the Caucasus Mountains are other earthquake regions, although the oil-bearing deserts of Arabia are relatively stable.

**Asia Minor**, historical term for Anatolia, the peninsula of land where the continents of Europe and Asia meet, and that today forms most of Asian Turkey.

**asphalt**, a solid or plastic variety of *bitumen. In its natural state it occurs in rocks of any geological age and particularly wherever oil is found. The largest sources are in Canada, Venezuela, Trinidad, and Cuba. Adhesive when heated, waterproof, and elastic, it can be used either on its own or mixed with sand.

**associativity** (in mathematics and computing). An *operation – is associative when, for any three elements of the set $a$, $b$, and $c$, it has the property that $(a - b) - c = a - (b - c)$. Multiplication over the set of real numbers, for example, is associative; division is not. The concept of association is needed for the definition of *group.

Excellent thermal insulation properties and resistance to burning make the fibrous minerals of the **asbestos** group ideal material for use in protective clothing.

**astatine** (symbol At, at. no. 85, r.a.m. 210), the heaviest member of the *halogens. All its isotopes are strongly radioactive; the most stable is astatine-210 with a *half-life of eight hours. The element is made by bombarding bismuth with alpha particles; its chemistry is similar to that of iodine.

**asthenosphere**   *Earth.

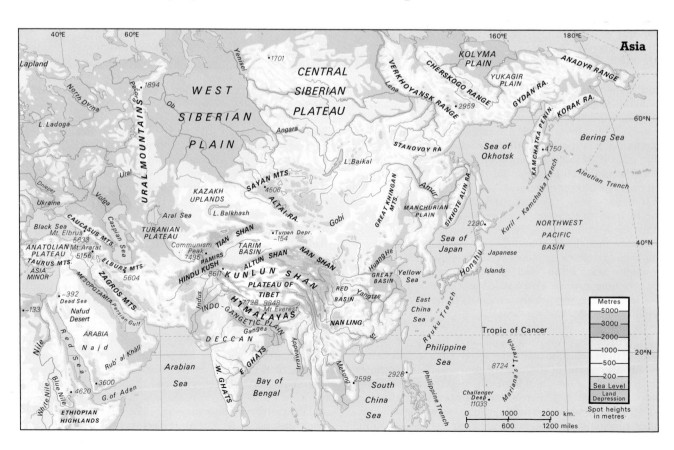

**asymptote**, a straight line in a plane which is approached arbitrarily closely by a curve but never actually touched. Alternatively an asymptote can be considered as the tangent that touches the curve an infinite distance away, so that the slope of the curve tends to that of the asymptote. By no means all curves have asymptotes, but the *hyperbola, for example, has two.

**Atacama Desert**, a cool and extremely arid region of northern Chile, running for more than 1,000 km (620 miles) north–south between the Andes and the Pacific coast. Standing at an average altitude of some 600 m (nearly 2,000 feet), it comprises in the main a series of dry salt basins where nitrates are abundant and copper and sulphur are also found. It has numerous volcanic cones and is subject to earthquakes. In some areas rain has never been recorded, and streams descending from the mountains evaporate long before they reach the sea. Vegetation is very sparse. In this century the desert has been steadily expanding southward, a continuing process .

**Athabasca, Lake**, Canada's fourth longest lake, straddling the Alberta–Saskatchewan boundary on the Canadian Shield in a thin crescent some 320 km (200 miles) long. In the south-west it receives the Peace and Athabasca Rivers, discharging northward by the Slave River into the Great Slave Lake, which connects it with the Mackenzie River system. Because of ice, it is navigable only in summer.

**Atlantic Ocean**, the expanse of sea which separates North and South America from Europe and Africa, its northern and southern boundaries being the Arctic and Southern oceans. Along each margin is a *continental shelf of varying width, while the *Mid-Atlantic ridge runs snake-like from north to south down the centre. The continents on either

*Atacama Desert* landscape with a sulphur ore lake in the foreground and, in the distance, one of the few nitrate factories still in existence in the area.

side have roughly interlocking shapes and provide early evidence of *continental drift; it is the youngest of the world's oceans, being some 200 million years old. Its deepest point is in the Puerto Rico Trench at nearly 8,300 m (27,200 feet). While water at the ocean bottom is at about 2 °C, the temperature of surface water near the Equator is about 27 °C (80 °F). This warm water is driven westward by the *trade winds, a process which initiates two giant circuits of *ocean currents. North of the Equator, the warm water moves clockwise into the Gulf of Mexico, which it leaves, off Florida, as the *Gulf Stream. Westerlies drive it north-east until it meets the cold, southward-flowing Labrador Current. Then it divides into the *North Atlantic Drift, which swings up to the Arctic, and the Canary Current, which turns east and afterwards south, back to the Equator. Meanwhile the southern circuit begins as the warm, westward-moving water is deflected by the huge bulge of South America and becomes the Brazil Current. This moves south into the zone of the *roaring forties, which drive the water eastward to the African coast. Here it is replaced by the cold upwelling of the *Benguela Current which travels north and thus completes the anticlockwise sequence. The contrasts in air and sea temperatures in the Atlantic are greater than in any other ocean. This is because it is open to the strong, chilling influences of both the Arctic and the Antarctic ice masses. The consequence is stormy weather, particularly in northern areas, which have some of the roughest seas found anywhere.

**Atlas Mountains**, a complex system of Tertiary ranges and valleys occupying the north-west corner of Africa. Pre-

(mmHg), or 14.7 pounds acting on 1 square inch. The pressure decreases with height as the air becomes less dense. At about 5,500 m (18,000 feet) it is so rarefied that man cannot breathe easily without an extra supply of oxygen. Over half of the atmosphere's total mass is below this height. Objects on Earth are not crushed by atmospheric pressure because air is a fluid, and so it exerts a pressure equally in all directions. This means that objects experience a pressure from air underneath, inside or around them, which counteracts the pressure of the air above them. An empty plastic bottle or tin can will crumple if the air is pumped out of it, because the pressure from the outside acting inward will be greater than the pressure on the inside acting outward. The size of atmospheric pressure was first indicated by Otto von Geuricke (1602–86) in Germany in the 17th century. He made two copper hemispheres which fitted together to form a sphere and pumped all the air out of the sphere. He then attached a team of eight horses to each hemisphere and drove the two teams apart. They were unable to part the hemispheres, because the atmospheric pressure outside was pushing the hemispheres together, and there was no longer any air inside the sphere to push them apart.

The atmosphere is divided into a number of spherical regions on the basis of the way its temperature varies with height (see figure). The lowest of these regions is the troposphere, followed by the stratosphere, mesosphere, and thermosphere. As well as providing air to breathe, the Earth's atmosphere acts as a barrier against harmful ionizing radiation (see *ozone layer) and as a blanket that traps the Sun's heat (see *greenhouse effect), and gives rise, in its *circulation close to the Earth's surface, to *weather.

**atmospheric dust**   *dust in the atmosphere.

**atoll**, a horseshoe-shaped or roughly circular coral reef enclosing or almost enclosing a lagoon. Generally, atolls are built on a volcanic base. Their ring-shaped structure may be due to the fact that coral on the outside of the mass gets more nourishment from the surrounding ocean than the coral inside; so the mass builds faster round the periphery. When the central lagoon is pushed above sea-level and drains, the atoll becomes a *coral island with a hollow in the middle. Sometimes some parts of the reef grow more quickly than others; then the atoll may look like a series of islands encompassing sea.

**atom**, the smallest particle that can be differentiated in chemical tests. Atoms of hydrogen are the simplest and lightest, and atoms of uranium are the heaviest to occur naturally. (Although atoms which are heavier than uranium can be made in the laboratory they are too short-lived to exist freely in nature.) All atoms consist of a central core called the *nucleus, which possesses a certain number of units of positive charge, and is surrounded by a cloud of *electrons each of which has unit negative charge. Their total negative charge is exactly equal to the positive charge on the nucleus; hence the atom as a whole is electrically neutral. The nucleus is composed of two types of particle which have almost the same mass. These are the protons, each of which carries one unit of positive charge, and the neutrons, which are uncharged. The electrons are very light, each having a mass only about 1/1,836 of that of the proton; and so nearly all the mass of an atom is concentrated in the nucleus. The arrangement of the electrons is described by Niels *Bohr's atomic theory. *Quantum mechanics gives a description of the behaviour of the electrons. Atoms of the various ele-

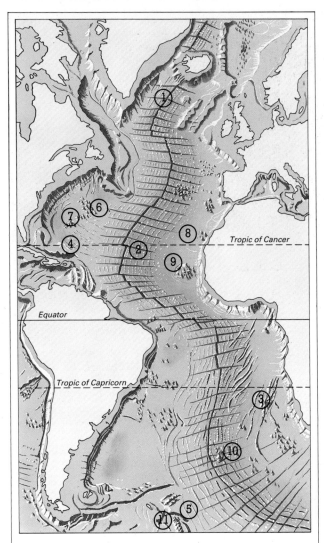

**Atlantic Ocean:** seabed topography

**Ridges**
1 Reykjanes Ridge
2 Mid-Atlantic Ridge
3 Walfisch Ridge

**Trenches**
4 Puerto Rico Trench
5 South Sandwich Trench

**Island groups**
6 Kelvin Seamounts
7 Bermuda Rise
8 Canary Islands
9 Cape Verde Islands
10 Tristan Da Cunha Group
11 Scotia Arc

dominantly *fold mountains of sedimentary rock, they are related to the Alpine system of the European *Alps. They run from the Atlantic coast through Morocco and Algeria into Tunisia, the main range being the High or Grand Atlas with its highest peak, Jebel Toubkal, at 4,167 m (13,671 feet). The Middle Atlas extends northward from the High Atlas and contains many high plateaux and deep gorges. On the north-east is the lower Saharan Atlas, while the Anti-Atlas runs south-westward.

**atmosphere**, the body of gas surrounding any planet or star and exerting a pressure on it. The pressure of the atmosphere is the force produced by the weight of the air above it. The Earth's atmosphere, composed of *air, extends upwards for over 1,000 km (600 miles) and exerts a *pressure at sea-level of approximately 101 kilopascals. This is equivalent to 1,013 millibars (mb), 760 millimetres of mercury

## Structure of the atmosphere

The heights of the various divisions shown in the diagram are representative rather than precise since the altitudes of the layers on fact vary depending on latitude, time of day, time of year, and level of solar activity (sunspots, solar flares).

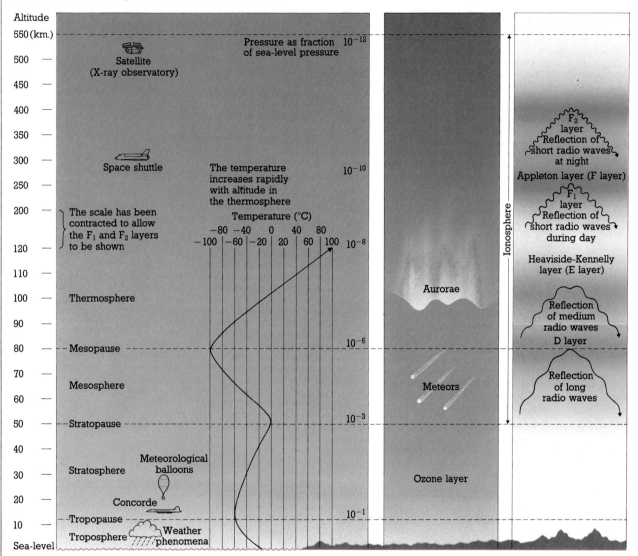

### Pressure

The atmosphere may be considered as a column of fluid in which the pressure at any level is due to the weight of all the fluid above it. The pressure is therefore greatest at sealevel and falls with increasing altitude.

### Temperature

Overall, the atmosphere is quite transparent to incoming short-wave solar radiation; it is heated mainly from below by long-wave terrestial radiation and, in the troposphere, by direct heat transfer from the Earth's surface. The temperature of the atmosphere therefore tends to fall with increasing altitude. In the stratosphere, however, the ozone which constitutes about 1 per cent of the stratospheric air absorbs ultraviolet solar radiation causing an increase in temperature in this region. Above the ozone layer, the temperature again falls with altitude.

The temperature rise in the thermosphere is due to absorption of short-wave radiation by ionization processes.

The temperature of the thermosphere can rise more than 1,500 °C during the day; at night, though, the region can lose heat rapidly as a result of recombination of ions and electrons, and the temperature may be as low as 250 °C.

### Composition

At a height of about 110 km the main mechanism determining the mixture of atmospheric gases changes. Below 110 km turbulent mixing maintains a relatively stable atmospheric composition (mainly $N_2 + O_2$). Above 110 km molecular diffusion becomes more important than turbulent mixing. Lighter molecules can diffuse more easily into the upper atmosphere than heavier molecules. Thus, above about 200 km atomic oxygen (O, relative molecular mass 16) becomes the main atmospheric constituent. Beyond about 600 km helium (He, r.m.m. 4) becomes the principal component; and higher still, atomic hydrogen (H, r.m.m. 1), which extends far into space.

A small coral **atoll** off the coast of New Guinea.

**Australia**, an island country and continent in the Southern Hemisphere in the south-west Pacific Ocean. Surrounding it are numerous islands, the largest being Tasmania, and off its east coast lies the *Great Barrier Reef. Much of the continent has a hot, dry climate, and a large part of the central area is desert or semi-desert; the most fertile areas are on the eastern coastal plains and in the south-west corner of Western Australia. The south-western coastal areas are undulating, their hills supporting forests of hardwood trees. They rise to a low plateau of ancient rocks, and this gives way in turn to the Great Sandy and Gibson Deserts. In the centre of the continent are the *Macdonnell Ranges, beyond which

ments are characterized by the charge on the nucleus, that is by the number of protons it contains (the *atomic number). Hydrogen, the lightest element, has a nucleus of one proton with a 'cloud' of one electron around it. The next lightest element is helium and it has a nucleus of two protons and two neutrons which is surrounded by two electrons. Uranium has a nucleus of 92 protons and 146 neutrons, surrounded by 92 electrons. Nuclei with *magic numbers (2, 8, 20, 50, 82 or 126) of either protons or neutrons are particularly stable.

**atomic energy**   *nuclear fission and fusion.

**atomic number**, the number of protons in the *nucleus of a particular element, being therefore equal to the positive charge on the nucleus. It is the basis for the classification of elements in the *periodic table.

**atomic weight**   *relative atomic mass.

**augite**, one of the chief members of the *pyroxene group of minerals. Essentially it is a calcium magnesium iron aluminosilicate. Its physical properties vary but crystals are usually hard, dense, and opaque. Black or greenish black in colour, it is a common mineral of igneous and metamorphic rocks.

**aurora**, a luminous electrical atmospheric phenomenon, usually of streamers of light in the sky above the northern or southern magnetic pole (respectively, aurora borealis and aurora australis). Auroras appear in the sky at latitudes where charged particles from the solar wind break through the Earth's magnetic field and hit gas molecules in the atmosphere. The collisions trigger the molecules to emit light. Controversy surrounds the mechanism by which the particles gain enough energy to break through the magnetic shield. The effect is of a streaming arch of flickering light from which coloured rays dart out. The illumination may last for several hours and shine like daylight in the sky.

---

### Atoms

It is impossible to give a true visual representation of atoms and their structure. Diagrams such as those presented here should be used simply as aids to intuitive understanding and should not be taken too literally.

### The Bohr model

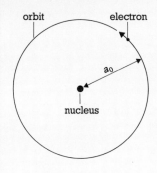

In the Bohr model, the hydrogen atom is considered as a nucleus (a proton) around which a single electron travels in a fixed orbit. In the ground state the radius of the orbit is $a_0$ (=0·53 Å), which is known as the Bohr radius. The electron can be excited into orbits of higher energy.

### The quantum mechanical model

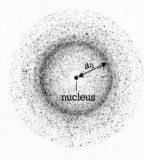

A cross-sectional view through the electron 'charge cloud' of a hydrogen atom in the ground state. The more dense the stippling, the higher is the probability of finding an electron there. The highest probability is at a distance $a_0$ from the nucleus.

### The sizes of atoms and nuclei

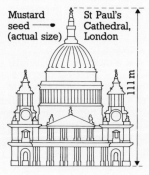

Atomic radii are of the order of 1 Å, while nuclear radii are of the order of $10^{-5}$ Å. A rough idea of the size of the nucleus in relation to that of the whole atom can be obtained by imagining a mustard seed (the nucleus) inside St Paul's Cathedral (the atom).

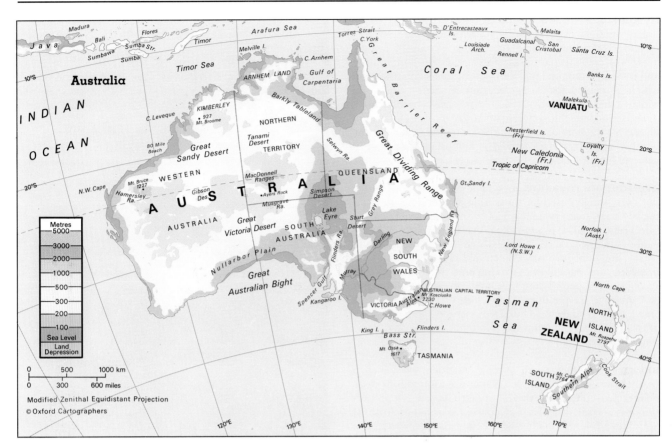

the land falls away to the Simpson Desert and Lake Eyre before gradually rising again to the Sturt Desert. The Murray–Darling basin is the country's largest water catchment area; its water supply for irrigation was greatly increased with the diversion of the Snowy River (1974) from its natural south-eastward course into the Murray River. Eastwards, the land rises to the *Great Dividing Range and then falls sharply to the sea. Moderate rain brought by depressions from the Southern Ocean is sufficient to support dense, evergreen forests and the cultivation of fruit and vegetables. Agriculture has always been of vital importance to the economy, with cereal crops grown over wide areas and livestock producing wool, meat, and dairy products for export. There are significant mineral resources: Australia is the world's leading exporter of aluminium, and its bauxite and high-grade iron-ore reserves are among the world's largest. Its energy resources, which include high-quality black coal, oil, natural gas, and uranium, constitute 18 per cent of global reserves.

**Australian Alps**, a part of Australia's Great Dividing Range of mountains. They lie to the south-east of the continent, and stretch some 480 km (300 miles) through Victoria and New South Wales. The Snowy Mountains and Australia's highest peak, Mount Kosciusko at 2,238 m (7,310 feet), are among them. They form the watershed between the Murray River system and streams flowing into the Tasman Sea. An intricate system of dams and tunnels directs water from the Snowy River to more than thirty generating stations. The rocks in the highlands are extensively mined for minerals. The area also has many nature reserves.

**Austria**, a country in central Europe, much of it mountainous, with the River Danube flowing through the northeast. It is bounded by Italy, Slovenia, and Croatia to the south, Hungary and Slovakia to the east, the Czech Republic and Germany to the north, and Liechtenstein and Switzerland to the west. Austria is the most densely forested nation in central Europe, with 40 per cent of its land covered by trees. In the Alpine regions, south facing mountain slopes have been cleared for pasture land and crops. In the Danube valley, arable land is characterized by very fertile soils. The warm, dry south wind, the *Föhn, affects vegetation and land use. The country's steep topography provides potential for hydroelectric development.

**avalanche**, a mass of earth, rock, ice, or snow dislodged from a mountainside by any sort of tremor or disturbance. Snow lying on a clear slope is poised for avalanche if the gradient is more than 22°; and if much steeper it may reach a speed of 300 km/hour (200 m.p.h.) or more. The material may be travelling on a trapped packet of air, like a hovercraft, or if the mass is huge the greatest danger may be from the air pushed ahead of it. This may fan out sideways like a *tornado, lifting trees, boulders, and rooftops in its path. In any case avalanches are responsible for much erosion, particularly in areas where they are almost seasonal events; and they frequently constitute a threat to both property and life. When falling mud on the slope of a volcano mixes with molten lava it can form an avalanche termed a nuée ardente, or burning cloud.

**average**, a single number intended as a representative of a set of numbers. There are several kind of average. Each kind preserves a particular feature of the parent set at the expense of other features. The *median and the *mode are averages which are picked from the set as being in some way typical of it. The *mean is calculated from all the members of the set, rather than being chosen from it. In everyday speech 'average' refers to the arithmetic mean.

**Avogadro, Amadeo, Conte di Quaregna** (1776–1856), Italian physicist best known for his hypothesis (or law), formulated in 1811 but ignored for the next fifty years, according to which equal volumes of gases at the same temperature and pressure contain equal numbers of molecules (the term which he coined for an aggregation of atoms), and from which it became relatively simple to derive both relative molecular masses and a system of atomic masses. A constant named in his honour is Avogadro's number, which is the number of molecules in 1 mole of a substance, and has a value of $6.02 \times 10^{23}$.

**avoirdupois measure**, a system of *units commonly, but decreasingly, used for measuring *mass. (The pound is the most familiar example.) The term is derived from the Old French *aveir de peis* meaning 'goods of weight', though in the strict scientific sense it is mass rather than weight which the units measure. Their abbreviations and relationships are as follows: 16 drachms = 1 ounce (oz.); 16 ounces = 1 pound (lb.); 14 pounds = 1 stone; 28 pounds = 1 quarter; 112 pounds = 4 quarters = 1 hundredweight (cwt.); 2,240 pounds = 20 hundredweight = 1 ton. The units are all based on the grain. By definition, 1 pound = 7,000 grains.

**axiom** (in mathematics), a basic statement on which a mathematical theory is built. Axioms are assumptions to be neither proved nor disproved, but taken as defining properties or self-evident truths. The concept is as old as Aristotle and *Euclid (fourth century BC). Following their example a distinction used to be made between axioms (for example, 'Things equal to the same thing are equal to each other') and *postulates (for example, 'Only one straight line can be drawn through a point parallel to a given line'). But modern mathematics does not make the distinction, and all statements taken as unproved assumptions are called axioms. To ask whether they are true or not may be irrelevant or even meaningless.

**axis of the Earth**, an imaginary straight line through the Earth's centre and both poles, about which it rotates. This is not at right angles to the plane of the Earth's orbit round the Sun, the *ecliptic, but at an angle of 66° 33′; and its direction relative to the stars is not fixed since it rotates very slowly round the perpendicular to the orbit plane, completing a revolution once every 26,000 years, and causing the *precession of the equinoxes. Thus, although for some centuries its northern end has pointed very nearly to the Pole Star (Alpha Ursae Minoris), this was not, nor will it be, always the case. The axis will in fact describe in due course a cone. Other minor deviations in its direction, and thus in the precise locations of the poles, are constantly being observed by astronomers all over the world, notably at the South Pole.

**Ayers Rock** (in Aboriginal, U luru), an *inselberg or rock mound in Northern Territory, Australia, rising 348 m (1,143 feet) in isolation above the flat, sandy desert. It has a long, rounded summit and measures over 8 km (5 miles) round the base. The Rock is composed of *conglomerate interbedded with layers of red sandstone, both tilted vertically. Parallel gutters show the erosional characteristics of the different rocks. It is between 400 and 600 million years old and is one of the largest rock mounds in the world. To several of the country's Aboriginal tribes it is a sacred place.

An **avalanche** of ice and snow pours down the north ridge of Karyolung in the Himalayas.

**azeotrope** (in chemistry), a mixture of two liquids whose boiling-point remains unchanged as the mixture vaporizes during distillation. The distillate has the same composition as the liquid, so the components cannot be separated by distillation. Ethanol and water form an azeotrope containing 95.6 per cent ethanol by mass, which boils at 78.2 °C (172.8 °F). If the liquids are mixed in any other proportion, the composition and boiling-point both approach these values as evaporation proceeds.

**Azerbaijan**, a country on the west coast of the Caspian Sea bordered by Armenia to the west, Georgia and Russia to the north, and Iraq to the south. The Apsheron Peninsula in the north contains the long-established Baku oilfields. The hot and arid Kura valley runs towards the south-east below the Caucasian foothills, cotton and tobacco being cultivated along the river banks. The Caspian coastal plain with a sub-tropical climate is more naturally fertile; and round it lie well-wooded hills with deep valleys. The mountainous south-west contains the large and scenic Lake Gyoygyol and numerous deposits of copper, iron, and lead.

**azimuth**, a true bearing usually measured eastwards from North. It can be obtained either by observation and calculation from two survey marks of known position, or by observations to the sun and stars taken at known times or with known altitudes.

**azonal soil**, a relatively young soil developed on recently laid down sediments, on rock which is very resistant to weathering, or on steep slopes where erosion removes most of the unconsolidated material. It has therefore only been exposed to the influence of the active factors of soil formation, such as climate and vegetation, for a relatively short time. As a result it has had insufficient time to develop the characteristics typical of *zonal soil at the same latitudes. It tends to be shallow and to lack well-defined *horizons. *Lithosols and *regosols are types of azonal soils.

**Azores**, a group of ten islands set out in three groups in the North Atlantic Ocean. Partially autonomous from Portugal, they are of volcanic origin and stand on the great *Mid-Atlantic Ridge, the largest being San Miguel some 66 km (41 miles) long and 15 km (9 miles) wide. Pico in the central group rises to 2,316 m (7,598 feet), and small volcanic eruptions still cause disturbances. Hot springs and *fumaroles are a feature on some of the islands, which are steep and heavily dissected by valleys. The winters are mild and the soil fertile, yielding fruit, grain, tobacco, and rich pasture.

**Azov, Sea of**, a gulf in the south of Ukraine, joined to the Black Sea by the Strait of Kerch, whose strong currents make navigation difficult. The Don, Kuban, and lesser rivers flow into the sea and make its waters almost fresh, although some secluded inlets are very saline. They also silt it up: with a depth of only 10 m (33 feet) it is the world's shallowest sea. Except for the southern shore, which is jagged with limestone rocks, the coastline consists of low-lying sandstones; and in some places alluvial spits extend across estuaries and bays. Annual freezing of the water begins in November–December and reaches a maximum extent in February before thawing in March–April. A combination of heavy frosts and thaws produces frequent fogs.

# B

**background radiation**, low intensity ionizing radiation which is always present in the environment. Most background radiation comes from natural sources such as cosmic rays and some types of rocks (for example granite in the Earth's crust); the rest—about 13 per cent—comes from artificial sources. Of the artificial sources the one that contributes most to the background radiation is the medical use of radioactive materials: other sources are the nuclear industry and fallout from weapons tests, television screens and luminous paint. When the radiation from a specific source is measured, the background radiation must be deducted from the result to make it accurate.

**backwash**, the flow of water down a beach under the influence of gravity after the breaking of a wave and its associated *swash. As this water returns to the breaker zone it carries beach material with it. Steep waves, which break almost vertically on to a beach, have an extremely powerful backwash and move much material out to sea. Backwash contributes to *longshore drift.

**Bacon, Roger** (c.1219–c.92), English scholar, educational reformer, and monk. Based at Oxford and Paris, he introduced the study of Aristotle in the West, as well as of languages, optics, and alchemy. He elucidated the principles of *refraction, *reflection, and spherical aberration, and described spectacles, which soon thereafter came into use. He developed many mathematical results concerning lenses, proposed mechanically propelled ships, carriages, and flying machines, and used a camera obscura to observe eclipses of the Sun. A proponent of experimental science, he produced, at the request of Pope Clement IV, treatises on the sciences (grammar, logic, mathematics, physics, and modern philosophy), but was confined to prison for his unorthodox views by his own monastic order, the Franciscan.

**badlands** (in geomorphology), areas of bare ground which have been intensely eroded by running water into a maze of miniature canyons and steep slopes. There may be hundreds of tiny stream channels within a single square kilometre or mile, with the channels containing water only after rainstorms. Common on clays and shales in areas where the climate is semi-arid, they occur also on the tip-heaps of mines, especially of china-clay workings, in areas where the climate is wetter. Resistant layers of rock are often left as cappings on pillars of softer rock; these structures are known as hoodoos, or pedestal rocks.

**Badlands National Monument**, an arid plateau in south-western South Dakota, USA. Volcanic ash from ancient eruptions covers several hundred square kilometres to a depth of some 90 m (300 feet), and deep gullies have exposed rocks of several hues. Herds of mammoths and other prehistoric animals were engulfed by the ash, and their fossil remains can be seen today. These original 'bad lands to cross' have given their name to other similar landscapes.

**Baffin, William** (c.1584–1622), English navigator and explorer who in 1616 discovered the largest island of the

Steep rock faces, deeply incised gullies, and a thin soil restricted to the gully bottoms, typify the barren scenery of the **Badlands National Monument** in south-west South Dakota, USA. The region has yielded some of America's most dramatic fossil finds.

Canadian Arctic and the strait between it and Greenland, named respectively Baffin Island and Baffin Bay in his honour. In the services of the Muscovy Company, he charted the waters north of Davis Strait. As a member of the East India Company from 1617, he served in the Persian Gulf where, in an expedition arranged by the Persian government to expel the Portuguese, he was killed in an engagement with the Dutch and Portuguese. He wrote accounts of most of his voyages.

**Baffin Island**, the largest and most easterly island in the Canadian Arctic and one of the largest in the world. West of Greenland, it lies largely within the Arctic Circle and is mostly Precambrian. It is 1,600 km (1,000 miles) long and 210–720 km (130–450 miles) wide, with an irregular coastline. The plateau rises to 1,000 m (3,280 feet) in the east; and mountains, glaciers, and snowfields rise to 2,440 m (8,000 feet), having permanent ice-caps. Precipitation is light and winter temperatures are very cold.

**Bahamas**, an archipelago of 700 mainly coral islands in the western Atlantic Ocean, set between Florida and Hispaniola and having Cuba to their south. Some thirty are large enough to live on, the largest being the Grand Bahama and New Providence islands. The climate is very warm in winter and also in summer, which is the rainy season.

**Bahrain**, a country comprising a group of islands 32 km (20 miles) off the Arabian coast of the Gulf, the largest being some 16 km (10 miles) wide and three times as long. The climate is hot and humid, although rainfall is very light. The islands contain large deposits of both oil and natural gas, and *bauxite from which aluminium is extracted.

**Baikal, Lake**, in south-east Siberia, Eurasia's largest freshwater lake, at some 640 km (395 miles) in length. At over 1,700 m (5,600 feet) in depth in places, it is also the world's deepest lake. It receives over three hundred streams from surrounding mountains and has only one outlet: the Angara River, a prolific source of hydroelectricity. It is frozen for four months of the year, but is otherwise navigable. It contains a number of large islands, the chief of which is Olkhon. The lake now suffers heavily from industrial pollution.

**Balearic Islands**, a Spanish archipelago in the western Mediterranean Sea comprising three large islands and several smaller ones. The largest, Majorca, has the best climate. Minorca is unprotected from the north and has cold winds, while Ibiza, the third in size, sometimes suffers from the *sirocco which blows up from the North African coast. Majorca has coastal highlands. Vineyards and olive groves flourish on the protected inland plain, as do oranges and figs. Pine trees on the hillsides are grown for timber.

**Bali**, east of Java in Indonesia, one of the world's most spectacular islands, covering an area of 5,700 km² (2,200 sq. mi.). In the north, volcanoes rise to over 3,200 m (10,000 feet) and

Lake **Baikal** contains about one-fifth of the fresh water on the Earth's surface. It is surrounded by mountains and lies on rock that is more than 500 million years old.

their craters contain lakes of great depth. In the south there is a large, fertile plain on which rice is grown. The coast has palm-fringed beaches facing the sea.

**Balkan Peninsula**, the great peninsula of south-east Europe, bounded by the Adriatic, Aegean, and Black Seas. It is very mountainous, taking its name from the Balkan Mountains south of the Danube. The Dinaric Alps of Croatia, the Pindus Mountains of Greece, and the Rhodope Mountains of Bulgaria, the other main ranges, all act as barriers to the mild climate of the Mediterranean, and winters, especially in the north-east, can be intensely cold. The scenery varies greatly, from the barren *karst country of Croatia, to the wooded slopes of the Rila Mountains in Bulgaria, and to the flat Danubian plains. Most of the principal rivers flow east or south-east, although the Morava provides a central outlet to the north. Earth tremors are fairly frequent, especially in the west and south, for the peninsula lies at a junction of crustal *plates.

**Balkhash, Lake**, a hook-shaped lake, curving for some 560 km (350 miles) through south-east Kazakhstan, central Asia. It is very shallow, saline in its eastern half, and is slowly evaporating. Across its centre a vast sand-bar separates its western half, which receives the fresh waters of the Ili River. There is no outlet, and the water is frozen for five months in the year. The northern shore rises to the Kazakh uplands through a region which is rich in copper.

**Balmer, Johann** (1825–98), Swiss physicist, who analysed the light emitted by hot hydrogen and discovered that the most prominent wavelengths in the *spectrum are linked by a simple formula. These wavelengths are seen as a series of lines, now known as the Balmer series. His formula is basic to the subsequent development of atomic theory and to the field of atomic spectroscopy.

**Baltic Sea**, the shallow inland sea of northern Europe. At the close of the last ice age it covered the central lake belt of Sweden, extended eastwards into Russia, and was joined to the North Sea by a broad channel. Now the Gulf of Bothnia marks its northern extremity and the Gulf of Finland and the Gulf of Riga its eastern ones, while in the west narrow channels lead to the Kattegat and Skagerrak and thence to the North Sea. This confinement, coupled with the flow into it of many rivers, such as the Oder and Vistula, makes its water less saline than ocean water. As it is cut off from the warm *North Atlantic Drift, large areas freeze in winter. Its average depth is only 36 m (120 feet), and sandbanks and shoals in many places make navigation difficult.

**Baltic Shield**    *Fennoscandian Shield.

**band theory**. In single atoms, the orbiting electrons have a specific energy (see *energy levels). When atoms come together to form a solid, the dense packing of so many atoms leads to interactions between the electrons, which cause their specific energies to spread across a range of values.

**Barchans** (crescent dunes) formed on the upper surface of a sand ridge in the Namib Desert, south-west Africa.

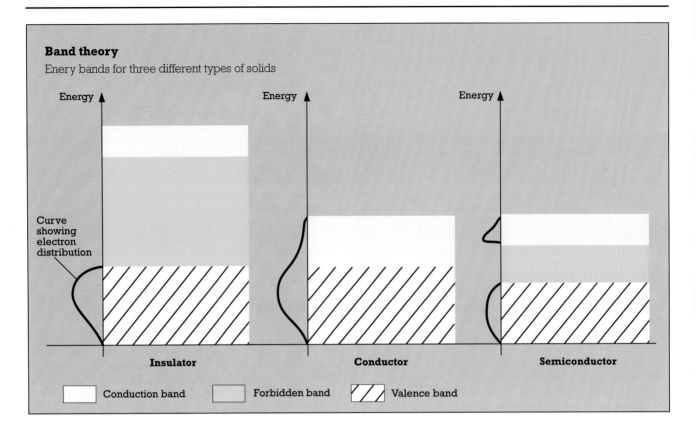

**Band theory**
Enery bands for three different types of solids

Energy

Curve
showing
electron
distribution

**Insulator**                    **Conductor**                    **Semiconductor**

Conduction band          Forbidden band          Valence band

This range of energy values is called an energy band. The two main bands are called the valence band and the conduction band. Electrons in the valence band are responsible for the *chemical bonds which hold atoms together to form the solid; electrons in the conduction band carry electric current (see *electricity). The conduction band is at a higher *energy level than the valence band. The separation of these two bands in the electronic structure of a solid determines whether the solid is a conductor, *semiconductor or insulator. In a conductor the valence and conduction bands overlap, so that valence electrons can easily move into the conduction band range of energies and conduct electricity. In an insulator the valence band is separated from the conduction band by a large gap called the forbidden gap. Electrons from the valence band cannot cross this gap to the conduction band, and so the solid does not conduct electricity. If the forbidden gap is small and some electrons can acquire enough energy to jump from the valence band to the conduction band, then the solid is a semiconductor.

**Bangladesh**, a tropical, low-lying Asian country at the head of the Bay of Bengal. Most of it is occupied by the deltas of the Ganges and the Brahmaputra. It is a land of rivers, which flood regularly in the *monsoon season, leaving fertile soil on their banks. The south-west delta area, the Sundarbans, is mainly swamp and jungle; the region is subject to frequent *cyclones which are funnelled up the Bay of Bengal and exacerbated by large-scale deforestation, thus causing immense damage and loss of life and crops. Jute is the main export. There are substantial reserves of oil, coal, and natural gas.

**bar, marine**, an elongated ridge of sediment (such as mud, sand, or shingle) that generally forms some distance off shore, parallel to a coastline. Bars are confined to areas where the sea-bed slopes very gently and form when waves break some distance away from the coast, excavating material from the sea floor; the material is redeposited nearer the

**Basalt** cliffs 40 m (135 feet) high almost completely encircle the tiny island of Staffa in the Scottish Hebrides. The lava flow cooled to form hexagonal columns.

shore as a ridge. Such ridges may or may not project above the sea at low tide and so are a hazard to shipping.

**bar, river**   *point bar.

**Barbados**, the most easterly of the Windward Islands in the Caribbean Sea. Of coral formation, it is about 34 km (21 miles) long by 22 km (14 miles) wide and rises in gentle stages to some 336 m (1,100 feet). The climate is very warm with heavy rain watering the sugar cane, from which molasses is produced.

**Barbuda**   *Antigua.

**barchan**, a *dune of sand or snow blown by wind into crescent shapes, with the horns trailing downwind on either side of a steep, downwind lee side.

**Barcoo River**   *Cooper's Creek.

**Barents, Willem** (c.1550–97), Dutch explorer and leader of several expeditions in search of a *North-East Passage to Asia, south of the Arctic Ocean. He discovered Spitsbergen and reached the Novaya Zemlya archipelago north of European Russia. His accurate charting and valuable meteorological data make him one of the most important of the early Arctic explorers. The Barents Sea is named after him.

**Barents Sea** (Murmean Sea), a part of the Arctic Ocean to the north of Russia, bounded by Spitsbergen, Franz Josef Land, and Novaya Zemlya. Navigation in the north is restricted by pack-ice; but the *North Atlantic Drift is just sufficient to keep the southern coasts clear. Once considered essential in the search for the North-East Passage, this southern region became a useful fishing-ground. The underlying sea-bed is believed to be rich in oil. A southern arm, more frequently frozen, is known as the White Sea.

**barite**, (or barytes, barium sulphate, $BaSO_4$), the chief ore of barium occurring in mineral veins with lead and zinc minerals. It is usually colourless with a vitreous or pearly lustre. Barite is used in paint manufacture and in paper-making as well as drilling for oil.

**barium** (symbol Ba, at. no. 56, r.a.m. 137.33), a silver metallic element, one of the *alkaline earth metals. It is reactive, combining with non-metals, water, and acids to form ionic salts. Barium compounds give a green colour in the flame test, and are used in flares and fireworks; they are also used in thermionic cathodes.

**baroclinicity**, a variation in atmospheric or oceanic density over a region of constant pressure; in such circumstances isobaric surfaces are inclined to surfaces of equal density. (This contrasts with barotropic conditions in which density and pressure surfaces are parallel.) Fronts in which such density variation occurs are said to be baroclinic. In the atmosphere the variation causes the air to be disturbed in two ways. Firstly, there is large-scale circulation when air is cooled and thereby becomes denser and sinks, undercutting warmer and lighter air, which is forced to rise and flow over the colder air. Secondly, smaller-scale circulations result from a turbulent mixing of air along the boundary between the denser and lighter masses. Both processes contribute to the formation of cloud in frontal zones. In the ocean, such fronts are often characterized by *meanders and *eddies.

**barrier island**, an accumulation of sand or a shingle forming bar roughly parallel to the coast but separated from it by a shallow stretch of water, or lagoon. Many barrier islands, such as Palm Beach, Florida, USA, and the Lido at Venice, Italy, are now seaside resorts. The Frisian Islands in the North Sea are also used for farming. Many smaller ones, such as the Outer Banks, North Carolina, USA, remain a hazard to shipping.

**barrier reef**, a large mass of coral that lies parallel to a coast or encircles an island but is separated from the land by channels or *lagoons, often of considerable depth and width. Most of the reef is shallowly submerged, but extensive coral sandflats may accumulate above sea-level. The *Great Barrier Reef is the most extensive; others exist in the Bermudas and elsewhere in tropical waters. As coral can only grow in clear, unmuddied water, there are usually gaps in barrier reefs opposite river mouths.

**Barth, Heinrich** (1821–65), German explorer of West Africa south of the Sahara. From Lake Chad he set out on a journey of 16,090 km (10,000 miles) to explore the area south and south-east of Lake Chad. He mapped the upper reaches of the Benue River and gave an accurate account of the River Niger. He published much valuable anthropological, historical, and linguistic data on Central Africa.

**baryon**, an elementary particle which undergoes reactions due to the strong force. It consists of three *quarks, and has a half-integral spin ($\frac{1}{2}$, $\frac{3}{2}$, and so on). Baryons are one group of *hadrons (the *mesons are the other). Protons and neutrons are baryons.

**barytes**   *barite.

**basalt**, a dark, fine-grained rock, the most common of the extrusive *igneous rocks, composed essentially of *plagioclase feldspar and *pyroxene. Having a low silica content, basaltic lava, when erupted from a volcano, quickly spreads out in a thin veneer before solidifying. Under the sea, basalt flows are also very extensive, being found along *mid-oceanic ridges as a product of upwelling lava; they solidify in pillow-like structures called pillow lavas. The *crust of *ocean basins is formed almost entirely of basalt lavas above and *gabbros beneath, and is overlain with *sediments ranging in thickness from a few metres to several kilometres. Most *sea mounts and oceanic islands (for example, the Azores, and Hawaii) are formed of basalts erupted from submarine volcanoes. The largest basalt flows on the Earth's surface are in the Deccan, India, and on the Columbia–Snake River plateau, USA, but extensive flows thousands of metres thick are also found in Greenland, Brazil, and Iceland. On cooling, basalts often shrink into polygonal pillars and can produce locally spectacular scenery; one of the most famous of these sites is the *Giant's Causeway, County Antrim, Northern Ireland. More than 90 per cent of all volcanic rocks are basalt. They are quarried for building stones and are crushed for building aggregates, road stone, and ballast.

**base**, any of a class of chemical compounds that can neutralize an *acid to give a salt and water. Typically bases are metal hydroxides, oxides, and carbonates. Like acids, bases can be poisonous and corrosive; strong bases such as sodium hydroxide (caustic soda) have to be handled with great care. An alkali is a base that is soluble in water. A basic solution has a *hydrogen ion concentration greater than 7 on the pH scale, and will turn litmus blue. Strong bases will completely dissociate and have high pH values. According to the Brønsted–Lowry theory a base is a substance which will accept protons in the form of hydrogen ions, H⁺. In the Lewis theory a base is a substance that can donate electron pairs; thus ammonia can be regarded as a Lewis base because it contains a *lone pair of electrons.

**baseflow** (rivers), the discharge which comes from the slow and steady drainage of water from natural reservoirs in rock and the deeper layers of the soil. It contrasts with a flood, which is produced by storms or melting snow. Rivers fed by large *springs in areas of limestone, sandstone, or lava have substantial, reliable baseflows, whereas those in areas of thin soil or on impermeable rock-like clay have little or no baseflow, drying up periodically. Rivers with large baseflows have always been very important for settlement, agriculture, and navigation.

**base level**, the lowest point to which rivers can cut their channels and, theoretically, the lowest point to which other agents can reduce the land's surface (that is, the depth below which erosion would be unable to occur). Sea-level acts as a grand base level for the denudation of entire land masses; lakes and major rivers represent local base levels for smaller, upland valleys. Because rivers and their tributaries require at least some gradient in order to flow, their effective base levels are actually very gently sloping surfaces, rather than horizontal ones like the base levels of seas and lakes. Whenever land lies above base level, agents of erosion that are driven by gravity will be at work lowering its surface, however slowly. Sometimes land lies below the expected base level. For example, the Dead Sea lies below sea-level, and this is because major faulting has depressed a large section of the Earth's crust. Earthquakes and faulting quite often cause depressions of base level; and erosion by moving ice or by wind can create small depressions below base level because both ice and wind can flow uphill. Even so, all depressions below base level are being filled in, however gradually, by the deposition of debris.

**baseline** (in surveying), one measured side of a triangle that, with other connected triangles, forms the basis of a framework from which are made the less accurate measurements required to map detailed features. It may be measured by pacing, or using a chain or tape, or in recent years by electronic distance measurement (EDM). The angles of the framework determine its shape, and the lengths of the baseline or baselines its size and scale.

**basement complex** (in geology), an extensive mass of very old (generally *Precambrian) igneous and metamorphic rocks overlain by sedimentary rocks that have not suffered *metamorphism. The term is used, for example, to describe the crystalline rocks of Africa and Arabia.

**batholith**, a very large *igneous rock mass that has been injected upwards, while still molten, into the surrounding *country rock. Some of the largest batholiths are more than 1,000 km (600 miles) long. They are steep-sided, generally cutting across any sedimentary structures, and are commonly aligned along mountain ranges associated with crustal plate activity (see *plate tectonics) as with, for example, the Coast Range batholith of western USA and the Andean batholith of South America. Composed usually of

granite, they are the source of many minerals, which are generally in workable deposits.

**bauxite**, a general term for mixtures of aluminium oxides. The chief commercial source of aluminium, it is soft, light, and earthy. Bauxite is produced by the weathering of rocks containing aluminium in hot climates where there are both wet seasons, when *leaching occurs, and long, dry periods when the aluminium ions are drawn back to the surface by capillary action. Constant repetition of this tropical weathering process removes other elements from the rocks and enables the bauxite to be formed. Regions in which such conditions occur are widespread, but exist notably in Jamaica, eastern Europe, the Balkans, and Hungary. The occurrence of bauxites at Les Baux, near Arles in the south of France, is the result of tropical weathering more than 60 million years ago.

**Bavaria** (German, 'Bayern'), a region of southern Germany, a plateau area with sandstone hills in the north-west and basalt hills and high plateaux in the north. Limestone

Alternating strata or **bedding** of limestone and shale form a sheer cliff on the coast of South Wales. Note how the soft shale is more deeply eroded than the harder limestone, and how vertical jointing has caused the limestone to break into regular blocks.

hills in the Franconian Jura along the River Danube separate North and South Bavaria. The Böhmerwald (Bohemian Forest) bordering the Czech Republic forms the eastern boundary, while south of the Danube the plateau merges into the Bavarian Alps at an average elevation of 2,000 m (7,000 feet).

**bay**, a curving indentation of the coastline between two promontories or headlands. Usually bays are wider at their seaward end than they are long. In general, therefore, they are a different shape from *gulfs; they are also generally smaller, although larger than coves. The term is sometimes also used for a recess in a mountain range.

**bayou**, in the southern USA, a sluggish backwater stream with little current, especially the lower Mississippi valley. Bayous often have extremely winding channels and occasionally form bayou or *ox-bow lakes.

**beach**, a narrow area along a coast (or along a shore of a lake or inland sea) where loose, unconsolidated material, particularly shingle and sand, has accumulated, particularly in the zone between low water mark and the highest point reached by storm waves. These loose sediments, which are derived either from the weathering of the adjacent areas of cliffs and headlands or from the erosion of material from the sea floor, are underlain by *shore platforms of solid rock. Extensive areas of sandflat, only fully uncovered at very low tides, such as those of Morecambe Bay, Lancashire, England, or Long Beach, Washington, USA, are typical of beaches forming in areas where the continental shelf is very wide, wave energy low, or the tidal range limited. Elsewhere, the presence of a beach will protect a backing cliff. Most beaches are gently sloping with concave profiles along which specific features occur in a regular order. Typically, the landward edge of the beach is marked by sand dunes. These give way to shingle ridges, deposited by storm waves, and then to sandy areas which are characterized by a series of small ridges, or berms, parallel to the shore. These form at the limit of wave action at each high *tide. As maximum tide height falls during the regular monthly cycle of spring to neap, a series of such ridges is produced down the beach; they are short-lived features which will be destroyed again when the height of the tide next increases. The seaward edge of the beach is frequently marked by low rocky ridges, which are often covered in seaweed.

**Beaufort scale**, a system for estimating wind speeds with reference to the behaviour of certain standard subjects, such as smoke, trees, and the surface of the sea. For example, if it is calm, smoke rises vertically; in a gale whole trees are in motion, and in a hurricane the surface of the sea foams and is white with driving spray. Devised by the British hydrographer, Francis Beaufort (1774–1857), it grades wind force on a scale 0–12. A breeze is in the range 2–6; a strong wind or gale is 7–9; and storm to hurricane conditions, with wind speeds of 48 to over 65 knots (88 to over 120 km/h, 55 to over 75 m.p.h.), are 10–12.

**Beche, Sir Henry Thomas de la** (1796–1855), British geologist who established the Geological Survey of Great Britain in 1835. His early work in Devon and Cornwall resulted in the description and illustration for the first time of the Jurassic and Cretaceous strata of those regions. He supervised the drawing up of a geological map of England, the first large scale methodological geological survey.

**becquerel** (symbol Bq), the *SI unit of radioactivity. The activity of a source is the number of nuclear disintegrations it undergoes per unit time—thus a source with an activity of 1 becquerel undergoes one disintegration per second. Laboratory sources may have activities of about $10^4$ Bq, whereas some medical or industrial sources might have an activity of approximately $10^{14}$ Bq. The unit is named after Henri *Becquerel, the French scientist who discovered nuclear radiation in 1896.

**Becquerel, Antoine César** and **(Antoine) Henri** (grandfather and grandson), French physicists who, each in his turn, made important scientific advances. While working as Professor of Physics at the Musée d'Histoire Naturelle in Paris, A. C. Becquerel (1788–1878) made an extensive study of the chemical effects of *electric current. He was awarded a Royal Society medal for this work. Henri Becquerel (1852–1908) carried out research into atmospheric polarization. He also investigated the properties of natural radiation from uranium salts and is chiefly remembered as the discoverer of *radioactivity. He shared the Nobel prize for Physics in 1903 with Marie and Pierre *Curie for this achievement.

**bedding** (stratification), in geology, the term for the layering that is present in most *sedimentary rocks, of which it is a characteristic feature. Usually, but not always, a bedding plane is parallel to the surface on which a sediment was laid down. Bedding occurs in rocks deposited in the sea, in a lake, or on land. It may be the result of a pause in the accumulation of sediment or of a change in the type of sediment deposited: shale within a coal-seam, for example. Generally it can be recognized by differences in colour, texture, or pattern. The layer of rock between two adjacent bedding planes is called a bed or stratum. In stratigraphy, bed (or beds) is also used in informal terms for rock units that are not strictly defined and are composed of several strata.

**bed load**, that part of the load of debris which is too big or too heavy to move smoothly within the current of a river. Instead, it is pushed and bounced along the bed of the channel and is the first to stop moving when the speed and force of flow decrease. The size of particles moved as bed load increases with the speed of the current: sand moves as bed load in gentle flows, while huge boulders may be shifted by large floods. Heavy minerals, such as gold, also move as bed load, which is why miners 'pan' river gravels.

**bedrock**, the solid rock that lies below loose sand, gravel, or soil. Where visible it is seen as an outcrop protruding through the superficial cover.

**Beilstein, Friedrich Konrad** (1838–1906), chemist born in St Petersburg of German parents, best known as the first editor of the *Handbuch der Organischen Chemie*, commonly referred to as 'Beilstein'. This major reference work, kept up to date by periodic supplements, is a compendium of all known organic compounds and now occupies more than a hundred volumes.

**Belarus** (Russian, 'White Russia'), a country bounded on the west by Poland, on the north-west by Latvia and Lithuania, on the north and east by Russia, and on the south by Ukraine. Gentle hills run through a series of low plains which are forested with conifer, oak, lime, and ash. Cold in winter and warm in summer, the climate is predominantly wet, and many rivers drain the land into the vast area of the

## Benzene rings

The Kekulé hypothesis for the structure of benzene has now been superseded by the orbital model.

### The Kekulé structure

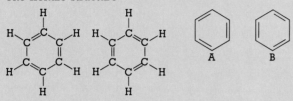

According to this structure the carbon–carbon single bonds and double bonds should be of different lengths (154 pm and 134 pm respectively). However, it is found that all the carbon–carbon bonds in benzene have the same length of 139 pm. Thus the benzene molecule can be thought of as changing continually between structures A and B.

### The orbital model

This model has superseded the Kekulé structure. Each carbon atom in benzene has four *orbitals available for bonding. The 2s orbital and two p orbitals are 'hybridized' to give three $sp^2$ orbitals. The remaining p orbital is not hybridized.

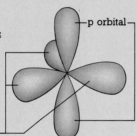

— p orbital —

$sp^2$ hybrid orbitals —

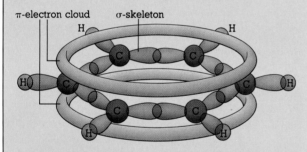

π-electron cloud   σ-skeleton

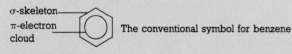

σ-skeleton
π-electron cloud   The conventional symbol for benzene

The $sp^2$ orbitals form three sigma bonds: two with other carbon atoms and one with a hydrogen atom. All these bonds are in the same plane. The six remaining p orbitals, one from each carbon atom, combine to form a delocalized pi electron cloud.

### The naming of benzene derivatives

functional group

1,2,3,4-tetramethylbenzene

benzoic acid

3-methylbenzoic acid, or
m-methylbenzoic acid

o, ortho-
m, meta-
p, para-

Pripet Marshes. Agriculture and animal husbandry are possible on a wide scale; and there are mineral deposits.

**Belgium**, a European country bordering the North Sea and bounded inland by The Netherlands, Germany, Luxemburg, and France. The coastal area comprises broad, sandy beaches backed by dunes. Inland, most of the rivers run across the flat, fertile Flanders Plain, north-eastward to The Netherlands. In the south-east the land rises from the Sambre–Meuse valley with its exhausted coalfields to the highlands of the Ardennes. Here the soil is poor, and the land generally forested. The Campine coalfield is in the east. Apart from coal and a little iron and copper, Belgium has almost no natural resources. The climate is cool and wet, with warm summers.

**Belize**, a small tropical country lying at the south of the Yucatán Peninsula in Central America. It is bounded by Guatemala to the west and the Caribbean Sea to the east, from which sea breezes temper the hot and humid rain forest; only in the south does it rise to pine forest and savannah. It is near an earthquake belt and is occasionally subject to hurricanes. Exports include sugar and citrus fruits.

**Bellingshausen, Fabian Gottlieb von** (1778–1852), Estonian-born Russian admiral who was the first to circumnavigate Antarctica. His discovery of islands within the Antarctic Circle (1821) was the first sighting of land there, and the Bellingshausen Sea was named after him.

**bench-mark**, a surveyor's mark cut in a wall, pillar, building or similar structure, and used as a reference point in measuring altitudes. In computing a benchmark is a task to be performed in a computer system, to measure the performance of the system under certain conditions, or undertaking certain classes of work.

**Bengal**, a region comprising Bangladesh and an adjacent part of India. It is dominated by the vast alluvial plains and deltas, which are still expanding from deposits of silt, from the Ganges and Brahmaputra Rivers. Rarely over 15 m (50 feet) in height, the centre of Bengal is an area of dead and dying rivers as a result of the joint delta migrating from west to east. West of the Hooghly River the swampy land rises to the Chota Nagpur plateau, while to the east the Lushai Hills form a boundary. The northern extremity is the Surma valley area. In the tropical climate, with heavy monsoon rainfall, rice and jute are grown.

**Benguela Current**, a broad, shallow, slow-moving body of cool water flowing northward along the west coast of southern Africa, part of the anticlockwise circulation system, or *gyre, of the South Atlantic Ocean. In this oceanic region, between latitude 15° S. and 35° S., the prevailing winds displace the surface waters away from the coast, a process which causes an *upwelling of subsurface waters to replace them. These subsurface waters are rich in nutrients which encourage the growth of plankton and other marine life, giving rise to fertile fishing grounds.

**Benin**, a West African country lying between Togo and Nigeria. It has a southern coastline of only 125 km (78 miles) but extends inland for 700 km (460 miles) to Niger. The coast is sandy with large lagoons and is hot and wet. Inland there is a fertile clay plain with thick tropical forest that rises to a sandy plateau with *savannah vegetation. In the north the land falls away to the middle Niger River valley. Small deposits of gold and chrome have been found. Cotton and vegetable oil are exported.

**Ben Nevis**, the highest peak in the British Isles, in the Grampian Mountains in western Scotland. It is composed of ancient *metamorphic and *igneous rocks. At 1,343 m (4,406 feet) it overlooks Glen Nevis on the west and south, while on its north-eastern side there is a sheer precipice of 442 m (1,450 feet).

**benthic**   *boundary layer (in oceanography).

**benzene ring**, the characteristic feature of most *aromatic compounds, of which the prototype is benzene itself. The molecular formula of benzene is $C_6H_6$; it is a colourless,

flammable, toxic liquid with an unpleasant aromatic odour. Its structure consists of a hexagon of carbon atoms, to each of which is bonded a hydrogen atom. All twelve atoms lie in the same plane. The bonding in this hexagon, the benzene ring, is as follows: within the plane of the ring are localized sigma electrons, and above and below the plane of the ring are two identical clouds of delocalized pi electrons (see *delocalized electrons). The effect of delocalization is to reduce the repulsions between electrons and thus to lower the energy of the molecule; for this reason, there are many naturally occurring compounds containing benzene rings. Moreover, benzene rings undergo reactions in which this delocalization is retained, namely substitution reactions, rather than those in which it is destroyed, namely addition reactions (see *chemical reaction). It was formerly thought that the bonding between the carbon atoms involved alternate double and single bonds (the *Kekulé structure). However, the existence of such double bonds would suggest, incorrectly, that benzene undergoes addition reactions. Also, all the carbon–carbon bonds are of identical length (see figure).

**Bergeron, Tor** (1891–1977), Swedish meteorologist, best known for his work on cloud physics. He was the first met-

The **Bering Sea** is linked to the Chukchi Sea by the relatively shallow Bering Strait separating the Chukotskiy Peninsula (Siberia) from the western tip of Alaska's Seward Peninsula. The International Date Line, which here coincides with the boundary between Russia and the USA, runs between Big Diomede and Little Diomede islands in the middle of the Strait.

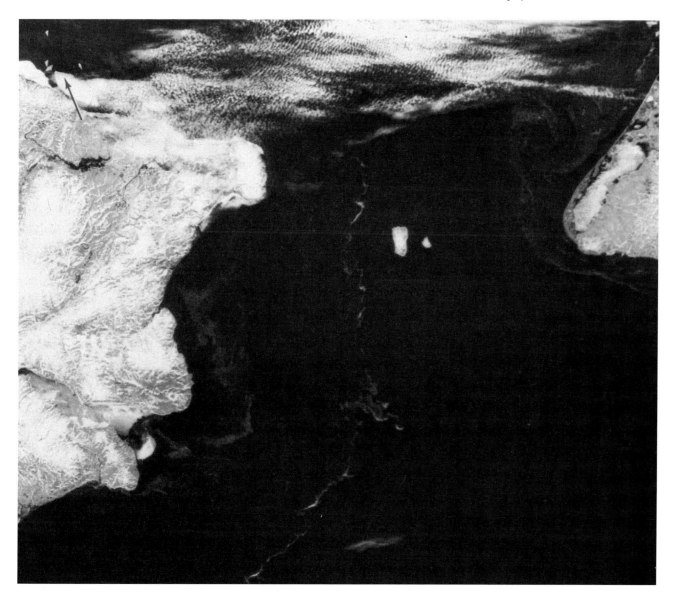

eorologist to take into account the upper atmospheric phenomena and their effect on climate. He demonstrated that raindrops can form in the upper parts of clouds, which contain little liquid water, through the growth of ice crystals. This happens at temperatures between −10 °C and −30 °C (14 °F and −22 °F) and is known as the Bergeron process.

**bergschrund**, a crack which occurs at the head of a *cirque glacier, between the main body of the ice and the rock of the back wall.

**Bering, Vitus Jonassen** (1680–1741), Danish navigator and explorer of Arctic Asia, who led several Russian expeditions aimed at discovering whether Asia and North America were connected by land. He sailed along the coast of Siberia and in 1741 reached Alaska from the east. On the return journey his ship foundered and he died on an island which now bears his name. Also named after him are the Bering Sea and Bering Strait (between Asia and America, connecting the Bering Sea with the Arctic Ocean).

**Bering Sea**, the northern arm of the Pacific Ocean between Siberia and Alaska. The volcanic Aleutian Islands ring its basin on the south, while the 90-km (55-mile) wide Bering Strait links it with the Arctic Ocean. A large proportion of the sea overlies one of the largest *continental shelves in the world, over 600 km (370 miles) wide in the north-east. In contrast to this there are areas as deep as 4,000 m (13,000 feet) in the south-west of it. It receives the Anadyr River from Siberia and the Yukon from Alaska, while through the Strait flows the ice which hampers all winter navigation. America and Asia were once connected where the Strait now separates them; and it is thought that people from Asia once crossed the isthmus, settling in North and South America to become the ancestors of the American Indians. As dry land it also provided an important migration route for plants and animals.

**berm** *beach.

**Bermuda**, a group of more than a hundred tiny coral islands, sometimes called the Bermudas, lying in the western Atlantic Ocean at latitude 32° N. They are composed of a layer 60 m (200 feet) thick of limestone, polyps, coral, and other marine organisms, capping an extinct and submerged volcanic mountain range rising 4,200 to 4,500 m (14,000 to 15,000 feet) above the ocean floor.

**Bermuda Triangle**, a region of the North Atlantic Ocean, centred on Bermuda and extending from 25° N. to 40° N. and from 55° W. to 85° W., credited since the mid-19th century with a number of unexplained losses of ships and, later, aircraft. Some ships were subsequently discovered abandoned, but others were never seen or heard from again. Scientific studies have revealed nothing to substantiate the arcane theories surrounding the disappearances, however recent advances in deep-sea diving technology have now enabled many of the wrecks to be located.

**Bernoulli**, family of Belgian origin that settled in Switzerland and produced many prominent mathematicians within three generations. Jacob, or Jacques, Bernoulli (1654–1705) was a founder of *probability theory and the calculus of variations, while his brother Johannes, or Jean, Bernoulli (1667–1748) developed many applications of the *calculus to physics. Daniel Bernoulli (1700–82) made important contri-

butions to *hydrodynamics and propounded a version of the *kinetic theory of gases. He outlined the principle, now known by his name, that the pressure in a fluid is inversely proportional to its speed. Three further members of the family became professors of mathematics and a fourth became Astronomer Royal at Berlin.

**Berthelot, (Pierre Eugène) Marcelin** (1827–1907), French chemist and statesman. He was one of the founders of thermochemistry, measuring the heats of reactions and devising a method for determining the *latent heat of steam. He also synthesized a number of organic compounds using inorganic materials, thereby refuting the classical division between organic and inorganic chemistry. A prominent statesman, he was appointed foreign minister of France in 1895.

**Berthollet, Claude Louis, Comte** (1748–1822), French chemist who discovered potassium chlorate and, although this did not provide the substitute for saltpetre in gunpowder that he had sought, it did enable the manufacture of coloured fireworks. In 1785 he demonstrated that chlorine can act as a bleaching agent. He was the first scientist to note that the completeness of chemical reactions depends in part on the masses of the reacting substances, and his work led to the law of definite proportions. This states that the proportions of the elements in a compound are always the same, no matter how the compound is formed.

**beryl**, a silicate of beryllium and aluminium that occurs in igneous rocks in the form of massive hexagonal crystals which are very hard but fracture readily. The crystals may be large; one from Maine, USA, was over 5.5 m (18 feet) long. Its main use is as the source of beryllium, although two of its coloured forms, *emerald and *aquamarine, are valued as gemstones.

**beryllium** (symbol Be, at. no. 4, r.a.m. 9.01), a metallic element in Group II of the *periodic table. It is a grey, light metal with a high melting-point; it reacts with acids and alkalis, showing valency 2 in its compounds, but is resistant to *oxidation. It transmits X-rays well because of its low mass and is used for windows in X-ray tubes; it is also used with copper to make alloys of great strength.

**Berzelius, Jöns Jakob, Baron** (1779–1848), Swedish chemist and inventor of the present system of representing chemical *elements by symbols. He discovered selenium, silicon, thorium, and cerium, and isolated zirconium. He tabulated *relative atomic masses and analysed many compounds, denoting the composition of molecules in the manner today. In 1812 he started to analyse organic compounds, examining blood, faeces, and other natural substances. It was probably he who named protein.

**beta particle**, the negatively charged particle emitted from some atomic nuclei during radioactive decay. It has now been demonstrated that beta particles are in fact electrons, but the term beta particle is still used in connection with radioactive phenomena. Rays of beta particles are called beta radiation, and are *ionizing radiation. Beta particles have a greater penetrating power than *alpha particles and can penetrate very thin metal foil.

**Bhutan**, a small Asian country lying in the Himalayas between Tibet in the north and, in the south, Assam in north-east India. In the north it is entirely mountainous with spectacular peaks rising to 7,300 m (nearly 24,000 feet). Deep valleys with fast-flowing rivers lead to warmer and lower land in the south, which is forested and offers soil for cultivation. Limestone and gypsum are present in large quantities.

**bicarbonate of soda**　*sodium hydrogencarbonate.

**Big Bend National Park**, a wilderness of some 2,800 km² (1,100 sq. mi.) in western Texas, USA. It is triangular in shape, and bounded on its south-western and south-eastern sides by a huge bend of the Rio Grande. With high mountains, desert plains, and deep canyons, it has much varied and spectacular scenery.

**binary** (in arithmetic), a way of representing numbers using only two different digits, 0 and 1. In ordinary decimal notation, a number such as 736 means 7 hundreds ($10^2$) + 3 tens ($10^1$) + 6 units. In a binary number powers of 2 are used; so, for example, 101 means $1 \times 4 (= 2^2) + 0 \times 2 + 1 \times 1$, that is, 5. The first eight binary numbers in order are: 1, 10, 11, 100, 101, 110, 111, 1000. Binary representation of numbers is widely used in digital computers: using an electric circuit, 0 is represented by 'off', and 1 by 'on'.

**binomial expansion**, an algebraic expression giving the *power of a sum of two elements in terms of powers of the individual elements. For example, $(x + y)^2 = x^2 + 2xy + y^2$. For any whole number $n$, $(x + y)^n = x^n + nx^{n-1}y + [n(n - 1)/2!] x^{n-2}y^2 + \ldots + y^n$. (The term 2! means *factorial 2.) The same form of expansion is valid for fractional or negative powers, but then the result is an infinite series rather than a finite number of terms and questions of *convergence arise. If $y/x$ is less than 1, the series converges and so the expansion can be used to obtain numerical approximations for such quantities as square roots and reciprocals.

**biotite**, a common rock-forming mineral, a member of the *mica group. It is found as dark brown plate-like crystals or as grains in both igneous and metamorphic rocks. It has a complex chemical formula (potassium magnesium iron

A classic **bird's foot delta** formed where the Tongariro River flows out into Lake Taupo in the North Island, New Zealand.

aluminium silicate). Crystals measuring 64 m² (76 square yards) have been found in Greenland.

**Biot–Savart law**, the result of investigations by two 19th-century French scientists, Jean-Baptiste Biot and Félix Savart, into the magnetic field produced by an *electric current. Measuring the strength of the field at various distances from a long, straight, current-carrying wire, they found (1820) that the field strength was, first, in direct proportion to the current and, second, in inverse proportion to the distance from the wire. This means, for example, that doubling the current in a wire, or halving the distance from the wire, will double the magnetic field strength.

**bird's foot delta**, a *delta formed by one outstretched river channel which has distributaries splayed out from it. The Mississippi River has a bird's foot delta.

**bismuth** (symbol Bi, at. no. 83, r.a.m. 208.98), a shiny metallic element in Group V of the *periodic table. It forms compounds in which it shows valencies 3 and 5, but is not very reactive. It is mixed with other low-melting metals to form fusible alloys, which are used in safety devices. It is a good absorber of gamma rays and is used as a gamma-ray filter.

**bitumen**, a general term for any of the various brown or black mixtures of tar-like hydrocarbons derived from petroleum, either naturally or by distillation. It is flammable and can range from a viscous oil to waxy substances and brittle solids. Bituminous *coal, which burns with a smoky flame, is transformed by pressure into anthracite. Bituminous tar or pitch is the basis of *asphalt. It is found in tar pits such as the Athabasca Tar Sands of Canada and the Trinidad Pitch Lake. Sometimes, as at Rancho El Brea in California, USA, it contains the relics of animals of the Pleistocene Epoch (10,000 to 2,500,000 years ago), trapped in it.

**Bjerknes, Vilhelm Friman Koren** and **Jakob Aall Bonnevie** (father and son), Norwegian meteorologists. V.F.K. (1862–1951), who was also a physicist, pioneered the science of dynamical meteorology, applying mathematics to describe motions in the atmosphere. His best known work was on the origin and characteristics of *depressions and on methods of weather forecasting. J.A.B. (1897–1975) discovered that depressions form, develop, and decay along the

*polar front and that large-scale atmospheric waves exist in the high westerly air-flow of middle latitudes.

**Black, Joseph** (1728–99), Scottish chemist who studied the chemistry of gases and formulated the concepts of *latent heat and *heat capacity. He developed accurate techniques for following chemical reactions by weighing reactants and products. In studying the chemistry of *alkalis he isolated a gas which he termed 'fixed air' (now known to be *carbon dioxide) and investigated its chemistry, including its characteristic reaction with *lime water.

**black-body radiation** (in physics), the energy radiated by a hypothetical body that has the property of being able to absorb all the radiant energy incident upon it. It is a perfect absorber and a perfect emitter of *radiation. The simplest example of such a body is the inside of a hollow sphere, because all the radiation it emits must strike the inner surface again and none of it can escape to the outside. The black body is an important concept because the radiation it emits (and absorbs) at each wavelength is dependent only on its temperature and not on the material from which it is made. The concept is therefore completely general and is used as a model for calculations of radiant energy, for while a perfect black body is difficult to realize in practice, there are many situations where a reasonable approximation to a black body can be achieved. The spectral distribution of black-body radiation has a characteristic form, with the maximum emission occurring at a wavelength inversely proportional to the temperature of the body. It was difficulties in accounting for the precise form of the spectrum that led *Planck to the idea of the *quantum.

**black earth**   *chernozem.

**Black Forest** (German, Schwarzwald), a forested mountain region flanking the east side of the Rhine *rift valley in south-west Germany. It extends north-east from Switzerland for 160 km (100 miles) and varies in width from 16 to 40 km (10 to 25 miles). Its steep, faulted, west-facing slopes look across the Rhine to the Vosges Mountains. Gentler gradients extend east to the Neckar Valley and contain the source of the Danube. Its surface is a dissected plateau dominated by round granite summits, the highest, in the south, rising to 1,493 m (4,897 feet). The valleys with their forests provide much picturesque scenery, now threatened by toxic pollutants such as *acid rain.

**Black Hills**, a rugged upthrust occupying an area of some 15,500 km² (6,000 square miles) in north-east Wyoming and (mainly) south-west South Dakota, USA. Rising above the semi-arid region of the Great Plains which surrounds them, they reach to their highest point at Harney Peak, and their forest-clad slopes appear at a distance as a dark mass. Following the gold-rush boom of the 1870s, other valuable minerals such as silver and uranium were discovered. On the granite side of Mount Rushmore the faces of four American presidents were carved as colossal sculptures by Gutzon Borglum (1871–1941).

**Black Mountains**, in the USA, a part of the Appalachians in western North Carolina, rising to 2,037 m (6,684 feet) at Mount Mitchell, the highest point east of the Rocky Mountains. The Black Mountains in Wales are part of the Brecon Beacons National Park in southern Powys, rising to 811 m (2,661 feet).

Niels **Bohr** visited Rutherford's Manchester laboratory for the first time in 1912, and published his theory of the atom the following year. In the 1930s he made important contributions to the theory of nuclear reactions, particularly with his liquid-drop model of the nucleus.

**Black Sea**, an inland sea bounded by Moldova, Ukraine, Russia, and Georgia on the north and east, Turkey on the south, and Bulgaria and Romania on the west, its only outlet being the Bosporus. Into its northern half, which contains the Crimea peninsula and the Sea of Azov, flow several great rivers: the Danube, Bug, Dniester, Dnieper, and Don. The salinity here is low, and the water brackish. There are sandbanks, shallow creeks, and lagoons; and it often freezes in winter. The southern half, with steep and rocky shores, is much deeper. Here there is a lower layer of water beneath the surface, like a huge underwater pool, so salty, stagnant, and lacking in oxygen that neither plants nor fish can live in it. The Black Sea is now the most polluted sea in the world. The tides are weak; but fierce winter storms and summer *waterspouts frequently disturb the surface.

**blizzard**, a storm with temperatures below 0 °C (32 °F), heavy snowfalls, and strong winds which keep drifting snow in suspension and reduce the visibility to less than 200 m (220 yards). The snow is driven by the wind, often at speeds in excess of 56 km/h (35 m.p.h.) and will form fresh drifts when meeting any obstacle. In contrast is the atmospheric condition known as a white-out. Daylight is diffused by multiple reflection between a snow-covered surface and a completely overcast sky. Contrasts vanish, there are no shadows, and it becomes impossible to distinguish the horizon or any snow-covered feature, though dark objects can be seen over a long distance.

**block mountains** (or fault-block mountains), large uplifted land masses (*horsts) bordered on two or more sides by faults. The Great Basin of western USA is broken by many of them, some rising to more than 3,000 m (9,800 feet). Mountains of this type (where a tilted block is bounded by a steep scarp on one side and a gentle slope on the other) have evidently been formed by vertical movements in the Earth's crust, but the exact mechanism involved is still debated.

**Blue Ridge**, USA, an eastern range of the Appalachian Mountains running from Maryland down to Georgia, generally some 900 m (3,000 feet) high. It receives heavy rain and is well timbered; its valleys are sheltered, and there are many scenic views. The section in northern Virginia forms the Shenandoah National Park.

**bluff**   *undercut bank of river.

**Bodensee**   *Constance, Lake.

**bog**, a generally flat area where the surface layers of the ground contain large quantities of water, either seasonally or all the year round. The mixture of soil, vegetation, and water is spongy and treacherous. It contains so much water and so little oxygen that the decomposition of vegetation is slowed down, allowing the development of peat. Other organic remains (including those of humans and their settlements) are also well preserved, so bogs provide information about climate and historical changes.

**Bohemia**, a region in the north-west of the Czech Republic. It is a dissected plateau rising to 1,602 m (5,256 feet) and composed of crystalline rock with rounded features that provides subdued highland scenery. Bounded by the Ore Mountains or Krušné Hory (German, Erzgebirge) in the north-west and the Bohemian–Moravian heights in the south-east, its chief wealth is mineral, including uranium. It is drained by the Labe (*Elbe) and its chief tributaries, the Vltava (Moldau), Jizera, and Ohře Rivers.

**Bohr, Niels Henrik David** (1885–1962), Danish physicist who successfully applied the *quantum theory to Ernest *Rutherford's model of the atom to produce a model known as the Bohr atom, and was able to explain how atoms emit light. Using *Planck's theory that energy exists only in 'packets' or quanta, he suggested that electrons orbit the nucleus of an atom at set distances or 'energy levels', changing level only when a quantum of energy is lost or gained, and emitting or absorbing radiation in the process. Many of his concepts are included in the theory of quantum mechanics. He was awarded the Nobel Prize for Physics in 1922.

**boiling-point**, the temperature at which the *vapour pressure of a liquid is equal to the pressure of its surroundings. Thus at high altitudes, where the air is thinner, boiling occurs with a lower vapour pressure and, therefore, at a lower temperature. This makes cooking difficult, since once boiling-point is reached all the heat goes into vaporizing the liquid, not into making it hotter.

**Bolivia**, an inland country in South America, bounded by Brazil and Paraguay to the north and east, Argentina to the south, and Peru and Chile to the west. In the south-west is a great plateau, the Altiplano, some 800 km (500 miles) long and 3,660 m (12,000 feet) high, set between two even loftier ranges of the Andes. At its northern end is the southern shore of a huge mountain lake, Titicaca, while in the south there are vast salt pans. The mountains offer large deposits of many minerals; more tin is found here than anywhere else in the world. The north-east by contrast has low plains with hot, wet rain forest and several navigable rivers. Here and in the east, the Gran Chaco, the soil is fertile and suitable for sugar cane, rice, coffee, coca, and cotton. Southward the ground rises to plains which are covered with lighter woodland and grass. Natural gas is the country's major export.

**Boltzmann, Ludwig Eduard** (1844–1906), Austrian physicist who made a fundamental contribution to *thermodynamics and the *kinetic theory of gases. He applied a statistical approach to give the *Maxwell–Boltzmann distribution for a large number of particles among the different energy states accessible to them. The Boltzmann constant ($k = 1.381 \times 10^{-23}$ joule/kelvin) is a universal constant in statistics.

**Boltzmann distribution**   *Maxwell–Boltzmann distribution.

**bond, chemical**   *chemical bond.

**bonding**   *chemical bond.

**Bonneville, Lake**, a vast expanse of water which covered the whole of north-west Utah, USA, during the *Pleistocene Epoch. At the end of the last ice age the lake shrank, leaving the Great Salt Lake as a remnant. Most of the former bed is now a flat plain, containing a number of *playas; but surrounding rivers left deltas with deposits of fertile valley soil. The different levels of the lake in the past are today marked by terraces.

**Boole, George** (1815–64), British mathematician. He wrote important works on differential equations and various other branches of mathematics, but is remembered chiefly for his development of an algebraic description of reasoning, now known as Boolean algebra. The branch of mathematics known as mathematical (or symbolic) *logic developed mainly from his ideas. Boolean logic employs the use of the logical operators 'and', 'or', and 'not' in retrieving information from a computer database. Entirely self-taught, Boole served as Professor of Mathematics in Cork in Ireland from 1849 until his death.

**Boone, Daniel** (c.1735–1820), American pioneer. From his native Pennsylvania, Boone made trips into the unexplored area of Kentucky from 1767 onwards, organizing settlements and successfully defending them against hostile Indians. He later moved further west to Missouri, being granted land there in 1799. As a hunter, trail-blazer, and fighter against the Indians he became a legend during his lifetime.

**bora**, a very strong, cold, dry, north-easterly wind which blows from the north-east, south through the mountains on the east coast of the Adriatic region of Italy and the Balkans. It is cold air flowing south in the wake of an eastward-moving *depression, like the *mistral of the western Mediterranean. When the weight of cold air from the mountains accelerates its flow, it can cause squalls at sea. The name bora is given to similar winds in other regions of Europe, including the Black Sea, Bulgaria, and the Arctic.

**borax** (sodium borate), the chief mineral containing *boron and the main source of boric acid. In its natural state it is usually massive, white, greasy to the touch, soft, and very light; and it has a sweet taste. It occurs in *evaporites found in salt-pans, and is particularly abundant in those of Death Valley, California, USA.

**bores, tidal**   *tidal bores.

**Born, Max** (1882–1970), German physicist who was instrumental in extending the *quantum theory to take account of the results of wave mechanics. In particular he introduced the concept of probability to describe the position of an electron in an *orbital to replace the fixed orbits of the *Bohr model of the atom. He also undertook extensive research into the properties of crystals. In 1933 he was forced to leave Germany and settled in Britain until 1953, when he returned to his homeland. He was awarded the Nobel Prize for Physics in 1954.

**Borneo**, the world's third largest island, containing Brunei and two parts of Malaysia (Sarawak and Sabah) in the north, and a part of Indonesia (Kalimantan) in the south. Set on the Equator and in the path of the two *monsoons, it is hot and one of the wettest places in the world. Tropical vegetation abounds. Much of the coast is swampy; there is luxuriant jungle inland; and evergreen forest covers even the central mountains, which rise to over 2,000 m (6,500 feet). The island is extremely well-rivered and is also rich in mineral resources.

**bornhardt** *inselberg.

**boron** (symbol B, at. no. 5, r.a.m. 10.81), a non-metal of Group III of the *periodic table which has colourless, brown and black forms. It does not resemble the other Group III elements closely; it reacts with the halogens, concentrated acids, and oxygen, forming covalent compounds. Its most important compounds are the borates, which are derived from boric oxide ($B_2O_3$); they are used in glasses, enamels, and glazes. Sodium borohydride ($NaBH_4$) is an important *reducing agent in organic chemistry. The boron-10 isotope is used in control rods in nuclear reactors as it is a strong neutron absorber.

**Bosnia–Herzegovina**, a country in south-east Europe, bordered by Croatia to the north and west, Serbia to the east, and Montenegro to the south-east. It has a short Adriatic coastline. Much of the country is mountainous and wooded. Mineral resources include coal, iron, and copper.

**boson**, an *elementary particle that has zero or integral number *spin. Photons and alpha particles are bosons. They are named after the Indian physicist Satyendra Nath Bose (1894–1974), who, together with Albert *Einstein, provided a statistical description of their behaviour.

**Bosporus**, the short and narrow strait separating Europe from Asia Minor and connecting the Black Sea with the Sea of Marmara. It is 29 km (18 miles) long and less than 0.65 km (0.4 mile) wide at its narrowest point, although there are several inlets for anchorages, the most famous being the Golden Horn. The current is strong, as the strait is the only exit for the waters of the Black Sea; its name, meaning 'ox ford', refers to classical Greek legend: the goddess Io is reputed to have crossed the Thracian Bosporus in the guise of a white heifer.

**Botswana**, a country in the hot, dry central region of southern Africa, surrounded by Namibia, Zimbabwe, and South Africa. The north-west, which has 600 mm (24 inches) of rain a year, drains into a swampy basin, the Okavango, the only surface water in the country. The centre and west is covered by the Kalahari Desert, while in the east is a large salt-pan, the Makgadikgadi, near which diamonds (now the country's chief export) have been found. Other minerals and fossil fuels include copper-nickel and coal.

**Bougainville, Louis Antoine de** (1729–1811), French explorer. Between 1766 and 1769 he led the first successful French circumnavigation of the globe, visiting many of the islands of the South Pacific and compiling a scientific record of his findings. The largest of the Solomon Islands is named after him as is the tropical plant, bougainvillaea.

**boulder** (in geology), defined as a block of rock exceeding 256 mm (10 inches) in diameter. Boulders may be found on or below the surface of the ground. They are usually weather-worn or water-worn into a rounded shape, and will either have been transported by gravity and/or ice or water or have been left by *spalling. In many parts of the world there are sedimentary boulder beds, consisting of large blocks of rock together with smaller particles.

**boulder clay**, a glacial deposit typically consisting of an unsorted mixture of boulders in a matrix of stiff clay. The material, which can range from large boulders to fine rock flour, is unstratified: it shows no layered structure. The word is more or less synonymous with *till.

**boundary layer**, a layer of flowing air or water whose characteristics are affected by the surface over which the fluid is flowing. In the atmosphere, the boundary layer defines the altitude at which airflow is affected by the ground. The greatest height at which airflow is affected by frictional drag and turbulence, 550 m (1,600 feet), is called the planetary boundary layer. At the other end of the scale is the surface boundary layer, below 50 m (160 feet).

In oceanography, the boundary layer (or benthic) defines the height above the sea-bed at which bottom currents cease to be affected by frictional drag and turbulence. The benthic boundary layer is typically of the order of 50 m (160 feet) thick and is best developed in the oceans and deeper waters of the *continental shelf. It is also more turbid than waters above, because of suspended bottom sediment stirred up by the turbulence. In shallow waters nearer shore, the benthic boundary layer, stirred by tidal currents, merges with the wind-mixed surface layer. The part of the atmosphere immediately above the ocean, and the uppermost part of the ocean, are referred to as the atmosphere-ocean boundary layer.

**'Bourbaki, Nicolas'**, the pseudonym under which a group of mathematicians, mainly French, attempted in the mid-1930s to publish an encyclopedic survey of pure mathematics. Their approach was highly abstract and strictly axiomatic in style and spirit, intending to lay bare the structure of the entire field. Volumes in different areas of mathematics began appearing in 1939 and were highly influential among mathematicians, not least in rendering Bourbaki's non-standard notation the norm. This approach also influenced the widespread reforms in school mathematics which took place during the 1960s.

**Boyle, Robert** (1627–91), Irish-born physicist, chemist, and founder member of the Royal Society who was largely responsible for establishing *chemistry as a serious scientific subject. He did much to advance the theory that matter consists of 'corpuscles', now identified as *atoms, and was the first to distinguish between mixtures and compounds. He made detailed studies of the behaviour of gases, performed experiments using the air pump, demonstrated that air has weight and, in 1663, published the law which now bears his name (see *gas laws).

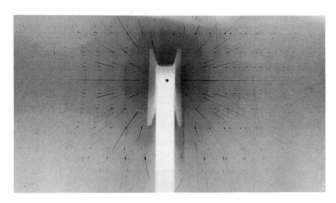

The technique of X-ray diffraction has undergone many refinements since the pioneering days of the **Braggs**. In this photograph of the pattern produced by the diffraction of X-rays from an oscillating crystal of sodium niobate ($NaNiO_3$), the positions and intensities of the spots give information about the configuration of atoms in the crystal.

**Boys, Sir Charles Vernon** (1855–1944), British physicist and prolific inventor, who developed a simple method of measuring the *refractive index (bending power) of the glass in a lens. Another of his achievements was a sensitive detector of radiation from hot objects called a radiomicrometer.

**Bragg, Sir William Henry** and **Sir (William) Lawrence** (father and son), British physicists who developed the X-ray spectrometer—a device for separating and measuring the wavelengths present in an *X-ray beam. Sir William (1862–1942), working with his son, analysed the arrangements of atoms in various crystals by measuring the patterns produced by X-rays reflected from them. Sir Lawrence (1890–1971) established a law, Bragg's law, which gives a simple link between the angles of reflection and the atomic spacing. The development of X-ray crystallography has enabled the structure of many complex substances to be identified, the double helix of DNA (deoxyribonucleic acid) being a famous example. In 1915, they were jointly awarded the Nobel Prize for Physics.

**Brahmaputra**, a river in the north of the Indian subcontinent. Its main source is a glacier 4,900 m (16,000 feet) up on a tableland north of the Himalayas in western Tibet, close to the headwaters of the south-west-flowing Sutlej and Indus Rivers. The Brahmaputra flows eastward, first as the Manan He (Tam Chok) and then as the Zangbo, for about 1,600 km (1,000 miles) before turning south through the Himalayas in its gorge section. It traverses the broad lowland of Assam and then turns south again to reach the main Ganges channel and the Bay of Bengal after a total journey of 2,900 km (1,800 miles). Navigable for less than half of this length, it is chiefly used for irrigation of the adjacent plains. The vast drainage basin extends to around 935,000 km² (361,000 sq. mi.).

**braiding** (in geomorphology), a process which occurs when a river channel becomes divided into two or more branches, with small islands or channel bars between them. Indeed, the subchannels may weave a wide and intricate basketwork pattern all over the valley floor. The phenomenon is usually caused by a combination of large, seasonal river flows, steep slopes, and large amounts of coarse-grained sediment such as sand or gravel. Many desert and mountain rivers are braided, especially those on the *outwash plains in front of melting glaciers. Frequent changes in the pattern of the subchannels make the building of bridges difficult and costly.

**Brazil**, the largest country in South America bordering ten countries and with a coastline 7,400 km (4,600 miles) long, and straddling the equator from latitude 4° N. to past latitude 33° S. The whole of the northern region lies in the vast Amazon basin with its tributary rivers. South of this are the Mato Grosso with its grassland plateau and the *campos*, mountain plateaux intersected by deep river valleys. In the region of great lakes the climate becomes suited to coffee-growing. Southward the land drops away to a vast plain suitable for livestock and plantation farming. Only about 7 per cent of Brazil's land area is considered arable. Brazil is rich in minerals: it has the third largest reserves of bauxite in the world, the largest reserves of columbium, high-grade iron ore, one of the largest reserves of beryllium, as well as gold, manganese and tin in large quantities. The destruction in recent decades of up to 12 per cent of the vast Amazonian rain forest is a cause for world-wide concern.

**breccia**, a term applied to rocks comprising mixtures of angular rock fragments cemented within a finer-grained deposit. These fragments may be sedimentary, igneous, or organic in origin, but by definition they must be angular; if they are rounded, the rock is called a *conglomerate. Breccias are known from all geological periods; they normally result from local processes: landslides of consolidated rock, cave collapse, or massive rock fracturing during faulting or folding.

**breeze**, a light local wind which is generated by differential heating across a coastline. On clear, sunny days the rapid rise in temperature over the land during the morning causes the air to expand and rise. Cooler air from above the sea flows in to replace it, causing a sea breeze. A sea breeze usually has a depth of about 1,000 m (3,300 feet) and a typical force of 4 to 7 m/s (9 to 16 m.p.h.). It can advance inland for many miles, but gradually ceases to blow at right angles to

Large volumes of sediment carried down from the mountains of South Island, New Zealand, are dumped as the Waimakariri River crosses the coastal plain to the sea. The result is a wide, heavily **braided** channel with countless sub-channels of coarse gravels and sands forming bars.

the coastline and by late afternoon is blowing parallel to it (and to the *isobars). It dies away when the land surface cools at night and the pressure gradient between the land and the sea is disrupted or reversed. Then it may be replaced by a lighter land breeze blowing out towards the sea. On the *Beaufort scale a breeze is a wind with a speed of between 4 and 27 knots (6–49 km/h, 4–31 m.p.h.).

**bremsstrahlung** (in physics), the *electromagnetic radiation produced by the acceleration, or especially the deceleration, of a charged particle after passing through the electric and magnetic field of a nucleus. When the velocity of a charged particle changes, the particle radiates energy in the form of electromagnetic waves. These waves are called bremsstrahlung (German for 'braking radiation'). The frequency of the bremsstrahlung depends on the size of the change in velocity of the particle. If a metal block is put in the path of a beam of high-energy electrons, the velocity of the electrons is changed when they hit the block. The bremsstrahlung produced by this change is in the form of X-rays. In nuclear reactors, charged particles produced by the nuclear reaction are slowed down by the cooling water which surrounds the reactor. This change in velocity produces bremsstrahlung in the form of a characteristic blue light. Bremsstrahlung is an important consideration in experiments which use high-energy electrons to investigate the structure and properties of matter.

**brine**, water which is saturated or nearly saturated with salt. It is used (now less often than previously) to preserve vegetables, fish, and meat. Sea water, particularly that of the *Dead Sea, is regarded as brine—as is that which penetrates freshwater rivers and lakes. Brine lakes develop as a result of high evaporation, the salt being derived either from the rock or from airborne sea-salt. Some of the most extensive occur in continental interiors, the Great Salt Lake in Utah, USA, being an example.

**Britain**   *Great Britain.

**British Columbia**, Canada's westernmost province, running the entire length of Canada's deeply indented Pacific coast. The Rocky Mountains form a natural border with Alberta in the south-east, while the Yukon Territory lies to the north. Evergreen forests cover the slopes of the Coast Mountains and provide enormous quantities of timber. All the major metals are found in the mountains, notably silver, lead, and zinc. Fringing the coast are numerous islands, a northern extension of the Coast Ranges of the USA, the largest of which is Vancouver Island. Behind the Coast Mountains (a different range) is an inland basin with many magnificent lakes and deeply incised by the Fraser River. The way out to the east through the Rocky Mountains goes through the Kicking Horse, Yellowhead, and Crow's Nest passes.

**British Isles**, a geographical region on the north-west shelf of the European continent, comprising two main islands Great Britain and Ireland, together with smaller islands near their coasts. Less than 32 km (20 miles) of shallow sea separates their nearest point from Europe, of which they are, geologically, the westernmost extension. Ireland, which was separated first from the continent by the rising sea-level at the end of the *Pleistocene Epoch, is little more than 20 km (12 miles) from Great Britain at the closest point. Between the two islands is the Irish Sea. Their geological history is very complex, and they contain a remarkably complete record of the major epochs of the Earth's history. The long and complicated sequence of Earth movements, *glaciations, and *erosion by rivers and the sea, acting on the great variety of rock types, has produced an extraordinary diversity of scenery for such a small area. To the north and west in both islands, old, hard rocks form uplands and mountains bearing many traces of the action of glaciers. These areas are generally wet and cool, with peat bogs, forests, and lush pastures. South and east of a line across England, from the River Tees in the north-east to the Exe in the south-west, lie younger, softer rocks arranged in broad, almost parallel, belts. Sandstones and limestones, including chalk, form uplands which are separated by broad clay vales. The relief is much gentler than in the north, and the climate is warmer and drier. These are the main areas where wheat, barley, and other crops are grown. Most mineral deposits are in the north and west, although there is coal and some iron ore in the south-east. Oil and gas deposits are exploited, notably off-shore in the North Sea.

**bromine** (symbol Br, at. no. 35, r.a.m. 79.90), a non-metallic element. One of the *halogens, it is a red-brown volatile liquid. It reacts with most metals and non-metals; and it dissolves in water, forming a reddish solution. Bromine occurs naturally in sea water and salt deposits in compounds with metals. It is used as an antiseptic; silver bromide is employed in the manufacture of photographic materials and 1, 2-dibromoethane ($C_2H_4Br_2$) is an *anti-knock additive in petrol.

**brown earth** (or brown forest soil), a rich type of soil found in temperate latitudes, in areas that were once covered with deciduous woodland. Most of these areas have been cultivated for a long time and the original forests have been cut down; nevertheless, the soil is often rich in organic matter and very fertile. The upper *horizons are grey-brown and often some *leaching takes place because of the high rainfall. The B-horizon is thick, dark brown in colour and generally clayey. Brown earths are found in the north-east United States, northern China, and north-west Europe.

**Brownian motion**, the incessant irregular movement of a suspension of tiny particles in a fluid, and it is due to the particles being continually bombarded by the molecules of the gas or liquid in which they are suspended. It can most easily be observed by examining under the microscope a droplet of liquid containing any fine material. The effect demonstrates that the molecules of a liquid or gas are in a state of continuous agitation. The effect was explained and studied in detail by the Scottish botanist Robert Brown (1773–1858) in 1827.

**brown soil**, a light- or greyish-brown type of soil containing little humus. Brown soils occur under sparse bunch grass or scrub vegetation in the semi-arid mid-latitude steppes of North America and Asia where rainfall is less than 350 mm (14 inches) a year. They are closely related to *chestnut soils, which form where rainfall is a little higher. Brown soils form marginal agricultural lands, suitable only for livestock grazing, in areas such as the Colorado piedmont, USA; central Turkey, and eastern Mongolia.

**Bruce, James** (1730–94), Scottish explorer in Africa and discoverer (1770) of the source of the Blue Nile at Lake Tana in Ethiopia. His *Travels to Discover the Source of the Nile* (1790)

Constant erosion by wind-blown debris, and the powerful down-cutting effect of flash floods caused by desert storms, have combined to produce the spectacular scenery of **Bryce Canyon** National Park in Utah, USA.

was for many years the best European source of information about Ethiopia, and remains one of the epics of African adventure literature.

**Brunei**, a small tropical country on the north-west coast of Borneo, comprising two enclaves surrounded by Sarawak (Malaysia). Its narrow coastal plain of alluvium and peat changes inland to rugged hill country of infertile lateritic soils, the highest point being Bukit Belalong at 913 m (2,997 feet) in the south-east. The coast is noted for its oil and natural gas, found both on shore and off-shore.

**Bryce Canyon**, south-western Utah, USA, a box canyon with white and orange limestone and sandstone walls. Extraordinary shapes have been carved by wind and water acting on alternate hard and soft strata of the rock. This spectacular scenery forms part of a large national park.

**buffer solution**, a solution in which the *hydrogen ion concentration (pH) is relatively insensitive to the addition of an acid or base. The pH changes only gradually and hence reactions take place at a known pH. Natural buffers play an important part in the chemistry of living organisms, where the reactions are sensitive to change in pH; in the laboratory they are usually prepared from the salts of a weak acid in the presence of the acid itself. In the case of sodium ethanoate, $CH_3COONa$, with ethanoic acid, $CH_3COOH$, the pH (or hydrogen ion concentration) is given by the *equilibrium constant, $K = [H^+] [CH_3COO^-] / [CH_3COOH]$, and it will change only slowly on the addition of hydrogen ions: the $CH_3COONa$ is fully dissociated and serves as a source of ethanoate ions; it will mop up the extra hydrogen ions. Similarly, the salt of a weak base in the presence of the base will act as a buffer solution which is insensitive to added alkali.

**Bulgaria**, a country of the Balkan Peninsula with Romania to the north, Serbia and Macedonia to the west, Greece and Turkey to the south, and a coast on the Black Sea. The northern boundary is the Danube River, except in the north-east, and about 80 km (50 miles) to the south the long Planina range of Balkan Mountains runs parallel to the river, dividing the country laterally. Further south the Rhodope ranges cut the country off from the mild climate of the Mediterranean Sea. Although its summers are very warm, winters are cold with snow and frost. There are deposits of coal and other minerals and the land is suitable for wine-growing, tobacco, and cotton.

**buoyancy**   *flotation.

**Burke, Robert O'Hara** (1820–61), Australian explorer and leader of an expedition in 1860–1 to cross the continent from south to north, using camels. With his associates William John Wills, George Grey, and John King, he was successful in reaching the estuary of the Flinders River.

**Burkina Faso** (formerly Upper Volta), a land-locked country in West Africa surrounded by Mali, Niger, Benin, Togo, Ghana, and Côte d'Ivoire. It lies on a plateau, rising highest in the west and cut in the centre by the north–south route of the Volta River. The soils are mostly coarse and sandy, based on hard rock; the climate is hot and arid, and the natural vegetation except in the river valleys is thorn-scrub and thin *savannah. There are few mineral deposits apart from manganese in the north.

**Burma**   *Myanmar.

**Burton, Sir Richard Francis** (1821–90), Anglo-Irish scholar and explorer. In 1857–9 he led an expedition to discover the source of the White *Nile. It reached the great lakes of East Africa, but it was Burton's companion John *Speke who made the final discovery. Later Burton explored West Africa and South America. He published over 40 volumes of his explorations and over 20 volumes of translations, including an unexpurgated translation of *The Arabian Nights*.

**Burundi**, a country on the east side of Lake Tanganyika in east central Africa, to the south of the Equator. It is bounded to the north by Rwanda, to the east and south by Tanzania and to the west by Zaire. It straddles the watershed of the Congo (Zaire) and the Nile Rivers, while the Ruzizi River in the west flows along the Great Rift Valley.

**butane** ($C_4H_{10}$), a gaseous *alkane, principally obtained from crude oil. It exhibits structural *isomerism: normal butane has the structure $CH_3CH_2CH_2CH_3$, while its isomer, 2-methylpropane, has the structure $(CH_3)_3CH$. Like other alkanes, it is fairly unreactive chemically. However, it is used extensively as a gaseous fuel because it readily undergoes combustion to give carbon dioxide and water.

**butte**, a residual hill formed by the erosion of a *mesa. Characteristically found in desert or semi-desert areas, the classic butte has a flat top of resistant rock overlying steep cliffs of softer rock; and the cliffs stand above straight and gentle slopes which fall away to the surrounding plains. It has little vegetation cover.

**Buys Ballot, Christoph Hendrik Didericus** (1817–90), Dutch meteorologist who formulated a law for locating areas of low pressure from the wind's direction. Buys Ballot's law states that, in the northern hemisphere, if one stands with one's back to the wind, low pressure lies to the left and high pressure to the right, while the reverse is true in the southern hemisphere. The effect is due to the *Coriolis force.

**Byrd, Richard Evelyn** (1888–1957), US admiral who began a career of exploration by being the first to fly over the North Pole in 1926. He was also the first to fly over the South Pole (1929). In addition he made four expeditions to the Antarctic and carried out geographical surveys of the south polar regions.

The red sandstone **buttes** of Monument Valley in north-east Arizona and south-east Utah, USA, tower as much as 305 m (1,000 feet) above the valley floor.

# C

**Cabot, John** and **Sebastian** (*c*.1450–98 and *c*.1485–1557), father and son, of Genoese origin, who at various times were in the service of Venice, England, and Spain as cartographers as well as explorers and navigators. John Cabot (Giovanni Caboto) was a successful merchant who settled in London in about 1495. In 1497 he set sail westwards in his small ship, *Matthew*, in search of a route to Cathay (China). On 24 June he reached the northern coast of North America, believing it to be north-east Asia, and took possession of the land for both the Venetian and the British kings. A second expedition in 1498 may again have reached America. His son Sebastian was cartographer to King Henry VIII, and in 1544 produced a notable map of the world as it was then known. He variously served in both the English and the Spanish armies and navies, and was expelled to Africa by the Spanish for disobeying orders. As Governor of the Merchant Adventurers in England, he organized an expedition to search for the *North-East Passage from Europe to Asia. His efforts were ultimately to lead to the establishment of trade between Europe and Russia.

**Cabrillo, Juan Rodriguez** (d. *c*.1543), Portuguese captain in the employ of Spain, one of the *conquistadors* of what is now Guatemala, El Salvador, and Nicaragua. In 1542 he discovered California. He sailed up the west coast of Mexico, hoping to open a route to the East Indies through Spanish waters, and entered San Diego and Monterey bays.

**cadmium** (symbol Cd, at. no. 48, r.a.m. 112.41), a silver *transition metal. It reacts readily with acids but otherwise resists corrosion, and is used for coating metals. Other uses are as a neutron absorber and in pigments; but its applications are limited as many of its compounds are toxic at low concentrations.

**caesium** (US, cesium, symbol Cs, at. no. 55, r.a.m. 132.91), a soft silvery metallic element, one of the *alkali metals. It reacts vigorously with non-metals and water; and its compounds closely resemble potassium compounds. It is used in photoelectric cells and in the caesium atomic clock.

**Cainozoic (Cenozoic) Era** (from the Greek, 'new animal'), the most recent of the four eras of *geological time, comprising the *Tertiary and *Quaternary Periods. It represents the period of time covering the last 66 million years to the present day. The Cainozoic was very much the age of mammals, which became dominant in the Tertiary Period. Great changes took place in the world's temperature, which increased and then decreased during the Tertiary and led to the Pleistocene ice ages of the Quaternary Period.

**Cairngorms**, a group of mountains forming part of the Grampian system of central Scotland, rising to 1,310 m (4,300 feet). The name Cairngorm is given to a form of *quartz that is yellow or wine-coloured and prized as a semi-precious stone. The Scottish mountains are among the places where it occurs.

**calamine** *smithsonite.

A crystal of Iceland spar, a transparent form of **calcite**, showing double refraction, an optical phenomenon in which a single incident light ray is split into two refracted rays, so forming a double image.

**calcite** (calcium carbonate), a common mineral and the main constituent of limestone rocks. Semi-hard and white or colourless, although it can be coloured by impurities, it occurs in several forms: crystalline, massive concretionary as in *stalactites, and spheroidal as *oolite. It can form by precipitation from sea water, by evaporation, or in veins by recrystallization. Good crystals are collectors' items; examples nearly 1 m (3 feet) in size have been found in Missouri and Oklahoma, USA. As limestone and in various other forms calcite is used as building stone and in the manufacture of cement.

**calcium** (symbol Ca, at. no. 20, r.a.m. 40.08), a silver metallic element, one of the *alkaline earth metals. It is a reactive metal; on treatment with non-metals, water, and acids it gives ionic compounds in which the metal has a valency of 2. It occurs in many minerals: as calcium carbonate in, for example, limestone, chalk, and marble, as calcium fluoride in fluorite, and as calcium sulphate in gypsum. It also occurs in seawater, and as calcium phosphate in bones and teeth. Calcium compounds are widely used in building materials such as plaster, cement, and concrete, in agriculture, and in the manufacture of paint, paper, and glass. The *hardness of water is due chiefly to calcium compounds.

**calcium bicarbonate**  *calcium hydrogencarbonate.

**calcium carbonate** ($CaCO_3$), a white solid that occurs widely in nature as calcite, chalk, Iceland spar, limestone, and marble. It is insoluble in pure water, but dissolves in water containing carbon dioxide, a process which causes the formation of caves. It reacts with acids, and gives off carbon dioxide on heating; it is used in blast furnaces and for making mortar and cement.

**calcium hydrogencarbonate** ($Ca(HCO_3)_2$), a compound that is formed when calcium carbonate reacts with a solution of carbon dioxide in water. Water containing calcium hydrogencarbonate is hard, the calcium forming a scum when soap is added; the hardness is temporary, and is removed by boiling, when carbon dioxide is driven off and insoluble calcium carbonate (familiar as the fur in kettles) is precipitated.

**calcium hydroxide** (or slaked lime, $Ca(OH)_2$), a white crystalline powder which results from the action of water on calcium oxide. It is slightly soluble in water, and in solution is known as *lime water. Mixed with sand and water it makes mortar.

**calcium oxide** (or quicklime, CaO), a white solid which is formed industrially by heating limestone, $CaCO_3$. It combines readily with water giving calcium hydroxide; it is used to make mortar and cement, and (as lime) as a cheap *base. When heated it gives out a bright white light; this was once used for lighting in theatres—hence the phrase 'in the lime-light'.

**calcium sulphate** ($CaSO_4$), a white crystalline solid. It occurs naturally as *anhydrite and *gypsum; on heating it loses water and becomes plaster of Paris, $CaSO_4 \cdot \frac{1}{2}H_2O$. When mixed with water the plaster can be moulded before it sets hard, as $CaSO_4 2H_2O$ re-forms. Calcium sulphate is found in some water supplies, and causes permanent *hardness. It is used in paint- and paper-making.

**calcrete**, also called caliche or hardpan, a hard crust of calcium carbonate occurring in desert and semi-desert regions. Usually white, although sometimes stained pinkish, yellowish, or brownish, it often has a rubble-like appearance. The material is extremely resistant to attack by weathering in dry environments and is largely impermeable to water movement, so calcretes develop only very thin soils and present a barren, inhospitable surface to vegetation. All calcretes are formed by a concentration of lime resulting from evaporation. This concentration occurs in different ways, however. In some cases the crust has been deposited by lime-rich waters flowing over the surface from another rock type. In others the intense heat of the ground surface has caused water carrying dissolved calcium carbonate to move upwards through the soil by capillary action; and as this water has evaporated, the lime has been deposited as a B-*horizon. In yet others, the activity of plants such as algae in shallow seasonal ponds is responsible.

**calc tufa**    *tufa.

**calculus**, the branch of mathematics concerned with the rates of change of dependent quantities relative to variations in other quantities. For example, the rate of growth of savings in a bank deposit account depends (among other things) on the interest rate. Calculus can show how a change of interest rate affects the rate of growth of the savings. Calculus was developed by Isaac *Newton and Gottfried *Leibniz in the 17th century, primarily to solve problems of motion. For example, does a moving body have a particular speed at a certain moment? The Greek mathematician Zeno had posed the problem in one of his *paradoxes, saying that an instant had no duration, so nothing could move or change at an instant. Calculus dodges the paradox by allowing an instant to have a small duration, over which an average speed can be defined. *Analysis shows that the average speed tends towards a limiting, instantaneous value, which can be calculated. Caculus is divided into two fields. Differential calculus is used for solving problems involving the

Crater Lake in southern Oregon, USA, occupies the **caldera** of the extinct volcano Mount Mazama. The lake is almost circular, nearly 10 km (6 miles) across, and 589 m (1,932 feet) deep.

rates at which processes occur and for obtaining maximum and minimum values for continously varying quantities. Integral calculus, which was initially concerned with the calculation of irregular areas and volumes by dividing them into regular fragments, is also used to solve other problems involving the summation of infinitesimals. Differential and integral calculus are connected by the processes of *differentiation and *integration, which are simply the reverse of each other. Calculus is an indispensable tool in science and engineering, affording a powerful method of solving numerous mathematical problems.

**caldera**, a very large volcanic crater. Calderas are formed either by huge, explosive eruptions which rip the whole top off a volcano or, more usually, by the upper part of a cone foundering and sinking down into the chamber from which the lava erupted. The largest calderas are formed by a combination of the two processes.

**caliche**, a lime-rich cemented deposit commonly found in the surface sediments and soils of semi-arid regions, especially under conditions of sparse rainfall. It is formed by the drawing of lime-rich waters to the surface by capillary action and the subsequent deposition of calcium carbonate in the pore spaces in the sediment when the water evaporates. Well-hardened caliches are known as *calcretes.

**California, Gulf of**, an arm of the eastern Pacific Ocean which reaches northward for some 1,100 km (680 miles) between the peninsula of Baja (Lower) California and the Mexican mainland. A flooded valley between an extension of the USA's Coast Range and the western Sierra Madre, it once stretched north to the Salton Sea in south California, but is now cut off by the *alluvium of the Colorado delta. Storms and strong currents hamper navigation, and it is subject to *tsunami, being at the unstable edge of the North American Plate on the San Andreas Fault. To the north is the Sonoran Desert.

**California Current**, a shallow, slow-moving body of water in the east Pacific Ocean, about 1,000 km (600 miles) wide, flowing southward along the west coast of North America, from Washington to California. It carries cool water derived from the Subarctic Current towards the Equator, and thus has an important role in modifying the climate of the regions it passes. Moist air moving towards the coast is cooled by passing over the California Current, and this causes dense sea fogs to form. The famous fog banks that roll into San Francisco harbour, USA, through the Golden Gate strait are formed in this way.

**Camargue, la**, a relatively flat region of approximately 560 km² (220 sq. mi.) of the Rhône delta in south-east France. It is characterized by alluvial deposits that give rise to marshlands containing numerous shallow salt lagoons. These are separated from the sea by well-developed sand bars. Reed-covered swamps occur in the south, but many areas elsewhere have been reclaimed as farmland. Free-roaming cattle and sheep are raised in the region, which is known also for its fighting bulls and wild horses, and as a reserve for rare species of birds.

**cambering** (in geomorphology), the downhill curving and bulging of hard rock layers caused by the very slow bending, or creep, of their edges under the force of gravity. It occurs particularly when beds of them lie almost horizontally above weaker layers at the top of steep slopes in deep valleys. When gorges are cut rapidly by streams or glaciers, the rocks on either side experience a sudden loss of support which encourages their outward and downward movement.

**Cambodia** (Kampuchea), a tropical country in south-east Asia flanked by Thailand, Laos, and Vietnam. Through it from the north flows the Mekong, while westward is a large lake, the Tonlé Sap. The climate is tropical monsoon, and most of the land marshy or forested, providing good crops of rice and timber. A short coastline faces south-west on the Gulf of Thailand.

**Cambrian Mountains**, a high and rugged plateau running from north to south along the length of the interior of Wales. The tallest peaks are in the north: Aran Fawddwy rises to 905 m (2,970 feet). There are numerous deep lakes and valleys, and the mountains contain the sources of many rivers, including the Severn and the Wye. The word Cambria is the medieval Latin name for Wales.

**Cambrian Period**, the oldest geological period of the *Phanerozoic Age, extending from 570 to 505 million years ago. Rocks of this age were first recognized in Wales (Cambria). The Cambrian Period was one of widespread seas. Cambrian rocks are the oldest in which *fossils can be used for geological dating. They contain trilobites (marine arthropods, now extinct), molluscs, and other marine invertebrates. Cambrian rocks are today exposed most notably in North Wales and Scotland, Norway, Spain, south-east Australia, and in the Appalachians and along the Saint Lawrence River in North America.

**Cameroon**, a country in the crook of West Africa, with Nigeria and Chad to its west and north, the Central African Republic to its east, and Gabon and Congo to the south. Most of the coastline is low, with creeks, lagoons, and swamps, although near Mount Cameroon, an active volcano, there are steep cliffs. The coastal plain is hot and very wet and covered with thick rain forest. Inland this becomes open woodland and then *savannah as the ground rises to the plateau that makes up most of the country. There are reserves of iron ore here, and coffee and cocoa are grown. Crude oil is a major export.

**Canada**, the second largest country of the world, occupying the whole of the northern part of North America except for Alaska and bounded by three oceans: the Pacific on the west, the Arctic on the north, and the Atlantic on the east. The southern boundary crosses the Rocky Mountains and continues eastward on latitude 49° N. to the Great Lakes and the Saint Lawrence, and then crosses the northern Appalachian Mountains to join the sea along the Saint Croix River. While the Saint Lawrence is Canada's most important river, the Mackenzie in the north-west is the longest and the Fraser in the south-west the most beautiful. Northern Canada is a land of lakes, wide and winding rivers, low tundra vegetation, and dark coniferous forests. Snow lies for six to nine months in the year and there is much *permafrost, making building and mining difficult and agriculture impossible. The west coast, with its mild climate and salmon rivers, is scored by fiords and over-hung by snow-capped mountains. Inland, the main Rocky Mountain chain yields rich mineral deposits, and its deep, sheltered valleys with hot, dry summers produce crops of vines and peaches. Through its eastern foothills, a major area of cattle-ranching and oil production, the land falls gently eastward to the prairies. This is the heart of the country and a vast grain-growing region, despite a harsh climate of very cold winters and very warm but short summers. Huge mineral deposits exist here too. To the east lies the lowland of the *Canadian Shield, also rich in minerals and covered by a mosaic of lakes and forest. Eastward again, between Lakes Huron, Erie, and Ontario, are rich farming lands. The land becomes more hilly in Quebec and the easternmost maritime provinces, and farmers concentrate on orchard crops. Fishing is an important activity as the waters of the North Atlantic Ocean are well stocked: this coast is less rugged than the west, but the cool, damp climate and poor, rocky ground limit agriculture. To the north are the plateaux of Labrador, and its huge deposits of iron ore and other minerals. Canada is the world's largest producer of zinc, nickel, and uranium. (See entries on the two territories and ten provinces: *Northwest Territories, *Yukon Territory, *Alberta, *British Columbia, *Manitoba, *New Brunswick, *Newfoundland, *Nova Scotia, *Ontario, *Prince Edward Island, *Quebec, *Saskatchewan.)

**Canadian Shield** (Laurentian or Precambrian Shield), a vast geological region occupying over two-fifths of the land area of Canada. It is the world's largest shield of Precambrian rock and the oldest part of the North American continent. From the Great Slave and Great Bear lakes in the Northwest Territories, it extends east to northern Manitoba, Quebec and Ontario, and the whole of Labrador. Most of the rock is metamorphic, that is, it has undergone structural, chemical, or mineralogical change by natural agencies (other than by weather or consolidation of sediments), especially heat and pressure. Uplifted and eroded continually through the ages, today it forms a generally low platform which was once much higher. Southward-moving Pleistocene ice-sheets depressed much of the land, formed the Great Lakes, and in withdrawing removed much of the soil. Today there are a few low mountain ranges on the east of the plateau, prairie in the west, tundra in the north, and good forests in the south. The shield is drained by rivers flowing into Hudson Bay, offering much scope for hydro-electric power, and it contains a variety of mineral wealth.

**Canary Islands**, a group of seven islands in Spanish possession, and volcanic in origin, which rise from the Atlantic Ocean floor some 108 km (67 miles) off the west coast of Africa at latitude 28° N. Their average temperature ranges from 10 °C to 35 °C (50 to 95 °F) and the rainfall is moderate. The main physical feature is the conical peak of Tenerife, at 3,717 m (12,195 feet), which is often ringed with cloud.

**candela** (symbol cd), the *SI unit of luminous intensity. It is defined as the luminous intensity emitted in a given direction from a source at the temperature of freezing platinum under a pressure of 101,325 newtons per square metre.

**Cannizzaro, Stanislao** (1826–1910), Italian chemist who discovered the reaction named after him: that two molecules of certain *aldehydes in the presence of dilute *alkalis will react to form the corresponding alcohol and acid. He was the first to appreciate the importance of *Avogadro's work on relative atomic and molecular masses and devised a method for determining relative atomic mass.

**Cantor, Georg** (1845–1918), Russian-born mathematician who spent most of his life in Germany. He developed a novel theory of the infinite based on the notion of *sets which was later to be adopted as a satisfactory medium in which to express most concepts of mathematics. His theory of transfinite cardinal and ordinal numbers was strongly resisted by many mathematicians of his time, and his attempts to obtain a position at the prestigious University of Berlin were blocked. Many of Cantor's results were counter-intuitive and he himself doubted some of them for a while. He suffered a series of mental breakdowns towards the end of his life, possibly influenced by the rejection of his work, but his ideas are now generally accepted and widely taught.

**canyon**, a spectacularly deep valley with almost vertical sides. Classic examples of canyons occur in the Colorado Plateau region, south-western USA; they have been caused by the Colorado River and its tributaries cutting down over hundreds of millions of years into some 2,000 m (over one mile) of almost horizontal rocks. Others almost as dramatic are found in other regions—the Blue Mountains, Australia; the Deccan Plateau, India; the Drakensberg, South Africa—where rivers have cut down for long periods through great thicknesses of sediments and lavas. For a canyon rather than a broad valley to be formed, a river must be powerful, the rocks resistant, and the climate so dry or so cold that little soil accumulates and the valley sides stay steep and angular. Moreover, the area must lie a long way above *base level, so that the river is able to cut a very deep vertical trench. Some canyons, such as that at Yosemite, USA, have also been occupied by glaciers; but glaciated valleys are usually much wider than true canyons. Canyons also occur underwater as *submarine canyons.

**canyon, submarine**   *submarine canyon.

**capacitance** (in electricity), the ability to store charge. Capacitors are devices which are used to store electric

The Grand Canyon at the junction of the Colorado and Little Colorado Rivers. Small stream beds channelling water from the plateau into the main **canyon** have cut deep notches in the far wall, and two have already begun to develop into side canyons.

charges in the same way as a sealed container is used to store gas. If the gas in the container is under pressure, the container can store more gas. The equivalent of pressure on a capacitor is the electrical potential across it: the greater the potential, the greater the amount of charge that can be stored. For a charge of magnitude Q and a potential difference of V, the ratio Q/V is the capacitance, which is a constant for that capacitor. For example, if a capacitor can store 1 Coulomb of charge when a potential of 2 volts is applied, then the capacitor has a capacitance of 0.5 farad. The *farad is a very large unit: in practice, values range between $10^{-12}$ and $10^{-6}$ farad.

**Cape Breton**  *Nova Scotia.

**Cape Province**, the largest and most southerly of South Africa's four provinces (the others are Natal, the Orange Free State, and Transvaal). Its area is over 721,000 km² (278,000 sq. mi.). The northern boundary is in the Kalahari Desert, which is always hot and arid. South of the Orange River, which drains into the Atlantic Ocean, a vast plateau lies at some 910 m (3,000 feet). This drops steeply to a lower plateau, the Great Karroo, which is clayey and lies between the escarpment and several ancient folded mountain ranges to the south. From the eastern end of the escarpment the Great Fish, Sundays, and Great Kei Rivers run into the Indian Ocean. Here the climate is of Mediterranean type and the coastal strip abounds with fruit and flowers.

**Cape Verde Islands**, an archipelago of volcanic islands forming a country in the Atlantic Ocean, 563 km (350 miles) west of Cape Verde Peninsula, Senegal, the most westerly point of Africa. The archipelago is in two groups, Windward and Leeward, and consists in all of ten islands and five islets. Sheer cliffs rise from the sea, and the inland slopes present a jagged landscape as a result of erosion by wind-blown sand. The prevailing winds are north-easterly trades, and the temperate maritime climate provides little temperature variation throughout the year. A dense haze containing Saharan sand often occurs.

**capillary action** (in physics), the process which is observed when liquids rise in very fine tubes (capillaries) or networks of fibre above the level of liquid in the main reservoir. It is responsible for the rise of the molten wax in the wick of a candle and for the action of blotting paper. It is caused by the attractive force between the molecules of the liquid and those on the surface of the capillaries. Liquids which have a high *surface tension will show a large capillary effect.

**carbolic acid**  *phenol.

**carbon** (symbol C, at. no. 6, r.a.m. 12.01), a non-metallic element in Group IV of the *periodic table. It exists in two *allotropes: diamond is extremely hard, colourless, and an insulator, whereas graphite is a soft, black solid which conducts heat and electricity. Although carbon is rather unreactive at low temperatures, on heating it reacts with oxygen, sulphur, and some metals. Carbon atoms can bond together in chains and rings, and carbon forms more compounds than any other element. Because many of them were first discovered in living organisms, their chemistry is called *organic chemistry, but there is no fundamental distinction between organic and other compounds. All life forms are based on carbon chemistry. Diamonds are used as jewellery

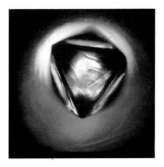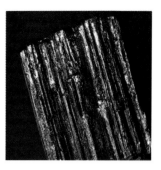

The two allotropes of **carbon**. Diamond has a different crystal structure to graphite where the crystal structure consists of carbon atoms arranged in layers. The diamond shown is an uncut stone; its colours are due to the dispersion of white light as it passes through the crystal.

and for cutting and grinding; graphite is used as a lubricant, in pencil leads, in nuclear reactors and as electrodes. Charcoal, which is an amorphous form of carbon, is used to absorb gases, as a decolorizer, and in paints and gunpowder; coal and coke consist mainly of carbon, and are important fuels. Carbon has a radioactive isotope, carbon-14, which is formed in the upper atmosphere from nitrogen and then incorporated into living things; radiocarbon (or carbon) dating is based on the decay of the carbon-14 isotope after the death of an animal or plant (see *radiometric dating).

**carbonate**, any of a class of basic compounds which contain the ion $CO_3^{2-}$. Carbonates are formed from the reaction of oxides with carbon dioxide; they give off carbon dioxide on addition of strong acids, and form hydrogen-carbonates when treated with carbon dioxide in water. They occur widely in nature: calcite, dolomite, and magnesite are all carbonate minerals.

**carbon cycle**, the movement of carbon through the atmosphere, surface, and interior of the Earth. The element exists in both the living and non-living environment and its circulation results from the processes of photosynthesis and respiration. Carbon (as *carbon dioxide) from the air is converted into more complex substances by photosynthesizing plants and is finally released again into the air by the respiration of plants and animals (which feed on the plants) or when organic substances decay. The rates of exchange are very small but over geologic time plants have concentrated large amounts of carbon mainly as *limestones and *fossil fuels. The combustion of fossil fuels releases carbon dioxide into the atmosphere (see *greenhouse effect).

**carbon dioxide** ($CO_2$), a colourless gas which is denser than air. It forms 0.03 per cent of the atmosphere by volume; this has an important effect on the Earth's temperature, as the carbon dioxide allows heat energy from the Sun to pass through it to the Earth, but absorbs energy radiated from the Earth's surface (this is known as the *greenhouse effect). Carbon dioxide is formed by the combustion of organic matter and carbon, by heating carbonates, by the addition of acids to carbonates, and in fermentation. Mammals breathe out carbon dioxide, but plants absorb it during photosynthesis. Carbon dioxide is quite unreactive although it is reduced to carbon monoxide by reactive metals, hydrogen, and carbon and it reacts with ammonia to form urea, which is used in the manufacture of fertilizers and plastics. It dissolves slightly in water, forming carbonic acid; fizzy drinks all contain carbon dioxide dissolved under pressure. Because it does not support combustion, it is commonly used in fire extinguishers; and liquid and solid carbon dioxide (*dry ice) are used as refrigerants.

**Carboniferous Period**, the fifth geological period of the *Palaeozoic Era, extending from 360 to 286 million years ago, so named because of the wide occurrence in rocks of this age of carbon, in the form of coal. Seed-bearing plants first appeared during the Carboniferous Period. Corals were widespread and extensive limestone deposits were formed. Rivers formed deltas and luxuriant vegetation developed on coastal swamps. This vegetation was later drowned and buried under mud and sand to form successive layers of *peat, which subsequently became coal. Rocks of Carboniferous age yield not only coal but also oil and iron ores. In the USA the Carboniferous Period is divided into the *Mississippian (Lower, or Dinantian) and the *Pennsylvanian (Upper). In Europe, North America, and Russia the terms correspond to differing geological epochs within the overall timespan of the period, and are still suject to debate.

**carbon monoxide** (CO), a colourless, poisonous gas produced by the combustion of carbon in an inadequate supply of oxygen. It burns with a characteristic blue flame to give carbon dioxide and acts as a *reducing agent. A component of domestic gas produced from coal (but not of natural gas) and of exhaust fumes and cigarette smoke, as little as 0.1 per cent by volume in air can be fatal. Haemoglobin (the carrier of oxygen in the blood) has a much higher affinity for carbon monoxide than for oxygen and rapidly forms carbonmonoxyhaemoglobin, which is useless as an oxygen carrier, thus depriving the body of oxygen.

**carbon tetrachloride** (or tetrachloromethane, $CCl_4$), a colourless volatile liquid which is a versatile organic solvent. It has been used in dry cleaning and in fire extinguishers, although it is toxic and is now being replaced by less hazardous chemicals.

**carbonyl group**, a carbon atom and an oxygen atom joined by a double bond. Such groups occur in aldehydes and ketones, and in carboxylic acids and their derivatives.

**carboxylic acid**, an organic compound containing a carboxyl group (−COOH) bonded to either hydrogen or an *alkyl, or *aryl group. If the latter group is denoted by R, the formula of a carboxylic acid can be represented by RCOOH. Carboxylic acids dissolve in water to form acidic solutions. The hydroxyl group can be replaced, resulting in a series of acid derivatives. These include acid chlorides (RCOCl), amides, *acid anhydrides, and *esters. Many carboxylic acids occur naturally, and they are formed by mild oxidation of most organic compounds.

**Caribbean Islands**, an archipelago bordered on the west by Central America and on the south by South America. Its islands sweep like a hook round the north and east, forming a barrier against the Atlantic Ocean. The Greater Antilles (Cuba, Hispaniola, Puerto Rico, and Jamaica) on the north are the largest. The Lesser Antilles comprise the Leeward Islands (Saint Kitts, Antigua, Monserrat, and Guadeloupe among them) and the Windward Islands (Dominica, Martinique, Saint Lucia, Barbados, Saint Vincent, and the Grenadines). To the north of Cuba are the Bahamas; and at the southern end of the hook are Tobago and Trinidad, off-

shore from the delta of the Orinoco River. The islands are the visible summits of a submerged mountain range which once connected North and South America. Some of them are of coral formation but most are of volcanic origin, with sulphur and other mineral springs. Trinidad is particularly rich in oil and asphalt. The climate is tropical, but the temperature is relieved by the north-east *trade winds, which bring heavy rain to windward slopes. Towards the end of the wet summer season there are sometimes hurricanes.

**Caribbean Sea**, a shallow sea, occupying two submarine basins between its island arc and Central and South America, with a mean depth of 2,500 m (8,200 feet). Its sheltered position protects it from the Atlantic tides, although not from *tropical revolving storms. A ridge running between Jamaica and the mainland separates the two basins, the northernmost of which is connected via the Yucatán Chan-

**Cartesian coordinates**

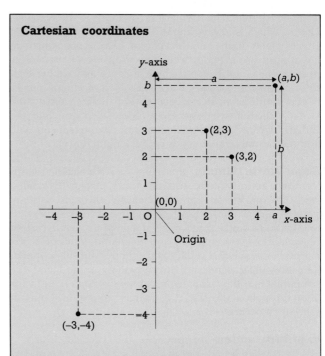

a) Two-dimensional coordinates.

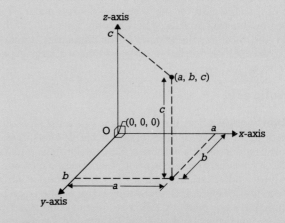

b) Three-dimensional coordinate. Any point in space may be defined uniquely by three ordered coordinates (a, b, c). As with two-dimensional coordinates, extension of the axes beyond the origin allows negative values to be plotted.

nel to the Gulf of Mexico. The current, entering from the east, exits through this channel and becomes the Gulf Stream. The water is warm and clear. The region takes its name from the Carib Indians, who inhabited the Lesser Antilbes and parts of the South American coast at the time of the Spanish conquest.

**Carlsbad Caverns**, a series of limestone caves occupying over 180 km² (70 sq. mi.) of south-eastern New Mexico, USA. Some chambers are more than 300 m (1,000 feet) below ground, and they are full of stalactites and stalagmites. The caves form part of Carlsbad Caverns National Park.

**Carpathian Mountains**, a mountain system curving like a sickle for some 1,400 km (875 miles) round the north and east of central Europe's Danube plain. The highest peaks are in the north, the granite Tatras in Slovakia rising to 2,663 m (8,737 feet). They have been carved by ice action into spectacular shapes which, snow-covered, tower above the forested slopes. Eastward the ranges are narrower and low, with easy passes and broad, fertile valleys. In Romania the system breaks up into several ranges, the highest of which is that of the Transylvanian Alps, where again the peaks rise above the tree-line, and the scenery is magnificent. The mountains here are of sandstone and crystalline rocks. Sheep are pastured on the high slopes in summer, and the clay valleys support a variety of crops: wheat, maize, fruit trees, and vines.

**Carpentaria, Gulf of**, a large but shallow inlet, part of the Arafura Sea, between Arnhem Land and the Cape York

When Jacques **Cartier** encountered some Iroquois seal hunters on Prince Edward Island, Canada, in July 1534, he raised a cross bearing the arms of France. The Indians' chief, Donnacona, had him arrested but later released him.

peninsula on the northern coast of Australia. Some 600 km (370 miles) from north to south, and almost as wide, the gulf contains three large groups of islands: Groote Eylandt with manganese deposits, the Sir Edward Pellew Group (named after a British admiral of the Napoleonic wars), and Wellesley Island. The low-lying shores, containing the mouths of many rivers, are fringed with mangrove swamps and mudflats; there are bauxite deposits at Albatross Bay. The climate is tropical monsoon.

**Carson, Kit** (1809–68), US soldier and scout, born in Kentucky, who established headquarters at Taos, New Mexico. In 1842–6 he guided *Frémont in mapping trips along the Oregon Trail and into California; and in 1849 he led emigrant convoys to the Pacific coast during the gold rush.

**Cartesian coordinates**, the most commonly used coordinate system for specifying numerically the location of points in a plane or in space, devised by the French philosopher and mathematician René Descartes (1596–1650). The basis of the system is a pair of lines at right angles to one another (see figure); they are called the coordinate axes. Points on these axes are numbered so that positive values increase to the right and upwards of the point of intersection, the origin, of these two lines. To give the Cartesian coordinates of any point, its perpendicular distances to the vertical line ($y$-axis) and the horizontal line ($x$-axis) must be computed. These numbers, placed in an ordered pair ($x, y$: just like the grid reference on a map), are the Cartesian coordinates of that point. The point (2, 3) is different from the point (3, 2). Each point has a unique pair of Cartesian coordinates. Many curves have simple Cartesian descriptions, that is, sets of points satisfying some algebraic equation which facilitates the study of their geometric properties. For example, the *parabola is $y^2 = 4ax$: the ($x, y$) coordinates of every point on a parabola satisfy this equation, given the right choice of coordinate axes. This system of reference can be extended to three dimensions ($x, y, z$) or, in mathematics, to spaces of higher dimensions. *Polar coordinates are another way of specifying the location of a point.

**Cartier, Jacques** (1491–1557), French navigator and explorer. Charged by François I to look for gold in the New World and for a *North-West Passage to China, he set sail from Saint Malo in 1534 and landed off Newfoundland twenty days later. On his second expedition (1535–6) he discovered one of the world's great rivers, the Saint Lawrence, a region which was to become the axis of French power in North America. He is credited with the discovery (1535) of an area around Québec, which he named Canada after the Huron-Iroquois *kanata*, meaning a village or settlement. Welcomed by the Iroquois Indians of Hochelaga, he renamed their village Mont Royal, the present site of Montreal city.

**cartography**, the science and art of making maps, by establishing and presenting in a suitable form the locations, shapes, and sizes of the features being mapped. (Normally these are features on the Earth's surface; but the term includes mapping geological strata, the surface of the Moon, and even nebulae with radio telescopes.) There are two stages: the science of collecting and determining positions and other data, and the art of presenting this information in an accurate and intelligible form. Surveying (the first stage) requires both the precise establishment of a framework of points, in relation to which the positions and shapes of features are fixed, and the detailed mapping of these by less precise methods. The basic framework is established by geodetic techniques using stars or satellites, together with the precise measurement of angles and distances between the points. The detailed survey may be done on the ground by similar methods, or by measurements from aerial photographs. The result is a basic plot which is accurate but is not attractive, easily intelligible, or suitable for copying. Cartographic presentation requires drawing with carefully designed and uniform lines, symbols, and lettering, and conversion to transparent film, printing plates, or digital tapes, from which copies can be made. A multicoloured map requires separate drawings for each colour. In simple line maps, black may be used for man-made features and names, blue for water, and brown for contours showing the shape of the ground, whereas in more elaborate maps various devices are used for depicting landforms. Such processes are used not only for the representation of physical features but also in thematic mapping of other distributions—for example, pollution, population, or disease.

**Cascade Range**, a series of mountains in the west of North America, ranging from 1,200 to 4,400 m (4,000 to 14,400 feet) high, running parallel to the Pacific coast. Volcanic in origin, they are a northern extension of the Sierra Nevada and reach through Oregon and Washington into British Columbia. Mount Rainier is the highest peak, and the range also contains the active volcano Mount Saint Helens. All the high summits are snow-covered, and many glaciers fall from them. The rainfall is heavy; lakes and torrents provide hydroelectricity, while fir forests are an important source of timber. The range embraces several national parks and is named from the cascades of the Columbia River which cut through the centre.

**Caspian Sea**, the world's largest lake, situated where Europe meets central Asia, between the Black Sea and the much smaller Aral Sea, to both of which it was once joined. Its present surface is some 90 m (295 feet) below sea-level, and only the waters of the Volga and Ural Rivers flowing in at the northern end prevent it from evaporating further. Whereas the northern part is shallow and contains comparatively fresh water which freezes in winter, in the south it is deep and very salty. To the west it is bordered by the snow-capped Caucasus and to the south by the forested Elburz Mountains of Iran. The sea was once noted for its sturgeon (the source of caviare), but the stock is now greatly reduced as a result of lower sea levels and the drying up of spawning grounds.

**cassiterite** (tin oxide, $SnO_2$), an ore of *tin. It is a hard and dense but brittle mineral, very dark brown or black in colour. Many of the deposits are alluvial and are found in river and marine sands, although it originally formed in veins associated with igneous rocks.

**catalyst**, a substance which changes the rate of a chemical reaction without undergoing chemical change itself. Positive catalysts (or just catalysts) increase the rate of reaction; negative catalysts (inhibitors) decrease the rate of reaction. Catalysts work in two ways: either they lower the *activation energy of the reaction or they make it possible for the reaction to proceed by an alternative pathway of lower activation energy. In both cases their effect is to reduce the amount of energy required to ensure the reaction takes place and they play an important part in many biochemical and industrial reactions. Enzymes are biochemical catalysts that enable specific reactions to take place. Industrially catalysts allow a reaction to take place without resorting to high temperatures and pressures. Catalytic converters are devices incorporated into the exhaust system of motor vehicles which use catalysts to convert pollutant gases into harmless products. The catalyst in this case is a metal catalyst with a large surface area which converts the carbon monoxide and oxides of nitrogen into carbon dioxide and nitrogen.

**cataract** *rapids, *waterfall.

**catastrophe theory**, the mathematical description of dynamical systems that undergo discontinuities, that is jumps or breaks where a continuous change in one *parameter gives rise to a discontinuous effect. This is in contrast to the main premise of continuity of cause and effect on which the Newtonian description of the world is based. At the heart of it is a classification theorem originated by the French mathematician René *Thom, which describes the various qualitatively different ways in which discontinuities arise. He described these in his book *Stabilité Structurelle et Morphogénèse* (1972). In systems with four dimensions or less, Thom identified only seven different types of catastrophe, called elementary catastrophes, the simplest two being the fold and the cusp. The theory has application in pure mathematics and in a surprisingly dissimilar array of applications in the real world. These include problems in physics (for example, phase transition), in engineering (for example, the buckling and failure of beams and bridges), in cell biology, and in the social sciences (for example, the instability leading to prison riots or the instability of a commodities market or the stock exchange).

**catena**, a related sequence of soils which occur in a regular succession as a result of changing conditions down a hillside. Even where the underlying bedrock is the same, environmental factors change dramatically as one goes down a hill. On top of the hill, soils are relatively stable and well drained. *Zonal soils are typically found here. On steep upper slopes, where erosion is pronounced, soil material is stripped away and soils tend to be shallow. Eroded material is carried downslope and redeposited to form thick soils which are comparatively young. At the base of the slope drainage is poor, and waterlogged or peaty soils form. Variations of this sequence are found on most slopes, although the specific characteristics of each soil catena differ according to the type of *bedrock, the amount of erosion, and the length of time over which the sequence has been forming.

**catenary**, the curve assumed by a flexible, inelastic chain when suspended freely from two points, and allowed to hang under the influence of gravity on its own weight. The Italian astronomer and physicist *Galileo Galilei thought the curve was a parabola, whereas it is, instead, generated by the focus of a parabola rolling along a straight line. Later, the Dutch physicist Christiaan *Huygens showed it was not even algebraic; its equation could not be a polynomial. In fact its equation is based on a *hyperbola and involves hyperbolic functions, that is $y = \frac{1}{2}a\left(e^{x/a} + e^{-x/a}\right) = a\cosh(x/a)$.

**cathode**, a negative electrode in such devices as electrochemical cells and thermionic valves. In *electrolysis *cations gain electrons at the cathode.

**cathode ray** *electrons.

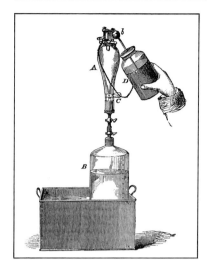

Henry **Cavendish** and the apparatus he used during his investigations into the composition of water. The apparatus, called a eudiometer, enabled Cavendish to determine the volume changes in the gas mixture when, by ignition with an electric spark, hydrogen was burned in air in the bulb A.

**cation**, a positively charged ion, so called because it is attracted by the cathode (negative electrode) in *electrolysis. Cations are formed from neutral atoms or molecules by the loss of one or more electrons. For example, the sodium atom loses one electron to form the sodium cation, $Na^+$.

**Catskill Mountains**, a range of the Appalachian system in south-east New York State, USA, covering an area of 2,600 km² (1,000 sq. mi.). It is a wooded region of gorges and waterfalls, with flattish summits generally about 900 m (3,000 feet) high. Slide Mountain at 1,281 m (4,204 feet) is the highest, acting as a watershed for the Hudson and Delaware Rivers.

**Caucasus Mountains**, a series of high, parallel ranges stretching for nearly 1,200 km (750 miles) south-eastward from the Black Sea to the Caspian Sea. In the west they are mainly limestone, elsewhere volcanic and crystalline, the two extinct cones of Mount Elbrus rising to over 5,630 m (18,480 feet). Permanent snow lies above 3,000 m (10,000 feet), and many glaciers exist. There are large deposits of iron, manganese, and oil, particularly in the east. More than 160 km (100 miles) broad at some points, these ranges contain lakes, limestone plateaux, narrow gorges, as well as broad fertile valleys where livestock is raised and vines are grown. Belts of pine and fir stand high on the mountainsides, and beneath them, beech; the lower slopes bear oak, ash, maple, and hornbeam. There are several accessible passes, which provide access from the north into both Georgia and Azerbaijan.

**Cauchy, Augustin-Louis, Baron** (1789–1857), French mathematician. It is said that more concepts and theorems have been named after Cauchy than after any mathematician. His textbooks and many of his original writings introduced new standards of criticism and rigorous argument in the *calculus from which grew the field of mathematics known as *analysis. He transformed the theory of complex functions by discovering integral theorems and introducing the calculus of residues. He founded the modern theory of elasticity in 1822, and contributed substantially in 1845 to the

founding of the theory of groups. He also contributed to astronomy, optics, and hydrodynamics.

**caustic soda** *sodium hydroxide.

**cave**, a large hollow of any shape or size, generally formed by the action of water. The most spectacular examples usually develop in regions with limestone rocks. Rain, mildly acid, attacks and dissolves the soft limestone; ever-widening cracks occur and the water streams in. As a river underground it cuts a gallery in the heart of the rock and sometimes vertical shafts or pipes through which it falls to make another gallery. Most of the action of the water is by now mechanical; but some is chemical, occasionally forming *stalactites and *stalagmites. If the limestone is thick enough and the local *base level low enough, huge vaults like those in the Carlsbad Caverns of New Mexico, USA, develop in time. River systems may remain within the complex, forming lakes; and if the roofs collapse, rugged gorges will result. Caves are also made by the action of seawater against cliffs. Fissures appear at first; incoming waves compress the air within them and then retreat, releasing the compressed air with explosive force. Growing salt crystals wedge rocks out of place and other rock dissolves. Tunnels are formed and extend, sometimes connecting with the Earth's surface inland; then a 'blow-hole' occurs, sea spray forcing its way up it like a fountain. Ice caves are hollowed out of glaciers and icebergs by streams of melt-water flowing into the ice from the surface. Volcanic caves are formed by lava flows; they often include large pockets of gas, which cause holes to be left when lava has cooled.

**Cavendish, Henry** (1731–1810), British scientist who in 1785 discovered the constitution of atmospheric air by passing electric sparks through it, and identifying the products formed. He also discovered 'inflammable air', now known as hydrogen, and established that it and oxygen are the constituents of water. He investigated electricity, and determined the *gravitational constant in order to measure the density of the Earth. As a grandson of the 2nd Duke of Devonshire he was a rich man, but he was a recluse, and most of his writings were not published until after his death. The Cavendish Laboratory in Cambridge, UK, is named after him.

**Cayley, Arthur** (1821–95), British mathematician and barrister who played a leading role in founding a modern British school of pure mathematics. His papers (of which there are almost 1,000) include articles on determinants, the newly developing *group theory, and the algebra of matrices. He also studied dynamics and physical astronomy. The Cayley numbers, a generalization of complex numbers, are named after him.

**Cayman Islands**, an archipelago in the Caribbean Sea, lying south of Cuba, north and west of Jamaica, comprising the Grand Cayman, Little Cayman, and Cayman Brac. Covering 259 km² (100 sq. mi.) in all, they have rocky coasts and reefs, with sharks and other tropical fish. The islands are a British dependency.

**Celebes** *Sulawesi.

**Celsius scale**, a scale of hotness, or *temperature, first established by the Swedish scientist Anders Celsius (1701–44) in 1742. On this scale, the unit of temperature is the degree

Tall narrow buildings with high centres of gravity and inadequate foundations may, should their foundations move, be tilted sufficiently for the line of action of their weight (acting through the **centre of gravity**) to fall outside the area of their base—a situation that could produce a turning moment large enough to topple them. The slant of the Leaning Tower of Pisa in Italy is due in part to the weakness of its foundations, though it remains standing because its centre of gravity is still above its base.

The speeding skateboarder is subjected to a **centripetal force** due to the reaction at the wall to the skateboard pressing on it. It is this force that allows him to 'climb' the wall so dramatically.

Celsius (°C); water freezes at 0 °C and boils at 100 °C (under agreed standard atmospheric conditions), although when Celsius originally devised the scale he made 0° the boiling-point and 100° the freezing-point. The Celsius scale is commonly known as the centigrade scale because of the 100 divisions between the freezing- and boiling-points of water. To convert from degrees Celsius to degrees *Fahrenheit multiply by $\frac{9}{5}$ and add 32. In scientific experimentation a scale based on thermodynamic temperature is more commonly used. This is measured in *Kelvin.

**Cenozoic Era**   *Cainozoic Era.

**centigrade**   *Celsius scale.

**Central African Republic**, a land-locked country stretching west-to-east from Cameroon to the Sudan and south-to-north from humid equatorial forests bordering Zaïre to the savannah plains of the Chad basin. The rock formation mainly comprises ancient shields or platforms, forming low plateaux, with the highest point at 1,420 m (4,660 feet) in the west. There is high ground also in the north, and from it streams flow south to the Oubangi River, which forms the southern boundary. Upstream of about 50 km (30 miles) of rapids, the Oubangi is navigable for four months in the year. There is a dry season from December to March, and temperatures are very warm at all times.

**Central America**, the southernmost extension of the North American continent joining it to South America. It stretches between the isthmuses of Tehuantepec, Mexico, in the north-west and Panama in the south-east, and it separates the Pacific Ocean from the Caribbean Sea. (Some geographers include the whole of Mexico in this region.) Mountains run along its spine, those in the south being an extension of the Andes; the highest is a volcano in Guatemala at 4,220 m (13,846 feet). Most are volcanic for the region is at a junction of crustal plates and an earthquake danger zone. The two great lakes of Nicaragua interrupt the chain. The climate is tropical, although above 760 m (2,500 feet) the temperature is mild and coffee grows. Cattle are bred, especially in Honduras. Elsewhere volcanic ash has weathered into fertile soil which yields bananas, sugar cane, maize, and fruit. The Pacific slopes fall steeply to the coast, while northward and eastward the Yucatán peninsula and broad coastal plains shelve gently to the sea. Rainfall in the east is heavy; the rivers bring down quantities of silt, and dense jungle flourishes behind the mangrove swamps of the seashore. The region contains substantial deposits of oil and gas, and of silver and gold.

**centre of gravity**, the point at which the weight of a body (an object) appears to act. In reality, the gravitational pull on an object is made up of a large number of small downward forces acting on the many particles of matter within it. The combined effect of these forces is equivalent to a single force—called the weight—acting at one point. For regularly shaped objects of uniform density, the point is at the centre. In other cases the point can be found by experiment, because an object will balance only if the point of support is in line with the centre of gravity.

**centrifugal force**, the 'force', often considered to be the one that causes a rotating object to pull away from the centre of the rotation. However, it is a fictitious force, as the only force acting on such a system is the *centripetal force which pulls the object into a circular motion rather than allowing it to continue in a straight line. In conjunction with the *Coriolis force, this fictitious force can be used to apply *Newton's laws of motion to rotating systems. A true centrifugal force is the reaction exerted by a rotating object to whatever is providing the centripetal force.

**centripetal force**, the force that makes an object move in a circular path. According to the first of *Newton's laws of motion, an object will continue to move in a straight line unless it is acted upon by an external force. Thus to make it move in a circular path a force must act upon it, and this is called the centripetal force. It acts towards the centre of a circular path and increases as the speed of the object increases or the radius of the circle decreases. For example, when some string is tied around an object and spun round, the centripetal force is represented by the tension in the string. If the string breaks, the object will continue in a straight line in the direction it had at the moment the string breaks; its path will be a *tangent to the circle. When a car goes round a corner, the centripetal force is represented by the friction between the tyres and the road. A ball lying on the back shelf of the car will roll across the shelf as the car corners. It appears that an outward force, called '*centrifugal force', is acting upon it. However, to an observer standing by the road, it will be apparent rather that the ball, uninfluenced by the centripetal force, is travelling in the same direction that it had before the car entered the bend.

**cesium**   *caesium.

**Ceylon**   *Sri Lanka.

**CFC**   *chloro-fluorocarbon.

**Chaco**   *Gran Chaco.

**Chad**, a land-locked country in north-Central Africa surrounded by Libya to the north, Sudan to the east, the Central African Republic to the south, and Niger, Nigeria, and Cameroon to the west. Out of the Sahara in its northern half rise the volcanic Tibesti Mountains, with reserves of tungsten, while in the east is the great depression surrounding Lake *Chad, with deposits of natron (hydrated sodium carbonate). The south has moderate summer rains which produce a *savannah and the seasonal Chari and Logone Rivers and their tributaries

**Chad, Lake**, the remnant of an inland sea on the southern edge of the Sahara in Central Africa. Four countries—Chad, Cameroon, Nigeria, and Niger—share its waters, which are seldom more than 7 m (23 feet) deep. Outside the rainy season its area shrinks by half and large areas of its northern and southern basins are no more than swamp. It is fed chiefly by the Chari (or Shari) River from the south; and its waters seep northward into the Soro and Bodélé depressions. Hundreds of mudbanks and small islands impede navigation, particularly along the eastern shore. The northern shore contains deposits of natron (hydrated sodium carbonate), which is used for curing and preserving hides and in the manufacture of soap.

**Chadwick, Sir James** (1891–1974), British physicist and pioneer of nuclear research who in 1932 discovered the *neutron, an uncharged particle from the *nucleus of the atom. He was awarded the Nobel Prize for Physics in 1935.

In World War II he was involved in the atomic bomb project, and afterwards stressed the importance of university research into nuclear physics.

**chalcedony**, a very finely crystalline (cryptocrystalline) variety of silica ($SiO_2$), found in various forms and colours, all with a wax-like lustre. Banded varieties (*agate and *onyx) are common; so too are the reddish-brown (*cornelian), green (prase), and red (jasper) varieties; these are all regarded as semiprecious stones. Chalcedony occurs in sediments, in cavities in lavas, and in veins associated with igneous rocks.

**chalk**, a fine-grained limestone which is friable and porous. It is often pure white in colour and commonly contains up to 97 or 98 per cent of calcium carbonate in the form of *calcite. This is generally composed of the shells of microscopic marine organisms, normally including foraminiferans such as *Globigerina*; algae known as coccoliths are also commonly present. Chalk is characteristically seen in the Upper *Cretaceous Period of western Europe and parts of North America. The most famous exposures are either side of the English Channel, where on the English side it forms the white cliffs of Dover. It contains *flint, and it is used for burning into lime.

The term 'Chalk' is also used as the *stratigraphical name for rocks of Upper Cretaceous age in Europe.

**Chamberlin, Thomas Chrowder** (1843–1928), US geologist who established the origin of *loess. He also discovered beneath the ice of Greenland *fossil forms which suggested an earlier, warmer climate, and he was one of the first to propose dating for the ice-sheets of the *Pleistocene Epoch. Much of his life was spent in developing a theory of the Earth's origin, formation, and growth.

**Champlain, Lake**, a lake close to sea-level in a long north–south valley in the Appalachians, which connects the middle Saint Lawrence and Hudson River valleys in southeast Canada and north-east USA. Only 10 km (6 miles) of its

The Seven Sisters **chalk** cliffs on the Sussex coast of England, showing the characteristic vertical cliff formed by wave erosion of this soft sedimentary rock. The fine horizontal lines in the cliff are bands of very resistant chert nodules, some of which can be seen projecting from the chalk in the foreground.

172 km (107 miles) lie in Canada. Fed by Lake George to the south-west and by streams from the Green and Adirondack Mountains, to east and west, it drains north to the Saint Lawrence River.

**Champlain, Samuel de** (1567–1635), French explorer and statesman. After an expedition to the Caribbean Sea, he made eleven voyages to Canada, following *Cartier's discovery of the site of Montreal. In 1608 he established the French colony of Quebec, of which he became Lieutenant General. From his base at Quebec he reached, over the years, lakes Champlain, Ontario, and Huron. Much of his career was spent exploring the Canadian interior and defending his settlements against hostile Indians. Lake Champlain, in the north-east USA, which he visited in 1609, is named after him.

**Chancellor, Richard** (d. 1556), English navigator who, in seeking a *North-East Passage to China, reached the northern Russian coast. His visit to Moscow (1553–4) laid the foundations for English trade with Russia. He was pilot to an expedition under Hugh Willoughby, who in a storm found shelter in Vardø, Norway (1553). Chancellor, whose ship was separated from Willoughby's by the storm, went on into the White Sea and was taken overland to Moscow. On a second voyage two years later, he discovered that Willoughby and all his men had perished from the Arctic winter; Chancellor himself lost his life in a shipwreck off the coast of Scotland a few months later.

**channel** (geomorphology), a clear, hollowed-out path cut by fresh or salt water, ice, or lava. Channels vary from shallow tracks of raindrops in a layer of dust to the huge dry channels in the Grand Coulée area, north-west USA, which were cut more than 10,000 years ago by the catastrophic draining of lakes dammed by glaciers. They are cut only when the force of flow (which increases with its depth and speed) exceeds the resistance of the surface. The most efficient cross-sectional shape for transferring flow is semi-circular, but natural channels are usually shallower and more irregular, so that much of the energy is lost by friction. They tend to be curved or irregular when seen in plan from

Jacques **Charles** reascending in his 'aerostatic globe'—a hydrogen-filled balloon—after its maiden flight of over two hours in December 1783. The balloon was made of silk impregnated with rubber to prevent hydrogen loss. It was similar in design to modern balloons.

above; and because they have ups and downs along the long profiles of their beds, the flow tends towards a corkscrewing motion, particularly in rivers. River channels have shallow, rather rectangular cross-sections, very curved courses and fairly regular pools and shallow sections along their long profiles, which fall in height as one travels downstream. Glacier channels resemble smooth parabolas in cross-section. They have few sharp curves but many very deep hollows and sharp rises along their course; and the outlet—as in the case of *fiords—is often higher than the up-valley sections. Sea channels are much the most irregular in all dimensions, since flow directions vary with winds, currents, and tides; and frequent changes of sea-level in the *Pleistocene Epoch have led to major differences in shapes and sizes. The English Channel, for example, has existed for less than 6,000 years and its water level is still rising.

**Channel Islands** (French, Iles Normandes), a group of nine islands 194 km² (75 sq. mi.) off the north-west coast of France. They are the only portion of the former dukedom of Normandy that still owe allegiance to England, to which they have been attached since the Norman conquest in 1066. They are rocky, but with a good covering of very fertile soil and a mild climate which together encourage much mixed farming. Jersey and Guernsey are famous for their breeds of cow, and for tomatoes, fruit, and flowers. The other islands are much smaller, but Alderney, Sark, and Herm are large enough to be habitable.

**chaos** (in mathematics). Newtonian or classical mechanics allows us to calculate the future behaviour of even complicated interactions provided we know enough about the conditions in which these interactions began. For example, if a ball is thrown into the air we can calculate how high and how far it will travel if we know how heavy it is, with what force it was thrown, and the forces acting on it as it travels through the air. However, there are many examples in the physical world, at many different levels of scale, of events or interactions which behave in a way which appears random, and which is different from what we would expect from such a calculation. This sort of behaviour is called chaotic, and the mathematical theory which describes it is called chaos theory. The behaviour is not actually 'chaotic' in the usual sense of the word; it appears chaotic because it does not follow our prediction. If we knew everything about the initial conditions we could predict even chaotic behaviour—though, because it followed our prediction, the behaviour would then appear orderly. Weather forecasting is an example of an activity in which it is impossible to find all the information required to make accurate long-term predictions because weather is the result of complicated interactions between a number of different factors. It is not due to any lack of knowledge about weather forecasting: the theory of chaos states that it is impossible to know the starting state of any system with complete accuracy, so we can never accurately predict future events. However, chaos theory can be used to analyse situations that other branches of mathematics cannot, for example the flow of oil through pipes or the pattern of traffic in a busy city. Chaos theory was developed during the 1970s and 1980s by researchers from a number of different fields: among them were biologists looking at the apparent unpredictability in the growth of animal populations; physiologists looking at irregular heart rhythms; and economists looking at stock prices.

**characteristic**    *logarithm.

**Charles, Jacques** (1746–1823), French mathematician, physicist, and inventor who pioneered the use of hydrogen-filled balloons and, around 1787, discovered the *gas law about expansion which now bears his name.

**charm** (particle physics), the term used to describe one of the six distinct types or 'flavours' of *quarks.

**Cheddar Gorge**, a narrow, rocky gorge 120 m (400 feet) deep in the Mendip Hills of south-west England. Erosion has exposed the grey limestones of the Lower Carboniferous Period. Water was the main agent of erosion, but the gorge is now dry. Numerous caves contain spectacular *stalactites and stalagmites, and relics of Stone Age man have been discovered there.

**chelation**, the process by which metal atoms or ions are held by organic molecules that loop round them, becoming attached at two or more places (hence the name, from the Latin word *chele*, 'claw'). Chelation occurs in soil, where organic compounds released by plants combine with metal ions such as iron and aluminium. Chelation increases the rate of weathering and is thought to promote *leaching, since the organo-metallic complexes, or chelates, tend to be more stable than the metal ions. Natural chelates are stable under acidic conditions but break down when the environment becomes more alkaline, releasing the metal ions.

**chemical analysis**    *analysis in chemistry.

**chemical bond**, the state in which two atoms are held closely together by an attractive force. There are two principal types of bond between atoms, the ionic bond and the covalent bond, although these two represent the extremes, and many compounds exhibit bonding of an intermediate character. See also *hydrogen bond. In forming an ionic bond, one atom loses one or more electrons from its outer shell to form a *cation, while the other atom gains electrons to form an *anion. The resulting electrostatic attraction of the oppositely charged ions holds them together in an *ionic compound. *Covalent bonding involves the sharing of electrons, rather than the complete transfer involved in ionic bonding. The reason that a bond forms is that the energy of the system is lowered by the process. The number of covalent bonds formed by an element is determined by the number of vacancies in its outer shell of electrons. Hydrogen, with one vacancy, can only form one covalent bond. Oxygen, on the other hand, has two vacancies in its outer shell and can thus form two covalent bonds. Thus, when oxygen reacts with hydrogen, the oxygen forms two covalent bonds, one to each hydrogen, forming water, $H_2O$. When two different atoms form a covalent bond, the resulting diatomic molecule possesses a *dipole moment, as the electrons in the bond are not shared equally. The greater the dipole moment, the more ionic the bond.

When two atoms combine to form a molecule, the bond that is formed between them results in the release of energy. To break the bond and reform the individual atoms requires the same amount of energy. This energy is the bond dissociation energy.

**chemical equation**, a representation of the substances formed and used up in a chemical reaction, and the respective proportions of these. Each substance is represented by its chemical symbol; the equation is then balanced so that each element has the same number of atoms on each side,

The photograph shows a copper (II) sulphate solution being added to a solution of sodium silicate already in the test-tube; a precipitate of copper silicate is formed immediately by the **chemical reaction** between the two solutions where they come into contact and mix.

showing that no atom has been created or destroyed. Thus for the formation of sulphur trioxide from sulphur dioxide and oxygen the equation is: $2SO_2 + O_2 \rightarrow 2SO_3$. In this reaction the volumes of sulphur dioxide and oxygen used are in the ratio 2:1. Substances which are not used up in a reaction (such as *catalysts or solvents) are not normally included in the chemical equation.

**chemical reaction**, a change in which one or more substances (the reactants) are converted into new substances (the products). Chemical reactions can be classified into different categories. They include, for example, synthesis reactions, which involve elements or small molecules being converted into larger, more complex, molecules; the reaction of aluminium and oxygen to form aluminium oxide, $Al_2O_3$, is a synthesis reaction. Decomposition reactions are the reverse, namely the breakdown of molecules into atoms or simpler molecules: for example, when calcium carbonate, $CaCO_3$, is heated, it gives off carbon dioxide, $CO_2$, and leaves a solid residue of calcium oxide, $CaO$. Neutralization reactions involve the complete reaction of an acid and a base to form a salt: for example, hydrochloric acid, $HCl$, is neutralized by sodium hydroxide, $NaOH$, to form sodium chloride, $NaCl$, and water. Precipitation reactions involve the formation of a solid, the precipitate, from the reaction of solutions; if, for example, silver nitrate solution, $AgNO_3$, is added to sodium chloride solution, a precipitate of silver chloride, $AgCl$, is formed. Other categories of reactions include addition reactions, elimination reactions, condensation reactions, and substitution reactions.

Addition reactions are ones in which one or more double or triple bonds in a molecule are converted to single bonds by the addition of further atoms or groups of atoms. They are the reverse of elimination reactions. The types of compounds that undergo these reactions are organic compounds such as alkenes, alkynes, aldehydes, and ketones. Condensation reactions are usually between organic compounds, in which two molecules join with the elimination of the elements of a small molecule, such as water, from between them. Elimination reactions involve replacement of a single bond with a double or triple bond by the removal of atoms, or groups of atoms, from adjacent carbon atoms. They are the reverse of addition reactions. Substitution reactions involve replacement of an atom, or group of atoms, in a molecule by another atom or group of atoms. There are two main types of substitution, for example, halocarbons undergo substitution involving *nucleophiles, one nucleophile displacing another. Whereas, *aromatic compounds undergo substitution involving *electrophiles, in which one electrophile displaces another.

Certain properties of a reaction are of interest. For example, the *enthalpy change is a measure of the heat given out, or taken in, by the reaction. The equilibrium constant is a measure of the extent to which the reaction proceeds; in other words, whether there is considerable or negligible conversion of reactants to products. The rate of a reaction, often the initial rate, can be measured. As a result, a relationship is sometimes found between rate and concentration of the reactant. This can lead to the proposition of a mechanism for the reaction, by which the reactants are converted to products.

**chemical symbol**, an internationally recognized abbreviation for the name of an element. Antoine *Lavoisier, Claude *Bertholet, and others first suggested a system of chemical nomenclature linked directly to the chemistry of the elements and John *Dalton proposed a series of circular symbols to represent these elements. The system now recognized, proposed by Jöns *Berzelius in 1813, uses the initial letter of the Latin name of the element (sometimes followed by an additional letter for clarity). This use of Latin names means that some symbols are not immediately clear (for example, sodium is represented by Na [natrium] and gold by Au [aurum]); the symbols for more recently discovered elements are derived from their English names (see *periodic table). A great advantage of symbols is that *molecular formulae can be shown by symbols which indicate both the elements present and the proportions in which they occur.

**chemistry**, the scientific study of the elements and their compounds, and the reactions they undergo. Inorganic chemistry is concerned with the elements and all their compounds except those of carbon, which are the subject of *organic chemistry. Physical chemistry studies their physical properties and structures and the relations between energy and physical and chemical change. Analytical chemistry is concerned with determining the composition of substances.

What began with the belief that earth, air, fire, and water combine to form all things, and proceeded through *alchemy to the scientific approach of Robert *Boyle in the 17th century, has now reached the point where elements can be made that are not found in nature. The discovery of *radioactivity and the electron, and theories such as those of *valency and the *chemical bond, have resulted in many chemical phenomena being explained in terms of atomic physics. The applications are wide. Industry, agriculture, medicine, are all supported by chemical research in specialist fields. Some 4 million chemicals have been identified, of which not more than 35,000 are in common use.

**chernozem**, or black earth, a *zonal soil found in the grasslands of the semi-arid mid-latitudes. The nearly black surface *horizons of chernozems, which may be over a metre (3 feet) thick, are rich in humus which is carried down the profile by worms and small animals. They have a loose, crumbly structure and are rich in soluble salts, particularly of calcium, because rainfall is insufficient to cause excessive *leaching. These soils are therefore extremely fertile. The chernozem areas of the United States, Canada, the Ukraine, and Argentina are important grain-producing areas, and are widely known as the bread-baskets of the world.

**chenier**, a beach ridge, usually composed of sand-sized material resting on clay or mud and formed by the reworking of these materials by waves. Muddy, marshy zones usually lie to the front and rear of the chenier. It is the term for the oak tree belts marking the distribution of the ridges in the Mississippi delta regions. The arrangement and composition of these cheniers are evidence of a fluctuation in sea level over time.

**chert**, a form of silica ($SiO_2$) that is cryptocrystalline, that is, the crystals are too small to be distinguished under the microscope at ordinary magnifications. Very dense and hard, it occurs in bands or nodules in limestone and other sedimentary rocks. Thicker deposits of chert also occur. They are thought to originate from the siliceous shells of marine organisms. *Flint is a dark-coloured variety of chert that when fractured shows a smoothly curved, shell-like surface (a conchoidal fracture).

**Chesapeake Bay**, the drowned mouth of the Susquehanna River, forming the largest inlet on America's Atlantic coast. Nearly 320 km (200 miles) long, it is sheltered from the ocean by the Delmarva Peninsula and contains the estuaries of the Potomac, Rappahannock, and James Rivers. As one of the world's largest *rias it provides innumerable anchorages and also provides an ideal and extensive habitat for crabs and oysters.

**chestnut soil**, a *zonal soil found in the drier parts of the mid-latitude short-grass prairies where rainfall is about 350–500 mm (14–20 inches) a year. Although the low rainfall limits plant growth, the chestnut soils are fairly rich in humus. They are a characteristic dark brown colour, becoming paler with depth. The low rainfall also inhibits *leaching and so they may be quite calcareous. Thus, although chestnut soils occur in regions subject to drought, they are fertile under conditions of adequate rainfall or irrigation; they are widely used for livestock grazing in the American High Plains, the Argentine *pampas, and the South African *veld.

**Chile**, a long and narrow country on the west coast of South America, occupying some 4,600 km (2,860 miles) between Peru in the north and Cape Horn. On average it is only 160 km (100 miles) in width from the Pacific to the high Andes, along which run the boundaries with Bolivia and Argentina. In the north is the arid Atacama Desert, while in the centre the climate is mild and conducive to most forms of agriculture. Here and in the south the lower slopes of the *cordilleras are well forested and there are short, fertile river valleys. Tierra del Fuego, in the extreme south, on the other hand is cold, very wet, and relatively barren, suitable only for sheep grazing. Inland, along the whole length of the country, stretch mountains, yielding a great variety of minerals, among them copper and iron in enormous quantities. Rivers supply a source for hydroelectric power.

**China**, the third-largest country in the world, occupying most of eastern Asia and bounded by North Korea, Kazakhstan and Mongolia on the north, Russia on the west, Afghanistan, Pakistan, India, Nepal and Bhutan on the south-west and Burma, Laos, and Vietnam on the southeast. Its coastline adjoins the South and East China Seas and the Yellow Sea. In the north-west lies Xinjiang (Sinkiang), an area of mountains and desert, and in the south-west is the mountainous region of Tibet. The remainder of China is divided laterally by the Yangtze (Chang) River. To the north-west is the high *loess region, supporting millet and wheat. The wind carries the loess eastward to the flat northern plain, while the eastward-flowing rivers carry yellow silt. The plain, with a monsoon climate of warm, wet summers and very cold, arid winters, is highly cultivable. In the northeast lies Manchuria, on higher ground and with many rivers and lakes. In the west are the mountains and plateaux surrounding the red clay basin of Sichuan, which is well watered and supports a mass of paddy fields. Huge lakes occupy low-lying land to the south of the Yangtze, while southward the terrain rises to many ranges of high hills. Here the climate is subtropical. The plateaux support tea plantations, many of the slopes are terraced for rice, and the deep valleys are full of natural forests of bamboo. The province of Gansu in the north-west region is the principal centre of earthquakes in China, where major earthquakes take place on an average of once every 65 years. China is rich in coal, oil, natural gas, and many minerals, notably iron, tungsten, tin, and phosphates; and the rivers have great potential for hydroelectricity.

**china clay**, one of the purest *clays, comprising a white powdery material arising from the decomposition of feldspar in granite. It is composed mainly of kaolin, a hydrous aluminium silicate. Known first in China and worked in Cornwall, UK, since 1746, china clay has long been used in the manufacture of fine porcelain. France and several places in the United States are other sources. It is also used as a filler in paint- and paper-making, and in plastics and fertilizers.

**China Sea**, a term used for the East and South China Seas, once known collectively as the China Seas. Divided by the island of Taiwan, they lie largely on the continental shelf to the east and south-east of Asia and are bounded by the Pacific along the arcs of the Ryukyu and Philippine Islands. They are both seas with weak tides. The East China Sea (Dong Hai) is the shallower, with a mean depth of 270 m (890 feet). It lies to the south of the Yellow Sea and receives the water and the silt of the Yangtze River. The South China Sea (Nan Hai), which is connected to it by the Taiwan Strait, has a mean depth of 1,060 m (3,480 feet) but is much shallower in the south, where it lies on the submerged Sunda platform, one of the largest sea shelves in the world. Its western shore forms the coast of south China and part of south-east Asia, indented by the Gulfs of Thailand and Tonkin. It covers rich reserves of oil and natural gas and contains many small islands and reefs. Its climate is generally humid, particularly during the season of the north-east *monsoon, and it is subject to extremely violent *typhoons.

**chinook** (in meteorology), either a warm, wet southerly wind which blows west of the Rocky Mountains, or a warm, dry *Föhn wind which blows east of them. It commonly produces a rise in temperature of as much as 10 °C (20 °F) within a few hours in spring, causing rapid thawing when the ground is snow-covered. It is a North American Indian word meaning snow-eater (it is also the name of a tribe and has been given to a species of salmon).

**chirality** (in chemistry), a property of a molecule lacking a centre or plane of symmetry and thus not superposable on its mirror image. In organic chemistry, this requires that a molecule contains a carbon atom, called the chiral centre, to which four different groups are bonded. Such a molecule exhibits optical *isomerism, and displays *optical activity; it occurs in two different forms called *enantiomers. A molecule can possess more than one chiral centre. Thus, if there are two chiral centres there will be four isomers, divided into two sets of enantiomers. If there are three chiral centres, there will be eight isomers, existing as four sets of enantiomers.

**chloride**, a compound which contains the element chlorine, Cl, showing valency 1; metal chlorides are ionic and contain the $Cl^-$ ion, whereas non-metal chlorides are covalent. Metal chlorides are salts of hydrochloric acid. The most abundant chloride is *sodium chloride, which occurs in sea water and rock salt.

**chlorine** (symbol Cl, at. no. 17, r.a.m. 35.45), a yellow-green choking gas; it is a reactive non-metallic element in Group VII, the *halogens, and in the free state consists of $Cl_2$ molecules. With metals it forms ionic compounds which contain the $Cl^-$ ion, and with non-metals covalent compounds; it also forms compounds with oxygen in which it shows valencies 3, 5, and 7. It occurs as *sodium chloride in seawater, from which it is obtained by electrolysis, and in rock salt. Widely used for disinfecting water supplies and swimming pools, and as a bleach and germicide, it is also

Paper **chromatography**: a sample of black ink on paper (*left*) is separated out into its constituents when the paper is suspended in a bath of water (*right*). The yellow and blue colours of the constituents can be clearly distinguished; the greyish staining indicates where water (the solvent) has risen up the paper.

converted into a variety of compounds, such as the solvent trichloromethane, $CHCl_3$, the plastic polyvinyl chloride PVC, and dyes and anaesthetics. Chlorine gas was used as a poison gas in World War I.

**chlorine water**, the solution obtained by dissolving chlorine in water; the chlorine reacts partially with the water, giving hydrochloric acid, HCl, and hypochlorous acid, HClO. It is acidic, and strongly oxidizing.

**chlorite**, a type of silicate mineral mainly of green colour; it contains varying amounts of aluminium, magnesium, iron, and other metals in combination with water. It is formed by the alteration of *micas in *igneous rocks, and is common in low-grade *metamorphic rocks. Hard, dense, and plate-like in form, chlorites are of little commercial value and not much industrial use.

**chloro-fluorocarbon** (CFC), any gaseous compound of carbon, hydrogen, chlorine and fluorine. CFCs are non-flammable, non-toxic, and have boiling-points below room temperature, which makes them ideal for use in *aerosols and refrigerators. They are also used in the manufacture of plastic packaging. However, there is concern over their effect on the environment for CFCs are known to cause damage to the *ozone layer, which protects us from the Sun's harmful *ultraviolet radiation. CFCs liberate chlorine in the presence of ultraviolet light, which then reacts with ozone to form oxygen leaving the chlorine atom free to attack ozone again.

**chromatography**, a technique for separating different compounds which depends on the distribution of a substance between a mobile phase and a stationary phase. In a typical experiment, a drop of a mixture of dyes is placed on a piece of adsorbent paper (the stationary phase), which is hung with its tip in a suitable solvent (the mobile phase). The solvent will rise up the paper. When it reaches the dyes, they will tend both to dissolve in the solvent and to remain bound to the paper. The different dyes will show these two effects to differing degrees. If a dye is strongly bound to the paper and sparingly soluble in the solvent, it will hardly move up the paper. On the other hand, if a dye is only weakly bound to the paper and is highly soluble in the solvent, it will move further in the same time. Thus the mixture of dyes will be separated. Regions of different colour, corresponding to each dye, will be observed at different heights on the paper. The solid phase can alternatively be a column of an adsorbent substance, such as silicon dioxide, or a thin layer on an inert glass support. This latter technique is called thin-layer chromatography. In gas chromatography, the stationary phase can be a solid with or without a viscous liquid. The mobile phase is a stream of unreactive gas, such as nitrogen. Volatile substances are separated according to the time taken for the gas to sweep them through the stationary phase. This is called the retention time. The usefulness of chromatography is that it can be carried out on very small amounts of substance. For example, it is used to detect nanograms of drugs in the blood of athletes.

**chromium** (symbol Cr, at. no. 24, r.a.m. 52.00), a hard, white metallic element, one of the *transition metals. It forms compounds, with the main valencies 3 and 6, but is rather unreactive. Electroplating is widely used to produce a thin layer of chromium on other metals, a method of protecting them from corrosion and wear. Chromium forms heat-resistant alloys with iron and nickel, and is added to

The glacial tarn of Marchlyn Mawr in the Snowdonia National Park of North Wales occupies the bottom of a small **cirque** on Elidir Fawr. The lake is retained by a barrier of glacial moraine debris, which is pierced by a small outflow stream.

other alloys to increase corrosion resistance and hardness. Its compounds are widely used as pigments; chromium oxide is green, and lead chromate yellow. Chromium salts are used for tanning leather.

**Churchill Falls** (until 1965 known as Grand Falls), a spectacular series of waterfalls and rapids extending for some 26 km (16 miles) along the upper Churchill River (until 1965 known as Hamilton River) in western Labrador, Canada. The single largest drop is 75 m (245 feet) into the McLean Canyon (named after John McLean who explored the region in 1839), along which the water continues to tumble between sheer cliffs. It is an important source of hydro-electric power.

**Cimarron**, a river of America's Great Plains. It rises near the Capulin Mountain National Monument in north-east New Mexico and flows eastward through the northern Oklahoma panhandle district before bending north through south-east Colorado and south-west Kansas, where for some 160 km (100 miles) the old Santa Fe Trail followed its course. The bed here is dry except in early summer and in periods of flash floods. The river re-enters Oklahoma as a permanent flow and enters the Arkansas River near Tulsa after a journey of 1,123 km (698 miles).

**cinder cone**, a small volcanic cone built by explosive eruptions of clinkery fragments of lava and ash. The cinder (or scoria) is loosely packed and absorbs rainwater like a sponge, so that it is difficult for soil and vegetation to develop and the slopes stay steep and bare. Some large volcanoes, such as Paricutin in Mexico, began as cinder cones. More usually, however, they grow rapidly for a short period, up to 300 m (1,000 feet) or so, and then the vent becomes blocked and a new one develops near by. As a result, cinder cones normally occur in small groups.

**cinnabar** (mercury sulphide, HgS), the chief ore of mercury. It has a distinctive cochineal red colour, and is soft, heavy, and fragile in crystal form. It is found in veins associated with igneous activity and is deposited by hot springs in volcanic regions. Important sources are Almaden (Spain), Monte Amiata (Italy), Idrija (Slovenia), and California (USA). The mineral pigment known as vermilion is prepared from cinnabar.

**circulation** (in climatology), the global patterns of air movement in the *troposphere and of currents in the ocean. The oceanic circulation can be divided into surface currents driven primarily by winds, and the vertical or deep circulation which is density-driven. As the properties which determine the density of sea water are its temperature and *salinity, this deep circulation is also known as the thermosaline circulation. Because they are deflected by land masses, and because they are acted upon by wind systems and the *Coriolis force, surface current systems tend to form *gyres. The subtropical gyres, which are driven by the mid-latitude anticyclones, are characterized by deeper, stronger currents along their western boundaries (for example, the *Gulf Stream in the North Atlantic and the *Kuroshio in the North Pacific). By contrast, the eastern limbs of subtropical gyres tend to be wide, slow and diffuse currents; these eastern boundary currents are often associated with coastal *upwelling. The main component of the deep circulation is cold, relatively saline water which sinks in polar regions and flows towards the equator at great depths in the ocean, but

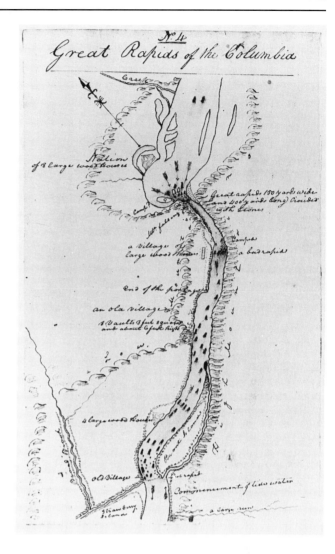

A sketch map of the Great Rapids on the Columbia River by William **Clark**. He and Meriwether Lewis left Saint Louis on 14 May 1804 to find a route to the Pacific Ocean and reached the mouth of the Columbia River in British Columbia, Canada, in November of the following year.

other *water masses sink at regions of *convergence of surface water. All water which is carried downward in the deep circulation is eventually, after tens, hundreds or thousands of years, mixed up to the surface again. Along the Equator, and in the vicinity of 65° S., are zones of divergence of surface water and hence enhanced upwelling of deeper water.

Atmospheric circulation consists of horizontal wind systems and vertical airflows. The horizontal wind systems are governed by the way atmospheric pressure varies from place to place. The vertical airflows are caused partly by large-scale *convection, partly by *convergence and *divergence at different levels, and partly by differences in the density of air masses. The driving forces are the atmospheric *energy budget and the transfer of heat from the equatorial zone towards the poles. The seasonal migrations of the *intertropical convergence zone north and south of the Equator is identified by areas of rising air and low pressure, which causes the monsoons. This rising air descends in the subtropics, giving areas of semi-permanent high pressure, and returns to the Equator in the *trade winds. In the mid-latitudes *westerlies blow from the subtropical areas of high pressure towards the *polar front, whose presence is marked by a westerly *jet stream. In the mid-latitudes the airflow aloft is a series of atmospheric *waves, while below it is dominated by cellular, migratory depressions and anticyclones. Temperatures over the South Pole are lower than over the North Pole, and consequently the thermal gradient and, therefore, the winds are strongest in the southern hemisphere, where the mid-latitude westerlies are termed the Roaring Forties.

**circumpolar vortex**, the two bands of mid-latitude westerly winds which encircle the poles in the middle and upper troposphere. The winds are strongest in winter, when there is the greatest temperature, and therefore pressure, difference between high and low latitudes. The westerlies of the middle latitudes are a manifestation of them at the Earth's surface.

**cirque** (corrie or cwm), a scoop-shaped steep-sided hollow formed in mountains or high plateaux by small, separate glaciers known as cirque glaciers. A classic cirque (such as Cwm Idwal on the side of Cader Idris, Wales) consists of very steep slopes of bare rock and *scree forming a semicircle cut into the mountainside. A low ledge of rock or *moraine stands at the head of the valley below, and a distinct hollow—which often contains a small lake or patch of snow—lies between this ledge and the back walls. A cirque begins to be formed when enough snow collects in a hollow to become compressed into ice, and this starts to flow, eroding the rock. As the hollow deepens, more and more bare rock is exposed and frost action prises off blocks which fall on to or into the ice and help further to erode the cirque floor. Cirques tend to form on the relatively shaded, downwind sides of uplands, where snowbanks collect best and last longest. If two cirques eat back into one ridge, *arêtes are formed, while three or more cirques developed round one mountain leave pyramidal peaks. The Matterhorn in the Alps is an example.

**cirrus**, a fine hair-like streamer of *cloud which forms in the upper troposphere, with a base generally between 8,000 and 11,000 m (25,000 and 35,000 feet) above ground level. Cirrus clouds are composed of ice particles. When newly developed they are well defined, but they become more diffuse and irregular as they grow older. Tangled masses of cirrus form when there is little wind at cloud level. More fibrous forms, the most wispy of which are commonly known as 'mares' tails', are indicative of strong winds aloft. Sometimes a thin film of cirrus in the night sky produces a halo round the moon; this is an almost certain indication of violent weather.

**Clapperton, Hugh** (1788–1827), British explorer, the first European to return from West Africa with a first-hand account of the topography of Nigeria. In 1822 he joined an expedition which crossed the Sahara in search of the source of the Niger. His companion having died, he proceeded alone and reached Kano, Katsina, Zaria, and Sokoto in 1823. Two years later he returned with his servant and companion, Richard Lander, reaching Yoruba in 1826, but civil war prevented them from reaching their goal, Timbuktu.

**Clark, William** (1770–1838), US army officer who jointly with Meriwether *Lewis commanded the Lewis and Clark expedition of 1804–6 across the American continent, a three-year trek from Saint Louis to the Pacific Ocean and back. Later he headed surveys, notably into the Yellowstone region, was governor of Missouri Territory (1813–21), and superintendent of Indian affairs.

**clastic sediments**, fragments of various sizes, ranging from clay and silt to large stones and boulders, derived from pre-existing rocks, which may have been of any type. Normally they were transported to the place where they were deposited by wind, water, or gravity. The corresponding rocks range from clays and shales through sandstones to conglomerates and breccias.

**Clausius, Rudolf Julius Emanuel** (1822–88), German physicist who established the mathematical explanation of the *kinetic theory of gases. He stated the second law of *thermodynamics in what is now its most familiar form: 'Heat cannot of itself pass from a colder to a hotter body', stressing the concept of entropy (dissipation of available energy).

**clay**, a *sedimentary deposit of very fine grain. The bulk of the microscopic particles of which it is composed are flaky. Their total surface area is correspondingly large, and they are able to take up relatively large amounts of water. When wet, the clay thus becomes plastic. The clay minerals that are the characteristic constituents of clays are hydrous aluminium silicates produced by the weathering of rocks. Some clays are rich in decayed plant and animal remains, which darken them; some contain iron and oxidize to brown colours when exposed to air. Residual clays are those that have formed in place by the weathering of rock. The sedimentary rocks termed clays are generally composed of material that has been transported, usually by water, and deposited elsewhere, often in a river estuary. Sometimes, when clay dries out, the surface cracks, peels off, and is carried away. Such flakes deposited in sand or other sediment are known as clay galls.

**cleavage** (in geology), the way in which a mineral or rock tends to split. In minerals, and particularly in crystalline materials, the natural lines of separation are determined by the internal arrangement, or lattice, of the atoms. There are planes of weakness in the atomic lattice, and the nature of the cleavage depends on the relative strengths of the bonds in these planes. In rocks, the cleavage is the result of partial or complete recrystallization during metamorphism. This produces a layered (foliated) structure that is independent of any original *bedding.

**cliff**, a steep, bare slope formed in rock, soil, *loess, or ice. Cliffs may be small, simple features where rivers have cut away their banks, or large, complicated forms 1,000 m (3,000 feet) or more high, running for long distances along an escarpment, a canyon, or a coastline. The shape and size of cliffs depend on three things. The first is the strength of the material forming them: soil or clay cannot support high cliffs as well as cemented sandstones or granite can. The arrangement of layers of different materials in the cliff face is also important: weak rocks near the bottom cause the whole face to collapse. Secondly, for slopes to stay steep and bare it must be difficult or impossible for soil and vegetation to develop. This depends largely on climate: in wet tropical areas, plants may cover slopes of 80°, whereas in deserts, slopes of 45° are barren cliffs. Finally, material must be prevented from piling up, smothering the bare surface: the sea, a river, or a glacier has to be actively moving debris away from the foot and keeping the face clear.

**Climatic types** A classification after Köppen and Thornthwaite

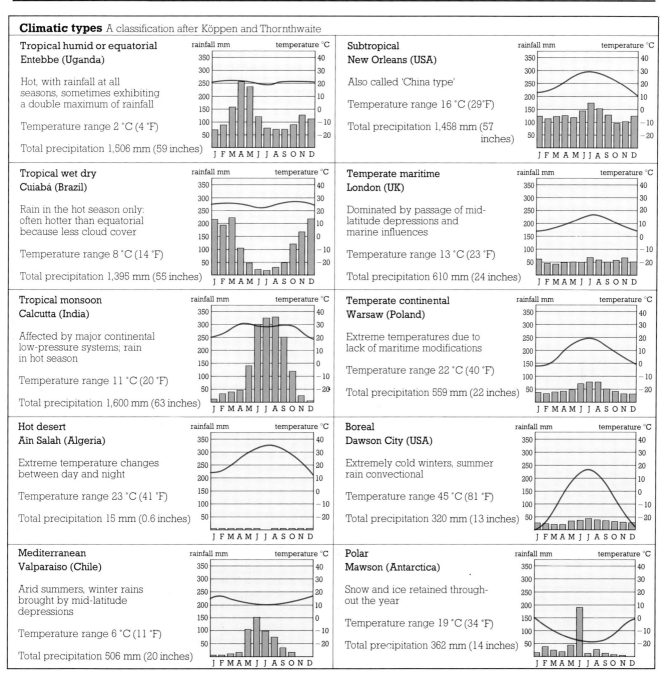

Tropical humid or equatorial
Entebbe (Uganda)

Hot, with rainfall at all seasons, sometimes exhibiting a double maximum of rainfall

Temperature range 2 °C (4 °F)

Total precipitation 1,506 mm (59 inches)

Tropical wet dry
Cuiabá (Brazil)

Rain in the hot season only: often hotter than equatorial because less cloud cover

Temperature range 8 °C (14 °F)

Total precipitation 1,395 mm (55 inches)

Tropical monsoon
Calcutta (India)

Affected by major continental low-pressure systems; rain in hot season

Temperature range 11 °C (20 °F)

Total precipitation 1,600 mm (63 inches)

Hot desert
Aïn Salah (Algeria)

Extreme temperature changes between day and night

Temperature range 23 °C (41 °F)

Total precipitation 15 mm (0.6 inches)

Mediterranean
Valparaiso (Chile)

Arid summers, winter rains brought by mid-latitude depressions

Temperature range 6 °C (11 °F)

Total precipitation 506 mm (20 inches)

Subtropical
New Orleans (USA)

Also called 'China type'

Temperature range 16 °C (29°F)

Total precipitation 1,458 mm (57 inches)

Temperate maritime
London (UK)

Dominated by passage of mid-latitude depressions and marine influences

Temperature range 13 °C (23 °F)

Total precipitation 610 mm (24 inches)

Temperate continental
Warsaw (Poland)

Extreme temperatures due to lack of maritime modifications

Temperature range 22 °C (40 °F)

Total precipitation 559 mm (22 inches)

Boreal
Dawson City (USA)

Extremely cold winters, summer rain convectional

Temperature range 45 °C (81 °F)

Total precipitation 320 mm (13 inches)

Polar
Mawson (Antarctica)

Snow and ice retained through-out the year

Temperature range 19 °C (34 °F)

Total precipitation 362 mm (14 inches)

**climate**, the sum total of weather conditions experienced over a long period of time. It includes extreme and variable conditions experienced, as well as average ones. The elements which it includes and which are recorded at weather stations are radiation, temperature, pressure, wind velocity, humidity, cloud types and amounts, precipitation, evaporation, hours of sunshine, and days with snow cover. It may refer to areas differing markedly in size, ranging from a small rural area or a town to a continent, or to the Earth as a whole. In any location the factors influencing the climatic conditions are latitude, altitude, topography, distance from the sea, ocean currents, type and density of vegetation, and soil conditions. Major *climatic change occurs naturally over only very long periods, the last great ice age ending nearly 10,000 years ago; but there is evidence that modifications are being caused by human activity. Atmospheric pollution, urbanization, and denudation of the landscape are all contributing to this process.

**climatic change**, a change caused by modifications to the Earth's atmospheric *energy budget, which may be the result either of a fluctuation in the output of energy from the Sun or a change in the heat budget of the *troposphere. Radical changes brought about the last ice age, after which temperatures in mid-latitudes rose very rapidly, so that by 4000 BC summer temperatures were several degrees higher than at present. This relatively warm period was then followed by cooler, wetter conditions around 700 BC. Conditions had ameliorated by AD 1100 but a marked deterioration followed, producing the so-called Little Ice Age between 1550 and 1700. Subsequently instrumental records, which became available in Europe from the 17th century, have revealed a general upward trend in temperature. Although in the last hundred years or so increased concentrations of atmospheric carbon dioxide have contributed to the *greenhouse effect, short-term fluctuations on a global scale (such as those experienced during the last 7,000 years) may result

Examples of **clouds** arranged according to the altitudes of their bases. From top to bottom: cirrus (high), altocumulus (medium), stratocumulus (low), and the low-based cumulonimbus that towers into higher levels.

more from an inherent instability in the atmospheric *circulation, together with miscellaneous factors such as an increase in atmospheric dust from volcanic activity. The longer-term, more dramatic, changes which result in ice ages will probably be the consequence of as yet unpredicted changes on a solar as well as global scale.

**climatic types**, the major kinds of climate that occur on the Earth. Classification enables the distribution of types to be described, although the boundaries are never sharply defined, since each type merges imperceptibly into its neighbours. While broad distinctions, as between desert, monsoon, and arctic climates, are easy to recognize, it is more useful to identify types in terms of biological response. Thus *Köppen recognized six major types on the basis of the relationship between temperature and plant growth, and *Thornthwaite later identified five major types on the basis of the availability of soil moisture in each month of the year. The distribution of global wind belts has also been taken into account. Most systems are complex, with subdivisions to accommodate all criteria. Broadly it can be said that the various elements are covered in ten basic categories, as typical in the global pattern: equatorial, or tropical humid (as at Entebbe, Uganda); tropical monsoon (Calcutta, India); tropical wet/dry (Cuiabà, Brazil); hot desert (Aïn Salah, Algeria); Mediterranean (Valparaiso, Chile); subtropical humid (New Orleans, USA); temperate maritime (London, Britain); temperate continental (Warsaw, Poland); boreal (Dawson City, USA), and polar (Mawson, Antarctica).

**climatology**, the study of climates. It involves mean values and the long-term variations which occur in meteorological phenomena, such as precipitation and temperature, and their distribution over the Earth's surface. Synoptic climatology attempts to relate actual weather conditions to patterns of airflow, and palaeoclimatology examines climates in the geological past.

Climatic trends are very slow. Even variations in a century of weather over a given region of the Earth may be insignificant in terms of long-term trends. The factors which determine general climate are complex, and the influence on them of human activity in the modern world (which is studied in applied climatology) is still uncertain.

**closure** (in mathematics), a condition in set theory which occurs if, for every two elements *a* and *b* in a *set, the result of some operation, −, *a* − *b* is also a member of the set. The set of *real numbers is closed under addition, since the sum of any two real numbers is also a real number. Closure is one of the necessary conditions for a set and an operation to form a *group.

**cloud**, a visible mass of condensed or frozen water vapour in the air. The former occurs when the air is cooled to its *dew-point and the relative humidity reaches 100 per cent. The air can be chilled in two ways: *advection over a colder land or sea surface, and expansion when raised to a greater height. The first leads to the formation of a low layer of cloud, the second to a layer or a heap, depending on atmospheric *stability. Layers form when stable air is forced to rise either up a hillside or over colder, denser air at a *front; heaps form when the upper air is unstable and *convection currents develop. Clouds exist only for as long as the condensation rate equals or is greater than the rate of evaporation of water droplets on their margins into the surrounding air. They are classified in two ways. The first is on the basis of their shape and structure: stratus is layered cloud in horizontal sheets; cumulus is heaped or lumpy, with a flat base and rounded top; cirrus is fibrous or feathery. The second way is according to the height of the cloud base: low means below 2,000 m (6,500 feet); medium means from there to 7,000 m (23,000 feet); and high may mean anything above 5,000 m (16,500 feet), for medium and high clouds are often lower in polar regions, and higher in tropical, than at the mid-latitudes. Cirrus cloud may occur at heights up to 13 km (8 miles). There are various combinations of form and height. Thus cirrostratus and cirrocumulus are both high clouds, altostratus (layered) and altocumulus (heaped) are medium-level clouds, and stratocumulus is a low, thick one. A nimbus cloud is a raincloud; nimbostratus is low and rain-bearing, while cumulonimbus towers up as a convectional thundercloud.

**cloud cover**, the amount of sky obscured by clouds. It is measured in eighths, or oktas, of the sky observed; and observers give estimates for the total cloud cover and for each type of high, medium, and low cloud seen.

**Clyde**, Scotland's most famous river and firth (or estuary). The river flows northward for 170 km (106 miles) from headwaters on the moorlands of the Southern Uplands. After the Falls of Clyde, where the river descends 76 m (250 feet) in only 6.5 km (4 miles), the valley opens out to Scotland's industrial 'heartland', centred on Glasgow. The Firth of Clyde passes through rolling country for 105 km (65 miles) before reaching the North Channel, which links the Irish Sea to the Atlantic Ocean.

**coal**, a black or blackish sedimentary rock of organic origin. It consists mainly of carbonized plant tissue that originally accumulated in swamps where there was little oxygen. It is now found in beds or underground seams, usually up to 2 m (7 feet) thick. *Peat represents the first stage in the formation of coal. The quality of a coal depends on its carbon content, and the term 'rank' is used to designate this. Coals with a high carbon content are thus referred to as of high rank. Subsequent heating and the pressure of overlying deposits increase the carbon content. *Lignite (brown coal) contains about 60 to 70 per cent carbon; bituminous coal, the dark shining variety familiar as a fuel, more than 80 per cent carbon; and *anthracite, the purest form, more than 90 per cent. Most lignites are of late *Cretaceous or *Tertiary Age, and most black coals are of *Carboniferous Age. North America contains more than half of the world's supply, but coal is plentiful also in Europe and elsewhere.

**coalescence** (in meteorology), the process whereby water droplets in a cloud combine to form larger drops. It occurs when large, free-falling, droplets, which have been produced by condensation, collide with and absorb smaller, slower, droplets lying in their path as they fall through the cloud.

**coast**, the border of the land nearest the sea. Coasts may be flat and low-lying, with gentle *beaches, *lagoons, or *mangrove swamps (as in the tropics), or they may be high with *cliffs (as is often the case elsewhere); but they are constantly changing with time. Some are altered by ocean currents and winds or by slow land movement such as *mountain building. Others are added to by rivers depositing silt in the form of deltas and mud-banks. Yet others are subject to erosion by the sea. When a coast is flooded, the result will depend on whether the land has sunk, leaving only islets and low headlands, or whether the sea has risen over ridges into valleys beyond, leaving the ridges as long, narrow islands. Valleys running towards the sea, as in glacier regions, form fiords when flooded which may be deeper than the sea-bed off shore. Some coasts may be affected by volcanic action, while others (in the Pacific) have been altered by the growth of coral reefs, either as straight barriers or in the circular form of *atolls. The accessibility of an area has always depended on its coasts. Whereas safe anchorages allowed the exploration and development of temperate regions, the inhospitable shores of many tropical ones have always had a contrary, inhibiting effect.

**Coast Mountains**, a range running parallel to the Pacific coast from British Columbia, Canada, to Alaska, a continuation of the Cascade Range, not to be confused with the (more westerly) Coast Ranges of the USA. It is composed mainly of metamorphic rock which has been heavily eroded, glaciers and rivers having cut deep and rugged valleys and gorges in all directions. The mountains themselves are majestic: Mount Waddington, the highest in Canada, rises steeply to 4,042 m (13,262 feet). Their melting snows and a superabundant rainfall provide hydroelectricity and from the forested slopes. Highest and broadest in the south, the range extends for over 1,600 km (1,000 miles).

**Coast Ranges**, a series of young, granite mountain formations running along North America's Pacific coast, from Alaska to southern California. Caused by folding at plate boundaries, they contain many escarpments, and their appearance is rugged. The *Saint Elias Mountains in the extreme north are the highest. The islands off British Columbia, the Olympic Mountains in Washington, and the Klamath Mountains in Oregon and California, all part of the chain, are heavily forested. Further south, below the Diablo and Santa Lucia ranges, the climate is much drier; and here the slopes are covered with coarse grass and scrub.

**cobalt** (symbol Co, at. no. 27, r.a.m. 58.93), a hard, grey metallic element; it is one of the *transition metals. Chemically resembling iron and nickel, it forms ionic compounds in which it shows valencies 2 and 3. It is commonly alloyed with other metals: with iron and nickel to make permanent magnets, and in steels to improve their cutting and wear resistance. Cobalt oxide is used in ceramics to give a blue colour, and to neutralize the yellow from iron compounds. The radioactive isotope cobalt-60 is used as a tracer and in cancer therapy.

**cobalt chloride** ($CoCl_2 \cdot 6H_2O$), a pale pink solid; on heating it loses *water of crystallization and turns blue. This can be used for invisible ink; writing in cobalt chloride solution becomes visible when warmed. The reverse change is used in anhydrous cobalt chloride papers, which are used to detect water.

**Cockcroft, Sir John Douglas** (1897–1967), British physicist who, with Ernest Walton, first brought about a nuclear disintegration ('splitting of the atom') by artificial means. In their classic experiment, performed in 1932, they used a high-voltage accelerator to speed up a beam of *protons (the nuclei of hydrogen atoms). The protons were directed at a plate of lithium metal, causing some of the lithium nuclei to break up into *alpha particles (helium nuclei). For their experiment, the two scientists were awarded the 1951 Nobel Prize for Physics.

**coherent radiation**, *electromagnetic radiation that is always in phase, with peaks and troughs all occurring in the same place. If you take a section across a coherent light beam, all parts of it would come to their maximum amplitude at the same instant and would continue to remain in step with each other. Such a type of beam is produced by a laser. An ordinary beam of light, by contrast, consists of a series of wave pulses that begin and end in a random manner so that there is no regular wave pattern between one part of the beam and another.

**col**, or saddle, a gentle depression in a mountain ridge, forming a pass between the valleys on either side. The term is also used to describe similar features on maps such as weather maps, particularly those showing variations in atmospheric pressure.

**cold fusion**    *fusion.

**colligative properties**, the properties that depend on the presence of a *solute in a liquid (solvent). These are *osmotic pressure, the lowering of the *vapour pressure and the *freezing-point of the solvent, and the raising of its *boiling-point. The amount by which any of these properties is altered is proportional to the number of particles of solute and is independent of their chemical identity. Thus, one *mole of any solute lowers the freezing-point of a fixed mass of a given solvent by an equal amount. Therefore, knowing the mass of added solute and measuring the consequent decrease in freezing-point, one can determine the relative molecular mass (molecular weight) of the solute.

**colloid**, a mixture in which there are two or more constituents (or phases). One constituent (the dispersion phase) is continuous and the other (the disperse phase) is present as dispersed minute particles. The particles are typically between $10^{-6}$ and $10^{-9}$ m in diameter. There are different kinds of colloid according to the phases involved. For instance solid particles in a gaseous continuous phase constitute a smoke, and liquid particles in a liquid continuous phase constitute an emulsion. Other types of colloid include *aerosols and gels. In lyophobic colloids, the particles show a marked tendency to coagulate: for example, colloidal gold precipitates in the presence of certain metal ions. In contrast, in lyophilic colloids, there is a high affinity between the continuous phase and the disperse phase, with the result that the latter tends not to coagulate readily: an example is the protein albumen, found in egg-white. Because of their size, particles in the disperse phase frequently scatter light, a property known as the Tyndall effect, first observed by John Tyndall (1820–93), an English physicist. Particles in a colloid often carry a net charge and thus they can be coagulated by oppositely charged ions. For example, colloidal mud precipitates at a river mouth, where it encounters ions dissolved in sea water.

**colluvium**, material which is loosened and moved by the various processes at work on hillsides, to pile up at their feet. A mixture of particle sizes can be represented depending upon the processes at work. Avalanches, rock falls, and frost shattering produce coarse, angular material, whereas the action of earthworms, needle ice, and soil creep give layers of fine, crumbly silt and loam.

**Colombia**, northernmost country of South America and the only one with coasts on both the Pacific and the Atlantic

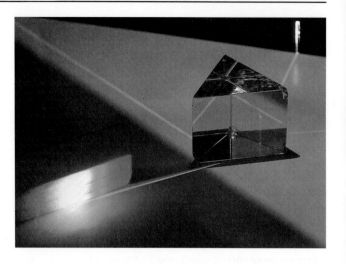

When a beam of white light passes through a prism it is split up into a spectrum of **colours**. White light is a mixture of all the visible wavelengths, which are refracted by different amounts in the prism, causing the various colours to separate.

oceans, separated by the isthmus of Panama. To the east is Venezuela, and to the south Brazil, Peru, and Ecuador. The northern end of the Andes occupies the north-western half of the country, here breaking into three great *cordilleras which enclose high, cool plateaux. Running from them are several large rivers to water the hot northern coastal plains. Coffee is the chief plantation crop here. South-east of the Andes, plains of rich pasture stretch away to the east and to the south, where the land falls in forested terraces towards the headstreams of the Amazon. About 5 per cent of Colombia's total area is arable, while 30 per cent is permanent pasture land. Colombia has large reserves of platinum, bauxite, and copper. Cannabis and coca are cultivated illicitly on a vast scale (73,000 hectares or about 180,000 acres of land) for the manufacture of illegal drugs.

**Colorado River**, the name of two major rivers of North America. (1) The greatest river situated in south-west North America, providing, with all its tributaries, hydroelectric power, and irrigation for vast areas. Rising among the highest peaks of the Rocky Mountains, it flows for over 2,320 km (1,400 miles) south-west, through numerous rugged canyons in the Colorado Plateau (including the Grand Canyon) to the head of the Gulf of California in Mexico. Here a huge delta has been formed by its silt; but so much of its water is now used for irrigation that it often dries up before reaching the sea. (2) The longest river in Texas, rising in the north-west of the state and flowing 1,450 km (900 miles) to the Gulf of Mexico. Along its length are many projects for irrigation flood control, and hydroelectricity.

**colour**, one of the qualities (another is brightness) that we attribute to *light, or to objects that reflect or emit light, when it produces the sensation of 'seeing' in the brain. The colour of light is determined by its wavelength: red light has a wavelength nearly twice as great as violet light, and in between come the other colours of the *spectrum in a continuous series. A mixture of all the visible wavelengths gives white light. Sources of light have characteristic spectra; these may be continuous (composed of a range of wavelengths), like those of sunlight or a light bulb, or discrete (containing only one or two wavelengths), like those of sodium or mercury street lamps. When an object is illuminated with white light some of the wavelengths in the light are absorbed by the object and others are scattered. It is the mixture of wavelengths in this scattered light which gives the sensation of colour and is called the hue. Thus an apparently red object is one which absorbs all wavelengths except those from the red region of the spectrum. Moreover, in this process of subtraction pigments can produce various subtle effects: certain parts of the spectrum may be scattered strongly and others weakly. Saturated hues mixed with white light produce tints; and the brain can distinguish many different degrees of saturation, perceiving depth and richness of colour. Many of the hues which we can discern, such as purple and brown, are not present in the 'rainbow' spectrum at all. They may be simulated by adding together a mixture of any three primary colours; these are a set of colours from which all the other colours can be produced by mixing them in suitable proportions; the usual three are red, green, and blue. If an object is illuminated by light which is not white, that is light in which certain wavelengths are absent, these wavelengths will also be absent from the scattered light, and so the object will change colour. The effect is very noticeable under sodium and mercury street lamps, because these emit only a very narrow range of wavelengths. Under weak illumination the eye does not distinguish colours well: on a moonlit night,

for example, there is only dark and light, and colours can scarcely be discerned.

In atomic physics colour is a property possessed by *quarks and *gluons. The word 'colour' and the names of the colours are used in this context in a purely metaphorical way: the quarks and gluons are not coloured in the usual sense. Colour is analogous to electric charge but comes in three varieties—red, green and blue—rather than the two varieties of electric charge. Three quarks make up a nucleon: one of each colour. Colour is believed to be the source of the *strong force, in the same way as electric charge is the source of the *electromagnetic force.

**Columbia Plateau**, a great, fertile region in the northwest of the USA between the Cascade Range and the Rocky Mountains. Originally a depression, it was filled by perhaps twenty basalt lava flows, mainly from fissure volcanoes. In parts the lava is 1,500 m (5,000 feet) thick. The plateau is drained by the *Columbia River and its tributary, the Snake, and contains the Blue and Wallowa Mountains, *cinder cones, and the barren landscape known as Craters of the Moon.

**Columbia River**, a great river rising in British Columbia, Canada, and entering the Pacific Ocean from Washington and Oregon, USA. Its course of over 1,930 km (1,200 miles) is a tortuous one. Flowing first north and then south among the Canadian Rocky Mountains, it enters the USA and is then forced west and south again before being joined by the Snake River. The combined flow then cuts westward

Two panels, depicting **Columbus**'s landing on Hispaniola, from *De Insulio Inventis*, a version of his 'letter', published in 1494, to Sanchez—an Aragon official, who raised a large part of the money for the voyage. The ship on the right is a more accurate representation than the one on the left.

through the Cascade Range to the ocean. Here it forms a fine natural harbour, having provided, on its inland course, the greatest hydroelectric potential of any river in the USA.

**columbium**   *niobium.

**Columbus, Christopher** (*c.*1451–1506), Genoese navigator who prevailed upon Ferdinand and Isabella of Spain to fund an expedition to 'the (East) Indies' for trade in spices. He proposed a westward passage, contrary to the general belief that none was possible, and set sail with three small ships in 1492. On reaching the islands of the Caribbean he named them the West Indies, believing himself to be near the Asian mainland. His published record was the first real evidence of the existence of the New World. A year later, for a second voyage, he was provided with seventeen ships and expected to trade for gold. He surveyed much of the Caribbean archipelago during the next three years, but then, with no gold forthcoming, he was recalled to Spain in disgrace. After months of lobbying, however, he was allowed again to search for Asia; and this time he took a more southerly route, discovering Trinidad and the mouth of the Orinoco. On his fourth voyage, in 1502–4, with four poorly equipped vessels, he explored the coast of central America, vainly seeking at Panama a strait that would lead him to Japan. He returned to Spain ill and discredited, and died in obscurity.

**columnar jointing**, a feature formed when lava cools and shrinks. Contraction results in tension in a layer of cooling lava, and this produces fractures that are more or less evenly spaced and are in all directions. Polygonal columns form as a result. These usually have from four to eight sides and are often hexagonal. They are characteristic in *basalt; fine examples can be seen at the Giant's Causeway, in County Antrim, Northern Ireland, and the Devil's Postpile in the Sierra Nevada, USA.

**combe**   *coomb.

**combustion**, or burning, the *exothermic reaction of an element or compound usually with oxygen. For example, magnesium burns in oxygen with an intense white flame to form magnesium oxide ($MgO$). When a compound is burnt, each element is separately converted to its oxide; thus hydrocarbons give carbon dioxide ($CO_2$) and water ($H_2O$) on combustion. A large proportion of the energy we use is obtained in this way, by the combustion of *fossil fuels such as coal and oil. Some combustion takes place without the flame and heat associated with the process, such as when body tissues are oxidized to give energy.

**commutativity** (in mathematics), a condition in set theory which occurs when, for any two elements $a$ and $b$ and an *operation, $-$, $a - b = b - a$. *Real numbers are commutative under addition ($3 + 7 = 7 + 3$) and multiplication ($3 \times 7 = 7 \times 3$). *Matrices are not, in general, commutative under multiplication.

**Comoro Islands**, or Comoros, a country consisting of a group of volcanic islands in the Mozambique Channel of the Indian Ocean, between the mainland of Africa and northern Madagascar. The chief islands are Great Comoro, Anjouan, and Mohéli. Mayotte remains a French possession. Exports include cloves and vanilla. Great Comoro is well forested.

**complementarity** (in physics). *Wave–particle duality is a feature of *quantum mechanics: elementary particles behave like waves in some situations and like particles in others. The *uncertainty principle is a mathematical statement of this dual nature. A consequence of the uncertainty principle is that there are some quantities, for example position and momentum, for which precision in the measurement of one precludes precision in the measurement of the other. According to the principle of complementarity, such pairs of quantities are complementary: that is, no possible measurement can determine them with greater accuracy than that allowed by the uncertainty principle. Experiments to determine complementary parameters therefore give results which, though real, cannot be assumed to be simultaneous: an experiment to obtain a precise measurement of momentum, for example, will give an imprecise measurement of position. The idea of complementarity was devised by Niels *Bohr to accommodate the uncertainty inherent in quantum theory. It is a philosophical explanation which satisfies most physicists—though not Albert *Einstein, who spent much of his life trying to refute it.

**complex numbers**, solutions of those quadratic equations which are insoluble in terms of *real numbers. They are defined as numbers of the form $a + ib$ where $a$ and $b$ are real numbers and $i = \sqrt{(-1)}$, a solution of the quadratic equation $x^2 + 1 = 0$. The real numbers can be seen as that subset of the complex numbers for which $b = 0$. Addition, subtraction, multiplication, and division of complex numbers can all be defined and obey the usual laws of arithmetic. The *Argand diagram gives a representation of complex numbers as points in the plane with *Cartesian coordinates $(a, b)$. In terms of *polar coordinates any complex number can be written equivalently as $r \cos \theta + ir \sin \theta$, where $r$ is the length of the line from the point to the origin and $\theta$ the angle that this line makes with the horizontal axis.

Complex numbers have wide practical application in science and engineering. Electronics and quantum physics, for example, use complex numbers extensively.

**components of a vector**, any two *vectors whose combined effect is equivalent to the original vector. Components do not have to be at right angles to each other, but for simplicity they are often chosen to be. A vector $x$ at an angle $\theta$ to the horizontal has a horizontal component of $x \cos \theta$ and a vertical component of $x \sin \theta$.

An almost perfectly spherical mineral **concretion** *in situ* in a sandstone cliff in New Zealand.

**compound**, a substance composed of molecules, formed when two or more elements combine chemically and in fixed ratios: for example, two molecules of hydrogen ($2H_2$) and one molecule of oxygen ($O_2$) react to give two molecules of water ($2H_2O$). Once formed, a compound can only be broken down to its elements by chemical means, unlike a *mixture, the components of which can be separated by physical means. Thus *electrolysis is required to decompose water into hydrogen and oxygen. The physical and chemical properties of a compound are different from those of its constituent elements. Water exhibits none of the characteristic properties of either hydrogen or oxygen: for example, it is a liquid at room temperature, while hydrogen and oxygen are both gases. In general terms, compound formation can be explained by considering the energy changes accompanying the process. In the formation of sodium chloride, sodium ions, $Na^+$, and chloride ions, $Cl^-$, have to be formed. In both cases, an input of energy is required. However, when these ions come together to form a crystal, the resulting attractions release so much energy as to outweigh the amount supplied in forming the ions. The formation of the compound is therefore accompanied by a net release of energy. Thus it is more favourable in energy terms for sodium and chlorine to exist as sodium chloride, rather than as the pure elements.

**Compton, Arthur Holly** (1892–1962), US physicist who discovered a phenomenon known as the Compton effect: an increase in wavelength which occurs when light, X-rays, or *electromagnetic radiation is scattered by electrons not attached to atoms. His discovery, made in 1923, provided support to the theory that light consists of *photons—tiny 'particles' of wave energy. In 1927, he shared with Charles *Wilson the Nobel Prize for Physics.

**concentration** (in chemistry), the weight of a substance in a known weight or volume of material. In solutions, it is usually measured in grammes per litre or moles per litre (*molarity).

**concretion** (in geology), a hard, compact, rounded nodule of mineral matter which may be found in sedimentary rocks, unconsolidated deposits, and soils. Concretions are generally formed by localized precipitation of minor mineral constituents such as manganese, or by, a cementing material—for example, silica, calcite, or iron oxide—round a solid object such as a fossil. Concretions vary in size from small pellets to great spheroidal bodies as much as 3 m (10 feet) in diameter.

**condensation nuclei**, atmospheric particles (of dust or ice, for example) around which water vapour condenses to form raindrops.

**condensation of vapour**, a process which occurs when a gas is cooled so much that it liquefies—very often in tiny droplets. For example, if steam is allowed to strike a cold plate, the surface of the plate becomes covered with water. When we exhale breath on a cold day we can see the condensation of the water vapour droplets from our breath. Vapour trails (or contrails) which appear to stream from the engines of high-flying jet aircraft are a result of the same effect, as is the formation of *dew. The reverse of condensation is *evaporation.

**condensation reaction**   *chemical reaction.

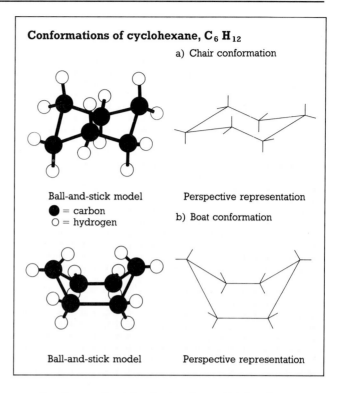

**Conformations of cyclohexane, $C_6H_{12}$**

a) Chair conformation

Ball-and-stick model
● = carbon
○ = hydrogen

Perspective representation

b) Boat conformation

Ball-and-stick model

Perspective representation

**conduction, electrical**, the flow of *electric current through matter. It occurs in three types of matter. In metals there is a bulk movement of electrons in the direction of an applied electric field. For a current to flow the electrons must be free to move and this occurs only if there are available energy levels just above the existing energy level of the electron; if these energy levels are too far above the existing levels then the material is an insulator. In solutions an electric current can be carried by electrolytes in *electrolysis. In *semiconductors the ability of the material to conduct is much less than in metals, but unlike metals, it increases as the temperature rises (see *band theory).

**conduction, thermal**, the flow of heat through matter. In order for it to flow from one point to another there must always be a temperature difference between the two points, the flow being from the higher to the lower temperature. The mechanism depends on the material. In metals the heat is transported by the same electrons that are responsible for electrical conductivity. In electrical insulators—that is, gases, some liquids, and non-metallic solids—no conduction electrons are available, and the heat is transferred from one atom to the next by the thermal vibration of the atoms. At room temperatures this mechanism is not as efficient as the transport of heat by electrons; and this is why metals tend to be much better conductors of heat than non-metals. In liquids and gases heat is transferred by direct collision between molecules, although this is less important than the bulk movement of fluid, *convection. The measure of a material's ability to conduct heat is called its thermal conductivity.

**configuration** (in chemistry), the different spatial arrangements that are possible in molecules containing the same atoms. In this respect it is like *conformation; the difference is that a change in configuration cannot occur by the simple rotation of a bond. Thus different configurations of a compound can be isolated. Cis- and trans-isomers are examples of compounds with different configurations (*isomerism).

## Conic sections

The standard conic sections, showing how they are derived and their equations. $F_1$, $F_2$, and $F$ are foci, and $e$ is the eccentricity, the parameter that determines the precise shape of the curves. The circle is a special case of the ellipse in which the eccentricity is zero.

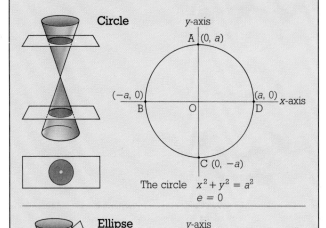

### Circle

The circle $x^2 + y^2 = a^2$
$e = 0$

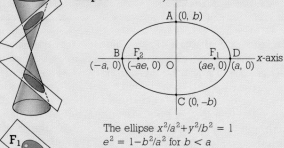

### Ellipse

The ellipse $x^2/a^2 + y^2/b^2 = 1$
$e^2 = 1 - b^2/a^2$ for $b < a$
$e < 1$
BD is the major axis
AC is the minor axis

### Parabola

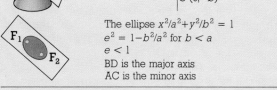

The parabola $y^2 = 4ax$ $e = 1$

### Hyperbola

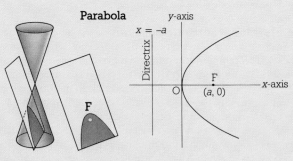

The hyperbola $x^2/a^2 - y^2/b^2 = 1$ $e^2 = 1 + b^2/a^2$
$e > 1$

**conformation** (in chemistry), the different spatial arrangements in a molecule that can occur by the twisting or rotation of single chemical bonds. Different conformations differ slightly in energy, and it is the one with the least energy that will tend to be the most stable form of the molecule. However, as it is relatively easy for a molecule to pass from one conformation to another, it is not usually possible to isolate one particular conformation of a compound. For example, cyclohexane ($C_6H_{12}$) consists of a non-planar ring of six carbon atoms. It exists in two conformations, named after the shapes they suggest. The boat conformation has two opposite carbon atoms above the plane of the remaining four carbon atoms, while in the chair conformation the two opposite carbon atoms are respectively above and below the plane of the other four carbon atoms. The chair conformation is more stable than the boat conformation.

**conformity** (in geology), the relationship shown by *sedimentary rocks in which the successive beds rest on each other without any evidence of interruption in the process of deposition. It is the opposite of *unconformity.

**conglomerate** (in geology), a *clastic sediment composed of rounded pebbles or boulders cemented into a matrix of finer sediment. If the fragments are angular rather than rounded, the rock is called a *breccia. Conglomerates can be formed in various ways. They may, for example, indicate an ancient marine transgression with an *unconformity; or storm deposition by floodwaters; or they may be of volcanic or glacial origin. They are widespread in occurrence and can be of any age. For example, in the eastern USA there are conglomerates of *Permian and *Triassic age which accumulated as gravel deposits after having been carried by rivers from the Appalachian Mountains. Accumulations of pebbles on present-day beaches may become conglomerates when cemented at some time in the future. Conglomerates are often used locally as building stone. Many contain minerals which are economically workable: the gold-bearing conglomerates of the Witwatersrand, South Africa, are an example.

**Congo**, an African country whose eastern boundary is the Congo River, bounded by Cameroon and the Central African Republic on the north and Gabon on the west. On its short stretch of Atlantic Ocean coast there are lagoons, large deposits of potash and oil. A small plain rises inland to a forest-covered escarpment, while most of the country comprises *savannah-covered plateaux. The climate is hot and generally very wet, the river valleys inland being marshy forest. Other mineral deposits include iron ore, zinc, lead, gold, bauxite, and phosphates.

**Congo**, the second longest river in Africa, flowing nearly 4,700 km (2,900 miles) from Zambia to the Atlantic. Its upper course, known as the Lualaba, runs northward through hills, savannah, and forest to the Boyoma (formerly, Stanley) Falls, a series of widely spaced rapids and waterfalls. Here it bends west, and becomes known as the Zaïre. Broadening, it passes in a navigable stretch through dense equatorial jungle, between sand-bars and round islands with evergreen forest. Then, turning south-west, it is joined by the Ubangi and later by the Kasai, the largest of many tributaries. From the lake-like Malebo (formerly, Stanley) Pool it descends by rapids called the Mateka and Livingstone Falls. Only for the last 140 km (87 miles) is it navigable from the sea.

**conic section**, the curve obtained by slicing a cone standing on a circular base with planes at various angles to its axis. Three distinct types of conic section exist: *ellipse, *parabola, and *hyperbola, the circle being a special form of ellipse. Although the study of these curves tends nowadays to be based on a *Cartesian coordinate description, in some respects the ancient Greeks' purely geometrical approach is simpler. Comets travel in orbits that are conic sections. Halley's comet has an elliptical orbit, but others, with greater speeds, follow parabolic or hyperbolic curves and so never return a second time to our solar system.

**Connecticut River**, rising in northern New Hampshire, USA, it flows south for 655 km (407 miles) to reach the Atlantic at Long Island Sound. Throughout most of its fairly direct course it runs in rapids down a wide, fertile valley between ranges of the northern Appalachian Mountains. It contains several falls, but for the last 80 km (50 miles) it is both navigable and tidal.

**conservation laws**. These relate the initial value of a physical quantity to its final value for a given process. If the quantity is 'conserved', it will be the same before and after the process. The idea that mass (that is, the quantity of matter) is conserved during chemical processes—the total mass of the reagents equals the total mass of the products—was the starting point of the modern theories of chemical reactions. The principle of the conservation of energy is fundamental to classical physics. Energy cannot be created or destroyed: one form of energy can be converted into another—for example the chemical energy in petrol is converted to the kinetic energy of a moving car—but the total energy will be the same after the process as before it. These two principles—the conservation of energy and of mass—had to be modified in the light of Albert *Einstein's proposition of the equivalence of mass and energy. In nuclear reactions, for example, mass and energy are considered together as a single quantity called the mass–energy: in such reactions it may be that mass and energy are not conserved, but, due to the conversion of one into the other, the overall result will be that mass–energy is conserved. Other quantities which are conserved include *momentum, *angular momentum, *charge, and *strangeness.

Antonio Snider-Pellegrini's maps proposed the concept of **continental drift**. These maps were published in 1858—more than 50 years before Alfred Wegener published his theory and more than 100 years before the concept of plate tectonics finally gave the idea scientific respectability.

**consistence** (in soil), the degree of cohesion between individual soil particles. It measures how easily the structure of the soil can be altered or destroyed, and is important in determining the shape and size of the *peds. If consistence is poor, then cultivation, particularly ploughing, may lead to a loss of structure, making the soil more subject to erosion and destroying its natural fertility.

**Constance, Lake** (German, Bodensee), a lake on the north side of the Swiss Alps, at the meeting point of Germany, Switzerland, and Austria, forming part of the course of the River Rhine.

**continental drift**, originally, a hypothesis which considered that the continental masses (composed largely of *sial) were floating on heavier oceanic material (*sima) and were drifting relative to each other. It was generally proposed that before the *Carboniferous Period there was one vast continental land mass, *Pangaea, which split up and drifted apart. This splitting occurred at different times to give, eventually, the present configuration of continents and oceans. The lateral displacement idea is ascribed to F. B. Taylor and H. B. Baker in America (1908) but mostly to A. *Wegener in Germany (1910). The idea was, however, first published in 1858 by Antonio Snider-Pellegrini. Wegener published his theory in 1915, but gained little support in early years since no satisfactory mechanism or motive force could be found. When, however, *plate tectonics became established as a theory in the 1960s the idea of continental drift became an accepted element of modern geological thought.

**continental rise**, a feature on the ocean floor which marks the extreme edge of a continent. A moderately sloping region between the oceanic *abyssal plain and the *continental slope. In some regions the rise is very narrow but in others it may be up to 600 km (370 miles) wide; and it may range in depth from 1,400 m (4,600 feet) to 5,100 m (16,700 feet). It takes the form of fans or aprons of sediment derived from the silts and clays of the continental shelf which have been carried downward by currents or under the influence of gravity.

**continental shelf**, the gently sloping margin of a continent at a shallow depth beneath the sea. It extends from the coast to a point where the seaward slope increases markedly, at which stage it gives way to a *continental slope. The depth at this point is generally somewhere between 100 m (330 feet) and 500 m (1,600 feet), while widths can vary considerably. The shelf off western Europe extends at least 320 km (205 miles) from the west coast of Britain; off the coast of Florida the shelf is 240 km (150 miles) wide, while that off the coast of Argentina is 560 km (350 miles) wide. It is much narrower or even absent, however, off some continents, particularly where fold mountains run parallel or close to the coast, as along the eastern Pacific Ocean. Most continental shelves represent land which has been inundated by a rise in sea-level. In some areas, like the Strandflat of northern Norway, they are thought to be the result of marine erosion; in other cases they are formed, or at least extended, by the building up of off-shore terraces or deltas by rivers. Off the coasts of regions which were once covered by ice sheets, they may consist of extensive glacial deposits: the area around the Grand Banks of Newfoundland was partly formed in this way. Under international law, the continental shelf is generally regarded as the extent of the territorial waters of nations it adjoins. Over the last few years the exact definition of these areas has become critically important, especially with regard to fishing rights and exploration for oil and gas.

**continental slope**, the relatively steep slope which marks the end of a *continental shelf. It is generally about 20 km (12 miles) wide but can extend for up to 100 km (65 miles) and contain many long canyons. Generally covered in clay and silty sediments carried down from the continental shelf by currents or under the influence of gravity, it gradually becomes less steep at its seaward end until it merges into the *continental rise.

**continents**, the major land masses of the world which constitute about 35 per cent of the Earth's crust if the submerged continental shelves are included. (Although submerged under shallow seas, the continental shelves belong to the continents rather than to the oceans.) Together with the oceanic plates the seven continental plates make up the Earth's *crust. In order of size the continents are Asia, Africa, North America, South America, Antarctica, Europe, and Australia. The rocks of the continents approximate to *granite in composition, and are of lower density than those of the oceanic crust, which are of *basaltic composition. Although subject to *continental drift, at no time do any of the great continental land masses appear to have been under more than shallow seas. (See also *plate tectonics.)

**contour**, a mapping line along which all points are at the same height above sea-level. Contours can be surveyed on the ground or from aerial photographs. In ground surveys the heights and positions of a number of points are determined by some combination of angle, distance, and height measurement, and the contours are interpolated between them. In aerial surveys the contours are traced directly in a photogrammetric instrument using pairs of overlapping aerial photographs, taken with a special survey camera whose axis in the aircraft is always near the vertical. These create a series of three-dimensional models of the ground on which the contours can be drawn while viewing each pair of photographs successively through a special stereoscopic device. The width of space between contours indicates the degree of slope on the land: the closer the contours the steeper the slope. Round hills appear as concentric circles; long ridges or valleys as roughly parallel lines. The complete pattern depicts the relief, or configuration, of the land.

**contraction of matter**, a process which occurs in most substances when they are cooled. Contraction occurs because, on cooling, the rapid motion of the atoms or molecules is reduced and this permits them to approach one another more closely; hence the volume of the material is reduced. Water is unique among liquids in undergoing *expansion as it is cooled from 4 °C to 0 °C.

**convection**, a process of heat flow and transfer that occurs in fluids, and involves movement of the medium itself. As the lower part of a fluid gets warmer it expands and thus becomes less dense than the fluid above it. It therefore rises, its place being taken by colder fluid which in its turn is heated, expands, and rises. The process continues so that heat is transferred throughout the fluid.

Air in the atmosphere above a warm land or sea surface will tend to rise, particularly so if it is moisture-laden. This is because the *latent heat released as the moisture condenses partly offsets the *adiabatic cooling which occurs as the air

Captain James **Cook**, portrayed at work in his study at Greenwich by the artist Nathaniel Dance-Holland.

rises and expands. In sea *breezes, air warmed by the land rises and is replaced by cooler air coming in from the sea. By contrast, convection in the ocean consists of surface water, which has become denser than the underlying water (usually through cooling, but sometimes also through increase in *salinity), sinking. This sinking water rises itself to become cooled and sinks in turn. The deep (thermohaline) *circulation can also be regarded as oceanic convection on a global scale. Transfer of heat by convection, involving the actual movement of water, occurs in all hot-water boilers.

**convergence**. Atmospheric convergence is a process which occurs whenever there is a net inflow of air into a region of the *atmosphere. Such an inflow results in the accumulation of air and an accompanying increase in density. The increase is relieved by a vertical motion, and in the lower troposphere this means an upward movement of air away from the convergence. In the upper troposphere, however, some movement is downward because upward movement is limited above the tropopause and stratosphere. In such circumstances, convergence above is associated with *divergence below and a decrease in cyclonic *vorticity. This encourages the development of anticyclones.

Oceanic convergences are found where surface waters are brought together and sink, as occurs in the centres of the subtropical oceanic *gyres under the influence of the mid-latitude anticyclonic wind systems. Convergence of water, and sinking, also occurs along oceanic *fronts.

**convergent series**, those number series such as $a_0 + a_1 + a_2 + a_3 + \ldots$ in which the successive partial sums obtained by taking more and more terms approach some fixed number or limit. For example, $3/10 + 3/100 + 3/1000 + \ldots + 3/10^n + \ldots$ is the series expansion of the decimal $0.333 \ldots$ and converges to $\frac{1}{3}$, a third.

**Cook, Frederick Albert** (1865–1940), US physician and explorer who claimed to have reached the North Pole in 1908, a year earlier than Robert *Peary. This and a similar claim to have climbed Mount McKinley in 1906 resulted in bitter controversy. Conviction for fraudulent use of the mail service led to his imprisonment from 1923 to 1929.

**Cook, James** (1728–79), British naval captain, navigator, and explorer. He charted the coasts and seaways of Canada (1759, 1763–7), and of New Zealand, eastern coast of Australia, and part of New Guinea (1768–71). On a second voyage (1772–5) he reached latitude 71° S. (being the first navigator to cross the Antarctic Circle) but was then driven back by ice. His third voyage (begun in 1776) was to find the *North-West Passage, which had eluded everyone from John *Cabot onwards. He was to seek it backwards, by entering the Pacific and sailing up the west coast of North America. He reached the Bering Strait and 70° N. before a wall of ice forced a retreat. On the way he had discovered Hawaii, a perfect place for refitting. Returning there his crew became engaged in a fight with the islanders over the stealing of a cutter, and he was stabbed to death. Cook had set new standards in the sea care of men exposed to lengthy voyages: in order to protect his crews from scurvy (a lethal disease caused by lack of ascorbic acid), he pioneered a diet that included cabbage, cress, and a kind of orange extract.

**Cook, Mount** (Maori, Aorangi, 'the cloud pieces'), the highest mountain in New Zealand, situated in the Southern Alps of South Island. Surrouded by 22 peaks exceeding 3,000 m (10,000 feet), at 3,764 m (12,349 feet) it is permanently snow-capped. The snowfields feed glaciers, particularly the Tasman Glacier, the largest, which descends on the south-eastern side.

**Cook Strait**, a stretch of water separating New Zealand's North Island from the South Island. Some 25 km (16 miles) wide at its narrowest point, it contains a deepish channel along the middle and is embayed on either side. The northern entrance faces north, the southern south-east; strong, gusty winds converge on it. The Strait lies within the main seismic region of New Zealand.

**coomb** (or combe), a short, steep-headed valley, not unlike a *cirque. (Indeed, the name is sometimes given to a small, shallow cirque in a mountain area.) The term is usually reserved for the steep-sided *dry valleys of such chalk areas as are found in southern England, and particularly for those which are cut into the face of an escarpment. These coombs are usually less than 5 km (2 miles) long and 100 m (300 feet) deep, with flat floors and side slopes at about 30° covered by short grass and a few bushes. Many have a spring near their mouths.

**Cooper's Creek**, the lower reaches, in Queensland and South Australia, of the Barcoo River. It is an intermittent stream flowing down from the Great Dividing Range to join its northern tributary the Thomson River, and meandering south-west to enter Lake Eyre. The total length is about 1,420 km (880 miles), but the Creek is generally a dry channel except after summer rains. The explorers Robert *Burke and William Wills died here.

**coordinates** (in mathematics), a means of specifying the location of points in space. Many different systems are possible, but the two most widely used systems in the plane are

The open-cast **copper** mine at Mount Morgan, eastern Queensland, Australia.

*Cartesian coordinates and *polar coordinates. The basis of any coordinate system is some collection of reference points or lines called axes. The coordinates of any point then reflect the distances or angles (or distances and angles) from it to the axes. Coordinate descriptions are usually ordered sets of numbers and contain the numerical information necessary to specify a particular point. Compass directions (N., S., E., W.) are a rudimentary coordinate system; it can be successively refined to NE, to NNE, and to the more precise numerical bearing system, which is based on angles in degrees from a fixed heading (North). On a sphere, such as the Earth, *latitude and longitude form one possible coordinate reference system.

**copper** (symbol Cu, at. no. 29, r.a.m. 63.55), a coloured metallic element which is a good conductor of heat and electricity, and is corrosion-resistant. It is a member of the *transition metals and forms ionic compounds in which it shows valency 2, or more rarely 1. Rather an unreactive metal, it is unaffected by water and acids; on long exposure to air it acquires a green protective layer of basic copper carbonate: verdigris. Its main use is for electrical wiring, but it is also used in building construction for roofing and piping, and in alloys for coinage. It is widely alloyed with other metals, and forms brasses with zinc, and bronzes with tin. Copper compounds, which are poisonous, are used as fungicides, fabric and wool preservers, and colouring agents. The main sources of copper are copper pyrites ($CuFeS_2$) and other copper sulphides, as well as *cuprite, from all of which the metal must be extracted, although it exists naturally. Major producers include the USA, Russia, Zambia, Zaïre, and Chile.

**copper(II) oxide** (CuO), a black solid which is insoluble in water. It is formed by heating copper in air, and by heat-

A small, heavily vegetated **coral island**, one of the thousands that fringe the Great Barrier Reef off the east coast of Australia.

ing copper hydroxide, nitrate, or carbonate. One of its uses is in anti-fouling paints for ships' hulls.

**copper(II) sulphate** ($CuSO_4$), a blue crystalline solid when in its hydrated form. On heating this loses water, forming the white anhydrous salt. It is readily reduced to copper on heating in a stream of hydrogen. It is used in agriculture as a soil additive and fungicide, and in electroplating.

**coral island**, an *atoll, or reef comprising rock which has been formed by the calcareous skeletons of myriad polyps, often building on a volcanic base. Because these coral animals can live only in clear, warm, and unpolluted water, the formations are found only between latitudes 30° N. and S. of the Equator, and generally in the Indian and Pacific Oceans, away from coastlines and river mouths. Once a formation is built up almost to the surface, waves break pieces off and pile them higher. Then sun, wind, and marine borers help the water to split and grind the coral to sand. Seeds of plants and trees are carried by water, wind, or bird and take root; and, lastly, drifting flotsam arrives with insect life.

**Coral Sea**, part of the south-western Pacific Ocean, lying in a basin between the coast of Queensland, Australia, and an island arc comprising New Guinea, the Solomons, and Tuvalu. It has a mean depth of 2,390 m (7,850 feet) and contains many coral islets and reefs; the Great Barrier Reef runs along the Queensland coast. Its deeper northern part is known as the Solomon Sea.

**cordillera**, a system or group of usually parallel mountain ranges together with intervening plateaux, applied originally by the Spaniards to the parallel chains of the Andes in Central America. The term is applied to the chain of mountain systems extending from Alaska to Nicaragua, including the Rocky Mountains, the ranges of the Great Basin, the Sierra Nevada, the Coast Ranges, and the Sierra Madre.

**Corfu** (modern Greek, Kerkira), northernmost of the Ionian Islands, a loose chain which runs down the western coast of Greece close to the Albanian coast. There is a great variety of scenery within its area of 593 km$^2$ (229 sq. mi.) of limestone structure.

**Coriolis force**, a fictitious force used to explain the movement of objects in a rotating system, for example, the movement of an air mass or the path of a rocket over the surface of the Earth. It was first described by the French mathematician and engineer, Gaspard Gustave de Coriolis (1792–1843). A point on the Equator travels about 1,670 km (1,050 miles) in one hour as a result of the Earth's rotation. A parcel of air above such a point will move with the same speed, and will keep this speed as it travels north. However, the further north it travels, the smaller the distance that a point on the Earth beneath it moves in one hour. To an observer on the Earth, therefore, it appears that the parcel of air is moving to the right. In this way wind and water currents are deflected to the right in the northern hemisphere and to the left in the southern, an effect which explains *Buys Ballot's law. The deflection is a direct result of the rotation of the Earth and not caused by any special force.

**cornelian**, a red and white or reddish-brown agate, which is a form of *chalcedony and a variety of silica. Cornelians are prized as semiprecious stones and are also used for making seals.

**corona**, a multi-coloured ring seen round the Sun or Moon. It is caused by the \*diffraction of light passing through droplets in the water vapour of the atmosphere, the radius of the ring depending on the size of the droplets. The outside of the ring is red, and the inside blue.

**corrasion** (in geomorphology), the mechanical pounding, scraping, and battering action of water or ice carrying pieces of rock, which wears away the land surface. Indeed it is the main process of erosion nearly everywhere, although it gives way in deserts to abrasion by sand and rock carried by the wind, and in areas of soluble rocks such as limestone to the dissolving action of fresh or salt water, termed corrosion.

**correlation** (in statistics), the interdependence of sets of data. The correlation coefficient measures in some sense the similarity between two scores, independently of the units in which the data is presented. The coefficient is usually a number between −1 and +1. Positive values imply that as one score increases so does the other, negative coefficients indicate a decrease in one score compared with an increase in the other. Coefficients of −1 and +1 are said to exhibit perfect negative or positive correlation. A zero value indicates no correlation, although it does not imply that the data sets are necessarily independent. Similarly, positive correlation does not guarantee a casual connection, as a classic example will illustrate. An American survey showed high correlation between the crime rate and the number of church attendances in a particular state. Both were on the increase, but it seems unlikely that either caused the other.

**corrie**   \*cirque.

**corrosion**, the formation of a surface compound on a metal by the action of air, moisture, or acid or alkaline pol-

A perfect lunar **corona** formed by the diffraction of moonlight passing through the minute water droplets in a veil of ground-level fog.

**Corrosion** of metals is seen in the wreck of the *Maria Schroeder* in the Red Sea. Constant exposure to moist air and the high salinity of this sea have rusted the entire ship and caused the lower hull to disintegrate.

lutants. If the compound is an oxide, the layer may protect the metal against further corrosion by air and merely tarnish it, as happens with copper and aluminium. Attack by moisture on the other hand may cause electrolytic corrosion with pitting and weakening of the metal. On iron and steel this is known as \*rust.

**Corsica**, a west Mediterranean island lying south of the Gulf of Genoa and just north of Sardinia, under French rule. Its north–south length is 183 km (114 miles) and its west–east width is 84 km (52 miles). A mountainous fragment of an old land mass, now submerged, it has high ridges separating secluded valleys, Mount Cinto rising to 2,710 m (8,891 feet). While the west coast is rocky and broken by deep bays, the east has an alluvial coastal plain which is very fertile.

**corundum**, an aluminium oxide mineral which is occasionally found in the form of brilliantly coloured gemstone varieties such as \*rubies and \*sapphires. More commonly it occurs in opaque grey or brown crystalline form; crystals weighing upwards of 170 kg (375 pounds) have been found in South Africa. It occurs chiefly in shales and limestones that have been subjected to contact metamorphism and in veins associated with igneous rocks. Being extremely hard, it is ground for use as an abrasive powder.

**cosine**, the ratio of the adjacent side to an angle, in a right-angled triangle, to the hypotenuse. Due to the properties of similar triangles, the value of this ratio is independent of the size of the particular triangle chosen. The term cosine is used because the cosine and \*sine functions are very closely related by means of the formula $\cos(\pi/2 - x) = \sin x$.

**cosmic rays**, high-energy charged particles which bombard the Earth from space. The primary cosmic rays which arrive in the upper atmosphere in a constant stream consist mainly of \*protons (alpha particles may also be present). They interact with the atoms of the atmosphere, producing secondary rays of generally short-lived particles such as \*pions. Sometimes these interactions cause a shower, either of electrons, positrons, or photons (a cascade or soft shower), or of nucleons and muons (a shower capable of considerable penetration). The origin of cosmic rays is not fully estab-

The snow-capped peak of the volcano **Cotopaxi** lies within 80 km (50 miles) of the Equator. A secondary cone known as the Cabeza del Inca (Spanish, 'Inca's head') can be seen on the slope to the left. Cotopaxi was climbed successfully in 1872 by William Reiss.

lished. Some come from the Sun, but most are the products of galactic and extra-galactic explosions.

**Costa Rica**, a small country on the Central American isthmus, between Nicaragua and Panama. It has a Caribbean coast on its north-east and a Pacific coast on its south-west. While the coastal lowlands have a tropical climate, a range of volcanic mountains occupies the centre of the country, providing plateaux which have a mild climate. There are several peaks over 3,350 m (11,000 feet). The soil is very fertile and supports livestock farming and some of the finest coffee in the world.

**Côte d'Ivoire** (Ivory Coast), a tropical West African country, bounded on the west by Liberia and Guinea, on the north by Mali and Burkina Faso, and on the east by Ghana. Its south-facing coastline is rocky in the west but elsewhere has sand-bars and lagoons. Three rivers run through the hot, rain-forested lowlands. In the central belt coffee is grown. In winter the drying *harmattan blows down from savannah-covered sandstone uplands. The Nimba Mountains in the west contain iron, and there are deposits of diamonds and manganese, cobalt, and uranium.

**Cotopaxi**, the world's tallest continuously active volcano, in the Cordillera (Mountains) of the Andes, rising to 5,897 m (19,347 feet) in north-central Ecuador. It has a snow-capped cone and a distinctive volcanic symmetry broken only by a

feature known as the Cabeza del Inca. The mountain's rich volcanic ash has created a fertile sediment of soil, with agricultural settlements concentrated in the Latacunga Basin.

**coulomb** (symbol C), the *SI unit of *electric charge. In magnitude it is equivalent to the charge on $6.24 \times 10^{18}$ electrons, though it is not defined in this way. By definition, a charge of one coulomb passes any point in an electric circuit when a current of one ampere flows for one second. It is named in honour of the French physicist, Charles-Augustine de Coulomb (1736–1806), who also established the basic law describing the force between electrical charges called Coulomb's law. This states that the force between two charges is proportional to the inverse square of the distance which separates them and to the product of the two charges. Thus if the separation of two charges is doubled, the force of one on the other is reduced to one quarter of the original force.

**country rock** (in geology), the rocks that enclose mineral veins or an intrusive mass of *igneous rock.

**covalent bond**  *chemical bond, *covalent compound.

**covalent compound**, a compound containing atoms joined by covalent bonds (see *chemical bond). If one pair of electrons is shared then a single bond is formed; with two pairs of electrons a double bond; and with three pairs of electrons a triple bond. In a molecular compound, such as carbon dioxide ($CO_2$) it may be possible to distinguish between individual molecules, since the distances between atoms in a given molecule are shorter than the distances between adjacent molecules. Furthermore, the covalent bonding within a molecule is usually considerably stronger than the *intermolecular forces. Therefore the individual molecules are relatively easily separated; in other words, such substances are often gases or liquids, or solids with low melting-points. Molecular compounds tend to be soluble. *Polar molecules, such as ethanol ($CH_3OH$), dissolve in polar solvents, such as water, while non-polar molecules, such as iodine ($I_2$), dissolve in non-polar solvents, such as hydrocarbons. In cases where compounds consist of covalent molecules bonded by intermolecular forces to form larger structures (such as silica, $SiO_2$), it is not possible to consider the properties of the individual molecules. All the bonding forces contribute to the properties of the compound. They have high melting-points and boiling-points, and tend to be hard and insoluble.

**crater**, a roughly circular, closed depression in the land surface, caused either by impact or by explosion. Impact craters, caused by meteorites, are rather broad, shallow, and flat-floored, with a small mound near the middle which marks the point of impact. The rim is steep on the inner side, but gentle or non-existent on the outer. Few meteorite craters survive for long on the Earth's surface because processes of weathering and erosion obliterate their shapes; but on the Moon, where there is no atmosphere, millions are preserved. Explosion craters form in the cones of volcanoes. They are usually well above the surface of the surrounding land and are ringed by distinctive volcanic rocks. Their shape is variable and irregular, since it depends upon the recent history of volcanic activity. *Cinder cones have rather smooth, gentle-sided craters (like a small scoop off the top of a boiled egg), whereas those of large volcanoes look far more ragged (like the top of a boiled egg smashed with its shell on). The centres of active craters contain vents leading down to their magma chambers, while craters of dormant or extinct volcanoes generally contain lakes.

**Crater Lake**, a flooded *caldera in Crater Lake National Park, high up in the Cascade Mountains in southern Oregon, USA. Nearly 10 km (6 miles) wide, and 604 m (1,983 feet) deep, it formed in the cone of an extinct volcano, Mount Mazama, at 1,830 m (6,000 feet) above sea-level. It is surrounded by cliffs rising another 600 m (2,000 feet) above its surface. Filled by rain and melted snow, it is very deep and, in sunlight, a clear blue. Wizard Island, in the middle of the lake, is part of the former volcano's cone.

**craton**    *shield in geology.

**creep of soil**, the slow downhill movement of soil particles disturbed for any reason, the force of gravity causing them to settle slightly downslope of their initial position. The disturbances arise in various ways: by the impact of raindrops; by swelling and shrinking, as the soil is wetted and dried; by the growth and melting of ice crystals; by the action of plant roots; by the burrowing and scratching of all kinds of animals; and by the tread of grazing animals. Even in areas with thick soil, vegetation cover, and gentle slopes, soil creep is an erosional process.

**Cretaceous Period** (from the Latin, 'chalk'), the last geological period of the *Mesozoic Era, spanning the period of time from some 144 to 66.4 million years ago. The climate was warm and the sea-level rose, and by the middle of the period marine transgression was widespread. *Chalk, a white limestone of great purity, is a characteristic deposit of the Upper Cretaceous in north-west Europe; it also occurs

in parts of the USA. In many places it is 460 m (1,500 feet) thick. Similar marine limestones were also deposited elsewhere. The Cretaceous saw the emergence of the first flowering plants and the dominance of dinosaurs, although these died out before the end of the Mesozoic Era.

**Crete**, a long, narrow island in the eastern Mediterranean Sea, under Greek rule. Its west–east length is 257 km (160 miles) and its north–south breadth 56 km (35 miles) at its broadest point. High limestone mountains rise in long chains along its centre, Mount Ida reaching 2,456 m (8,058 feet), and enclose a number of small, elevated plains, formerly the basins of lakes which dried up or drained away. These plains once were centres of ancient Greek civilization.

**crevass**, a deep, gaping crack in a *glacier or moving ice-sheet (although the term is also used to describe cracks in river banks, especially in the *levees of the lower Mississippi, USA). Crevasses are caused by stresses which build up within the ice as it meets obstacles and as different parts move at different rates. They open and close as it moves and may be hidden by crusts of snow, making travel on the ice both difficult and dangerous. Glaciers show distinctive patterns of crevasses along their length. At the head of the *cirque glacier lies a deep arcuate crevasse, or bergschrund,

Alpinists thread their way through a maze of deep **crevasses** on a steep section of the Bossons glacier in the Mont Blanc massif, France.

which is caused by movement away from the back wall. As ice flows over the lip of the cirque, an ice-fall is produced; and massive crevasses break the ice into huge, unstable blocks. Along the main glacial valley, sets of crevasses run out diagonally from the walls, reflecting the strains set up as ice at the centre moves faster than at the sides. Obstructions in the bed, under the ice, cause transverse crevasses; and the snout may have curved patterns, pointing down valley.

**Crimea, the**, a peninsula in southern Ukraine, bounded on the west and south by the Black Sea and on the east by the Sea of Azov. Northward the 8-km (5-mile)-wide Perekop Isthmus joins it to the Ukraine mainland. The northern area comprises a low, flat plain of steppe grassland which has only 250–380 mm (10–15 inches) of precipitation a year. In the south mountain ridges rising to 1,545 m (4,769 feet) extend for 160 km (100 miles) in length and 48 km (30 miles) in width and protect the south coast from cold northerly winds, giving this coast a Mediterranean climate. The north-east shoreline is noted for its stagnant, shallow, but mineral-rich lagoons.

**critical point**, the moment at which the properties of the liquid and gaseous phases of a fluid become identical. It is defined by the fluid's critical temperature and critical pressure. The temperature above which it is impossible to liquefy a gas merely by compressing it is called the critical temperature, and the pressure which is necessary to produce liquefaction at this temperature is the critical pressure. The critical points for both oxygen and nitrogen are below −100 °C (−148 °F) and this is why air at room temperature will not liquefy however much it is compressed. Carbon dioxide, which has a critical temperature of approximately 31 °C (88 °F), can be liquefied by compression and is often used in demonstration experiments of the critical point.

**Croatia**, a country in south-eastern Europe bounded by Slovenia, Hungary, Bosnia-Herzegovina, Serbia, and the Adriatic Sea. In the south-west, the Dinaric Alps form a rugged chain, while the north-eastern part is mostly flat and fertile and well suited to agriculture. Grapes are grown mainly on the off-shore islands. Natural resources include hydraulic power, coal, bauxite, and oil.

**Crookes, Sir William** (1832–1919), English physicist and chemist whose wide-ranging researches included the identification of the element thallium and the discovery of cathode rays produced by electrical discharge in a vacuum tube. His detailed studies of the properties of cathode rays (now known to be streams of *electrons) led to the discovery of *X-rays by Wilhelm von *Röntgen and of the electron by Joseph *Thomson. He also designed a device to measure radiation, the Crookes' radiometer, which contains a series of vanes in an evacuated glass bulb, one side of each vane being silvered, the other matt black. He was president of various societies, including the Royal Society.

**crust** *Earth.

**crystal**, a solid three-dimensional form of a substance in which a regular internal atomic structure is expressed by a regular arrangement of plane (flat) faces. For each crystalline form of a substance the angles between particular crystal faces are always the same. The angles remain constant even when the growth of the crystal is distorted, as is often the case in nature. The crystal structure is one of the characteristic properties of a mineral identified by its X-ray diffraction pattern. All crystals can be assigned to one of the seven crystal systems, according to their degree of symmetry. Crystals may be described in terms of the groups of faces (forms) that bound the solid crystal. Thus, a cube-shaped crystal (such as

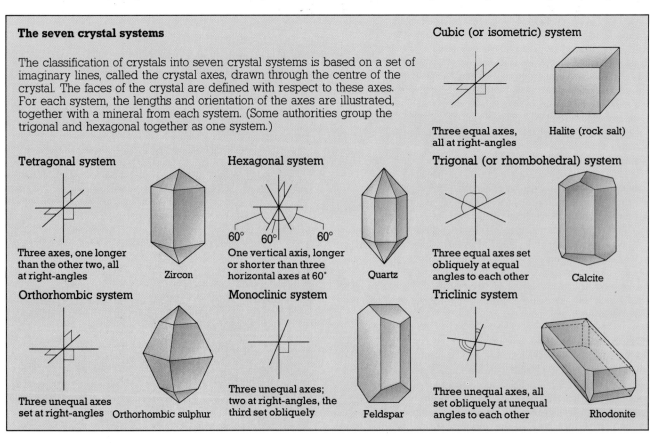

**The seven crystal systems**

The classification of crystals into seven crystal systems is based on a set of imaginary lines, called the crystal axes, drawn through the centre of the crystal. The faces of the crystal are defined with respect to these axes. For each system, the lengths and orientation of the axes are illustrated, together with a mineral from each system. (Some authorities group the trigonal and hexagonal together as one system.)

Cubic (or isometric) system
Three equal axes, all at right-angles
Halite (rock salt)

Tetragonal system
Three axes, one longer than the other two, all at right-angles
Zircon

Hexagonal system
60° 60° 60°
One vertical axis, longer or shorter than three horizontal axes at 60°
Quartz

Trigonal (or rhombohedral) system
Three equal axes set obliquely at equal angles to each other
Calcite

Orthorhombic system
Three unequal axes set at right-angles
Orthorhombic sulphur

Monoclinic system
Three unequal axes; two at right-angles, the third set obliquely
Feldspar

Triclinic system
Three unequal axes, all set obliquely at unequal angles to each other
Rhodonite

halite) with (in the ideal development) all its faces identical is a simple cubic structure. Quartz, with its characteristic hexagonal columnar shape capped by a pyramid, exhibits two forms, the prism and the pyramid. Well-formed crystals may be used for a variety of purposes. Some are used as gemstones; others, such as calcite or quartz, have commercial uses. Crystallization is the process which results in the formation of crystals and occurs either by cooling a melt or by cooling or evaporating a solution. As crystallization proceeds the randomly moving molecules of the melt or solution become stabilized in definite positions relative to each other, establishing long-range order in the solid crystal. In solution *water of crystallization is frequently incorporated into the crystal structures. The growth of a crystal occurs in an orderly fashion, reflecting the crystal structure of the substance and external conditions. Apart from the many crystals that occur in nature there are many important industrial applications of crystallization—sodium chloride crystals are formed by the evaporation of seawater, sugar crystals by cooling hot, saturated solutions, and synthetic gemstones and diamond under extreme conditions of temperature and pressure.

**Cuba**, an island country, the largest of the *Caribbean Islands. It is long and narrow—about 1,280 km (795 miles) from west to east yet rarely more than 160 km (100 miles) from north to south. Most of it is flat, with plains rising southward to heights seldom greater than 90 m (295 feet), except in the south-east, where the Sierra Maestra reaches 2,000 m (6,560 feet) and more. The climate is tropical, with heavy rain and easterly winds which often become hurricanes. Sugar, molasses, and high-quality tobacco are the chief crops, while iron, nickel, and manganese are the main mineral resources.

**cuesta**   *escarpment.

**cumulonimbus clouds**, or thunderclouds. These have towering, diffuse tops consisting of ice crystals, rather than the cauliflower-like domes of the large cumulus clouds from which they develop. The difference is associated with the development of excessive *precipitation within the cloud mass. Growth is enhanced by the strong vertical convection currents which occur within the cloud; and if the top of an upward-growing cumulonimbus encounters a stable layer of air above, it is drawn out downwind beneath it, so that the upper portion of the cloud mass develops into a smooth, fibrous streamer which commonly resembles an anvil.

**cumulus clouds**. These develop over regions of strong upward *convection, such as heat sources (for example, volcanoes or the ocean in the *trade wind belt). Cumulus clouds are especially characteristic of the *intertropical convergence zone. They form at various altitudes in response to unstable conditions and exhibit a fluffy, heaped appearance and swelling cauliflower-like tops, which provide evidence of *convection in the atmosphere. They are composed of water droplets and possess well-defined outlines and horizontal bases, the height of the base depending on the humidity of the air when it leaves the ground. High humidities result in a low cloud-base because little cooling is required before the air becomes saturated, and vice versa. At medium and high levels cumulus clouds often extend downwind in long, tufted rows. If on a summer's day cumulus cloud evaporates and disappears in the heat of the sun, the weather will be fine and settled. If on the other hand it accumulates towards the end of day, then a weather change is probable. A formation that towers up into the shape of a cumulonimbus cloud is a sign of thunder.

**cuprite**, a red copper oxide ($Cu_2O$) mineral which is found in very hard, dense masses and as crystals. It is produced in copper vein deposits where the copper becomes oxidized from weathering. Such deposits occur in many localities, including Chessey (France), Cornwall (UK), and Arizona (USA). It is an important source of copper, and as perfect crystals it is prized as a semiprecious gemstone.

**Curie, Marie** (1867–1934) and **Pierre** (1859–1906), pioneers of radioactivity. Born Marja Sklodowska in Poland, Marie had been active as a girl in the 'free university' for Polish women workers in Warsaw. At the age of 24, she began to study physics at the Sorbonne in Paris and married Pierre in 1895. In 1898 they discovered polonium (so named by Marie in honour of her native land), and radium. For this, and for the discovery of radioactivity, they shared the 1903 Nobel Prize for Physics with Henri *Becquerel. Marie succeeded to her husband's chair of physics at the Sorbonne (becoming the first woman to teach there) after his accidental death, and continued her work on radioactivity. She received a second Nobel Prize in 1911, this one for Chemistry, for her isolation of pure radium; she was the first scientist to be awarded two Nobel Prizes. She also studied radioactive decay and the applications of radioactivity to medicine, pioneered mobile X-ray units, headed the French Radiological Service during World War I, and afterwards worked in the newly established Radium Institute, which was to become a universal centre for nuclear physics and chemistry. Pierre's early researches were on the *piezoelectric effect (which he discovered with his brother Jacques in 1880) and on the effects of temperature on magnetism. He discovered that at a certain temperature (the Curie point) ferromagnetic substances lose their magnetism and exhibit paramagnetism. In 1934, the Curie's daughter and son-in-law, Irene and Frederic *Joliot-Curie, discovered artificial radioactivity. Several months later, Marie died of leukaemia

Pierre and Marie **Curie** in their laboratory at the Ecole de Physique et de Chimie, Páris, in 1903.

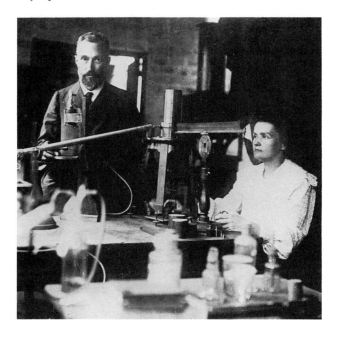

caused by the action of radiation. The curie, a unit of radioactivity, was named after Pierre and the element curium after Marie and Pierre Curie.

**current, electric**   *electricity.

**current, ocean**   *ocean current, *circulation.

**cut-off grade** (geology), the minimum concentration (*grade) of metal or other useful element in an *ore, at which the metal or element can be extracted at a profit. Cut-off grade varies according to the market price, distance from market, economics of extraction and processing, and so on.

**cut-off river**   *ox-bow lake.

**cwm**   *cirque.

**cyanide**, a molecule containing the CN group or CN$^-$ion. Organic cyanides are called *nitrites and have the general formula R$-$C$\equiv$N, where R is an *alkyl or *aryl group. All cyanides are extremely poisonous because the cyanide ion is able to coordinate with the ion in haemoglobin and so block the uptake of oxygen.

**Cyclades**, a part of the Greek archipelago in the Aegean Sea. There are over two hundred islands in the group, the largest being Andros and Naxos and the smallest being uninhabitable. Many are mountainous, yielding iron, marble, and manganese. With a Mediterranean climate, the chief crops are olives, grain, and grapes for wine.

**cycle of erosion**, a theoretical sequence of events which, it has been proposed, would occur if various types of large land mass were suddenly to be lifted above sea-level, erosion continuing until their surfaces were reduced to nearly flat *peneplains at *base level. The resulting cycles, it has been thought, would correspond to different climatic situations. The 'normal' cycle would apply in areas like the eastern USA, where rivers are dominant; the 'arid' cycle in areas like the south-western USA; the 'tropical' cycle in the seasonally wet tropics; the 'glacial' cycle in mountains like the Alps; and the 'periglacial' cycle in the northern tundra zones. As each cycle progressed from 'youth' through 'maturity' to 'old age', there would be particular changes in the shape of the land surface and in its weathered mantle. By looking carefully at any landscape, one could work out the stage it had reached in the appropriate cycle. These ideas were first proposed by William *Davis and have gained

---

### Cycles of erosion

Although the 'classical' erosion cycles for desert, temperate, tropical and polar regimes are imperfect, they do help our understanding of the natural processes shaping the earth's surface. Similarly, these individual cycles can be viewed as part of a much greater cycle in which geological forces deep in the crust play a major role.

**Erosion:** Uplifted land areas are immediately attacked by frost, ice, wind, running water, and by chemicals dissolved in rainwater.

**Transportation:** Eroded particles are carried to lower altitudes by the combined forces of gravity, wind, ice action, and rivers.

**Deposition:** As winds lose their energy and rivers slowly meander across lowland plains to the coast, eroded particles are deposited. Eventually they are carried into the sea where coarse particles sink close to land, finer material being carried farther afield.

Magma

**Uplift:** Large-scale geological processes (mountain-building, isostasy) raise areas of the crust high above sea-level, so completing the cycle.

**Alteration and addition:** Rising magma from the mantle adds new material to the cycle, while intense heating and pressure may radically alter the chemistry of existing rocks.

**Lithification:** Compacted under its own accumulated weight, the mass of sediment undergoes complex chemical and physical changes and becomes rock.

much currency, but are no longer highly valued. Land masses are not suddenly uplifted and climate is not constant for the millions of years necessary to produce a peneplain, nor is the land surface likely to remain stable.

**cyclone**, a term sometimes used for any travelling low-pressure system. It is seldom now used for mid-latitude *depressions, being reserved chiefly for *tropical revolving storms.

**Cyprus**, an island country in the north-east corner of the Mediterranean. It is 225 km (140 miles) long and 97 km (60 miles) in breadth at its widest point. The Kyrenia coast on the north has a range of steep limestone mountains along most of its length. South of that is a treeless plain, hot and arid in summer, while further south still are igneous mountains rising to 1,950 m (6,400 feet). Here seasonally heavy rainfall has caused erosion, for winter torrents rush down unchecked. Lack of consistent rainfall is ameliorated by a high water-table which allows the use of wells. Vineyards and orchards flourish, and sheep and goats graze the hills. Cyprus (Greek, 'copper') still has some copper, as well as iron pyrites and asbestos.

**Czech Republic, the**, a landlocked country in central Europe covering an area of 78,864 km² (30,442 sq. mi.), comprising Bohemia and Moravia. It is bordered on the west by Germany, on the south by Austria, on the east by Slovakia, and on the north and east by Silesian Poland. The country lies in the headwater area of the main European watershed; the Labe–Vlatava (Moldau–Elba) river system flows in the Bohemian basin towards the North Sea, and the Odra (Oder) flows northwards towards the Baltic. Rich alluvial soils alongside river courses are characteristic. The country is rich in mineral springs. The Bohemian highlands form a large elevated basin encircled by mountain ranges that at Sněžka reach an altitude of 1,602 m (5,256 feet). South of the central Sudety (Sudeten) Mountains, which border on Germany, is found the spectacular Moravian karst. A moderate climate prevails. The country has mineral reserves, including uranium, as well as brown coal (lignite).

**Da Gama, Vasco** (c.1460–1524), Portuguese navigator who was the first European to find a sea route to India. Selected to pursue the discovery by Bartholomeu *Diaz of an ocean east of the Cape of Good Hope, he successfully rounded the Cape (1497) and sailed up the east coast of Africa, thence crossing the Indian Ocean to Malabar. Laden with spices, da Gama returned home in 1499. Two years later he was given command of a punitive expedition, Muslim traders having massacred a Portuguese settlement left at Calicut. He made a third voyage to India when he was recalled from retirement and appointed viceroy in 1524. Da Gama was instrumental in breaking the monopoly of trade with India and other eastern states which the Muslims had enjoyed, and he succeeded in establishing Portugal as a world power.

**Dalton, John** (1766–1844), British scientist renowned as the originator of the atomic theory of matter. He received no formal education, but he developed an interest in mathematics and the physical sciences while working in a school in Kendal. As a young man he studied the weather and recorded his meticulous observations in a journal, and it was this interest in meteorology which led him to investigate the behaviour of gases and to formulate his law of partial pressures: the total pressure of a mixture of gases is equal to the sum of the partial pressures of its components. He was the first to recognize the existence of colour blindness, a disability from which he suffered and which became known as Daltonism. His greatest contribution to science, however, was his development of the theory (now known as the Dalton hypothesis) that all matter is composed of small, indestructible particles called *atoms, which are indivisible by ordinary chemical means.

**Dampier, William** (1652–1715), English navigator and surveyor. After an adventurous career of piracy, he professed reform and received an admiralty commission to explore the west coast of Australia, as then unknown. Although a good hydrographer, he proved incompetent in command and was court-martialled. On another voyage there were constant mutinies. It was after a quarrel with him that the master of one of his ships, Alexander Selkirk, was put ashore at his own request on an uninhabited island west of Chile. He spent five years there before being discovered by a ship belonging to another of Dampier's privateering expeditions, and his experiences provided the inspiration for Defoe's *Robinson Crusoe* (1719).

**Dana, James Dwight** (1813–95), US geologist, mineralogist, and naturalist. His *System of Mineralogy* (1837) presented a classification of minerals based on mathematics, physics, and chemistry. It established his reputation and became the first of a series of standard reference books with that title which have continued into the 20th century. His *Manual of Geology* (1862), in which he investigated the origin and structure of continents and ocean basins, likewise has gone through many editions. Dana accompanied Charles *Wilkes in his circumnavigation of the world, and made important studies of coral reefs.

**Daniell, John Frederic** (1790–1845), British scientist who began his career in a sugar-refining factory. He was an outstanding research worker and at the age of 23 he became a Fellow of the Royal Society. He invented the hygrometer in 1820. Appointed as the first Professor of Chemistry at King's College, London, he shortly afterwards invented an electric cell (now named after him) having copper and zinc electrodes. This was the first reliable source of electricity, producing a constant voltage over a considerable period of time.

**Danube River**, the second longest river in Europe, at more than 2,820 km (1,750 miles), it flows through Germany, Austria, Slovakia, Hungary, Romania, and Ukraine, and is a major avenue for freight transport. Rising in the Black Forest, it winds eastward through the highlands of Germany and Austria, varying in width according to the resistance of the hard rocks of its bed. The current is so strong that navigation upstream is very slow, but as it enters the central European plain it changes in character, becoming sluggish and muddy. In Hungary it turns south and collects the drainage of the Carpathian Mountains from the Tisza and its tributaries. Bending eastward it passes between the Transylvanian Alps and the mountainous area of the north

Below the industrial city of Linz, Austria, the valley of the upper **Danube** widens and then passes through the Wachau Gorge, with its castles and picturesque villages, before reaching Vienna.

Balkans to the lowlands of Romania, where, after more meandering, it finally reaches its vast delta on the Black Sea. The Danube is linked by canal to the Rhine and thus forms the most important commercial waterway in Europe. Like the Saint Lawrence waterway, the joint Danube–Rhine is designated an international waterway to ensure that vital traffic, mostly vast barge-trains, can move freely.

**Dardanelles** (Hellespont), a strait separating Europe from Asiatic Turkey and uniting the Sea of Marmara with the Aegean. It is 76 km (47 miles) long and up to 5 km (3 to 4 miles) wide, with an average depth of 55 m (180 feet). A rapid surface current flows to the Aegean Sea, more saline waters returning as an undercurrent. The waters contain many kinds of fish, which migrate between the Black and Aegean Seas.

**Darling River**, the longest river in Australia, and an erratic tributary of the *Murray. Its headstream, the Macintyre, rises from sources near the boundary of Queensland and New South Wales, in the Great Dividing Range. The general course is south-westward, across the vast interior plain, for 2,757 km (1,712 miles). Its waters are essential for irrigation, yet during times of drought, and sometimes for more than a year, it dries to a mere trickle.

**date-line**    *international date-line.

**datum plane**, a theoretical horizontal plane above which terrestrial heights are measured, but only in areas small enough for the Earth's curvature to be ignored. For larger areas the precise nature of the Earth's shape, defined as the *geoid, has to be taken into account.

**Davis, John** (*c.*1550–1605), English navigator who continued Martin *Frobisher's work in seeking a *North-West Passage through the Canadian Arctic to the Pacific, in 1585 and again in 1586 and 1587. The Davis Strait between Baffin Island and Greenland was named after him. He fought against the Spanish Armada (1588) and sailed with Henry *Cavendish on his last voyage (1591). In exploring a passage through the Strait of Magellan, Davis discovered (1592) the Falkland Islands. He sailed with Walter *Raleigh to the Azores (1596–7) and accompanied expeditions to the East Indies in 1598 and 1601. On a further voyage in 1605, he was killed by Japanese pirates. Davis invented a quadrant which remained in use until the 18th century, and wrote the first English manual on navigation, *The Seaman's Secrets* (1594).

**Davis, William Morris** (1859–1934), US geographer and geologist who was an authority on *cycles of erosion and greatly advanced the science of *geomorphology. Many of his articles are collected in the wide-ranging *Geographical Essays* (1909).

**Davisson, Clinton Joseph** (1881–1958), US physicist. With Lester Germer in 1927, he demonstrated that electrons possess wave-like properties (see *wave–particle duality). In his experiment, electrons bouncing off a nickel surface produced wave patterns similar to those formed by light reflected from a diffraction grating. For his work on electron diffraction he shared the 1937 Nobel Prize for Physics.

**Davy, Sir Humphry** (1778–1829), British chemist, a pioneer of electrochemistry and the inventor of a miner's safety lamp. After an apprenticeship with a surgeon he became an assistant at the Pneumatic Institution at Bristol, which had been set up to examine the medical properties of gases. He investigated the respiratory properties of nitrogen monoxide or 'laughing gas', and almost died while testing the effects of methane. His *Researches, Chemical and Philosophical* (1799) led to his appointment as lecturer at the Royal Institution in London. Large audiences were attracted to his public lectures, the most famous of which was 'Some Chemical Agencies of Electricity'; but his most important legacy was his discovery of the existence of several new metals, including potassium, sodium, calcium, and magnesium. The young Michael *Faraday became his assistant and together they studied *electromagnetism. Davy was elected President of the Royal Society in 1820.

**DDT** (dichloro-diphenyl-trichloro-ethane), a chlorinated hydrocarbon contact insecticide. It was first synthesized in 1873, and its insecticidal properties were discovered by the Swiss scientist Paul Müller in 1942. DDT was more powerful than previously known insecticides, and was effective against a wide range of insects. Its most spectacular use was in the eradication of malarial mosquitoes. However, in the 1950s doses of DDT and other insecticides had to be doubled or trebled as resistant insect strains developed, and evidence began to grow that the chemical was concentrated in the food chain. Questions were raised about the chemical's safety, and in over twenty countries (for example, Norway in 1970 and the UK in 1984) DDT was banned.

Humphry **Davy** demonstrating his safety lamp. In this lamp, the flame chamber was surrounded by an envelope of wire gauze, which prevented the flame from passing outwards to ignite explosive gases in a mine.

The **Dead Sea** contains within its southern depths the sites of the ancient cities of Sodom and Gomorrah. Centuries later, the Jewish sect that left the biblical manuscripts known as the Dead Sea Scrolls was to take shelter in caves near the lake.

However, it is still widely used for malaria and pest control in some Third World countries.

**Dead Sea** (Arabic, Al-Bahr Al Mayyitt), a landlocked salt lake, 70 km (44 miles) long, between Israel and Jordan; its northern half belongs to Jordan; its southern half is divided between Israel and Jordan. Since 1967 Israel has occupied the entire west shore. Set in the *Great Rift Valley and flanked by steep hills, it has the lowest surface level in the world, 400 m (1,300 feet) below sea-level, and is five times as saline as the open ocean. The River Jordan feeds it, but it has no outlet; it is much deeper at the northern end than at the southern, and evaporation causes a heat haze during most of the year. It is rich in potash and other chemicals. With the exception of bacteria, no animal or vegetable life can exist in its salty waters, while bathers float on it very easily.

**Death Valley**, a desert in eastern California, USA, lying within the Great Basin 85 m (280 feet) below sea-level. It is a long and forbidding desert of alkaline flats and briny pools, with deposits of borax. Summer temperatures reach to above 55 °C (130 °F), but winter nights can be very cold.

**de Broglie waves**, waves of matter whose existence was first predicted by the French physicist Louis de Broglie (1892–1987) in 1924. He suggested that all particles of matter possess wave-like properties, the wavelength being shorter the more massive the particle and the greater its speed (see *wave–particle duality). His prediction was confirmed in 1927 by the *Davisson–Germer experiment on electron diffraction, and forms the basis of the present-day theory of wave mechanics.

**Deccan**, the triangular-shaped plateau of south-central India, bounded by the Satpura Range in the north and by the Western and Eastern Ghats on the other two sides. Tilting eastward, from about 900 m to 450 m (3,000 feet to 1,500 feet), it is drained by the Godavari, Krishna, and Cauvery rivers flowing into the Bay of Bengal. The lava beds in the north-west are characterized by water-retaining black soil, and cotton is grown.

**decibel** (symbol dB), a measure of the relative intensity of a wave, especially a *sound wave. The intensity is usually compared with the intensity of the smallest sound ($I_0$) that can be detected by the human ear. Although the ratio of these two intensities could be used as a measure, it would usually involve a wide range of very large numbers and this would be inconvenient. Instead, ten times the logarithm of the ratio is used to give the value of the relative intensity in decibels. Expressed mathematically, if $I$ and $I_0$ are the two intensities, their relative intensity in dB is given by the expression $10 \log(I/I_0)$. A very loud sound, such as a pneumatic drill, is about 80 dB, conversation in the home is about 60 dB, and a scarcely audible one, like the rustle of leaves, is about 10 dB. Decibels are also commonly used to express the strength of electrical signals.

**decrepitation**, the crackling of crystals of certain substances when they are heated. This is caused by the rapid evaporation, and consequent expansion, of the *water of crystallization within the crystals. The colourless crystals of lead nitrate, $Pb(NO_3)_2$, decrepitate on heating.

**definite integral**   *integration.

**deflation** (in geomorphology), a type of erosion with the removal of loose particles of rock by wind. Although gravel and small round pebbles can be rolled short distances by strong winds, deflation mostly involves the lifting and blowing of sand, silt, and clay. Very shallow deflation hollows, or blowouts, each up to 1 or 3 km (a mile or two) across, are thus produced. Most common in deserts and in semi-arid areas where the vegetation cover is scanty, deflation also occurs on dry farmland elsewhere: for example, the 'fen blows' of eastern England, or the infamous Dust Bowl of the midwestern USA.

**degrees** (of latitude and longitude), units of circular-arc measurement used to measure distances and specify positions on the Earth's surface, each one degree ($1°$) comprising sixty minutes ($60'$), and a minute comprising sixty seconds ($60''$). A degree of *latitude is determined by a length along a *meridian that subtends one degree at the Earth's centre. It averages about 110 km (70 miles), being slightly shorter near the Equator ($0°$) than at either pole ($90°$ N. or S.) due to the *oblateness of the Earth. A degree of longitude (see *latitude and longitude) is measured at right angles to latitude, round the *axis of the Earth. It varies from about 110 km (70 miles) at the Equator to zero at the poles.

**Delaware River**, a river of the north-east USA, rising in the Catskill Mountains in New York state and flowing south-east for 450 km (280 miles) before entering the Atlantic at Delaware Bay, which is itself an estuary over 80 km (50 miles) long. The Delaware Aqueduct is a circular tunnel which forms part of the system supplying fresh water to New York City, running to a depth of 750 m (250 feet).

**deliquescence**, the property of some crystalline substances of dissolving in water that they absorb from the air. Thus they dry the surrounding air, and for this reason they are sometimes used when dry air is required for a process in industrial chemistry. An example of a deliquescent compound is sodium hydroxide, NaOH, or caustic soda.

**delocalized electrons**, electrons that are not located solely in one atom. When two atoms form a covalent bond (see *chemical bond), two or more electrons are spread, or delocalized, between them. Delocalization can extend over more than two atoms: for example, six in benzene and the entire crystal in a metal.

**delta**, a deposit of silt, sand, and gravel laid down by a river as it enters a body of relatively still water. The name comes from the Nile, which extends into the tideless Mediterranean in a roughly triangular shape resembling the Greek Δ (delta). Such deltas, with one edge bulging beyond the shoreline, and built by a fan of minor channels, are called 'arcuate'. The Mississippi, in contrast, has one main, outstretched channel with short bunches of distributaries splaying out from it, giving a 'bird's foot' pattern; while the Tiber's 'cuspate' form has smooth, concave wings of sediment swept shorewards by currents on either side of the central river mouth. Finally, many deltas such as the Mackenzie's are built within the confines of a former estuary; and such long, narrow forms are 'estuarine'.

Deltas range in size from tiny features formed in small lakes by mountain streams, up to the enormous constructions of the Ganges–Brahmaputra and the Yangtze; but all are established in the same way. Coarse material is dropped first, forming horizontal 'top-set' beds; medium-sized debris is carried further out and deposited as sloping 'fore-set' beds, parallel to the shore; and the finest grains settle slowly in deep water in front of the delta, giving horizontal 'bottom-set' beds.

**Democritus** ($c$.460–370 BC), Greek philosopher and scientist who was the first to suggest that all matter consists of atomic particles. He argued that they are in constant movement, that the Earth is composed of heavy aggregations and the heavenly bodies of lighter ones, and that materials differ in quality according to their atomic arrangement. Only fragments of his work survive.

**De Moivre's theorem**, the easy computation of any power of a *complex number, $z$. If $z$ is written in polar form, $z = r(\cos\theta + i\sin\theta)$, then De Moivre's theorem states that $z^n = r^n(\cos n\theta + i\sin n\theta)$; in other words, that the distance from the origin has been scaled to $r^n$ and the original angle has been multiplied by $n$. The solutions of the equation $z^n = 1$ (the $n$th roots of unity) are shown by De Moivre's theorem to be equally spaced around the unit circle at whole-number multiples of the angle $\theta = 2\pi/n$. The theorem was established by the French-born mathematician Abraham de Moivre (1667–1754).

A small **delta** formed where the Eglinton River flows into Lake Te Anau in the South Island, New Zealand. Silt carried from the surrounding mountains is steadily increasing the size of the promontory, on which can be seen the traces of several earlier river courses.

**De Morgan, Augustus** (1806–71), British mathematician and logician who wrote many textbooks on analysis and symbolic logic; among them are *Formal Logic* (1847) and *Trigonometry and Double Algebra* (1849). He became Professor of Mathematics at University College London at the age of 22, and helped to found the London Mathematical Society (1865).

**Denmark**, a Scandinavian country in northern Europe, situated between the North and Baltic Seas and comprising most of the peninsula of Jutland together with many islands, the largest of which are Sjaelland (Zealand), Fyn (Funen), Lolland, and Bornholm. The northern end of the peninsula has coasts on the Skagerrak and Kattegat channels, while to the south there is a boundary with Schleswig-Holstein in Germany. It is a flat and low-lying country, the sea twisting into it at many points and *outwash sand forming much of the subsoil. The climate is temperate and well suited for dairy-farming, as an abundant rainfall encourages the growth of good pasture. Kaolin is almost the only underground resource. Greenland and the Faeroe Islands are part of the Danish political realm.

**density**, the ratio of the mass of a body to its volume, and hence it is a *scalar quantity. The standard units are kilograms per cubic metre, or pounds per cubic foot. Different substances have different densities. Lead has a density of $11.35 \times 10^3$ kg/m$^3$ (709 lb./ft.$^3$), greater than that of water, which is $1 \times 10^3$ kg/m$^3$ (62.4 lb./ft.$^3$), and of cork, which is $0.24 \times 10^3$ kg/m$^3$ (15.0 lb./ft.$^3$). It is this relationship which allows lead to sink in water while cork floats. Most substances shrink or expand under changes of pressure and temperature and thus their density will also change. Standard measurements for gases are made at 0 °C (32 °F) and at a pressure of one atmosphere (101 kilopascals or 760 mm of mercury), while liquids and solids are measured at 4 °C (40 °F), which is the temperature at which water has greatest density. Relative density is often a more useful measure than density itself. It is the ratio of the density of a substance to the density of water (at 4 °C, 40 °F). Aluminium, for instance, has a density of 2,700 kg/m$^3$ compared with 1,000 kg/m$^3$ for water, so the relative density is 2.7. Other values are 11.4 for lead, 0.8 for petrol and 1.0 for water itself (by definition). Relative densities of liquids can be measured with a hydrometer. This is a small weighted float with a numbered scale on a stem which projects above the liquid surface. The denser the liquid, the higher the hydrometer floats, and the greater the reading on the scale where the surface of the liquid crosses it. Measured values can be a useful indicator of other properties—the quality of beer or milk, for example, or, in the case of battery acid, the state of charge of the battery: the relative density of the acid falls as the battery loses charge. In everyday usage density can also refer to 'quantity per unit length or area'. Population density means the number of people living in some unit of area—for example, 2,000 people per square mile. Similarly, in physics, terms such as 'energy density' are coined to refer to the amount of energy in a unit volume.

**denudation**, the whole process of lowering of the land surface, by all the agents of *weathering and *erosion combined. Once rocks or sediments appear above sea-level, because of volcanic or tectonic forces or a drop in the sea-level itself, they become subject to the full force of gravity, to changes in heat and moisture and pressure, which produce chemical and mechanical changes in their composition, and

**Density**. The ice floats on the surface of the lake because water, unlike most liquids, expands on freezing; the ice is therefore less dense than the water in the lake.

to the disintegrating and eroding actions of wind, rain, frost, ice, running water, waves, plants, animals, and man. These processes combine to alter and sculpt the surface. They produce landforms by erosion and the deposition of the material eroded. Slowly, but very surely, this leads to material finding its way back into the sea or lakes, where new sediments and rocks are formed. Ultimately, the process will begin again. Although denudation is universal and unceasing over the Earth's surface, it is very irregular in its intensity in time and space. Young, high mountains like the Karakorams and the Andes, still being actively pushed upwards, lose phenomenal quantities of material every year by the action of glaciers and rivers cutting deep valleys which are scarred by avalanches and landslides. In contrast, the old, hard, flat continental shield areas of north-east Canada or western Australia now show almost no denudation at all. It is therefore difficult to talk of denudation rates, although there is some evidence that denudation processes are unusually active at the present day. Certainly man has accelerated their operation by bad farming and construction practices in many areas.

**deposition** (in geology), the laying down by nature of inorganic or organic material. The deposits may be short-lived or endure for hundreds of millions of years, like the swamp vegetation of the *Carboniferous Period which is preserved as coal-seams. Deposition is of three kinds: mechanical, chemical, and organic. Material larger than clay particles transported by wind, water, ice, or *mass movements on slopes will be mechanically deposited, or dropped, when the transporting medium loses speed. Wind and water deposits are described as 'sorted', since the heaviest particles are dropped first, giving parallel layers of differently sized material. Ice, on the other hand, deposits unsorted *till, in which all sizes of debris may be churned together. Avalanche and landslide deposits are also unsorted. Dissolved material is chemically deposited, either when the fluid becomes saturated, or because of concentration by organisms such as coral polyps. Limestones are the major group of chemical deposits. Finally, organic deposits are laid down by the preservation after death of vast numbers of plant or animal remains, giving peat or lignite, and ultimately coal or oil, and bone or shell beds.

**depression, atmospheric**, an area of low pressure in the mid-latitudes which forms, in the lower levels of the troposphere, beneath areas of upper-air *divergence. The outflowing air aloft is replaced by rising air from below in the lower levels, and this results in a low centre pressure, into which there is *convergence. The wind blowing into a depression is deflected by the Earth's rotation and turns anticlockwise in the northern hemisphere and clockwise in the southern. Depressions commonly form along boundaries between cold and warm air. The warm air begins to rise over the denser cold, and as the central pressure falls, a wedge of cold air pushes into the rear of the warm air, causing it to rise more rapidly and to greater heights. This results in the formation of increasingly thick layers of frontal cloud, from which rain or snow may eventually fall. Often some 1,600 km (1,000 miles) wide, depressions travel at variable speeds but commonly at 10–30 km/h (6–18 m.p.h.), usually in a north-easterly direction in the northern hemisphere and south-easterly in the southern. They are sometimes heralded by the appearance of high cirrus cloud (the 'mare's tail' sky of seamen) and sometimes by a halo round the Sun or Moon. Their lifetime is measured in days; but occasionally they travel in families of three or four, with ridges of high pressure between them bringing fair weather.

**derivative** (in mathematics), the result of *differentiation of a function. The derivative expresses the rate of change of one variable quantity to another. If the function is one of several variables and only one of them changes, the rest being held constant, then the derivative is called partial. If a derivative can be expressed in terms of a series of partial derivatives, one for each variable, then it is called a total derivative. Equations that contain derivatives are called *differential equations. The derivative of $f(x)$ with respect to $x$ is written $df(x)/dx$; and the partial derivative of $f(x, y)$ with respect to $x$ is $\partial f(x, y)/\partial x$.

**desert**, an arid and generally almost barren region of the Earth, occurring in all continents except Europe. Deserts cover over a quarter of the world's land surface, occurring mainly in the interior of continents where atmospheric pressure is high and rainfall low, restricting plant growth. Most have little cloud cover and experience great extremes of temperature. The surface of sandy deserts absorbs the Sun's heat quickly, and during the day the air which rises from it shimmers; but after sunset it gives up the heat equally quickly, and the air becomes cold and clear. The sand is frequently piled by wind into *dunes. Rocky deserts, which are more widespread, present a great range of scenery, from bare mountains to plateaux scored by *wadis, to vast plains of closely packed pebbles. Wind erosion is less apparent,

although it can sandblast rocks near the ground into weird flutings: it is the rare but torrential thunderstorm which is mainly responsible for carving the rocky landforms. These hot deserts (such as Sonoran, Atacama, Sahara, Kalahari, Thar, and the Arabian and Australian deserts) lie generally on the western sides of continents between 10° and 30° North and South of the Equator. Some get no rain for years on end. Although the cold deserts in mid-latitude regions (such as Patagonia, Turkmenistan, and Gobi) have hot summers, they experience bitterly cold winters with some snow. Some are at high altitudes or set in basins below mountains, from which chilling air rolls down in winter. The circumpolar deserts of the high Arctic and Antarctic *dry valleys have short summers and long, dark and intensely cold winters. On the ice-caps themselves, absolute deserts exist, in which nothing can survive year-round. Desert soils form in areas characterized by low, irregular rainfall, where only drought-resistant shrubs can grow. Since vegetation in such areas is scarce and grows only slowly, these soils are low in organic matter. They tend to be shallow, with only poorly developed *horizons, and are often coarse in texture and stony. Desert soils are generally a pale reddish grey to deep red, because of the presence of iron oxides. Like soils in most dry climates where evaporation exceeds precipitation, they contain accumulations of soluble salts such as calcium carbonate, as a result of *salinization. The spread of desert-like conditions, a process called desertification, occurs in semi-arid areas where there is climatic change or, more frequently, as a result of human interference. Population growth forces overuse of semi-arid regions for cultivation and grazing. This leads to reduced vegetation cover and increased *soil erosion.

**desertification** *desert.

**desiccant** *drying agent.

**Desmarest, Nicholas** (1725–1805), French doctor, geologist, and mineralogist. In 1771 he was among the first to recognize that igneous rocks like basalt are the products of volcanic eruptions and were not formed by sedimentation from primaeval oceans.

**De Soto, Hernando** (c.1500–42), Spanish *conquistador* and explorer who took part in the conquest of Central America and Peru. In 1531 he joined Francisco Pizzaro's command, and befriended the Inca King Atahualpa. On the latter's brutal execution by Pizzaro he parted company with the Peruvian expedition and began to explore southern North America, where he discovered the Mississippi River (1540).

**determinant** (in mathematics), an array of numbers like *matrices, but is capable of being evaluated by recognized procedures to give a single number. The value of the determinant of a 2 × 2 matrix which contains the elements $a$ and $b$ in its first row and $c$ and $d$ in its second is given by the expression $ad - bc$.

**deuterium** (symbol D or $^2$H), the isotope of hydrogen of mass number 2; its nucleus consists of a proton and a neutron. Deuterium occurs naturally in all hydrogen compounds with an abundance of 0.015 per cent. Its compounds are physically almost identical with the corresponding hydrogen compounds, but their chemical reactions are often slower and their *spectra differ. Pure heavy water, $D_2O$, does not support life. Lithium deuteride is used in hydrogen

**Desert** scenery viewed across the Ahaggar Mountains of Algeria. Here, wind and flash-flood erosion have created a harsh landscape of ridges and gullies with rock-strewn surfaces and sparse drought-resistant vegetation. In the background the conical hills are volcanic plugs.

bombs: neutrons convert the lithium into tritium, $^3$H, which then undergoes *nuclear fusion with the deuterium releasing much energy.

**Devils Tower National Monument**, in north-west Wyoming, USA, the remains of an ancient lava intrusion. The surrounding sedimentary strata have been eroded by wind and water, leaving the massive, fluted tower which stands 264 m (865 feet) tall. It narrows from 300 m (1,000 feet) at its base to 76 m (250 feet) at its summit, and is composed of columns characteristically formed as a result of the cooling and crystallization of molten lava. It is essentially the neck of a former volcano.

**Devonian Period**, a geological period of the *Palaeozoic Era, extending in time from 408 to 360 million years ago. It contains the oldest widespread continental deposits in Europe (those of the 'Old Red Sandstone' continent) and North America. The period was one in which several groups of plants and animals showed great evolutionary development. Devonian marine deposits contain armoured fish, corals, ammonites, clams, and the last graptolites. On land, the first forests appeared and the first amphibians evolved.

**dew**, water droplets which are deposited on exposed surfaces during calm, clear nights, when the ground loses heat by radiation to the sky and causes the air in contact with it to become saturated. It usually forms on the tops of plants, especially the tips of grass, in places where there is a continuous vegetation cover. This is because the vegetation insulates the soil and therefore the temperature of the plant tops falls more rapidly, and to a lower level, than that of the ground surface. The water vapour is derived partly from the air and, for as long as the ground temperature remains above the dew-point, partly by evaporation from the soil. The dew-point is the temperature at which the water vapour in the air becomes saturated (the maximum amount of water vapour that the air can hold) and condenses on an available surface to form tiny droplets of dew. If a parcel of unsaturated air is cooled at constant pressure, the dew-point tem-

The spectacular sheer columns of **Devils Tower** are covered in lichens which give them a light grey and buff colouring; moss and grasses grow on its summit. Devils Tower National Monument was established in 1906.

perature will be that at which it becomes saturated. The more water vapour present in the air, the higher will be this temperature. The air becomes saturated more quickly at lower temperatures, and so dew is formed more easily.

**diagenesis**, the processes, mainly chemical, by which changes in *sediments are brought about after deposition but before their final conversion into rock. Changes in the water composition or temperature of the sediments usually leads to chemical alteration of the minerals present. An example of diagenesis is the alteration of a *feldspar to form a new *clay mineral.

**diamond**, a crystal of pure *carbon found usually in the form of an octahedron, the hardest substance known. Formed under intense heat and pressure, often in volcanic conduits at great depth, crystals occur in igneous rocks and in gravels, in regions as far apart as South Africa, Brazil, and Siberia. Colourless diamonds are the hardest and cut cleanest, being highly valued as gemstones. So-called black diamonds are used mainly for industrial purposes.

**diatomic molecule**, a molecule of two atoms which are so tightly bound together by covalent bonds that they can exist under normal conditions only as a molecule rather than as individual atoms. Particularly important are those in which both atoms are the same, such as oxygen, $O_2$, nitrogen, $N_2$, and hydrogen, $H_2$. But there are also many pairs of different atoms which form molecules, as for example carbon monoxide, CO, hydrogen chloride, HCl, and nitrogen monoxide, NO, and these molecules usually possess a *dipole moment.

**Diaz de Novaes, Bartholomeu** (c.1455–1500), Portuguese explorer who led the first European expedition (1488) to round the Cape of Good Hope, thus opening the sea route to Asia via the Atlantic and Indian Oceans. On a voyage surveying the West African coast he had sailed to latitude 26° S., off Namibia, when his ships were caught in a storm and swept further south for thirteen days. His landfall (1488) was near the southernmost tip of Africa: coasting eastwards, he found that the land turned north. He is attributed with having named it variously as the Cape of Storms and the Cape of Good Hope. He participated in Vasco da Gama's discovery of Brazil (1497).

**dielectric constant**   *permittivity.

**differential equation**, an equation that involves *derivatives as well as *functions. If $y$ is a function of $x$, then $(dy/dx) + y = 0$ is a differential equation of order 1. The order of the equation is given by the highest order of the derivative. Thus $(d^2y/dx^2) + n^2y = 0$ is a second order equation and describes *simple harmonic motion. These examples are ordinary differential equations since they involve only one independent variable. Sometimes partial derivatives occur: $\partial^2 y/\partial t^2 = a^2 (\partial^2 y/\partial x^2)$ is a partial differential equation of order 2. A differential equation is linear (see *linearity) if terms in $y$, or derivatives of $y$, are of power 1, and if there are no products of $y$ and its derivatives. Differential equations arise from problems in many areas other than pure mathematics. The most common is probably that of motion, since if the distance $y$ is given as a function of time $t$, then $dy/dt$ gives the velocity and $d^2y/dt^2$ the accleration. Oscillations can be described by differential equations which take into account *resonance or damping by friction;

and these equations can provide information which could be crucial, for instance, in the design of bridges. Electric currents, heat conduction, various chemical reactions, and rates of growth and decay can all be analysed with the help of differential equations.

**differentiation** (in mathematics), the process of finding the rate of change (derivative) of a function. It is one of the two central operations of infinitesimal *calculus. Both Gottfried *Leibniz and Isaac *Newton claimed to have invented the calculus, although their approaches were different and expressed in different notations. Newton's was via fluxions, the rate of change with time of a 'fluent' or variable $y$, written $\dot{y}$. Leibniz introduced the symbol d for differentiation; the rate of change of $y$ with respect to $x$ being written $dy/dx$. This latter notation has proved more useful in further mathematical developments, since $x$ need not necessarily be time. For example, if $y = 3x^2 + 2x + 1$, then the rate of change of $y$ with respect to $x$ is $dy/dx = 6x + 2$. Based on the theory of infinitesimal changes, there are many standard algorithms for differentiation, and *differential equations, involving derivatives, occur in many areas of mathematics.

**diffraction**, the spreading or bending of waves as they pass through an aperture or round a barrier. Diffracted waves subsequently interfere with each other producing regions of reinforcement and cancellation (see *interference). Diffraction occurs with sound waves, electromagnetic radiation (including light), X-rays, gamma rays, and with very small moving particles (such as *atoms, *neutrons, and *electrons) which show wave-like properties. For example, when light strikes an object the edges of the shadows produced do not have sharp edges; when a stream of fast particles (such as

The Oranjemund **diamond** mine on the coast of Namibia. The diamonds are found in the thick alluvial deposits which can be seen in the background. The deposits are worked right down to the bedrock, which is carefully scoured so that no diamonds are overlooked.

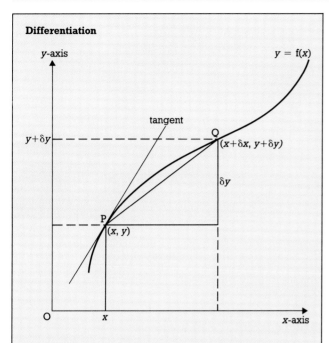

**Differentiation**

The rate of change of a curve at a point is given by the gradient of its tangent at that point. Point P, with coordinates $(x, y)$, and point Q, with coordinates $(x+\delta x, y+\delta y)$ lie on a curve. The gradient of the straight line PQ is $\delta y/\delta x$. From the graph $\delta y = (y+\delta y) - y$ and $y = f(x)$. Thus $\delta y$ can be written as $f(x+\delta x) - f(x)$ and

$$\frac{\delta y}{\delta x} = \frac{f(x+\delta x) - f(x)}{\delta x}$$

As Q moves closer to P, $\delta x$ becomes smaller and is said to 'tend to zero'. PQ now approximates to the tangent at P and its gradient to that of the tangent, which is thus defined as the limit of

$$\frac{f(x+\delta x) - f(x)}{\delta x} \text{ as } \delta x \text{ tends to zero}$$

This is written as $dy/dx$ and is called the derivative of the function $y = f(x)$. Many derivatives can be calculated from this expression. For example, if $f(x) = 3x^2 + 2x + 1$, then it is found that $dy/dx = 6x+2$. This result gives the gradient at any point $(x, y)$ on the curve $y = 3x^2+2x+1$. A more convenient way of calculating derivatives is to use the empirical rule which states that the derivative of an expression of the form $x^n$ is $nx^{n-1}$

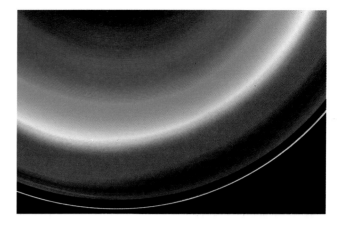

The grooves on the surface of a video disk can produce **diffraction** effects. Since the angle at which a diffraction band occurs depends on the wavelength of the light involved, white light can be dispersed by the surface of the disk into its constituent colours, giving rise to coloured bands as in this photograph.

root of the molecular mass of the gas. At temperatures exceeding half the melting-point in Kelvins, even solid particles can diffuse.

There is also a second meaning of the term: the scattering of beams of radiation. Diffusion occurs when light passes through fog or frosted glass, or is reflected from a rough surface. Then the normal laws of *reflection and *refraction do not apply.

**dikes** *dykes.

**dimension**. The common usage, as in 'the dimensions of the room', is as a measurement of spatial extent. This is related to the 'three dimensions' of space: length, breadth, and thickness (or depth, or height). Three *coordinates are needed to locate a point in space. A flat surface has two dimensions, and two coordinates are enough to define a point on it. A straight line has one dimension, and a point none. In *relativity theory time is treated as a fourth dimension, giving a four-dimensional *space–time, and in mathematics many results can be generalized to 'spaces' of any number of dimensions. Another meaning in mathematics has to do with equations. A product of two unknown quantities such as $xy$ is said to be of two dimensions; $x^2y$ is of three (two in $x$ plus one in $y$), and $x^3$ is also of three dimensions. In physics a quantity can be expressed in terms of other, more fundamental, quantities and these are called its dimensions. For example, speed is distance (length) divided by time, $[L]/[T]$, also written $[L][T]^{-1}$, and is said to be of dimension $1$ in length and $-1$ in time. Density is mass divided by volume: $[M][L]^{-3}$. This concept is useful in relating units of measurement to one another.

**diorite**, a coarse-grained igneous rock of intermediate composition (that is, with up to 10 per cent of quartz), composed essentially of plagioclase feldspar and ferro-magnesian minerals, typically hornblende. It occurs mainly as minor intrusions.

**dioxin** (2,3,7,8-tetrachlorodibenzo-$p$-dioxin), a poisonous compound produced as a by-product of the manufacture of certain insecticides and defoliants. In 1976 it was the active pollutant in an industrial accident at a chemical plant in

X-rays) impinges on the atoms of a crystal, their paths are diffracted into a regular pattern (as recorded in X-ray diffraction); and when sound is emitted from a loudspeaker, the loudspeaker itself acts as a barrier and casts a shadow at its rear, allowing only the longer base notes to be diffracted there.

**diffusion** (in physics and chemistry), the process whereby small particles which are released, or produced, in one part of a gas or a liquid spread out to form an even distribution throughout the whole volume of the gas or liquid. For example, a drop of ink added to a bucket of water will disperse and eventually colour all the water in the bucket, even if the water is not stirred. The process is usually slower in liquids, whereas the rate of diffusion of a gas is described by *Graham's law: the rate is inversely proportional to the square

Seveso, Italy. An area of 30 km² (12 sq. mi.) had to be evacuated and turned into a no-go area, which still exists today. Dioxin resists washing out by water or organic solvents and is taken up by fatty tissue in the body. It is known to cause chronic skin diseases, muscular dysfunction, cancers, birth defects, genetic mutations, and disorders of the nervous system. Small quantities of dioxin found in *bleached paper products have caused public concern, and there has been a move towards the use of paper products made using non-chlorine bleaches.

**dip** (geological), the angle at which a bed of rock or some other surface (such as a cleavage plane) is inclined to the horizontal plane. The angle measured in the direction where the slope is greatest is the true dip. If this is not known, the angle measured in an exposure is referred to as the apparent dip. The true dip is always at right angles to the *strike.

The magnetic dip is the inclination of the Earth's magnetic field to the Earth's surface.

**dipole**, two equal and opposite charges that are separated by a distance. Dipoles arise in molecules in which the electric charge is unevenly distributed, for example the water molecule. If one element in the molecule is more *electronegative than the others, it becomes a centre of negative charge. Since molecules are neutral overall, a concentration of negative charge at one place in the molecule must leave a concentration of positive charge in another place. Thus the molecule has a positive and a negative pole: together these form a dipole. The magnitude of this dipole is given by the dipole moment, which is the product of the magnitude of either charge and the effective distance between them. The unit of the dipole moment is the debye (D), where 1 debye is $3.3356 \times 10^{-30}$ coulomb metre.

The equivalent in magnetism, the magnetic monopoles, also come in two varieties: usually called north and south. However, while positive and negative electric charges can exist separately, magnetic poles appear to be unable to do this. If a magnet which has a north and south pole is broken in half, each half has both a north and south pole. This seemingly inseparable pair of poles is called a magnetic dipole. Some attempts at *grand unified theories require that the magnetic dipole be separable into two monopoles, and that magnetic monopoles with a particular set of physical properties exist in the universe. It should be possible to detect them, but very little evidence has yet been found to indicate that magnetic monopoles actually exist.

**Dirac, Paul Adrien Maurice** (1902–84), British theoretical physicist who worked on *quantum theory; in particular he worked to develop a version of quantum theory which took account of special relativity. He found theoretical evidence for many new aspects of particle behaviour, including electron *spin and the magnetic monopole (see *dipole). Dirac also found that there ought to exist an 'opposite' to the electron, that is a particle which has the same mass as the electron but is positively charged. The same idea also applied to the proton, so that an opposite of the proton ought also to exist. The idea of 'anti-particles', as these opposites were known, seemed far-fetched when Dirac published his work in 1930, but the anti-electron (or 'positron') was discovered soon after, and a variety of anti-particles have been discovered since (see *anti-matter). For his work on the relativistic version of quantum mechanics Dirac shared the 1933 Nobel Prize for Physics with Erwin *Schrödinger.

Despite its heavy load of silt and mud, the left-hand stream may have a small **dissolved load**, whereas the right-hand stream could have a very high dissolved load reading. Only laboratory analysis can reveal the dissolved load of chemical ions carried in the water.

**direct current**  *electric current.

**discharge** (of rivers), the volume of water passing through a given cross-section of a channel in a unit of time. It is now measured as cubic metres per second (cumecs) or cubic feet per second (cusecs); older observations were sometimes in gallons, or acre-feet. Measurements can be made at intervals, or recording gauges used to give a continuous record. The volume depends upon the cross-sectional area occupied by the flow and the speed at which it moves, although different threads of water will move at different speeds, so that an average velocity must be calculated. The *base flow is the regular discharge of a river, while *floods are high, or peak, discharges.

**dissociation** (in chemistry), the reversible splitting of a molecule into two or more smaller molecules. Often these smaller molecules are of different kinds, but sometimes they are of the same kind. The extent of dissociation is measured by the dissociation constant, $K$; this is defined as the product of the concentrations of the fragments, divided by the concentration of the parent molecule. Dissociation is an important process in chemistry, for nearly all the reactions which take place in solution are between the ions from dissociated molecules. Acids and bases reversibly ionize in solution ($HA \rightleftharpoons H^+ + A^-$; $B + H_2O \rightleftharpoons BH^+ + OH^-$), and the dissociation constant is then a measure of the acid or base strength respectively.

**dissolved load**, the proportion of the sediment being carried in a river which has been reduced to chemical ions and is invisibly mixed with the water. It comes from rainwater falling on the river surface, from solution within the soil and rock of the river basin, and from the breakdown of material in the channel itself, by *corrasion. All rivers have some dissolved load, although it is sparse in tropical areas of hard rocks. The largest quantities occur in areas of soluble limestone, in swampy channels, and where rivers are polluted.

**divergence,** a depletion of air in the *atmosphere, and consequent reduction in density resulting from a net outflow of air from a particular region, such as that of a trough in the upper westerly *jet stream. This is compensated by a vertical motion as air flows up (or down) to the depleted region.

A divergence in the upper troposphere results from an upward movement of air, which is limited by the existence of the tropopause and stratosphere. Divergence above is associated with *convergence below and an increase in cyclonic *vorticity. This encourages the development of depressions. In the oceans, divergence of surface water results in deeper water rising to take its place (*upwelling).

**divergent series**, a series in which the addition of further terms does not produce a sum which approaches some fixed value: for example $1 + 2 + 3 + 4 + \ldots + n + \ldots$. The partial sum to $n$ terms is $n(n + 1)/2$, which gets larger without bound as more terms are added. Less obviously the harmonic series $1 + \frac{1}{2} + \frac{1}{3} + \frac{1}{4} \ldots + \frac{1}{n} \ldots$ is also divergent, even though each individual term $\frac{1}{n}$ gets smaller and even tends to zero.

**divide** (in geomorphology), a watershed or 'water-parting'—an area from which rivers or glaciers flow outwards, in different directions and sometimes to different seas. Every *drainage basin is surrounded by a divide, separating its sources of surface water from those of its neighbours. However, not all divides are sharp, clear-cut features. On plateaux or floodplains they may be wide, boggy tracts. Major divides often occur in mountains and are used as political boundaries, but this can cause problems because, as in the southern Andes, the line of the highest peaks is not always the line of the watersheds.

**Djibouti**, a small country of north-east Africa, on the south coast of the Gulf of Aden at the narrow entrance to the Red Sea, opposite Yemen. It lies on the Great Rift Valley: Lake Assal lies at 155 m (509 feet) below sea-level. The climate is harsh and much of the country is semi-arid desert.

**Dnieper River** (Russian, Dnepr), the third longest river in Europe, flowing 2,300 km (1,430 miles) in a general southerly direction from its source in the Valdai Hills in Belarus, to the Black Sea, which it enters west of the Crimea. It is the main river of Ukraine and is joined by many tributaries. In its lower reaches it takes a great turn eastward and then turns back again—the Dnieper bend—before entering its large estuary. When free of ice—that is, for eight or nine months in the year—it is navigable for most of its course.

**Döbereiner, Johann Wolfgang** (1780–1849), German chemist who invented a lamp in which hydrogen ignited on contact with a platinum sponge. Although the lamp had limited application, the use of finely divided platinum had wider significance in the development of chemical catalysis. Also significant was his observation that certain triads of elements possess a periodicity related to their relative atomic masses. This helped pave the way to the *periodic table.

**Dodecanese Islands**   *Rhodes.

**Dogger Bank**, an extensive shoal in the North Sea, approximately 100 km (62 miles) east of the English coast. Some 240 km (150 miles) long, its sandbanks lie at depths varying from only 12 m (40 feet) to 36 m (120 feet). It is a good breeding ground for fish.

**Dokuchaiev, Vasilii Vasiliievich** (1846–1903), Russian geographer, who is widely regarded as the founder of modern soil science. He believed that soil forms because of the interaction through time of climate, vegetation, parent material and relief. Since climate and vegetation vary in a predictable fashion over the Earth's surface, Dokuchaiev suggested that different types of soil would show a similar zonal distribution. This concept of *zonal soils, which was developed by Nikolai *Sibertsev, is fundamental to our present understanding of soil formation. In 1899 Dokuchaiev founded the pedological journal *Soil Science*, which has been international since 1910.

**doldrums**, the hot and humid belt of ocean which lies in the equatorial low-pressure trough between the trade winds of the northern and southern hemispheres. Generally it is a region of calm, but sometimes there are intense, squally thunderstorms along the *intertropical convergence zone. The areas immediately north and south of the trade winds were once included but are now known as variables, areas mostly of uncertain light breezes.

**dolerite** (US, diabase), a medium-grained basic igneous rock, dark green in colour, usually with an interlocking texture of plagioclase feldspar and pyroxene crystals, giving the rock a mottled appearance. Common as *sills and *dykes, dolerites are found throughout the world. They are mainly of scientific interest but are frequently associated with valuable concentrations of copper.

**doline**, a depression in the surface of a limestone region. Dolines are formed by running water which has dissolved the rock and then found its way underground, carrying the calcium carbonate with it in solution and leaving the insoluble material as a clayey deposit in the bottom of the hollow. Medium-sized depressions up to about 1 km (0.62 mile) across, they are larger than *sink-holes and smaller than *poljes. While some have flat floors and steep, bare rocky sides, most are gently funnel-shaped.

**dolomite** (calcium magnesium carbonate), a mineral closely associated with calcite and often found replacing it.

'Half **Dome**'—one of the many huge glacially eroded granite intrusions that dominate the scenery of the Yosemite National Park in California, USA.

It is relatively light in colour and weight. The word 'dolomite' is also used for rock containing more than 50 per cent carbonate, of which more than one-half is the mineral dolomite. To prevent confusion dolomite rock is also known as dolostone. It is used in the building, metallurgical, and chemical industries. The Dolomite mountains are a range of Alps in northern Italy, so named because the characteristic rock of the region is dolomitic limestone.

**dome** (in geology), a structure shaped like the dome of a building. Domes may be on a very large scale. In structural geology a dome is an *anticline in which the beds dip outwards in all directions. The word 'dome' is also used to describe bodies of igneous rock: either the curved upper surface of an *igneous intrusion or a volcanic dome, a mass of lava pushed up above the crater of a volcano: Lassen Peak (California) is an example. Small domes of yet another type are produced by *exfoliation. Ayers Rock in Australia is a famous example.

**Dominica**, the second largest of the Windward group of the Caribbean Islands, some 750 km² (290 sq. mi.) in area. The loftiest island in the region, it has a mountainous ridge rising to Morne Diablotin, at 1,447 m (4,747 feet). Of volcanic origin, it offers beautiful scenery, with forests, waterfalls, craters, and springs. Only the coastline is cultivable on any scale; here bananas and other tropical fruits form the main crops.

**Dominican Republic** *Hispaniola.

**Dongbei** *Manchuria.

**Doppler effect**, the effect on sound waves and electromagnetic radiation of relative motion between the observer and the source of the waves. If the motion is towards the observer the waves get packed closer together so that more of them reach the observer in any interval of time. Hence the *frequency appears to be greater. If, however, the source is receding, the waves are more spread out and the frequency appears to be less. The effect is readily heard when the siren of a police car is sounded. As the car approaches the pitch rises and immediately it has passed the pitch drops. While the Doppler effect is most noticeable in the case of sound, it occurs with any type of wave motion. With light waves it is responsible for the wavelength of light from a receding star shifting towards the red end of the spectrum—that is to lower frequencies. The speed at which the star is receding can be calculated from the amount of the shift. The phenomenon was first described in 1842 by the Austrian physicist Christian Johann Doppler (1803–53), as an attempt to explain the colouration of stars. The Doppler effect also occurs if a source is stationary and the observer moves either towards or away from it.

**Doughty, Charles Montagu** (1834–1926), British traveller in Arabia who joined a pilgrimage to Mecca (1876) and later a group of nomadic Bedouin to explore the Arabian desert, where he made his most important geographical, geological, and anthropological observations. These were published in 1888 as *Travels in Arabia Deserta* which has come to be regarded as a masterpiece of travel writing.

**downthrow**, the side of a *fault that has been thrown down in relation to the rocks on the other side (the upthrow block).

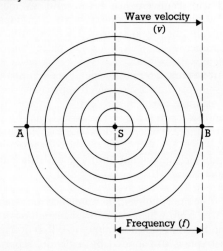

**Doppler effect**

**Stationary source**

In one second, a number of waves (f) of velocity (v) are emitted by a stationary source at S. To observers at A and B the wavelength ($\lambda$) of the waves will be $v/f$ and the frequency will be $f$.

**Moving source**

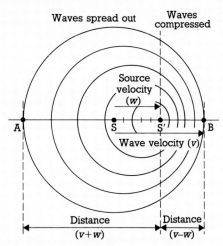

If, in one second, the source moves a distance (w) from S to S′, measurements made at A and B will give different values for $\lambda$ and $f$.

At A, the wavelength $\lambda_A$ will be $(v+w)/f$ (i.e. longer) and the frequency $f_A$ will be $f \times v/(v+w)$. In the case of a sound wave, the pitch would drop.

At B, the wavelength $\lambda_B$ will be $(v-w)/f$ (i.e. shorter) and the frequency $f_B$ will be $f \times v/(v-w)$. In the case of a sound wave the pitch would rise.

**drainage basin**, an area which contributes surface water to a river. The basin of a single stream, with no tributaries, is often roughly pear-shaped, narrowest at the mouth; the zone separating it from its neighbours is the *divide. While rivers may gain some water from *springs, drawing on underground reservoirs fed by precipitation which fell a long distance away, drainage basins generally operate as self-contained units of water collection and transmission. Termed catchment areas, they are almost entirely carved by processes involving the movement of water, and their slopes and channels function interdependently. Some of the precipitation falling on a basin is intercepted by vegetation (or buildings) and evaporates back into the atmosphere; some, however, sinks into the ground and, if not used by plants, will move slowly downhill within the soil or rock and finally seep into the river channel. If it rains long or hard, or if snow melts quickly, the soil and rock become saturated and water flows directly to the channels as *runoff. So the river gathers a proportion of the precipitation that falls all over the basin and transfers it downstream and into a larger river, a lake, or the sea (although some will evaporate from the river's surface and some may soak into rocks along its course). In areas of bare impermeable rock, thin soil, poor vegetation cover, steep slopes, and heavy, sudden rainstorms, very little water is lost to seepage or to *evapotranspiration, and individual drainage basins can be very small. With permeable rocks, deep soils, thick vegetation, gentle slopes, and moderate precipitation, more water is lost, so basins are larger. The length of channel divided by the basin area is the 'drainage density': this is usually between 1 and 10, but it may be as high as 1,000 in *badlands.

**drainage pattern**, the arrangement of river channels, as seen on maps or from the air. There are three different aspects of the pattern that can be defined: the density of channels, the way large and small rivers are fitted together into a network or hierarchy, and the general arrangement of the drainage lines. Density is the length of channels in a unit area. In limestone regions anywhere, it may be zero; in temperate areas such as Britain and eastern USA the density is usually between one and ten, while in semi-arid regions like the south-west USA it is larger. Networks of channels result from the ways in which single, unbranched streams join larger streams or rivers. The simplest description of a network is of its magnitude, or of the number of unbranched headwater streams it contains. The overall arrangement of channels tends to reflect the influence of underlying geological structures. Dendritic patterns, like the veins of a leaf, are commonest and suggest there is no geological control. Straight channels, meeting roughly at right angles, are trellised or rectangular, reflecting bands of alternating hard and soft rocks or major 'joint' patterns. On *domes, outward-flowing radial drainage develops; while enclosed basins have inward-flowing centripetal patterns.

**Drake, Sir Francis** (*c*.1540–96), English sailor and explorer, the most daring and successful of Elizabethan privateers in the Spanish West Indies. He was backed by Elizabeth I in his successful circumnavigation of the globe (1577–80). Having passed through the *Magellan Straits he plundered the Spanish South American settlements before sailing his ship, the *Golden Hind*, up the Californian coast, which he named New Albion. He was the first European to sight the west coast of Canada. From there he traversed the Pacific, sailed round the Cape of Good Hope, and arrived back in Plymouth in 1580 a rich man, being knighted in the following year. He was the first captain ever to sail his ship around the world. His successful raid on Cadiz in 1587 (the operation known as 'singeing the king of Spain's beard') delayed the sailing of the Armada by a year by destroying its supply-ships, and the next year he played an important part in its defeat in the *Channel by organizing the use of fire-ships to drive the Armada out of the port of Calais, France, and into a devastating storm. Drake died at sea with his cousin John Hawkins (1532–95) during an unsuccessful expedition to the West Indies.

A portrait of Francis **Drake**, the most renowned seaman of the Elizabethan Age. The son of an impoverished farmer, his navigational skills were excellent and he became the first captain ever to sail his own ship around the world.

**Drakensberg Mountains**, the great mountain chain of south-east Africa. It extends some 1,100 km (700 miles) from the north-east to the south-west through the Transvaal, Natal, the Orange Free State, and the Cape, and contains the whole of Lesotho. It has peaks rising to Thabana Ntlenyana's 3,482 m (11,425 feet), and in some places the escarpment alone rises sheer for over 2,100 m (7,000 feet) from foot to crest; but there are numerous passes. The water-eroded edge of an ancient plateau, it is South Africa's main watershed, being the source of the Orange River and its tributaries, the Vaal and Caledon, flowing west to the Atlantic Ocean, and the Tugela to the Indian Ocean in the east. The Natal National Park has splendid mountain scenery, including the gorge and falls of the Tugela River.

**drawdown**, the lowering of the level of a *water-table. The effect is usually caused by artificial pumping.

**drift** (in geology), a term with several meanings. It can refer to *continental drift; to the gradual movement of any surface material, such as sand; or, more usually, to glacial and fluvio-glacial deposits such as *till. This glacial drift, transported and deposited by glaciers and retreating ice-sheets, is generally unsorted and unstratified, a jumble of material ranging from large boulders to fine particles. Fluvio-glacial deposits, laid down by water resulting from the melting of the ice, are usually better stratified. They may be up to 100 m (330 ft.) thick, their composition depending on the nature of the bedrock.

**Driftless Area**, part of the central lowlands of the USA, south-west of the Great Lakes, over which continental glaciers did not pass. It stands as a vast island surrounded by regions which were covered with glacial *drift, and differs greatly from them. Weathering and stream erosion have dissected it time and again, so that much of the sedimentary rock cover has been removed, leaving some unusual rock features. There are caves and *sink-holes and much residual well-drained soil. Mainly in Wisconsin, the area extends into Illinois, Iowa, and Minnesota.

**drizzle**, very fine atmospheric *precipitation falling in drops of less than 0.5 mm (0.02 inch) in diameter from low stratus (layered) cloud. It occurs when the rate of precipitation is matched by the rate of condensation in the cloud.

**drought**, lack or insufficiency of rain for an extended period that causes a considerable hydrological imbalance. Drought occurs when evaporation and transpiration exceed precipitation of rain. When prolonged it causes damage to agriculture, depletion of ground and soil water, and limits water available for drinking, sanitation and industry. Streams and lakes dry up, and *water-tables fall. Any area in the world, except the true deserts, may experience a drought; but the definition varies from place to place. The larger the amount of rain expected, the shorter is the period of deficiency to be accounted as a drought. For example, whereas throughout much of Africa and the interior of Australia several months without rain may occur before a drought is officially declared, in Britain and along the eastern seaboard of the USA three weeks in summer without rain may cause lawns to turn brown and the use of garden hoses to be banned. Nowhere in the world is climate entirely constant from one year to the next, and so it is often difficult to say whether a particular drought is simply a freak occurrence or whether a series of droughts is due to a long-term

The **drought** conditions that ravaged Niger, south of the Sahara, have in recent years been caused by the repeated failure of the meagre annual rains, exacerbated by the loss of vegetation cover through overgrazing of livestock.

and more serious alteration in global wind and precipitation patterns. *Anticyclones over the Atlantic in summer occasionally deflect rain-bearing depressions away from Britain and western Europe. Persistent periods of drought, such as occurred south of the Sahara in the 1970s and in central Australia in the early 1980s, lead, on the other hand, to speculations about *climatic change. Disturbance of global wind patterns is apparently responsible for monsoon failure in Asia and Africa, causing devastating series of droughts such as those which the Bible describes as affecting Egypt.

**drumlin**, a small, ice-moulded hill whose shape resembles half a hard-boiled egg, cut lengthways. Drumlins almost always occur in groups in valleys or lowlands, producing what has been called 'basket-of-eggs topography'. Produced by the pressure of moving ice, they are good evidence for the past existence of glaciers or ice-sheets in any area: their blunt ends point towards the source of the ice and their long axes are roughly parallel to its direction of movement. They are usually made of *till, although some have rock cores.

**dry ice**, *carbon dioxide which has been solidified by cooling it below $-78$ °C ($-108$ °F). At atmospheric pressure it turns straight into carbon dioxide gas on warming, with no intervening liquid state (a process known as *sublimation). The liquid state can exist only at pressure above 50 atmospheres. If warm air is blown over dry ice, then a dense white cloud forms, which settles at floor level; this effect is sometimes used in the theatre. Dry ice is also used as a coolant.

**drying agent** (in chemistry), a compound used to remove undesirable water from a substance. For example, a gas contaminated with water vapour can be passed through an appropriate drying agent—concentrated sulphuric acid will dry an acidic gas such as hydrogen chloride, while calcium oxide will dry an alkaline gas such as ammonia. Organic solutions frequently contain unwanted traces of water which can be removed by adding a drying agent; an anhydrous salt is often used. It removes water from the solution and thus becomes hydrated. The salt is then removed by filtration.

**dry valley**, a linear depression which does not contain a surface river channel. Although temporary streams may flow after heavy rain or as snow melts, no definite channels are cut. Thus dry valleys differ from *wadis and *arroyos, whose watercourses are obvious. Most dry valleys occur on highly permeable rocks, especially limestone, chalk, and lava, and were cut by rivers either when the water-table was

higher or when *permafrost made the surface less permeable. Thousands of dry valleys in the British Isles and in Europe were cut during the Pleistocene Epoch. An extraordinary group also exists in Antarctica; they are the homes of the Earth's most southerly ecosystems.

**Dumas, Jean Baptiste André** (1800–84), French chemist who established a method for determining vapour density by weighing a known volume of the vapour. He also developed a technique for estimating the nitrogen content of an organic compound and derived a correct composition for chloroform after observing the action of chlorine on alcohol.

**Dumont d'Urville, Jules Sébastien César** (1790–1842), French navigator and explorer who twice circumnavigated the world. His voyages of exploration to the South Pacific (1826–9) and the Antarctic (1837–40) resulted in extensive revisions of charts of those regions. In 1820 he was instrumental in gaining possession of the Greek sculpture the Venus de Milo, from the Aegean island of Mílos. From Micronesia, Polynesia, and Malaysia he brought to France about 1,600 plant specimens, 900 rock samples, and information on the languages of those regions.

**dune**, a heaped accumulation of sand-size particles, shaped by the wind. Although the overwhelming majority of dunes are made of sand, they can also form from dry soil, gypsum, or hard, dry snow; but there must be plenty of dry material of the right dimensions, strong winds, and a fairly flat surface with slight protrusions such as small rocks or plants round which the moving particles can collect. While these conditions obviously occur in many of the world's hot deserts, circumstances are often favourable also in other places, such as along coasts, where small dune fields and isolated dunes frequently form. The shape of a dune is determined by how often winds of different strengths blow from different directions, the direction of the dominant wind, and the amount of material available. On a surface covered by a thick layer of sand, transverse dunes may form in a series of giant asymmetric ripples, their crests at right angles to the wind and with gentle slopes on the windward faces and steep ones on the lee. Sand is blown up the gentle slope and falls down the sharp one, so that the dune is moving slowly. Crescent dunes, or *barchans, move similarly. Wind eddies may scoop out hollows and spread out tongues of sand in a series of parabolic shapes. These may be stretched into long hairpins and then into longitudinal dunes running end-on from the dominant wind and with roughly equal slopes on each side. Cross winds may form *seif dunes. When winds blow almost equally from various directions, either star-shaped or pyramid-shaped dunes may result. All move with the wind unless stabilized by vegetation. Plants arrest their progress; and a static dune will absorb whatever rainfall occurs and help to form an oasis.

**duricrust**, a very hard layer in the ground which contains high concentrations of iron, aluminium, magnesium, calcium carbonate, or silica. Formed at the surface in areas where wet and dry seasons alternate, especially in the tropics and subtropics, it can be several metres (7 feet or more) thick. The colour depends upon the particular mineral of which it is composed. The concentration of minerals— which is what makes it so hard—is often produced by the capillary rise of water in the soil during hot, dry periods; when the water evaporates, the minerals are precipitated as coatings on soil particles.

**dust bowl**, an area in which a combination of drought and strong winds has removed the topsoil from land which has been intensively farmed, leading to erosion. The removal from a surface of natural vegetation such as grass, the roots of which bind soil together, is necessary for cultivation; but earth so exposed has to be protected. In the mid-western USA, a long period of prairie-ploughing was followed by a return to grazing, and the hooves of the livestock pulverized the loose earth to dust. This has been described as one of the worst ecological blunders in history. Several years of drought were followed, in 1934, by a season of winds which blew the dust in clouds over many areas in Kansas, Oklahoma, and elsewhere, a disaster which was repeated in several successive seasons. The result was the Great Dust Bowl, a graphic and moving description of which is given in John Steinbeck's *The Grapes of Wrath* (1939).

**dust in the atmosphere**. This can exert a profound influence both on atmospheric behaviour and on human life. It enters the atmosphere naturally as a result of dust storms, volcanic eruptions, and the passage of meteorites. Its natural occurrence can cause *haze. It also comprises increasing quantities of solid pollutants such as compounds of carbon and sulphur which have been injected, over the last hundred years or so, as a result of human activity in urban and industrial areas. The effects of these solid particles on human life range from the symptoms associated with hay fever to more serious respiratory diseases such as bronchitis; and the reduction of visibility in *smog is well known. The net impact on climate is less well documented, however. On the one hand, dust particles both absorb and scatter sunlight, thus reducing the amount of radiation reaching the Earth's surface; on the other, they absorb and re-radiate the Earth's outgoing energy, enhancing the *greenhouse effect. The formation of cloud and rain also appears to be affected by dust particles acting as *condensation nuclei, but again the net impact is unknown: the occurrence of clouds may be increased or diminished by their presence.

**Dutton, Clarence Edward** (1841–1912), US-born geologist who made his name in the US Geological Survey of the Rocky Mountain region, reporting on the structure of the high plateaux of Utah (1879–80) and the Tertiary history of the Grand Canyon district (1882). He was a pioneer of the theory of *isostasy to explain certain earth movements.

**dyke** (in geology), a sheet-like igneous body which cuts across the bedding of the host rock (unlike a *sill, which develops concordantly to the existing rock). Most dykes have been injected under pressure into the surrounding rock while still in a molten state and often occur in large numbers (dyke swarms). They are usually composed of basic *igneous rocks. One of the longest known dykes is the 'Great Dyke of Zimbabwe', which is more than 480 km (300 miles) long and about 8 km (5 miles) wide. Typical dykes are usually less than 30 m (100 feet) wide.

**dynamic equilibrium** (in geomorphology), the concept that a landform will evolve until a state of balance between the erosional and depositional forces acting on it has been achieved. Subsequently, the landform will not change its shape, although the landscape may be lowered by erosion. If factors affecting erosion and deposition rates change, the landform will adjust its shape until a new state of equilibrium has been achieved.

**E**

**Earth, the**, one of the smaller planets of the solar system. It has a mass of nearly $6 \times 10^{24}$ kilograms ($6 \times 10^{21}$ tonnes) and has the shape of a slightly flattened sphere with a mean radius of 6,371 km (3,960 miles). Its age, and that of the solar system as a whole, is estimated at 4,600 million years. The Earth is composed of three parts: the crust, the mantle, and the core. The crust is a thin layer of rock with an average thickness of about 40 km (25 miles) in the continental areas but only about 6 km (4 miles) under the oceans. The continental crust, which varies from about 10 to 70 km (6 to 43 miles) in thickness, is not only thicker but is less dense than that below the oceans. It is also more permanent: the oldest parts are about 3,800 million years old, whereas the oceanic crust is nowhere more than 200 million years old. Chemically, the continental crust is richer in such elements as silicon, potassium, sodium, uranium, and thorium. Below the crust is the mantle, the boundary between the two being marked by the *Mohorovičić discontinuity or moho. The mantle extends to a depth of about 2,900 km (1,800 miles) and constitutes the bulk of the Earth—about 84 per cent by volume. The material of which it is composed is believed to have a composition close to that of *peridotite, a basic igneous rock consisting largely of magnesium-rich silicates.

## The structure of the Earth

A sectional view of the Earth showing the main structural elements. The lithosphere (not shown to scale) consists of the crust and the solid outer-most layer of the upper mantle. This zone of rigid material is underlain by the asthenosphere, a thin layer of structurally weak and mobile partially molten rock within the upper mantle. The density of the mantle increases with depth until a sudden sharp increase, the Gutenberg discontinuity, marks the boundary with the liquid outer core.

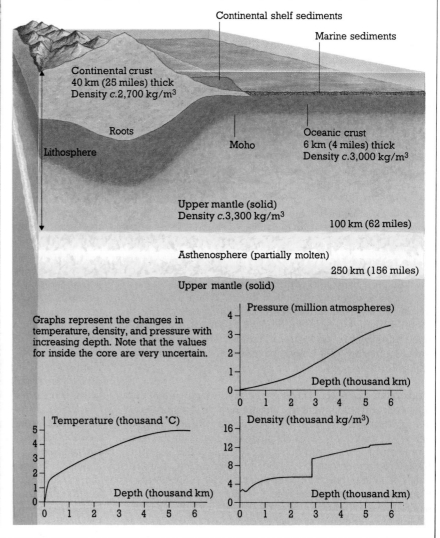

The light granitic rocks of the continental crust 'float' on the denser basaltic material below, the upstanding masses of mountain ranges being compensated by deep 'roots'.

Crust
Mohorovičić discontinuity
Lithosphere
Asthenosphere

Mantle (solid)

Gutenberg discontinuity
2,900 km (1,800 miles)

Outer core (molten)

5,200 km (3,250 miles)

Inner core (solid)

6,371 km (3960 miles)

Continental shelf sediments
Marine sediments
Continental crust
40 km (25 miles) thick
Density c.2,700 kg/m³
Roots
Moho
Lithosphere
Oceanic crust
6 km (4 miles) thick
Density c.3,000 kg/m³
Upper mantle (solid)
Density c.3,300 kg/m³
100 km (62 miles)
Asthenosphere (partially molten)
250 km (156 miles)
Upper mantle (solid)

Graphs represent the changes in temperature, density, and pressure with increasing depth. Note that the values for inside the core are very uncertain.

Pressure (million atmospheres)
Depth (thousand km)

Temperature (thousand °C)
Depth (thousand km)

Density (thousand kg/m³)
Depth (thousand km)

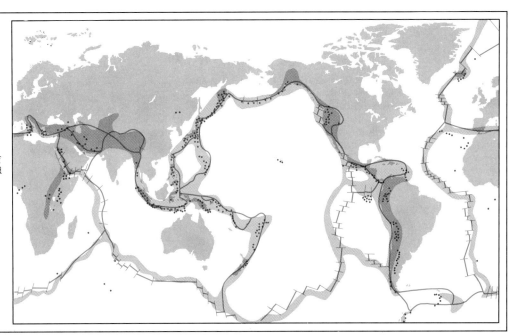

## Earthquake activity and major volcanoes

 Plate boundaries

Zones of shallow- and deep-focus earthquakes

Major volcanoes

Note the concentration of activity around the margins of the Pacific plate: the so-called 'Pacific Ring of Fire'

The oceanic and continental crust, together with the upper and stiffer part of the mantle immediately below, constitute the lithosphere, which extends up to a depth of 100 km (62 miles). This is divided into a number of rigid *plates that move very slowly in relation to one another and in relation to the Earth's poles, most probably as a result of large-scale convection currents in the mantle. These movements, their cause, and their consequences are the study of *plate tectonics. Below the mantle is the central region of the Earth, the core, with a radius of about 3,500 km (2,200 miles). It is generally agreed that iron constitutes about 90 per cent of the core. The other constituents are uncertain; nickel, sulphur, oxygen, and silicon are possibilities. The pressure within the core is extreme; it is estimated at between 1.3 and 3.5 million atmospheres. The temperature is also very high: 4,000 to 5,000 °C (7,200 to 9,000 °F). Evidence from earthquakes shows that the inner core, with a radius of about 1,200 km (750 miles), is solid, but that the outer core is molten.

**earthquake**, a rapid, often violent, oscillation of the Earth's surface (the land or the sea floor) caused by internal friction between moving parts of the Earth's crust. While gentle earth tremors can occur in any region of the globe, large earthquakes usually occur near the edges of the major *plates that make up the crust and along the *mid-oceanic ridges, where new crust is forming. The greatest concentration is on the 'ring of fire' round the Pacific and on a belt from the Mediterranean eastwards into the Himalayas and China. In coastal areas earthquakes often give rise to *tsunamis. The severity of earthquakes depends on the energy released in them. The point of origin is usually at a depth not exceeding 30 km (20 miles) and is termed the focus. The epicentre is the point on the Earth's surface vertically above the focus. Shock waves travel outwards from the epicentre at different speeds in different layers of the *crust. Surface and shear waves arrive together within about 2,000 km (1,250 miles) of the epicentre; compressional waves travel deeper, more slowly, and arrive later. The magnitude of an earthquake is measured on the *Richter scale. Major earthquakes can cause much damage to property and loss of life. One in Assam in 1897 devastated many villages in

north-east India; one on the *San Andreas Fault in 1906 devastated San Francisco; and another in Japan in 1923 resulted in a fire in Tokyo in which nearly 150,000 people died. Since then developments in *seismology have led to attempts at predicting earthquakes by the analysis of minor shock waves in the areas most at risk.

**earth sciences**, a general term for all the sciences that study the Earth, its atmosphere and ocean. They include geology, geomorphology, geophysics, geochemistry, glaciology, oceanography, meteorology, and parts of astronomy relating to the Earth as a member of the solar system. Increasingly, earth scientists are considering the Earth as a complex system, the various components of which—the solid earth, the ocean, the atmosphere and the biosphere—cannot be considered in isolation.

**East China Sea**   *China Sea.

**easterlies**, winds blowing from the east or nearly from the east. They occur in equatorial regions as the *trade winds or tropical easterlies. In polar regions there are transient easterlies. They blow between weak areas of high pressure which develop over the poles and the subpolar low-pressure belts.

**eastings**, distances—or angles of *longitude—measured eastward from either a defined north–south grid line or a meridian.

**East Timor**, the largest and most easterly of the Lesser Sunda Islands of Indonesia, lying between the Savu and Timor Seas and part of the Malay Archipelago. The coastal plains often inundated with mangrove swamps gradually rise to a mountainous interior, Mount Ramelau at 2,960 m (9,711 feet) being the highest point. The volcanic nature of the island is displayed by mud geysers but the volcanoes are not active. It is part of the *island arc which stretches eastward from Sumatra and Java.

**ebb, tidal**, part of the tidal cycle of horizontal water movement near coasts, caused by the rise and fall of the sea surface. Flood-tides occur as the water rises and comes in ('flows') and ebb-tides when it retreats ('ebbs'), the periods between being known as *slack water. In places where *tides are semidiurnal, each ebb lasts about six hours, being strongest in the middle two.

**echo**, a wave reflected from a surface and directed back towards its source. If a short pulse is initiated, such as a cry or a shot, the echo will be heard a certain time later. This time will be that which is taken by the waves to travel to the reflecting surface and back again. If the surface is a distance $d$ away and the wave velocity is $v$, then the time interval for the echo will be $2d/v$. Thus, if the time interval is measured and the velocity of the waves is known, the distance of the reflecting surface can be determined. This is the principle used in radar, which sends out and detects short radio waves, and in echosounding, which uses sound waves to reveal sea-floor topography.

**Ecuador**, an equatorial country on the Pacific coast of South America, bounded by Colombia on the north-east and Peru on the east and south. Palms flourish on the sandy, salty parts of the coast, and there are also mangrove swamps. Inland is a rich tropical plain, drained by several meandering rivers, and higher valleys where cocoa and coffee are grown; they extend into the foothills of the

Steep-sided valleys, fast-flowing rivers, and a thick covering of rain forest are typical of the scenery in the interior of **Ecuador**, where the Andes give way to the westernmost reaches of the Amazon basin.

*Andes, where there are cinchona and great mahogany trees. The Andes run north to south through the middle of the country. The peaks are lofty, *Cotopaxi, at 5,897 m (19,347 feet), being the highest active volcano in the world, and between the peaks are high but fertile valleys where the climate is temperate and tall eucalypts grow. The rivers provide hydroelectric power. The eastern slopes fall away into tropical forest and form a region in which there are large deposits of oil, the chief export. Ecuador is also the world's leading exporter of bananas.

**efflorescence**, the process by which crystals of certain hydrated salts lose some or all of their *water of crystallization to the air, turning into a powder as they do so. The rate of efflorescence depends on the humidity of the air and the nature of the salt. Hydrated sodium carbonate and copper(II) sulphate are examples of salts which effloresce under normal atmospheric conditions. The latter compound is sometimes used in barometers to show humidity, since its colour changes from blue to white as water is lost to the surrounding dry air.

**Egmont, Mount** (Maori, Taranaki), a symmetrical volcanic cone, rising from sea-level to 2,518 m (8,260 feet) on a peninsula in the west of North Island, New Zealand. It has been dormant since the 17th century, and meltwater from summit snowfields feed streams which have cut deep incisions into it. Thick forests mask most of the slopes but give way to open, fertile land at the base. Egmont National Park is centred on the summit of the Mount at altitude upwards of 360 m (1,180 feet).

**Egypt**, a country in the north-east corner of Africa, bounded by its Mediterranean and Red Sea coasts, Israel in the north-east, Sudan in the south, and Libya in the west. It is generally hot and arid—the south experiences some years with no rain at all—and civilization depends on the waters of the Nile, which are regulated by the Aswan Dam. To the west of the Nile valley is a desert of rock, sand, and gravel, with a few *oases, the great Qattara Depression, and deposits of oil. To the east is a range of hills with limestone and sandstone plateaux dissected by *wadis. Here there are phosphates, manganese, and iron. There is oil also in the Sinai desert, on the east bank of the Gulf of Suez. The fan-shaped Nile delta in the north, where the climate is wetter, is very fertile and is the main source of the finest cotton in the world. Egypt's climate has only two seasons: summer, lasting from April to September, and winter, lasting from October to March.

**Einstein, Albert** (1879–1955), German-born mathematical physicist whose *relativity theory altered ideas about space, time, and the nature of the universe. Educated in Switzerland, he first took employment in a patent office in Berne. The work was undemanding, however, and he quickly turned his mind to problems in theoretical physics. In 1905, he successfully used the *quantum theory to explain the *photoelectric effect. He received the Nobel Prize for Physics in 1921 for this achievement. Also in 1905 he put forward the special theory of relativity, describing the effects of motion on observed values of length, mass, and time. One consequence of his theory is that mass, $m$, is equivalent to energy, $E$, a concept expressed by the equation $E = mc^2$, where $c$ is the *speed of light. This is the basis of all calculations of the energy released by nuclear reactions. He extended his ideas in the general theory of relativity, published in 1915, which is concerned with gravitation and the effects of accelerated motion. In 1913 he returned to his native Germany to take up a professorship at the University of Berlin. As a Jew, however, he later experienced Nazi persecution, and in 1932 was forced to leave the country. After a brief stay in the UK he settled in the USA, and eventually became an American citizen. In a famous letter to President Roosevelt in 1939 he outlined the military potential of nuclear energy and the dangers of a Nazi lead in this field. His letter influenced the decision to build an atomic bomb, the use of which he greatly regretted. His last years were spent attempting to develop a *grand unified theory—a single mathematical system incorporating the laws of gravitation and electromagnetism.

**Eire**   *Ireland.

**elastic collision** (physics), an ideal collision between two or more bodies in which the initial total *kinetic energy is equal to the final total kinetic energy. Such collisions do occur, but only on an atomic scale; usually some of the initial kinetic energy is converted to another form, such as heat or sound.

**elasticity**. A solid is elastic if it returns to its original size and shape after it has been deformed. If a small weight suspended from a frame wire produces an extension of the wire, the wire will recover and return to its original length when the weight has been removed. However, this recovery will not occur if the weight is too great. If a large force is applied to the wire it will acquire a permanent stretch—that is, it will have been plastically deformed. The maximum force which

Albert **Einstein**, photographed in 1944. Although his explanation of the photoelectric effect in 1905 made him one of the pioneers of quantum theory, Einstein remained unhappy with the fundamental role played by probability concepts in quantum mechanics, summarizing his view neatly in the famous statement that 'God does not play dice with the Universe'.

can be applied without plastic deformation occurring is called the elastic limit. *Hooke's law, which states that strain (deformation) is proportional to the stress producing it, holds only within this limit. The point at which the material begins to 'give' is called the yield point.

**Elba**, the largest island of the Tuscan archipelago, 10 km (6 miles) off the west coast of Italy in the Tyrrhenian Sea. Its towering and rugged coast rises to a mountainous interior dominated by Monte Capanne, 1,019 m (3,343 feet) high. Extensive iron-bearing strata earned it the Greek name Aethalia, 'Smoky Place', on account of the smelting work that was carried out.

**Elbe** (Czech, Labe), a river providing one of Europe's chief waterways, being navigable for 845 km (525 miles) of its 1,170-km (725-mile) course from central Europe to the North Sea. It has its source in the mountains of eastern Bohemia, in the Czech Republic. After cutting through steep sandstone cliffs, it descends northward on to the North European Plain. Here it is joined by its main tributaries. It splits briefly into two channels, which come together again at the start of an estuary some 90 km (56 miles) long. Its mouth, in the Heligoland Bight, is 14 km (9 miles) wide. It is connected by canal to the Baltic Sea and Oder (Odra) River.

**electric charge**, a basic property of certain particles of charge which causes them to attract or repel each other. There are two types, called negative and positive: *electrons carry a negative charge and *protons an equal quantity of

This girl's hair is standing on end because of repulsion between hairs carrying the same type of **electric charge**. Not only the girl's hair, but her whole body, has acquired a charge from touching this van der Graaff generator (a machine that can store electric charge).

positive charge. Charges of the same type repel one another, while opposite charges attract. The force between charges obeys *Coulomb's law. It is the attraction between protons and electrons which holds the latter in orbitals round the nucleus of each atom, and, on a wider scale, it is similar attractions which bind atoms and molecules together to form solids and liquids. Atoms are usually electrically neutral because they possess electrons and protons in equal number, and the overall charge is zero. Rubbing materials together can upset this balance, and the materials are then said to be charged with static electricity. Chemical action, as in a battery, can cause a flow of charge, as can the motion of a wire in the magnetic field of a generator. A flow of charge—usually in the form of electrons—is an electric current. Quantities of charge are measured in *coulombs.

**electric current**, a flow of electric charge, usually in the form of electrons. In a circuit, it is measured using an ammeter, and the *SI unit of measurement is the *ampere (A). It may be direct current (d.c.), in which case the charge flow is one way, as from a battery. Or it may be alternating current (a.c.), as from a mains supply. Here, the charge flows alternately backwards then forwards in a circuit many times every second.

**electric field**, the region around an electric charge in which another charged particle experiences a force. The strength and direction of an electric field can be represented by *lines of force. The strength (or intensity) for any given point in the field is given by the force per unit charge at that point and is measured in volts per metre.

**electricity**, the collective term for the phenomena resulting from an *electric charge and the effects it produces when travelling as a current. Experiment has shown that there are two types of charge. These are now associated with sub-

atomic particles: the negatively charged electron and the positively charged proton. The phenomena associated with stationary, or static, charges are the concern of electrostatics. This branch of physics deals, for instance, with the cause of lightning in thunderstorms, the generation of high voltages for particle accelerators, and the technology of photocopying systems. The ability of a charge to pass through a conductor (which is usually a metal) has provided the most important applications of electricity. Electrons are driven through the conductor by a source of potential which may be a generator or a cell. A common type of cell consists of two rods, one of zinc and the other of carbon, in a solution of ammonium chloride. When the rods are connected by a wire, a current passes through the wire. In a generator, a wire is moved through the field of a magnet, and this causes the electrons in the wire to move along it as a current. In both cases the wire presents resistance to the electron flow; the electrons are scattered and lose energy, which is given up in the form of heat. The relation between the potential difference $V$ (in volts) between any two points, the current $I$ (in amperes), and the resistance $R$ between the points (in ohms) is given by *Ohm's law: $V = IR$. The flow of an electric current in a liquid can produce *electrolysis, which is used in electroplating and many other chemical applications. Of even more widespread use is the interaction between a current and a magnetic field, the study of which is *electromagnetism.

**electrochemical series**, an example of an *activity series. In it metals are listed in order of their ability to act as *reducing agents. When a metal acts as a reducing agent, it is itself oxidized; it loses one or more electrons and becomes a *cation. The elements at the top of the electrochemical series are stronger reducing agents than those lower down. For example, zinc is higher in the series than copper. Therefore, if zinc is added to a solution of a copper salt, it will displace the copper, which will precipitate as the metal; the zinc now be present in solution as a salt. An abbreviated form of the electrochemical series, listing the most reactive first, is: potassium, sodium, calcium, magnesium, aluminium, zinc, iron, copper, lead, and silver.

**electrolysis**, the process of decomposing a compound by the passage of an electric current. The compound must be a conductor of electricity for electrolysis to occur; this usually means either making a solution of the compound, or melting it. For the passage of an electric current two conductors called electrodes are dipped into the solution or melt. At the negative electrode (the cathode), metal ions and hydrogen gas collect, while at the positive electrode (the anode) negative ions collect. *Faraday formalized the laws of electrolysis by noting that the mass of metal atoms deposited at the cathode depends on the quantity of electricity flowing; in particular, one *mole of electrons (called the faraday) is needed to deposit one mole of silver atoms. At the cathode metal ions gain electrons to become metal atoms and are deposited on the cathode; this *reduction process has important industrial applications for reducing the ore of an impure metal to the metal itself. Aluminium, magnesium, sodium, and zinc are manufactured in this way. However, these processes often require special cells, inert electrodes, cooling systems, and large electric currents, and are therefore very expensive.

**electrolyte**, a compound which when molten or in solution conducts electricity and is simultaneously decomposed by it. An electrolyte may be an acid, a base, or a salt. It con-

## The electromagnetic spectrum

The following abbreviations are used: UHF, ultra-high frequency; VHF, very high frequency; SW, short wave; MW, medium wave; LW, long wave; LF, low frequency.

The spectrum of electromagnetic radiation covers a vast range of wavelengths, extending even beyond the limits shown: for instance, photons in cosmic-ray showers can have wavelengths of less than $10^{-15}$ m, while the electromagnetic waves produced by alternating-current generators in power stations can have wavelengths of more than 10,000 km.

Only radiation in the near-UV, visible, and near-IR wavebands, and the radio waveband from about 10 cm to 10 m, reaches the Earth's surface from outer space. The advent of satellites equipped to detect radiation outside these wavebands (for example X-rays) should greatly increase our knowledge of the universe.

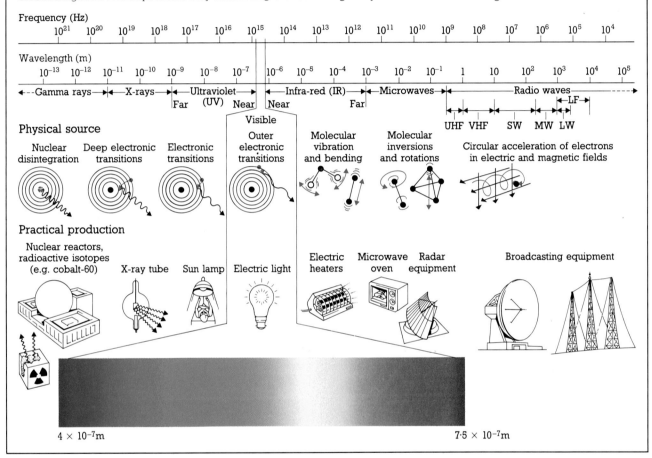

ducts because it consists of separate positive and negative *ions; these act as charge carriers for the current in a manner similar to electrons in a metal. A few substances, such as silver iodide (AgI), are electrolytes in the solid state.

**electromagnetic force** (in atomic physics), the *force responsible for atomic structure, chemical reactions, and all electromagnetic *interactions.

**electromagnetic radiation**, the general term for wave-like fluctuations in electric and magnetic fields travelling through free space or a material medium. This radiation is produced by the acceleration of electric charges. The electromagnetic waves travel at a constant speed in a vacuum, called the *speed of light, which is close to 300,000 km/s (186,000 m.p.s.): this may be slower if the waves are travelling in a medium. They may be considered as a type of wave with a wide spectrum of frequencies and wavelengths (see *transverse wave). The wavelength of the radiation varies inversely with the frequency of oscillation, which is usually measured in hertz (Hz). In some situations, such as *photo-electric effects, electromagnetic radiation behaves as if it consisted of a stream of particles, called *photons (see also *wave–particle duality). The shortest known electromagnetic waves are *gamma rays, with a wavelength of less than $10^{-11}$ m. *X-rays have a wavelength up to $10^{-9}$ m. Next in the electromagnetic spectrum comes *ultraviolet radiation ($10^{-9}$ to $10^{-7}$ m), then visible *light ($10^{-7}$ to $10^{-6}$ m), *infra-red radiation ($10^{-6}$ to $10^{-3}$ m), and *microwaves (1 mm to 30 cm). The spectrum is completed by *radio waves with wavelengths up to several kilometres. *Solar radiation, for example, has its maximum energy in the visible part of the spectrum, and hardly any radiation with a wavelength of less than $3 \times 10^{-7}$ m reaches the surface of the Earth since it is absorbed in the outer layers of the *atmosphere. Solar radiation that does reach the surface of the Earth is re-emitted as infra-red radiation.

**electromagnetism**, the study of the effects which arise from the interplay of an electric current with a magnetic field. The most straightforward phenomenon is the production of a magnetic field by a current. Any conductor which carries a current is surrounded by a magnetic field whose *lines of force form circles with the conductor at the centre. The strength of the field is proportional to the current. If the conductor is wound into a coil (often called a solenoid) the

**Electronic Configuration:** the arrangement of atomic shells and subshells

| Shell | Number of subshells | Number of orbitals in each subshell | | | | | Total number of orbitals in shell | Maximum number of electrons in shell |
|---|---|---|---|---|---|---|---|---|
| | | s | p | d | f | g | | |
| $n = 1$ (K) | 1 | 1 | | | | | 1 | 2 |
| $n = 2$ (L) | 2 | 1 | 3 | | | | 4 | 8 |
| $n = 3$ (M) | 3 | 1 | 3 | 5 | | | 9 | 18 |
| $n = 4$ (N) | 4 | 1 | 3 | 5 | 7 | | 16 | 32 |
| $n = 5$ (O) | 5 | 1 | 3 | 5 | 7 | 9 | 25 | 50 |

field is concentrated along the inside, and in many respects the coil behaves like a bar magnet. If the charge moving through the conductor accelerates, then the magnetic field changes along with the associated electric field. By making the fields fluctuate *electromagnetic radiation can be produced, in which the fluctuations are propagated through space.

**electron**, an elementary particle that possesses one unit of negative charge ($-1.602 \times 10^{-19}$ coulomb). Electrons are a constituent of all *atoms, forming *orbitals which surround the positively charged nucleus. In a free atom the number of electrons is equal to the number of positive charges (*protons) in the nucleus, so overall the atom is electrically neutral. When atoms combine to form molecules, some electrons in the *valence shell are transferred to or are shared with a neighbouring atom. This is the basis of *chemical bonding. In *metals and *semiconductors the outermost electrons in the valence shell are able to detach themselves and are free to move through the material. These electrons are responsible for the conduction of electricity and heat. A heated wire filament can be made to emit electrons, and if this is done in a vacuum their paths can be controlled by electric or magnetic fields. Such beams of electrons are used to operate television picture tubes and electron microscopes. Electrons are also emitted at high energy from the nuclei of radioactive atoms, and they are then known as beta particles. In some circumstances electrons behave as waves; that is, they exhibit *wave–particle duality.

**electronegativity**, a measure of the ability of an element to acquire electrons. Different atoms in a stable molecule have different affinities for electrons. In the covalent molecule, hydrogen chloride, HCl, for example, the electrons are found to be much closer to the chlorine atom than to the hydrogen atom, and chlorine is said to be the more electronegative atom. The most electronegative element is fluorine and the least is caesium. There has been some attempt to assign numerical values to electronegativity, but only relative values can be quoted. In general, electronegativities increase from left to right across each row of the *periodic table, and decrease down each group.

**electronic configuration**, the pattern in which electrons are arranged around the nucleus of an atom. Mention is often made of electron 'orbits', but this suggests a set of sharply defined paths and is not a good description. Rather, electrons are grouped in shells. A shell represents a region of space surrounding the nucleus and a certain average distance from it. Each shell contains electron clouds called *orbitals which are themselves grouped into subshells (labelled s, p, d, f, . . . according to the *quantum number $n$

of the electrons). Since an orbital can contain at most two electrons, there is a limit to the number of electrons in each shell. The shells are numbered outwards from the nucleus beginning with the K shell ($n = 1$), which can contain two electrons (in the 1s subshell, written $1s^2$). The L shell ($n = 2$) can contain eight electrons, the M shell 18 electrons, and so on. Thus the electronic configuration of hydrogen, with one electron, is $1s^1$ (one electron in the s subshell of the $n = 1$ shell) while sodium, with 11 electrons, has the $n = 1$ shell and the $n = 2$ shells completely filled and the remaining electron in the $n = 3$ shell (configuration $1s^2 2s^2 2p^6 3s^1$).

**electron spin**   *spin.

**electron-volt** (symbol eV), a unit of work or energy, being the work done when the charge on one electron moves

This photograph shows the path of an **electron** in a bubble chamber (a device used to record the trajectories of subatomic particles). The electron enters the chamber at the bottom left-hand corner, and then, under the influence of a magnetic field, follows a curved path whose curvature decreases as the electron loses its energy.

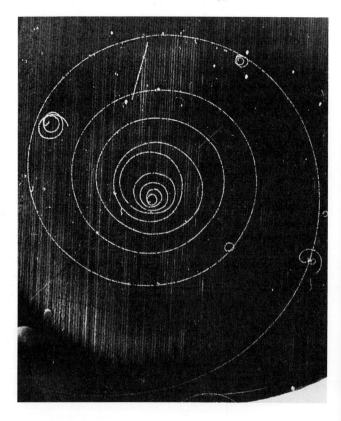

through a *potential difference of one volt. It is commonly used in atomic and nuclear physics because energy values are conveniently calculated in this way. For example, if electrons in an X-ray tube are accelerated by applying a potential difference of 10,000 volts, the work done on each is 10,000 eV and each gains 10,000 eV of energy. One electron-volt is equal to $1.602 \times 10^{-19}$ J.

**electrophile**, a reagent which reacts with a centre of high electron density. The word means 'electron lover' and implies that it will react with any region of high negative charge. Some electrophiles possess an overall positive charge, examples being the hydrogen ion, $H^+$, and the nitronium ion, $NO_2^+$. Others are neutral molecules containing atoms of different *electronegativity. An example is iodine monochloride, $ICl$, in which chlorine is the more electronegative element; there is a reduction in electron density on the iodine atom with the result that it acquires a partial positive charge: the iodine is thus the electrophilic atom.

**electropositivity**, a measure of the extent to which atoms will part with electrons. It is thus the converse of *electronegativity. Weakly electronegative elements such as the alkali metals are said to be strongly electropositive. However, even the most electropositive of metals, such as caesium, give up their electrons reluctantly. Electropositivity decreases across a period in the *periodic table and increases down a group.

**element**, a substance which cannot be broken down into simpler substances by chemical means. All chemical compounds are made up from different combinations of elements. The smallest particle of an element is an *atom, which consists of a dense *nucleus surrounded by clouds of *electrons. The nucleus consists of protons and neutrons; it is the number of protons, the atomic number, which determines the chemical identity of the atom. Although the number of electrons may be changed during a chemical reaction, the number of protons and neutrons does not, and so elements can neither be created nor destroyed in chemical reactions. It is possible for two atoms to have the same number of protons but a different number of neutrons; these are atoms of the same element, but have different masses, and are called *isotopes or nuclides. There are just over 100 known elements, of which about 90 occur naturally. Hydrogen is much the most abundant element in the universe, with helium second; all others are present in relatively small quantities. Elements with even atomic numbers are generally more abundant than those with odd atomic numbers; this reflects the relative stabilities of their nuclei. The relative abundances of elements on Earth itself are quite different from those in the universe as a whole, and depend on whether account is taken of those in meteorites and at the core. When the elements are arranged in order of their atomic numbers, those with similar properties occur at regular intervals. This is shown in the *periodic table, in which the elements are arranged horizontally in order of atomic number, and show vertical relationships in their properties. The periodic table reflects the *electronic configuration of the elements. The elements discovered most recently are *transuranic elements and do not occur naturally. Research into them continues, and it is possible that more will be discovered.

**electrostatics**, the study of the effects of positive and negative charges. The fundamental charges are the electron, which is negative, and the proton, which is positive. These two charges are the same size. Like charges repel; unlike charges attract. Particles with unequal numbers of electrons and protons are said to be charged. Ions are charged atoms or molecules. Larger charged particles are formed when ions or electrons become attached to bits of solid and liquid matter. Atoms or molecules can be charged by putting them in a strong electric field, or by irradiating them with ionizing radiation; certain substances can be charged by rubbing or heating them. The basic electrostatic law is *Coulomb's law: two electric charges attract or repel each other with a force which is proportional to the product of their charges and inversely proportional to the square of the distance between them. This force has practical applications: for example, for collecting waste ash from power station chimneys. If the ash is negatively charged at the bottom of the chimney, and the upper part of the chimney is positively charged, the ash will be attracted to the walls of the chimney, from where it can be collected. This prevents the ash from escaping into the environment. (See also *electricity.)

**elementary particle** (in atomic physics), a term originally used to denote any of the small number of particles, such as the proton, neutron, and electron, which were thought to be constituents of the atom and the basic building blocks of the universe. With the development of high-energy particle accelerators many hundreds of new particles have been discovered. It is clear that they cannot all be 'elementary': most of them are quite short-lived and decay into other particles. The belief now is that there are two main classes of particle—the *hadrons, which are strongly interacting and are made of various combinations of quarks, and the *leptons, which are weakly interacting and include the electron, the muon, and the tau, with their neutrinos. All known 'elementary' particles can be accounted for within this classification; and its great success has been the prediction of the existence of other particles, later confirmed by experiment.

**Ellesmere Island**, the northernmost island of North America, lying north-west of Greenland in the Arctic Ocean. Part of Canada's Northwest Territories, it is 800 km (500 miles) long, 40–480 km (25–300 miles) wide, and covers some 196,400 km² (75,800 sq. mi.). Its coastline is deeply indented and its surface is mountainous, rising to over 3,350 m (11,000 feet) in the north. It is largely under permanent ice, but in ice-free regions there is some vegetation.

**ellipse**, a closed curve commonly called an oval. More precisely an ellipse is a locus of points the sum of whose distance from two fixed points (foci) is constant. The major axis is the line joining the foci. The paths of the planets as they go round the Sun are ellipses. Alternatively, ellipses, being *conic sections, can be considered as the shapes obtained by slicing a cone obliquely.

**Ellsworth, Lincoln** (1880–1951), US civil engineer, explorer, and scientist who led the first transarctic and transantarctic air crossings in 1926 and 1936 respectively. He and the Italian explorer Umberto Nobile had made the first crossing of the North Polar Basin in the dirigible *Norge*, a 5,463-km (3,393-mile) journey from Spitsbergen to Alaska, in 1925. In 1936 he accomplished the first flight over Antarctica from the Weddell Sea to the Ross Sea. In 1939 he flew into interior Antarctica from the Indian Ocean side, claiming previously unseen land for the USA.

## The Elements

| Name (symbol) | Derivation of name/ Year of discovery | Atomic Number | Relative atomic mass | Number of naturally occuring stable (long-lived) isotopes | Density at 20 °C (g/cm³) | Melting-point (°C) | Abundance in the Earth's crust (grams per tonne of Earth's crust) |
|---|---|---|---|---|---|---|---|
| **Actinium (Ac)** | Gk, *aktis*, ray / 1899 | 89 | (227) | 0 | 10.07 | 1,050 | — |
| **Aluminium (Al)** | L, *alumen* alum / 1827 | 13 | 26.98 | 1 | 2.70 | 660.4 | 83,600 |
| **Americium (Am)** | America / 1944 | 95 | (243) | — | 13.67 | 994 | — |
| **Antimony (Sb)** | Medieval L, *antimonium*, origin unknown; Sb, L, *stibium*, antimony / Before 1600 | 51 | 121.75 | 2 | 6.68 | 630.7 | 0.2 |
| **Argon (Ar)** | Gk, *argos*, inactive / 1894 | 18 | 39.95 | 3 | 1.784* | −189.2 | — |
| **Arsenic (As)** | Gk, *arsenikon*, yellow orpiment / 1250 | 33 | 74.92 | 1 | 5.73 (grey) | 817 (grey) | 1.8 |
| **Astatine (At)** | Gk, *astatos*, unstable / 1940 | 85 | (210) | 0 | — | 302 | — |
| **Barium (Ba)** | Gk, *barys*, heavy / 1808 | 56 | 137.33 | 7 | 3.5 | 725 | 390 |
| **Berkelium (Bk)** | Berkeley, California / 1950 | 97 | (247) | — | 14 (est.) | 986 | — |
| **Beryllium (Be)** | Gk, *beryllos*, beryl / 1798 | 4 | 9.01 | 1 | 1.85 | 1,287 | 2.0 |
| **Bismuth (Bi)** | Ger, *wismut*, latinized to *bisemutum* / 1753 | 83 | 208.98 | 1 | 9.8 | 271.3 | 0.008 |
| **Boron (B)** | Ar, *burak*, Per, *burah*, borax / 1808 | 5 | 10.81 | 2 | 2.35 | 2,079 | 9 |
| **Bromine (Br)** | Gk, *bromos*, stench / 1826 | 35 | 79.90 | 2 | 3.12 | −7.2 | 2.5 |
| **Cadmium (Cd)** | Gk, *kadmeia*, calamine, from Cadmus, legendary founder of Thebes / 1817 | 48 | 112.41 | 8 | 8.65 | 320.9 | 0.16 |
| **Caesium (Cs)** | L, *caesius*, bluish grey / 1860 | 55 | 132.91 | 1 | 1.88 | 28.4 | 2.6 |
| **Calcium (Ca)** | L, *calx*, lime / 1808 | 20 | 40.08 | 6 | 1.54 | 839 | 46,600 |
| **Californium (Cf)** | California / 1950 | 98 | (251) | — | — | — | — |
| **Carbon (C)** | L, *carbo*, charcoal / Prehistoric | 6 | 12.01 | 2 | 2.25 (graphite) 3.51 (diamond) | 3,550 | 180 |
| **Cerium (Ce)** | The asteroid *Ceres* / 1803 | 58 | 140.12 | 3(1) | 6.77 | 799 | 66.4 |
| **Chlorine (Cl)** | Gk, *khloros*, green / 1774 | 17 | 35.45 | 2 | 3.214* | −101 | 126 |
| **Chromium (Cr)** | Gk, *khroma*, colour / 1797 | 24 | 52.00 | 4 | 7.2 | 1,857 | 122 |
| **Cobalt (Co)** | Ger, *kobold*, goblin / 1735 | 27 | 58.93 | 1 | 8.83 | 1,495 | 29 |
| **Copper (Cu)** | L, *cuprum*, from *Cyprium aes*, Cyprus metal / Prehistoric | 29 | 63.55 | 2 | 8.92 | 1,083.4 | 68 |
| **Curium (Cm)** | Marie and Pierre Curie, Polish and, French scientists / 1944 | 96 | (247) | — | 13.5 (est.) | 1,340 | — |
| **Dysprosium (Dy)** | Gk, *dysprositos*, hard to get at / 1886 | 66 | 162.50 | 7 | 8.55 | 1,412 | c.0.3 |
| **Einsteinium (Es)** | Albert Einstein, German-born, theoretical physicist / 1952 | 99 | (254) | — | — | — | — |
| **Erbium (Er)** | Ytterby, town in Sweden / 1843 | 68 | 167.26 | 6 | 9.07 | 1,529 | 3.46 |
| **Europium (Eu)** | Europe / 1896 | 63 | 151.96 | 2 | 5.24 | 822 | 2.14 |
| **Fermium (Fm)** | Enrico Fermi, American physicist / 1952 | 100 | (257) | — | — | — | — |
| **Fluorine (F)** | Fluorspar, from L, *fluere* 1771 | 9 | 19.00 | 1 | 1.696* | −219.6 | 544 |
| **Francium (Fr)** | France / 1939 | 87 | (223) | 0 | 2.4 | 27 | — |
| **Gadolinium (Gd)** | Gadolin, a Finnish chemist / 1880 | 64 | 157.25 | 7 | 7.9 | 1,313 | 6.14 |
| **Gallium (Ga)** | L, *Gallia*, France / 1875 | 31 | 69.74 | 2 | 5.9 | 29.8 | 19 |
| **Germanium (Ge)** | L, *Germania*, Germany / 1886 | 32 | 72.59 | 5 | 5.36 | 937.4 | 1.5 |
| **Gold (Au)** | OE, *gold*; Au, L, *aurum*, gold / Prehistoric | 79 | 196.97 | 1 | 19.32 | 1,064.4 | 0.004 |
| **Hafnium (Hf)** | L, *Hafnia*, Copenhagen / 1923 | 72 | 178.49 | 6 | 13.3 | 2227 | 2.8 |
| **Hahnium (Ha)** | Otto Hahn, German physicist / 1970 | 105† | — | — | — | — | — |
| **Helium (He)** | Gk, *helios*, sun / 1895 | 2 | 4.0 | 2 | 0.178* | −272.2 | — |
| **Holmium (Ho)** | L, *Holmia*, Stockholm / 1879 | 67 | 164.93 | 1 | 8.8 | 1,474 | 1.26 |
| **Hydrogen (H)** | Gk, *hydor*, water, + *genes*, producing / 1766 | 1 | 1.01 | 2 | 0.09* | −259.1 | 1,400 |
| **Indium (In)** | From the indigo line in its spectrum / 1863 | 49 | 114.82 | 1 (1) | 7.31 | 156.6 | 0.24 |
| **Iodine (I)** | Gk, *iodes*, violet / 1811 | 53 | 126.90 | 1 | 4.94 | 113.5 | 0.46 |
| **Iridium (Ir)** | L and Gk, *iris*, rainbow / 1803 | 77 | 192.22 | 2 | 22.42 | 2,410 | 0.001 |
| **Iron (Fe)** | OE, *iren*; Fe, L, *ferrum*, iron / Prehistoric | 26 | 55.85 | 4 | 7.87 | 1,535 | 62,200 |
| **Krypton (Kr)** | Gk, *kryptos*; hidden / 1898 | 36 | 83.80 | 6 | 3.743* | −157.3 | — |
| **Kurchatovium (Ku)** | Igor Kurchatov, Soviet nuclear physicist / 1964 (1969) | 104 | — | — | — | — | — |
| **Lanthanum (La)** | Gk, *lanthanein*; to escape notice / 1839 | 57 | 138.91 | 1 (1) | 6.15 | 921 | 34.6 |
| **Lawrencium (Lr)** | Ernest O. Lawrence, American physicist / 1961 | 103 | (256) | — | — | — | — |
| **Lead (Pb)** | OE, *lead*; Pb, L, *plumbum*, lead / Prehistoric | 82 | 207.2 | 4 | 11.35 | 327.5 | 13 |
| **Lithium (Li)** | Gk, *lithos*, stone / 1817 | 3 | 6.94 | 2 | 0.53 | 180.5 | 18 |
| **Lutetium (Lu)** | *Lutetia*, ancient name for Paris / 1907 | 71 | 174.97 | 2 | 9.84 | 1,663 | 0.5 |
| **Magnesium (Mg)** | *Magnesia*, district in Thessaly / 1808 | 12 | 24.31 | 3 | 1.74 | 648.8 | 27,640 |
| **Manganese (Mn)** | Medieval Italian alteration of L, *magnesia* / 1774 | 25 | 54.94 | 1 | 7.3 | 1,244 | 1,060 |
| **Mendelevium (Md)** | Dmitri Mendeleyev, Russian chemist / 1955 | 101 | (258) | — | — | — | — |
| **Mercury (Hg)** | The planet *Mercury*; Hg, L, *hydrargyrum*, liquid silver / Prehistoric | 80 | 200.59 | 7 | 13.55 | −38.8 | 0.086 |
| **Molybdenum (Mo)** | Gk, *molybdos*, lead / 1778 | 42 | 95.94 | 7 | 10.22 | 2,617 | 1.2 |
| **Neodymium (Nd)** | Gk, *neo*, new + *didymos*, twin / 1885 | 60 | 144.24 | 6 (1) | 7.00 | 1,021 | 39.6 |
| **Neon (Ne)** | Gk, *neos*, new / 1898 | 10 | 20.18 | 3 | 0.9* | −248.7 | — |
| **Neptunium (Np)** | The planet *Neptune* / 1940 | 93 | 237.05 | — | 20.45 | 640 | — |
| **Nickel (Ni)** | Ger, *kupfernickel*, demon's copper / 1751 | 28 | 58.71 | 5 | 8.9 | 1,453 | 99 |
| **Niobium (Nb)** | *Niobe*, daughter of Tantalus in Gk myth / 1801 | 41 | 92.91 | 1 | 8.6 | 2,468 | 20 |
| **Nitrogen (N)** | *Nitre* (18th C.), saltpetre, + *−genes*, producing / 1772 | 7 | 14.01 | 2 | 1.25* | −209.9 | 19 |
| **Nobelium (No)** | Alfred Nobel, Swedish inventor and industrialist /1958 | 102 | (255) | — | — | — | — |
| **Osmium (Os)** | Gk, *osme*, smell / 1803 | 76 | 190.2 | 7 | 22.5 | 3,045 | 0.005 |

| Name (symbol) | Derivation of name/ Year of discovery | Atomic Number | Relative atomic mass | Number of naturally occuring stable (long-lived) isotopes | Density at 20 °C (g/cm³). | Melting-point (°C) | Abundance in the Earth's crust (grams per tonne of Earth's crust) |
|---|---|---|---|---|---|---|---|
| **Oxygen (O)** | Gk, *oxys*, acid, + -*genes*, producing / 1774 | 8 | 15.9994 | 3 | 1.429* | −218.4 | 456,000 |
| **Palladium (Pd)** | The asteroid *Pallas* / 1803 | 46 | 106.42 | 6 | 12.16 | 1,554 | 0.015 |
| **Phosphorus (P)** | Gk, *phosphorus*, light-bearing / 1669 | 15 | 30.97 | 1 | 1.82 (white) | 44.1 (white) | 1,120 |
| **Platinum (Pt)** | Spanish, *plata*, silver / 1735 | 78 | 195.09 | 4 (2) | 21.4 | 1,772 | 0.01 |
| **Plutonium (Pu)** | The planet *Pluto* / 1940 | 94 | (244) | — | 19.8 | 641 | — |
| **Polonium (Po)** | Medieval L, *Polonia*, Poland / 1898 | 84 | (210) | 0 | 9.4 | 254 | — |
| **Potassium (K)** | E, *potash*; K, modern L, *kalium*, alkali / 1807 | 19 | 39.10 | 2 (1) | 0.87 | 63.3 | 18,400 |
| **Praseodymium Pr** | Gk, *prasios*; green, + *didymos*, twin / 1885 | 59 | 140.91 | 1 | 6.77 | 931 | 9.1 |
| **Promethium (Pm)** | *Prometheus*, character in Gk myth / 1945 | 61 | (145) | 0 | 7.26 | 1168 | — |
| **Protactinium (Pa)** | Gk, *protos*, first, + *actinium* / 1917 | 91 | 231.04 | 0 | 15.37 | 1,200 | — |
| **Radium (Ra)** | L, *radius*, ray / 1898 | 88 | 226.03 | 0 | 5 | 700 | — |
| **Radon (Rn)** | From *radium* / 1900 | 86 | (222) | 0 | 9.96* | −71 | — |
| **Rhenium (Re)** | L, *Rhenus*, Rhine (river) / 1925 | 75 | 186.2 | 2 | 21.02 | 3,180 | 0.0007 |
| **Rhodium (Rh)** | Gk, *rhodon*, rose / 1803–04 | 45 | 102.91 | 1 | 12.44 | 1,966 | 0.005 |
| **Rubidium (Rb)** | L, *rubidus*, red / 1861 | 37 | 85.47 | 1 (1) | 1.53 | 38.9 | 78 |
| **Ruthenium (Ru)** | L, *Ruthenia*, Russia / 1844 | 44 | 101.07 | 7 | 12.36 | 2,310 | 0.01 |
| **Rutherfordium (Rf)** (*see* Kurchatovium) | Ernest Rutherford, New Zealand-born physicist / 1964 (1969) | 104† | — | — | — | — | — |
| **Samarium (Sm)** | Mineral samarskite, named after Col. Samarski, Russian mine official / 1879 | 62 | 150.4 | 6 (1) | 7.52 | 1,077 | 7.02 |
| **Scandium (Sc)** | L, *Scandia*, Scandanavia / 1879 | 21 | 44.96 | 1 | 2.99 | 1,541 | 25 |
| **Selenium (Se)** | Gk, *selene*, moon / 1817 | 34 | 78.96 | 6 | 4.8 (grey) | 217 (grey) | 0.05 |
| **Silicon (Si)** | L, *silex*, flint / 1823 | 14 | 28.09 | 3 | 2.3 | 1,410 | 273,000 |
| **Silver (Ag)** | OE., *seolfor*, Ag, L, *argentum* / Prehistoric | 47 | 107.87 | 2 | 10.49 | 961.9 | 0.08 |
| **Sodium (Na)** | E, *soda*; Na, modern L, *natrium* / 1807 | 11 | 22.99 | 1 | 0.97 | 97.8 | 22,700 |
| **Strontium (Sr)** | Strontian, town in Scotland / 1808 | 38 | 87.62 | 4 | 2.6 | 769 | 384 |
| **Sulphur (S)** | L, *sulfur* / Prehistoric | 16 | 32.06 | 4 | 2.07 (rhombic) 1.96 (monoclinic) | 112.8 (rhombic) 119 (monoclinic) | 340 |
| **Tantalum (Ta)** | *Tantalos*, character in Greek myth / 1802 | 73 | 180.95 | 2 | 16.63 | 2,996 | 1.7 |
| **Technetium (Tc)** | Gk, *tekhnetos*, artificial / 1937 | 43 | 98.91 | 0 | 11.5 | 2,172 | — |
| **Tellurium (Te)** | L, *tellus*, earth / 1782 | 52 | 127.60 | 8 | 6.25 | 450 | <0.01 |
| **Terbium (Tb)** | Ytterby, town in Sweden / 1843 | 65 | 158.93 | 1 | 8.23 | 1,356 | 1.18 |
| **Thallium (Tl)** | Gk, *thallos*, green shoot / 1861 | 81 | 204.37 | 2 | 11.85 | 303.5 | 0.72 |
| **Thorium (Th)** | *Thor*, Scandinavian god of thunder / 1828 | 90 | 232.04 | 0 (1) | 11.73 | 1,750 | 8.1 |
| **Thulium (Tm)** | L, *Thule*, Northland / 1879 | 69 | 168.93 | 1 | 9.32 | 1,545 | 0.5 |
| **Tin (Sn)** | OE, *tin*; Sn, L, *stannum* / Prehistoric | 50 | 118.69 | 10 | 7.3 (white) | 232 | 2.1 |
| **Titanium (Ti)** | Gk, *Titanes*, giants in Gk myth / 1791 | 22 | 47.90 | 5 | 4.51 | 1,660 | 6,320 |
| **Tungsten (W)** | Sw, *tung sten*, heavy stone; W, Ger, *wolfram* / 1781 | 74 | 183.85 | 5 | 19.3 | 3,410 | 1.2 |
| **Uranium (U)** | The planet *Uranus* / 1789 | 92 | 238.03 | 0 (3) | 19.05 | 1,132 | 2.3 |
| **Vanadium (V)** | *Vanadis*, Scandinavian goddess / 1801 | 23 | 50.94 | 1 (1) | 6.09 | 1,890 | 136 |
| **Xenon (Xe)** | Gk, *xenos*, strange / 1898 | 54 | 131.30 | 9 | 5.896* | −111.9 | — |
| **Ytterbium (Yb)** | Ytterby, town in Sweden / 1907 | 70 | 173.04 | 7 | 6.97 | 819 | 3.1 |
| **Yttrium (Y)** | Ytterby, town in Sweden / 1828 | 39 | 88.91 | 1 | 4.47 | 1,522 | 31 |
| **Zinc (Zn)** | Ger, *Zink* / Before 1300 | 30 | 65.37 | 5 | 7.1 | 419.6 | 76 |
| **Zirconium (Zr)** | Ger, *zirkon* / 1789 | 40 | 91.22 | 5 | 6.5 | 1,852 | 162 |

## Notes

**Column 1** The name 'hahnium' has not been officially adopted for element 105. The names 'kurchatovium' and 'rutherfordium' have been proposed for element 104, but neither has been officially adopted.

The claims for the discovery of element 104 (kurchatovium/rutherfordium) have still not been settled between the Soviet researchers at Dubna who performed their experiments in 1964 and the American group at Berkeley, California, who performed their experiments in 1969.

**Column 2** The following abbreviations are used: Ar, Arabic; E, English; Ger, German; Gk, Greek; L. Latin; OE, Old English; Per, Persian; Sw, Swedish.

**Column 4** The values in parentheses are the atomic mass numbers of the isotopes with the longest known half-life, except for polonium, where the atomic number of the most readily available isotope is given.

**Column 5** The figures in parentheses give the number of naturally occurring long-lived radioactive isotopes. For example, potassium has two stable isotopes ($^{39}$K and $^{41}$K) and one long-lived radioactive isotope ($^{40}$K) with a half-life of 1.3 × 10⁹ years.

**Column 6** The densities of gases (*) are given in grams per litre at standard temperature and pressure (0 °C and 101,325 N/m²). Where a value applies to a particular allotrope, this is named in parentheses. The abbreviation 'est.' indicates an estimated value.

**Column 7** Where the melting-point of a particular allotrope is given, this is named in parentheses. Grey arsenic melts at 817 °C under a pressure of 28 atmospheres; at atmospheric pressure it sublimes at 613 °C. The melting point given for helium is for a pressure of 26 atmospheres; helium does not exist as a solid at atmospheric pressure.

**Column 8** The noble gases helium, neon, argon, krypton, and xenon occur in very small quantities in the Earth's crust. Technetium and promethium do not occur naturally in the Earth's crust; however, their spectral lines have been observed in the light from certain stars. Polonium, astatine, radon, francium, actinium, and protactinium do occur naturally, but only as short-lived radio-active products in decay chains beginning with the long-lived radioactive products in decay chains beginning with the long-lived radioactive elements thorium and uranium. Trace quantities of neptunium and plutonium occur naturally in uranium ores as a result of transmutation reactions produced by neutrons present in the ores. The transuranic elements with atomic numbers above 94 have only been produced artificially.

† Names formed systematically and without attribution are preferred by IUPAC for numbers from 104 onward, and are used exclusively for numbers from 106 onward. Names based on the atomic number are formed on the numerical roots nil (=0), un (=1), bi (=2).

**El Niño-Southern Oscillation event (ENSO)**, a climatic change that occurs on average every four to five years in the eastern South Pacific Ocean, whose impact may be felt throughout the world. El Niño (Spanish, the Child, in association with the Christ Child) is a phenomenon which usually begins at Christmastide. It brings with it a reversal of winds and ocean currents across the Pacific, causing drought in normally wet islands of the tropical western Pacific and floods in the desert Pacific coasts of the Americas. The cause of ENSO events is unclear, but it is related to the difference in atmospheric pressure between the *low over Indonesia and the *high in the south-east Pacific. This pressure oscillates seasonally. When it is large, the south-east trade winds are strong and surface water is 'piled up' in the western tropical Pacific, causing the sea surface along the Equator to slope to the west. During an El Niño event, the south-east trade winds are very weak and the sea surface slope collapses, allowing warm water from the western Pacific to flow along the Equator to the eastern Pacific. The severest El Niño of this century occurred in 1982–3; that of 1991–2 brought drought to southern Africa and Australia, and storms to California.

**El Salvador**, a Central American country on the Pacific coast. Only some 80 km (50 miles) wide, it is bounded on three sides by Guatemala, Honduras, and Nicaragua and has a 258-km (160-mile) southward-facing coastline. A hot, very wet coastal plain supports crops of cotton and sugarcane, and on wooded inland slopes, coffee. Above the slopes rise volcanic mountains with cratered lakes; and as the country is at a junction of two crustal *plates, earthquakes occasionally occur.

**eluviation**, the washing out of soluble salts, organic matter, and clay particles in suspension from the upper *horizons of soil, by water moving down through the profile. It is part of the process of *leaching.

**emerald**, a green variety of *beryl, chromium being present as an additional element. The crystals are brittle and often cracked; unflawed stones are rare, especially the deep green ones which retain their colour in artificial light. The finest stones come from high-altitude, open-cast mines in metamorphic rocks in Colombia. Other sources include India, the Urals, Siberia, and New South Wales.

**empirical formula** *molecular formula.

**enantiomer**, two forms of a compound which have the same molecular structure except that one form is the mirror image of the other, like a pair of gloves. A characteristic property of enantiomers is that they exhibit *optical activity, and this is due to the asymmetry of the molecules. An example is lactic acid, $CH_3$*$CH(OH)COOH$, the starred carbon atom has four different groups attached to it, and the two ways in which these may be arranged in space are mirror images of one another. The molecule is said to exhibit *chirality and the starred carbon atom is the chiral centre. The two forms of the acid have the same physical and chemical properties, except for the way they rotate *polarized light. In some cases enantiomers also have different physiological effects.

**endothermic reaction**, a chemical reaction in which heat is removed from the surroundings—that is, there is an increase in the *enthalpy of the reaction mixture. An example of an endothermic process is the dissolving of ammonium nitrate, $NH_4NO_3$, in water. As the solid dissolves, the temperature of the container decreases as heat is removed from it. The resultant solution has a higher enthalpy than the separate solid and water. An endothermic compound is one which absorbs heat as it is formed.

**energy**, the capacity to do work and, therefore, a measure of the state of a physical system. Light energy, heat, and electrical energy all form part of the two main classes of energy: potential energy, due to position, and kinetic energy, due to motion. The SI unit of energy is the *joule, and *power is the rate at which energy is delivered or converted. The total energy of an isolated system remains constant, although the energy may change from one form to another within the system. This is the law of the *conservation of energy. As with money in business, energy forms the basis of an accounting system in which exchanges and transfers balance. In some circumstances, it appears that energy is not conserved: this apparent discrepancy is explained by Einstein's equation $E = mc^2$, which says that energy ($E$) and mass ($m$) are equivalent and interconvertible. If energy and mass are considered as a single quantity called *mass–energy, then mass–energy is always conserved.

**energy budget** (in the atmosphere), the reception (as *insolation), transmission, and storage of *solar radiation by the Earth's atmosphere. Incoming radiation is of three general kinds: sunlight (the visible light waves), ultraviolet rays (which are of shorter wavelength), and infra-red rays (which are of longer wavelength than visible light). On entering the atmosphere, about 27 per cent of all this radiation is reflected directly back into space by, for example, clouds and the ground surface. About 25 per cent is scattered or diffused in the atmosphere, of which some 4 per cent is redirected into space and 21 per cent is directed back down to the Earth's surface. Some 24 per cent is absorbed by *ozone, clouds, and *dust in the atmosphere, and is converted to heat. The remaining 24 per cent, together with the 21 per cent of scattered radiation, is what reaches the ground, where it is absorbed, only to be re-radiated back into the atmosphere eventually as longer-wave radiation. Unlike most of the incoming short-wave radiation, this long-wave radiation is readily absorbed by the carbon dioxide and water vapour in the atmosphere, and only a small proportion of it is emitted directly into space. Of the remainder, much is absorbed by clouds and diffuse water vapour, and some of this is later radiated back to Earth, giving the *greenhouse effect. In this manner a continuous exchange of heat energy is maintained within the *troposphere, although eventually about 70 per cent of all the original solar radiation escapes back into space. There are variations within this global energy budget, smaller insolation being experienced at the poles than at the Equator. Consequently latitudes between the poles and 40° N. and S. experience a net heat loss, while lower latitudes experience a net gain. It is this imbalance and the resultant transfer and attempted equalization of heat across the globe that drives the general *circulation.

**energy levels** (in atomic physics), the set of permitted energies which an electron can have in any particular system. They can be calculated using *quantum or *wave mechanics. The electrons in the orbitals around the nucleus of an atom have a relatively small set of fairly widely spaced energy levels, giving the characteristic *electronic configura-

## Energy Budget of the atmosphere

Although there are local variations, on a global scale there is no net energy loss or gain by the atmosphere at the border with space or at the Earth's surface, so that an overall energy balance is maintained. At the Earth's surface, the energy balance is not purely radiative: about 6 units of energy are lost to the atmosphere by conduction and convection, while a further 23 units are used in evaporating water from the Earth's surface. This latter energy warms the atmosphere by the release of latent heat when the water vapour condenses to form clouds. The energy gained by the atmosphere by absorption of solar radiation and by heat transfers from the earth's surface is eventually lost to space as long-wave radiation. This long-wave radiation (64 units) together with direct radiation from the earth's surface (5 units) and reflected insolation (31 units) maintain an energy balance with the incoming solar radiation (100 units) at the atmosphere–space border.

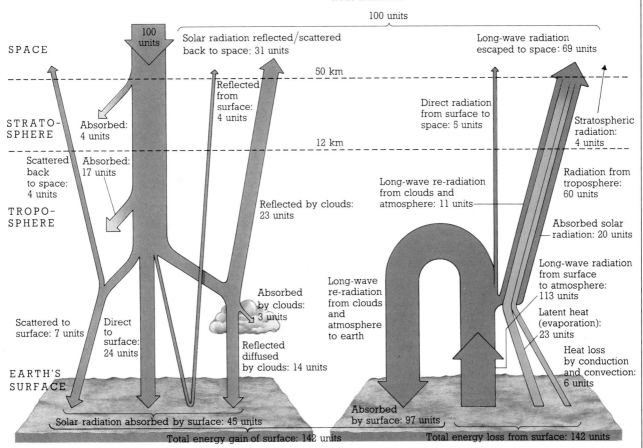

Solar radiation (short-wave, $0.2-4 \times 10^{-6}$ m.)

Terrestrial radiation (long-wave, $4-100 \times 10^{-6}$ m) and heat transfers

100 units

SPACE — 100 units — Solar radiation reflected/scattered back to space: 31 units — Long-wave radiation escaped to space: 69 units

50 km

Reflected from surface: 4 units

STRATO-SPHERE — Absorbed: 4 units — Direct radiation from surface to space: 5 units — Stratospheric radiation: 4 units

12 km

Scattered back to space: 4 units — Absorbed: 17 units — Long-wave re-radiation from clouds and atmosphere: 11 units — Radiation from troposphere: 60 units

TROPO-SPHERE — Reflected by clouds: 23 units — Absorbed solar radiation: 20 units

Absorbed by clouds: 3 units — Long-wave re-radiation from clouds and atmosphere to earth — Long-wave radiation from surface to atmosphere: 113 units

Scattered to surface: 7 units — Direct to surface: 24 units — Latent heat (evaporation): 23 units

Reflected diffused by clouds: 14 units — Heat loss by conduction and convection: 6 units

EARTH'S SURFACE — Solar radiation absorbed by surface: 45 units — Absorbed by surface: 97 units

Total energy gain of surface: 142 units — Total energy loss from surface: 142 units

---

tion of the element. The energy of these levels depends largely on the distance of the electron from the nucleus. In electrical conductors, however, where the electrons are able to move freely throughout the whole material, the energy levels are compressed into bands in which the levels are extremely close together. According to the *exclusion principle put forward by Wolfgang *Pauli in 1925, two electrons can occupy the same energy level if they have opposite *spin but otherwise share equal *quantum numbers.

**energy resource**, any available natural source of useful energy. *Fossil fuels have provided the world's main energy resources for more than a century. However, consumption of these non-renewable resources has continued to rise and serious consideration is being given to alternatives to these fossil fuels. Concern over the impact on the environment from burning fossil fuels (see *greenhouse effect) has added impetus to this search for alternative energy resources. Nuclear power and hydroelectricity are the most fully devel-

oped alternatives. However, hydroelectric power could not satisfy total world demand in the long term, and nuclear power is controversial because of fears concerning safety and undesirable environmental consequences. Other renewable resources such as geothermal energy, solar power, tidal power, and wind power offer potential alternatives but they are not yet technologically proven on a world scale, and their economic viability remains to be established.

**England**, the largest part of the island of Great Britain in north-west Europe, bounded by Scotland on the north and Wales on the west. Roughly triangular in shape, it has a coastline of 3,200 km (2,000 miles); the land mass extends for some 560 km (or 350 miles) from the Cheviot Hills in the north to the South Downs, and from The Wash on its east coast to Land's End in the south-west. The highest point is Sca Fell at 978 m (3,209 feet), among the Cumbrian Mountains in the Lake District of the north-west, although there are peaks also in the central Pennine chain. The variety of rock structure, sediments, and superficial deposits make for great scenic differences. On either side of the Pennines, drain the rivers Mersey, Tyne, and Ouse. The long eastern plain is broken only by the Yorkshire Moors and the lower Yorkshire and Lincolnshire Wolds. The Midlands comprise a central plain with reddish soil of brick earth. To the west are the Severn valley and the Malvern Hills, while in the east the land sinks to the Fens and East Anglia. Southward the limestone Cotswold and the Chiltern hills are separated by the upper Thames valley with its rich clay soil. In the south chalk downlands run east–west. The hilly south-west peninsula includes Exmoor and Dartmoor; the coastline is rocky and indented.

**English Channel** (French, la Manche), the channel separating Britain from France. An arm of the Atlantic Ocean, it is some 560 km (350 miles) long. In width it tapers eastward to the 35-km (22-mile) Strait of Dover, linking with the North Sea. Near France are the Channel Islands, while the Isle of Wight is separated by the Solent from the English coast. Tides meet at the western, Atlantic end, where the water can be choppy. The prevailing winds are westerlies, and the tidal currents are fairly strong.

**enthalpy**, a measure of the internal energy of a substance; it is a *thermodynamic property and is usually measured in kilojoules per mole. It is difficult to measure enthalpy directly; it is considerably easier to measure the enthalpy change accompanying a chemical reaction. In an *exothermic reaction, there is a decrease in enthalpy for the reaction mixture; in other words, heat is given out. In an *endothermic reaction, there is an increase in enthalpy; heat is taken in by the reaction mixture.

**entisol**, an immature soil which has had insufficient time for distinct B-*horizons to form. Entisols occur on recent deposits, such as loess, till, or alluvium. The upper horizons are distinguished from the weathering parent material largely because they contain humus and are therefore darker in colour. They tend to be relatively shallow. Entisols, though not widely distributed, can occur in any climatic zone. They are the most important soil type both in the glaciated Ungava region of Quebec and Labrador, and in the Kalahari Desert of south-western Africa.

**entropy**, a measure of disorder. It is used in *thermodynamics to determine the way in which a system will change when it is compressed or expanded, heated or cooled. Mathematically, entropy can be calculated from measurements of the heat required to raise the temperature of a body a certain amount, divided by the temperature of the body. Its significance lies in its relation to disorder: the random manner in which the energy of the particles in the system is distributed. The greater the spread in energies, the greater is the disorder, and hence the entropy is higher. At low temperatures, where particles have only low energies, many of them will have the same energy and thus the entropy of the system will be small. At high temperatures the particles will have a wide range of energies and hence a high entropy. One of the fascinating deductions of thermodynamics is that the entropy of a system can never become smaller but, if changed at all, must always increase. Applied universally this deduction leads to the idea that all matter is becoming more disordered. Thus there is significance in the difference between the negative and positive directions of time. In much of physics it is not important whether we regard time

as a negative or a positive quantity, provided we are consistent. If, however, we are dealing with an assembly of many particles then the entropy will be quite different for negative and for positive time. In one case it will decrease whereas in the other it will increase. For this reason the British astronomer Arthur Eddington (1882–1944) called entropy 'the arrow of time'.

**Eocene Epoch**, the second of the five geological epochs of the *Tertiary Era, representing the interval of time from 57.8 to 36.6 million years ago. The temperature was rising at this time. Mammals flourished in great variety: primates, rodents, and other types on land; whales and sea-cows in the seas. Eocene deposits generally show great variation, from continental to marine.

**eon** *aeon.

**epochs, geological**, arbitrary units of time used in geology. They are subdivisions of *periods. The Pliocene and Pleistocene Epochs are examples.

**equation**, an algebraic expression which expresses equality between quantities or functions. They can be used to describe sets of points or to find solutions for variables under certain prescribed constraints. If $a$, $b$, and $c$ are any numbers, then $y = ax + b$ is a linear equation representing the set of points lying on a particular straight line, and $y = ax^2 + bx + c$ is a quadratic equation giving the set of points on a parabola. Solutions, or roots, are those values of the variables for which the equation is true. Thus $5x + 1 = 11$ is true if $x = 2$; and $2x^2 - x - 3 = 0$ has roots $x = -1$ and $x = \frac{3}{2}$. To solve equations involving many variables at least as many equations are needed as there are variables. Such groups of equations are called simultaneous.

**equations of motion**, the equations in classical physics which completely define the movement of an object with relation to space and time. For a body undergoing constant acceleration $a$, a series of four equations relate its initial velocity $u$, its final velocity $v$, its displacement $s$, and time $t$. These equations, $v = u + at$, $s = \frac{1}{2}(u + v)t$, $s = ut + \frac{1}{2}at^2$, and $v^2 = u^2 + 2as$, enable the motion of the body to be described. More generally, the basic equation of motion is derived from the second of *Newton's laws of motion, which states that the applied force $F$ is equal to the rate of change of momentum, or $F = d(mv)/dt$, where $m$ is the mass of the body and $v$ its velocity. For constant mass this gives $F = ma$, where $a$ is acceleration. A second equation gives the rate of change of angular momentum $H$ about a fixed point as equal to the moment of the resultant force about the same point: $H = r \times mv$ and so $dH/dt = rF$ where $r$ is the displacement. Boundary conditions for position and velocity and knowledge of the *forces in operation at any instant are necessary to solve completely these equations of motion.

**Equator**, the imaginary *great circle, 40,076 km (24,902 miles) round, whose plane is at right angles to the Earth's axis of rotation. All points on it are by definition at latitude 0° and equidistant from both poles: it divides the Earth's surface into the northern and southern hemispheres. At all points on it the Sun will be approximately overhead twice a year, at the *equinoxes; and the Sun at midday is never more than 24° from the vertical. That is why places on or near the Equator are very hot unless they are at high altitudes, and this applies to all the *tropical zones.

**Equatorial Guinea**, a relatively small country in equatorial West Africa on the Gulf of Guinea. It includes the plateau of Río Muni bounded by Cameroon and Gabon, and the more mountainous and fertile, but smaller, island of Bioko (Fernando Póo).

**equilibrium** *dynamic equilibrium.

**equilibrium** (in physics), the state of a system in which all the forces are balanced. A system is in stable equilibrium if, following a small disturbance, it returns to the equilibrium position. A ball-bearing in a spoon given a small push will settle down after a short while in its original position. Unstable equilibrium is when that state of affairs fails to occur: for example, if the ball-bearing were balanced on the back of the spoon. A juggler balancing spinning balls on top of one another is illustrating his skill in keeping a system in unstable equilibrium. For stable equilibrium to occur, the potential energy $P$ of the system must be at a minimum. That is to say, $dP/dt = o$ and $d^2P/dt^2$ is positive. The situation of constant potential energy, such as when the ball-bearing rolls along a horizontal table, is sometimes called neutral equilibrium, although by the above definition it is actually unstable.

In chemistry, the equilibrium is the state of balance in *chemical reactions, when there is no further tendency for the reactants or their products to change their concentrations: reactant + reactant product + product. The effect of a change in conditions (such as addition to, or removal of, one of the substances; a rise or fall in temperature; or an increase or decrease of pressure) destroys the equilibrium, and the reaction moves in a way indicated by the equilibrium constant. The equilibrium constant provides a measure of whether reactants or products are favoured by the reaction at equilibrium. These constants have important industrial applications as they can be used to calculate the heat exchange accompanying a chemical reaction.

**equinox**, the time when the Sun appears to cross the celestial Equator, which occurs twice a year. At the spring or vernal equinox, about 21 March, the Sun appears to cross from south to north, and at the autumnal equinox, about 23 September, it appears to re-cross from north to south. In theory, on these days night and day are of equal length; and at each pole the Sun is either rising or setting for the next six months. In practice, however, the Sun's rays are bent by refraction in the atmosphere, so that it appears to rise earlier and set later than theory has it, making day slightly longer than night.

**equipartition of energy**, the manner in which the energy is shared between a very large number of particles in a system which is in thermodynamic equilibrium, that is, when all parts of the system are at the same temperature. At any particular temperature a system will have a certain total energy and this will be divided so that there is a certain average energy per particle. In essence the equipartition principle states that the total energy is shared on average by all the particles roughly equally, and that it is highly unlikely (if not impossible) that most of the energy will go to a few particles while the remainder have very little.

The equipartition principle actually goes further than this and states that if each particle has different types of motion or excitation then the energy must be shared equally among each of them. For example, the molecules in a gas can move independently in each of the three perpendicular directions

Antarctica's Mount **Erebus**, discovered and named by Sir James Ross, the Scottish explorer, in 1841, was first climbed by members of Shackleton's 1907–09 polar expedition.

in space and we might envisage all of them travelling in the same direction. This does not happen. The energy must not only be shared equally among all the particles; it must also be shared equally between all the different motions of which each particle is capable.

**era, geological**, the second largest of the time divisions used in geology. The Earth's *Phanerozoic history (that is, the last 570 million years) is divided into three eras: the Palaeozoic, the Mesozoic, and the Cenozoic. Each era is subdivided into a number of *periods.

**Eratosthenes** (*c.*276–194 BC), Greek geodesist who calculated the Earth's circumference based on the north–south distance between Aswan and Alexandria and their difference in latitude (obtained from the midday position of the Sun). He compiled a map of the inhabited world as known in his time and calculated the magnitude and distance of the Sun and Moon.

**Erebus, Mount**, an active volcano on Ross Island in Antarctica. It lies approximately 1,450 km (900 miles) from the South Pole and is 3,743 m (12,280 feet) high; it is often visible from 160 km (100 miles) away. Its lower slopes rise from the sea in gentle curves seamed with glaciers, while above is a typically volcanic profile. Steam is continually emitted from the summit, where there are three extinct craters as well as the current active one.

**erg**, a sandy desert, especially one in which the climate is hot and the whole land surface is covered by a *sand sea.

The heavy **erosion** of the banks of this Amazon tributary in the Peruvian rain forest demonstrates the destructive power of running water—especially in times of flood, when the suspended load of abrasive debris is at its greatest.

The name comes from the northern Sahara, but is applied also to sandy deserts in Arabia and elsewhere.

**ergodic theory** (in mathematics), the probability of the recurrence of phenomena. This branch of mathematics deals with questions of long-term equilibrium and the stability of a varying system. It has its origin in much of the classical theory of statistical mechanics, exploring such thermodynamic properties as temperature and *entropy. Ergodic theory also deals with questions such as whether the solar system as a whole is stable.

**Eric the Red** and **Leif Ericsson** (father and son), Viking explorers. Exiled from Iceland for manslaughter Erik ( *fl.* 984) explored the land to the west, which had been skirted earlier on the 10th century by the Norwegian Gunnbjörn Ulfsson. He founded the first European settlement there, calling the region Greenland. His son Leif (*fl.* 1002), hearing of land to the south-west of Greenland, became the first European known to have set foot in North America, landing at a region he called Vinland (possibly Nova Scotia) in *c.* 1000.

**erosion**, the removal by natural forces of material from any point and its transportation elsewhere on the Earth's surface . While it is the principal cause of *denudation of the land surface, it occurs also in lakes and in the sea, and *soil erosion is only one particular case. The main influence is gravity, the force of which is proportional to the sine of the angle of the surface slope. The most effective agents are rivers; they are responsible for carving the basic pattern of hills and valleys. On steep upland slopes the effect is chiefly vertical, boulders in a torrent wearing away at the channel bed and producing steep-sided valleys. On lowland plains, on the other hand, rivers meander and the pebbles cut laterally at the banks. Ice too erodes, glaciers depositing

A small-scale **escarpment** and dip slope formed at an outcrop of gently dipping limestone strata.

\*moraines both vertically and laterally. Avalanches and landslides are more ephemeral agents, with more localized effects. The waves and currents of the sea erode the land by pulling away pebbles, hurling them back at cliffs in times of storm, by solution, and by hydraulic action. The action of wind, \*deflation, is more limited, although it can carry fine particles vast distances. Erosion by plants is achieved by the removal of material through their roots to their tissues, by animals by trampling and burrowing and throwing up soil, which then gets blown or washed away, and by man in many ways.

**escarpment**, a steep slope of a cuesta—asymmetric upland block varying enormously in size. Made of tilted sedimentary or volcanic rock, a cuesta has a scarp face—the escarpment—and an opposite, gentler one—the dip slope, which declines generally at a gradient roughly equal to the dip of the layers of rock. Often cuestas occur in sets, one behind the other (rather like books which are laid overlapping), giving a sequence of scarp, dip slope, valley; scarp, dip slope, valley. Examples occur in southern England, especially on either side of the Weald, and in the south-east USA, where the belted coastal plain stretches south-east from northern Mississippi, Alabama, and Georgia in a series of north-facing escarpments. Some were formed by the faulting, uplift, and tilting of blocks—but many more were created by rivers in a very slow process of erosion. The rivers picked out softer layers of rock, forming valleys, and left the harder layers as escarpments. These main valleys run roughly at right angles to the dip of the rocks, parallel to the scarp faces and parallel to the strike of the strata. They are called strike vales.

**esker**, a low, steep-sided, sinuous ridge of sand and gravel which can wind for long distances across a lowland or valley floor. Eskers were formed underneath glaciers, by streams of melt-water flowing in tunnels within the ice. Because they are deposits laid down by running water, the sands and gravels are roughly sorted and bedded. Since the water was confined under pressure, it could flow uphill; and so eskers wind up and down, as well as from side to side.

**Espy, James Pollard** (1785–1860), meteorologist to the US government who gave the first essentially accurate explanation of the thermodynamics of cloud formation. He pioneered scientific weather forecasting, and was the first to use the telegraph for collecting meteorological information. His *Law of Cooling of Atmospheric Air* is a classic in the field.

**ester**, any of a class of compounds with the general formula $RCOOR'$, where R and $R'$ are either \*alkyl or \*aryl groups. If R and $R'$ are small groups, the resulting esters are volatile liquids, insoluble in water. They frequently possess characteristic sweet smells. For example, the smell of pear drops is caused by the ester pentyl ethanoate, $CH_3COOC_5H_{11}$. There are many naturally occurring esters. For example, fats are esters of glycerol and carboxylic acids with long carbon chains.

**Estonia**, a country of northern Europe, bounded on the north by the Gulf of Finland, on the east by Russia, on the south by Latvia, and on the west by the Baltic Sea. Two large islands and numerous small ones lie off the coast, which is occasionally ice-bound in winter although the summers are warm. On the mainland, a low-lying plain encompassing lakes of glacial origin, there are forests yielding high-quality timber. A limestone plateau in the north contains rich oil-shale deposits; while among the territory's other resources are dolomite, phosphorite, and clays.

**estuary**, the broad, lowest, tidal section of a river. All rivers flowing into the sea or very large lakes have either estuaries or *deltas at their mouths. The extent of an estuary depends upon the river's slope, the shape of the valley, and the range of the *tidal stream of the water body into which it flows; shallow estuaries of rivers with strong currents often develop *tidal bores. Because estuaries are tidal and relatively sheltered, they are often important harbours, although the tendency of rivers to deposit sediments as their currents are checked means that dredging is frequently needed to keep channels open.

**ethane** ($C_2H_6$), a colourless, odourless gas which burns readily in air; it is the second member of the *alkanes. Occurring with methane in natural gas, much of it is burnt directly without separation. It can be separated by liquefaction under pressure and can then be passed through hot tubes, forming hydrogen and ethene, a major petrochemical feedstock.

**ethanoic acid** (or acetic acid, $CH_3COOH$), the *carboxylic acid which is found in vinegar; it is formed when alcoholic drinks go sour, by *oxidation of the ethanol. It is used as a solvent, as a preservative, and in the manufacture of flavourings and plastics. The pure acid freezes, giving ice-like crystals, and is called glacial ethanoic acid.

**ethanol** (or ethyl alcohol, $C_2H_5OH$), a colourless, flammable, liquid *alcohol with a pleasant smell. As the intoxicating ingredient in all alcoholic drinks, it is commonly called alcohol and is produced in the fermentation of sugars by yeast. Industrially it is also manufactured from steam and ethene. Produced in dilute solution in these ways, it can be concentrated by distillation. It is widely used as a solvent, usually with methanol added to make it undrinkable and to remove its liability to tax. It burns readily in air; and in some countries where sugar can be grown easily it is employed as a fuel for cars by mixing it with petrol. Ethanol is toxic to humans; in small quantities it produces drunkenness, but larger quantities are fatal.

**ethene** (or ethylene, $C_2H_4$), the first member of the *alkenes; it is a colourless gas which burns readily in air. It occurs in natural gas, and is produced in the cracking of oil. It undergoes *polymerization to form polyethene (polythene), which is widely used in packaging; and it is also employed in the manufacture of ethanol, styrene, and ethylene oxide. Ethene produces ripening in fruit, but also inhibits growth in plants.

**ether**, any of a class of organic compounds with the formula $ROR'$, where R and R' are either *alkyl or *aryl groups, which need not necessarily be identical. Ethoxyethane (or diethyl ether), $C_2H_5OC_2H_5$, is the most common ether. This is a volatile, highly flammable liquid, insoluble in water. It is used as a solvent, mainly for organic compounds. It also possesses anaesthetic properties.

**Ethiopia**, a country lying in the eastern 'horn' of Africa, a north-eastern coast on the Red Sea. Sudan is on its eastern border and Kenya on its southern, while Somalia reaches round it on the east. The coastal region, Eritrea, is very hot and arid, as is the low-lying Ogaden region in the east; but the entire centre of the country is a group of volcanic mountain ranges with high plateaux where the air is mild and there is moderate summer rain. The Great Rift Valley runs through these, and the whole area is cut about with ravines and fertile valleys. In the north-west lies Lake Tana, the source of the Blue Nile, while in the south-west forests rise along the slopes of the mountain ranges. No great mineral deposits are yet known, though this is the fabled country of King Solomon's mines.

**ethyl alcohol** *ethanol.

**ethylene** *ethene.

**ethyne** (or acetylene, $C_2H_2$), the first member of the *alkynes; it is a colourless gas which is formed from calcium carbide, $CaC_2$, and water or by the partial *oxidation of methane. Burning readily in air, it is used in lamps, and in oxy-acetylene torches which can reach 3,000 °C (6,000 °F). It is used in the manufacture of a wide variety of products, including ethanal, synthetic rubbers, vinyl fabrics, and solvents.

**Etna**, in eastern Sicily, at 3,340 m (10,958 feet), Europe's highest volcano. It is also one of the world's most active, eruptions occurring every six or seven years. Round its barren summit, which is snow-covered for much of the year, are several hundred subsidiary cones; and it is from these, and especially from a number in a huge chasm on its eastern side, that the lava usually spreads. Clinker and ash cover the slopes down to the tree-line, while below forests of pine, chestnut, oak, and acacia the lava-rich soil is intensely cultivable. The circumference of the base of this great mountain is nearly 160 km (100 miles).

**Euclid** (*fl.* 300 BC), Greek mathematician who taught in Alexandria, home of the great ancient library. Although the author of several texts, including *The Optics* and *The Data*, he is known primarily for compiling one of the most famous works in all mathematics, *The Elements*. The oldest surviving copy dates from AD 876. The work consists of thirteen books, each containing many propositions on geometry. Book I contains results about familiar plane polygonal figures, including the famous Theorem of *Pythagoras. The subjects of some of the other books are number theory, proportions, circles, and solid figures. The treatise is systematically organized and later propositions use earlier results without mentioning them explicitly. Nowhere are any of the methods of discovery revealed. Euclid used a uniform style of setting out a result, which was followed for the succeeding two millennia. Many commentaries have been written on *The Elements*, and Euclid is frequently referred to as *the* geometer.

**Euler, Leonhard** (1707–83), Swiss mathematician who was the most creative and productive mathematician of the 18th century. His work exhibited a widespread use of algebraic methods for treating problems in many different areas; it runs to 70 volumes and includes essays on the tides, shipbuilding, and navigation, as well as on mainstream topics in pure and applied mathematics. Euler invented many mathematical notations which are still employed today. He used e for the base of natural *logarithms, i for $\sqrt{(-1)}$, and $f(x)$ for a function of $x$.

**Euphrates**, the greatest river of south-western Asia, 2,700 km (1,700 miles) long. Its source is the confluence of the Kara and the Murad in the mountains of Erzurum, Turkey. Running generally southward, it cuts through rugged canyons and carries great quantities of silt on to its

Syrian floodplain. Here it swings sluggishly south-east and into Iraq, where it enters the broad valley of ancient Mesopotamia, which it shares with its twin river, the Tigris. Its channels shift and part and come together again, forming small islands. The land becomes marshy and very fertile, with rice fields and date plantations. Lowest in September, the river reaches its highest in May, when it forms many seasonal lakes. Just north of Lake Hammar it joins the Tigris, a union known as the Shatt al-Arab—a muddy waterway extending south-eastward through a vast delta to the Gulf.

**Eurasia**, a term used for Europe and Asia combined; they are sometimes considered to be a single continent.

**Europe**, the smallest continent of the northern hemisphere, stretching westward from the Ural Mountains and surrounded on three sides by sea. Its structure is complex. In the north-west, mountains of old, hard rock occupy most of the Scandinavian Peninsula, the north-west of the British Isles, and Brittany in France; much of this area is covered by barren rocks and moorland. Most of it is separated by the shallow North and Baltic seas from the North European Plain, which spreads from England and France across the north of the continent to Finland and the Baltic states and down to the Black Sea. The greater part of this plain is well watered and extremely fertile, although the climate and vegetation vary, the west being temperate maritime, with meadowland and deciduous woodland, whereas the east is temperate continental with much coniferous forest and only small clearings for agriculture. Throughout there are scattered rich deposits of coal, oil, and natural gas. Southern Europe is hilly or mountainous, except for two plains: a triangular plain in northern Italy and the broad one of the middle Danube. From west to east is a curving chain of ranges—the Pyrenees, Alps, and Carpathians—while pointing southward are the Apennines and the parallel ranges of the Balkan Peninsula. They form barriers, yet are so cut by rivers and valleys that no part of Europe is completely isolated. Some of their northern slopes are forested, and in certain areas there are workable deposits of iron. In the south, a Mediterranean climate of mild winters and hot summers provides for the cultivation of vines, olives, and citrus fruits; but the soil is generally too dry for more than a little grain. The extreme south is volcanic, being close to the edge of the Eurasian *plate.

**eustatic change** (or eustatic movement), change relating to worldwide variations in sea-level, as distinct from regional change caused by earth movements in a particular area. 'Change' is a more appropriate word than 'movement' for events of this kind. Eustatic movements are taking place at the present time. The sea-level has, for example, risen slowly

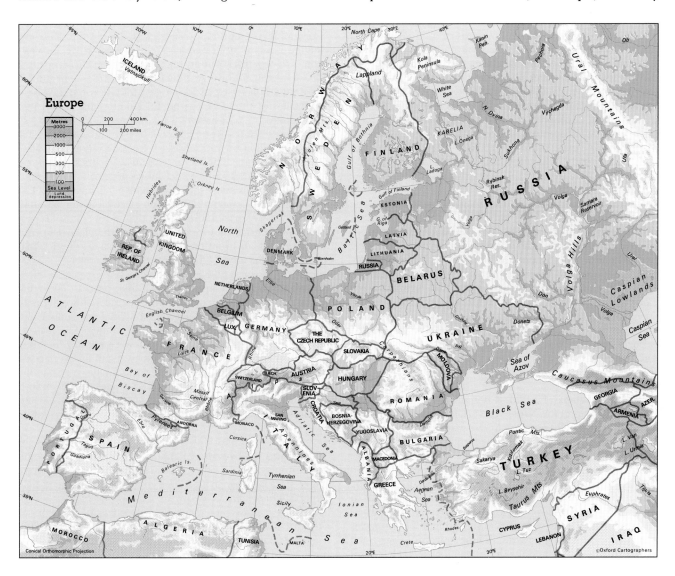

throughout the world since the middle of the 19th century. A likely cause for such changes is the advance or recession of the polar ice, which would affect the amount of water in the oceans. Global warming as a consequence of the *greenhouse effect may accelerate sea-level rise, partly through increased melting of polar ice, partly through thermal expansion of ocean surface waters as they warm.

**evaporation**, the conversion of a liquid to a vapour which occurs at the free surface of the liquid. It arises because the more energetic particles in the liquid are able to escape when they reach the surface. Once this has occurred there is very little chance of their returning to the liquid again and thus the volume of the liquid is continually reduced. Evaporation increases at high temperatures because the molecules have a higher energy and therefore they can escape from the liquid surface more easily. Because it is the lower-energy particles that are left behind, the liquid tends to become cooler.

**evaporites**, deposits which form by the precipitation of dissolved solids, especially salt, from water. Since the precipitation of salts is due to evaporation of the water the residue is known as an evaporite. Common evaporitic substances include *halite or rock-salt (NaCl) and *gypsum ($CaSO_4 \cdot 2H_2O$). Most evaporites are interpreted as having been formed by the evaporation of an arm or portion of the sea. Others result from the evaporation of inland lakes. Many evaporite deposits are hundreds of metres (or yards) thick. This poses a problem. Sea water contains only about 3 per cent of dissolved salts, and the evaporation of, say, 100 m (330 feet) of seawater would produce an evaporite bed only about 1.5 m (5 feet) thick. Replenishment of the sea water has therefore to be invoked in order to explain the formation of the thicker deposits. Ancient evaporites on a large scale occur near Salzburg, Austria, and in the north of England (halite), Texas and New Mexico, USA (gypsum), the Mojave Desert, California, USA (borax and potash), and elsewhere.

**evapotranspiration**, the movement of water from the soil to the atmosphere by means of the combined processes of *evaporation and *transpiration. It is essentially the opposite of *precipitation. On a global scale, approximately 66 per cent of the precipitation which falls on the land surface is returned to the atmosphere in this way, with the remaining third contributing to *runoff and *groundwater. Locally it is controlled by such factors as temperature, wind speed, and the availability of moisture. Potential evapotranspiration is the amount of evapotranspiration that would occur if there were an unlimited supply of water available and is a concept which is employed in the determination of the atmospheric *water balance.

**Everest, Mount** (Tibetan, Chomolungma), the highest point on Earth, on the Nepal–Tibet (China) border situated at 8,847 m (29,028 feet) among the eastern Himalayas—a range that is still rising. Named after George Everest (1790–1866), surveyor-general of India, it is joined to lesser peaks by cols. Tenzing Norgay of Nepal and Edmund Hillary of New Zealand were the first climbers to reach the summit (1953). Junko Tabei of Japan was the first woman to reach the summit (1975). Below the ridges are ice-bound *cirques, called cwms, glaciers with toppling ice pinnacles and deep, moving crevasses. These hazards apart, the southerly monsoon in June to September, which causes

heavy snowfall, and westerly gales from November to March, leave scant time in the year for expeditions to approach the summit.

**Everglades, the**, a low-lying, marshy and subtropical area of some 13,000 km² (5,000 sq. mi.) covering the greater part of southern Florida, USA. Mangrove swamps are on the coast and saw-grass inland, with cypress and other trees growing densely out of black mud formed by plant decay in stagnant water. In a national park 4,500 km² (1,720 sq. mi.), flora and fauna are preserved, and the bird life especially is varied and abundant.

**excitation** (in physics), a process in which a physical system acquires a higher energy level (an excited state) than that of its lowest energy level (its ground state). For an isolated atom in the ground state the electrons fill, in order, the orbitals of lowest energy round the nucleus. Excitation can occur if the atom is irradiated with electromagnetic radiation of suitable frequency or if it is bombarded with electrons. The extra energy enables the atomic electrons to occupy permitted states of higher energy. In a solid, excitation can also be provided by heat energy, which will increase the amplitude of vibration of the atoms, that is, put them in higher vibrational states.

**exclusion principle** (in physics), a principle which states that the electrons in the same atom must differ in at least one aspect of their quantum properties. It governs the electronic configuration of atoms, which is the way in which the electrons are organized within the atom. The exclusion principle was discovered by Wolfgang *Pauli in 1925. He studied the atomic spectra of various atoms to determine the quantum states of the electrons in the atoms. Pauli found that some states in some atoms were missing, and worked out that if these states were present they would have to have the same quantum properties as electron states that were already present. The total absence of these identical states implied that states which were present must be non-identical. Studies made since the exclusion principle was first proposed have confirmed that each electron within an atom is in a state which is unique within that atom. Thus it is possible to construct an accurate picture of the electronic configuration of an atom, which is useful since this is what determines the atom's chemical behaviour.

**exfoliation** (in geomorphology), the process occurring when curved layers of rock fall from the steep, bare slopes of cliffs or summits; it leaves large hollows or alcoves on the cliff faces, and it rounds summits to form domes. The process occurs in fine-grained rocks with few *joints or *bedding planes. When steep slopes are cut by rivers or by glaciers, lateral pressure is reduced and the rocks 'bulge' very slightly, creating fine fractures which curve parallel to the surface. The sheer weight of the slabs may cause them to fall; or their *spalling may be encouraged by frost and by percolating water.

**existence theorems** (in mathematics), the claims, and their proofs, that something postulated to exist actually does. Since it is possible to postulate and discuss mathematical objects which cannot exist (for example a regular seven-sided object), existence theorems are necessary as checks or as correctives. An existence theorem for *transcendental numbers was proved by the German mathematician Georg Cantor (1845–1918).

Mount **Everest** and the distant saddle of the South Col,
viewed across the north-west ridge of Nuptse.

**exothermic reaction**, a chemical reaction in which heat
is given out to the surroundings—that is, there is a decrease
in the *enthalpy of the reaction mixture. An example of an
exothermic reaction is the neutralization of an acid by a
base. If sodium hydroxide solution, the base, is added to
hydrochloric acid, the container becomes warm. This rise in
temperature is brought about by the heat energy released by
the reaction; and the products of the reaction, namely
sodium chloride and water, therefore have a lower enthalpy
than the reactants. *Combustion reactions are exothermic.
For example, energy is released when *fossil fuels are
burned. The combustion of carbohydrates by living cells, to
form carbon dioxide and water, is a biochemical example of
an exothermic reaction and represents a major way in which
many cells obtain their energy. An exothermic compound is
one whose formation is accompanied by the liberation of
heat.

**expansion** (of matter), the increase in size of a body, be it
a solid, a liquid, or a gas. Expansion can most readily be
brought about by heating the body, in which case the expansion is called thermal expansion. This is an effect which is
used in many devices, particularly in those which measure
or regulate temperature. For example, the expansion of a
liquid is used in the mercury thermometer and the expansion of a solid is the basic mechanism in many thermostats.
The expansion of a gas is used in a hot-air balloon. When
the gas in the balloon is heated it expands and thus becomes
less dense than the cooler air outside; hence the hot gas rises,
bearing the balloon with it. However, although such uses
can be made of thermal expansion, it can also cause problems; and the effects of expansion must always be considered
in the design of any object which is going to operate over a
range of temperatures. Uniquely among liquids, *water
exhibits a strange and exceedingly important behaviour:
between 0 and 4 °C (32 and 39 °F) it contracts on heating;
only above 4 °C (39 °F) does it start to expand. This means
that when it is cooled below 4 °C it expands, becoming less
dense than less cold water and so floating on top of it. The
expansion continues until the top layer of water freezes; and
it is for this reason that ice always first forms on the surface
of water, protecting to some extent the water beneath it, and
then extends downwards. In all other liquids freezing starts
at the bottom.

**explosions**. These occur when exothermic chemical reactions take place at a very high rate, producing almost instant

aneously a very high pressure, which causes a loud noise and possibly destruction of the surroundings. Explosions usually occur because the heat given out by the reaction increases the temperature and makes the reaction go faster; this in turn gives out more heat, and so on. The reaction rate increases rapidly, and the explosive is all consumed in a very short period of time. The first explosive mixture to be widely used was gunpowder, a mixture of potassium nitrate, charcoal, and sulphur. Many other explosives have been manu-

factured on a large scale, such as nitroglycerine, picric acid, trinitrotoluene (TNT), and mixtures of *oxidizing agents such as potassium chlorate with combustible materials such as petroleum. Mixtures of ammonium nitrate and fuel oil are widely used. Explosions can also be produced readily in gaseous mixtures. The internal-combustion engine relies on explosions in petrol–air mixtures, while methane–air explosions have caused many mining accidents. Most combustible gases or powders form an explosive mixture with air within limited composition ranges; outside these ranges reaction is slow and smooth. Nuclear reactions have also been used to create explosions; here the explosion is caused by a chain reaction. A neutron causes the fission of one atomic nucleus, which produces energy and three more neutrons. Each of these neutrons can then cause further fission, producing more energy and more neutrons, so that within a short period of time all the nuclear fuel has reacted. As nuclear reactions give out more energy than chemical reactions, nuclear explosions are extremely powerful.

**exponential function**, a function that varies according to the *power of another quantity (see figure). Exponential functions are written as $y = a^x$ (where $a$ can be any positive number) and their common property is that as $x$ increases by $1$, $y$ is multiplied by the value of $a$. Every such function has the property that $a^x$ is positive for all values of $x$ and its graph passes through the point $(0, 1)$. Each function is the *inverse of the corresponding *logarithm to base $a$. The function $e^x$ is often called *the* exponential function, where e is an *irrational number defined as the limit of $(1 + 1/n)^n$ as $n$ tends to infinity, and is approximately equal to 2.718. The inverse of this function, $\log_e x$, is called the natural logarithm of $x$. The derivative of $e^x$ is itself, and the *Taylor expansion for $e^x$ is $1 + x + x^2/2! + \ldots x^n/n! + \ldots$, which converges for all values of $x$, even complex ones. Exponential functions are ubiquitous in all branches of science. They are used, for example, to describe the growth of bacterial colonies and the *half-life of radioactive substances.

**extrusive rock**, a rock that has been poured out on to the Earth's surface. Some are extruded as molten magma; others as solid fragments. They are also termed 'volcanic' and are most commonly found as *basalts or *pyroclasts.

**Eyre, Edward John** (1815–1901), British explorer and colonial statesman. Having emigrated to Australia at the age of 17, Eyre established himself as a sheep-farmer and in 1840–1 undertook explorations in the interior deserts of the continent. He later served as Lieutenant-Governor of New Zealand (1846–53), Governor of Saint Vincent (1854–60), and of Jamaica (1864–6). He was recalled from the last post for putting down an indigenous revolt with undue severity, but was eventually cleared of all charges.

**Eyre, Lake**, a vast centre of internal drainage in northern South Australia. In dry seasons it is a salt marsh; after flooding it is a saline lake with a depth of 2–4 m (7–14 feet). It occupies two basins totalling some 8,800 km² (3,400 sq. mi.) at about 10 m (36 feet) below sea-level—the lowest point in Australia. Streams from Northern Territory and Queensland drain their muddy waters into it, which it then loses by evaporation. Only once in every fifty years or so is it really full; when this occurs, it is the largest lake in Australia.

## Exponential functions and series

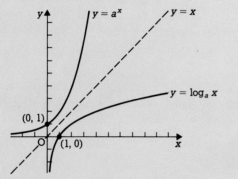

The function $y = a^x$ is the mirror image or reflection of its inverse, $y = \log_a x$, in the line $y = x$.

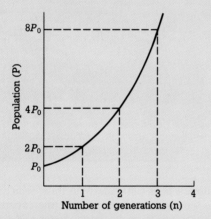

The population ($P$) of a colony of bacteria grows exponentially according to the equation $P = P_0 2^n$ where $P_0$ is the original population.

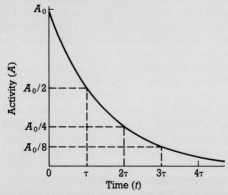

The activity ($A$) of a sample of radioactive material decays according to the equation $A = A_0 e^{-0.693\, t/\tau}$ where $A_0$ is the original activity and $\tau$ is the half-life, the time taken for the activity of the sample to decay by half.

# F

**fabric** (in geology), the appearance of a rock, and the way minerals are arranged in it. Fabric is related to the texture of the rock, and the terms are more or less synonymous. Thus it is possible to speak of metamorphic fabrics or textures as distinct from igneous or sedimentary ones; and to make more subtle distinctions within the categories, for example, schistose or gneissic fabric (texture) in metamorphic rocks.

**factorial**. The factorial for any whole number, $n$, is the product of all the whole numbers from 1 up to and including $n$, and is written $n!$. For example: $10! = 1 \times 2 \times 3 \times 4 \times 5 \times 6 \times 7 \times 8 \times 9 \times 10$. A quick inspection shows that factorials rapidly become very large. Factorials occur in many power series, including that produced by the *binomial expansion, where the coefficient of the term $a^r\, b^{n-r}$ in the expansion of $(a + b)^n$ is shown to be $n!/[r!\,(n - r!)]$.

**Faeroe Islands** (Faeroes), a group of islands in the North Atlantic between Iceland and the Shetland Isles, belonging to Denmark, but partly antonomous.

It was Michael **Faraday** who first proposed the idea of the magnetic 'field' to explain why a magnet can act on a distant object. The field concept has since proved of great value in physics, for instance in gravitation and electromagnetic theory.

**Fahrenheit scale**, a scale of temperature, first established by the German physicist Gabriel Fahrenheit in 1715. The unit of temperature is the degree Fahrenheit (°F), and 0 °F was originally the coldest temperature Fahrenheit could achieve using a freezing mixture of salt and ice. On his scale, water freezes at 32 °F and boils at 212 °F (under set atmospheric conditions). No longer used in scientific work, Fahrenheit temperatures still feature in everyday language; hot days 'in the eighties', for example. To convert a Fahrenheit temperature to *Celsius (centigrade), subtract 32, then multiply by $\frac{5}{9}$.

**Falkland Islands** (Malvinas), two main islands and nearly a hundred smaller ones, belonging to the UK, lying some 480 km (300 miles) off the coast of Argentina in the South Atlantic Ocean at latitude 50° S. Inland from the jagged coastlines of East and West Falkland the ground rises to heights of about 690 m (2,260 feet), bare of trees and windswept. The moors are the home of many species of bird and hundreds of thousands of sheep, no cultivation being possible. Winters are long, with much snow, and even summer temperatures seldom rise above 10 °C (50 °F). South Georgia is an even bleaker island 1,290 km (800 miles) away to the east and further south. The South Sandwich, South Shetland, and South Orkney Islands lie more southward still, only just outside the Antarctic Circle. They are covered with snow and ice all year.

**fan, alluvial**    *alluvial fan.

**farad** (symbol F), the *SI unit of capacitance, such that one coulomb of charge causes a potential difference of one volt. The unit is too large for most applications and the microfarad ($10^{-6}$ F) is more frequently used. The unit is named after Michael *Faraday.

**Faraday, Michael** (1791–1867), British physicist and chemist who made major advances in the study of *magnetism, *electricity, and the chemical effect of a current. He started his working life as a bookbinder, but later became laboratory assistant to Humphry *Davy at the Royal Institution, ultimately succeeding him as Director. Fascinated by electrical phenomena, he constructed a simple form of electric motor in 1821, applying Hans Christian *Oersted's discovery that electric currents produce a magnetic effect. After much research he discovered how to use magnetism to produce or 'induce' an electric current, publishing his laws of electromagnetic induction in 1831. In the same year he constructed two other 'firsts'—the first transformer and the first dynamo. His laws of *electrolysis, published in 1834 and named after him, described the changes caused by electric current passing through liquids. Other discoveries included the chemical compound *benzene, diamagnetism (a weak magnetic effect present in all materials), and the rotation of light waves by strong magnetic fields. Arguably the most outstanding experimental scientist ever, he refused a knighthood and the Presidency of the Royal Society because he feared that such honours would undermine his integrity and his intellectual freedom.

**Fata Morgana**    *mirage.

**fault, geological**, a plane surface fracture caused when stresses within the earth break and dislocate bodies of rock. The relative movement may be vertical or nearly so (as in normal faults) or horizontal (tear or wrench faults). In areas of extreme compression, rocks may be pushed up and over the fracture (overthrusting). Faults are recognized by the displacement of layers of rock and by the crushing and alteration of material along the fault surface itself. Displacement can be a matter of centimetres or many kilometres. Some fault-lines (like the *San Andreas Fault) continue to move jerkily for thousands or millions of years; and although the movement at any one time may be small, the cumulative displacement may be considerable. Major faults can create significant features of the landscape, such as *block mountains and *rift valleys, while even minor faults provide lines of weakness which are subjected to weathering and erosion.

**feldspar** (felspars), a highly important group of rock-forming minerals: they constitute about half the rocks seen at the Earth's surface and are essential constituents of

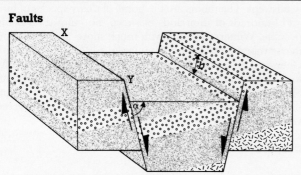

Faults

Normal faults, caused by crustal extension. Angle α is the dip of the fault-plane; XY is the strike of the fault; *b* is the displacement or dip-slip.

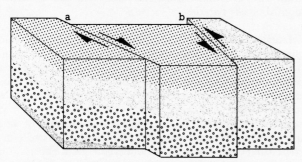

Tear (wrench or transcurrent) faults release compressional forces by sideways displacement. Dextral faults (a) displace to the right; sinistral faults (b) to the left. One of the best-known tear faults is the huge San Andreas Fault in California.

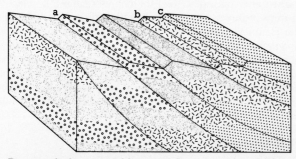

Reverse faults, caused by crustal compression; (a) is a high-angled reverse fault; (b) and (c) are low-angled reverse or overthrust faults, a common feature in areas of intense compressional deformation.

*igneous rocks of all types. The amount and type of feldspar is an important factor in giving a name to a rock. The various types of feldspar are all aluminosilicates containing varying proportions of sodium, potassium, calcium, and barium. The most common types are orthoclase and *plagioclase.

**felsenmeer**, or 'block' or 'boulder' field, the jumbled expanse of sharp-edged rocks found on flat surfaces near sea-level in the High Arctic and Antarctic, and on high mountain plateaux and flat areas in lower latitudes. Felsenmeer are produced by water freezing in the joints or cracks in the rocks and prising blocks loose. Ice crystals can grow underneath blocks as well as round their edges and so the blocks become tipped and tilted on top of each other.

**fen**, a swampy, low-lying area of freshwater *peat formed along and between sluggish river channels. The soil is rather alkaline, unlike the acid peat of bogs. When drained, fens make good farmland, as in the fenlands of eastern England.

**Fennoscandian Shield**, a geological name for the exposed portion of the *Baltic Shield which occupies part of Norway, Sweden, and Finland, in northern Europe. Made up of Precambrian crystalline rock—the oldest in Europe—it is dominated by granites and gneisses, any horizontally bedded or slightly inclined *sedimentary rocks being restricted to a small area in the interior. In places along the shield's frontier there are great faults, where there has been displacement. The old, eroded rocks have yielded a great variety of minerals, especially copper and iron.

**Fermat, Pierre de** (1601–65), French mathematician and physicist who developed the modern theory of numbers, laid the foundations upon which Isaac *Newton was to build the *calculus, and founded, with Blaise Pascal (see *pascal), the theory of *probability. He put forward the principle that light, when *reflected or *refracted, always takes the path for which its travel time is least. However, his most famous assertion, or 'Fermat's Last Theorem', is that simple relationships of the form $3^2 + 4^2 = 5^2$ are not possible with higher powers than 2. This attracts more attention than any other mathematical problem, but nonetheless, it still remains neither proved nor disproved.

**Fermi, Enrico** (1901–54), Italian-born US physicist who masterminded the design and construction of the first nuclear reactor, the 'Fermi pile', in 1941. His contributions to nuclear physics were many and varied. Working at first in his native Italy, he established the statistical laws—found independently by Paul *Dirac—which apply to the particles forming the *atom. Later, in 1934, he predicted the existence of the *neutrino, a small uncharged particle released in certain radioactive decay processes. In 1938 he was awarded the Nobel Prize for Physics for his research into nuclear reactions caused by neutron bombardment. Fleeing fascist persecution in Italy, he settled in the United States, where his continuing research led to the building of the 'pile', and ultimately the construction of the first atomic bomb in 1945.

**fermion** (in atomic physics), a particle with half-integral *spin, such as a proton, neutron, positron, electron or muon.

**Ferrel, William** (1817–91), US meteorologist, known for his law of atmospheric *circulation, which states that bodies on the Earth's surface are deflected to the right in the northern hemisphere and to the left in the southern. He studied the movements of tides, currents, and storms, and invented a machine to predict highest and lowest tidal variations.

**ferric oxide**    *iron oxide.

**ferrisol**, an iron-rich soil occurring in tropical climates with high temperature and rainfall. In these conditions soluble minerals are removed from the soil by *leaching, leaving behind only the iron and aluminium compounds which cause the characteristic red colour of the soil. The soil material is often highly weathered and may be extremely deep. Ferrisols are found in the Amazon and Zaïre basins, along the east coast of Brazil, and in Indonesia.

**ferromagnesian minerals**, rock-forming minerals rich in iron and magnesium: biotite, hornblende, augite, hypersthene, and olivine. They are generally dark in colour. They are primary constituents of basic igneous rocks.

**ferromagnetism**    *magnetism.

**ferrous oxide**    *iron oxide.

**fetch of waves**, the distance of open water over which wind is blowing in a constant direction, generating a wave system. In general, the longer the fetch the higher the waves and the longer the swell lasts after the wind has dropped. Easterly winds blowing across the narrow Strait of Dover, for example, can only raise waves to a height of some 3 m (10 feet). The height determines how much energy is available for erosion or deposition along a coast; wave attack is greatest on headlands exposed to long fetches.

**Feynman, Richard** (1918–88), US physicist who worked for the Manhattan Project to develop the atomic bomb. After the war he worked briefly at Cornell University and then went to the California Institute of Technology. In the late 1940s he was a major contributor to the development of quantum electrodynamics (see *quantum mechanics), and shared the 1965 Nobel Prize for Physics for this work. He is also well known for 'Feynman diagrams', which he invented to illustrate the interactions between elementary particles, and for his skill as a lecturer and writer.

**Fibonacci numbers**, a sequence starting 1, 1, 2, 3, 5, 8, 13 . . . in which each number is the sum of the two preceding numbers. The series of numbers is named after the Italian mathematician Leonardo Fibonacci (*c.*1200). This mathematical sequence frequently occurs in nature. A male bee has only a mother whereas a female has both parents. Tracing back the family tree of a male bee reveals that the numbers of ancestors in each generation form a Fibonacci sequence. The number of sepals, petals, and stamens of flowers often form such a sequence, as do the successive number of shoots on a branching flower stalk. Natural spirals such as a nautilus shell or a spider's web seem to be related to a curve based on the Fibonacci numbers, as is the exponential curve. The ratio of successive terms of the sequence approaches the *golden ratio and any two successive terms are relatively prime (have no factors in common).

**field**, a region in which a force acts. Thus a gravitational field is a region in which objects experience a gravitational force; an electric field is a region in which charged bodies experience an electric force; and so on. Fields can be imagined as a pattern of lines. The number of lines in a given

The type of spiral that occurs in the nautilus shell is related to the **Fibonacci numbers**.

space represents the strength of the field. Arrows on the lines represent the direction of the force (see *lines of force).

**Fiji**, a country comprising a group of two islands, Viti Levu and Vanua Levu, and several hundred smaller ones in the south-west Pacific Ocean. Being situated some 400 km (248.6 miles) from a *plate boundary, they are volcanic. Mountains rise to some 1,300 m (4,265 feet) and have thick rain forest on the wetter slopes. The climate is hot, though not unpleasantly so, and sugar cane and coconut are the main crops. The islands lie in a hurricane belt, and there is periodic devastation by *tornadoes.

**finger lake**, a body of water formed in a rock basin scraped out by the ice of glaciers or ice-sheets. Long and thin in shape, finger lakes occur usually in mountain or upland areas. Many of the lochs of Scotland and Ireland are finger lakes, and there is a famous group in western New York State, USA. As former river valleys which were overdeepened by ice, they are often entirely cut in rock but sometimes have a dam of *moraine or *till at their lower end. If drowned by the sea, they become *fiords.

**Finland** (Suomi), a Scandinavian country bounded by Norway on the north, Sweden and the Gulf of Bothnia on the west, and Russia on the east. A long coastline round the west and south, studded with over 6,000 Åland islands, thrusts into the Baltic Sea. Of the rolling, granitic land area, of which the *Fennoscandian Shield forms part, only a tenth is cultivable, some 70 per cent being coniferous forest, 11 per cent tundra, and 9 per cent lakes. Its 60,000 lakes are linked by short rivers, sounds, or canals to form busy waterways. A third of the country lies north of the Arctic Circle and is part of *Lapland.

**fiord**, a long, narrow, steep-sided coastal inlet found in previously glaciated areas such as western Scotland, Norway, Greenland, Alaska, southern Chile, and New Zealand. Fiords were formed by glaciers which moved down valleys to the sea, carving deep gorges; and they show many of the characteristics of glacial valleys on land, such as U-shaped profiles and *truncated spurs. A rock sill, often covered with boulders and clay debris which may have been deposited as a terminal *moraine, often marks the seaward end of these deep troughs. As the sea-level rose after the retreat of the glaciers, such valleys were drowned and became coastal inlets. One of the best-known fiords is *Sogne Fiord; but the world's longest is Nordvest Fiord in eastern Greenland, which extends for 314 km (195 miles). Fiords are excellent natural harbours. In many areas their openings are protected by low hill-like islands known as skerries. These lie parallel to the coast, and behind them is a stretch of sheltered water which forms a quiet channel for shipping.

**Fiordland National Park** (formerly Sounds), an area forming the south-west corner of the South Island, New Zealand. It extends for 320 km (200 miles) along a coastline so indented as a result of glacial action that it resembles the Norwegian fiords. It is mainly mountainous, with valleys providing great scenic beauty. Mount Tutoko stands at 2,746 m (9,010 feet); Lake Manapouri is New Zealand's deepest lake, and the Te Ana-au Caves are inhabited by glow-worms. There is much virgin forest on the slopes.

The view west from the head of the Geiranger **Fiord** in Norway. The surrounding mountains have been smoothed and rounded by the great ice-sheets that covered them.

**fire**, the effect produced when a chemical reaction yields gas or vapour accompanied by heat. The visible flame occurs because the atoms or molecules in the vapour are excited to high energies. The excited atoms then release some of this energy in the form of light. In most fires the chemical reaction is one in which the burning material combines with the oxygen in the air. The more air there is available, the more rapid is the reaction and the hotter is the flame. The light of flames is due to electrons falling from higher *energy levels to lower ones, and so it can be analysed to tell us something about these levels and hence about the nature of the substances present in the flame. This is the basis of flame tests, which are used to detect an element by observing the colour it produces when put in the colourless flame of a Bunsen burner.

**firn**, (French Alpine dialect, *névé*), granular snow which is half-way to becoming glacier ice. Often buried by new falls, it is old snow which has been partly melted and re-frozen. This process joins the particles together into granules, but still leaves air pockets between them.

**fission** *nuclear fission.

**Fitzgerald-Lorentz contraction**, a postulate used to explain the negative result of the *Michelson–Morley experiment and which helped to lead to the development of *relativity theory. It predicts that when a body is moving away from or towards a stationary observer, its length will contract in the direction of its motion. The effect is extremely small and considered negligible unless the motion is close to the speed of light. It is named after the Irish

physcist George Fitzgerald (1851–1901) and the Dutch physicist Hendrik *Lorentz, who both postulated it independently in 1892.

**fixed-point arithmetic**, normal decimal arithmetic, usually only referred to by its full name to contrast it with *floating-point arithmetic. Rounding-off is usually done to a certain number of decimal places. Although this rarely causes problems for addition and subtraction, errors may well occur in multiplication and division.

**Fizeau, Armand Hippolyte Louis** (1819–96), French physicist, who in 1849 made the first reliable measurement of the *speed of light. He directed light at a distant mirror and estimated its travel time by spinning a toothed wheel in the path, so that the beam departed through a gap and was blocked by the following tooth.

**flavour** (in atomic physics), a term for a set of distinguishing properties of *quarks and *leptons. Quarks have any of six flavours: u (up), d (down), c (charm), s (strangeness), b (bottom or beauty), and t (top); the last one has not been experimentally confirmed yet but is confidently predicted. (All these names, like flavour itself, are arbitrary choices, and have nothing to do with the ordinary meanings of the words.) By extension the three kinds of leptons and their three neutrinos are regarded as flavours. Ordinary objects have qualities such as mass, momentum, and energy, which obey conservation laws, for example the *conservation of energy, when they interact. Similarly quarks and leptons are believed to have qualities called flavours which are subject to conservation laws; they have become significant in the study of fundamental *interactions in particle physics. (See also *colour).

**Flinders**, an Australian river 837 km (520 miles) long, flowing intermittently across Queensland. It rises in the eastern highlands and runs initially south, swinging in a great arc, through wide rolling plains, before entering the tropical lowlands of the north. Here it picks up its main tributaries, the Cloncurry and the Saxby, before flowing into the Gulf of Carpentaria.

**Flinders, Matthew** (1774–1814), British navigator and surveyor. In the company of George Bass, he explored the coast of New South Wales in 1795–1800, before being commissioned by the Royal Navy to circumnavigate Australia. Between 1801 and 1803 he charted much of the west coast of the continent for the first time, but was wrecked on his voyage home and imprisoned by the French on Mauritius until 1810. His *Voyage to Terra Australis* was written on retirement in England and appeared on his death. Flinders Island, the Flinders Range in South Australia, and Flinders River in Queensland are named after him.

**Flinders Range**, a highland belt in South Australia that runs northward from the eastern side of Gulf Saint Vincent for some 800 km (500 miles) before it peters out in the low country south-east of Lake Eyre. It consists of resistant rocks of Precambrian age that were severely crumpled early in the Palaeozoic Era. Subsequent block-faulting has given the range its character, but this is modified in detail by erosion, which has cut fine valleys such as the Alligator Gorge. Down-faulting has given rise to marginal zones of subsidence, two of which are now occupied by the Spencer and Saint Vincent Gulfs.

**flint**, a type of *chert: a hard material consisting of nearly pure silica ($SiO_2$) in cryptocrystalline form (the common crystalline form being quartz). It occurs as roundish nodules, usually steely-grey and encrusted with white. The silica was originally the skeletons of sponges; these dissolved and the silica was redeposited in the rocks. The nodules are found in regular layers in chalk and other limestone, and when broken open usually disclose a fossil sponge. Flint breaks into flakes and sharp-edged fragments which spark when struck with steel. Heated in kilns, it produces a soft white silica powder. It has in the past been much used as a building material in the south-east of the UK. Apart from the well-known occurrences in the chalk (Upper *Cretaceous) of Britain and western Europe, similar concretions are known in limestones of the *Jurassic and *Tertiary Periods.

**floating-point arithmetic**, a method of calculation which at times ignores the correct position of the decimal point. For instance, in the common *algorithm for multiplying decimals, the numbers are treated as whole numbers. Rules are then applied after this calculation to ascertain the correct location for the decimal point in the answer. The Babylonians some 5,000 years ago had such an arithmetic based on a numeration system to base 60 with only two symbols, one for 10 and the other for 1 and their repetitions. Computers have limited storage space and thus the length of fixed-point numbers which can be handled is restricted. The acceptable length can be considerably increased by writing the number $n$ in the form $n = x \times 2^y$, where $x$ is the mantissa (see *logarithm), and $y$ is the exponent. Using binary notation, the number $0.0000001101 = 0.1101 \times 2^{-7}$. This requires a 4-bit word for the mantissa and a 4-bit word for the exponent ($-111$ in binary notation), whereas the original fixed-point number representation needs an 11-bit word.

**flood**, an inundation of dry land, by a river, lake, or the sea. A river flood occurs when there is too much water to be accommodated within the channel or when the flow is enough to burst the bank, the likelihood of either event depending largely on the permeability of the *drainage basin which feeds the river. Lakes flood when they receive more water than can be disposed of by seepage and evaporation; spectacular floods occur when water in lakes dammed by glaciers finds outlets through melted ice. Sea floods are caused by high tides driven on shore by strong winds, as in the North Sea in spring; and the incidence increases if the land is sinking relative to sea-level, as at the head of the Thames estuary. They also result from tidal waves, or *tsunamis, produced by earthquakes. The term 'flood' is also used for the inflow of tides and the high flow of rivers which may or may not inundate the land. The frequency of occasions on which the flow of a river will reach a flood peak can be calculated using probability theory. The larger the peak the longer the recurrence interval, a 'ten-year flood' for example being the flow to be expected once every ten years on average.

**floodplains**, flattish areas alongside river channels which are covered by water during floods. Made of alluvium deposited in former floods or as channels shifted their course, they are particularly associated with meandering rivers. These cut their channels sideways, leaving new alluvium inside each bend. The curved ridges, or 'meander scrolls', thus formed are best seen from the air. Over the years meanders change their course, and *ox-bow lakes may form. Rivers with large loads of fine sediment, like the

Mississippi, build their channels above their floodplains and run between *levees. When such rivers flood, water flows long distances along the floodplain before re-entering the channel. As the layers of deposited alluvium build up, the land becomes increasingly fertile for farming.

**Florida Keys** (Spanish, *cayo*, shoal, barrier-reef), a chain of islands that curve in a long arc for some 240 km (150 miles) south and west of Biscayne Bay, Florida, USA. They are made of *coral reefs and shoals of oolitic limestone that have been uplifted above sea-level; so they are quite different from the offshore beaches of North Carolina and Texas with which they are sometimes confused.

**flotation** (in physics), a technical word meaning 'the state of floating'. An object in a *fluid (liquid or gas) experiences an upward force equal to the weight of the fluid it displaces (but acting in the opposite direction). This upward force is the buoyancy. If the object is in a liquid, the buoyancy increases as it sinks lower, and if it is less dense than the liquid there will come a point before it is entirely submerged when the buoyancy equals the weight and they cancel one another out. When this state of equilibrium is reached, the object floats. That a floating object displaces its own weight of fluid is called *Archimedes' principle.

**fluorescence**, the emission of light by a substance as a result of its simultaneously absorbing radiation of another wavelength. The electrons of the atoms or molecules of the substance are excited by the radiation and emit the excess energy in returning to their original state. This emission, unlike *phosphorescence, ceases as soon as the source of excitation is removed, and so the glow disappears. The light emitted is generally of a lower frequency than the radiation absorbed, which may be visible light of a different colour or ultraviolet light. The effect is used in dyes and paints. Biological matter which exhibits fluorescence can be illuminated with ultraviolet radiation, thus making microscopic examination of it easier.

**fluorine** (symbol F, at. no. 9, r.a.m. 19.00), a yellow-green gas and one of the *halogens. The most reactive non-metal, it forms compounds with all the elements except helium, argon, and neon, and reacts explosively with many substances. It occurs widely in the minerals fluorite (fluorspar) and cryolite, but can only be obtained pure by the electrolysis of a molten mixture of hydrogen fluoride, HF, and potassium fluoride, KF. The pure form is used in some rocket fuels. Its compounds are less reactive and find many applications. Sodium fluoride is added to drinking water to prevent tooth decay in children. Uranium hexafluoride is employed in gaseous diffusion plants to separate the isotopes of uranium. Organic fluorine compounds, fluorocarbons, can be polymerized; an example is polytetrafluoroethene (teflon or PTFE) used as a non-stick coating. Others containing carbon, fluorine, and other halogens have been widely used as aerosol propellants and as coolants in refrigerators (see *CFC).

**fluorite** (or fluorspar), a very common fluoride mineral (calcium fluoride, $CaF_2$) and the main source of fluorine. Its crystals are hard, fragile, and typically blue or purple in colour. In ultraviolet light it fluoresces. It is found in veins and pockets associated with igneous activity. Fluorite is used in the production of hydrofluoric acid, which is a vital raw material for the plastic and optical industries.

**fog**, a suspension of minute water droplets in the air at ground level which reduces visibility to less than 1,000 m (3,300 feet). A dense fog will reduce visibility to around 200 m (650 feet). It occurs when the temperature of the air and the *dew-point coincide. Radiation fog forms when the ground and air close to it cool rapidly at night, giving a foggy layer up to about 100 m (330 feet) in depth which is frequently cleared by the heat of the sun during the day. Advection fog forms when a warm wind blows over a cold sea, steam fog when a cold wind blows over warm water, and frontal fog when rain increases the moisture in the air. Excessive dust or smoke particles in the air will turn fog into a *smog, while dust without water droplets gives a *haze. *Mist is formed in similar ways to fog, but it is thinner.

**Föhn wind**, a dry, warm, strong, and gusty wind occurring when moist, stable air is forced to rise over a mountain range. As the air rises it cools by expansion, without utilizing energy from the surrounding air, at a constant rate called the the low saturated adiabatic *lapse rate (of 9.8 °C km⁻¹). Condensation occurs, clouds develop, and precipitation falls on the windward side of the mountain range. While descending to regain its original level in the lee of the range the air warms at the higher dry adiabatic lapse rate; it is commonly 5–10 °C (9–18 °F) warmer than the air at the same height on the windward side of the mountains. The greater the amount of precipitation on the windward side, the warmer is the descending air on the lee side. Föhn winds are characteristically associated with the Alps, but are locally known as *chinook in the Rockies, zonda in the Andes of Argentina, and as northwesters on the east side of South Island, New Zealand.

**folds, geological**, bends or flexures in layered (stratified) rocks. *Anticlines (arch-shaped) and *synclines (trough-shaped) are the most common types (see figure). Many other types of fold exist and they can be found on many different scales, ranging from a few centimetres across to many kilometres. They are normally caused by compression or uplift.

**foliation** (in geology), the layered appearance of a *metamorphic rock in which particular groups of minerals are arranged in parallel layers as a result of extreme pressure and temperature. It is typically seen in *schists. The word also describes layers of glacial material formed as a result of shearing processes during ice movement.

**forbidden gap**  *band theory.

**force**, the agent that causes a change in the momentum of a system: it is a *vector quantity. If the speed of the system is small compared with that of light, the second of *Newton's laws of motion states that the force is proportional to the mass times the acceleration or, equivalently, to the rate of change of momentum. Both these phrases are used as definitions of force. The *SI unit of force is the newton: one newton causes a one-kilogram mass to accelerate by one metre per second each second. There are four fundamental forces in nature: the *gravitational force, the *electromagnetic force, the *strong force and the *weak force.

**formaldehyde**  *methanal.

**formic acid**  *methanoic acid.

**Formosa**  *Taiwan.

**fossil**, the remains of a once-living organism, generally taken to be one that lived prior to the end of the last *ice age, that is, fossils are older than 10,000 years. The term includes skeletons, tracks, impressions, trails, borings, and casts. Fossils are usually found in consolidated rock, but not always (for example, woolly mammoths living 20,000 years ago were recovered from the frozen *tundra of Siberia). The impression of skeletal remains in surrounding sediments constites a 'mould'. Filling of a mould cavity by mineral matter may produce a 'natural cast'. Tracks, trails, burrows, and other evidence of organic activity may also be preserved. These are called trace fossils. The process whereby a fossil is formed is called fossilization. Generally the soft parts of organisms decay and it is the hard parts that undergo various degrees of change. Fossilizing processes include carbonization where chemical action reduces tissues to carbon; permineralization (petrification) where tissues such as bones and shells are made more dense by deposition of mineral matter; and recrystallization where tissues of one composition are recrystallized into more stable composition.

**fossil fuels**, a collective term for coal, oil and natural gas; natural fuels developed from the remains of living organisms. Oil and gas were formed from the slow decomposition and burying of planktonic marine plants and animals which sank to the muds of the sea floor. Coal is derived from the accumulation of partially decayed land plants. Fossil fuels are essentially finite, or non-renewable and are currently the world's primary *energy resources.

**Foucault, Jean Bernard Léon** (1819–68), French physicist chiefly remembered for the huge pendulum which he used to demonstrate the rotation of the Earth. He obtained the first accurate determination of the *speed of light by using the rotating mirror technique developed by Charles *Wheatstone in the 1830s, introduced the modern technique of silvering glass for the reflecting telescope, pioneered astronomical photography, discovered eddy currents (the Foucault currents induced in cores of electrical equipment such as generators), and improved devices such as the arc lamp and the induction coil.

**Fourier analysis**, the study of functions expressed in terms of a Fourier series. Unlike the terms of a *power series, the terms in a Fourier series are *sine and *cosine terms. Thus the terms are periodic, usually having frequencies that are simply related to a fundamental frequency—just as musical sounds contain harmonies of the fundamental note. The French mathematician Joseph Fourier (1768–1830) developed these series, and mathematical techniques for dealing with them, in his analytic theory of heat, in which he attempted to describe the changing distribution of heat as bodies of different shapes cool. Fourier analysis is widely used in many branches of physics and in electronics, control theory, and engineering.

**fractal**, a geometrical shape or pattern made up of identical parts which are in turn identical to the overall pattern. The shape of the overall pattern can be found repeated in miniature within the overall pattern itself; and within the miniature version a smaller version of the pattern can again be found. The structure of a fractal is therefore recognizably similar (but not necessarily identical) near all points in the shape and under all magnifications. It is therefore difficult to define the size of a fractal, since it exists within itself on many different scales: however, the basic repeating unit may be

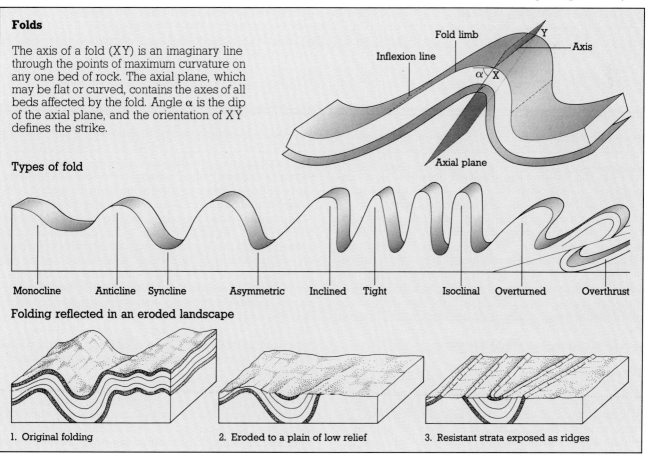

**Folds**

The axis of a fold (XY) is an imaginary line through the points of maximum curvature on any one bed of rock. The axial plane, which may be flat or curved, contains the axes of all beds affected by the fold. Angle α is the dip of the axial plane, and the orientation of XY defines the strike.

Fold limb
Inflexion line
Y
Axis
α X
Axial plane

**Types of fold**

Monocline    Anticline    Syncline    Asymmetric    Inclined    Tight    Isoclinal    Overturned    Overthrust

**Folding reflected in an eroded landscape**

1. Original folding    2. Eroded to a plain of low relief    3. Resistant strata exposed as ridges

## Fractal

### The Koch snowflake

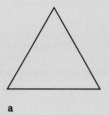
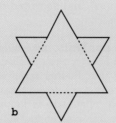

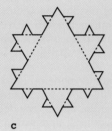
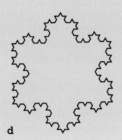

To construct the Koch snowflake,
(a) start with an equilateral triangle.
(b) Place a smaller equilateral triangle
on each side. (c) Place yet smaller
equilateral triangles on each side.
(d) Continue indefinitely.

### Julia sets

Julia sets are generated by following the behaviour
of the iteration $z \to z^2 + c$, where c is an arbitary
constant and z is a complex variable.
(In the iteration, a value is chosen for z, then $z^2 + c$
is calculated, and this becomes the new value for
z in the next iteration.) Two sorts of behaviour
are possible: either the modulus of z tends to
infinity or it remains bounded. The Julia set is
the set of z-values on the boundary between
these two behaviours. Computers are usually
used to perform the iterations and create pictures,
as here.

defined. The basic unit of the Koch snowflake, first constructed by the mathematician Helge von Koch (1870–1924),
is the equilatorial triangle which can be built up into a much
larger but still similar pattern. Any part of the snowflake is
equally crinkly, whatever scale it is viewed at. Some of the
most remarkable fractals are the Julia sets, devised by the
French mathematician Gaston Julia (1893–1978). The fractal here (see figure) has been drawn according to mathematical rules of fractal geometry. The many fractals to be found
in nature appear to be random patterns, but they can be
called fractals because their parts are identical to the whole
on a statistical level. Coastlines are an example of a fractal
pattern in nature. (See also *Mandelbrot.)

**France**, a country in western Europe, bounded on the
north by the English Channel (la Manche), on the west by
the Atlantic Ocean, on the south by the Pyrenees and the
Mediterranean, and on the east by Belgium, Germany, Luxemburg, Switzerland, and Italy. It is Europe's second largest
country after Russia covering an area of 544,000 km²
(210,039 sq. mi.). In the north-west the Brittany peninsula

with its low granite hills, Normandy with its fertile uplands,
the broad Loire valley, and the Seine Basin, all enjoy a temperate climate. The north-east can be colder; but here there
is agricultural land on chalk or limestone well drained by
rivers. There are also deposits of coal. Southward the
ground rises to the Massif Central, a region of high plateaux
and rolling country set on volcanic rock. To the west lie the
Bordeaux lowlands and the Gironde Estuary, to the south
the plains of Languedoc, and to the east the Rhône valley.
Extending from south to north along France's eastern border are the Jura Mountains, the Vosges, and the western
Alps, falling away on their northern slopes to Alsace-Lor-
raine with its resources of potash and iron ore. France also
has sizeable reserves of tungsten, bauxite, antimony, copper,
lead, and zinc.

**francium** (symbol Fr, at. no. 87, r.a.m. 223), the heaviest of
the *alkali metals. All its isotopes are radioactive, the most
stable being francium-223, with a *half-life of 21 minutes; it
is formed by bombardment of thorium with protons. Francium appears to resemble the other alkali metals chemically.

**Franklin, Sir John** (1786–1847), English naval officer and Arctic explorer who served under Matthew *Flinders as a surveyor and at the battle of Trafalgar. In 1819–21 and 1825–7 he commanded explorations of Canada's Northwest Territories by land and sea; the first of these two expeditions suffered appalling hardship. During 1836–43 he was governor of Tasmania; and then, when nearly 60, he set out to discover the *North-West Passage which had eluded everyone from John *Cabot onwards. His two ships became icebound, and all 134 officers and men perished.

**Fraser**, the chief river of British Columbia, Canada. Some 1,370 km (850 miles) long, it rises in the Selwyn Range of the Rocky Mountains, at the Yellowhead Pass. Its direct route to the sea is blocked by the Cariboo Mountains, so it skirts them by flowing first north-west and then south through forested valleys in a great, sharp-angled detour, picking up its major tributaries on the way. In its lower reaches the river has cut a dramatic canyon up which Pacific salmon pass to spawn. For the last 160 km (100 miles) of its course to the Strait of Georgia it is navigable, and the sediment of its delta provides many thousands of acres of fertile soil.

**free oscillation**, the frequency of periodic motion at which any body, for example, the Earth, tends to vibrate or resonate most freely. There are two fundamental types: torsional (vibration with motions perpendicular to the Earth's radius); and spheroidal (vibrations that are both radial and tangential to the Earth's surface). The study of such resonances, for example, those induced by major earthquakes have been so large that sensitive detectors have continued to record the oscillations for weeks after the event (see *seismology). The decay of the vibrations gives valuable information about the elastic layering of the Earth.

**free radicals** (in chemistry), atoms or molecules with one or more unpaired electrons available to form a bond. The term includes mainly short-lived species in complex chemical reactions, particularly those initiated by light, namely *photochemical reactions. A few free radicals, such as nitrogen oxide (NO) and nitrogen dioxide ($NO_2$) are stable. For instance, in the *ozone layer, *ultraviolet radiation from the Sun splits a chlorine atom from a *chloro-fluorocarbon molecule. This attacks ozone making oxygen molecules, but leaving the chlorine atom free to attack ozone again.

**freezing-point**, the temperature at which solid and liquid forms of a substance can exist together in equilibrium. It is also known as the *melting-point. The value of the freezing point depends on outside pressure. For water, it is 0 °C (32 °F) at a pressure of 101 kilopascals (1 atmosphere), and falls by about 0.01 °C for each atmosphere increase in pressure. Water is unusual in this respect; most substances contract on solidifying, and a pressure increase raises their freezing-point.

**Frege, Gottlob** (1848–1925), German philosopher and mathematician, founder of modern logic. His aim was to introduce rigour into mathematical proofs and establish the certainty of mathematical truth, and he developed a logical system for the expression of mathematics which was a vast improvement on the syllogistic logic which it replaced; he also worked on general questions of philosophical logic and semantics. His theory of meaning, based on his use of a distinction between what a linguistic term refers to and what it expresses, is still influential. Frege attempted to provide a

rigorous foundation for mathematics on the basis of purely logical principles, but decided to abandon the attempt when Bertrand Russell (1872–1970) pointed out that his system was inconsistent.

**frequency** (physics), the number of cycles occurring within an oscillating system or wave motion in a unit of time. The frequency of a wave motion is in inverse proportion to the *wavelength. Frequency is measured in hertz (symbol Hz), where 1 Hz is equivalent to one cycle per second: a string vibrating 440 times a second has a frequency of 440 Hz.

**Fresnel, Augustin Jean** (1788–1827), French physicist and civil engineer. He took up the study of polarized light in 1814 and postulated that light moved in a wave-like motion, which had already been suggested by, among others, Christiaan *Huygens and Thomas *Young. They, however, assumed the waves to be longitudinal, while by 1821 Fresnel was sure that they vibrated transversely to the direction of propagation, and he used this to explain successfully the phenomenon of double refraction. He invented a large lens, made up of a series of concentric rings, for lighthouses and searchlights.

**friction**, the force which acts to resist the relative motion of two bodies when they are rubbed together or when one moves over the other. Even if the surfaces are highly polished some friction arises because the atoms on one surface are attracted to those on the other and work has to be done to move one past the other. If the surfaces are rough the friction is greater because the ridges in the surfaces get caught up with one another. The harder the surfaces are forced together the greater is the friction; and the work that is done in overcoming it is converted into heat energy at the interface. Frictional forces also operate in liquids and gases, and give rise to *viscosity.

**Friendly Islands**    *Tonga.

**Frisian Islands**, a chain of low, sandy islands including Helgoland, extending for some 420 km (260 miles) along the coasts of the Netherlands, Germany, and Denmark. Between 7000 and 5000 BC they were the continuous dune-covered shoreline of the south-east sector of the North Sea. Since that time they have been broken up by periodic storms, forming the *Zuider Zee, and have experienced subsidence and flooding. Consequently much coastal defence and reclamation work has been carried out. The West Frisian Islands belong to the Netherlands; the East Frisian Islands belong to Germany; the North Frisian Islands are divided between Germany and Denmark.

**Frobisher, Sir Martin** (c.1535–94), English navigator and explorer, inspired by Sir Humphrey Gilbert's vision of a North-West Passage, who commanded three expeditions (1576–8) to the North American coast, discovering what became known as Frobisher Bay and landing in Labrador. He discovered the Hudson Strait, which he named Mistaken Strait, together with mica and iron pyrites ('fool's gold')—a poor substitute for the gold he and his backers sought. Abandoning the search after the 1570s, he joined Francis *Drake's expedition to the West Indies and in 1588 distinguished himself in the action against the Spanish Armada. In 1594 he was mortally wounded in an assault on a Spanish fort near Brest, but took his squadron safely back to Plymouth before he died.

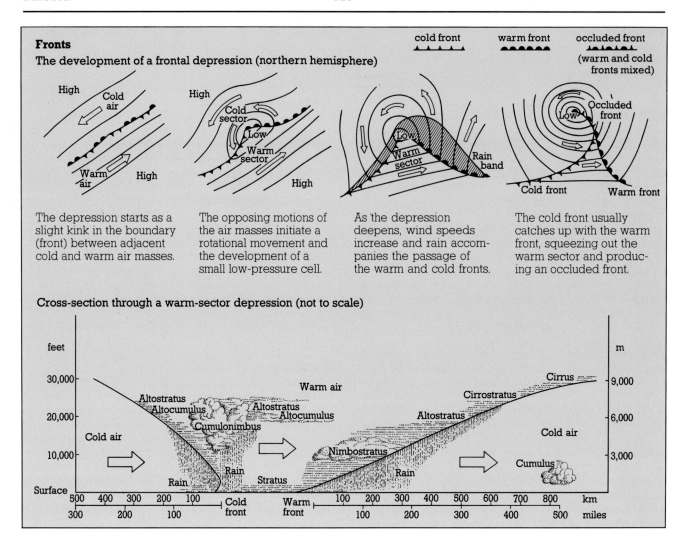

**Fronts**

The development of a frontal depression (northern hemisphere)

cold front    warm front    occluded front
(warm and cold fronts mixed)

The depression starts as a slight kink in the boundary (front) between adjacent cold and warm air masses.

The opposing motions of the air masses initiate a rotational movement and the development of a small low-pressure cell.

As the depression deepens, wind speeds increase and rain accompanies the passage of the warm and cold fronts.

The cold front usually catches up with the warm front, squeezing out the warm sector and producing an occluded front.

Cross-section through a warm-sector depression (not to scale)

The delicate ice crystals on this grass were deposited from a gently moving current of air in freezing fog conditions. The build-up of **frost** is on the upwind side of the grass stems.

**front**. In meteorology, an inclined boundary between *air masses of different temperatures. The boundary is really a frontal zone, 1 to 2 km (0.6 to 1.2 miles) thick, in which the two types of air are mixed as a result of turbulence. Such a zone may be 100 to 200 km (60 to 120 miles) long at the Earth's surface, which it intersects at an angle of only 3 to 7°. At a front the warmer air rises over the denser, colder air. A front is called 'warm' when warmer air is replacing colder at the surface, and 'cold' when the reverse happens. Cold fronts usually travel faster than warm ones and, when they catch them up, the warmer air is lifted above the Earth's surface. The front is now called 'occluded', with cold air both ahead of and behind it. A warm front has layers of cloud up to 800 km (500 miles) wide and 10 km (6 miles) deep associated with it, the cloud thickening towards the surface and often giving a period of continuous precipitation. A cold front has a steeper gradient than a warm one, with a narrower belt of clouds often including cumulonimbus, which give heavier and more intense precipitation.

In the ocean, a front is an inclined boundary or boundary region between two different *water masses, which may have contrasting temperatures, salinities and (commonly) nutrient concentrations. Oceanic fronts are regions where conditions are strongly *baroclinic and may be associated with strong surface currents such as the Gulf Stream or the Antarctic Circumpolar Current. They are also regions of *convergence of surface water in which a denser water mass sinks beneath a lighter water mass.

**frost**, frozen dew which occurs when the temperature falls to 0 °C (32 °F) or below. When the water vapour in the atmosphere freezes, which is due usually to radiational cooling of the ground or to the arrival of a cold *air mass, the result is an air frost. Hoar-frost, the fluffy deposit of minute ice crystals on grass and brickwork, occurs on calm, clear nights when condensation takes place after freezing. A ground frost is recorded when the temperature of the tips of short blades of grass is below 0 °C. When rain falls and spreads over frozen ground it produces a film of ice called glazed frost, or glaze, which is harder and more transparent than hoar-frost.

**Fujiyama** (Japanese, Fuji-san), a dormant volcano, at 3,776 m (12,388 feet), the highest peak in Japan. Situated in south central Honshu, it stands alone, its summit crowned almost throughout the year with snow. In the flattened top is a great crater whose floor is covered with cinders and jagged lava; the last eruption was in 1707. Mount Fujiyama is considered sacred in Japan; its name is of Ainu origin and means 'everlasting life'.

**fuller's earth**    *montmorillonite.

**fumarole**, a volcanic vent from which steam and other hot gases emerge. Fumaroles are characteristic of a late stage of volcanic activity when violent eruptions have ceased. The Valley of Ten Thousand Smokes in Alaska is well known for its fumaroles.

**functional groups** (in chemistry), atoms or groups of atoms in an organic molecule which cause it to react in a particular way. All the members of a *homologous series possess the same functional group, and differ only in the number of atoms in the carbon chain. For example, the carboxylic acids all have the general formula RCOOH, where R is either hydrogen or an *alkyl or an *aryl group, and the functional group is the carboxyl group, $-COOH$. The chemical properties of an organic compound are largely determined by the functional group, or groups, that it contains. Thus the reactions of all the carboxylic acids are very similar, the relatively small differences resulting from differences in the size and shape of the R group. Where a molecule contains more than one functional group, its chemical properties are generally the sum of the separate properties associated with each group. However, when the two groups are very close, they modify each other. For example, the carboxyl group can be viewed as a *hydroxyl group bonded to a *carbonyl group, but the properties of the carboxyl group are different from those of the two constituent groups.

**functions** (or mappings), a central concept in contemporary mathematics. Gottfried *Leibniz in 1694 first used the word for line segments whose lengths depended on lines related to curves. Today it has a meaning that is precisely defined but difficult to articulate. Three conditions must be fulfilled. A function f exists if (i) it acts on the elements of some set D, called the domain, (ii) it produces elements in some set T, not necessarily a different one, called the range, and (iii) it has a rule which assigns a unique element in the range to every element in the domain. Written symbolically this is $f: D \rightarrow T$; if variable $x$ is an element of D and variable $y$ the corresponding element of T, then we write $y = f(x)$. The following are all examples of functions: 'sine of' with domain the real numbers and range the reals between and

Steam and other gases pouring from **fumaroles** at Noboribetsu on the southern coast of Hokkaido Island, Japan.

including $-1$ and $+1$; 'log of' with domain the positive real numbers and range all the reals; 'square of' with domain the imaginary numbers and range the negative real numbers; and 'integer part of' with domain the real numbers and range the integers (for example the integer part of both $3\frac{1}{2}$ and $3\frac{3}{4}$ is 3). As can be seen in the last example, functions can map more than one element to a single element of the range. Such functions produce a many-to-one correspondence as opposed to the one-to-one correspondence of the log function. One-to-one correspondence allows the inverse of a function to be defined as that function g for which $g[f(x)] = x$, g being sometimes written as $f^{-1}$. The exponential function is the inverse of the logarithmic function. The many properties of functions are studied in the field of mathematical analysis.

**Fundy, Bay of**, an arm of the North Atlantic Ocean that separates Nova Scotia from New Brunswick, Canada. It is about 240 km (150 miles) long and about 80 km (50 miles) wide, and occupies the central portion of a downfolded trough. It is best known as the site of the highest tidal range in the world, owing to its funnel-like shape, which accentuates the high tidal ranges of this part of the Atlantic. The high tide at Minas Bay, an inlet, may be up to 16 m (50 feet) over a period of six hours. A further consequence is *tidal bore, which may be 1.2 m (4 feet) high.

**fusion**    *nuclear fusion.

# G

**gabbro**, a coarse-grained igneous rock composed of light-grey or greenish minerals: pyroxene, plagioclase feldspar, and occasionally olivine. There are many varieties, but gabbro is the coarse-grained or *plutonic equivalent of *basalt, so all gabbros have crystallized at depth and are basic rocks (low in silica). The rock is too fragile for use as a construction material, but it often contains valuable quantities of chromium, nickel, cobalt, platinum, and copper.

**Gabon**, an equatorial country on Africa's Atlantic coast, bounded inland by Equatorial Guinea, Cameroon, and Congo. Along the coast are lagoons, mangrove swamps, and large deposits of oil and natural gas. A broad plain covered by thick rain forest rises gradually to a plateau which surrounds a central river valley, and near the head this vegetation gives way to *savannah. Here uranium is found, and manganese. The country is also rich in a soft timber, *okoumé*, used for making plywood.

**Gaia hypothesis**, the proposition that surface conditions on planet Earth have been maintained so as to provide an

**Galena**, one of the principal ores of lead. This group of crystals, approximately 10 cm (4 inches) across, shows several of the physical shapes characteristic of the cubic crystal system.

environment suitable for life as a result of the interaction of processes occurring in the ocean, atmosphere and solid earth, including biological processes themselves. In essence, that the Earth as a whole is a complex system which may be regarded as a self-sustaining organism. The proposition was presented by the British scientist James Lovelock (1919–   ) in his book *Gaia: A New Look at Life on Earth* (1979).

**Gairdner, Lake**, the largest of a cluster of salt lakes to the north of the Eyre Peninsula in South Australia. It is 155 km (96 miles) long and 48 km (30 miles) wide when full; but it is very shallow and becomes partly dry in summer.

**Galápagos Islands**, a group of thirteen large islands and many small ones spread across the Equator in the Pacific Ocean, about 1,000 km (600 miles) west of Ecuador. They consist mainly of volcanoes that have developed on an east–west-trending fracture zone and which rise up to 3,000 m (10,000 feet) from the sea floor. They then stand a further 1,800 m (6,000 feet) above sea-level. The resulting scenery is striking: large summit craters, fresh lava flows, and impressive sea cliffs diversify a generally rugged topography. There is a rich wildlife with many endemic species including birds (some flightless), iguanas, and giant tortoises.

**gale**, a wind blowing at speed of 34–47 knots (63–87 km/h, 39–54 m.p.h.) on the *Beaufort scale, anything faster being a storm or a hurricane. Gales arise in *depressions and are usually accompanied by rain. At sea, waves reach 7 m (23 feet) in height during a strong gale; there are white streaks of foam, and the crests topple and roll over.

**galena** (lead sulphide, PbS), an ore mineral and an important source of lead. The crystals are shiny lead-grey cubes which blacken with time. It is very dense but rather soft. Deposits are widespread, the most extensive being in Missouri, Oklahoma, and Kansas (USA).

**Galilee, Sea of** (Lake Tiberias), a slightly saline lake lying in northern Israel near the head of the Great Rift Valley. Its surface is nearly 210 m (700 feet) below sea-level and its salinity is caused by hot mineral springs whose waters enter the lake. The River Jordan flows through it from north to south and is the main source of water; from biblical times it has been used for fishing. The lake is 21 km (13 miles) long and up to 11 km (7 miles) wide.

**Galileo Galilei** (1564–1642), Italian astronomer and physicist and the founder of dynamics, the science of moving bodies. He was the first person to make extensive use of experiments to investigate natural phenomena. He studied medicine and then mathematics at the University of Pisa and became well known in 1586 when he published details of his new invention, the hydrostatic balance. He then disproved Aristotle's idea that objects with different weights fall at different speeds (though not, as legend has it, by dropping objects off the Leaning Tower of Pisa). He worked on the problems of motion, and determined that a moving object will continue to move with a constant speed and in a straight line unless acted on by an outside agent (see *conservation laws). In 1592 he became Professor of Mathematics at the University of Padua, and did most of his important work there. In 1604 he proved theoretically that falling bodies accelerate uniformly with time, and formulated the law which describes parabolic motion. In 1609 he went to Venice and heard about a new invention—the telescope. He

Minerals of the **garnet** family show a wide range of form and colour and many are used as semiprecious stones. The uncut specimen at the top of the picture is almandine garnet from Alaska, still embedded in the mica schist in which it was formed.

made himself a telescope, and became the first person to use one for astronomical work. He discovered that the surface of the Moon is not smooth, and that the Milky Way is a collection of stars. He also found the moons which orbit Jupiter, which led him to question the then firmly held belief that the Earth was fixed at the centre of the Universe, and that all the motion of the heavens was around the Earth. Further astronomical work led Galileo to propose that the Sun was the fixed body at the centre of motion, and that the Earth orbited the Sun along with all the other planets. He presented his case in a book which was written as an argument between a supporter and an opponent of his views: the *Dialogue concerning the Two Chief World Systems* (1638). Galileo's work was considered heretical by the Church of Rome, and he was tried by the Inquisition and forced to spend the last years of his life under house arrest.

**gallium** (symbol Ga, at. no. 31, r.a.m. 69.74), a metallic element in Group III of the *periodic table. It is rather unreactive, but forms ionic compounds in which it shows a valency of 3. Its most important compound is gallium arsenide, GaAs, which is widely used as a *semiconductor.

**Galois, Évariste** (1811–32), French mathematician who founded an entire branch of mathematics known now as Galois theory. This gave conditions for the solvability of *polynomial equations, but was abstract, highly innovative,

and unappreciated by his contemporaries. It introduced the notion of a group to mathematics (see *group theory). His bids for recognition and access to higher education were dogged by lost and rejected manuscripts. A strong republican, after several spells in prison he died aged only 20, as the result of a duel.

**Gambia**, a country on the West African coast, it runs west to east along the lower 320 km (nearly 200 miles) of the River Gambia, entirely surrounded inland by Senegal. Its territory on either bank is no more than about 24 km (15 miles) in width. The river is broad and navigable, though its banks are marshy; and its valley is fertile, groundnuts being grown in the upper region. Climatically the country is warm and arid between November and April, when the *harmattan blows from the interior. Summers are hot and very wet.

**game theory**, a branch of mathematics concerned with the analysis of conflict in war, economics, games of skill, etc. It represents conflicts as mathematical problems (often modelled on real games like chess and bridge), so as to decide optimal strategies. An early difficulty in the theory was how to quantify desirable results. At first personal gain was used as an index of desirability. Later, moral factors were acknowledged to affect judgements of desirability. The theory was first developed by John von *Neumann in 1928. In 1944, with Oskar Morgenstern, he applied it to economics.

**gamma rays**, one of the products emitted from the decaying nuclei of radioactive atoms. They are very short electromagnetic waves, with wavelengths of less than $10^{-11}$ m, and therefore carry a lot of energy. This enables them to pass a long way through matter before being absorbed.

**Ganges** (Hindi, Ganga), a great river of north India, flowing over 2,500 km (1,550 miles) from the southern Himalayas to the Bay of Bengal. Issuing from an ice cave, it first tumbles south-west through the mountains in a series of rapids interspersed with long, deep pools. It then swings south-eastward to enter its floodplain, where it is eventually joined by its main tributary, the Yamuna (or Jumna). Now flowing broadly, and swollen by other tributaries, it spreads its silt in summer monsoon floods, fertilizing large areas of the plain. It becomes navigable and, still 350 km (220 miles) inland, turns south to split into a number of sluggish rivers, the chief being the Hooghly. The delta (the world's largest) is joined in the east by the great Brahmaputra, forming the Padma River, and together they pass through the Sundarbans, a series of marshy islands, before reaching the sea.

**gangue**, the term applied to the valueless minerals or earthy matter associated with the valuable minerals in *ores. Many ores are of very low *grade, less than 1 per cent, which means that over 99 per cent of the rock consists of gangue material. This poses a major problem of disposal when the ore is mined.

**Garda, Lago di**, the largest of the Italian Lakes (370 km² or 143 sq. mi.) bodering Lombardy to the west and south-west, Veneto to the east and south-east, and Trentino-Alto Adige to the north. In the Alpine regions it is surpassed in area only by Lakes Geneva and Constance, and lies at an altitude of 65 m (213 feet).

**Garibaldi Provincial Park**, a region of scenic beauty in south-west British Columbia, Canada, lying in the Coast Mountains 64 km (40 miles) north of Vancouver. It has high peaks, such as Wedge Mountain at 2,891 m (9,484 feet), glaciers, mountain lakes, and broad meadows.

**garnet**, any one of a group of silicate minerals (orthosilicates) occurring principally in metamorphic rocks, although found also in sediments as rounded grains. The deep red varieties are known as Bohemian garnets, Cape rubies, or Arizona rubies, according to their place of origin. Purplish red ones are called carbuncles and come from Brazil or Sri Lanka, as do the golden or cinnamon hessonites. Bright green ones are demantoids, from the Urals.

**gas**, one of the three *states of matter commonly encountered, the other two being solid or liquid. Like liquids gases have no fixed shape, but in addition they have no fixed volume either: they fill whatever space they are in. Gases represent the high-temperature form of substances, when the atoms or molecules have sufficient thermal energy to break away from their neighbours and move around freely. Most gases can be turned into liquids and then solids by cooling them sufficiently; similarly many solids and liquids can be turned into gases by heating, though in some cases they decompose or burn before the temperature gets high enough. Gases can also be liquefied by pressure alone, but their temperature must be less than the *critical point for this to be possible. The gaseous form of substances which are solid or liquid at room temperature is often called a vapour at temperatures up to the critical point, and a gas only at higher temperatures. In thermodynamics the concept of an *ideal gas is used to describe the behaviour of gases. The gas laws describe the behaviour of gases under different conditions of temperature and pressure. *Charles' law provides a description of the expansion of gases when they are heated: it states that the volume of a fixed mass of gas is directly proportional to its temperature (in *kelvin) if the pressure is constant. *Boyle's law describes the behaviour of gases under pressure: it states that the volume of a fixed mass of gas is inversely proportional to its pressure if the temperature is constant. The pressure law, which describes the relationship between pressure and temperature, says that the pressure of a fixed mass of gas is directly proportional to its temperature (in kelvin) if the volume is constant.

**gas, natural**, a mixture of gaseous hydrocarbons, chiefly *methane ($CH_4$). It is often found in sedimentary rocks in association with oil, and commonly forms a 'gas cap' in an oil field, on account of its lower density. This gas, like the oil, was formed originally from organic matter (the remains of *planktonic marine plants) in *sedimentary rocks and has migrated upwards to accumulate in rocks that can act as a reservoir. It can be recovered either under natural pressure or in a condensed form as a liquid. Large amounts of natural gas, again mainly methane, are also found in association with *coal, formed from the breakdown of terrestrial plant material in sedimentary rocks, and migrated upwards to accumulate in reservoir rocks. This type of natural gas is normally too 'light' to be recovered in liquefied form. Vast fields of natural gas have been found, particularly in the northern hemisphere, many of them under the sea. Smaller quantities of natural gas occur at the Earth's surface in isolated pockets and are termed marsh gas. They are not normally commercially viable resources.

**gas constant**, the equivalent for an *ideal gas, of $pV/T$, where $p$ is pressure, $V$ is volume, and $T$ is absolute temperature. It is constant for all gases if equal numbers of gas molecules are considered for each gas. If the amount of gas studied is one *mole ($6.022 \times 10^{23}$ molecules) then the gas constant is referred to as the universal gas constant (symbol $R$) and has the value of 8.314 joule per kelvin. It is used in the equations of state used to describe the behaviour of gases.

**Gauss, Karl Friedrich** (1777–1855), German mathematician, astronomer, and physicist. He laid the foundations of number theory, producing the first major book on this subject in 1801. In the same year he rediscovered the lost asteroid Ceres using computational techniques too advanced for most astronomers. He contributed to many areas of mathematics (his name is attached to a number of important results), and refused to distinguish between pure and applied mathematics, applying his rigorous mathematical analysis to such subjects as geometry, geodesy, electrostatics, and electromagnetism. He was involved in the first world-wide survey of the earth's magnetic field. Two of Gauss's most interesting discoveries, which he did not pursue, were non-Euclidean geometry and quaternions (a kind of complex number later developed by the mathematician W. R. Hamilton, 1805–65).

**Gay-Lussac, Joseph Louis** (1778–1850), French physicist and chemist who was one of the first airborne researchers, making atmospheric and magnetic measurements from a balloon above Paris in 1804. He is chiefly remembered, however, for his work on the behaviour of gases. In 1802 he re-established a law of gas expansion, first suggested by Jacques *Charles. Six years later, he published a law which now bears his name, stating that gases which combine chemically do so in volumes which are in a simple ratio to each other (see *gas).

**Geikie, Sir Archibald** (1835–1924), British geologist of Scottish extraction who pioneered the study of Britain's volcanic past, publishing seminal works in 1888 and 1897. He was also famous for his insistence that *erosion by glaciers and rivers has been the main influence on the Scottish landscape as it appears today.

**gemstones**, the general name given to precious or semiprecious stones or crystals of flawless quality that are cut and polished to accentuate either their colour, clarity, or lustre. Diamonds, sapphires, emeralds, and rubies are typical gemstones.

**geochemistry**, the study of the chemistry of the *Earth. It is concerned with the distribution of elements and their *isotopes in the Earth, in the mantle and core as well as the crust, and including those elements (trace elements) that are present only in very low concentrations. It is also concerned with the relationships between these elements; with the chemical processes that take place on and in the Earth; and with the evolution of the Earth and the solar system. The commercial applications of geochemistry are mainly in geochemical prospecting, in which the chemical analysis of soils and stream sediments is one of the chief methods used to detect the presence of ore bodies.

**geochronology**, the science of dating rocks or geological events in absolute terms, that is, in numbers of years. The time-spans of *geological time are extremely large by ordinary standards, and geochronological measurements are expressed in correspondingly large units: millions or billions of years for most of geological time, although tens of thousands of years are convenient for the *Pleistocene Epoch. The chief method used is *radiometric dating. Other methods are used for the *Quaternary, such as dendrochronology or tree-ring dating, in which the rings formed annually by trees are counted. Varve-counting, which uses the annual layers deposited in glacial lakes, can similarly be used for parts of north-west Europe and the USA for the past 10,000 years.

**geodesy**, the scientific study of the *geoid, or shape of the Earth's equipotential or level surface, as defined by mean sea-level and its presumed continuation under the land. The first geodetic observations are generally attributed to *Eratosthenes, who, supposing that the Earth is spherical, made a calculation of its circumference. The *oblateness of the Earth was postulated by Isaac *Newton; and increasingly accurate measurements of long arcs and astronomical positions were later made to determine the degree of oblateness. By 1970 one long arc had been measured near longitude 30° E., from Archangel to Capetown, and another across Africa on latitude 12° N., in order to provide a scale for the Earth: its shape could be obtained from accurate measurements of the orbits of artificial satellites. Slight irregularities in these orbits can be used to calculate how the actual shape differs from a geometrically perfect ellipsoid of revolution. Geodetic surveys have to be of very great accuracy and extent to contribute to this study of the figure of the Earth, while less accurate surveys are used to determine the *topography of the actual physical surface. The areas studied are vast, so not only gravitational force but the Earth's curvature has always to be taken into account. Related matters, such as the effect of the *rotation of the Earth, are also observed. Geodesy today is mainly concerned with the improvement and correction of past measurements.

**geoid**, a surface of gravitational equipotential (that is, of equal gravitational *potential energy) around the Earth; of necessity the *acceleration due to gravity acts at right angles to such a surface. The 'marine geoid' is that equipotential surface that corresponds to what mean sea-level would be in the absence of winds and currents. The geoid has large-scale undulations of up to about 200 m, as a result of variations in the thickness of the Earth's crust and density variations in the crust and upper mantle. Smaller scale anomalies in the geoid over the oceans result from bathymetric features such as seamounts and trenches. Because the geoid is a surface of equal potential energy, movement from a geoid 'low' to a geoid 'high' does not involve a change in potential energy and so does not involve 'going uphill' in the usual sense. The study of the geoid is known as geodesy. The shape of the marine geoid has been determined using satellite altimetry, in which a satellite in a known orbit measures its own height above the sea surface.

**geological timescale**, a scale that subdivides all time since the Earth first appeared into named units of abstract time. The current estimate of the age of the Earth is 4,600 million years. As would be expected, we have no direct evidence of the earlier periods of the Earth's history; the earliest known rocks are estimated to be about 3,800 million years old, and they are found only in a few places. The evidence becomes more abundant about 1,000 million years later: in the continental shields rocks up to 2,800 million years old are not uncommon. The two great divisions of geological time are the *Precambrian and the *Phanerozoic; the dividing-line between them is dated at about 570 million years ago. The Precambrian thus represents the great bulk of geological time, though our knowledge of the Phanerozoic is much more detailed. The Phanerozoic is divided into three eras: the *Palaeozoic, the *Mesozoic, and the *Cainozoic, each of which is in turn divided into a number of geological periods: the Palaeozoic into the Cambrian, Ordovician, Silurian, Devonian, Carboniferous, and Permian Periods; the Mesozoic into the Triassic, Jurassic, and Cretaceous Periods; the Cainozoic into the Tertiary and Quaternary Periods. The geological periods are further divided into epochs, ages, and chrons. The divisions of geological time were established by studying *sedimentary rocks and the fossils they contain, which make it possible to correlate rocks in different places. This development, the study of stratigraphy, rests on the discovery by William *Smith early in the nineteenth century that stratified rocks occur in a constant sequence and that certain fossils are found only in particular strata. Using these principles, it was possible to build up a picture of the succession of strata for the whole of the Phanerozoic. To avoid confusion, a separate terminology is used for the rocks. Thus a system corresponds to a geological period: the rocks of the Cambrian System, for example, are those deposited during the Cambrian Period. A series similarly corresponds to an epoch; a stage to an age; and a chronozone to a chron. The rocks of the ocean floors are nowhere more than about 200 million years old, and it is only on the continents that the earlier history of the Earth can be traced.

**geology**, the study of the Earth, its composition, structure, processes, and history. As such it deals with the rocks and minerals of the Earth's crust, the fossilized remains of plants and animals, and the history of the Earth since its formation some 4,600 million years ago. This definition is based on the work of Charles *Lyell in 1830 and has changed little except

**Geological timescale**

| Aeon | Era | Period | | Epoch | Time before prese (10⁶ years) |
|---|---|---|---|---|---|
| Phanerozoic | Cainozoic (Cenozoic) | Quaternary | | Holocene | |
| | | | | Pleistocene | 0·01 |
| | | Tertiary | Neogene | Pliocene | 1·6 |
| | | | | Miocene | 5·3 |
| | | | Palaeogene | Oligocene | 23·7 |
| | | | | Eocene | 36·6 |
| | | | | Palaeocene | 57·8 |
| | Mesozoic | Cretaceous | | | 66·4 |
| | | Jurassic | | | 144 |
| | | Triassic | | | 208 |
| | Palaeozoic | Permian | | | 245 |
| | | Upper | Carboniferous | Pennsylvanian | 286 |
| | | | | Mississippian | 320 |
| | | Devonian | | | 360 |
| | | Silurian | | | 408 |
| | | Lower | Ordovician | | 438 |
| | | Cambrian | | | 505 |
| Proterozoic | Pre-Cambrian | | | | 570 |
| Archaean | | | | | 2,500 |
| | | | | | 4,600 |

| Some features of continental movement | Mountain building | Positions of the continents at various periods |
|---|---|---|

**Some features of continental movement**

The Mid-Atlantic ridge is still spreading at up to 2 cm (0.8 inches) per year.

The Atlantic basin continues to move outwards from its central ridge, causing the Americas to drift westwards. The Red Sea starts to open.

Africa pushes northwards against N. Europe to produce the later folding of the Alps.

Most of N. Europe and Britain continue to move northwards.

The N. Atlantic continues to widen. The folding and uplift of the Himalayas begin as India, moving northwards, starts to push against Asia.

Greenland and Europe begin to separate as the Arctic/N. Atlantic Ocean opens up.

The continents continue to move apart at rates between 1 and 10 cm (0.4 and 3.9 inches) per year. By the end of the period Africa and S. America have separated, and Australia has broken away from Antarctica.

Much of Europe, including Britain, continues to move northwards. With the appearance of the main N. Atlantic basin, Pangaea begins to break up. North America separates from Africa, while Africa, S. America and India separate from Antarctica.

Asia joins with Euramerica to form Laurasia. Pangaea is formed from Laurasia to the north and Gondwanaland lying around the southern polar region.

Africa moves against the joined continent of Europe and N. America (Euramerica) to produce the Hercynian orogeny. Britain crosses the Equator in mid-Carboniferous times and remains in the northern arid zone until the end of the Triassic Period.

A continent consisting of N. America, Greenland and N.W. Scotland becomes joined to Europe. British Isles lies south of the Equator.

A continent, including parts of Europe, moves against the mass of N. America and Greenland, continuing the Caledonian orogeny.

The Caledonian orogeny begins. The drift of the Canadian, European and Siberian shields widens the seas between them. North America, N. Greenland, Britain and Central Europe lie near the Equator, while Africa and S. America are near the S. Pole.

Most of the continents lie south of the Equator at the start of the period. Later, the area including British Isles and N. Europe moves slowly northwards.

The Earth is formed about 4,600 million years ago. The oldest known crustal rocks, from Greenland, date from 3,800 million years ago; between this date and the end of the Archaean eon, the Earth's continental crust is formed. Continental movements probably begin about 700 million years before the present.

**Mountain building**

Western Cordillera of America

Alps

Himalayas

Andes
Rocky Mountains

Caucasus

Urals

Appalachians

Scottish Highlands
Northern Appalachians
Mountains of Scandinavia and eastern Greenland

**Positions of the continents at various periods**

Present

Palaeocene Epoch

Early Cretaceous

Early Jurassic

Laurasia

Tethys

Gondwanaland

Pangaea

Tethys

Triassic

that we now include the study of other planets in geology. Like the other major sciences, geology has a number of branches. The chief of these are: mineralogy (the study of minerals), petrology (the study of rocks), geochemistry (the chemistry of the Earth), geophysics (the physics of the Earth), stratigraphy (the study of the sequences and ages of sedimentary rocks), palaeontology (the study of fossils), structural geology (the study of the deformation and configuration of rocks), and geomorphology (the study of landforms). The practical applications of geology draw upon all these branches of the subject. Exploration for oil and minerals is perhaps the most apparent contribution that geology has made to technology. The search for minerals and ores had been carried out for many centuries before the development of geology as a science, but it has been greatly aided by geological knowledge.

**geomagnetic dating**, a method of determining the age of a core obtained from the sea floor. (Cores of this type are obtained in large numbers by survey ships using special equipment.) The Earth's magnetic field has reversed (that is, its north and south poles have changed places) at intervals of about 200,000 to 300,000 years. Rocks deposited during periods of reversed magnetic polarity are correspondingly magnetized in the reverse direction. By making *radiometric dating determinations on sequences of lava flows having known palaeomagnetic directions, it has been possible to work out a detailed sequence of polarity changes for the past 4.5 million years. This is called the magnetic polarity sequence. If magnetic polarity measurements are made on a core sample, the sequence of reversals of magnetization can be matched with the sequence obtained from the rocks on land, and the core can thus be dated. Measurements of this kind have been used to estimate rates of sedimentation in the oceans, and for other purposes.

**geomagnetism**, the branch of *geophysics that is concerned with the Earth's magnetic field and the location of its magnetic North and South Poles. Although the magnetism of the Earth has been present throughout much of geological time, the positions of the poles have varied quite considerably. This polar wandering can be calculated from the magnetic indicators present in ancient rocks; indeed, it is known that the magnetic poles have exchanged their positions—or reversed—on many occasions in the past. There are local variations in the strength of the Earth's magnetic field because of variations in the nature and structure of the rocks. Such magnetic anomalies are used in exploring and prospecting for mineral and oil reserves. There are also variations over time that are caused by the interference of *plasma in the solar wind, emitted from the Sun.

**geometric series** (or progression), a succession of numbers each of which is a constant multiple of the previous one—for example, 2, 4, 8, 16, 32, . . ., where 2 is the constant, or common ratio. A common ratio greater than 1 produces an increasing series, while for a ratio less than 1 the terms decrease.

**geometry**, a branch of mathematics traditionally concerned with the properties of points, lines, solids, and surfaces, and with the way they relate to each other. Thus geometry is concerned with the notions of length, angle, parallelism and perpendicularity, similarity and congruence, area and volume, ratio and proportion, but without the idea of measurement. Traditional geometry is called Euclidean

geometry after Euclid, whose book the *Elements* (c.300 BC) both detailed the extensive results obtained by Greek mathematicians and used the language of geometry for their proof. The *Elements* begins with definitions of terms, followed by five postulates and five assumptions. The subsequent propositions, theorems and proofs are supposed to employ no other factual information than is contained in these preliminary *axioms. Geometry was thus an overtly axiomatic branch of mathematics, and other branches have taken it as a model—even though the *Elements* falls short of its own rigorous programme. Euclid's axioms were based on an idealized view of the real world (lines are assumed to have no thickness, points are assumed to have no area). More recent geometries have axioms that are not necessarily based on ordinary experience. Thus in the 19th century, rejection of one of Euclid's axioms, the *parallel postulate, led to the development of non-Euclidean geometries such as those of Nikolai *Lobachevsky and Bernhard *Riemann in which, for instance, parallel lines may intersect. These geometries have found application in relativity theory. Transformation geometry, which considers the effects on shapes of transformations such as reflection and rotation, has now largely replaced Euclidean geometry in schools. Turtle geometry, which can be explored using the computer language LOGO, and finite geometry, are two recent developments in this field.

**geomorphology**, the science that interprets and studies the *landforms of the Earth's surface and, increasingly, those of other planets, notably Mars. It is sometimes regarded as a branch of physical geology (particularly in the USA) and sometimes as a part of physical geography (particularly in Britain, Canada, and Australia). On the whole, the subject is concerned with the processes which take place at or near the Earth's surface, questions relating to deep-seated tectonic forces or to the formation of rocks being regarded rather as part of geophysics or geology, respectively. The subject-matter is the shape of landforms, the processes producing the shape, and the changes that have taken place through time. Geomorphologists begin with description and mapping of landforms; increasingly, satellite photographs are used to help in this task. Maps can be produced to show such things as changes in the ground's slope, or the material of which it is made. In order to understand the changes, study is made of the processes of weathering, erosion, transportation, and deposition. Although investigations take place both in the field and in the laboratory, most conclusions are matters of inference, since it is difficult to conduct realistic experiments and because observation over short periods can give misleading ideas about the rates at which slow or irregular processes operate. However, the radiometric dating of an increasing range of geological and biological materials is helping enormously in the interpretation of land-form development. As a science, geomorphology derives from the work of James *Hutton and John *Playfair in the late 18th century. Many other contributions were provided in the 19th and early 20th centuries, notably by Americans, and on these the modern subject is based.

**geophysics**, the science of the structure, dynamics, and physical properties of the Earth. Taken in its broadest sense, the term includes the study of the atmosphere and the oceans. It borrows much of its theory from physics and includes a variety of subjects: seismology (the study of earthquakes), geomagnetism (the study of the Earth's magnetic field), geodynamics (the study of large-scale movement affecting the Earth's crust), meteorology (the study of the atmosphere), and the study of the Earth's gravitational field and heat flow. Geophysics is thus a very broad discipline. Its commercial applications have been largely in oil and gas exploration.

**Georgia**, a mountainous country in south-east Europe. It is separated from Russia in the north by the Caucasus Mountains. It has a coast on the Black Sea, shares a border with Turkey to the west, and is bounded by Azerbaijan and Armenia to the east and south. The climate is subtropical, with cool winters and hot summers, very wet in the west and arid in the east. On the coastal plain and in the central valley fruit trees, palms, and eucalypts flourish. Vines, tobacco, and tea are cultivated. The east by contrast is treeless grassland, but it is rich in manganese, coal, and oil.

**geosyncline**, a term invented by James *Dana in 1873 for elongated basins in the Earth's crust in which great quantities of sediment accumulate. Geosynclines were considered to be downwarped areas which formed parallel to the continental masses and, as a result of receiving vast amounts of land-derived sediments, developed under the sheer weight of sediment accumulation. An elaborate terminology was developed for geosynclines, based largely on their shape, size, and proximity to land masses. This terminology has now fallen into disuse since their mechanism of formation is now best explained with reference to the more unifying theory of *plate tectonics.

High-temperature, high-pressure steam produced naturally in the upper layers of the Earth's crust can be tapped directly into turbines and used to generate electricity. This **geothermal** power station at Wairakei is one of several in the hot springs region of the North Island, New Zealand.

**geothermal energy**, energy extracted in the form of heat from within the Earth. The source for this interior heat is thought to be radioactive decay together with the general slow cooling of the Earth. On average the rise in temperature downwards into the crust is approximately 25 °C/km (100 °F/mile), but mapping of heat flow using thermic probes in boreholes shows considerable variation from one area to another. Areas of ancient hard rocks such as in Western Australia show low values, while areas which are geologically active, such as *plate margins, have much higher values. Geothermal energy has been exploited for such purposes as electrical power generation and domestic heating in areas of natural *hot springs and *geysers, as for example in the Yellowstone National Park, USA, Wairakei in New Zealand, Iceland, and Larderello in Italy. Methods being tried in other areas to extract geothermal energy from hot igneous rocks below the surface include the use of twin boreholes to pump cold water down and hot water up; the energy obtained can be used to desalinate water or precipitate mineral salts.

**germanium** (symbol Ge, at. no. 32, r.a.m. 72.59), a brittle whitish *metalloid element in Group IV of the *periodic table. It is sometimes present in coal and can be found in chimney soot. Industrially it is extracted from the flue dust of zinc smelters and used as a *semiconductor. Compounds, except for the oxide, $GeO_2$, are rare.

**Germany**, a central European country covering an area of 357,000 km² (138,000 sq. mi.). In the west it extends across the Rhine valley, in the south it includes the central Alps, and in the east it is bounded by the River Oder in part only. Bordering countries are Denmark, Poland, Czech Republic, Austria, Switzerland, France, Luxemburg, Belgium, and the Netherlands. The whole of northern Germany, through which run the Weser, the Elbe, and smaller rivers, is set in

Castle **Geyser**, in the Yellowstone National Park in Wyoming, USA, spouts steam and near-boiling water from a vent at the bottom of its cone of hardened mud and mineral salts.

the North European Plain. The Rhine Basin encompasses some of the most beautiful landscape and best wine-growing regions in Europe. Towards the east, this consists of morainic hills containing fertile *loess soil. More than a quarter of the whole of Germany is covered with forest. Among the major ranges of the mid-German highlands are the Teutoburger Wald, the Harz Mountains, the Sauerland, Westerwald, and Taunusgebirge. In the west are the Ruhr coalfields, while in the east there are large lignite deposits. Southward the ground gradually rises to the Black Forest (Schwarzwald), and the Swabian Jura, with dense pine forests and moorland, and potash, salt, and other minerals. In Bavaria, further south, the land becomes rugged. Here are patches of mountain pasture and lakes; to the east is the deep Danube valley.

**geyser** (Icelandic, 'to rush forth'), a natural spring which intermittently spouts hot water and steam out of the ground. Where volcanic action has cracked the crust, and water in the depths has boiled, it erupts like a fountain, squirting violently to heights of 60 m (200 feet) and more. The regularity of eruption depends on the time it takes for the underground gusher system to fill. Mineral salts blown out with the water deposit mounds of lime and silica round the vents, in time forming fantastic rock formations which may contain pools,

terraces, and waterfalls. The most spectacular geysers are those of Iceland and western USA, the most famous being Old Faithful in the Yellowstone National Park. In California their geothermal energy has been harnessed for the production of electricity. In New Zealand geothermal energy for power production comes from geothermal bores.

**Ghana**, a West African country with a south-facing coast, bounded by the Côte d'Ivoire on the west, Burkina Faso on the north, and Togo on the east. Its flat and sandy coast is backed by a rolling plain of scrub and grass, except in the west, where moderate rains produce thick forest. The forest extends northward to the Ashanti plateau, which produces cocoa and tropical hardwoods, as well as manganese, bauxite, and gold. Further north, up-country of the valley of the Volta, it is very hot even in winter, though the *harmattan brings relatively cool (and dusty) conditions from the interior of West Africa.

**Giant's Causeway**, a promontory of columnar *basalt on the coast of County Antrim, Northern Ireland. Caused by rapid cooling of a sheet of lava from an eruption in the *Tertiary Period, its several thousand mainly hexagonal pillars are set together in a honeycomb formation and resemble a huge but irregular staircase leading down to the sea.

**Gibbs, Josiah Willard** (1839–1903), US mathematical physicist whose *On the Equilibrium of Heterogeneous Substances* (1876–8) was one of the foundations of physical chemistry.

His later work in statistical mechanics, describing the properties of collections of particles like atoms and molecules, is also enduring, applying to *quantum mechanics as well as to the classical physics from which it had been derived. He also wrote on the mechanical action of heat and on the electromagnetic theory of light.

**Gibraltar**, a fortified town and rocky headland, 5 km (3 miles) long, near the extreme south of Spain. A British dependency, its northern end is a low-lying sandy isthmus, south of which is the famous limestone Rock, containing caves and with a precipitous eastern face. Westward it slopes more gently towards a magnificent bay, which is a natural harbour. The Strait of Gibraltar to the south is the channel, from 15 km (9 miles) to 37 km (23 miles) in width and 56 km (35 miles) long, linking the Atlantic Ocean with the Mediterranean Sea. A surface current flows east and a deeper one west. The Rock of Gibraltar and Almina Point on the facing Moroccan coast are the ancient Pillars of Hercules, marking the limit of the known western world of antiquity.

**Gibson Desert**, an arid wasteland occupying some 340,000 km$^2$ (130,000 sq. mi.) of east-central Western Australia, along the Tropic of Capricorn. Although surrounded by seasonal lakes, it is an area of salt marshes and moving sand dunes, treeless and without vegetation apart from scrub and desert grass.

**Gilbert, Grove Karl** (1843–1918), US geologist and geomorphologist whose detailed and painstaking work on many problems laid the foundations for much 20th-century earth science. His monographs, *Geology of the Henry Mountains, Utah* (1877) and *The Transportation of Debris by Running Water* (1914), contain outstanding descriptions of the work of rivers as well as major contributions to geological theory. Other studies, on the evidence of climatic changes in inland lake basins, glaciation, the formation of lunar craters, and the methodology and philosophy of science, are also widely quoted today.

**Gilbert, Sir Humphrey** (*c*.1539–83), English soldier and navigator who first suppressed uprisings in Ireland and later intercepted Spanish galleons carrying American silver to Spain. But his real interest was seen in his *Discourse of a Discovery for a New Passage to Cataia* (Cathay, or China), published in 1576 to announce Martin *Frobisher's first voyage. With the help of his half-brother Walter *Raleigh, he raised money to sail with five ships to Newfoundland, which in 1583 he claimed in the name of Elizabeth I as the first English colony in North America.

**Gilbert, William** (1544–1603), English physicist and physician who established the scientific study of *magnetism, publishing his results in *De Magnete* in 1600. This book gives an account of his detailed experimental work with loadstones, including studies of how their magnetism could be improved or lost, and of his proposal that the Earth should be considered as a giant magnet with a north and south pole. He was also a highly respected doctor, becoming physician to Elizabeth I and to James I.

**glacial mills** *moulins.

**glaciation**, the action of moving ice on the land surface, and the state of being covered by ice. Ice-caps, ice-sheets, and glaciers each produce characteristic landforms, both while the ice remains (sometimes called glacierization) and after it melts. The impact of glaciation depends upon the kind of ice, the nature of the landscape being covered, how long the cover lasts, how the ice moves, and the number of episodes which occur within a particular geological period. It also depends on the length of time which has elapsed since the ice melted and how active other, subsequent processes have been. Upland glaciation is largely erosional. It leaves steep, shattered peaks and *arêtes, *cirques, flat-floored, steep-sided valleys, some of them hanging, rock basins and *finger lakes, *striations and lines of *moraine. Lowland glaciation varies in impact, according to whether the rocks are more or less resistant. On hard rocks, as in the Canadian Shield, it smoothes, polishes, and flutes the bedrock, leaving millions of small, irregular basins. In other areas, the surface is blanketed by *till and *outwash deposits, producing irregular but rather flat surfaces, pitted by *kettle-holes, or ridged by *eskers and *drumlins.

**glacier**, a body of land ice which flows or once flowed. If glaciers originate in *cirques in mountain areas and extend down valleys cut by rivers, they are termed 'alpine', whereas those formed where ice-caps spill over the edge of high ice plateaux are 'outlet' forms. Huge ice-sheets are sometimes called 'continental' glaciers. Ice develops from snow and *firn by melting, freezing, and compression, as more snow piles up at low temperatures. When it is approximately 65 m (200 feet) thick, the lower layers become plastic and start to flow. As long as new ice forms in the accumulation zone, flow will continue; it stops when ablation (melting and evaporation) exceeds accumulation. The snout, or 'terminus', will halt when it loses more ice by melting than is supplied by the flow. Flow is not smooth, especially in cold-based, polar glaciers where the bottom layer or 'sole' is frozen to the rock below: the build-up of pressure causes temporary thawing and a very jerky movement. Warm-based, temper-

A diagram from William **Gilbert**'s *De Magnete*, illustrating the alignment of a magnet at different positions around the Earth's North Pole (A).

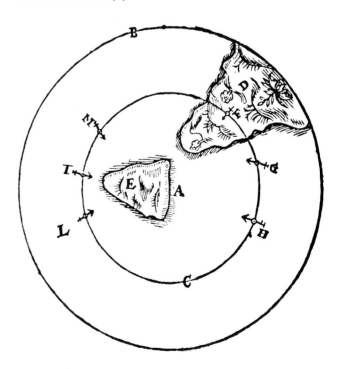

ate glaciers have a thin layer of water at the sole, especially in summer, and move more continuously. The upper layers of ice flow faster than the lower ones, causing shear planes to develop; and the middle moves faster than the sides, creating *crevasses. Meltwater from the surface finds its way into the ice, lubricating the flow and building *kames at the bed, and *eskers in tunnels. Glaciers erode by plucking and shearing rock from their beds and by grinding their channels with this material and with shattered debris fallen from the valley walls. They deposit unsorted material and the streams flowing from their snouts are milky with *rock flour.

**Glacier National Park**, name shared by two national parks in western North America. One, in the USA, lies in the mountains of north-west Montana, USA, adjacent to the Canadian Waterton Lakes National Park, with which it combines to form the Waterton–Glacier International Peace Park. The Glacier National Park of Canada, in south-east British Columbia, is in the Selkirk Mountains. The American park contains scores of glaciers, waterfalls, lakes, and snow-capped peaks and precipices. The Canadian park is smaller, but is also famous for its glaciated mountain scenery. In both parks dense forests cover the lower slopes.

**Glaisher, James** (1809–1903), British meteorologist who laid down standards for meteorological observations and instrument testing and manufacture. Between 1862 and 1866 he made a series of balloon ascents in an attempt to determine the temperature and humidity of the atmosphere at different altitudes.

## Glaciation

Glaciated uplands display a wide range of erosional features caused by the grinding action of rock fragments held in the ice, the plucking action of the moving ice, and by the shattering effect of water freezing, and expanding, in rock crevices.

Lowland features are predominantly depositional, consisting of unsorted debris dumped by melting ice and debris that has been reworked and sorted by running water both on and beneath the ice and on lower ground beyond the ice-front.

| | | | |
|---|---|---|---|
| 1 | Arête | 9 | Crevasses |
| 2 | Bergschrund | 10 | Glacier snout |
| 3 | Cirque | 11 | Terminal moraine |
| 4 | Pyramidal peak | 12 | Moraine-dammed lake |
| 5 | Ice-fall | 13 | Braided stream |
| 6 | Valley glacier | | |
| 7 | Lateral moraine | | |
| 8 | Medial moraine | | |

| | | | |
|---|---|---|---|
| 1 | Tarn | 8 | Kame consisting of sorted debris washed into a crevasse and later dumped |
| 2 | U-shaped valley | | |
| 3 | Hanging valley | | |
| 4 | Waterfall | 9 | Drumlins, consisting of boulder clay shaped by moving ice |
| 5 | Truncated spur | | |
| 6 | Outwash fan | | |
| 7 | Esker deposited by sub-glacial stream | | |

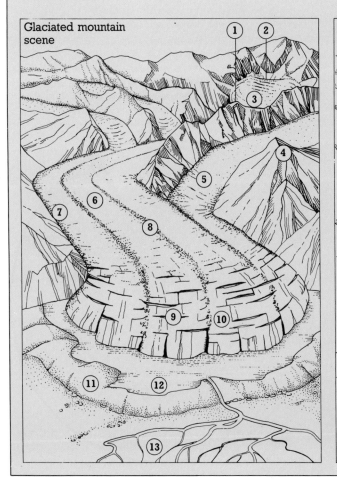

Glaciated mountain scene

Same scene after glaciation

**glass, volcanic**, the material produced by the rapid cooling of molten lava. Rapid cooling prevents crystals from forming and the resultant glass lacks crystal structure. It is commonly black with a conchoidal (shell-like) fracture. Glassy rocks include *obsidian, or pitchstone. Volcanic glass was once used industrially as a raw material for rock wool.

**glauconite**, a potassium iron silicate mineral related to *mica, a common mineral in sedimentary rocks of marine origin (such as *greensands). It usually occurs as small grains which are olive green, soft, and lustrous. It is used in the textile, sugar, and brewing industries (as a non-toxic colorant) and in fertilizers (for its potassium content).

**gleying**, a process which occurs when soils become waterlogged, causing some substances, particularly iron compounds, to become reduced or depleted of oxygen by soil bacteria. The reduction of iron gives a characteristic blue-grey colour to the soil. Soils may be waterlogged either because they are formed on impermeable clays or because they are low-lying and poorly drained. If they are only seasonally waterlogged a partially gleyed, mottled horizon forms. The *mottling is caused by the oxidation of iron along cracks and channels when air enters the soil as it dries out. Gleying is a common feature of meadow and tundra soils and of some *podzols.

**global warming**, a gradual increase in the average temperature of the Earth's atmosphere attributed to the *greenhouse effect.

**globe**, a *map of the world in the form of a sphere on which all its continents and features are shown at the same scale and with their correct shapes and areas. A globe presents information in a form which no map *projection on to a plane can achieve, except for small areas. The form is used mainly, however, to show the relationship between different countries and continents rather than to give their details. Certainly the ordinary school globe of about 30 cm (1 foot) in diameter is too small to give many details, as it has a scale of only 1/40,000,000 (or 700 miles to the inch) and many countries appear as tiny patches. It offers particular facilities even so: for example, *great circles can be represented by stretching round it pieces of string or thread. Whereas globes were originally made by hand, now they are mass produced by covering a plastic sphere with a specially drawn map divided into gores. These are strips bounded by *meridians of longitude a few degrees apart and tapering to points at the poles. When pasted on the sphere they fit exactly along their eastern and western edges.

**gluon** (in nuclear physics). Theories of fundamental interactions require that the fundamental forces have associated with them a particle to carry the force. Gluons are the carriers of the *strong nuclear force, which binds together *quarks to form hadrons, such as protons and neutrons, and holds hadrons together to form nuclei. There are eight different types of gluon: they have no mass, travel at the speed of light and have *colour and anti-colour. Their behaviour is described by the theory of quantum chromodynamics (see *quantum mechanics).

**glycol** (or ethylene glycol, $CH_2OH \cdot CH_2OH$), a colourless viscous liquid which is miscible with water. It is manufactured from ethene, and is widely used as an *antifreeze, and in the production of solvents.

A boulder of **gneiss** showing the characteristic segregation of the constituent minerals into alternating light and dark bands.

**gneiss**, a coarse-grained banded rock formed as a result of recrystallization under intense heat and pressure. Gneisses are high-grade *metamorphic rocks. The banding is caused by the segregation of light- and dark-coloured minerals during metamorphism.

**Gobi Desert** (Mongolian, *gobi*, waterless place), a desert region in southern Mongolia and northern China, stretching for 1,600 km (1,000 miles) east from Xinjiang to Manchuria and 800 km (500 miles) south from the Altai Mountains to the Huang He (Yellow River). Lying between 900 and 1,500 m (3,000 and 5,000 feet) above sea-level, it contains a series of shallow alkaline basins, where streams created by occasional short, sharp storms quickly disappear. In the main it is rocky, edged with scanty pastureland and treeless short-grass steppe; fierce sandstorms are common and have eroded the topsoil. Climatic conditions are acutely continental and dry. Winters are long and cold, summers short and hot.

**Gödel, Kurt** (1906–78), Austrian-born US mathematician who worked extensively on the problem of whether the *axioms for arithmetic are consistent with one another. His incompleteness theorem, which he proved in 1931, showed that any consistent axiomatic description of the natural numbers must include undecidable propositions. There must exist certain well-formulated claims about numbers which can neither be proved nor disproved from the axioms in a finite number of steps. His proof used mathematics in a reflexive way to explore its own foundations and was the inception of a major development in metamathematics.

**Godwin Austen**   *K2.

**Golan Heights**, uplands north-east of the Sea of Galilee (Lake Tiberius), overlooking the Jordan Valley, part of south-west Syria but occupied by Israel. The predominant feature is the number of volcanic cones; these were active until the Pleistocene Epoch, and their gaping craters are found in many of the hills. Other evidence of volcanic activity can be seen in the great basalt boulders and the basaltic–lacustrine deposits. The highest cone is Tell-a Shaikha, which stands at over 1,280 m (4,200 feet).

**gold** (symbol Au, at. no. 79, r.a.m. 196.97), a soft, yellow, metallic element, one of the *transition metals. It is very unreactive, though attacked by halogens and *aqua regia. Occurring in nature as small particles of the free metal, in quartz or in *alluvium, it caused the 19th-century gold-rushes in America and Australia; today it is produced mainly in Russia and South Africa. Its rarity, appearance, and lack of reactivity have led to its being highly valued throughout history. Its value is thought to be more stable than that of many currencies, and it is widely held as an investment. Another major use is as jewellery; it is easily beaten into ornaments which are attractive and do not tarnish. A good conductor of heat and electricity, it is used widely in electronics. Pure gold is too soft for most applications and is generally hardened by alloying it with copper or silver. The gold content of alloys is measured in carats, with 24 carats corresponding to pure gold.

**golden ratio** or section, the name given to a division of a line or figure in such a way that the ratio of the smaller section to the larger is the same as the ratio of the larger to the whole; this common ratio is $(\sqrt{5} - 1)/2$, or about 0.618. To the Greeks it was known as dividing a line in extreme and mean ratio, or merely as *the* section, and a construction for so dividing a line is given in Euclid's *Elements*. The pentagram, formed by joining all the diagonals of a regular pentagon, has the property that the point of intersection of two diagonals divides both of them in the golden ratio. It is claimed that objects or shapes in such proportions are particularly pleasing to the eye.

**Gondwana** (or Gondwanaland), the postulated supercontinental mass which once included Australia, Antarctica, India, Africa, and South America, separated as a result of *continental drift, before the Carboniferous Period. It was named Gondwanaland by the German meteorologist Alfred Wegener in 1912, who named the northern supercontinent *Laurasia.

**Good Hope, Cape of**, a headland on the south-west coast of Cape Province, South Africa. Rising to 256 m (840 feet), it is a southern spur of Table Mountain and shelters False Bay on the western side from the Atlantic. *Diaz named it the Cape of Storms; it was renamed by *Henry the Navigator because its discovery promised a sea route to the east.

**gorge**, a deep, narrow valley with very steep sides. Gorges tend to be narrower and more V-shaped than *canyons, and have craggy, irregular walls, although the distinction between the two terms is rather arbitrary. They form in areas of resistant rocks where rivers are able to cut their channels downwards very rapidly. This is common in high mountains, where heavy snow cover melts quickly and the usually heavy rainfalls create high flood peaks. Such mountains are often still being uplifted, a process which continually lowers the *base level of erosion and encourages further down-cutting.

**Goudsmidt, Samuel Abraham** (1902–78), Dutch-born American physicist who, with George Uhlenbeck in 1925,

first suggested that the electron possesses *spin. The concept proved to be of fundamental importance in the development of *quantum mechanics.

**graben**, a rift valley in which elongated blocks of rock, usually of great size, have dropped down between two parallel *faults. Graben are geologically complementary to *block mountains or horsts.

**grade** (in geology), the concentration of a metal or other useful element in an *ore. The *cut-off grade is the lowest grade at which the ore can be extracted at a profit.

**Graham, Thomas** (1805–69), Scottish chemist who is regarded as one of the founders of physical chemistry. He studied the molecular *diffusion of gases and formulated the law that the rates of diffusion of gases vary inversely as the square root of their densities or relative molecular masses: thus, a light gas such as helium will diffuse more rapidly than a heavy one. His investigation of the diffusion of molecules in solution across a membrane was the basis for understanding *colloids and the invention of dialysis.

**Grampian Mountains**, a series of much eroded mountain ranges stretching north-east–south-west across the central highlands of Scotland. They contain the *Cairngorms and many isolated bens (Gaelic, 'peak'), including *Ben Nevis, and lochs (long, narrow lakes produced by glacial *erosion). Down the straths (valleys) flow the rivers: the Spey and Findhorn to the north, the Don and Dee to the east, and the Esk, Tay, and Forth to the south. The superficial deposits are mainly brick earth and hill peat, providing forest and the widest expanses of heather in the UK.

The name is also applied to a mountain range in Australia, extending south-west from the Great Dividing Range, where the highest peak Mount William, rises to 1,166 m (3,827 feet).

**Gran Chaco**, a lowland plain of south-central South America which includes parts of Argentina, Bolivia, Brazil, and Paraguay, and which has an area of some 518,000 km² (200,000 sq. mi.). It slopes to the east and is developed on gravel, sand and clay which have been washed from the Andean foothills. Marshes have accumulated where deposits of clay have hindered drainage, and elsewhere the landscape shows fragments of ancient river channels. It is crossed by only four permanent rivers: the Pilcomayo, Bermejo, Salado, and Dulce.

**Grand Banks**, the upper part of a submerged plateau lying south-east of Newfoundland, with an area of about 93,000 km² (36,000 sq. mi.). It is part of the submerged continental shelf of eastern North America. The warm water of the Gulf Stream meets the cold water of the Labrador Current in the vicinity of the Banks, and the favourable conditions that result have made it one of the world's greatest fishing grounds. However, the convergence of contrasting *air masses has also made it one of the world's foggiest areas.

**Grand Canyon**, one of the world's natural wonders, in north-western Arizona, USA. It is the largest of a series of gorges cut by the *Colorado River and is a continuation of the Marble Canyon; their combined lengths total over 480 km (nearly 300 miles). A mile deep in places and varying from 6.4 to 29 km (4 to 18 miles) in width, it is a magnificent display showing the action of millions of years of

An aerial view of part of the Great Rift Valley in Kenya. The straight, parallel, faulted valley sides separate the **graben**—the block of rock strata forming the valley floor—from the flanking blocks of uplifted strata.

erosion by wind and water. Some 175 km (110 miles) of its length forms a national park. There are towers and cliffs, ledges, steep *scree slopes, gullies, and tributary gorges. The multicoloured rock strata—white limestone and green to grey or rusty sandstones, with reddish iron deposits—are rendered brilliant in the sunshine.

**grand unified theory**, the name for attempts to describe, using a single theory, all the interactions governed by the four fundamental forces. Grand unified theories (GUTs) are also called unified field theories or theories of everything, and have occupied physicists for some time. The theory of electromagnetism was a first step: *Maxwell's equations unified the electric and magnetic forces into a single electromagnetic force. Current attempts at unification are motivated by the belief that there is a unity in nature—a single principle governing all natural phenomena. So far, theories have been proposed which provide unifications of *weak and *strong nuclear forces and the electromagnetic force. The inclusion of the gravitational force is proving extremely difficult, although proponents of *string theory hope to make some progress here.

**granite**, a coarse-grained intrusive igneous rock that commonly contains orthoclase feldspar, quartz, and mica. Hornblende may be present in addition to, or in place of, mica. The general colour is light: grey, pink, yellow, or green. Granites are of all geological periods and are the most widespread rocks on the continents. They are particularly common in the ancient Precambrian shields of Russia, Africa, Canada, and South America; and well-known examples occur in the western Coastal Range of North America (from California to Alaska). They are widely used as building stones and for road surfacing. Only rarely are they a source of valuable minerals.

**granulites**, *metamorphic rocks having a granular texture: that is, a texture in which the mineral grains are all more or less of the same size. Granulites are usually composed of quartz, feldspars, and the ferromagnetic minerals garnet and pyroxene. They are formed by regional metamorphism of high grade and may originate either as sediments or as igneous rocks. They occur extensively in the north-west highlands of Scotland.

**graph**, a way of representing statistical, experimental or mathematical information diagrammatically, usually to make the information easier to interpret. A simple example is a bar chart of monthly rainfall (see figure). The top of each bar embodies two pieces of information: a quantity of rainfall, read from the vertical scale; and a month of the year, read from the horizontal scale. (The scales are called axes.)

The three main mineral constituents are clearly identifiable in this **granite** specimen: pale pink orthoclase feldspar, small black crystals of biotite mica, and glassy quartz.

Because graphs show how one quantity varies in relation to another, they are used to display *functions—a function being a mathematical statement of how two variables are related. For example, a graph of $y = x^2$ (see figure) shows how $y$ (usually measured along the vertical axis) varies in relation to $x$ (measured along the horizontal axis). The steps on graph axes do not always represent equal increments. In science they often represent *logarithmic increments. Such axes enable wide-ranging data to be compressed on to a reasonably sized graph. They also transform *exponential functions (often encountered in science) into straight-line graphs, which are easier to interpret. Mathematicians and scientists look for particularly significant features of graphs. These include: whether the graph is straight or curved, smooth or ragged; whether it has a repeating pattern; whether and where it crosses the axes; whether it has the shape of a hill top or a valley bottom anywhere; whether it tends *asymptotically to a steady value; and so on.

Graph theory, despite its name, has little to do with the graphs described above, but is concerned with the study of diagrams involving points, lines, and paths. It arose from the investigation of puzzles, properties of electrical circuits, and representations of chemical structures.

**graphite**, a dark (black or grey) mineral that is one of the *allotropes of carbon. Found in metamorphic rocks, it has a greasy feel and is very soft. It is an excellent conductor of electricity and is used mainly as a dry lubricant, for electrodes, and in paint manufacture; in the home it is familiar as the 'lead' in pencils.

**gravel**, an unconsolidated deposit in the form of pebbles laid down by melting ice, rivers, or the sea. The pebbles in ice-laid gravels are generally angular; those of river-laid ones smoother and sometimes flat; and those of wave-beaten ones (shingle) rounder. The pebbles in glacial gravels typically show the greatest variety; those of river gravels the least. A more specific use of the word gravel is for deposits made up of particles in the range 2 to 60 mm (just under 0.1 inch to about 2.4 inches). Some gravels contain gemstones or gold; others, metals such as tin, washed from neighbouring regions.

**gravitation**, one of the four fundamental forces of nature. It is an attractive force, and is always present between any two bodies which have mass. The strength of the gravitational force is proportional to the product of the masses of the two bodies. It is an *inverse square law: it is also inversely proportional to the square of the distance between the two bodies; so that if their separation is doubled the gravitational attraction will be one-quarter of its original strength. An object falls to the ground because of the gravitational attraction between it and the Earth (see *acceleration); and the planets are maintained in their orbits round the Sun by the gravitational force between them and the Sun. Even so, compared with the other forces which exist in nature—for example, electromagnetic forces—the gravitational force is extremely weak. It is significant only if at least one of the bodies has a sizeable mass. The gravitational force between individual atoms or molecules, even when very close together, is insignificant compared with the other *interactions that occur.

**graviton** (in atomic physics). Theories of fundamental interactions require that the fundamental forces have associated with them a particle which carries the force. The

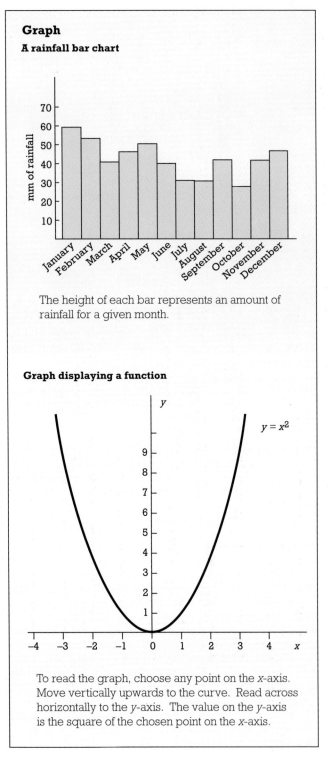

**Graph**

**A rainfall bar chart**

The height of each bar represents an amount of rainfall for a given month.

**Graph displaying a function**

$y = x^2$

To read the graph, choose any point on the $x$-axis. Move vertically upwards to the curve. Read across horizontally to the $y$-axis. The value on the $y$-axis is the square of the chosen point on the $x$-axis.

graviton is the carrier of the gravitational force. The graviton has no mass, is stable, has a spin of 2, has no electrical charge and travels at the speed of light. The graviton interacts only very slightly with matter and so it is extremely hard to detect; the experimental evidence for its existence is inconclusive.

**graywacke** *greywacke.

**Great Australian Bight**, a wide and shallow bay on the southern continental shelf of Australia. Its generally inhospitable coastline extends for 1,100 km (700 miles) from Cape

Pasley in the west to Cape Carnot in the east, and comprises for much of its length the cliffs of the Hampton Tableland and Nullabor Plain. Many islands dot the eastern end, but there are few safe anchorages. Set on the edge of the South Australian Basin, part of the Indian Ocean, it offers no protection from the *westerlies, which in winter can be stormy.

**Great Barrier Reef**, off Australia's north-east coast, the largest single system of coral *reefs and the largest living structure in the world. Stretching southward for 1,930 km (over 1,200 miles) from the Torres Strait to Swain Reefs, the 2,500 reefs are concentrated in a band 50–60 km (30–37 miles) wide along the margin of the continental shelf. Over the years it has suffered considerable damage from increased numbers of the crown of thorns starfish. There are many channels through the Reef, which is pounded by surf on its outer edge. A broad and sheltered but shallow channel twists between the reefs and islets a few miles off shore.

**Great Basin**, a vast semi-arid region in the western USA, between the Sierra Nevada, to the west, and the Wasatch range south of Great Salt Lake. Its rugged north–south ranges are divided by deep valleys—including *Death Valley in the south—with wide sedimentary floors. It contains about a hundred *drainage basins and many deserts, the Mojave, Black Rock, and Colorado Deserts among them. Most of its rivers, finding no outlet to the sea, either disappear in alkaline sinks or drain into saline lakes such as the Great Salt Lake in the east. As well as salt, there are deposits of various metals, including silver and copper.

**Great Bear Lake**, a lake in the Northwest Territories, on the Arctic Circle and on the edge of the *Canadian Shield, covering an area of 31,792 km² (12,275 sq. mi.). With surface ice even in summer, it is navigable for only four months of the year. It is irregular in shape, with five arms, and contains many small, sparsely forested islands. Drained to the west by Great Bear River, it contributes to the waters of the Mackenzie River. The long days of summer provide a short growing season on its shores.

**Great Britain**, the largest of the *British Isles, a large island off Europe's north-west coast and containing England, Scotland, and Wales. The distance from Land's End on its south-west corner to John o' Groats in the far north is 971 km (603 miles); yet such are the coastal indentations that no part is more than 160 km (100 miles) from the sea. Of its mountains, which lie in the north and west, few are higher than 1,000 m (3,300 feet), while of its rivers none is longer than the Severn at 354 km (220 miles). Within this small compass, however, the geological differences are great. The rocks are of many periods and kinds, with granite and slate, basalt, sandstones, and hard limestone all included. Generally lower in the west than the north, the rocky masses underlie much moorland, generally bare of trees and having for vegetation peat moss, heather, and acid grass in varying proportions. The south of the country, which is warmer and drier than the rest, has hills of chalk and flint or limestone rising to 300 m (less than 1,000 feet). Here the valleys are broad, with sandy soil or clay supporting oak, ash, beech, and chestnut trees. In the east, which is lower and flatter, river gravels and alluvium from the North Sea have produced dark, rich soils. Its principal river, the *Thames, flows into the North Sea. Once famous for its tin and later for its iron, the country still has reserves of coal together with deposits of oil and natural gas, both on shore and off shore.

**great circles**, the circles that can be described on the surface of a sphere with their planes passing through its centre: they are the largest circles it is possible to draw on a sphere. Round the Earth, opposite meridians meet at the poles and thus form great circles; and the Equator is one, although other parallels of latitude are not. When a great circle passes through two particular points it represents the shortest distance between them and is generally followed by ships and aircraft when unimpeded by bad weather, mountains, or other obstacles. It may not appear, however, as the shortest distance on a two-dimensional map.

**Great Dividing Range**, the crest of the eastern highlands of Australia, curving roughly parallel to the coast for almost its entire north–south length and forming a folded inner arc of the series of mountain chains in the western Pacific. Generally it is some 240 km (150 miles) across but varies greatly in height. The Queensland ranges, Darling Downs among them, are the lowest, gently rising to no more than 1,000 m (3,300 feet) or so. The more southerly New England Range and Blue Mountains are higher, while the Snowy Mountains (Australian Alps), including Mount Kosciusko, near the southern end of the chain are about twice that height. There are many gaps, exposing rocks of all ages, and much fertile soil derived from weathered volcanic basalt. The Range catches moderate rain from the great atmospheric depressions of the Southern Ocean and acts as a watershed for the rivers. The many tributaries of the Darling and the Murray flow inland, while the Burnett, Brisbane, Hunter, Shoalhaven, and many more have shorter journeys to the sea.

**Great Lakes**, in North America, the largest body of fresh water in the world, forming a natural boundary between Canada and the USA. Lake Superior, the most extensive, is also the highest. South of it, and within the USA, is Lake Michigan, which connects with Lake Huron to the east, from which the Saint Clair River leads into Lake Erie. The Niagara River flows over its famous falls from Lake Erie to Lake Ontario. All the lakes are subject to sudden and violent storms and freeze over in winter. Even so, for eight months in the year they constitute a magnificent waterway, which is linked by the Saint Lawrence River to the Atlantic. Together the lakes span 1,870 km (1,160 miles). Their basins were formed during the Pleistocene ice ages by a combination of processes. First there was the grinding action of enormously thick ice-sheets which eroded basins in the rocks. Second, the weight of the ice was so great that it caused the *Earth's crust to sag slightly, enlarging the basins. Although the ice with its weight has long since vanished, the crust is still adjusting to the removal of the load in a process known as *isostasy. At present northern Canada is slowly but steadily rising, tilting the whole continent very gently southward. Unless the ice-sheets reappear, Lake Michigan will eventually drain into the Mississippi valley, and the Great Lakes will eventually disappear.

**Great Plains**, the gently sloping plateaux of west-central North America, reaching from Alberta in the north to Texas in the south. The western elevation of around 1,800 m (6,000 feet) runs along the foothills of the Rocky Mountains; the slope, of over 640 km (400 miles), is to an eastern elevation of around 600 m (2,000 feet). In its central section they merge with the prairies of the American Middle West. The surface is largely made up of material transported from the Rockies and covers mineral-rich sedimentary rock deposited by what was once a vast inland sea. Rivers such as the North and South Saskatchewan, the Missouri, Yellowstone, Platte, Arkansas, Cimmaron, and Pecos still cut through it, their broad, shallow valleys contrasting with *badlands such as the plateau east of the Black Hills. The climate is semi-arid, with a wide range of seasonal temperatures, and high winds make it a potential *dust bowl country. Trees are sparse away from the rivers, and the prairie grassland is the home of great herds of livestock or is ploughed for wheat.

**Great Rift Valley**, the world's largest *rift valley system, extending south from the River Jordan to the Zambezi. It is not a continuous valley, for plateaux and mountains interrupt it, but it is traceable on a map by the seas and lakes which fill its elongated pockets. In the Red Sea area crustal *plates are diverging, while east Africa has been bowed upwards to form a crest which is slowly splitting; in both areas as the rift widens the floor of the valley sinks. In east Africa there are two main branches of the valley: the Eastern Rift runs through the Ethiopian Highlands to Lake Turkana, then past Mount Kenya and Mount Kilimanjaro, which are associated volcanoes, to Lake Malawi; the Western Rift branches off from Lake Turkana to Lake Albert and Lake Tanganyika. The heights of the valley's floors and walls vary considerably. The Dead Sea in the north and the floor of Lake Tanganyika in the south are well below sea-level, while the surface of the Eastern Rift is well above it in many places. The walls of the Western Rift fall between 500 and 800 m (1,600 and 2,600 feet) from the plateau on either side, the floor here being up to 100 km (60 miles) across. Its surface is generally flat, with a good deal of sedimentary cover.

**Great Salt Desert** (Iranian, Dasht-e-Kavir), an area stretching some 800 km (500 miles) across north-central Iran, south-east of the Elburz Mountains, at about 760 m (2,500 feet). It is a huge basin with interior drainage, though almost entirely rainless. Evaporation has created a salt crust which covers the marsh and mud. This surface is dangerous to travellers because it acts like quicksand.

**Great Salt Lake**, the largest body of water in the west of the USA. Situated in northern Utah, it is 120 km (75 miles) long, yet smaller than the ancient Lake Bonneville, of which it is but a remnant. It has no outlet. Its salt density has become six times that of the sea, and the human body cannot sink in it. It contains many islands, the largest being Antelope Island, while the only life it supports are brine shrimp.

**Great Sandy Desert**, a tract of waterless country in north-central Western Australia some 390,000 km² (150,000 sq. mi.) in area. It lies to the south-west of the Kimberley Plateau and stretches to the coast. With a rainfall of less than 200 mm (8 inches) a year, its surface consists mainly of westward-pointing sand *dunes and *salt marshes. Waterholes exist only at infrequent intervals, but despite the aridity the coarse, spiny-leaved grass, spinifex, is often seen, and there is some scrub.

**Great Slave Lake**, situated in the Northwest Territories, Canada's second largest lake, being 480 km (300 miles) long but of an irregular shape. At 614 m (2,015 feet) it is also the deepest lake in North America. Its long northern and eastern arms extend into tundra country, while its western shore is forested. The Hay and Slave Rivers run into it from the south, while in the west it gives rise to the Mackenzie River.

It is navigable from July to October. Valuable deposits of lead and zinc ores are exploited on its southern shore; gold, sulphur, and gypsum are among the other minerals found.

**Great Smoky Mountains**, a national park on the boundary between Tennessee and North Carolina, USA. It is part of the southern Appalachian Mountain system, with peaks rising to over 2,000 m (6,500 feet) which are often surrounded by haze. They are among the oldest mountains in the world. The foothills are famous for their forests, which are inhabited by bears.

**Great Victoria Desert**, the vast arid region which straddles the boundary between Western Australia and South Australia. Lying north of the Nullarbor Plain, the access route between west and east, it stretches for some 725 km (450 miles) across and reaches heights of 300 m (1,000 feet) above sea-level. The borderline between the scrub of the desert and the flat, treeless Nullarbor is very sharp, and is marked by sand-ridges several hundred metres high. The interior consists of sand *dunes, *salt-marshes, and dried-up lakes and is almost entirely barren.

**Greece**, a maritime country in south-east Europe, bounded by Albania, Macedonia, and Bulgaria to the north, and by Turkey to the east. The many islands round its long coastline include Corfu, Crete, the Cyclades, and the Sporades. The peninsula is bounded by the Ionian, Mediterranean, and Aegean Seas. Thrace in the north-east is mainly low-lying, as are the river deltas of Macedonia. Most of the mainland, however, is a peninsula of mountains, the highest being Olympus. These continue southward beyond the Gulf of Corinth and its isthmus and on to the high Peloponnese peninsula. In winter the northern plateaux are cold and suitable only for sheep grazing. One-third of the country can be cultivated; in areas where the climate is truly Mediterranean, crops include tobacco, tomatoes, and vines.

**Greely, Adolphus Washington** (1844–1935), US army lieutenant who explored and mapped parts of Greenland and Ellesmere Island. Trapped in Smith Sound during a winter of 250 days with food rations for only 40 days, he and his party were reduced to eating their own leather clothing. Only Greely and six others survived. In later years he established telegraphic communications in outlying US posessions and in 1888 helped found the American Geographical Society.

**Green, George** (1793–1841), British mathematician and physicist who was self-taught and started work as a miller. His work in applied mathematics, particularly the theory of electricity and magnetism, was only circulated in a privately produced pamphlet and was largely ignored until after his death. In it he proved the theorem named after him, relating the integral of potential functions over a closed curve to the integral of their partial derivatives over the region inside the curve.

**greenhouse effect**, the retention of heat by the lower layers of the Earth's atmosphere. Just as the glass of a greenhouse lets in short-wave radiation from the Sun while trapping the longer-wave radiation emitted within, so gases in the atmosphere (such as water vapour, *carbon dioxide, *methane, and *chloro-fluorocarbons) reflect long-wave radiation from the Earth's surface. (The term 'greenhouse effect' is slightly misleading as it refers only to the trapping of long-wave radiation and not to the fact that the glass of greenhouses also prevents the dispersal of warm air within into the atmosphere.) With the addition of solid pollutants, the capacity of the lower layers to absorb and re-radiate heat is increased. The average concentration of carbon dioxide in the air has increased by over 15 per cent in the last hundred years or so, due mainly to the burning of coal, gas, and oil. This, coupled with deforestation, is reducing the planet's ability to maintain the carbon dioxide balance. It is expected that the original level of carbon dioxide will be doubled within the next hundred years. This is likely to result in a 3 °C (5 °F) increase in mean air temperatures. This global warming may be accompanied by a melting of polar ice and thermal expansion of the ocean's surface waters, resulting in accelerated rise of mean sea-level. Other considerations are the possible long-term changes in weather patterns.

**Greenland**, the world's largest island, lying more than two-thirds within the Arctic Circle and extending from the Arctic Ocean into the North Atlantic. It measures 2,670 km (1,659 miles) in length and 1,288 km (800 miles) in breadth at its widest. Separated from Canada's Ellesmere Island to the north by only 25.6 km (16 miles), it is the most northerly land in the world, its interior covered by great sheets of ice which may be more than 2,000 m (6,500 feet) thick and conceal 90 per cent of the land area. The coasts are mountainous but are cut by long fiords and surrounded by many smaller islands. Although beset by snow and fogs, the southerly coasts have temperatures above freezing for most of the year, and it is here that cryolite (an aluminium ore) is found. Other resources include uranium, zinc, and lead. A part of Denmark, it has internal autonomy.

**greensand**, a marine *sandstone containing the green mineral *glauconite, of which it is the main source. Common in *Cretaceous and *Eocene sediments, it is found especially in New Jersey and Delaware on the coastal plains of the eastern USA. Modern greensands are forming off the coasts of Africa, Australia, and northern America, among other places.

In Europe the term Greensand is used as the name of a stratigraphical division of the Cretaceous Period.

**Greenwich meridian**, the prime meridian of longitude with the arbitrary value of 0°. All other longitudes are measured eastward or westward from it, until the international date-line is reached on the other side of the world. Greenwich, England, was chosen for this base line by international agreement in 1884, partly as a result of the pioneering work in astronomy conducted at the Royal Observatory there, much of which was concerned with providing a navigational standard for ships at sea. Greenwich Mean Time (GMT) is the local time on this meridian from which times to the east and west are calculated. The time at a place east of Greenwich is always ahead of GMT, while at a place west it is always behind, the difference in general being one hour for every 15° of longitude.

**Grenada**, a state comprising the southernmost of the Windward Islands in the Caribbean and several small islands, part of the Grenadines archipelago. The island of Grenada is 310 km² (120 sq. mi.) in area and contains rugged, forested mountains, rising to Mount Saint Catherine at 838 m (2,749 feet), with crater lakes and springs. The mountains are of volcanic origin and enclose valleys where bananas, spices, and sugar cane are grown.

**greywacke** (US, graywacke), a special type of impure *sandstone that is formed in regions where sediments are being deposited while mountain-building is in progress. These sediments, called *turbidites, are transported by strong currents of water. Greywackes are dark in colour, consisting of angular and subangular fragments of various sizes in a matrix of clay. They occur extensively; examples can be seen in the Lower Palaeozoic rocks of Wales and the Lake District in Britain.

**Grignard, François Auguste Victor** (1871–1935), French chemist who discovered the alkyl magnesium halides, which are prepared by reacting magnesium with a halocarbon in dry ether. These reagents facilitate a number of chemical reactions and extremely important in organic syntheses. Grignard spent much of his life working on them and for his discovery he shared the 1912 Nobel Prize for Chemistry with Paul Sabatier (1854–1941).

**grit**, a term used to describe a coarse sandy deposit, either consolidated or unconsolidated. The predominant mineral is usually, but not necessarily, subangular or angular *quartz.

**groundwater**, a subsurface water that lies in a zone of rock that is completely saturated with water. Most of it comes from rain or other precipitation, or by infiltration from streams and rivers: this is called meteoric water. A small proportion (called connate water) is water that was present in sedimentary rocks when they were deposited. Some groundwater also comes from igneous intrusions: this is juvenile water. Where groundwater levels reach the surface, springs develop, as on the lower edges of *chalk escarpments. Groundwater levels fluctuate according to rainfall. In areas near the sea, groundwater can often be polluted by seawater. Porous sedimentary rocks provide the best reservoirs for groundwater storage.

**group theory**, the study of the properties of mathematical groups. A group consists of a set of elements (for example, real numbers) and an *operation (for example, addition) which together satisfy the conditions of (i) *closure, (ii) *association, (iii) existence of an *identity, and (iv) existence of an *inverse for every element. Finite groups are those with a finite number of elements; the number of elements in a group is called its order. A subgroup is a subset of the elements which themselves form a group under the same operation. For example, the set of integers forms a subgroup of the set of real numbers under addition. Of particular interest are cyclic groups, in which all the elements are generated by repetition of the operation on one element. The group of clockwise right-angle turns of a square is cyclic, since if $R^0$ is zero right-angle turns, then $R^1$ is one 90° turn, $R^2$ is 180°, $R^3$ is 270° and $R^4 = 360°$, which is the same as $R^0$. Groups capture the notion of symmetry algebraically and have been used widely in all branches of mathematics, both pure and applied.

**Guam** (US), largest and southernmost of the Marianas island chain in the Pacific Ocean which, situated at the junction of the Philippine and Pacific *plates, is on a ridge beside the *Mariana Trench, deepest in the world. The northern islands are volcanic and very mountainous; Guam, itself, whose volcanic base is limestone-covered, rises to 400 m (over 1,300 feet). The interior is jungle. Despite its size— 540 km² (210 sq. mi.)—it has few natural resources.

**Guatemala**, a Central American country, bounded by Mexico on its north and west and by Honduras and El Salvador on its south-east. It has a southern coast on the Pacific Ocean and access to the Caribbean Sea on the east, where it is also bounded by Belize. A very high range of volcanic mountains crosses it from east to west and rivers water the lower slopes, which support crops of coffee. The plateaux have a mild climate, the lowlands a hot one. Earthquakes are frequent, the country lying near a junction of crustal *plates.

**Guernsey** *Channel Islands.

**Guettard, Jean Étienne** (1715–86), French geologist who publicly proposed that the Earth is older than contemporary Christian belief held, a view which he was compelled at the time to recant. He pioneered the study of the distribution of different kinds of rocks, minerals, and fossils, and showed that strata in Brittany are similar to those in south-west Britain. His correct suggestion that some fossil forms are those of extinct marine species, and his view of mountains in the Massif Central as ancient volcanoes, were received with derision.

**Guinea**, a West African country with an Atlantic coast, bounded on the north by Senegal and Mali, on the east by the Côte d'Ivoire, and on the south by Liberia and Sierra Leone. Inland from the marshy coast is a plain with large bauxite deposits. This rises to a sandstone plateau, the Fouta Djallon. Southward is the source of the Niger River; and further south still (the country bends like a hook) are large reserves of iron ore. The climate is hot; the southernmost part is drier than the coast.

**Guinea–Bissau**, a small tropical country on the coast of West Africa, bounded by Senegal on the north and Guinea on the south. Off-shore is the Bijagós archipelago with a score of inhabitable marshy islands. The deeply indented coast, stretching for some 240 km (150 miles) from north to south, is marshy and contains the mouths of three major rivers. The interior, which extends eastward for some 300 km (185 miles), consists mainly of river valleys filled with rain forest; it rises to above 200 m (650 feet) only in the south.

**gulf**, an extensive inlet of the sea into the land, usually larger, more enclosed, or more deeply indented than a *bay. They vary much in shape and size, however, as does the Gulf of Mexico from the Gulf of Bothnia, or the *Gulf from the Gulf of Saint Lawrence.

**Gulf, the** (formerly, Persian Gulf), the arm of the Arabian Sea lying between the deserts of Arabia and Iran. Nearly 970 km (600 miles) in length, it is very shallow, with a mean depth of only 100 m (330 feet). At its north-western end it receives the waters of the Euphrates and Tigris through the Shatt al-Arab; at its south-eastern end it connects with the Gulf of Oman through the Strait of Hormuz. The temperature of its waters can reach 35 °C (95 °F) in summer, and it was once famous for its pearl-bearing oyster beds. Now its vast oil reserves are more important. Of its many islands, Bahrain is the largest.

**Gulf Stream**, a North Atlantic Ocean current bringing a temperate climate to western Europe. Its warm waters originate in the North Equatorial Current (which, in the Atlantic Ocean, crosses the Equator). These then flow into the Caribbean and Gulf of Mexico and out through the Straits of Florida as a narrow, fast, intense current, whose surface velocities can be of the order of 2 m/s (this is fast for current flow). Because of flows along the boundary of the cold coastal water and the warm *Sargasso Sea, the stream is a *frontal region. It is the western limb of the North Atlantic sub-tropical *gyre. After following the *continental slope up as far as Cape Hatteras (35° N.) it flows eastward, becoming more and more diffuse until it is known as the North Atlantic Drift. Much of this eventually turns southwards to become the Canary Current, the eastern boundary current of the gyre. As it leaves the coast at Cape Hatteras the stream begins to meander considerably. Sometimes meanders are cut off (rather in the manner of *ox-bow lakes) to form isolated eddies or rings. Those cut-off to the north of the stream are warmer than the surrounding water (which is influenced by the cold waters of the *Labrador Current), and those cut off to the south are colder than the surrounding Sargasso Sea water; for this reason, the former are referred to as warm-cone eddies. These eddies are hundreds of kilometres across (approximately 125 miles) and, like the current from which they form, extend to considerable depths; they are known as 'meso-scale' (that is, intermediate-scale) eddies, and similar ones are formed along intense frontal currents elsewhere in the world.

**gully**, a steep, bare-sided miniature valley or gorge which is cut in soil or weak rock by surface *runoff, especially after heavy rainstorms. Gullies are frequent in semi-arid areas and can easily develop into *badlands. The most spectacular gullying, however, occurs in wet tropical areas if the vegetation has been removed and the soil is exposed to intense rainfall. Gullies often destroy valuable farmland and

Satellite photography using heat-sensitive film shows a clear demarcation between the warm waters (purple/red) of the **Gulf Stream** and the cold waters (blue) of the US Atlantic coast between Cape Hatteras and Cape Cod. As the main current sweeps out into the Atlantic it is flanked by swirling eddies and isolated cut-off cells of water of intermediate temperatures.

The 'desert rose' form of the mineral **gypsum**. Each petal is about 5 cm (2 inches) wide.

threaten to undermine housing; and the sediment eroded from them will choke river channels and, if spread over valley floors, ruin crops, fill drainage ditches, and bury roads. Once formed, gullies are difficult and expensive to stabilize.

**gusher** *geyser.

**Guyana**, a country on the north-east coast of South America, with a maximum length from north to south of 800 km (500 miles) and maximum width from east to west of about 460 km (285 miles). It is bordered by the Atlantic Ocean to the north, Surinam to the east, Brazil to the south and southwest, and Venezuela to the west. Much of the country is covered with dense rain forest. Sugar is a major export, the province of Demerara having given its name to a type of sugar that originated there. Bauxite mining is becoming increasingly important.

**gypsum**, is a light-coloured, soft *evaporite mineral composed of calcium sulphate ($CaSO_4 \cdot 2H_2O$). It is found as crystals, scattered nodules, and as vein deposits. Transparent crystals (selenite), granular masses (*alabaster), and rosette-shaped nodules ('desert roses') are well-known varieties. It occurs in large quantities in sedimentary rocks formed by evaporation of seawater or salt-rich lakes, together with calcite and clays. It is a common deposit in the USA in rocks dating from the *Ordovician to the present. Essential for making plaster of Paris, it is also used as a flux for pottery and as a filler material for the building industry.

**gyre**, a circular or spiral motion of water, usually in a current system. Gyres are generated mainly by surface winds and move clockwise in the northern hemisphere and anticlockwise in the southern hemisphere. (See also *ocean current, *circulation.)

**Hadley, George** (1685–1768), English lawyer and climatologist who first formulated the theory describing the trade winds and the associated meridional circulation pattern now known as the Hadley cell. He realized that the additional heat from the Sun received by equatorial regions explains the global pattern of surface and high-level winds. Warm air which rises near the Equator becomes colder and denser as it flows aloft towards the poles. This air then sinks to the surface, causing the *trade winds which blow back towards the Equator, thus completing the cell circulation.

**hadron**, an elementary particle subject to the *strong force. Hadrons are formed of a combination of *quarks. There are two main groups: the *baryons, which have half-integral spin, and the *mesons, which have zero or integral spin. Particles not subject to the strong interaction are called *leptons.

**haematite** ($Fe_2O_3$), the most important ore mineral of iron; the iron content is over 70 per cent. Commonly found as dark-brown kidney-shaped nodules, it is very dense and moderately hard. The largest deposits are found round Lake Superior, Quebec, and in Brazil. Crushed haematite (red ochre) is used as a pigment and as a fine abrasive powder.

**hafnium** (symbol Hf, at. no. 72, r.a.m. 178.49), one of the *transition metals; it closely resembles zirconium and is usually found in zirconium minerals. It is rather unreactive, and shows valency 4 in most of its compounds. A strong neutron absorber, it is used for control rods in nuclear reactors.

**Hahn, Otto** (1879–1968), German chemist, co-discoverer of nuclear fission, for which he shared the 1944 Nobel Prize for Chemistry with the German analytical chemist Fritz Strassmann (1902–80). He started the study of radiochemistry during a brief work period outside Germany to study English, first with William *Ramsay in London and then

'Kidney ore' is one of the main varieties of **haematite**. This specimen is approximately 4.85 cm (1.9 inches) across.

An almost-complete solar **halo**, with the vertical and horizontal components of a 'sun cross' and well-developed parhelia ('sun dogs'). The latter are bright patches of light formed where the halo and the arms of the cross intersect.

with Ernest *Rutherford in Manchester, identifying various radioactive isotopes of thorium. His fruitful partnership with Lise *Meitner began shortly after his return to Germany and ended when she, a Jew, fled from the Nazis in 1938. They discovered the new element protoactinium in 1917, but the culmination of their collaboration occurred in 1938 when, with Strassmann, they discovered neutron-induced nuclear fission, so named by Meitner's nephew, the physicist Otto Frisch (1904–79).

**hail**, *precipitation in the form of small pellets of ice, or occasionally larger pieces—hailstones with a diameter of several centimetres have been recorded. They form usually in cumulonimbus clouds, when the air is so unstable that intense convection currents reach levels as high as the *tropopause. When the temperature of the cloud tops is below −10 °C (14 °F) some of the water droplets they contain freeze. As these ice particles are carried upwards in the strong air currents they grow when they collide with other water droplets, the liquid of which spreads round them and freezes to produce a layer of clear ice. If carried to higher levels where the cloud temperature is below −30 °C, frost accretes to form a layer of opaque ice. Several layers of each kind of ice may accumulate when the hail is carried up and down a number of times. Growth continues until the effect of gravity is greater than that of the convection currents; then the hailstone falls out of the clouds. Hailstones have been known to weigh 2.5 kg (5 lb.) or more. During summer they are prevalent in the interiors of continents in temperate latitudes, when intense surface heating triggers thunderstorm activity.

**Haiti** *Hispaniola.

**Hakluyt, Richard** (1552/3–1616), English geographer and chronicler whose *Principall Navigations* (1589) contains accounts from manuscript sources and from personal interviews with mariners, of famous voyages of discovery up to his time of writing and gave great impetus to discovery and colonization.

**half-life**, the time it takes for half of the radioactive atoms in a sample to decay. This can range from small fractions of a second to billions of years: for example, the half-life of the most abundant uranium *isotope (uranium-238) is $4.5 \times 10^9$ years, that of radium (radium-226) is 1,600 years, and that for radioactive iodine (iodine-128) is 25 minutes. Any other phenomenon in which numbers or intensity diminish in accordance with an *exponential function can be said to have a half-life. For example, a drug injected into the body has a certain half-life; after this time its concentration in the body's tissues is halved.

**halide**, a chemical compound of a *halogen with another element or group. The halides are typically ionic, for example, sodium fluoride ($Na^+F^-$), but there are examples that exhibit covalent bonding, such as aluminium chloride ($AlCl_3$). There are many naturally occurring mineral forms including *halite and *fluorite, which frequently occur as precipitates resulting from the evaporation of saline waters.

**halite** (rock-salt), an *evaporite mineral formed by the evaporation of *brine. It is the chief source of table salt. It is sodium chloride (NaCl) occurring as crystals which are soft, light, and fragile and usually colourless or white. It is found worldwide, notably in Stassfurt (Germany) and Louisiana and Texas (USA); and although soluble it occurs also beneath the sea, notably the Mediterranean and Red Seas, where it is protected by overlying impervious sediments, and where it provides incontrovertible evidence that at some time in their history these seas were repeatedly evaporated to dryness to form *evaporite deposits well over 1 km (0.62 mile) thick.

**Hall, James** (1811–98), US geologist who provided an acceptable theory of mountain-building based on a study of the elevation of *geosynclines. It arose out of work on the sedimentary origin of the Appalachians, to which he was led by his lifelong ambition: a composite record of all fossils found below Upper Carboniferous strata throughout the USA.

**halo**, atmospheric: a short-lived, incomplete ring of bright light, with the Sun or Moon at its centre, caused by the random refraction of light by ice crystals in high cloud. More complete rings and other complex features such as mock suns and sun pillars may be formed if the ice crystals have a preferred orientation and concentrate the light. Examples of these are prisms of ice with their long, horizontal axes and plates with horizontal bases. The shape and appearance of haloes vary with the Sun's elevation and the orientation of the ice crystals.

**halocarbon**, an organic compound derived from a *hydrocarbon, in which one or more hydrogen atoms are replaced by *halogen atoms. Examples are the *chlorofluorocarbons, and the fluorocarbons. The latter are chemically unreactive and tetrafluoroethene, $C_2F_4$, forms a *polymer, polytetrafluoroethene, known as teflon or PTFE; Teflon is a suitable material for containers of corrosive substances such as hydrogen fluoride, HF. In contrast, halocarbons containing the other halogens are more reactive and toxic. The main reaction they undergo is nucleophilic substitution, in which the nucleophile displaces the halogen as the halide ion. For example, chloromethane, $CH_3Cl$, reacts with hydroxide ions, $OH^-$, to form methanol, $CH_3OH$, and chloride ions, $Cl^-$.

**halogen**, an element of Group VII in the *periodic table, namely fluorine, chlorine, bromine, iodine, and astatine. They are all non-metals, fluorine and chlorine being gases, bromine a volatile liquid, and iodine a solid, at room temperature; astatine is a radioactive element, with a *half-life too short to permit detailed study of its chemistry. Halogens are reactive elements. They do not occur free in nature, but in compounds such as sodium chloride (common salt). They react with most elements, forming the corresponding *halide, their reactivity decreasing down the periodic group.

**Hamersley Range**, the main mountain range of Western Australia, lying between the Fortescue and Ashburton Rivers. It stretches for some 274 km (170 miles) west–east and reaches heights of 1,226 m (4,024 feet) at Mount Bruce and 1,236 m (4,056 feet) at Mount Meharry. Brightly coloured sandstone rock covered sparsely with vegetation predominates, and there are dramatic gorges with sides that descend step by step. The rock is mainly sedimentary, but igneous intrusions have resulted in rich deposits of iron ore and blue asbestos.

**Hamilton, Sir William Rowan** (1806–65), Irish mathematician and physicist who made influential contributions in optics, particularly in the study of *refraction, and in the foundations of algebra. He produced a rigorous treatment of

The Yellowstone River cascading over the Lower Falls in Yellowstone National Park, Wyoming, USA, forms a **hanging valley**. The photograph was taken by William Jackson on the Hayden Expedition, 1871.

*complex numbers as pairs of real numbers and discovered an algebra of quadruples (quaterions) that described the transformation of vectors in space. His approach to mathematical physics was the only classical approach that met the needs of *quantum theory. He was appointed Professor of Astronomy at Trinity College, Dublin, while still an undergraduate, but later he became a recluse.

**hanging valley**, a (usually tributary) valley which has not had its floor cut down to the level of the valley or plain it joins. In glaciated mountains hanging valleys represent the former channels of small glaciers which could not dig their beds as deeply as the main glacier they merged with. They also occur along fault lines where blocks of land have been suddenly uplifted, disrupting river channels. The step below a hanging valley is often the site of a waterfall.

**hardness of water**, the presence of calcium or magnesium compounds in water. When soap is added to hard water, an insoluble scum is formed instead of a lather; this is because soap contains sodium stearate, which reacts with calcium and magnesium ions, forming the insoluble calcium or magnesium stearate. This leaves less stearate available for combining with the dirt it is meant to remove. Hard water is often found in areas containing chalk or limestone. If hard water contains calcium or magnesium hydrogencarbonate, then it can be softened by boiling, as the soluble hydrogencarbonate decomposes to the insoluble carbonate, which is precipitated out and is the fur found in kettles. The water is called temporarily hard. Water containing calcium or magnesium chlorides or sulphates cannot be softened by boiling, as these compounds do not decompose; such water is called permanently hard. Permanent hardness can be removed by the addition of sodium carbonate or washing-soda, or by the use of *zeolites.

**hardpan** (duricrust), a hardened or cemented layer which occurs in or below the soil *profile. Hardpans are formed when material is washed out of the upper part of the soil by eluviation and redeposited as a distinct horizon lower down. Nodules of cemented material, or *concretions, formed by the same process may represent the beginning of hardpan formation. Hardpans vary in thickness from a few millimetres to a metre or more, depending on how long they have been forming. Many different substances can act as cementing agents. The most common are iron, silica, calcium carbonate, clay, and humus. Thick ironpans are formed by iron and aluminium oxide accumulation in *latosols, producing a material known as laterite. Laterite is used in Indo-China as a building material, because cut blocks become very hard when dried. Calcium carbonate hardpans are known by many names, such as calcrete, caliche, kunkar, and travertine. They are common in desert soils and *sierozems. Humus-cemented hardpans, which are also called orstein and coffee rock, are found in *podzols, where they occur above thin pans of iron and clay. Most hardpans are impermeable and so they profoundly affect the drainage of water through the soil profile.

**Hare, Robert** (1781–1858), US chemist who is mainly remembered for the apparatus he devised for comparing the densities of two liquids. The liquids are drawn up separate vertical tubes by sucking on a mouthpiece connected to both. The densities of the liquids are in inverse proportion to the heights raised.

**harmattan**, a parching, dry wind which blows southwestward in winter from the Saharan centre of West Africa towards and over the tropical Atlantic coasts. Sometimes it is accompanied by dust storms, picked up in the desert, and generally it feels cooler than the hot, humid climate of the coasts.

**Harz Mountains**, a wooded range that straddles the former border between Lower Saxony and Magdeburg about 58 km (36 miles) south of Brunswick (Braunschweig) in Germany. It trends from north-west to south-east and is about 100 km (60 miles) long and 30 km (18 miles) wide. Geologically the mountains are the eroded stumps of a faulted block of ancient resistant rocks. They reach their highest elevation in the Brocken, which is developed on granite and which reaches to 1,142 m (3,759 feet). Legend has it that the bleak summit of the Brocken is the scene of a witches' gathering on Walpurgis Night, 30 April.

**Hawaii** (US), the largest of a score of volcanic islands lying on a ridge in the central Pacific Ocean at around latitude 21° N., longitude 157° W. Together they comprise the US state of the same name. They lie in what is known as the Molokai fracture zone. Only seven islands (Hawaii, Oahu, Maui, Kaui, Molokai, Lanai, and Nihau) are inhabited, and of these Hawaii and Maui are very mountainous. Mauna Kea and Mauna Loa on Hawaii rise to more than 4,160 m (13,650 feet). The volcanic soils, produced from old lava-flows, are very fertile, and the climate is wet and very warm. These natural conditions yield a variety crops, including sugar cane, bananas, pineapples, and coffee.

**Hayden, Ferdinand Vandiveer** (1829–87), US geologist, who was largely responsible for creating Yellowstone National Park. He began with a series of investigations of the Far West in 1856, and for twelve years from 1867 was geologist-in-charge of surveys in the Rocky Mountain region, where he found extensive mineral resources. His works, such as the *Geological and Geographical Atlas of Colorado* (1877), covered all aspects of natural history.

**haze**, a suspension of solid particles, such as smoke and dust, in the atmosphere. Normally it does not reduce visibility to less than 1 km (0.6 mile), but when encountered in deserts or in industrial areas the density of the dust may obscure objects closer at hand. It differs from mist in appearing bluish or yellowish.

**heat**, a form of energy which manifests itself in a system or a body by imparting extra motion to its constituent atoms or molecules. In a gas or a liquid additional heat makes the molecules move around more rapidly; in a solid, in which the atoms vibrate about fixed points in space, extra heat increases the amplitude of these vibrations. Heat may be generated in many ways. It can be produced in chemical reactions, for example when a fuel reacts with oxygen in the air, and by *friction. The passing of an electric current generates heat, because the electrons carrying the current collide with imperfections in the conductor and at each collision heat results. Energy carried by electromagnetic waves as infra-red radiation is converted into heat when absorbed: so the rays of the Sun warm the Earth. The kinetic energy of particles emitted by radioactive substances can be converted into heat when they are slowed down; this process is used in nuclear power stations. Heat may be transferred from a point of high temperature to one of low temperature by *conduction, *convection, or *radiation. It may melt a solid into a liquid and evaporate a liquid. Heat generally causes *expansion of matter.

**heat capacity**, the quantity of heat energy required to raise the temperature of a body by one degree Celsius. It depends on the material of which the body is made and on its mass. The heat capacity for unit mass (1 kg), the specific heat capacity, is tabulated for most materials; and the heat capacity of any body can be calculated by multiplying this by the mass of the body.

**heat waves**, prolonged spells of unusually hot, dry weather, are usually associated with stable, anticyclonic conditions. In mid-latitudes in the northern hemisphere they are normally caused by *anticyclones blocking the eastward movement of depressions, while on the western side of such anticyclones tropical continental or tropical maritime air is transported polewards from low latitudes. It is a phenomenon of summer. When temperatures reach 30 °C (86 °F) people suffer the risk of heatstroke or sunstroke, given lengthy exposure with physical activity. The actual temperature at which the risk of heatstroke occurs depends, however, on the relative humidity of the air; and this is largely a function of general climate. A temperature of 27 °C (81 °F) with a relative humidity of 100 per cent causes as much stress as one of 35 °C (95 °F) and a relative humidity of 10 per cent. In many parts of the world intense desiccation accompanies prolonged heatwaves. It creates conditions favourable to widespread fires, such as the devastating ones which affected thousands of square kilometres of bush and cropland in eastern Australia in 1982.

**Heaviside–Kennelly layer**, the region of the *ionosphere between about 90 and 120 km (60–75 miles) above the Earth. Discovered in 1902 independently by Oliver Heaviside (1850–1925) in the UK and Arthur Kennelly (1861–1939) in the USA (where it is more commonly known as the Kennelly layer), it reflects medium-frequency waves and makes possible long-distance radio communication by reflecting *radio waves. At night the layer becomes considerably weaker.

**heavy water**   *water.

**Hebrides**, two groups of islands (Inner and Outer) off the north-west coast of Scotland. The Inner Hebrides include Skye, Mull, Jura, and Islay (the four largest), and Rhum, Eigg, and the island of Iona among many others. The Outer Hebrides or Western Isles, which lie in an arc beyond the Little Minch channel and the Sea of the Hebrides, include Lewis and Harris (the name of a single island), North and South Uist (two islands), Benbecula, and Barra in the south. Formed of Lewisian *gneiss, they are one of the oldest rock formations in the world. Over a hundred out of the total of some 500 are habitable. All have been fashioned and scoured by glaciation. There are few trees anywhere. The climate is mild, the scenery is beautiful, and there are rare geological structures.

The coastline of Kauai—one of the islands that make up the island chain of **Hawaii**. The high rugged cliffs contrast with beaches of black volcanic sand.

**Heisenberg, Werner Karl** (1901–76), German physicist who, following James *Chadwick's discovery of the neutron in 1932, was the first to develop a detailed theory of the *nucleus of the atom, using the idea that it consists of neutrons and protons. He is chiefly remembered, however, for the *uncertainty principle, which he proposed in 1925, and for which he won the Nobel Prize for Physics in 1932. The principle plays a key role in quantum *mechanics—the present-day theory which describes the behaviour of the elementary particles in the atom.

**Helgoland**, two small islands in the Deutsche Bucht (German Bay) of the North Sea, off the coast of Germany. An important German naval base in both World Wars, the island area consists of a level, sandstone cliff plateau and a low sandy island eastwards.

**helium** (symbol He, at. no. 2, r.a.m. 4.0), a colourless, odourless gas; it is one of the *noble gases, and forms no true chemical compounds. Although it occurs to a small extent on Earth, it was first discovered in the Sun from the analysis of the solar spectrum; and it is widespread in stars, where it is formed from hydrogen by nuclear fusion. Helium liquefies at −268 °C (−514 °F), and remains a liquid down to absolute zero; it can only be solidified under pressure. At −271 °C (−520 °F) it becomes a superfluid; its viscosity disappears, and its thermal conductivity becomes very high. Helium is found in ores of uranium and thorium but the main source of the element is natural gas, from which it is obtained by liquefaction of all the other components; it is

Its low relative molecular mass of only 4 and its chemical inertness, which precludes the risk of fire, make **helium** the most suitable gas for providing buoyancy in modern airships.

used to provide an inert atmosphere in welding, for buoyancy in balloons, and as a coolant. Mixed with oxygen, it forms a breathing mixture which reduces the danger of 'the bends' for divers.

**Helmholtz, Hermann Ludwig Ferdinand von** (1821–94), German scientist who, during a distinguished and varied career in both physics and physiology, invented the ophthalmoscope used by opticians, did much to advance the study of *thermodynamics and the law of *conservation of energy, and developed a theory of *sound. He devised a two-coil system for producing a uniform magnetic field, and carried out research into the properties of oscillating electric currents. This research was continued by his assistant, Heinrich *Hertz, who discovered radio waves as a result.

**hematite**    *haematite.

**henry** (symbol H) the *SI unit of inductance, defined as that which gives an electromotive force of one volt in a closed circuit with a rate of change of one ampere per second. It is named after the US physicist Joseph Henry (1797–1878).

**Henry's law** (in chemistry), a gas law which states that at a constant temperature the mass of gas dissolved by a given volume of liquid is proportional to the pressure of the gas in equilibrium with the solution. The law, which is named after William Henry (1774–1836), is valid only if there is no chemical reaction between the gas and the liquid.

**Henry the Navigator** (1394–1460), Portuguese prince, son of John I, who inspired many voyages of exploration among the Atlantic islands and down the west African coast. As governor of the Algarve he established a school of navigation, astronomy, and cartography for his captains, the search for a new route to the Indies being his objective. The efforts of his captains, who reached as far south as Cape Verde and the Azores, laid the groundwork for later Portuguese exploration south-east round Africa to the Far East.

**Hercynian episode**, an *orogeny, a period of land movements in Europe in late Palaeozoic times (from the *Carboniferous to the *Permian) that caused the uplift and formation of a series of mountains in Europe (including the Harz, from which it takes its name).

**hertz** (symbol Hz), the SI unit of *frequency: one hertz is one cycle every *second. The unit is named after Heinrich Hertz, the German physicist who in 1888 first demonstrated the existence of radio waves, theoretically predicted several years earlier by James Clerk *Maxwell.

**Hertz, Heinrich Rudolf** (1857–94), German physicist and a pioneer of radio communication, who was the first to broadcast and receive radio waves. He worked for a time as Hermann *Helmholtz's assistant in Berlin. He began his world-famous study of electromagnetic waves in 1886. James Clerk *Maxwell had predicted the existence of these waves in his electromagnetic theory; Hertz demonstrated this experimentally, and also the fact that these waves behaved like light and radiant heat, thus proving that these phenomena, too, were electromagnetic. In 1889 he was appointed professor of physics at Bonn, where he continued his research on the discharge of electricity in rarefied gases.

**Hess, Germain Henri** (1802–50), Swiss-born Russian chemist, who applied the first law of *thermodynamics to the heat changes accompanying a chemical reaction and formulated the law of constant heat summation. This states that the net heat evolved or absorbed during a chemical reaction is independent of the path taken and depends only on the initial and final stages.

**Hess, Victor Franz (Francis)** (1883–1964), Austrianborn US physicist who divided his academic career between Austria and the USA. His research interests in atmospheric *electricity and *radioactivity culminated in the discovery of *cosmic rays, which led to the discovery of the positively-

A portrait of **Henry the Navigator** taken from a detail of the painting *At the Altar of Saint Vincent*, by the Portuguese artist Nuno Goncalves. In 1419 Henry the Navigator established a school of navigation in the Algarve close to Cape Saint Vincent overlooking the Atlantic Ocean.

The world's highest mountain system, the **Himalayas** stretches across several Indian states and the kingdoms of Nepal and Bhutan. The mountains are associated with many legends in Asian mythology. On their isolated slopes are found the retreats of *rishis* (sages), *gurus* (teachers), and Tibetan monks.

charged electron or positron by the American physicist Carl Anderson (1905–  ). They shared the 1936 Nobel Prize for Physics.

**heteroatoms** (in chemistry), atoms of any elements, other than carbon and hydrogen, which occur in organic molecules. The most common heteroatoms are the halogens, oxygen, nitrogen, sulphur, and phosphorus. Most *functional groups contain at least one heteroatom. For example, the carbonyl group in aldehydes and ketones consists of a double bond between a carbon atom and an oxygen atom, as, for instance, in the molecule of methanal (or formaldehyde), $H_2C=O$.

**high** (in meteorology), a region of relatively high atmospheric pressure, as measured at ground level. Highs occur either in the form of the migratory anticyclones of the mid-latitude regions or as semi-permanent centres of high pressure. The *Siberian High and the *subtropical highs are examples of the latter.

**High Plains**, the higher part of the Great Plains of North America, extending along the eastern foothills of the Rocky Mountains. They coincide closely with the distribution of *Tertiary formations, and are covered with a mantle of river- and wind-borne deposits which vary in depth. It is a rolling landscape, much given to prairie farming, although until the mid-19th century it was considered too arid to be habitable and was known as the Great American Desert.

**Hilbert, David** (1862–1943), German mathematician who epitomizes, and did more than anyone else to produce, the changes in mathematics that occurred around the turn of the century. He proved fundamental theorems about rings and their ideals, he collected, systematized, and extended all that was then known about algebraic numbers, he reorganized the axiomatic foundations of geometry, he set potential theory and the theory of integral equations on its modern course with his invention of Hilbert space (an infinite-dimensional analogue of Euclidean space), and he formulated the formalist philosophy of mathematics and mathematical logic. At the International Congress of Mathematicians in Paris in 1900 Hilbert proposed 23 problems which, as he had hoped, crystallized mathematical thinking for the next few decades.

**hill**, a low upland, smaller than a mountain (but whether an upland is considered a hill or mountain depends on the scale of the local scenery: most mountains in the UK would be classified as hills in North America or New Zealand). Most hills are formed by the erosion of the weaker strata of rock mainly by rivers and glaciers, although they can also be created by volcanic eruptions or through the deposition of material by glaciers, glacial melt-water, or the wind. In *permafrost areas, small hills known as 'pingos' are formed by the growth of large lenses of ice, doming up the ground surface above.

**Himalayas** (Sanskrit, 'abode of snow'), the highest mountain system in the world, forming the southern rim of the Tibetan plateau in central Asia. Extending in an arc some 2,400 km (1,500 miles) long, the mountains began to be formed by folding 40 million years ago when the Indian subcontinent thrust northward against the main Asian land mass. The northern range is the highest: it contains Nanga Parbat in the extreme north-west and Everest, the world's highest mountain, and Kanchenjunga towards the east. South of centre is Annapurna. On clear days their ice-covered summits shine brilliantly in the rarefied air; but gales and storms are frequent, blowing long trails of ice particles off the peaks and ridges. The snow-line descends to about 4,600 m (15,000 feet), while glaciers descend below it for around 1,200 m (3,900 feet). The mountains comprise *granites, *gneisses, and ancient *sedimentary rocks The ranges form a climatic barrier: the rain-bearing winds of the south-west *monsoon rarely cross into Tibet, nor can winter winds from north Asia reach India. Whereas the glaciated southern slopes feed the Indus, Ganges, and Brahmaputra with melted snow, the northern slopes are comparatively dry, the smaller rivers here being the Sutlej which runs west and the Tsangpo (the upper reaches of the Brahmaputra) running east. The vegetation of the southern valleys varies from coniferous and alpine around the beautiful Vale of Kashmir, with its fruit trees and lakes, to temperate and sub-tropical rain forest in the east. While access to the system's mineral deposits is severely limited, the full and fast-flowing southern rivers offer much scope for the development of hydroelectricity.

**Hindu Kush**, the mountain range of northern Pakistan and Afghanistan, an extension of the Himalayas, running for some 800 km (500 miles) south-westward from the Pamirs. One of the world's highest ranges, its loftiest peak is Tirich Mir at 7,692 m (25,236 feet). The region is glaciated and receives heavy snowfall; the mountains are permanently snow-covered, and their melt-waters feed the headstreams of the Indus and Amu Darya Rivers. There is little vegetation and the foothills are generally barren except in wooded Nuristan. The Hindu Kush is crossed by passes, one or two of which are over 5,000 m (16,400 feet) high. Among the major routes are the Baroghil, Dorah, and Khawak Passes, and the Shikar Pass, which is a gorge.

**Hispaniola**, the second largest of the Caribbean Islands, divided between two countries (the Dominican Republic and Haiti), and lying between Cuba and Puerto Rico. In the centre, mountains rise to about 3,000 m (9,900 feet), and north-east *trade winds bring heavy rain to the windward slopes. On the coastal plains the climate is tropical, a hot and wet 30 °C (86 °F) for much of the year. Sugar cane, coffee, cocoa, and tobacco are grown, while bauxite is the main mineral resource.

**histogram**, a type of diagrammatic graph in which data are grouped in some way, and columns of equal width are drawn such that their heights represent the relative frequency of occurrence within each group. For example, in a sample of 100 people, one-tenth (0.1) of the sample may have heights in the range 180–190 cm (36–38 inches). Thus the relative frequency of heights in this range is 0.1, and this would be represented by a column of height 0.1. The column would be centred on the mid-point of the range (185 cm; 37 inches) on a horizontal axis. The range is indicated by the column width. A histogram consists of the complete set of such columns for a particular sample.

**histosol**, a highly organic soil which forms on poorly drained sites. Peaty histosols occur in cold climates where the soil is saturated with water for most of the year and the decomposition of plant remains is therefore extremely slow. They tend to be very thick, acidic, and low in plant nutrients. Such soils commonly occur in the Canadian muskeg and in central Siberia. Histosols are also found in mid-latitudes, typically on former glacial lake-floors. Commonly called mucks, these are relatively thick accumulations of fine-grained, sticky black material. Muck soils tend to be nutrient-rich and are often used intensively for agriculture.

**hoar-frost**  *frost.

**Hofmann, August Wilhelm von** (1818–92), German chemist who discovered several organic compounds, isolated benzene from coal-tar, and gave his name to a number of reactions, including the conversion of *amides to primary *amines. When the Royal College of Chemistry was established in London in 1845 he was appointed superintendent, and was later chemist at the Royal Mint. After twenty years of invaluable work in England, he became Professor of Chemistry at Berlin.

**hogback**, a long, steep hill which falls away abruptly on either side, resembling the back of a wild boar. Hogbacks are related to *escarpments, but occur on rocks which are dipping nearly vertically on both sides; some escarpments become hogbacks as the dip slope steepens. The valleys on either side of hogbacks are cut by rivers wearing away softer layers of rock.

**Hokkaido**, the northernmost and second-largest of the four main islands that make up Japan. It is separated from Honshu Island by the Tsugara Strait and from Sakhalin

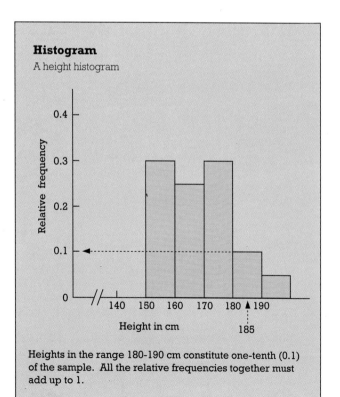

**Histogram**

A height histogram

*Height in cm*

*Relative frequency*

Heights in the range 180-190 cm constitute one-tenth (0.1) of the sample. All the relative frequencies together must add up to 1.

**Hofmann**'s *Introduction to Modern Chemistry* (1865) was a classic textbook that led to great reforms in the teaching of chemistry. His research contributed greatly to the development of the aniline dye industry.

Island in Russia by the Soya Strait. Volcanic and mountainous, its interior rises to 2,289 m (7,511 feet) in Asahi-dake. The Ishikari, the second longest river of Japan, crosses western Hokkaido. The island is heavily forested and has coal, iron, and manganese. Hokkaido is one of the major fishing centres of the world.

**Holocene Epoch**, or Recent Epoch, the later of the two geological epochs into which the *Quaternary Period is divided: the period of geological time from 10,000 years ago to the present. During this period, human intervention has considerably modified the landscape.

**homologous series** (in chemistry), a group of organic compounds with the same general molecular formula. Each member of a series has one more carbon atom than the previous one. An example is provided by the *alkanes, for which the general molecular formula is $C_nH_{2n+2}$, where $n$ is a whole number.

**Honduras**, a Central American country with a long, north-east coast on the Caribbean Sea and a short, south-west coast on the Pacific Ocean. It is bounded on the north and west by Guatemala and El Salvador and on the south by Nicaragua. Most of it is mountainous and heavily forested, and it is rich in minerals yielding zinc, lead, and silver. The soil is generally poor and acid, but it yields some tropical crops. The climate varies with altitude but is predominantly tropical.

**Hong Kong**, collective name for a small part (Kowloon and the New Territories) of the south-east coast of China, the island of Hong Kong itself, and nearly 200 outlying islands of which Lantau is the largest. It is situated at the mouth of the Xi Jiang (Pearl River) and has a total area of 1,060 km² (410 sq. mi.). Hong Kong island rises steeply to a series of peaks, the highest being Victoria Peak at 560 m (1,840 feet). The New Territories have higher mountains and much of the land is too steep for agriculture or settlement. The climate is subtropical: spring is usually humid, summer is hot and very wet, *typhoons sometimes occurring, while autumn is cooler and drier, and in winter the temperature can drop below 10 °C (50 °F).

**Honshu**, the largest island of Japan, being about 320 km (200 miles) wide and about 1,600 km (1,000 miles) long. Its generally mountainous relief results from its formation in an island arc. In the north are chains of young folded mountains rising to 2,400 m (8,000 feet), with many volcanoes. In the central region several structural trends meet to produce the highest mountains of Japan, rising to 3,776 m (12,388 feet) at Mount Fujiyama. The Shinano-gawa, the longest river of Japan, crosses central Honshu. The climate ranges from snowy winters in the north to the subtropical in the south. Rice, cotton, fruits, and cereals are grown, and the bulk of Japan's tea and silk come from Honshu. Running north–south through this region is the great *fault trough of the Fossa Magna. The high relief and narrow width combine to produce steep, energetic streams, feeding many hydroelectric plants.

**hoodoo**   *pedestal rock.

**Hooke's law**, the law of elasticity which states that when a material is stretched, the change in length of the material is directly proportional to the stretching force applied. If an object can be deformed under pressure and then regains its original shape when the pressure is removed, then the object is elastic. Hooke's law describes this elastic behaviour: it was first used to describe the deformation of a spring. It only holds for forces up to a particular value—beyond this limit the material will not return to its original length when the force is removed. The limit beyond which the law does not apply is called the elastic limit.

Hooke's law was named after its discoverer, Robert Hooke (1635–1703), who was assistant to Robert *Boyle at the Royal Society, still the most prestigious society of scientists in the UK. It was at the Royal Society that he developed his law of elasticity. He also proposed an early theory of gravitation, and the idea that light might be in the form of waves. Isaac *Newton later presented fuller and more developed treatments of both these ideas. Hooke developed many pieces of apparatus which enabled others to make fundamental discoveries: his air pump enabled Boyle to do the experiments which led to Boyle's contribution to the *gas laws.

**horizon**, the apparent boundary between the sky and the visible surface of the Earth, from the Greek *horizōn kuklos*, 'limiting circle'. Obstructions such as buildings and nearby hills are usually ignored and regarded as concealing the horizon rather than determining it. At sea the distance to the horizon depends on the height of the observer. If his eyes are $h$ m above sea-level, the distance $d$ of the horizon (in km) is given by the simple formula $d = 3.6\sqrt{h}$. (If $h$ is in feet then $d$ in miles is $1.2\sqrt{h}$.) In practice one can see a little further

The **Huang He**, or Yellow River, loaded with the yellow silt from which it gets its name. The river's many changes of course across the lowland plains of China have laid down fertile deposits over more than 14 million hectares (35 million acres) of land.

because of the *refraction of light by the atmosphere. In astronomy a different definition of horizon is used. An elevated observer, instead of looking slightly down to the sea-level horizon, looks exactly horizontally to the celestial horizon; this is not the visible horizon, but is a useful concept in astronomical and navigational work.

**horizon, soil**, a distinct layer, roughly parallel to the surface of the land, within the soil *profile. Horizons can normally be distinguished one from another by characteristic differences in physical or chemical composition, organic content, texture, or structure. The formation of horizons results from the action of soil-forming processes on weathered rock material through time. There are three major horizons. The near-surface mineral layer, in which organic matter tends to accumulate, is known as the A-horizon of the soil; but because clay and minerals such as iron and aluminium are often washed out of it by *eluviation, it is sometimes also called the E-horizon. Beneath this is the B-horizon; here the minerals washed out from above accumulate. Lastly, the partially weathered rock material at the base of the soil is termed the C-horizon. Distinct layers within each of these major horizons are identified by means of numerical subscripts. The A-horizon, for example, can often be subdivided into a highly organic layer (an $A_0$-horizon), a less organic and partially leached region ($A_1$),

and a bleached zone from which most of the iron and aluminium has been washed out ($A_2$). The recognition of horizons is an important step in understanding the formation of different soils.

**Horn, Cape**, the southernmost point of South America. It is a headland in the archipelago of *Tierra del Fuego, south of the Strait of Magellan. Standing 424 m (1,391 feet) high, it is part of the ancient volcanic chain which extends from the Andes to South Georgia. It is infamous for the violence of the sea, 'rounding the Horn' at any time of the year meaning having to face the bitterly cold winds—the *roaring forties—and strong currents which sweep from the Pacific Ocean into the Atlantic. The name is taken from Cape Hoorn, the home in Holland of the chief financial backer of a trading expedition which used the route in 1616.

**hornblende**, a common dark green or black mineral, one of the *amphiboles: a silicate containing calcium, sodium, iron and aluminium. It occurs as hard, lustrous crystals in igneous rocks and in metamorphosed calcareous rocks. It is found notably in Edenville, New York (USA), and Kotaki (Japan), but is of no commercial interest.

**horse latitudes**, ocean belts which lie between the generally westerly winds of the higher latitudes and the *trade winds. They correspond to the zone of *subtropical highs located between 20° and 30° North and South of the Equator. They move northwards in the northern summer and southwards in the southern summer and are characterized by fine, clear weather and light variable winds. The name is believed to come from the practice of throwing the effigy of a dead horse overboard, after sailing for a month or two out of England. This was done to celebrate the end of the 'dead horse' period from signing on, for which seamen had been paid in advance and during which it was no use flogging them for extra work.

**horst**, a long plateau with a geological fault on each side. Horsts can form *block mountains and are the geological opposites of *grabens.

**Horton, Robert Elmer** (1875–1945), US engineer, hydrologist and geomorphologist. His work on the infiltration theory of *runoff formed the basis of modern theories of basin hydrology and of river, valley, and slope development. He was one of the first to develop ways of describing landscapes in quantitative terms.

**hot spring**, a spring where hot *groundwater emerges from the land surface, either as a steady trickle into a pool or in a more spectacular way as a *geyser, shooting into the air. Hot, or thermal, springs are caused through the penetration by underground water deep into the Earth, where it is heated to the temperature of the rocks or volcanic magma (molten rock) that it encounters. Hot springs are rich in dissolved minerals and may be classified as sulphate-, chloride-, carbonate-, or acid-bearing water depending on the dissolved mineral. Their healing properties have been recognized since earliest times.

**Hot Springs National Park**, in central Arkansas, USA, a beautifully situated park in the Ouachita Mountains containing over forty thermal springs. Other US resorts with the name 'Hot Springs' are in south-west South Dakota, south-west New Mexico on the Rio Grande, and western Virginia in the Alleghenies. Hot Springs District in New Zealand is in north-central North Island; its chief resort is Rotorua.

**Huang He** (Hwang Ho, Chinese, 'Yellow River'), the great river of north China, flowing for some 4,700 km (2,900 miles) from its source in the Kunlun Mountains of the Tibetan autonomous region to a northern gulf of the Yellow Sea. It runs turbulently at first, through a series of gorges, and once off the plateau turns north to skirt the Ordos desert in a great bend. Forced south again by the Lang Shan highlands it enters *loess country, picking up huge quantities of yellow silt. After receiving its two main tributaries, the Fen He and the Wei He, it turns east through the Sanmen Gorge and so emerges on to the North China Plain. Here it broadens out to become fan-shaped, the yellow silt forming a vast delta which has become one of China's most fertile regions.

**Hudson**, a river rising in the Adirondacks in north-east USA, and flowing south for over 500 km (300 miles) to enter New York Bay. The scenic grandeur of its upper reaches, with their falls and rapids, gives way to wider vistas south of Lake Champlain where it is joined by the Mohawk. From here on it is navigable. The final stretch, called the North River, is linked by the Harlem River to the East River and Long Island Sound.

**Hudson, Henry** (d. 1611), English explorer, discoverer of the North American bay, river, and strait which bear his name. He conducted two voyages in 1607–08 for the English Muscovy Company in search of the North-East Passage to Asia, reaching Greenland and Spitzbergen on the first and Novaya Zemlya on the second. In 1609 he explored the north-east coast of America for the Dutch East Indies Company, sailing 240 km (150 miles) up the Hudson River to Albany. In 1610 he set out on his last voyage, again under English colours, and reached Hudson('s) Bay in the north of Canada. He attempted to winter in the Bay, but when food ran out his men mutinied and set him adrift in a small boat with a few companions—none of them were ever seen again.

**Hudson Bay**, a penetration of the Arctic Ocean, well over 1,000 km (600 miles) into the north-east of the North American continent. Its depression was created when that part of the *Canadian Shield was crushed by Pleistocene ice-sheets. Only the coasts and islands of the southern half are forested. The western shores tend to be low and marshy, the eastern ones rocky and more barren. Many rivers run into the Bay, which is generally navigable from July to October. It connects with the Atlantic Ocean through the Hudson Strait and with the Arctic Ocean through the Foxe Channel. A southern extension, James Bay, intrudes between Ontario and Quebec for nearly 450 km (280 miles) and provides sanctuary for many wild animals.

**Humboldt, Friedrich Heinrich Alexander, Baron von** (1769–1859), German explorer and scientist who travelled for five years in Central and South America (1799–1804) and wrote extensively on natural history, meteorology, and physical geography, financing his expeditions and scientific work out of his own pocket. Accompanied by the French botanist Aimé Bonpland, he proved that the Amazon and Orinoco river systems are connected. He took measurements in the *Peru or Humboldt Current that showed the coldness of the flow in relation to the sea around it. He climbed a number of peaks in the Andean Highlands and was the first to ascribe mountain sickness to lack of oxygen. He established the use of isotherms in map-making and pioneered investigations into the relationship between geographical environment and plant distribution. In 1827 Humboldt returned to his birthplace, Berlin, serving in various capacities at the Prussian court. He wrote a popular work in several volumes, *Kosmos* (1845–62), describing the structure of the universe as it was then known.

**Humboldt Current** *Peru Current.

**humidity**, the degree to which air is moist or damp; it can be measured as absolute humidity or relative humidity. Absolute humidity is the actual mass of *water vapour in a given volume of air and is expressed in terms of $g/m^3$ or grains per cubic foot. Relative humidity is the proportion of this quantity to the mass that would be present if the air were saturated (containing the maximum amount of water vapour) at the same temperature. It is usually expressed as a percentage, completely dry air having a relative humidity of 0 per cent, and fully saturated air one of 100 per cent. In terms of the Earth's atmosphere, relative humidity is the more significant quantity, especially with regard to meteorological processes, biological response, and human comfort. This is because the body's perspiration does not evaporate as readily when the relative humidity is high, so to keep cool in humid heat humans perspire more profusely. In hot weather a fall in humidity can bring as much relief as a fall in temperature. The amount of water vapour which the air is capable of holding before condensation occurs depends on temperature: warm air can contain more water vapour than cold air.

**Hungary**, a central European country, bounded by Czech Lands on the north, Romania on the east, Croatia and Serbia on the south, and Austria on the west; it is also conterminous with Ukraine in the north-east. From north to south through the centre flows the Danube, in a broad plain (the puszta) which extends eastward to the river Tisza across pastureland and areas suited to agriculture. West of the river is the Bakony Forest of mainly deciduous trees, Lake Balaton (the largest and shallowest lake in central Europe), and a fertile plateau with granite hills. There are deposits of lignite, bauxite, and natural gas; and the climate, with cold winters and hot summers, is continental.

**Huron, Lake** *Great Lakes.

**hurricane**, a severe *tropical revolving storm, in particular one in which the wind reaches a speed of 65 knots or more (120 km/h, 75 m.p.h.). A hurricane is also the name sometimes given to a wind of hurricane force on the *Beaufort scale, with a minimum speed as above. Such a wind is not necessarily associated with a tropical revolving storm.

**Hutton, James** (1726–97), British geologist of Scottish extraction who put forward certain views, controversial at the time, that became accepted tenets of modern geology. In opposition to Abraham *Werner's Neptunian theory he emphasized heat as the principal agent in the formation of land masses, and held that rocks such as granite were igneous in origin. He described the processes of deposition and denudation and proposed that such phenomena, operating with roughly equal intensity over millions of years,

A satellite photograph of **hurricane** 'Frederic' crossing the southern states of the USA. The swirling cloud bands and the clear eye of the storm are easily visible.

would account for the present configuration of the Earth's surface; it therefore followed that the Earth was very much older than was generally believed at the time. These conclusions were presented in his *Theory of the Earth* (1785), and met with the hostility of those who accepted the biblical account of the creation of the world. Hutton's writing style was poor, however, and his views did not become widely known until a concise account of them was published by his friend John Playfair in 1802.

**Huygens, Christiaan** (1629–95), Dutch physicist mathematician and astronomer, best known for his pendulum regulated clock invented in 1656. He improved the lenses of his telescope, discovered a satellite of Saturn, and also the latter's rings, which had eluded *Galileo. In dynamics he studied such topics as as centrifugal force and the problem of colliding bodies, but his greatest contribution was his wave theory of light, made public in 1678. He formulated what has become known as 'Huygen's pinciple', that every point on a wave front is the centre of a new wave, and this allowed him to explain the *reflection and *refraction of light, including its double refraction in Iceland spar.

**Hwang Ho** *Huang He.

**hydrate**, a compound which contains *water of crystallization. Hydrates are crystalline solids which contain a definite proportion of water molecules. The water may be held in the crystal in various ways but is loosely bonded, and on warming is driven off, leaving an anhydrous salt. Some common examples include copper(II) *sulphate ($CuSO_4 \cdot 5H_2O$) and washing soda ($Na_2CO_3 \cdot 10H_2O$). If the salt contains a *transition metal, then there is often a colour change when the water of crystallization is removed: copper(II) sulphate changes from blue to white.

**hydrocarbon**, a compound containing only carbon and hydrogen. Hydrocarbons are classified into the following homologous series; *alkanes, *alkenes, and *alkynes. The principal large-scale source of these is crude oil, containing predominantly alkanes. These can be broken down to smaller alkanes, and also converted to the more industrially useful alkenes by the process of cracking, in which the alkane vapour is passed over a heated catalyst. In general, the type of reactions undergone by hydrocarbons varies from one *homologous series to another.

**hydrochloric acid** (HCl), a strong, corrosive *acid formed when hydrogen chloride gas, HCl, is dissolved in water. Hydrogen chloride gas, which is poisonous and acrid, is prepared commercially by reacting sulphuric acid, $H_2SO_4$, with sodium chloride, NaCl. The acid formed when the gas is dissolved in water reacts vigorously with metals and metal oxides and hydroxides. Hydrochloric acid is widely used in the laboratory as a reagent and in industry in the manufacture of dyes, drugs, and other chemicals.

**hydrodynamics**, the study of the motion of bodies in any fluid, not necessarily water. The fluid is usually an incompressible liquid, motion in gases being the concern of aerodynamics. It is customary to treat the liquid as a continuous medium for the purpose of modelling real situations: for example, the flow of oil in a pipeline, or the performance of submarines. *Archimedes formulated his famous law of flotation while studying the properties of solid bodies immersed in fluids, giving rise to the notion of fluid pressure. Other phenomena that are studied include fluid density, viscosity, and turbulence.

**hydrogen** (symbol H, at. no. 1, r.a.m. 1.01), a colourless, odourless gas which burns readily in air; in its free state it consists of diatomic molecules, $H_2$, and has the lowest density of all gases. It is by far the most abundant element in the universe; the energy of stars comes from the conversion of hydrogen to helium by nuclear fusion. Interstellar space is filled with extremely rarefied hydrogen, mostly in the form of single atoms or ions. On Earth it is less abundant, although it occurs in water, petroleum, coal, and all living matter. Except in negligible quantities, it does not occur naturally as a free element. It reacts with metals to form compounds which contain the $H^-$ ion, and with non-metals to give covalent compounds; in this respect it is similar to the *halogens. However, some of its compounds when dissolved in water give $H^+$ ions; and here hydrogen resembles the *alkali metal elements. In consequence it is not placed in a group in the periodic table. $H^+$ ions cause acidity; the pH of a solution is related to the *hydrogen ion concentration. Hydrogen is formed industrially from steam or oxygen and methane, or from steam and coke. It is used in the manufacture of ammonia, methanol, and petrochemicals, and in the hydrogenation of foodstuffs, such as the manufacture of margarine. It is no longer used for filling large balloons; it has been replaced by helium, which has less lifting power, but is not flammable.

**hydrogen bond**, a weak bond between a hydrogen atom in one molecule and an atom in a second molecule (or a different part of the same molecule). Hydrogen bonds only form in certain circumstances: both the atom to which the hydrogen atom is linked in its own molecule, and the atom in the second molecule, must be strongly *electronegative (fluorine, oxygen, or nitrogen). The resulting attraction is a

The exceptionally low density of **hydrogen** made such gas very attractive to the designers of airships, but the tragic end of the *Hindenburg* as it approached its mooring mast, at Lakehurst, New Jersey, in 1937 demonstrated another, less welcome property of the gas: it is also highly flammable.

hydrogen bond, the strongest of the *intermolecular forces. A result of hydrogen bonding is a high melting-point and boiling-point. A compound is likely to dissolve in a solvent with which it can form hydrogen bonds. Ethanol can form a hydrogen bond with water, so it mixes readily with water. In contrast, ethane cannot, so it is insoluble. The complex structure of many biological molecules is a result of hydrogen bonding. For example, the helical structure of many proteins results, to a large extent, from hydrogen bonding between different parts of the helix.

**hydrogen ion concentration**, a measure of the number of hydrogen ions present in a litre of solution. Although these ions are produced by the *dissociation of acids, the concentrations are still small. They are therefore expressed as the logarithm of the reciprocal of the actual hydrogen ion concentration $[H^+]$. This measure is called the pH (an abbreviation for 'potential of Hydrogen'), and is expressed mathematically as $pH = -\log [H^+]$. It can be determined absolutely using a glass electrode, or less accurately by using coloured *indicators and a calibrated scale. In alkali solutions the concentration is so small that very sensitive equipment is needed to obtain a meaningful measurement. The rate of many chemical reactions in solution, particularly those in the body, depends critically on the hydrogen ion concentration; it is carefully controlled and stabilized in *buffer solutions. In neutral solutions the pH works out at 7; a greater concentration of hydrogen ions means that the solution is acidic and has a pH less than 7, while a lesser concentration makes it alkaline with a pH greater than 7. The digestive juices have a pH of about 1.4, rainwater (mildly acidic) about 6.5, and lime water 10.5.

**hydrogen peroxide** ($H_2O_2$), a colourless liquid which is miscible with water. It is a strong *oxidizing agent; when concentrated it is used in rocket fuels, and in dilute solution as a disinfectant and as a bleach for textiles and hair. It decomposes on heating, or in the presence of a catalyst, giving water and oxygen. With organic compounds it reacts to give peroxides, which are used to initiate polymerization.

**hydrogen sulphide** (H$_2$S), a colourless, poisonous gas. Natural gas and volcanic emissions contain hydrogen sulphide, and it is produced by putrefying organic matter, such as bad eggs. Its foul smell is characteristic of stink bombs.

**hydrograph**, a graph which records river discharge. The quantity of water passing through a measured cross-section is gauged at fixed time intervals—every minute, every hour, or every day—and its value is then plotted on the vertical axis of the graph, while the time is plotted on the horizontal one. The shape of hydrographs varies with the state of flow: *floods give sharp peaks; *base flow gives only gentle variations in form. 'Unit' hydrographs are specially standardized versions which allow hydrologists to compare the behaviour of *drainage basins of different sizes.

**hydrography**, the science of surveying and charting all the Earth's surface waters. Charts of the sea and the navigable parts of rivers show for shipping not only the depth of water but also the range of tides, the speed and direction of currents, the shape of the shoreline with its shelf, and sometimes the nature of the bottom. Submarine developments, such as the search for oil and natural gas, have latterly increased the need for oceanographic data of all kinds.

**hydrological cycle**, the continuous, cyclic movement of water molecules between oceans, atmosphere, and land, little water being gained from volcanic eruptions or lost to the upper atmosphere. The transfers involve changes of state between vapour, liquid, and solid, and the energy producing these changes comes from heat derived from solar radiation. Water itself is a major heat store, so its cycling involves transfers of heat. The oceans store 97 per cent of all the water in the system. This moves slowly between the Equator and the poles, and between the surface and abyssal depths, as currents driven both by winds and by differences in temperature and salinity. Of the remaining 3 per cent of global water stores, 2.25 per cent is locked in glaciers and ice-caps, perhaps for thousands of years. A further 0.75 per cent is stored in rivers, lakes, and as groundwater, while only 0.001 per cent is stored in the atmosphere. Movement of water between these stores ensures a world-wide annual average of 86 cm (34 inches) of precipitation. Water evaporates from the sea and is carried by winds until it falls as rain, hail, or snow. If it falls into the ocean, the cycle is completed; but if it falls on land, more complex processes occur. Snow must melt into water. Some of the rain is intercepted by plants or buildings and may evaporate. Of that which reaches the surface, some is stored for short periods in hollows and may either evaporate or undergo *infiltration. Some will infiltrate immediately and be stored in the soil. It may subsequently be lost by *evapotranspiration, or it may either travel through the soil as 'throughflow' to rivers or sink to the *water-table and become 'groundwater'. Heavy rain or melting snow may pass as surface *runoff into rivers and lakes. River channels transfer runoff, throughflow, and groundwater from springs, to lakes or the sea, thereby completing the cycle.

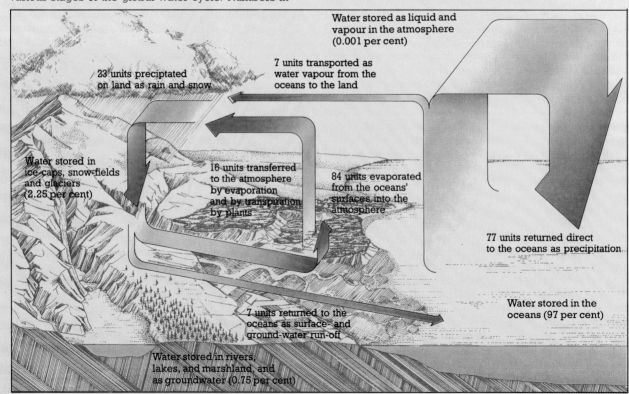

**The hydrological cycle**

Taking the average total exchange of water between the earth's surface and the atmosphere as 100 units, the diagram shows the relative amounts involved in the various stages of the global water cycle. Numbers in parentheses give the approximate percentages of the Earth's free water stored in the oceans, on land, and as water vapour in the atmosphere.

Water stored as liquid and vapour in the atmosphere (0.001 per cent)

23 units precipitated on land as rain and snow

7 units transported as water vapour from the oceans to the land

Water stored in ice-caps, snow-fields and glaciers (2.25 per cent)

16 units transferred to the atmosphere by evaporation and by transpiration by plants

84 units evaporated from the oceans' surfaces into the atmosphere

77 units returned direct to the oceans as precipitation

7 units returned to the oceans as surface- and ground-water run-off

Water stored in the oceans (97 per cent)

Water stored in rivers, lakes, and marshland, and as groundwater (0.75 per cent)

**hydrology**, the science concerned with all water on or near the Earth's surface and especially with the behaviour of fresh water. In planning dams, irrigation schemes, methods of flood control, hydroelectric power projects, or indeed any use of lakes and rivers, understanding is required of variations in the supply and flow of water in a particular place, and of the sediment it carries. Measurements of the changing volume and chemical composition of surface water are related to variations in climatic and ground conditions. Predictions are made of the occurrence of *floods and low flows in rivers. The changing yields of *aquifers and springs are monitored. Modern hydrology dates from the early 20th century, with the development of recording gauges and better understanding of the global energy balance.

**hydrolysis**, a chemical reaction in which a molecule is broken down by water, and the water itself is also decomposed. For example, an ester, such as ethyl ethanoate, $CH_3COOC_2H_5$, reacts with water in the presence of an acid catalyst to form ethanoic acid, $CH_3COOH$, and ethanol, $C_2H_5OH$. One of the hydrogen atoms in the water is incorporated into the ethanol, and the oxygen and the other hydrogen into the ethanoic acid.

**hydrosphere**, the whole body of water that exists on or close to the surface of the Earth. This includes the oceans, seas, lakes, and the water in the atmosphere.

**hydroxide ion** ($OH^-$), an ion found in metal hydroxides. In solution hydroxide ions give rise to alkalinity, and when they are added to the $H^+$ ions present in acidic solutions they form water molecules, and neutralize the acid.

**hydroxyl group**, an oxygen atom covalently bonded to a hydrogen atom. Hydroxyl groups are characteristic of alcohols, phenols, and carboxylic acids. Oxygen has a higher *electronegativity than hydrogen, so a hydroxyl group has a *dipole moment, the hydrogen being the positive end of the dipole. This polarity determines much of the chemistry of the hydroxyl group. For example, under certain circumstances, the hydrogen dissociates as an $H^+$ ion; in other words, the molecule acts as an acid. Because of the high concentration of negative charge on the oxygen, it can act as a *nucleophile, as in the formation of esters.

**hyperbola**, a curve with two distinct but identical sections, called branches, each bounded by *asymptotes. It is obtained by slicing a cone at a steep angle, so is one of the three kinds of *conic section. Alternatively it can be regarded as the locus of points in a plane such that the difference between their distances from two fixed points, the foci, is constant. The simplest algebraic equation for a hyperbola is $x^2/a^2 - y^2/b^2 = 1$; and the asymptotic lines are solutions of $x^2/a^2 - y^2/b^2 = 0$, that is, $y/x = \pm b/a$. If $a = b$ then the asymptotes are at right angles to each other and the curve is called a rectangular hyperbola. The shock wave known as a sonic boom, created by aeroplanes exceeding the speed of sound, is cone-shaped and hits the Earth in a hyperbolic curve. No sound is heard outside this curve, but all places within it will eventually hear the boom.

Hyperbolic functions are analogues of the trigonometric functions *sine, *cosine, and *tangent, but are based on the hyperbola rather than the circle. They are widely used in hyperbolic non-Euclidean geometry in formulae analogous to those using sine and cosine in elliptic geometry. Their definition is in terms of the *exponential function: the hyperbolic sine, $\sinh x = \frac{1}{2}(e^x - e^{-x})$, and $\cosh x = \frac{1}{2}(e^x + e^{-x})$. $\tanh x = \sinh x/\cosh x$, and sech, cosech, and coth are derived on the same basis as the related trigonometrical ratios. The terminology was introduced by the Swiss mathematician Johann Lambert (1728–77) in the 18th century, although not in the context of non-Euclidean geometry despite his intensive studies of that topic.

**hypothesis**, a proposition or assumption, initially not claimed to be true but offered as a basis for further mathematical or scientific deduction. Some of the deductions should be testable. If the test results are consistent with the hypothesis, it is upheld. If the hypothesis is upheld by many different tests, it may become accepted as a theory. This happened to *continental drift. In statistics, a null hypothesis which denies a main hypothesis may be proposed and investigated. For instance, the hypothesis that boys are born with a greater frequency than girls may be tested by proposing the null hypothesis that boys and girls are born with equal frequency. The criterion for rejection of the null hypothesis must be declared. If the null hypothesis is rejected, the main hypothesis is upheld.

# I

**Iberian Peninsula**, the great peninsula of south-west Europe, containing Spain and Portugal. It is separated from the rest of Europe by the Pyrenees and from Africa by the narrow Strait of Gibraltar; its west coast is on the Atlantic Ocean, its east on the Mediterranean Sea. Two-thirds of it comprises a faulted plateau, the Meseta, containing several rugged mountain ranges and drained by five major rivers (among them the Ebro, from which the name of the peninsula is derived). Arid and with hot summers, although cold winters, the climate of the Meseta resembles that of North Africa.

**Ibiza**   *Balearic Islands.

**Ibn Battutah** (*c*.1304–68), Berber explorer, the greatest medieval Arab traveller and author of one of the most notable travel books, the *Rihlah* (Travels), in which he describes his journey of some 120,000 km (75,000 miles) through almost all the Muslim world and many non-Muslim countries. Part of his travels were conducted by caravan to central Asia, where he visited the ancient cities of Bukhara, Samarkand, and Balkh, and continued on to Afghanistan and across the Hindu Kush mountains into India. Ship-

wrecked off the coast of Coromandel, he journeyed on to China, reaching Beijing. On his return to Morocco, he dictated his reminiscences to a writer, Ibn Juzayy, who ornamented his prose style. Deeply rooted in orthodox Islam, Ibn Battuta's observations shed important light on the social, cultural, and political history of the Muslim world of his day.

**ice ages**, periods when the Earth, or part of it, experienced repeated *glaciation and mean temperatures were about 6 °C (13 °F) lower than at present. There is geological evidence for several distinct periods when one or more continents were permanently covered in ice; the most recent began about ten million years ago and often called 'the Ice Age'. Ice ages may be initiated as a result of fluctuations in solar radiation and associated variations in meteorological parameters and *circulation patterns, in combination with tectonic processes and *continental drift. Evidence for the significance of these mechanisms is, however, inconclusive.

**iceberg**, a floating mass of ice, usually a detached portion of a polar *ice-sheet or glacier. As they consist of ice formed on land they are made of freshwater, not frozen seawater. Icebergs may drift for hundreds of kilometres on ocean currents and last for two years or so before melting. Only a ninth of each mass projects above the surface and the coldness of the surrounding sea encourages fog, so they are a great hazard to shipping. But they can be of entrancing beauty: dazzling white pinnacles, caves and cliffs and ledges shadowed blue.

**ice-cap**, a vast, thick dome of land ice which builds up when low temperatures and heavy snowfalls encourage the transformation of snow into ice. The major examples today are in Antarctica and Greenland, now more properly called *ice-sheets because of their great size, but more existed in

The tabular **icebergs** that break away from the shelf ice of Antarctica are characteristically massive, sheer-sided and flat-topped. Large bergs may drift in the ocean currents for many years, gradually being carved into fantastic shapes by melting and wave erosion.

cold periods of the Pleistocene Epoch and they do not necessarily form over high ground: the Greenland cap—more than 3,000 m (10,000 feet) thick at the centre—is located largely over lowland, with mountains at its eastern edge. The sheer weight of the ice depresses the surface beneath, and the ice moves very slowly except where outlet *glaciers spill over mountain rims.

**ice-fall**, a jumbled slope of glacier ice which occurs when a *glacier moves over a sharp drop in the ground surface. The step where a *cirque hangs above a main valley is a common place for ice-falls to develop. The ice is effectively 'stretched' as it moves down the slope and it fractures into large, jagged, unstable blocks. These frequently break away, with explosive cracks or deep rumblings, and shatter when they land. The changing surfaces of ice-falls make them extremely dangerous to cross; the areas at their feet are hazardous too, from falling ice.

**Iceland**, an island country just south of the Arctic Circle in the north-east Atlantic Ocean. It is approximately 460 km (285 miles) long by 280 km (174 miles) wide; but only its coastal areas can be used for settlement and agriculture because the rest is a wasteland of ice, ash, and lava flows. It lies at the edge of the Eurasian *plate, on the *Mid-Atlantic Ridge. A hundred volcanoes rise from it—several to over 1,500 m (5,000 feet)—and there are *geysers and *hot springs. The climate is ameliorated by the *North Atlantic Drift. Sheep graze in the coastal areas, while off the rugged shores there are rich fishing grounds.

**ice-sheet**, a thick mass of moving land ice at least 50,000 km² (19,500 sq. mi.) in extent. The only remaining ones (which are also, colloquially, termed *ice-caps) are in Antarctica and Greenland; but during the cold periods of the Pleistocene Epoch, enormous areas of North America were covered by the Laurentian ice-sheet, and of Europe by the Scandinavian one, each being over 1,000 m (3,000 feet) thick. Formed by a coalescence of ice-caps and glaciers in very cold conditions, when heavy snowfalls encourage the transformation of snow into ice, they can extend out to sea in the form of floating ice-shelves.

**ice-wedge**, a tapering, vertically layered mass of ice appearing in regions of frozen subsoil, and forming a lattice-work of cracks, low ridges, and shallow ponds. Fine-grained material is frozen suddenly in autumn, and its shrinkage causes networks of contraction cracks which extend down into *permafrost. In winter and particularly in spring, water freezes in the cracks and, although the *active layer thaws in summer, renewed cracking occurs in autumn. Tapering wedges of ice gradually build up in the cracks, pushing up as ridges so that shallow ponds form in summer at the polygon centres. If the wedges melt, 'thaw ditches' result.

**ideal gas** (in physics), a hypothetically 'perfect' gas used to represent the gases which exist in nature. In an ideal gas the atoms or molecules are assumed to be so small as to be negligible in volume, and there are no forces between them. They travel at high speed and occasionally collide with one another, but these collisions are elastic collisions—that is to say, none of the energy of motion of the particles is converted into any other energy form: the total energy of motion of two particles before they collide is exactly the same as it is after the collision. Using these ideas it is possible to derive a very simple relationship between the pressure of a gas, its volume, and its absolute temperature (see *gas laws). The conclusions that can be deduced from the formula describe the behaviour of most real gases to a good approximation. The ideal gas model is therefore important and useful. Only when a gas is close to liquefaction or at a very high pressure is the model not satisfactory.

**identity element**, in set theory, an element, $e$, of a *set which, for an *operation, $-$, for every element, $a$, in that particular set, has the property that $a - e = e - a = a$. The identity element in the set of real numbers under addition is 0. Under multiplication, however, it is 1. An identity must exist for a set and an operation if they are to form a group.

**igneous intrusion**, a body of *igneous rock that has made its way into pre-existing rock (country rock). Igneous intrusions are emplaced as *magma, which is less dense than solid rock and therefore tends to move upwards. It can then force its way through cracks in the rocks and can wedge them apart or, if it is hot enough, it can melt and replace them. Igneous intrusions can be of a variety of shapes and sizes, ranging from huge *batholiths to bodies only 1–2m across. The general term 'pluton' can be applied to any of these. Intrusions may cut across the bedding of the country rock. They are then termed 'discordant' or 'transgressive'; *dykes and *laccoliths are examples. Intrusions that follow the bedding of the country rock, such as *sills, are termed 'concordant'.

**igneous rock**, rock that has originated from molten or semi-molten *magma. Igneous rocks are composed almost entirely of silicate minerals. Of many different types, they can be classified in various ways: by composition, crystal size, or mode of occurrence. One method is to divide them according to their silica ($SiO_2$) content into three main groups: acid rocks, basic rocks, and intermediate rocks. There is, however, continuous gradation from acid to basic. ('Acid' and 'basic' are here used in a special sense, not with their ordinary meanings.) Acid rocks are characterized by the presence of 10 per cent or more of quartz, usually accompanied by lighter-coloured minerals such as ortho-clase feldspar and muscovite. This acid group includes rocks such as granite and rhyolite. Molten acid lava is very viscous, and its viscosity prevents the molten lava flowing very far and produces tall, conical volcanoes of the Vesuvius type. Intermediate rocks have less than 10 per cent quartz; diorite and andesite are typical of this group. Basic igneous rocks are characterized by the absence of quartz and the predominance of dark minerals such as ferromagnesian minerals (amphiboles, pyroxenes). Common basic igneous rocks include gabbros and basalts. When extruded on to the Earth's surface these low-viscosity basic lavas form flat plateaux such as the Columbia Plateau, USA. Those igneous rocks that crystallize below the Earth's surface are termed intrusive or plutonic, according to whether they were formed at shallow depths, like dolerite, or deeper down, like granite. All these rocks have relatively large crystals produced by slow cooling of the molten magma. Igneous rocks that are extruded at the Earth's surface are termed extrusive or volcanic: basalt is an example. The rapid cooling that occurs at the surface does not allow large crystals to form, and these rocks are glassy or contain only small crystals.

**ignimbrite**, a solidified deposit from hot, dense, incandescent clouds of dust and ash (*nuées ardentes) which roll down the slopes of active volcanoes after an eruption. It contains very small crystals together with fragments of rock. The particles are often welded together, and the rock is then called a welded tuff. Ignimbrites occur at sites of ancient volcanic activity, as in Iceland, New Zealand, and the Caribbean.

**Iguaçu Falls**, one of the great sights of Brazil, on the Iguaçu River just east of its junction with the Paraná, in south-central South America. Hundreds of waterfalls, interspersed among rocky islands along an escarpment of approximately 5 km (3 miles) long, each drop 60 m (200 feet) and more. They provide tremendous potential for hydro-electric power.

**illite**, a clay mineral group consisting of potassium aluminium silicates. Illites comprise minerals of extremely fine grain size that are formed by the alteration of micas and feldspars under alkaline conditions. Illites are common minerals in most sedimentary rocks.

**illuviation**, the accumulation or deposition in the lower soil *horizons of soluble salts, organic matter, or clay particles (either from suspension or solution) which have been washed down from the upper part of the profile in the process known as *leaching.

**ilmenite**, a black mineral iron *titanium oxide.

**imaginary numbers**, a subset of the *complex numbers $a + ib$ in which $a = 0$. All numbers of the form $ib$, where $i = \sqrt{(-1)}$, are imaginary because $i^2 = -1$ does not have a real-number solution. In terms of the *Argand diagram, they are located on the vertical axis through the origin. The term 'imaginary' is one of several which have been used since the 16th century to describe these numbers; other terms, indicating greater doubt about their acceptability within mathematics, have been 'impossible' or 'absurd' numbers. Imaginary numbers are widely used in science, electronics and engineering.

**imperial unit**   *unit.

**inceptisol**, a soil which occurs on young land surfaces and has therefore been subject to the processes of soil formation for a relatively short time. As a result it still contains an abundance of weatherable minerals and tends to lack a distinct *horizon. The upper part of the profile may be modified by the presence of organic matter. Inceptisols occur in a wide range of latitudes, but are most common in mountainous areas.

**India**, a South Asian country occupying most of the southward-pointing peninsula of the Indian subcontinent. It is bounded by Pakistan on the north-west, China, Nepal, and Bhutan on the north, and Myanmar (Burma) on the east. It is roughly triangular in shape, most of the northern frontier

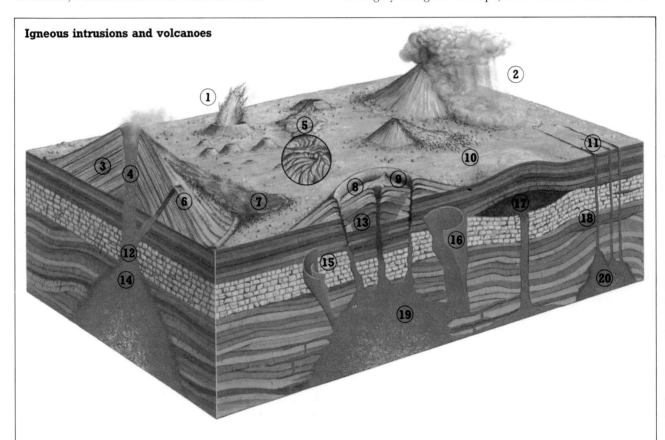

**Igneous intrusions and volcanoes**

| 1 Lava fountain (Hawaiian type) | 5 Ropy lava (*pahoehoe*) | 10 Block lava (*aa*) | 15 Cone sheets |
| 2 Nuée ardente (glowing cloud eruption) | 6 Parasitic volcano | 11 Dike swarm | 16 Ring dikes |
| 3 Layered tethra and lava | 7 Lava flow | 12 Boss | 17 Laccolith |
| 4 Pipe or neck | 8 Collapsed caldera | 13 Radial dike | 18 Sills |
| | 9 New dome and spire | 14 Magma chamber | 19 Magma reservoir |
| | | | 20 Batholith |

following the Himalayas, the world's highest mountains. The two southern sides are formed by a coastline on the Arabian Sea and another on the Bay of Bengal: they are backed by the ranges of the Western and Eastern Ghats. In its north-east corner are the *Brahmaputra valley and the wet, tea-bearing hills of Assam, bounding Bangladesh. In the extreme north is Kashmir, embraced by the Karakoram range. Then, across a northern belt of the Himalayas, are the Thar (or Great Indian) Desert, the central Punjab watershed with its fields of wheat, the Ganges *floodplain, and Bengal which produces jute. In the west are the cotton-growing areas of Gujarat. From here the land rises to the middle of the country, Madhya Pradesh, and the forested hills of Orissa. Extending southward is the Deccan plateau, terminating in the Nilgiri Hills where tea and coffee are grown. The southern coasts, Malabar and Coromandel, are famous for their paddy fields and citrus fruit. The country is also rich in coal, iron ore, and other minerals. India has two *monsoons: the south-west, which brings moderate-heavy rain to most of the country from June to September; and the north-east, which blows from October to February.

**Indian Ocean**, the third largest sea area in the world. Extending from Africa on the west to Australia on the east, it is bounded by Asia on the north and broadens southward to the Southern Ocean. A mid-oceanic ridge runs north–south along a junction of crustal *plates, splitting into two ridges running south-west and south-east at about 23° S. Together with other ridges and plateaux these ridges give rise to a number of small islands, while other islands (including the largest: Madagascar, Sri Lanka, and Sumatra) are structural extensions of Africa and Asia. Deepest in the east, the ocean also contains a number of basins; but its northern arms (the Red Sea, Persian Gulf, Arabian Sea, and Bay of Bengal) are generally shallow.

The current system in the Indian Ocean varies with the *monsoon winds. During the north-east monsoon (dry air blowing from the Eurasian continent) there is a strong flow southwards down the coast of East Africa in the Somali Current; this mostly turns eastward to form the Equatorial Counter Current, flowing between the westward-flowing North Equatorial Current and South Equatorial Current. During the south-west monsoon, the Somali Current reverses and now flows very strongly northwards, turning eastwards in the Arabian Sea to become the south-west monsoon Current; Meanwhile the North Equatorial Current and the Equatorial Counter Current have disappeared. While passing over the ocean the winds of the south-west monsoon pick up moisture which is released over the continent as the monsoon rains.

**indium** (symbol In, at. no. 49, r.a.m. 114.82), a soft, silver, metallic element in Group III of the *periodic table. It reacts readily with acids, the halogens, and sulphur with a principal valency of 3. It is used in the manufacture of semiconductor devices, and to monitor neutron fluxes near nuclear reactors.

**Indo-China**, the south-east Asian peninsula occupied by Myanmar (Burma), Thailand, peninsular Malaysia, Laos, Cambodia, and Vietnam; or, more often, a term used to describe only the latter three countries. When used generally it is in recognition of a physical entity and describes the existence of both Indian and Chinese culture there.

**Indonesia**, a country composed of hundreds of tropical islands in south-east Asia, in the region where the Pacific and the Indian Oceans meet. Its east–west length is greater than the width of Australia or the USA, for among its larger islands are included parts of New Guinea (Irian Jaya) and Borneo (Kalimantan) and all of Sumatra, Java, and Sulawesi (once Celebes). Among its smaller islands are Bali, Timor, Flores, and the Moluccas. This vast area lies at the edge of the Eurasian *plate. It contains over seventy volcanoes, some periodically active like Krakatoa; and it is subject to severe earthquakes. While many of the beaches are black with volcanic mud, others are coral, with very clear water. With both a north-west *monsoon (December to March) and a south-east one (April to October), the natural vegetation inland is dense rain forest and the main crop is rice. Rubber, tobacco, tea, and coffee plantations also flourish, and the country is rich in palm products, kapok, and various hardwoods. Spices, the traditional crops of the islands, are still grown. Oil resources are plentiful, and there are deposits of coal, tin, bauxite, kaolin, phosphates, and sulphur.

**induction** (in mathematics), a technique for proving generalized results, such as $1 + 4 + 9 + \ldots + n^2 = \frac{1}{6}n(n+1)(2n+1)$, in which the $n$th term is a function of $n$. The technique involves three stages: (i) assume that the formula is true for some value of $n$, say $k$; (ii) show that, if this assumption is true, the formula also holds for $n = k + 1$; (iii) show that the assumption is true for a particular value of $n$, usually $n = 1$, and thus that it is true for all subsequent values of $n$. Different arguments, generalizing from particular results, are often required to derive the formula to be proved. *De Moivre's theorem can be proved by induction.

**Indus**, the great waterway of Pakistan, in the west of the Indian subcontinent of south Asia. Rising in the Kailash Mountains of Tibet, it first flows north-west for several hundred miles, collecting water from glacial streams. Skirting Nanga Parbat, it then turns south-west and enters its great valley, heavy with silt but now navigable. The five rivers of the Punjab (or Panjab)—the Jhelum, Chenab, Ravi, Beas,

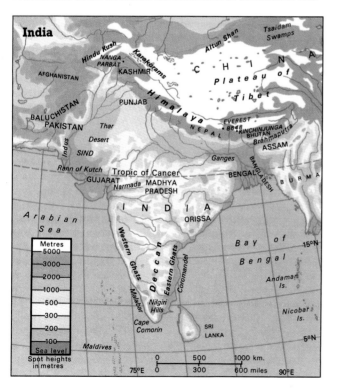

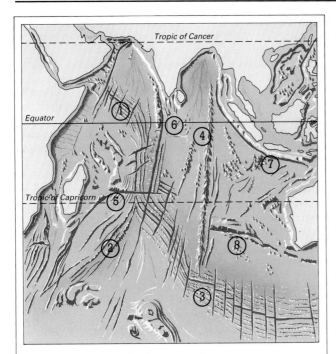

**Indian Ocean:** sea-bed topography

| Ridges | Trenches |
|---|---|
| 1 Carlsberg Ridge | 5 Mauritius Trench |
| 2 Southwest Indian Ridge | 6 Chagos Trench |
| 3 Mid-Indian Ocean Ridge | 7 Java Trench |
| 4 Ninety East Ridge | 8 Ob Trench |

and Sutlej, all rising in the Himalayas—join it as the flow continues southward to the desert plain of Sind. Here, after spreading broadly, it enters a narrow gorge and its waters can be used for power and irrigation. Emerging into a wide delta of infertile clay, it again becomes navigable for small boats and at last reaches the Arabian Sea, its total journey being some 2,700 km (1,700 miles).

**inert gases** *noble gases.

**inertia**, a property of all objects such that they remain still or continue to move at a constant velocity when no external forces are acting. Any force applied to a body will be resisted by the inertia of that body. The principle of inertia is fundamental to the first of *Newton's laws of motion and those laws only apply in systems in which inertia is maintained (inertial frames of reference). In a rotating system inertia is not maintained, as a force has to be applied to keep a body rotating at a constant angular velocity. Thus, strictly, the Earth should not be considered as an inertial frame of reference but, as the speed of rotation is slow, it is thought of as one except in special circumstances, such as *Foucault's pendulum, where the swing of the pendulum is altered by the rotation of the Earth.

**infiltration** (in hydrology), the passage of water through the surface of the ground and into soil or rock (or drains) beneath. The depth of water absorbed by the surface in a given time is termed the infiltration rate, the infiltration capacity being the maximum rate which ground in a given condition can absorb. Both are measured in centimetres (or inches) per unit time. Infiltration rates are controlled by the kind of precipitation, particularly whether it is rain or snow; the quantities intercepted by vegetation; the character of the

surface and its slope; the depth and permeability of the soil; and the amount of empty storage capacity. Actual rates correspond to the lowest value imposed by one of these different controls. During infiltration, water percolates downwards to the *water-table and, on sloping ground, some moves downslope as 'throughflow'. Intense rain, melting snow, a frozen surface, or large quantities of moisture already in the soil, lead to the infiltration capacity being exceeded and the occurrence of surface *runoff. Runoff erodes soil; so good land management encourages high infiltration capacities to prevent it.

**information theory** (in mathematics), a theory of communication that concerns the transmission of information by signals. It covers the capacity of communication channels, the corruption of messages (by 'noise' or interference), and the detection and correction of errors. It is much used in electronic communications, but the theory is not specifically electronic. A simple application is the parity check code for error detection. Suppose each letter of a message is coded as a *binary number. For example, the number 1000 might represent A, and 1001 represent B. The A code has an odd number of ones (this is odd parity) and that for B has an even number (even parity). A fifth digit could be attached to each code to make the parity even. So the code for A would be 10001 and that for B (already even) 10010. A single error in the transmission of these codes (making a one into a zero or vice versa) would alter the parity to odd. The receiver could detect the wrong parity and request retransmission. With more sophisticated codings the receiver can correct errors, if there are not too many. All error detection and correction uses the concept of redundancy. This is the inclusion of more information in a code than is necessary for the message (for example, the inclusion of the extra digits above). Human language is highly redundant, as shown by the intelligibility of this corrupt message: mst ppl cn rd ths (most people can read this). Much pioneering work on information theory was done by Claude Shannon in the USA during the 1940s. Practical applications range from the International Standard Book Number (ISBN) on all books, which incorporates a check digit, to the reception of messages from satellites.

**infra-red radiation**, *electromagnetic radiation with a wavelength of $10^{-6}$ to $10^{-3}$ m, which is slightly longer than that of visible light. It lies in the spectrum between red light and microwaves, is emitted by hot bodies (most intensely if they are red or white hot), and is sometimes called thermal *radiation. Its energy is in the same range as that of atomic and molecular vibrations in solids; when it enters a material it is therefore able to impart its energy to the vibrating atoms so that their *amplitude of oscillation is increased. Hence it is often used as a means of heating. Indeed, it is by infra-red radiation from the Sun that the Earth is heated, the rays having the power to penetrate the atmosphere, haze, and fog. Aerial photography using infra-red film together with coloured filters is used in preparing geological maps. The technique, called infra-red remote sensing, distinguishes various types of vegetation, rocks, water, and even certain types of alteration in the landscape.

**Inland Sea** (Japanese, Seto-Naikai), an arm of the Pacific Ocean in south Japan, about 440 km (270 miles) long, between the islands of Honshu, Shikoku, and Kyushi, linked to the Sea of Japan by a narrow channel. It is famed both for the scenic beauty of its 950 islands some of which constitute the Seto-Naikai National Park, and for its flourishing trading and fishing ports. The outer shores are heavily populated and a series of major cities along it form Japan's most important industrial belt.

**inlier** (in geology), an outcrop of older rocks which are surrounded by younger rocks. Inliers are usually formed when folded or faulted rocks are eroded, leaving an area of the older rock exposed with an eroded surface of the younger rocks all round it. *Outliers are the opposite of inliers.

**inorganic chemistry** *chemistry.

**inselberg**, a steep-sided, isolated hill, the term being generally used in the seasonally dry tropics, especially the great savannah plains of Africa. It is not clear whether inselbergs are fundamentally different from other residual hills, such as *buttes and *mesas: all are thought to be the remnants of larger upland areas that have been eroded away by the action of rivers, although it may be, as some think, that inselbergs are large blocks of unweathered rock that are slowly being excavated from a covering of weathered material. Probably both processes are at work.

**insolation, atmospheric**, the radiation received by the Earth from the Sun, or more precisely, the rate at which solar energy is received at any given point. It varies both in time and space, depending upon the degree of exposure to the sun and the angle of incidence of the Sun's rays. The outer limits of the Earth's atmosphere receive approximately 8.2 joules (1.95 calories) per square centimetre per minute. On a global scale, the uneven distribution of insolation is the fundamental cause of atmospheric *circulation and many weather phenomena, through the mechanism of the poleward transfer of heat. Variations in insolation can also cause *climatic change.

**insulation, electrical** *band theory.

**integration**, the reverse of *differentiation. That is, given a function (say the squared function, $y = x^2$), the object is to find another function, the integral, which when differentiated yields the original ($x^2$). (This problem frequently occurs in mathematics and science.) The integral of $x^2$ is $(x^3/3) + K$ where $K$ is an arbitrary constant number. This is written $\int x^2 \, dx = (x^3/3) + K$. There are several techniques for integrating functions, such as integration by substitution, integration by parts, and so on. The type of integration described above is indefinite integration. It is distinguished from definite integration, where the answer is always a number rather than a function. Definite integration developed separately from indefinite integration as a method for calculating irregular areas and volumes. For example, the area between the curve $y = x^2$ and the $x$-axis, over the interval from $x = 1$ and $x = 3$ is irregular (see $a$ in the figure). By thinking of an irregular area as divisible into numerous rectangular strips, each of calculable area (see $b$ in the figure), one can get an approximate value for the irregular area by adding together all the strips' areas. Letting the strips be narrower (and using more of them) improves the approximation. The result of letting the strips become infinitesimally wide and infinite in number (a theoretical rather than a practical proposition) is to make the approximation exact. Techniques of *analysis can be used to calculate what the answer would be. They show that the *in*definite integral (without its arbitrary constant $K$) corresponds to the area between a curve and the $x$-axis over the interval from $x = 0$

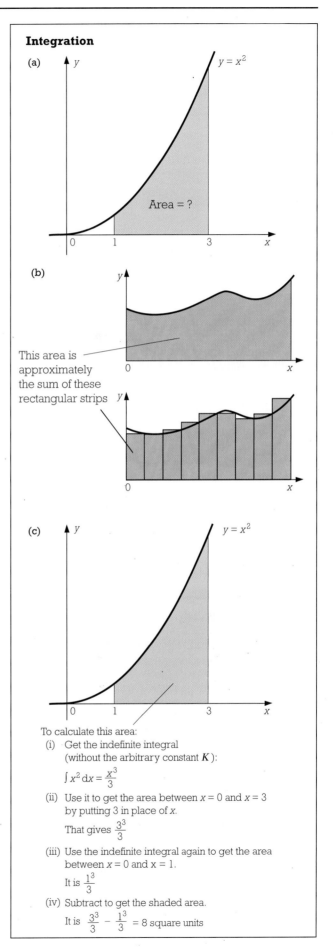

**Integration**

(a) $y = x^2$

Area = ?

(b) This area is approximately the sum of these rectangular strips

(c) $y = x^2$

To calculate this area:
(i) Get the indefinite integral (without the arbitrary constant **K**):

$$\int x^2 \, dx = \frac{x^3}{3}$$

(ii) Use it to get the area between $x = 0$ and $x = 3$ by putting 3 in place of $x$.

That gives $\frac{3^3}{3}$

(iii) Use the indefinite integral again to get the area between $x = 0$ and $x = 1$.

It is $\frac{1^3}{3}$

(iv) Subtract to get the shaded area.

It is $\frac{3^3}{3} - \frac{1^3}{3} = 8$ square units

Ayers Rock is a huge **inselberg** of conglomerate and sandstone that dominates the plains of Australia's Northern Territory.

to any chosen value of $x$. Thus to calculate the area over an interval (see $a$ in the figure), where $x$ is not zero at one end, requires a double use of the indefinite integral (see $c$ in the figure). This way of calculating an area is called definite integration. The notation for a definite integral is $\int_1^3 x^2 dx$ . The integral sign $\int$ is an elongated 's', standing for summation. The term $x^2\, dx$ represents the area of an infinitesimally wide rectangular strip. Thus the notation symbolizes the summation of infinitesimal strips. The numbers at the top and bottom of the integral sign (that is 1 and 3) are the limits of integration.

**interactions** (in physics), the ways in which one particle has an effect on another. They result from the four fundamental forces. On the human scale the most obvious is *gravitation, which makes objects fall to the ground under the gravitational attraction of the Earth. On the atomic and subatomic scale, however, gravity is so weak that it is much less important than the other three kinds of interaction that are known: the strong, the electromagnetic, and the weak. All three, unlike gravity, act only on certain classes of particle. Strong interactions result from the *strong force. They occur over a very short distance and in a very short time—typically of the order of $10^{-23}$ second—the time it takes for light to cross an atomic nucleus. In these interactions the *flavour of the particles remains unchanged (is 'conserved'). It is thought that the gluons which bind *quarks together are the agents of strong interactions. Electromagnetic interactions result from the *electromagnetic force. They occur in times of $10^{-15}$ to $10^{-20}$ second between charged particles, such as when an electron and a positron collide to form photons. The photon is the agent of electromagnetic interactions, and it operates over all distances. The weak interaction results from the *weak force. It has been the subject of intense interest, and was first noted as the agency

responsible for the beta decay of radioactive nuclei. It can occur over a very wide range of times—from $10^{-13}$ second to $10^{10}$ years. The process occurs by the exchange of very heavy *bosons, and flavour is not conserved. Although it is called weak, at sufficiently high energies it can be as strong as an electromagnetic interaction. Its range is the shortest of all the interactions. It is the goal of some physicists to combine the theories for each of these interactions into one single *grand unified theory. So far, a joint theory of electromagnetic and weak interactions has been developed; it appears satisfactory, but a full unified theory has yet to come.

**interference** of wave motions, a phenomenon that occurs when two or more wave motions with the same *wavelength overlap one another. When this happens the waves reinforce each other at some points, where their crests coincide, and cancel at others, where a crest coincides with a trough. Light of a single wavelength can be used to demonstrate interference. If the light is made to pass through two slits which are close together, a pattern of light and dark bands called interference fringes is produced when the light strikes a screen; the fringes represent points of reinforcement and cancellation. The interference of light was first demonstrated in this way by Thomas *Young in 1806. Interference may sometimes be observed when two stones are dropped into a pond and their ripples overlap.

**interglacial**, the comparatively warm periods which separated periods of glaciation during the *Pleistocene Epoch. Characterized by similar flora and fauna to those of the present day, although maximum temperatures may have been 2–3 °C (4–5 °F) higher, they varied between about 20,000 and 70,000 years in length.

**intermolecular forces**, the forces that act between adjacent molecules. In liquids and some solids it is the intermolecular forces that keep the molecules from dispersing as they do in a gas. They are weaker than the covalent bonds within the molecules; and therefore, when a molecular substance is heated, it is the intermolecular forces that are overcome. *Van der Waals' forces are a type of intermolecular force. They exist between all molecules and arise from the uneven distribution of electrons in a molecule at any time. The resulting instantaneous electric *dipole induces similar dipoles in neighbouring molecules. These dipoles attract each other weakly. An example of a substance in which only these forces operate is nitrogen. If the molecule has a permanent *dipole moment, dipoles in adjacent molecules will attract each other. The resulting dipole–dipole forces are stronger than, and thus mask, the weak van der Waals' forces. An example of a compound in which these forces operate is hydrogen chloride. The strongest intermolecular force is the *hydrogen bond. It is so strong as to mask the van der Waals' forces completely. Water ($H_2O$) is a compound which forms hydrogen bonds.

**internal energy**, the total energy possessed by the atoms or molecules in a system by virtue of their motion and their interactions with one another. In a gas the molecules are in continuous rapid motion. They are constantly colliding with one another; and although in these collisions energy is transferred from one molecule to another it can never be lost. The hotter a gas is, the more rapidly the molecules move and the greater its internal energy. Thus temperature is a measure of internal energy.

**international date-line**, nominally the meridian of *longitude 180°, which fortunately runs through the Pacific Ocean over very little land. At this line the date is deemed to change when a ship or aircraft crosses it. For convenience to the inhabitants of Fiji, Tonga, and some of New Zealand's islands, the line is made to deviate eastwards by 7° between latitudes 10° and 50° S.

**interstitial compounds**, crystalline solids that contain additional atoms in between the regular sites of the crystal lattice. They form between the *transition metals and elements with small atoms, especially hydrogen, carbon, and nitrogen. Graphite also forms interstitial compounds. They resemble metals in that they are shiny and are good conductors of electricity. They do not have definite chemical formulae, as not all the gaps in the metal are always filled; but they are stable over quite wide composition ranges.

**intertropical convergence zone (ITCZ)**, the boundary between the *trade winds and tropical air masses of the Northern and Southern Hemispheres, along the axis of the *doldrums. It is generally marked by a belt of cumulonimbus clouds and heavy precipitation often owing to the *convergence of air masses with different temperature and humidity characteristics. These differences are very pronounced when, as in West Africa, there is the convergence of dry continental and humid maritime air. Over the ocean the zone is characterized by vigorous upward convection of moist air brought in from north and south by the *trade winds. The intertropical convergence zone is a region of *low atmospheric pressure; and it is thought that *tropical revolving storms are generated by small low pressure centres associated with it. Between January and July the zone migrates northward from close to or south of the Equator, sometimes reaching 30°–35° N. in south and east Asia in July. Between July and January it migrates southward, as far as 23° S. in East Africa and Australia. In southern Asia, northern Australia, and East and West Africa, its movement is associated with the *monsoon.

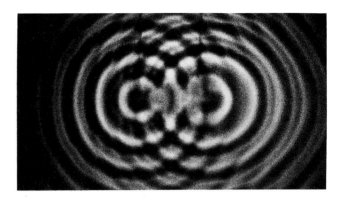

The pattern that is produced by the **interference** of water waves in a ripple-tank. The picture shows clearly the equal wavelengths of the waves, which were generated by two spheres vibrating at the same frequency.

**intrazonal soil**, a soil whose main characteristics are determined by local conditions, related to topography, drainage, or the nature of the bedrock, rather than to regional factors such as climate and vegetation. *Rendzinas and *andosols, which form on limestone and basic volcanic deposits respectively, are examples of intrazonal soil; with them the character of the parent material is the most important influence on the formation of the soil. Intrazonal soils also form under conditions of poor drainage, such as in bogs, on river floodplains, or in the playa lake basins of deserts. *Solonchaks and *solonetz are examples of intrazonal soils of this type.

**intrusion** (in geology)   *igneous intrusion.

**inverse elements** in set theory, pairs of elements, $a$ and $a'$, in a given set, such that $a - a' = a' - a = e$, where $e$ is the *identity element and $-$ is an *operation. Every element of the positive rational numbers has an inverse, under multiplication: for example, $7 \times \frac{1}{7} = \frac{1}{7} \times 7 = 1$. With the exception of 1, however, the positive integers do not have inverses under multiplication: $\frac{1}{7}$ is not an integer. The existence of an inverse for every element is a necessary condition for a set and an operation to form a group.

**inverse function** (in mathematics). The inverse of a *function is another function which cancels out the effect of the original one. Some examples are square and square root, logarithm and exponential, and addition and subtraction. Symbolically, f and g are inverses if and only if, for all appropriate $a$ and $b$, $f(a) = b$ and $g(b) = a$, so $f[g(b)] = b$.

**inverse square law**, a law describing the behaviour of physical phenomena which spread out equally in all directions from a single source. For example, objects exert a gravitational force which acts outwards equally in all directions. The strength of the gravitational force decreases with distance, so at a distance $r$ away from the object, the strength of the force is inversely proportional to $r$. As the intensity of the force is spread out over the surface of a sphere radius $r$, this surface area is proportional to $r^2$, therefore the intensity of the force at any point is inversely proportional to $r^2$. Thus the intensity of the field is related to distance by an inverse square law.

**inversions** (in meteorology), the reversal of the usual decrease of temperature with height within the troposphere, temperature increasing with height within limited zones. They commonly develop at night near the Earth's surface, as the ground cools due to conduction and long-wave radiation. The result is the creation of an inversion, with the greatest fall in air temperature nearest to the ground, and the rate and amount of cooling decreasing with height. Because of the inverse temperature gradient of such inversions, atmospheric pollutants are unable to escape beyond the inversion layer, causing the concentration of pollutants to increase close to the surface of the Earth and helping in the formation of *smog. Inversions also develop when warm air flows over a cold land or sea surface. The warm air rises over the cold. A further instance is when air, sinking from higher in the troposphere, is warmed by compression.

**iodine** (symbol I, at. no. 53, r.a.m. 126.90), a black shiny solid in Group VII (the *halogens) of the periodic table. On gentle warming it sublimes to a violet vapour; both the solid and the vapour contain $I_2$ molecules. It dissolves in many organic solvents and in potassium iodide solution, but it is not very soluble in water. Less reactive than the other halogens, it forms compounds with most metals and non-metals; and it also forms compounds in which it has the valencies 1, 3, 5, and 7. Sodium iodide is a minor constituent of sea water and is concentrated in seaweed, which has been used as a source of iodine. Tincture of iodine is used as an antiseptic. Iodine is also an essential element in the body; it occurs mainly in the thyroid gland. The radioactive isotope iodine-131 is widely employed in medicine.

**Ionian Islands**, a region of modern Greece consisting of a chain of seven islands, lying in the Mediterranean to the west of the mainland, and extending from Corfu in the north to Zante in the south. They are famous for their mountainous, gaunt, and rugged scenery, developed for the most part on limestone rocks. They may result from variable subsidence in the area of the surrounding Ionian Sea, which locally is deeper than 4,600 m (15,000 feet); and earthquakes still occur.

**ionic bond**   *chemical bond, *ionic compound.

**ionic compound**, a compound formed when a metal reacts with a non-metal; the metal atoms give away one or more electrons, forming positively charged *ions, and the non-metal atoms accept the electrons, becoming negatively charged ions. The product is a solid which consists of a regular arrangement or lattice of positive and negative ions, and it is held together by the forces of attraction between them. These are called ionic bonds. Ionic compounds have high melting-points because of the high attractive forces in the bond. When the solid is melted or dissolved, the ions are no longer arranged in a regular pattern, but move about independently of each other. Cations are formed most easily by metals, and anions by either single non-metal atoms or groups of them. It follows that the simple requirement for ionic bonding is that the compound should contain both a metal and a non-metal. For example, sodium chloride is ionic and has the ionic formula $Na^+Cl^-$. However, cations containing only non-metals do exist, for instance the ammonium ion, $NH_4^+$. Thus, the ionic formula of ammonium chloride is $NH_4^+Cl^-$. Not all ionic compounds consist just of a single metal and non-metal: for example, ammonium chloride contains $NH_4^+$ ions and $Cl^-$ ions, and sodium carbonate contains $Na^+$ ions and $CO_3^{2-}$ ions. Ionic compounds are typically crystalline solids, with high melting-

and boiling-points. They are typically soluble in water but insoluble in organic solvents such as toluene. Whereas they are electrical insulators when solid, they conduct electricity when molten, or in solution. This conduction is accompanied by chemical decomposition, and is called *electrolysis.

**ionization**, the process by which an electrically neutral atom or molecule becomes either positively or negatively charged due to the removal or addition of one or more electrons. Once an atom or molecule has been ionized, it is called an *ion. The amount of energy needed to remove an electron from an atom or molecule is called the ionization potential. Whether the ion is positive or negative depends on the *electronic configuration of the original atom. If the atom has only a very small number of electrons in an outer shell which could accommodate a much larger number, it tends to lose those electrons to form positive ions. For example, aluminium atoms have three electrons in an outer shell which could accommodate up to eight electrons. When ionized, aluminium atoms lose these three electrons to form ions with three positive charges. Chlorine atoms, which have seven electrons in an outer shell which could accommodate eight, gain an electron to form ions with a single negative charge. Ionization can be caused by the passage of electric currents, in chemical reactions, during collisions between atoms and by electromagnetic radiation (which is then known as ionizing radiation).

Ionizing radiation is any type of *electromagnetic radiation which causes the ionization of atoms or molecules. For most atoms and molecules, only high energy radiation from the ultraviolet region of the electromagnetic spectrum and beyond can ionize them; but even relatively low energy radiation such as visible light can ionize some substances. The ionizing radiation responsible for the ions in the Earth's atmosphere is ultraviolet radiation from the Sun. Ionizing radiation can be dangerous for living organisms because it can damage molecules responsible for vital functions.

**ionosphere**, electrically charged zone of the Earth's *atmosphere, extending from a height of about 50–80 km (30–50 miles) for some 400–600 km (250–370 miles) into space. X-rays and ultraviolet radiation from the Sun cause nitrogen and oxygen molecules in the air there to ionize, producing free electrons. The resulting layer of charged particles enables radio waves to be reflected round the Earth. The ionosphere is not uniform throughout. The layer nearest the Earth has the lowest concentration of free electrons and reflects low-frequency waves. The *Heaviside–Kennelly layer reflects medium waves, while the still higher *Appleton layer has the highest concentration owing to the lower density of its gases (its electrons collide with ions less frequently) and reflects short waves. The thicknesses of these layers vary with latitude, season, and time of day, ionization in the lower layers falling when night comes.

**ion**, an atom or group of atoms which are electrically charged as a result of losing or gaining electrons. Ionization can be produced if atoms are passed through a high electric field, as in an electrical discharge tube, or if they are bombarded by energetic particles; and those which are accelerated to high speeds can be stripped of electrons when they pass through thin sheets of material. Gaseous ions are produced by high-energy electromagnetic radiation such as X-rays. Many compounds when in solution separate into groups of ions. For example, copper(II) sulphate, ($CuSO_4$), when dissolved in water dissociates into $Cu^{2+}$ ions, which

The northern lights (aurora borealis) pictured here occur when electrically charged particles from the Sun interact with molecules of gas high in the **ionosphere**, exciting them and causing them to glow and undulate like a giant curtain in the sky. The same phenomenon occurring in the southern hemisphere is called the aurora australis.

are positively charged, and $SO_4^{2-}$ ions, which are negatively charged. In solids, electrons are often transferred to a neighbouring atom, thereby forming a negative–positive pair of ions which attract one another. This is one of the mechanisms of *chemical bonding in solids. In a sodium chloride (NaCl) crystal, a typical ionic compound, when the sodium atoms lose an electron to the chlorine atoms, a network of $Na^+$ and $Cl^-$ ions is formed. If ions are mobile, as in a gas, a solution, or a liquid, they can act as carriers of electricity and the material becomes an electrical conductor. This is termed ionic conductivity. The *activity and mobility of an ion can influence chemical reactions in solution.

**Iran** (formerly Persia), a country of the Middle East in central-west Asia. Bordering on Turkey and Iraq on the west, Turkmenistan on the north, and Afghanistan and Pakistan on the east, it has a northern coast on the Caspian Sea and a southern coast on the Gulf and Arabian Sea. It is mostly arid tableland surrounded by mountains (the Elburz in the north and the Zagros in the south-west) and containing extensive salt deserts: the *Great Salt Desert or Dasht-e-Kavir in the north and the Dasht-e-Lut in the south-east. The climate varies from hot to cool according to season and altitude. Parts of the country provide sparse pasture for camels, sheep, and goats, and parts are cultivable for grain and fruit, while its greatest present-day resource is the oil-fields of the south-west. There are substantial deposits of coal, copper, and iron.

**Iraq**, a West Asian country bordering on Turkey on the north, Iran on the east, Syria and Jordan on the west, and

Saudi Arabia and Kuwait on the south. A waterway, Shatt al-Arab, at the delta of the Euphrates, gives it access to the Gulf in the south-east. The Euphrates and its tributary the Tigris traverse the whole country from north-west to south-east, bringing silt to a vast depression which would be widely cultivable were it not for salinity and *erosion. This land, once known as Mesopotamia, was the site of early civilizations. To the north are mountains and desert plateaux, to the west all is desert; and the climate is one of extremes. Date palms flourish in the delta. Oil is found there too, as it is in the north, in Kurdistan, and in several other areas.

**Ireland**, an island off the north-west coast of Europe, the furthest west of the British Isles. Situated on the continental shelf, it is surrounded on three sides by the Atlantic Ocean and is separated from Great Britain by the Irish Sea. About 370 km (230 miles) long by 225 km (140 miles) wide, four-fifths of the country comprises the Republic of Ireland, with the remainder, Northern Ireland, a part of the UK. A flat and fertile plain surrounds a central lake, Lough Ree, and the basin of the River Shannon. It is surrounded by coastal areas of great beauty: the Wicklow Mountains in the south-east reach to nearly 1,000 m (3,300 feet); the Connemara Mountains in the west stand up above great lakes, while those of Kerry in the south-west reach to over 1,000 m (3,282 feet) and point like rugged fingers to the sea. Many islands, among them Aran, lie in the deep bays of the western coast, where there are sandy beaches among the rocks. Warm, damp winds from the Atlantic keep the country largely free of frost, while rainfall is moderate to heavy. The countryside stays very green and livestock flourish, as do all root crops. Minerals are rare, peat rather than coal being the major fuel.

**iridium** (symbol Ir, at. no. 77, r.a.m. 192.22), an unreactive silver metallic element; it is one of the *transition metals. Alloyed with platinum it is used in pens, electrical contacts, and crucibles; the standard kilogram mass is a platinum –iridium alloy.

**iron** (symbol Fe, at. no. 26, r.a.m. 55.85), one of the *transition metals. It is greyish white in colour, and hard and strong though malleable and ductile. The ancient Egyptians knew it, and its strength has been employed in Europe for some three thousand years. Now it is the most widely used of metals, being the major constituent of steel. In nature the purest iron is generally found in meteorites. It is a good conductor of heat and electricity, but its properties are affected strongly by the presence of other elements. Its melting-point is 1,535 °C (2,795 °F), and it is believed to be the main component of the earth's core. Iron ores are found in many kinds of rock throughout the world, the chief among them being haematite, magnetite (loadstone), and siderite (ironstone). The yellow iron pyrites ($FeS_2$) is known as fool's gold. Iron reacts with acids and non-metals, and forms *rust in moist air. It forms two sets of compounds: iron(II) compounds (ferrous compounds), which contain the $Fe^{2+}$ ion, and iron(III) compounds (ferric compounds), which contain the $Fe^{3+}$ ion. Iron(II) compounds are often pale green, and iron(III) compounds yellow-brown; the colours of many rocks are caused by the presence of iron. Iron is an essential element in diet and in the human body. It is present in enzymes, which control oxidation reactions, and in haemoglobin, which transports oxygen in the blood. Haemoglobin also binds other inorganic molecules, including carbon monoxide, which prevents uptake of oxygen.

**iron oxide**, any one of three different compounds. Iron(II) oxide (or ferrous oxide, FeO) is a black powder; it forms iron(II) salts when treated with acids, but gives iron(III) oxide on heating in air. It is used as a pigment in glass. Iron(III) oxide (or ferric oxide, $Fe_2O_3$) in the form of *haematite is the commonest *ore mineral of iron. When ground to powder it is used as a red pigment and for polishing diamonds. It forms a number of hydrates of varying compositions; one is *rust, produced by the action of water, oxygen, and carbon dioxide on iron. Iron(II) di-iron(III) oxide (ferroso-ferric oxide, $Fe_3O_4$) occurs as the mineral *magnetite, the second most important ore mineral of iron; it is also formed when steam is passed over hot iron. It is used as a black pigment.

**irrational number**, a number which cannot be written as a fraction, $p/q$, where $p$ and $q$ are integers. That such numbers exist was known to the Greeks at least 2,200 years ago, when it was shown that the side of a square cannot be expressed as a fraction of the diagonal (they are incommensurable). For a square with sides of unit length, the diagonal is $\sqrt{2}$, which is irrational. Irrational numbers have infinite, non-repeating decimal expansions, and examples include $\sqrt{7}$, $\sqrt{2}$, $\pi$, e, and many more.

**Irrawaddy**, the great river of Myanmar (Burma), about 1,600 km (1,000 miles) in length. From its source in Tibet, it rushes southward through great gorges before reaching its main valley and becoming navigable. In the heart of Myanmar it receives its chief tributary, the Chindwin, and further south passes through a region of oil-bearing rocks. The delta, which its silt is building out into the Bay of Bengal, has become a vast paddy field some 300 km (nearly 200 miles) wide; only the coast is swampy, with mangroves and crocodile-infested jungle.

**Ischia**, a volcanic island near the Bay of Naples on the west coast of Italy. In an area of 48 km² (18 sq. mi.) it consists

The open cut mines at Iron Knob, in the Middleback Range, South Australia, provide an important source of **iron** ore to several steel-producing centres in Australia.

almost entirely of volcanic rock, Monte Epomeo rising to over 780 m (2,560 feet). There are hot springs, vineyards, olive groves, and an attractive coast; and in spring and early autumn the climate is mild.

**island**, an area of land which is smaller than a continent and totally surrounded by water in an ocean, sea, or lake. Although Australia is sometimes known as the island continent, Greenland is generally considered to be the largest island in the world. Other large islands in order of size are New Guinea, Borneo, Madagascar, Baffin, Sumatra, Honshu, and Britain. There are many thousands of smaller ones. Islands are formed in several different ways. Those in relatively shallow seas just off a continental coast generally have very similar geology to areas on the mainland, and this shows that they were once part of the continent but were cut off when the sea-level rose at the end of the last great ice age. The *archipelagos of the Aegean Sea are islands formed in this way, as are the many islands along the New England coast of America, such as Long Island and Martha's Vineyard. Other islands near the shore have risen out of the sea as *barrier islands. Further out in the oceans there are *coral islands, volcanic islands thrown up by eruptions, and island arcs. Volcanic islands, which may be small but are usually high, are common and are being created all the time. They tend to occur in groups along zones of weakness in the earth's crust, sometimes as parts of island arcs at the junction of crustal *plates. Japan, the Marianas, and the Aleutians are examples of island arcs; others occur in the Caribbean and Indonesia. Most border ocean *trenches, some in a double arc, the outer one generally non-volcanic.

**island arc**, an archipelago in the form of a curved chain; examples are the Philippine and Marianas islands of the

Pacific. The convex side of the chain faces the ocean, and on the same side there is a deep oceanic trench. They are of significance in the theory of *plate tectonics. Associated with them are gravity anomalies and magnetic anomalies; so also are deep-focus earthquakes, and they may exhibit volcanic activity. These facts are interpreted to mean that the arcs are places where the plates of the oceanic crust are subducted, that is, carried down to great depths and melted. (See also *subduction.)

**isobar**, a line or contour drawn on a weather map to link places with the same barometric *pressure. Isobars usually represent the sea-level pressure distribution. Before they can be drawn the pressures measured at weather stations must be adjusted to sea-level by allowing for the decrease of pressure with altitude. Moreover, the pressure at the various places must be that at a given time or the average value over a given period.

**isomerism** (in chemistry), the existence of two or more molecules, isomers, with the same molecular formula but different three-dimensional structures. There are two main types of isomerism, structural isomerism and stereoisomerism. In structural isomerism, the isomers differ in the arrangement in which the atoms are joined. For example, there are two structural isomers of $C_2H_6O$. Ethanol is an alcohol, and has the structure $CH_3CH_2OH$, while its isomer, dimethyl ether, has the structure $CH_3OCH_3$. They have different physical and chemical properties. There are two kinds of stereoisomerism. Geometrical isomerism occurs in structurally rigid molecules such as alkenes, in which rotation about a particular bond is restricted. The alkene but-2-ene, $CH_3CH=CHCH_3$, forms two geometrical isomers. In the cis-isomer, the two hydrogen atoms are both on one side of the carbon–carbon double bond, while the two methyl groups ($-CH_3$) are both on the other side. In the trans-isomer, the two hydrogen atoms are on opposite sides, as are the two methyl groups. The cis- and trans-isomers differ in all their physical and many of their chemical properties. The other form of stereoisomerism is optical isomerism. If an organic molecule contains a carbon atom to which four different groups are joined, the compound can exist in two isomeric forms differing in the sequence in

A curving line of conical volcanoes jutting through cloud picks out the shape of the Indonesian **island arc**, part of the geologically active western margin of the Pacific crustal plate.

---

### Isomerism

Examples of the principal forms of isomerism: structural isomerism and the two forms of stereoisomerism – geometric and optical.

**Structural isomerism**: the two structural isomers of $C_2H_6O$.

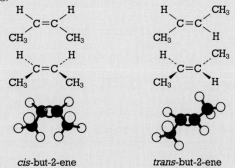

ethanol          dimethyl ether

**Geometric isomerism**: formulae, graphical and ball-and-stick representations of the stereoisomers of but-2-ene.

*cis*-but-2-ene          *trans*-but-2-ene

**Optical isomerism**: the mirror-image enantiomers of lactic acid.

L-lactic acid          D-lactic acid

*Note*: in graphical representations, --- indicates a bond directed into the plane of the paper, ➤ indicates a bond directed towards the reader.

---

which the groups are joined. These two isomers are termed *enantiomers. They have identical physical properties, and most chemical properties are identical. The most important way in which they differ is that they rotate the plane of plane-polarized light in opposite directions, that is, they exhibit *optical activity.

**isomorphism** (from the Greek *isos* 'equal' and *morphē* 'form'), the existence of two or more systems that have the same structure. In crystallography the term describes two minerals of similar chemical composition which have the same crystal structure. In mathematics the term means that results obtained from working in one system can be applied to the other system. Thus there must be a one-to-one correspondence between the elements which preserves the results of the operations. An example using two groups is as follows. The set of four complex numbers 1, i, −i, and −1 under the operation of multiplication forms a group. The rotations of a rectangle through multiples of 90° also forms a group. The function f which takes i to R, −1 to $R^2$, −i to $R^3$, and 1 to $R^4$ is a one-to-one function between these two groups which preserves the result of any multiplication; and hence it is an isomorphism, since for example i × −i = 1, while f (i) = R, f (−i) = $R^3$, and R × $R^3$ = $R^4$, which is f (1).

**isostasy** (in geology), the state in which large blocks of the *Earth's crust are in equilibrium, as if they were floating in a liquid, without any tendency for them to move up or down. For this equilibrium to exist, the mountains must have deep roots that are less dense than the mantle below; in other words, the highest parts of the continents must be the places where the crust is thickest. A further consequence of isostasy is that the continents will tend to subside when they are loaded by ice-sheets and will rise again when the load is removed. This, in fact, is what is found to have happened during the ice ages.

**isothermal change**, a change in which the temperature of a body or a system is maintained constant throughout the change. This very often means that for an isothermal process to occur heat must be allowed to enter or leave the system. For example, if a gas is compressed under normal conditions, it will heat up; if this is done isothermally, the gas must be compressed sufficiently slowly for the heat produced to have time to leak away, so that the temperature remains constant. This is in contrast with an *adiabatic change, in which no heat is allowed to enter or leave a system.

**isotope**, one of two or more forms of an *element which differ in relative atomic mass (atomic weight) and nuclear properties, but are chemically identical. Atomic nuclei are composed of protons and neutrons. It is the number of protons (the atomic number) that determines which element a particular atom is, but the number of neutrons can also vary, and this is the explanation of isotopes: they have the same number of protons in their nuclei, but different numbers of neutrons. For example, uranium-238 ($^{238}$U), the common isotope of uranium, has a nucleus containing 92 protons and 146 neutrons (92 + 146 = 238); uranium-235 ($^{235}$U) has 92 protons and 143 neutrons. All elements have at least two isotopes. Some exhibit radioactivity, and over a period decay into an isotope of a different element. Knowing the rate of decay one can sometimes calculate the age of an object from the proportion of isotopes present in it. This is the basis of the *radiometric carbon-14 dating of organic material and potassium–argon dating of rock (potassium-40 decays into argon-40). Radioactive isotopes are important technologically, and many are produced by artificial means for use in medicine, weaponry, and the nuclear power industry.

**isotopic dating**  *radiometric dating.

**Israel**, a country of south-west Asia at the eastern end of the Mediterranean Sea. It is bounded on the north by Lebanon, on the east by Syria and Jordan, and on the south by Egypt. The coastal plain is very warm in summer and suited particularly to the growth of citrus fruits. The north includes the Sea of Galilee and part of the River Jordan, while the east extends to the Dead Sea with its deposits of potash and reserves of natural gas. Southward is a hot and arid *rift valley (part of the Great Rift Valley system) running down the eastern side of the rocky Negev Desert. Here oil is found, together with some copper. Massive irrigation programmes have brought large areas of former desert under cultivation.

**isthmus**, a narrow neck of land with water on either side, connecting larger pieces of land. The term is usually applied to areas separating different seas, as do the isthmuses of Corinth, Panama, and Suez. They are obvious places to cut canals.

**Italian Lakes**, glacial lakes in north Italy, including Maggiore and Lugano (both shared with Switzerland), Como, Garda, and other smaller ones. They are long glacial lakes blocked largely by *moraines and famed for their beauty. Maggiore, Como, and Garda (the largest) are each 50 km (30 miles) or more long and surrounded by mountains of the Alps in the north and foothills in the south. The climate of the lakes is cool to mild.

**Italy**, a country bounded on the north by France, Switzerland, Austria, and Slovenia, the mainland forming a peninsula in the Mediterranean Sea, and including the islands of Sardinia, Sicily, Ischia, and Capri. Among the southern foothills of the Alps in the north of the mainland are the Italian Lakes. Below them the River Po runs west–east across the fertile Lombardy Plain to the Adriatic Sea. The Apennines are the backbone of the peninsula itself. To their west are the hills and plains of Tuscany; further south the Tiber flows across the Pontine Marshes to the Tyrrhenian Sea. Further south still the coastal plain is enriched by the debris of Vesuvius and the climate becomes warmer. To the south is Calabria, where the mountains fall steeply to the sea and in summer the land bakes brown. Eastward, stretches a wide and arid limestone plain. Here the land has little to offer by way of mineral deposits; but it is suitable for cultivating the tough wheat grain from which pasta is made.

**iterative methods** (in mathematics), repetitive methods of obtaining solutions to equations $f(x) = 0$ which produce ever closer approximations to the true value. The equation is first rewritten in the form $x = g(x)$. An estimated solution is then substituted into it, which leads to the output of a second approximate solution. This output is then used as the input for the equation on the next iteration. If the successive outputs of this cyclic process tend to converge then the iterative process is of value. For many engineering equations, iterative methods are the only way to reach a solution. The repetitive work is usually done by computer.

**Ivory Coast**  *Côte d'Ivoire.

# J

**jade**, a mineral of two types that are usually whitish to dark green. Jadeite or Chinese jade, the rarer, is a silicate of sodium and aluminium found not only in the East but also in Guatemala. It has a slightly greasy lustre and is tough and fibrous. Nephrite, a calcium, magnesium, iron silicate, comes mainly from New Zealand, America, and Russia. It glistens and is brittle. So-called Indian jade, aventurine, is a form of quartz.

**Jamaica**, a Caribbean island country lying south of Cuba. It is about 235 km (146 miles) from west to east and 80 km (50 miles) from north to south at its widest point. Along its spine is a range of limestone hills which rises to 2,256 m (7,400 feet) in the Blue Mountains in the east. Streams flow both north and south, the northern rivers reaching a coast which is very beautiful, with palm-fringed beaches and long, sandy bays. Temperatures are hot, and rainfall exceeds 1,000 mm (40 inches) a year. Sugar and Blue Mountain coffee are the main crops. Bauxite is more plentiful than almost anywhere else in the world, and there are also deposits of gypsum and oil.

**James River**, either of two rivers in the USA. The first runs for over 1,130 km (700 miles) southward through the Dakotas to join the Missouri. It is useful for irrigation but is not navigable. The second runs eastward from the Allegheny Mountains through Virginia to Chesapeake Bay, a distance of 550 km (340 miles). Its upper reaches have rapids and falls; its lower reaches are navigable for 160 km (100 miles) inland from Hampton Roads, a fine natural harbour.

**Japan** (in Japanese, Nihon or Nippon), a country occupying an archipelago off the coast of east Asia. It stretches about 2,400 km (1,500 miles) from Hokkaido in the north-east through Honshu, Shikoku, and Kyushu to the Ryukyu Islands in the south-west. The islands curve along the edge of the Eurasian *plate, one of the Earth's geologically most active zones, creating almost perpetual earthquake and much volcanic activity. Japan is separated from China to the south-west by the East China Sea, from Siberia and Korea to the west by the Sea of Japan, and from the islands of Sakhalin and the Kuriles to the north and north-east by the Sea of Okhotsk and the Nemuro Strait. The deeply indented coastlines are surrounded by many smaller islands, with the Inland Sea forming an important constituent of the country. Mountains cover two-thirds of Japan's surface, and less than 20 per cent of the land is arable. The latter is intensively cultivated through the use of irrigation, terracing, and multiple cropping. Fishing is highly developed. Rice on the coastal plains is the chief crop. Mineral resources are scarce, with the exception of coal. The rivers are generally unsuited for navigation. Generally the climate varies from the long Hokkaido winter of deep snow to subtropical conditions of the south, influenced by the Kuroshio and the Tsushima Currents. During the seasonal periods of heavy rainfall and typhoons, flooding becomes a major problem. Large-scale irrigation schemes have been developed, and hydro-electric plants provide much of the country's energy.

**Japan, Sea of**, a sea of the western Pacific Ocean separating the islands of Japan and of Sukhalin from Korea, China, and Siberia. It covers about 1,048,950 km² (405,000 sq. mi.) and at its deepest is 3,742 m (12,276 feet). One of the major epicentres of the Eurasian *plate runs along its seabed faults, so that offshore tremors may trigger *tsunami seismic sea waves and cause severe coastal damage. Natural gas and petroleum deposits lie off Japan and Sakhalin island. A branch of the relatively warm waters of the *Kuroshio Current flows north-west through the sea, contributing greatly to the mild climate of Japan.

**Japan Current** *Kuroshio.

**jasper** *chalcedony.

**Jasper National Park**, on the eastern slope of the Rocky Mountains in Alberta, Canada, the largest scenic and recreational park in the country, covering some 10,900 km² (4,200 sq. mi.). As almost its entire area exceeds 1,500 m (5,000 feet) in height, there is much spectacular scenery, including Mount Columbia at 3,747 m (12,294 feet), many glaciers, and the remarkable Maligne Gorge. The Miette Hot Springs are among its attractions, and it is one of the greatest wildlife sanctuaries of North America.

**Java**, an Indonesian island between the larger island of Sumatra, to the west and the much smaller one of Bali. It is over 1,000 km (620 miles) long but only some 120 km (75 miles) wide for much of its length. Extending for almost all its west–east length is a chain of volcanic mountains, many of them densely forested. Short, swift rivers run north and south to plains fertile with volcanic soil, where rice and other tropical crops can be cultivated. In the north-east there are oilfields, while deposits of other valuable minerals are widespread.

**Jenolan Caves**, a complex of tunnels and caverns on the western margin of the Blue Mountains, Australia, 113 km (70 miles) west of Sydney. They were eroded by underground streams in a thick bed of limestone, and subsequently fine *stalactites have developed. The caves are at different levels.

**Jersey** *Channel Islands.

**jet**, a hard, black variety of *lignite or brown coal, light in weight and capable of being carved and highly polished. There are deposits in the USA, Spain, France, and Germany, but the chief source is Yorkshire, UK, where it can be found on the shore, having been dislodged by waves from the seaside cliffs.

**jet stream**, a narrow meandering band of very strong wind which generally exceed 100 knots (187 km/h, 116 m.p.h.) and encircles the globe in the upper and middle troposphere. Jet streams are caused by the extremely large temperature contrasts between adjacent air masses such as those which occur along the *polar front. The polar front jet stream is of fundamental importance to the formation of the migratory *depressions and *anticyclones of mid-latitude regions, because strong, localized accelerations and decelerations which occur within it generate *divergence and *convergence respectively. Its track also steers these surface pressure systems in their eastward passage across the Atlantic and Pacific oceans. Jet streams also have an important effect on air travel across the Atlantic and Pacific oceans. Rapid west–east travel times can be achieved by riding the easterly flowing jet; conversely, east–west journey times may be retarded by the strong headwinds.

**joint** (in geology), a fracture in rock that has not undergone any movement—if it had it would then be a *fault. Joints may be formed by shrinkage (on cooling) of an igneous rock, by *sheeting (pressure-release), or by tectonic forces (the brittle fracture of rocks during flexure).

**Joliot-Curie, Jean-Frédéric** (1900–58) and **Irène** (1897–1956), French nuclear physicists. Frédéric gave up a career in engineering to study radioactivity and in 1925 became Madame *Curie's assistant at the Radium Institute in Paris. There, he worked with her daughter Irène, whom he married, both taking the name Joliot-Curie; their joint discovery of artificial radioactivity earned them the 1935 Nobel Prize for Chemistry. This research led James *Chadwick to discover the neutron when he reviewed their experiments in Cambridge. Shortly before World War II Jean-Frédéric demonstrated that a nuclear chain reaction was possible, and after the war both he and his wife became involved with the development of nuclear energy and the establishment of the French Atomic Energy Commission, but were removed from this government body because of their commitment to communism. Irène, like her mother, died of leukaemia.

**Jordan**, a mainly inland country, part of historical Palestine, bordering on Syria on the north, Iraq on the east, Saudi Arabia on the south-east, and Israel on the west. Its natural resources are meagre, and its only outlet to the sea is the port

Deep **joints**, usually made more pronounced by weathering, are a characteristic feature of massive granite outcrops.

of Aqaba at the north-east end of the Red Sea. Most of the country is on a desert plateau which has only about 250 mm (10 inches) of rain a year; but in the west is the Jordan River valley (whose West Bank is occupied by Israel) where some crops can be grown. The main mineral resource is phosphates, while near the Dead Sea potash is found.

**Jordan, River**, a river flowing southward from Syria across Israel into Jordan. From a height of 2,700 m (nearly 9,000 feet) on Mount Hermon it runs for 360 km (223 miles), first to the Sea of Galilee and then down the *rift valley to the Dead Sea, some 400 m (1,300 feet) below sea-level. Turbulent during winter rains, the flow of the river is sluggish during summer and it becomes quite salty. Irrigation has been increased through the construction of canals and water supply grids.

**Jostedalsbreen**, a sheet of ice north of the Sogne Fiord in Norway. The largest ice-mass in Europe outside Iceland, it has shrunk quite appreciably to its present area of some 477 km² (184 sq. miles). If its neighbouring smaller ice-masses are included, the total area becomes 830 km² (320 sq. mi.). It mantles a number of mountain peaks, the highest of which rises to over 2,000 m (6,500 feet), and it feeds glaciers that flow into a number of adjacent valleys.

**joule** (symbol J), the *SI unit of *energy or work. It is defined as the work done when a force of 1 newton moves a distance of 1 metre in the direction of the force. A joule per second is a *watt. The joule is named after the British physicist, James Prescott Joule (1818–89). He was the first to determine the mechanical equivalent of *heat, that is the work required to produce a given amount of heat energy. Joule's research on the nature of heat led to the development of thermodynamics by Rudolf *Clausius and William *Thomson. He also contributed to the *kinetic theory of gases. Joule's law, which he proposed in 1841, concerns the heating effect of an electric current in a wire. It states that the heat produced in any given time is in direct proportion to the

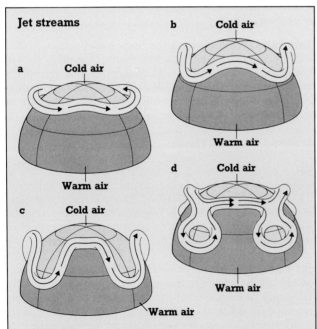

**Jet streams**

a  **Cold air**

**Warm air**

b  **Cold air**

**Warm air**

c  **Cold air**

**Warm air**

d  **Cold air**

**Warm air**

Jet streams form at altitudes of 10–15 km (6–9 miles) in the middle and upper troposphere, along the boundary between warm moist and cold dry air masses (a). Undulations in these 'tubes' of fast-moving air increase in amplitude (b and c) until rotating cells of warm and cold air become detached (d). These gradually die away as the original wave pattern is re-established.

square of the current: for example, doubling the current gives four times the heat.

**Jungfrau**, a mountain in the Bernese Oberland, part of the Alps, in central Switzerland, 18 km (11 miles) south-east of Interlaken. Standing at 4,158 m (13,642 feet), it dominates its surroundings, and from its summit can be viewed the peaks of the Bernese Oberland, the Alps of the Valais, including Monte Rosa and the Matterhorn, and Mont Blanc. It is pyramidal in shape, and on its southern side is the beginning of the Aletsch Glacier.

**Jura Mountains**, a system of limestone and sandstone ranges, running for 260 km (160 miles) along the French–Swiss border. Lying in an arc parallel to the Alps but much lower, its rounded ridges rise no higher than 1,723 m (5,652 feet) at Crêt de la Neige. The eastern slopes are the steeper, and the three main rivers flow down the longer western slopes into France. The ranges are pine-covered but contain their own valleys and provide good pastureland. There are many gorges, waterfalls, and limestone caves. Fossils abound in the rocks, and it is from them that the *Jurassic Period takes its name.

**Jurassic Period**, the second of the three geological periods that constitute the *Mesozoic Era, and spanning the interval of time from 208 to 144 million years ago. It follows the *Triassic and precedes the *Cretaceous Period. In the Jurassic, reptiles attained their maximum size and were found on land, in the sea, and in the air. The shallow Jurassic seas were rich in marine life: ammonites and clams proliferated. On land the flora included ferns and conifers; and the small rat-sized mammals and the first birds (*Archaeopteryx*) appeared.

**Jutland**, the peninsula of northern Europe that forms continental Denmark. Its gentle relief—the highest point is 173 m (568 feet)—reflects the generally soft underlying rocks which include pre-Quaternary sediments and a mantle of *Pleistocene drifts. The major scenic contrast is between the landscape of west Jutland, with its extensive sandy plains and occasional hill, and that of the east, which is more undulating. The character of the former area was fashioned by glacial meltwater, while the scenery of the latter is a result of the dumping by decaying glaciers of their load of debris. The boundary between the two regions marks the glacial limit of the last ice age. The coast is dominated by the effects of subsidence in the north, and by extensive *dune systems in the west.

**K2** (known locally as Dapsang and Chogori, also as Godwin Austen after the peak's first surveyor), a peak in the Karakoram range of the Himalayas presently under Pakistani administration. At 8,611 m (28,250 feet) it is the world's second highest mountain and probably the most difficult to scale, although the summit was reached by an Italian expedition in 1954, led by the geologist Ardito Desio.

**Kabylie**, a mountainous coastal region comprising the Great Kabylia, the Kabylia des Babors, and the Kabylia de Collo. The Kabylie is joined on the west to the Tell Atlas Mountains. The highest peak is Tamgout de Lalla Kredidja, at 2,308 m (7,572 feet). The region embraces the Djurdjura and Akfadon National Parks, and in its mountain strongholds the Berber people and their culture survive in their purest form.

**Kalahari**, an arid plateau, largely desert, some 900–1,200 m (3,000–4,000 feet) high between the Zambezi and Orange Rivers in southern Africa; it forms the western part of Botswana. With annual rainfall varying between 130 mm (5 inches) in the south-west and 500 mm (20 inches) in the north-east, the only perennial river is the Okavango, which flows from the north into the swampy Okavango Basin north of Lake Ngami. The plateau is covered mainly by reddish sand and the vegetation comprises dry grass, scattered acacias, and thin thorn-scrub. In the south is the Kalahari Game Reserve.

Scattered acacias and a small herd of wildebeest are all that break the monotony of this view over the vast red sand plain of the **Kalahari** desert.

**Kamchatka**, a peninsula extending southward for 1,200 km (750 miles) in the far-eastern republic of Russia, lying between the Sea of Okhotsk on the west and the Pacific Ocean and Bering Sea on the east. It has a backbone of folded mountain ranges, some containing extinct volcanoes, that runs for almost its entire length. To the east are a number of active volcanoes; these are due to its position on the *plate margin that rims the west Pacific. The highest volcano is Mount Klyuchevskaya at 4,750 m (15,580 feet), which has erupted some thirty-five times in the last 250 years. West of the central spine is a wide and sandy coastal plain.

**Kamchatka Current**, a continuation of the Aleutian or Subarctic Current, flowing south-westward along the shores of the Kamchatka Peninsula and eventually bringing cold water into the North Pacific Ocean. Much of its water is derived from melting of the polar ice; icebergs which have broken off the Arctic ice mass are often carried south by this current.

**kame** (esker, or osar), a fairly small mound of sand and gravel laid down by running water accompanying the ice of glaciers or ice-sheets. Kames can be almost any shape: long and sinuous, or short, dune-like mounds. While some represent the infilling of crevasses—deep cracks—in the ice (by debris brought in from the glacier surface by meltwater streams), the origin of others is not very clear. The term is often used as a general description of any small heap of poorly sorted fluvioglacial material.

**Kangaroo Island**, an island just off the south Australian coast, 4,351 km² (1,680 sq. mi.) near the mouth of the Murray River. Cliffs rise to a low plateau, which is developed across block-faulted structures that continue those of the Mount Lofty and Flinders ranges to the north.

**kaolin** *china clay.

**Karakoram**, a great chain of mountains in central Asia, stretching for about 480 km (300 miles) between the Pamirs and the Himalayas and standing mainly in Kashmir. In the centre is *K2; some sixty other peaks rise to over 6,700 m (22,000 feet), and the only passes are in regions of perpetual snow. The Karakoram Pass at 5,800 m (19,000 feet) is the old route between Kashmir and Xinjiang, while the slightly lower Khunjerab Pass is the one now used. The ranges contain many huge glaciers, and the southern slopes give rise to tributaries of the Indus, which flows along the foot of the Ladakh range to the south.

**karren** (lapiés), a small, often intricate channel on the bare surface of hard limestone. Different names are given to different shapes and sizes of karren. Those which are quite shallow, but have very sharp ridges between the channels, are termed rillenkarren. These are formed by the action of rainwater, seawater or melting snow dissolving the calcium carbonate in the limestone when it is exposed on the surface, especially if there is a steep slope which allows the water to run off rapidly. Larger, more rounded flutings are called rinnenkarren. These often form under a layer of soil, where the limestone is attacked more slowly and deeply by percolating water carrying dissolved acids from the soil. When rinnenkarren are exposed to the atmosphere, rillenkarren can develop on their slopes. Fields of karren on limestone 'pavements', such as those of the Burren, western Ireland, have a superficially desolate appearance; but the cracks and chan-

nels provide a sheltered, moist environment for many plants. Extremely intricate and dangerously sharp-edged sets of karren develop on coral rocks exposed to solution along tropical coastlines; while giant forms, more than 1 m (3 feet) deep and tens of metres long, are formed on soluble gypsum in the Canadian Arctic.

**karst**, the distinctive type of landscape developed on and within limestone. The name comes from the Dalmatian area of Croatia and Bosnia, but is applied to other regions of similar landforms. The term 'pseudokarst' describes corresponding features on non-limestone rocks, particularly silicate forms in the wet tropics; and 'thermokarst' is produced when ice in *permafrost layers melts, causing collapse of the surface. Karst develops on thick layers of fairly hard limestone which have well-developed systems of joints and bedding planes. Water percolates down and along the cracks, dissolving the calcium and magnesium carbonate as it goes and enlarging the cracks into passages, tunnels, and caves. As the underground channels grow larger, it is more and more difficult for rivers to continue to flow on the surface. Finally, they disappear into sinkholes, leaving a surface of dry valleys or closed depressions such as *dolines and *poljes. The bare limestone surfaces may be weathered into flat 'pavements' criss-crossed by shallow channels, or *karren; pillars and 'tombstones' of rock, excavated from a layer of soil, may stand like prehistoric monuments on the slopes. Steep-sided, residual hills, shaped like cones or turrets, develop on the divides, especially in wet tropical areas. Sometimes the roof of a cave collapses, forming a gorge. Underground, solution and *corrasion combine to create highly intricate labyrinths of passages, chutes, caves, and underground lakes. Water dripping slowly from fine cracks allows tiny amounts of carbonate to be re-deposited on the roofs and floors of caves and passages, forming *stalactites and *stalagmites, and great pillars and curtains of stone. Water moving sluggishly on the floors of the caves and passages deposits *travertine terraces. Solution may go on both above and below the *water-table, but it is most efficient when the flow is rapid, allowing replacement of saturated films of water on the rock faces.

**katabatic wind**, a light, local wind which is generated when a sloping ground surface cools during the night. The air in contact with the ground is cooled by radiation, increases in density, and flows downhill and along the valley bottom. (See also *anabatic wind.)

**Kavir Desert** *Great Salt Deasert.

**Kazakhstan**, a country of western Asia, stretching for some 3,200 km (2,000 miles) from the Caspian Sea to Xinjiang. It is bounded by China on the east, Kyrgyzstan and Uzbekistan on the south, the Caspian Sea and Turkmenistan on the west, and Russia on the north. In the north a belt of fertile steppe with rich, black earth provides scope for cultivation. Southward, however, it becomes more arid, degenerating into the Kara-Kum desert. Kazakhstan has rich and varied mineral deposits, including tungsten, lead, uranium, diamonds, and iron ore. On the east Caspian coast, oil and natural gas are found. Further east, towards the Aral Sea, is a clay desert plateau; east and south-east of it, sand desert. To the east of this are the stony Kazakh uplands with huge coal deposits in their northern slopes and copper in their southern ones. Here is the extensive and partly saline Lake Balkhash, which is slowly evaporating.

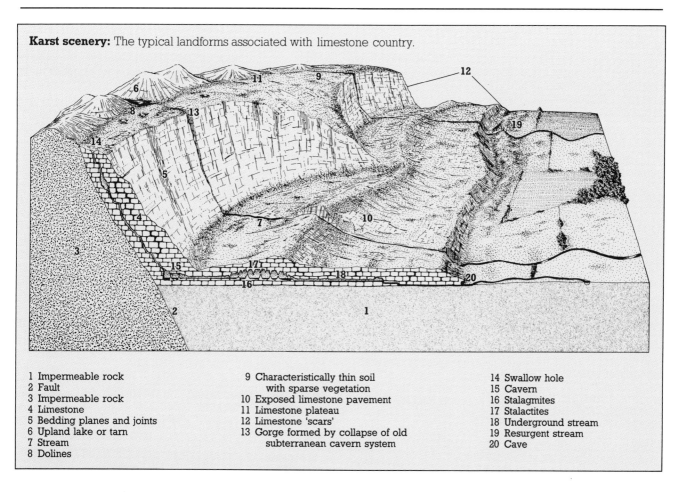

**Karst scenery:** The typical landforms associated with limestone country.

| | | |
|---|---|---|
| 1 Impermeable rock | 9 Characteristically thin soil | 14 Swallow hole |
| 2 Fault |    with sparse vegetation | 15 Cavern |
| 3 Impermeable rock | 10 Exposed limestone pavement | 16 Stalagmites |
| 4 Limestone | 11 Limestone plateau | 17 Stalactites |
| 5 Bedding planes and joints | 12 Limestone 'scars' | 18 Underground stream |
| 6 Upland lake or tarn | 13 Gorge formed by collapse of old | 19 Resurgent stream |
| 7 Stream |    subterranean cavern system | 20 Cave |
| 8 Dolines | | |

**Kekulé von Stradonitz, (Friedrich) August** (1829–96), German chemist who is regarded as one of the founders of structural organic chemistry. His training as an architect may have prompted his interest in the structure of molecules and in 1857 he proposed that the carbon atom can form four bonds with other atoms, furthermore, they could combine with other carbon atoms and form complex chains. In 1865 he suggested a structure for the *benzene ring in which the six carbon atoms are arranged in the form of a regular hexagon, and thus established a basis for the study of *aromatic compounds.

**Kelvin** *Thomson, William, Lord Kelvin.

**kelvin** (symbol K), the *SI unit of thermodynamic temperature, equal in magnitude to the degree Celsius. The kelvin scale is a temperature scale based on the idea that temperature is a measure of internal energy. Thus the zero point on the kelvin scale is the point at which a substance has no internal energy. This point is called *absolute zero, and is equivalent to $-273$ °C on the Celsius scale. Since the degrees on the kelvin scale are the same size as degrees Celsius, 0 °C = 273K. The kelvin scale is based on energy considerations, and is, therefore, more appropriate for most physics problems than the Celsius scale. It is named after William *Thomson, Lord Kelvin.

**Kennelly layer** *Heaviside–Kennelly layer.

**Kenya**, an equatorial country in east Africa, bounded inland by Somalia on the east, Ethiopia and Sudan on the north, Uganda on the west, and Tanzania on the south. In

August **Kekulé**'s hypothesis of a hexagonal ring structure for the benzene molecule allegedly arose out of a waking dream he had in which he pictured linked carbon atoms 'twisting and twining in snakelike motion' until one of the snakes seized its own tail.

the south-east is a hot, damp coast on the Indian Ocean, into which run two long rivers, the Tana and the Galana. They rise in the central highlands, a region containing Mount Kenya and cool slopes and plateaux suitable for farming of various kinds, particularly the cultivation of tea and coffee. The highlands are split by part of the Great Rift Valley, a region of lakes, and to the west fall away to the eastern shore of Lake Victoria. Northward is a rift-valley lake, Turkana (once called Rudolf), and to its east is a vast, hot, dry region with thorny scrub. In the south there is a smaller lake, Magadi, with major deposits of soda.

**Kenya, Mount**, a gigantic extinct volcano lying south of the Equator in central Kenya (the country is named after the mountain). It reaches a height of 5,199 m (17,058 feet) and is Africa's second highest mountain. Its slopes reveal evidence of numerous explosive episodes, and the central core is eroded to form several snow-capped, rocky peaks. Numerous glaciers emerge from *cirques on the upper slopes, which are covered with glacial debris. Tropical forests on the lower slopes, the home of much wildlife, are threatened by the advance of agriculture.

The 'Big Hole' of the Kimberley diamond mine. The diamond-bearing volcanic pipe of **kimberlite**, or 'blue ground', was discovered in 1871; by the time working ceased in 1914, more than 25 million tonnes of rock had been excavated from the 460 m (1,500 feet) wide shaft and the mine had yielded 14,504,567 carats (3 tonnes) of diamonds.

**ketone**, an organic compound in which the carbon atom of a *carbonyl group is bonded to two other carbon-containing groups, namely *alkyl or *aryl groups. These need not necessarily be identical. If these two groups are denoted by R and R′, the general formula for a ketone is RCOR′. Like the *aldehydes, the principal reactions of ketones are addition and condensation reactions (see *chemical reaction). However, unlike the aldehydes, they are not easily oxidized to carboxylic acids. Thus, they fail to produce a positive reaction with chemical tests for detecting reducing compounds.

**kettle-hole**, a small, enclosed depression found in areas of glacial deposits and which may contain ponds or marshes. If a large number occur close together, they give the surface an irregular, pock-marked appearance. They are thought to be formed by large blocks of ice which became detached from a glacier or ice-sheet and were covered and surrounded by rock debris, which insulated them. As the blocks slowly melted, the covering subsided to fill the depression, creating a kettle-hole.

**Keuper**, the uppermost division of the *Triassic System. It is represented by marine deposits in central Europe, but in Britain by continental deposits: barren red mudstones (Keuper Marl) and sandstones, and salt.

**khamsin**, an oppressive, hot, south or south-east wind occurring in North Africa and the Arabian Peninsula intermittently in late winter and early spring. The name is

derived from the Arabic, *khamsun*, meaning fifty, for the approximate period of days during which it blows.

**Khyber Pass**, a route through the eastern end of the Himalayas, between north-west Pakistan and the Kabul plain of Afghanistan. For part of its length it runs through a gorge cut by stream erosion, and for a distance of 8 km (5 miles) it narrows to a defile little more than 180 m (600 feet) wide. It is the most northerly and most important of the passes between Pakistan and Afghanistan.

**Kicking Horse Pass**, a routeway through the eastern ranges of the Canadian Rocky Mountains on the border between Alberta and British Columbia. The highest point of the Canadian-Pacific Railway, it stands at 1,627 m (5,339 feet). The Trans-Canada Highway came through the Pass in the 1960s.

**Kilimanjaro**, in north-east Tanzania, Africa's highest mountain. An extinct volcano, it rises at Mawenzi Peak to 5,149 m (16,896 feet) and at Kibo Peak to 5,895 m (19,340 feet). The two peaks are snow-capped and joined by a broad *col. The mountain is drained by a number of streams that form a radial pattern, some feeding the Galana and Pangani rivers, while others peter out on the plains below. The lower slopes are intensively cultivated, but there are forests and grassland above.

**kilogram** (symbol kg), the SI base unit for *mass. It is defined as the mass of a particular cylinder of platinum–iridium alloy held by the International Bureau of Weights and Measures at Sèvres, France. One kilogram is equal to 2.205 pounds.

**kimberlite**, a type of *peridotite containing mica in addition to olivine. The name of the rock comes from the Kimberley district of South Africa, where *volcanic necks filled with kimberlite are mined for diamonds.

**Kanchenjunga**, (Kinchinjunga), a mountain in the Himalayas on the border between Nepal and Sikkim. At 8,598 m (28,208 feet) it is the third highest mountain in the world. The combination of its height, its position on the edge of the Himalayas, and its relative isolation make it a fine spectacle when viewed from the hill station of Darjeeling, 74 km (46 miles) to the south. Its summit is split into five separate peaks, hence its name, 'the five treasures of the snows' in Tibetan.

**kinetic energy**, the ability of a body to do work as a result of its motion. For a body of mass $m$ and velocity $v$, its kinetic energy is equal to $\frac{1}{2}mv^2$, and in the *SI system is measured in joules. For a rotating body the kinetic energy is given by $\frac{1}{2}Iw^2$, where $I$ is the *moment of inertia and $w$ the angular velocity. Many energy changes involve the interconversion of kinetic energy and *potential energy, the energy resulting from the position of a body. For example a child's swing has its greatest kinetic energy as it moves through the lowest point on its path; here it is moving fastest. As the swing rises it loses kinetic energy (it slows down) but gains potential energy as it rises from the ground. The swing has its greatest potential energy where it has its least kinetic energy: at its highest point above the ground.

**kinetic theory**, a theory concerned with the movement of molecules in a gas, developed in order to calculate the properties of gases when their pressure, temperature, or volume is changed. It assumes that all the molecules in a gas are tiny, elastic spheres in rapid motion and that they collide with one another in a random manner. From such a simple description it is possible to account convincingly for many properties, such as the *specific heat and the *thermal conductivity of gases.

**King, Clarence** (1842–1901), US geologist, who was the first director of the US Geological Survey. In 1867–72 he led the Fortieth Parallel Survey, which mapped the cordilleran ranges from Colorado into California; and he exposed the 1872 diamond fraud in which jewels were strewn over rocky areas in northern Utah in order to attract investors.

**Kings Canyon National Park**, a national park in eastern California, USA, high in the Sierra Nevada, taking its name from the Kings River, whose canyons traverse it. A wilderness of snow-capped peaks, huge *cirques, and precipices, it is largely inaccessible except to climbers. In the south-west, where it adjoins the Sequoia National Park, there are groves of giant sequoia trees.

**Kingsley, Mary Henrietta** (1862–1900), British traveller in western and equatorial Africa who alone and in uncertain health made two long journeys for the collection of zoological specimens. In Gabon she made a hazardous journey up the Ogooué River through the country of the Fang, a tribe reputed to practise cannibalism. Returning to Britain, she lectured widely about her work, and her *Travels in West Africa* (1897) records her experiences. In South Africa during the second Boer War, she died of typhoid fever contracted while nursing sick prisoners.

**Kirchhoff, Gustav Robert** (1824–87), German physicist who worked with the German chemist Robert Bunsen (1811–99) and made major advances in the study of light spectra, thermal radiation, and electric circuit theory. His name is given to a law linking the radiating and absorbing powers of a surface. He also established two laws used in analysing electrical circuits, and discovered the elements caesium and rubidium (1850–1).

**Kirghizia**, a mountainous country, lying mostly in the Alai and *Tian Shan ranges of central Asia, which rise to 7,439 m (24,406 feet) at Pobedy on the border with China. Bounded also by Kazakhstan, Uzbekistan, and Tajikistan, it is a mass of snowfields, glaciers, forests, and deep lakes. The lower slopes provide pasture for millions of sheep, while in the spacious valleys cotton, tobacco, sugarbeet, and corn can all be cultivated. Among the mineral deposits are coal, mercury, antimony, tin, lead, and gold.

**Kiribati** (formerly Gilbert Islands), an island country comprising a widely scattered archipelago in the Pacific Ocean, lying either side of the Equator and between longitudes 169° W. and 147° E. There are over thirty islands, many of them mere coral atolls not more than 1 km (0.5 miles) across. The main resource is the coconut palm, although Ocean Island has phosphates.

**Klein, (Christian) Felix** (1849–1925), German mathematician and educator who disapproved of the increasing tendency towards abstraction in mathematics. An important mathematician in his own right, he used the concepts of *group theory to unify and classify the disparate geometries which were being studied at the time. He claimed that every geometry was nothing more than the study of those properties of figures which remained invariant under a particular group of transformations.

**Kola Peninsula**, a large peninsula on the far north-west coast of Russia, separating the White Sea from the Barents Sea; it covers some 100,000 km² (40,000 sq. mi.) and extends across the Arctic Circle about 305 km (190 miles) north–south. The area is nearly all tundra and swampy forest, with the world's largest deposits of phosphor-rich minerals. Nephelinite (a source of aluminium), zirconium, and columbium are also mined. The peninsula contains the world's deepest bore hole (12,261 m, 40,241 feet). The area is notorious for its heavy pollution caused by the huge nickel-smelter industry. A dead zone of some 700 km² (270 sq. mi.) is reported, where all forests, fish, grass, mushrooms, moss, reindeer, insects, and berries have perished.

**kopje** (koppie, Afrikaans, 'hill'), a steep-sided, isolated land-form, usually occurring on granite outcrops.

**Köppen, Wladimir** (1846–1940), German climatologist and biologist who in 1900 classified *climatic types by relating them to the Earth's natural vegetation zones and defining them in terms of mean annual temperature and precipitation. His system of classification remains one of the most easily understood and widely used.

**Korea**, a southward-pointing peninsula in east Asia, between the Sea of Japan to the east and the Yellow Sea to the west. It is divided into two countries. North Korea is bounded inland by China. Here it is largely mountainous,

A valley in the mountains of **Kurdistan** in north-east Iran, where a shepherd tends his mixed flock of sheep and goats on land which is poor in topsoil.

with narrow valleys, fine forests, and rivers which freeze in winter. Iron, lead, and zinc are to be found underground. Southward on the peninsula, the hills are lower, the valleys wider, and the climate warmer. South Korea, which is roughly all that part below latitude 38° N., is mainly agricultural, and it has one of the largest reserves of tungsten in the world. Numerous islands lie off its western coast in the Yellow Sea.

**Kosciusko, Mount**, in south-east New South Wales, the highest peak in Australia, rising to 2,228 m (7,310 feet). It is a crustal block or *horst lying on a lofty plateau in the Muniong Range of the Australian Alps, here known as the Snowy Mountains, and is the centre-piece of a national park. The name is that of the Polish patriot and leader, Tadeusz Kociuszko (1746–1817).

**Kotzebue, Otto von** (1787–1846), German-born Russian naval officer who circumnavigated the Earth three times (1803–6; 1815–18; 1823–6), charted much of the Alaskan coast, discovered and named Kotzebue Sound, as well as discovering several islands in the Pacific.

**Krakatoa**, an island volcano in the Sunda Strait between Sumatra and Java, Indonesia. It exploded in 1883 in one of the greatest volcanic eruptions recorded. The explosion left three small islands, which within fifty years had forests and were colonized by many species of insects and birds. A fourth island has appeared and disappeared several times since then; and whenever the sea laps over the edge of the low crater fresh eruptions are liable to occur.

**krypton** (symbol Kr, at. no. 36, r.a.m. 83.80), a colourless unreactive gas which is used together with other *noble gases in discharge lamps. Although a member of the inert gases, it forms a few unstable compounds such as krypton difluoride, $KrF_2$.

**Kubiena, Walter L.** (1897–1970), German soil scientist who developed a natural classification system for the soils of Europe. This classification emphasized both the relatively young soils of the continent, and the importance of wetland soils in the region.

**Kurdistan**, a mountainous region of the Middle East, lying partly in Turkey and Iraq, but mainly in Iran. Many of the mountains are over 2,000 m (6,600 feet) high, the highest rising to 4,168 m (13,675 feet), and they form a watershed between the Tigris in the south and the inland lakes of Van, Urmia, and the Caspian Sea in the north. The terrain generally is difficult, the climate hot and dry in summer, and the pasture poor. Oil is the main natural resource.

**Kurile Islands** (in Japanese, Chishma-Retto), an archipelago of 56 islands extending for 1,200 km (750 miles) from the Kamachtka Peninsula in Siberia to Hokkaido Island in Japan. The islands lie within the geologically unstable circle of the Pacific Ocean, and contain 35 active volcanoes and many hot springs. Parallel to the islands on the ocean floor runs the Kurile Trench 2,900 km (1,800 miles) long, which itself marks the beginning of a chain of oceanic trenches extending from the Bering Sea to the Philippine Trench. Thickly forested and rich in gold, silver, and other precious metals, the southern Kuriles are washed by some of the richest fishing grounds in the world.

**Kuroshio** (Japanese, 'black stream'), a strong fast-moving current flowing north-eastward from the northern Philippines up the east coast of Japan. As a continuation of the North Equatorial Current, it carries warm waters into the North Pacific Ocean, much as the Gulf Stream does in the Atlantic. It is about 80 km (50 miles) wide but only 400 m (1,300 feet) deep.

**Kutch**, a part of Gujarat in west-central India. In the north is the Rann (marsh) of Kutch, an area of saline mudflats that was formerly an extension of the Arabian Sea but which has been filled by sediment. The Great Rann has an area of 18,000 km² (7,000 sq. mi.).

**Kuwait**, a small country in the north-west corner of the Gulf, flanked by Iraq and Saudi Arabia. It is mainly low desert, very hot in summer but cool in winter, and very arid. It has enormous reserves of oil, on land and off-shore.

**Kyrgyzstan**, a country in central Asia bounded by Kazakhstan on the north and north-west, Uzbekistan on the south-west, and Tadjikistan on the south. On the south-east its Kokshaalatu range of mountains shares a border with china. A mountainous country, its lower plains are exposed to hot desert winds. Its middle reaches are forested. There are substantial mineral reserves, including coal, petroleum, and natural gas.

**Kyushu**, the most southerly of the four main islands of Japan. It occupies a junction between two volcanic arcs, one from *Shikoku to the east and the other from the Ryukyu Islands to the south-west. As a consequence it is dominated by volcanic rocks, with a rugged relief of dissected ash and lava plateaux; there are fine individual volcanoes and several small alluvial plains. Structural disturbance is common: the important coalfield in the north lies in a *tectonic basin, and the complicated bays of the west partly result from *faulting.

**Labe** *Elbe.

**Labrador**, the easternmost part of the Canadian mainland, a vast, cold region drained by rivers flowing into the Atlantic Ocean. Its bleak coast is seldom free of the ice carried south by the Labrador Current, and the mountains which curve round its snowy interior are themselves glaciated. They contain several vast lakes, from the largest of which issues the Churchill River at the start of a long eastward course to its estuary in Goose Bay. Hydroelectricity is obtained from Churchill Falls. Labrador is on the *Canadian Shield, and is rich in iron ore and other minerals, many of which await exploitation. Most of its surface is undulating or low-ridged plateaux which are poorly drained but forested in the valleys. The forests constitute one of the largest sources of virgin softwood (primarily conifers) remaining in North America.

**Labrador Current**, a slow-moving body of cold surface water in the North Atlantic Ocean, flowing southward off the coast of Labrador and Newfoundland to meet the northward-flowing Gulf Stream. Being denser, it dips beneath the warmer water. In summer the Current extends only to Cape Cod, Massachusetts, USA; but it may penetrate as far south as Virginia in winter, and icebergs are often carried down into the New York–Europe shipping lanes at such times. The influence of these cool waters on the climate of North America's eastern seaboard is very noticeable: New York, for example, is at the same latitude as southern Italy, but it has a much cooler climate because of the Labrador Current.

**laccolith**, an intrusive body of *igneous rock, more or less circular in plan, with a flat floor and a domed roof. Laccoliths have been injected as molten rock (*magma) into the surrounding rock, mostly along bedding planes. First described by Grove *Gilbert, an American geologist, from the Henry Mountains of Utah, they can be many miles across. Some are mined as a source of economically important minerals.

**Ladoga, Lake**, Europe's largest lake, lying at the southeast edge of the *Fennoscandian Shield in the north-west of Russia. Formerly a part of Finland, it is rocky in the north and swampy in the south; it extends for over 200 km (120 miles) in length and is 130 km (80 miles) wide. From December to March it is frozen, and navigation at other times is hampered by storms and fog. It receives the waters of Lake Onega and other lakes and is drained into the Gulf of Finland by the River Neva. With Lake Onega it helps to link the White Sea and the Volga with the Baltic Sea.

**lagoon**, a relatively shallow sheet of salt water which is more or less separated from the open sea. Lagoons may be formed behind banks of sand or shingle, as are the lagoons of Venice; behind *barrier reefs such as the Great Barrier Reef; or within *atolls. Sand lagoons are excavated by the action of currents and waves. Coral lagoons are developed as the polyps flourish and die: those on the seaward side of a

A small **lagoon** (right foreground) on the coast of Oman. Cut off from the sea by a broad sand-bar, it lies at the exit of the *wadi.

reef are nourished while those inside are not, and the cycle of life and death thus extends the reef outwards, forming the lagoon within. Although lagoons are connected to the sea by channels, the water is generally sheltered, providing moorings and occasionally coastal shipping routes. Tidal action is limited, and only overwashing storms or tidal waves disturb the surface of the sea.

**Lagrange, Joseph Louis, Comte de** (1736–1813), French mathematician and astronomer. He is remembered for his proof that every positive integer can be expressed as a sum of at most four squares, and for his study of the solution of algebraic equations which, many years later, provided the inspiration for the founding of the theory of groups and of the *Galois theory. But his greatest and most influential work was the *Traité de mécanique analytique* (1788) which was the culmination of his extensive work on mechanics and its application to the description of planetary and lunar motion.

**lake**, a body of water surrounded by land formed either when hollows fill with water or when natural drainage is obstructed so that water piles up behind the barriers. Some freshwater lakes are the result of earth movement, as in *rift valleys. Others, long and narrow like the Scottish lochs or broad like some in the USA and Canada, are caused by *glaciation. Yet others are the water-filled craters of extinct volcanoes or the result of water seeping into limestone rocks and forming caves, the roofs of which then collapsed. Sometimes the lava from a volcano or the moraine of a glacier blocks a valley, and a river then fills the land behind the barrier. Many lakes are fed by melting snow and become larger in the spring. Saltwater lakes may be parts of oceans or seas cut off by earth movement, or their salinity may have resulted from evaporation. Shallow lakes with flat shores may vary greatly in depth from season to season, reducing to swamp after a dry spell. Fresh or salt, they are useful in many ways—checking the flow of rapid rivers, absorbing floodwater, providing routes for travel, serving as reservoirs, and supplying headwater for irrigation and the generation of electricity.

**Lake District**, a scenic region of mountains and lakes in the north-west of England, UK. It includes fifteen lakes, several falls, and some of England's highest peaks. Composed of rocks of the Palaeozoic Age, the region was the centre of intense volcanic activity over 350 million years ago. It is a domed structure with a radial drainage pattern; streams have cut deep gorges and ancient ice-sheets are responsible for the development of broad U-shaped valleys. Crags, bare fells, and ravines add to its rugged beauty.

**Lake of the Woods**, a scenically attractive shallow lake on the border between Canada and the USA, at the junction between the provinces of Ontario and Manitoba and the state of Minnesota. It has a long, highly irregular shoreline and is reputed to contain some 14,000 islands. It lies in a region of pine forests on the hard granitic rocks of the *Canadian Shield, and was eroded by glaciers.

**Lander, Richard Lemon** (1804–34), English explorer in Africa who accompanied Hugh *Clapperton on his last journey, and then undertook a fresh expedition which successfully explored (1830) the course and termination of the Niger. Encouraged by the British government, he trekked with his brother John overland to the point where Mungo *Park had died and set off in canoes downstream. Surviving rapids and capture by Ibos, they eventually emerged in the Bight of Biafra at the outlet of the River Quorra (the Arabic name of the Niger River). In 1882 Lander was financed by

Liverpool merchants to ascend the Niger and open up trade with the countries of central Africa. Ascending the river once more in canoes, he died from wounds received from a musket-ball.

**landforms**, the separate features that make up the Earth's surface topography. Most are formed by natural processes like uplift or erosion; but man, too, can create landforms by building such works as Silbury Hill, UK; by opencast mining or allowing collapse of the surface over underground workings; by damming rivers and estuaries; or by draining and reclaiming land, as in the great Dutch reclamation works along Holland's North Sea coast. The largest landforms—mountains, volcanoes, and deep ocean trenches—are created by forces within the Earth's crust, driving the movement of crustal *plates; these are termed endogenetic or primary features. Smaller forms are cut by running water, ice, wind, and the sea, or are built out of the deposits of these agents; they are called exogenetic or secondary features. A comparatively minor group of forms—of which coral reefs, coral islands, and coral atolls are the most important members—are biological in origin. Fossil landforms are those created by processes which no longer modify them. The old dunes which are now covered by rain forests in the Amazon basin, and the glaciated valleys of much of northern Europe, are landforms that reveal to major changes in climate.

A huge **landslide** on New Zealand's South Island was caused by an earth tremor in 1968. The tangled mass of earth, rock, and shattered beech trees blocked the Buller River gorge for several hours.

**landslide** (or landslip), a sudden movement of rock and soil which happens when the ground surface is shaken, overloaded, or inadequately supported. Shaking occurs during earthquakes, blasting operations, and the passage of heavy vehicles. Overloading is caused by heavy snow or rain or by building roads, reservoirs, or houses at the top of slopes. Poor support occurs where rivers, glaciers, the sea, or building operations have cut away the lower sections of hillsides. Water is a major and particular factor in the incidence of landslides. It adds to the weight on the slope when it soaks into the surface and it also acts as a lubricant. As a result, material which has been saturated by heavy rain can slip a long way down even gentle slopes. The most dramatic and devastating landslides occur in mountainous areas and can involve the collapse of entire hillsides. Sometimes a cushion of air is trapped under the falling mass. Then it will travel a very long way, even uphill, like a hovercraft. More often a semicircular chunk of the slope rotates backwards as it gives way, leaving a cliff or scar above a lobe of debris. The area of debris remains dangerous as further slipping and sliding may easily be triggered.

**Langmuir, Irving** (1881–1957), US chemist who studied the surface properties of solutions and in 1917 devised a method for measuring directly the surface pressure exerted by surface films on liquids. He derived an expression relating the amount of gas adsorbed at a plane solid surface to the pressure of gas in equilibrium with the surface. His many inventions included the gas-filled tungsten lamp and the atomic-hydrogen welding torch. In 1932 he won the Nobel Prize for Chemistry for his work on surface chemistry.

**lanthanide** (or lanthanoid, rare-earth element), any of a series of silvery-white metallic elements in the *periodic table with atomic numbers from 57 (lanthanum) to 71 (lutetium), although some authorities exclude lanthanum itself from the series. The series is also called the rare-earth elements because their oxides (earths) were formerly thought to be rare; in fact even the rarest, thulium, is more common than silver. All the lanthanides have very similar chemical properties, and this is because they all have the same number of electrons in their outer shell; the additional electron added to each element across the series goes to fill an incomplete inner shell and is not greatly involved in *chemical bonding. The lanthanides are predominantly very *electropositive elements which give ions with a charge of +3. They occur together in monazite and certain other minerals, mainly in the USA, Russia, India, and Scandinavia, and are separated from other elements by *precipitation and from each other by ion exchange. Cerium is used in cigarette lighter flints and the europium ion as the red phosphor in colour television tubes.

**Laos**, a long, thin, land-locked country in south-east Asia, bordering China and Myanmar (Burma) on the north, Thailand on the west, Cambodia on the south, and Vietnam on the east. It is mostly high and hilly, with evergreen forest, this terrain also supporting maize. The Mekong River runs through the north of the country, down the western boundary, and through it again in the south; and its wide valley, swept by a summer monsoon, is ideal for rice growing. Rain forests in the valley provide teak.

**lapis lazuli**, a deep blue or bluish gemstone consisting of a sodium aluminium silicate with other minerals. It is found in metamorphosed limestones. The main deposits are in

Afghanistan and Chile, although the USA, Russia, and Myanmar (Burma) also have workings.

**Lapland**, a region in the far north of Europe, stretching from Norway's Atlantic coast, across northern Sweden and Finland, to the White Sea and the Kola peninsula in Russia. Lying mainly within the Arctic Circle, it has long dark winters and short mild summers. The west is mountainous and there is a wide belt of tundra inland from the northern coast; the south on the other hand is densely forested. Reindeer are farmed. Innumerable rivers and lakes, some of them very large, yield fish. The region lies on the *Fennoscandian Shield, and iron ore, copper, nickel, and apatite are found.

**lapse rate**, the rate at which atmospheric temperature decreases with height. The temperatures recorded at selected pressure levels by a climbing aircraft or by a radiosonde weather balloon are plotted on a graph to show the actual rate at which temperature decreases with height at a particular time and place. This is called the environmental lapse rate. When a parcel of air rises it expands and so cools adiabatically. If it is unsaturated the rate of cooling is approximately 1 °C per 100 m (5.5 °F per 1,000 feet); and this is called the dry adiabatic lapse rate. When a rising parcel of air is cooled to its *dew-point the resultant condensation of water vapour leads to the liberation of latent heat. This causes the air to cool more slowly than when unsaturated, the rate being approximately 0.6 °C per 100 m (3.3 °F per 1,000 feet). This is called the saturated adiabatic lapse rate.

**La Salle, René Robert Cavelier, Sieur de** (1643–87), French explorer. A settler in French Canada, La Salle sailed down the Ohio and Mississippi Rivers to the Gulf of Mexico in 1682, naming the valley of the latter river Louisiana in honour of Louis XIV. He returned to France and was appointed Viceroy of North America, returning in 1684 with a colonizing expedition. This venture went disastrously wrong, landing in Texas by mistake and squandering time

A specimen of **lapis lazuli** with white calcite and dark speckles of iron pyrites.

**La Salle's** successful expedition of 1682, which traced the Mississippi to the sea, was followed in 1684 by a disastrous one in which he failed to relocate the river's mouth. It was not until some seventeen years after his original claim that the French actually founded the colony of Louisiana.

and resources in fruitless attempts to get back to the Mississippi. Eventually La Salle's followers, embittered by their wanderings and his harsh discipline, mutinied and killed their leader.

**Lascaux Cave**, a large underground hall and several steep galleries in the Dordogne, central France, formed in the Tertiary Period, when water percolated through joints in the limestone rock of the plateau above and dissolved the rock. Discovered during World War II, it contains some remarkable displays of prehistoric art from the Upper Palaeolithic Period in the form of friezes depicting engraved, drawn or painted animals such as red deer, aurochs, oxen, horses, stags, and a unicorn-type animal.

**Lassen Volcanic National Park**, a region in northern California, USA, sited at the southern tip of the Cascade Range. It contains spectacular lava formations, hot sulphur springs, and other evidence of volcanic action. Lassen Peak, a volcano whose most recent activity occurred during the period 1914–21, rises to 3,187 m (10,547 feet).

**latent heat**, the energy released from a substance when it changes from a vapour to a liquid, or from a liquid to a solid, without a change in temperature. The energy released as latent heat is equal to the energy absorbed when such a change of state occurs in the reverse direction. Values can be large. For example, ice at 0 °C absorbs almost as much energy in changing to liquid water as is needed to heat this water from 0 °C to 100 °C; and it takes over six times as much energy again to change water at 100 °C into steam at the same temperature. Thus the latent heat of vaporization is the energy a substance absorbs from its surroundings in order to overcome the attractive forces between its molecules as it changes from a liquid to a gas and in order to do work against the external atmosphere as it expands.

**laterite**, the upper layer of soil in which large quantities of iron and aluminium oxides are concentrated by seasonal fluctuations of the *water-table. Laterites form in tropical areas, particularly on plains and plateaux. When fresh, they are mottled in red, yellow, and grey, but after exposure to the atmosphere, the sand and clays they contain are washed out by *leaching and the reddish material which remains hardens to form a very tough crust. Iron-rich laterites contain up to 30 per cent iron oxide, while those enriched with aluminium—bauxites—may have over 40 per cent concentration and are mined commercially. Most iron laterites are used only as roadstones at present, although more may be mined in the future. A typical exposed laterite *profile shows a layer of pea-sized iron-rich nodules (pisolitic gravel) overlying the thick, hard, reddish layer. Below this is a pale zone containing quartz and aluminium silicates washed down from the laterite capping: this layer has lost exchangeable *cations like calcium, potassium, and magnesium. Laterites are very common indeed in tropical areas. If vegetation and the thin top soils are removed, the laterites harden and cultivation becomes just about impossible.

**latitude and longitude** (mapping), a conceptual grid of lines covering the Earth's surface and used on *maps to enable positons to be accurately specified. Latitude lines (parallels) run east to west with their centres on the Earth's axis and their planes at right angles to it. The latitude of any of these circles, in degrees, is the angle that a line from it to the centre of the Earth makes with a similar line from the Equator, which has latitude 0°. The greatest possible latitude is 90°, that of the poles. Due to the *oblateness of the Earth the length of a *degree of latitude increases slightly towards the poles. Lines of latitude are generally shown according to scale; on world maps at intervals of 5°, with the Arctic and Antarctic Circles and the tropics of Cancer and Capricorn intervening. Together with lines of longitude they form a grid on which the position of any place can be specified. Longitude lines (meridians) run from north to south meeting at the Poles: a longitude is expressed as as the angle made at the Earth's centre by the plane of the meridian withthat of the prime or Greenwhich meridian at 0°. Lines of longitude thus range from 0° to 180° east or west of the prime meridian (180° E. and 180° W. being the same: the *international date-line). The distance between lines of longitude at any point depends on the degree of latitude; but because longitude is proportional to the time it takes the Earth to rotate through the angle subtended with the prime meridian, the longitude of any place can be found once the time is known.

**latosol**, a general name for *zonal soils found in the humid tropics, including *ferrisols, yellow *laterite soils, and black acidic soils. These soils share many common features because they develop in climates with high temperatures and heavy rainfall. They are highly weathered and may be extremely deep. Soluble bases and silica are removed from the profile by intensive *leaching, which leaves behind only iron and aluminium compounds. The organic content of these soils is low because humus is rapidly destroyed at high temperatures. Although the soils support luxuriant natural rain forests, they quickly lose their fertility under cultivation.

**Latvia**, a country lying on the shores of the Baltic Sea and the Gulf of Riga. 63,688 km² (24,590 sq. mi.) in area, it borders on Estonia to the north, Russia to the east, and Lithuania to the south. It is generally flat, though hilly in the lakelands of the east and well forested with fir, pine, birch, and oak. A modified continental climate provides for horticulture and dairy-farming, while the Dvina and its tributaries are the source of hydroelectric power.

**Laue, Max Theodore Felix von** (1879–1960), German physicist who devised the first practical method of analysing the wavelengths present in an *X-ray beam. The experiment was performed in 1913 by his assistants who directed a narrow beam of X-rays at a crystal and measured the pattern formed on a photographic plate by waves scattered from the regularly arranged atoms (see *interference). This technique, called X-ray diffraction, was further developed by William and Lawrence *Bragg and is now used extensively to study crystal structures. Von Laue won the Nobel Prize for Physics in 1914.

**Laurasia**, a vast supercontinent, so-named by the German meteorologist Alfred *Wegener in 1912, who presented the theory of *continental drift. He deduced that late in the Palaeozoic Era, which ended 225 million years ago, all the continents were united into a vast supercontinent which he called Pangaea. Later, this broke into two supercontinental masses: Laurasia, which existed in the northern hemisphere and contained North America (formerly Laurentia) and Eurasia, and *Gondwana.

Von **Laue**, photographed between 1910–15 while he was working on X-rays; he also contributed to the study of electromagnetism, thermodynamics and relativity.

**Laurentian Shield**   *Canadian Shield.

**Laurentides**, a provincial park in south-central Quebec, Canada. Part of the Laurentian Plateau, it occupies some 10,000 km² (4,000 sq. mi.) and rises to an elevation of 1,158 m (3,800 feet). It contains 1,600 lakes and a vast network of streams.

**lava**, a very hot, molten rock emitted from a volcanic vent or from a fissure (before it is emitted it is *magma). The same word is used to describe the rock that is formed when this material has cooled and solidified. Its chemical composition affects the way it moves and the type of scenery it produces. Acidic lava rich in silica moves slowly as a thick mass and cools quickly, producing upstanding peaks like Etna or Mount Saint Helens. Lavas containing less silica are more fluid and can flow appreciable distances before cooling. Basic, silica-poor lavas such as *basalts tend to form broad shield volcanoes with gentle slopes—as in the Hawaiian Islands—or to 'flood' wide areas, producing vast plateaux like the Deccan, India, or the Columbia Plateau in northwest USA. The tendency of acid lavas to cool rapidly often causes a plug to form in the vent of the volcano. Pressure builds up under it and a violently explosive eruption can result, as at *Krakatoa. The emission of basic lava is much less dramatic. The places where lava is emitted at the Earth's surface are in many instances related to the movement of the *plates that constitute its crust.

A basalt **lava** flow in the Galapagos. The wrinkled surface is caused by cooling of the outer 'skin' while the bulk of the lava is still mobile—a feature characteristic of very fluid silica-poor lavas.

**La Vérendrye, Pierre Gaultier de Varennes, Sieur de** (1685–1749), French-Canadian soldier and fur trader, one of the greatest explorers of the Canadian West. With his sons Louis-Joseph and François Gaultier he opened the country from Lake Superior to the Saskatchewan and Missouri Rivers to the French fur trade. The effect of this was to break the monopoly of the London-based Hudson's Bay Company and strengthen French claims to North America.

**Lavoisier, Antoine Laurent** (1743–94), French scientist, regarded as the father of modern chemistry. He initially studied law, but his first interest was science which, apart from chemistry, included for him agriculture, geology, and experimental physics. The chemical revolution which he caused was to describe the true nature of combustion, to introduce rigorous methods of analysis, and to develop a new rational chemical nomenclature, published in 1789. He realized in 1774 that it was Joseph *Priestley's 'dephlogisticated air' that combined with substances during burning, renamed this gas 'oxygen' in 1779, because he thought it a constituent of all acids and, in 1783, suggested that water was made up of the gases of oxygen and hydrogen; but in this he was anticipated by Henry *Cavendish. The holder of a number of important public offices, he supplemented his private income by becoming a member of a consortium that gathered the indirect taxes for the government, and it was this position that led to his death by guillotine during the Reign of Terror of the French Revolution.

**leaching**, a process which occurs when weakly acidic solutions from rainwater or plant acids are washed downward through the soil. This causes elements such as sodium, potassium, magnesium, and calcium to be released from the soil. These substances form alkaline compounds which are then carried down through the soil *profile in solution, a process known as *eluviation. As a result of the removal of these elements the upper horizons of the soil become increasingly acidic. The effects of leaching can be seen in the formation of the white salty deposits that often appear on the outside of earthenware flowerpots.

**lead** (symbol Pb, at. no. 82, r.a.m. 207.2), a soft, dense, grey metal which occurs in Group IV of the *periodic table. It is unreactive; it dissolves slowly in nitric acid but resists other acids, water, and oxygen. In its compounds it shows the *valencies 2 and 4. Because it is cheap and corrosion-resistant, it has been employed widely for roofing and for protecting cables and pipes underground; and as it absorbs radiation, it is used to shield X-ray equipment and nuclear reactors. It is also made use of in storage batteries, as ammunition, and in low-melting alloys such as solder—but not in pencils, the 'lead' in which is a mixture of graphite and clay. Tetraethyl lead, $Pb(C_2H_5)_4$, is extensively used as an *antiknock additive in petrol, although like all other lead compounds it is toxic, and it has been suggested that its use may be a significant health hazard. Four lead isotopes occur naturally: $^{204}Pb$, $^{206}Pb$, $^{207}Pb$, and $^{208}Pb$. Each is the end-product of a radioactive decay chain. The isotopic composition of lead therefore varies from place to place, and the relative atomic mass of lead is not constant. Galena, the sulphide (PbS) is the main natural source and is mined extensively in the USA.

**lead oxide**, any of three different compounds. Lead(II) oxide (PbO) is a red solid used in making lead storage batteries, and in glass-making. Lead(IV) oxide ($PbO_2$) is a

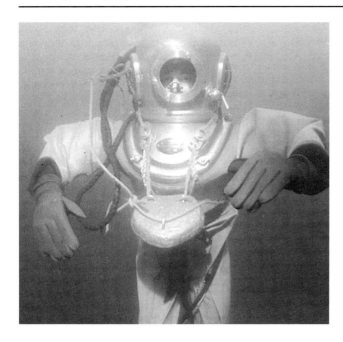

A **lead** weight slung round a diver's neck reduces his buoyancy and helps him to remain submerged. This use of lead relies upon its high density of approximately 11,400 kg/m³ (709 pounds per cubic foot);though several elements, including gold and tungsten, are more dense than lead.

strong *oxidizing agent, and on heating gives off oxygen. It is used in the manufacture of safety matches. Red lead ($Pb_3O_4$) is formed by oxidation of PbO; it is used in corrosion-resistant paints, especially to prevent rust.

**lead sulphide** (PbS), a blackish compound, occurring naturally in cubic crystals as galena, from which lead is extracted commercially. It is used in rectifiers and in detectors of infra-red radiation.

**least squares method**, a means of ascertaining the line or curve of 'best' fit for a set of data points. If the data points are plotted on a graph and a smooth line is drawn through the midst of them, the distance of the points from the line gives the difference between the observed and predicted results. The average of the squares of these distances gives a measure of 'goodness of fit' for the line. The line of best fit is that for which this mean square deviation is least. It can be shown that this line must pass through the *arithmetic mean $(\bar{x}, \bar{y})$ of the array, and its equation can be expressed as $y = \bar{y} + r(s_y/s_x)(x - \bar{x})$, where $r$ is the *correlation coefficient and $s_x$ and $s_y$ are the sample *standard deviations of the $x$- and $y$-values respectively. This technique for curve-fitting was developed by Adrien *Legendre in the context of geodesy and by Karl *Gauss in that of computing approximate orbits for planets from only a few observations of varying accuracy.

**Lebanon**, a country of south-west Asia at the eastern end of the Mediterranean Sea, bounded by Syria on the north and east and Israel on the south, which the latter has controlled since 1982. Lebanon is some 200 km (125 miles) from north to south and 50–80 km (30–50 miles) from east to west. On the narrow coastal plain summers are sunny and warm; fruits of all kinds grow well. Inland the ground rises quickly, to two ranges of high mountains, where there is much winter frost and snow. Between them is the fertile Bekaa Valley,

well suited to agriculture, while much of the eastern boundary resembles steppe.

**Lebesgue, Henri Léon** (1875–1941), French mathematician whose primary achievement was to extend the notion of *definite integrals. By generalizing the ideas of length and area to a general concept of the measure of a set, he allowed an integral to be assigned to a much broader class of functions. A superb teacher and popularizer of mathematics, he also wrote on its history.

**Le Châtelier, Henri-Louis** (1850–1936), French chemist who formulated the principle that if a system is subjected to a change in conditions, the system will respond in a way that tends to counteract the change. Thus, if a reversible reaction gives out heat, increasing the temperature will tend to reverse the reaction.

**Leeward Islands** *Caribbean Islands.

**Legendre, Adrien Marie** (1752–1833), French mathematician noted for his work on the theory of numbers and the publication *Theorie des Nombres*, 1830. He devised, independently of Karl *Gauss, the method of *least squares which he applied to the elliptical movement of planets. He taught in Paris and also published a geometry textbook.

**Leibniz, Gottfried Wilhelm** (1646–1716), German philosopher, mathematician, inventor and political adviser. He worked on the problem of the continuum and the laws of motion, and invented the infinitesimal calculus independently of Isaac *Newton. In 1673 he constructed a calculating machine and presented it to the Royal Society in London. Leibnitz was one of the creators of geology proposing the hypothesis that the Earth was at first molten. In 1679 he perfected the binary number system and also proposed the basis for general topology. In philosophy, he argued that the world is composed of single units (monads) which are simple yet each in its own way mirrors the whole universe; each is self-contained, but acts in harmony with every other, and they form a continuously ascending series from the lowest (which is next to nothing) to the highest (which is God; though in some places he speaks as though God were outside the series).

**Leichhardt, Friedrich Wilhelm Ludwig** (1813–48), German-born explorer of Australia. Having emigrated to Australia in 1841, Leichhardt began a series of geological surveys of that continent, crossing from Moreton Bay to Port Esslington in 1843–5, but disappearing without trace in the area of the Cogoon River on another attempt at an east-west crossing in 1848.

**lemma** (in mathematics), an auxiliary result which is often required in the course of proving a more important theorem, but is proved separately in order not to break the thread of ideas in the development of the main argument. Lemmas tend to be unimportant mathematically in their own right and frequently are of a technical nature. If it were not for their role in helping to establish the main theorem, they would probably not be worth noting.

**Lena**, the most easterly of the great Siberian rivers and, at 4,350 km (2,700 miles) in length, one of the longest in the world. Rising west of Lake Baikal it flows first north-eastward and then makes a huge bend northward to the

Arctic Ocean. In its main valley beneath the Verkhoyansk Range it reaches a width of over 13 km (8 miles); and its islanded delta, which thrusts out into the Laptev Sea, is nearly 400 km (250 miles) wide. The delta is ice-bound from October to July and its middle reaches from November to May or June; otherwise it is navigable for four-fifths of its entire length. Its banks and those of its tributaries contain deposits of oil, coal, and gold. In 1968 *permafrost to a depth of 1,500 m (4,900 feet) was measured in its basin.

**Leo, Johannes** (Al-Hasan Ibn Muhammad Al-Fasi) (c.1494–1552), known as Leo Africanus, Arab diplomat and scholar, born in Granada. Widely travelled in north Africa, he was captured by Christian pirates in the Mediterranean and presented as a gift to Pope Leo X. He was persuaded to receive (1520) a Christian baptism (in later years he returned to north Africa and is believed to have died a Muslim). In Rome, Leo completed his greatest work, *A Geographical History of Africa* (1526). This, together with his other writings, remained one of Europe's principal sources of information about Islam for some 400 years.

**lepton**, originally the term given to a light particle such as the electron, as opposed to a heavy particle (a *baryon). Nowadays the term encompasses the particles which participate in the electromagnetic interaction and weak *interaction but not the strong. These are the electron, the muon, and the tau, their respective *neutrinos, and the *antiparticles of each of these, giving a total of twelve. All leptons have a *spin of $\frac{1}{2}$, the anti-leptons having the same spin but in an opposite direction.

Natural **levees** on the banks of the Missouri River in the Three Forks region, Montana, USA.

**Lesotho**, a small country entirely surrounded by South Africa. It lies in the central and highest part of the Drakensberg Mountains, where summer rains cause severe soil erosion and in winter the temperature can be as low as −16 °C (2 °F). The Orange River rises here, in a terrain most suitable for grazing sheep and mountain goats, and only in its lower valley and to the west is there much scope for cultivation. Diamonds are the chief mineral resource.

**levee**, a low ridge running along the edge of a channel cut by a river, mudflow, or lava flow. (By extension, the term is also used for artificial embankments built to prevent flooding, especially those along the Mississippi.) Levees are formed by deposition of *alluvium during overbank flooding, when the force of the current slackens as it spills over on to the broad floodplain from the narrow, faster-flowing channel. Those along mudflows and lava flows form as the flow edges harden on drying or cooling. Once flow spills beyond the levees, it has obvious difficulty returning to its channel and therefore cuts a completely new course, a process termed 'avulsion'.

**Lewis, Gilbert Newton** (1875–1946), US chemist who proposed that a bond between two atoms could be formed not only through the complete transfer of electrons but also through the sharing of electrons to form a covalent bond (see *covalent compound). He extended the definition of an *acid to include all substances capable of accepting a pair of electrons from another compound; similarly he defined a *base as a substance capable of donating a pair of electrons—the so called Lewis acid-base theory. He also investigated thermodynamic properties and wrote an influential book, *Thermodynamics and the Free Energy of Chemical Substances* (1923). Ten years later he became the first person to prepare

heavy water ($D_2O$), formed from oxygen and *deuterium, an isotope of hydrogen. (See also *water.)

**Lewis, Meriwether** (1774–1809), US explorer. Formerly private secretary to President Jefferson, he was named by the President to lead an expedition to explore the newly acquired Louisiana Purchase, and chose William *Clark as co-leader. Between 1804 and 1806 the Lewis and Clark Expedition successfully crossed America from Saint Louis to the mouth of the Columbia River and returned (once again by land). During the last two years of his life (1807–9) Lewis served as Governor of the Louisiana Territory.

**Liberia**, a tropical country on the Atlantic coast of West Africa, flanked by Sierra Leone, Guinea, and Côte d'Ivoire. The climate is hot and very wet. Rain forest and swamp cover the coastal plain, which is traversed by several rivers flowing down from savannah-covered uplands. Diamonds are found here, and there are major reserves of iron ore, manganese, and bauxite. Rubber is the main plantation resource, though cocoa, coffee, and sugar-cane are also grown.

**Libya**, a country on the north coast of Africa, bounded by Tunisia and Algeria on the west, Niger and Chad on the south, and Sudan and Egypt on the east. The north-west region, Tripolitania, is cultivable near the coast, which has a Mediterranean climate; while inland the ground rises to a high desert of mainly limestone rocks. In Cyrenaica, the north-east region, some of the coast is high tableland, with light rain supporting forests. Southward the ground is low and sandy, though studded with oases. Here there are reserves of oil in huge quantities. The south of the country lies within the *Sahara; but to the west, in the Fezzan region, there are a few large oases among the otherwise bare, stony plains and scrub-covered hills.

**Lie, (Marius) Sophus** (1842–99), Norwegian mathematician who worked to establish a *Galois theory of differential equations, namely criteria for deciding when a differential equation is solvable. With his friend Felix *Klein, he strove to popularize the concepts of *group theory.

**Liebig, Justus, Baron von** (1803–73), German chemist and one of the founders of modern organic chemistry. He established at Giessen the first practical chemical teaching laboratory; and in 1832 he founded the *Annalen der Pharmazie*, later called the *Annalen der Chemie und Pharmazie*, an important journal of chemistry. His work in pure chemistry was of great importance. It included new techniques of organic synthesis and analysis, the invention of a simple condenser, and his famous investigation of benzaldehyde with Friedrich *Wöhler. This established the concept of a *functional group, the benzoyl group (in this case) which forms a constituent of an extensive series of compounds. With Wöhler also he examined uric acid, and he published an elaborate survey of organic acids. His work on the composition of ether, ethanol, and their derivatives led him to discover chloroform, chloral, and the aldehydes. He investigated the constituents of body fluids, and among his many findings showed that body heat results from the combustion of food in the body. Turning to vegetable physiology, he found that plants obtain their carbon and nitrogen from carbon dioxide and ammonia in the atmosphere, and their minerals from the soil, leading him to experiment with artificial fertilizers.

G. N. **Lewis** in 1944 at work in his laboratory at the University of California at Berkeley, USA.

**Liechtenstein**, in central Europe, one of the smallest countries in the world, with an area of 160 km² (62 sq. mi.). It lies between Austria and Switzerland, to the south of Lake Constance. Its western section occupies part of the flood-plain of the upper Rhine, while to the east it extends up the forested and then snow-covered slopes of the Rätikon Massif, part of the central Alps. Its mild climate is significantly affected by the warm *Föhn wind from the south.

**ligand** (in chemistry), a molecule or negative ion which can bond to a metal forming a *complex ion. Ligands all possess a *lone pair of electrons; $H_2O$, $NH_3$, and $CN^-$ are common examples. Ligands which have several atoms each of which can bond to a metal are called polydentate or *chelating, EDTA (ethylene-diaminetetraacetic acid) is the most important polydentate ligand.

**light**, *electromagnetic radiation with a wavelength between approximately $7.5 \times 10^{-7}$ (red) and $4 \times 10^{-7}$ m (violet), that is, the visible region of the spectrum. The corresponding frequencies are $4 \times 10^{14}$ hertz and $7.5 \times 10^{14}$ hertz. The wave nature of light is demonstrated by the phenomena of *diffraction and *interference. White light is a mixture of all the colours, consisting of a continuous range of wavelengths. Light is produced when electrons in solids and gases which have been excited to higher energies by heat or an electrical discharge return to their original ground state; the excess energy is then released as radiation, although not all of it needs be in the visible range. For true white light to appear, the temperature of the body emitting it must be about 6,000 °C. The *speed of light (sometimes wrongly called the velocity of light) in a vacuum is approximately $3 \times 10^8$ m/s ($9.85 \times 10^8$ feet) and is the maximum speed that can be obtained in the universe. The radiation travels in a straight line for as long as the medium through which it passes is homogeneous. If, however, it passes into another medium, part of it may be subject to *reflection at the boundary and the remainder subject to *refraction as it enters the new medium—that is, the direction of its path is

Multiple **lightning** flashes photographed during an intense thunderstorm over Tucson, Arizona, USA. Each flash is initiated by a 'leader stroke': this creates an ionized path through the air, which is then followed by the main electrical discharge.

altered. The action of light on the chlorophyll in plants (photosynthesis) converts carbon dioxide from the air into starches and sugars; and its action in initiating various chemical reactions (such as those that occur on photographic film) is studied in *photochemistry. In the *photoelectric effect light gives rise to an electric current.

**lightning**, an enormous spark which is generated by the discharge of static electricity between two clouds, or between a cloud and the ground. If the flash takes a zigzag or branching path through the atmosphere it is known as forked lightning, while if the flash is diffused by clouds it is known as sheet lightning. The presence of ice in the upper portions of a *cumulonimbus cloud is particularly associated with the generation and separation of *electric charges, which are probably produced by the preferential migration of *protons under the influence of a temperature gradient. A flash occurs when a large enough charge has built up within the cloud, and it heats the air so rapidly that the air along it suddenly expands, producing thunder.

**lignite**, an organic sedimentary rock, brown in colour, that tends to crumble on exposure to the air. It is a low-grade *coal made up of accumulated plant material and wood. It contains about 60 to 70 per cent carbon and burns with a smoky flame. Extensive deposits occur in the *Cretaceous and *Tertiary coalfields of North America and Europe.

**lime**, any of various compounds of calcium, especially *calcium oxide or *calcium carbonate but also other basic (alkaline) substances, used to correct soil acidity.

**limestone**, a sedimentary rock, consisting mainly of calcium carbonate but also of magnesium carbonate. It can be of organic or inorganic origin, or it may be detrital (derived from an earlier limestone). Most limestones are organic: *chalk and *oolite are examples. Pure limestones are usually white or whitish, and consist of the calcium carbonate remaining from the secretions, shells, or skeletons of plants and animals (such as corals, molluscs, and crustaceans). Chemically formed limestones are precipitated from water containing dissolved calcium carbonate. They are generally less soluble and more resistant to weathering. Travertine is a type of limestone deposited by springs, and is used as an ornamental material. All limestones may be coloured by impurities such as sulphur, carbon, and iron. Limestones have important commercial uses as building materials and in cement manufacture.

Fossiliferous **limestone** from the Silurian Period (438 to 408 million years ago). The main constituents are sponges, bivalves, and fragments of crinoid stems cemented into a calcium carbonate matrix.

**lime water**, a solution of calcium hydroxide, $Ca(OH)_2$, in water used as an antacid or more commonly to detect the presence of carbon dioxide, $CO_2$. When carbon dioxide is passed through lime water, the solution will turn milky as calcium carbonate, $CaCO_3$, is precipitated.

**limonite** (laterite), the general term given to any rock rich in iron oxides that cannot be identified without complex laboratory tests. It is always of secondary origin and is often the product of tropical weathering of iron ore. It is rarely found in old rocks but is common in bogs.

**Limpopo**, a river 1,770 km (1,100 miles) long in south-east Africa. It rises in the high veld of the Transvaal and flows in a great arc, first north-east (forming South Africa's bound-ary with Botswana) in a stretch which is also known as the Crocodile River; then east (forming the boundary with Zimbabwe), and south-east on to its floodplain in Mozambique, where it is joined by its main tributary the Oliphants or Elephants River. Here it becomes navigable for the last 200 km (120 miles) of its journey to the Indian Ocean. This last stretch is through a hot, wet, and extremely fertile area of tropical growth.

**linearity** (in mathematics), a relationship between two variables ($x$ and $y$, say) which if plotted as a *graph is a straight line. Direct proportionalities, such as that between speed and distance travelled in a certain time, are examples. All linear relationships are described by equations like $y = mx + c$, where $m$ and $c$ are arbitrary constants.

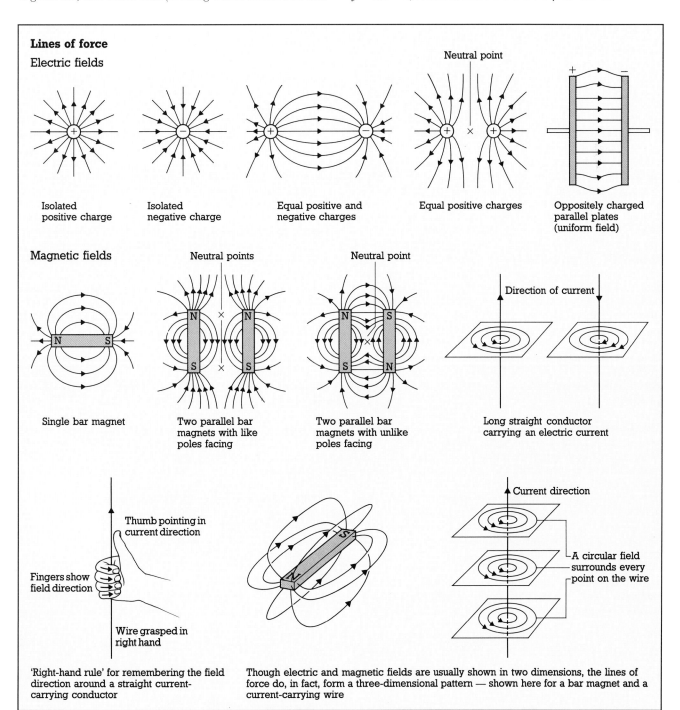

**Lines of force**

Electric fields

Isolated positive charge

Isolated negative charge

Equal positive and negative charges

Equal positive charges

Neutral point

Oppositely charged parallel plates (uniform field)

Magnetic fields

Single bar magnet

Neutral points

Two parallel bar magnets with like poles facing

Neutral point

Two parallel bar magnets with unlike poles facing

Direction of current

Long straight conductor carrying an electric current

Thumb pointing in current direction

Fingers show field direction

Wire grasped in right hand

'Right-hand rule' for remembering the field direction around a straight current-carrying conductor

Though electric and magnetic fields are usually shown in two dimensions, the lines of force do, in fact, form a three-dimensional pattern — shown here for a bar magnet and a current-carrying wire

Current direction

A circular field surrounds every point on the wire

Linearity has another meaning in the context of *differential equations. For linear differential equations, if functions $F(x)$ and $G(x)$ are each solutions, then $aF(x) + bG(x)$ is also a solution. (Here $a$ and $b$ are arbitrary constants, and this way of combining functions is called a linear combination.) An exact analogy is with a tuned string on an instrument. It can vibrate at several frequencies, all related to a fundamental (or lowest) frequency. Equally, its mode of vibration can be any combination of those frequencies. (This partly accounts for the richness of musical sounds.) Nonlinear equations lack this property. They are often insoluble without a computer, and are intimately connected with *chaos. The concept of linearity (in its second sense) is widely used in mathematics, physics and engineering.

**lines of force**, the imaginary patterns in space which represent the strength and the direction of a magnetic or electric field at any point. They are usually represented in diagrams as sets of lines which are close together in some places and further apart in others (see figure on page 195). The direction of the lines indicates the direction of the field and the density of lines in a particular area is a measure of the strength of the field there.

**Lipari Islands**, once called the Aeolian Islands, a group of seven Italian islands and ten islets in the Tyrrhenian Sea off the north coast of Sicily. They are the summits of a submerged chain of volcanoes, reaching a maximum height of 962 m (3,156 feet) above sea-level on Salina. Only the eastern volcanoes are still active; Stromboli's last major eruption was in 1921, and Vulcano erupted in 1890. There are hot springs on Lipari, largest of the islands.

**liquefied natural gas**, natural gas (see *gas, natural) which has had its *liquid petroleum gas fraction removed, and has then been cooled and pressurized to make it liquefy. Natural gas (largely *methane) liquefies at about −160°C at normal pressure, whereby its volume is reduced by a factor of 600. Despite this advantage, the low temperature involved has made it impractical to produce and move large quantities of liquefied gas, although specialist tankers have now been developed to carry liquefied gas cargoes to areas or countries where pipeline gas delivery would be impractical.

**liquid**, one of the three most common *states of matter, the others being solids and gases. Like gases, liquids have no fixed shape, but they do have a fixed volume (as long as the temperature does not vary): they do not expand to fill the space available, and they are very difficult to compress into a smaller volume. The molecules or atoms in a liquid have sufficient thermal energy to move around freely, but there is also considerable intermolecular attraction between them. Liquids may be turned into solids by cooling them, and into gases or vapours by heating.

**liquid crystal**, a *state of matter, in addition to the more common solid, liquid, and gas. A small proportion of organic compounds, of which the *esters of cholesterol are the best known, can be obtained in the liquid crystal state. Their solids melt to form a turbid fluid, the liquid crystal, and this fluid changes into a clear liquid, the true liquid state, at a higher temperature. The characteristic of liquid crystals is that although they are fluid, like ordinary liquids, they possess a far greater degree of ordering of their molecules than liquids, somewhat similar to that in a crystal.

The temperature display on a **liquid-crystal** thermometer strip.

They contain long molecules which lie parallel to one another but which can move over each other. They have unusual optical properties, and these have given rise to important applications. A thin clear layer of liquid crystal placed between two glass surfaces becomes opaque when a voltage is applied across it, and this is used in electronic displays, such as in digital watches. Some liquid crystals have colours which are highly temperature-sensitive, and these have been used in medicine, electronics, and the production of simple thermometers.

**liquid petroleum gas** (LPG), a mixture of gases obtained from petroleum or natural gas (see *gas, natural), and stored as a liquid. The gases are kept in liquid form either by dissolving them in solvent oils or by storage in pressurized containers. The two main LPG gases are *propane ($C_3H_8$) and *butane ($C_4H_{10}$), which are either extracted from natural gas or produced in petroleum refining. LPG will stay liquid at much lower pressures than unprocessed natural gas, and is therefore easier and safer to store and transport. It is used in pressurized bottles as a fuel in caravans, boats, and homes without piped gas supply. LPG is also a viable alternative to petrol for powering vehicles. (See also *liquefied natural gas.)

**lithium** (symbol Li, at. no. 3, r.a.m. 6.94), a soft, metallic element in Group I of the periodic table, the *alkali metals. Lithium is reactive, and is stored under oil; it combines with non-metals, water, and acids, forming ionic compounds in which it has the charge +1, and a few covalent compounds. Lithium carbonate is used in glasses and ceramics, and as a tranquillizer; lithium hydride is used as a source of hydrogen, and lithium hydroxide is used to absorb carbon dioxide in submarines. The isotope lithium-6 forms *tritium when bombarded with neutrons.

**lithosol**, a soil which forms in mountainous regions on steep slopes where erosion removes loose, weathered material very rapidly. Lithosols tend to be thin, generally less than 10–15 cm (6–12 inches). They are stony and lack distinct *horizons. They contain little organic matter because vegetation is sparse in rocky, upland areas. Other characteristics, particularly the texture and composition of the material, reflect the nature of the parent rock.

**lithosphere**  *Earth.

**Lithuania**, a Baltic country, lying between Latvia to the north, Belarus to the east, and Poland to the south. Its area measures 65,201 km² (25,174 sq. mi.). It has just some 25 km (15 miles) of Baltic Sea coast, and is predominantly flat, though hilly in the east, where there are many lakes. The lowland plain is forested and fertile, supporting dairy herds and a variety of crops. It is drained by the Nemen and its tributaries. Mineral resources are varied, including unexploited off-shore oil deposits.

**litmus**, one of the oldest acid–base *indicators: when added to acidic solutions it turns red, but in alkaline solutions it is blue. It is a mixture of dyes extracted from lichens, and is commonly absorbed on to filter paper to make litmus papers. Blue litmus papers are used to test for acidity, and red ones for alkalinity.

**Livingstone, David** (1813–73), British missionary and explorer. He first went to southern Africa as a missionary in 1841, travelling extensively in the interior, discovering Lake Ngami (1849) and the Zambezi River (1851), before undertaking a great journey from Cape Town to west central Africa (1852–6) on which he discovered the Victoria Falls. Welcomed back to the UK in 1855 as a popular hero, Livingstone returned to Africa as consul at Quelimane (1858–64), and made further expeditions into the interior in the Zambezi region, before returning once again to the UK to attempt to expose the Portuguese slave trade. He returned

The explorer David **Livingstone** experienced a not-uncommon childhood for his times: he was reared as one of seven children in a single room in a tenement building for the workers of a cotton factory on the River Clyde, and was himself sent to work in the mill by the age of 10.

to Africa for the last time in 1866 to lead an expedition into central Africa in search of the source of the Nile. His disappearance became a Victorian *cause célèbre* and he was eventually found in poor health by the explorer Stanley at Ujiji on the eastern shore of Lake Tanganyika, in Tanzania, in 1871. He died in Africa and his body was brought home and buried in Westminster Abbey.

**Llanos**, level, mostly treeless plains or steppes in the northern part of South America. Stretching from the Andes Mountains to the north and west, the Rio Guaviare and the Amazon Fair Forest to the south, and the lower Orinoco River and the Guiana Highlands to the east, they cover an area of 570,000 km² (220,000 sq. mi.). The Llanos economy is based on cattle-raising, but petroleum finds in the Venezuelan region have greatly enhanced the importance of the region.

**load** (of rivers), the amount of debris in a river, which varies with the volume of water, its speed, and its turbulence. The load has three components: *dissolved load, *suspended load, and *bed load. Dissolved materials, carried by ions, are only detectable by chemical analysis. Suspended particles range in size from the microscopic to pebbles, or large cobbles in powerful currents. Bed material, the largest and heaviest part of the load, is pushed or rolled along the channel floor. Whereas dissolved load tends to move without interruption to the sea or a lake, larger particles may move in suspension or on the bed, or be immobilized, as the flow of a river varies.

**loadstone** (or lodestone)   *magnetite.

**loam**, a spongy or crumbly soil formed from mixtures of sand, silt, and clay in roughly equal proportions. They can hold water without becoming waterlogged, are rich in organic matter, and are thus good for growing plants.

**Lobachevsky, Nikolai Ivanovich** (1792–1856), Russian mathematician who developed hyperbolic geometry, one of the non-Euclidean geometries in which the parallel postulate of Euclid does not hold. In this geometry there is an infinite number of lines through a given point parallel to a given line, and the angle sum of any triangle is less than 180°. Although quite revolutionary, this work produced very little reaction during his lifetime.

**loess**, a wind-blown deposit of coarse *silt, and containing a high proportion of calcium carbonate if derived from areas with limestone bedrock. It is pale yellow and has a very uniform consistency, without internal structure apart from thin, vertical hollows which are the impressions of old plant roots. The particles are so small that slight electrical forces develop between them. This allows the formation of steep and even vertical *cliffs, which is surprising, given its otherwise soft and often slightly crumbly consistency. The faces of loess cliffs are often fluted by rain into intricate columns. Loess deposits cover vast areas of China—where in places they are 90 m (300 feet) thick—and parts of central Europe, central USA , Argentina, and New Zealand. The deposits often blanket former landscapes, producing plains. Although it is still being laid down today, particularly at the edges of deserts or outwash plains, most of it was formed during cold periods in the Pleistocene Epoch, when ice-sheets and glaciers were more extensive and vegetation cover thinner, providing ideal conditions for *deflation by winds. The chemistry and texture of loess allows the development of soils which make very fertile farmland if there is adequate rainfall or irrigation.

**Logan, Mount**, Canada's highest and North America's second highest mountain, in the south-west corner of Yukon Territory. Part of the Saint Elias Mountains, it rises steeply to 6,050 m (19,850 feet). It caps a vast tableland and stands at the centre of the largest glacial expanse on the North American continent. The great Seward Glacier falls 4,300 m (14,000 feet) below the peak.

**Logan, Sir William Edmond** (1798–1875), Canadian geologist who was the first to map the *Canadian Shield. On appointment as first director of the Geological Survey of Canada he set out by canoe to map the country. The result, twenty years later, was his *Geology of Canada* (1863).

**logarithm**, the *inverse of an *exponential function. If $y = a^x$, then $x$ is said to be the logarithm of $y$ to base $a$ (written $y = \log_a x$). Thus 2 is the logarithm of 100 to base 10, because $100 = 10^2$. Logarithms are not always positive, nor always whole numbers; in which case the decimal part is called the mantissa and the whole number part is called the characteristic. The logarithm of 3 to base 10 is about 0.477; the logarithm of 30 is about 1.477; and for 300 it is about 2.477. This sequence of numbers shows that adding numbers to logarithms corresponds to multiplication of the number whose logarithm is being added to. (In the sequence above, adding 1 to the logarithm corresponds to multiplication by 10.) Before cheap electronic calculators existed, complicated multiplications and divisions were done by consulting tables of logarithms and adding or subtracting logarithms, and converting the answer back from logarithms. (John *Napier devised this technique.) Slide rules do the same job mechanically. Logarithms are widely used in science and mathematics, not so much for computation as for representing phenomena, which often obey logarithmic laws (the response of the human ear to sound intensity is approximately logarithmic). In these fields, base $e$ rather than 10 is often used ($e$ is an *irrational number, approximately equal to 2.7183). This is because *differentiation and *integration of logarithmic functions to base $e$ is tidier than to any other base. Logarithms to base $e$ are called natural logarithms. Axes of *graphs are often divided logarithmically to allow wide-ranging data to be plotted. For instance, an axis marked in steps from 0 to 6 could, using logarithms to base 10, represent numbers in the range 1 to 1,000,000.

**logic**, the science of reasoning and proof. In the 19th century there was an increasing distrust of intuition and experience in mathematics. It led to greater reliance on formal mathematical logic, starting from stated and accepted *axioms, or logical propositions, and providing rules for determining the accuracy of arguments and truth of conclusions. Aside from this use of logic to put mathematics on a more secure foundation, there developed in the 19th century the new branch of mathematical logic. This was instigated mainly by George *Boole. His Boolean algebra uses algebraic symbols and operations to represent propositions and the relationships between them. His ideas became the basis of symbolic logic, which has found application in some branches of computing and electronics.

**Loire**, the longest river in France, flowing for 1,010 km (627 miles) in a great arc to the Atlantic Ocean. It rises at about 1,350 m (4,430 feet) on Mont Mézenc in the south-east of the Massif Central and runs in a torrent northward through numerous basaltic gorges before emerging from the mountains. South of the Paris Basin it swings west and enters a broad, fertile valley which supports many vineyards. It is joined by many tributaries, the Cher, Indre, Vienne, and Mayenne among them, and readily floods. Its estuary on the Bay of Biscay is 55 km (35 miles) long but much silted and, in summer, shallow enough to impede navigation.

**Lomonosov, Mikhail Vasilyevich** (1711–65), Russian scientist who proposed a theory of gases, similar to *kinetic theory, which he developed by applying Newton's laws of motion to particles of gases, and studied the mechanical equivalent of heat. He did much to further the study of science in Russia and constructed the first chemistry laboratory in the country.

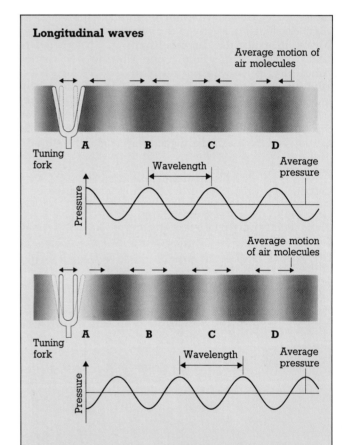

**Longitudinal waves**

Sound waves in air are longitudinal waves consisting of alternating zones of compression (high pressure) and rarefaction (low pressure). The upper picture shows the sound wave produced by a tuning fork vibrating in air, while the graph shows the variation of air pressure about the average value (the amplitude of this variation is small: about $10^{-5}$ atmospheres). At the particular instant depicted, there are zones of compression at A, B, C, and D, corresponding to the crests of the sound wave. A short time later (*lower picture*) the air molecules, on average, have changed direction and there are zones of rarefaction at A, B, C, and D, corresponding to troughs of the wave, while the crests have travelled to the right. Thus the wave travels from left to right, while the air molecules oscillate with small amplitude (about 0.1 mm) about their average positions in the same direction.

**lone pair**, a pair of electrons in a molecule which are not part of a *chemical bond—that is, not shared between two atoms. There are eight electrons round the oxygen atom in a water molecule; two pairs of electrons form the bonds to the hydrogen atoms, and the other four electrons form two lone pairs. Lone pairs are important in determining the shapes of molecules and are used for forming new bonds in many reactions.

**Long Island**, the USA's fourth-largest island, extending for 190 km (118 miles) along the coast eastward from the mouth of the Hudson River. At its eastern end are two tail-like peninsulas, parts of *moraines left by the ice age. Low, wooded hills lie to the north of the moraines, a flat plain to the south. Wide bays, long beaches, and lagoons form the south coast. The land is fertile enough for farming, and there are glacial deposits of gravel and sand.

**Long Island Sound**, the channel between Long Island, USA, and the Connecticut mainland to the north, formed as a result of the deposition of Long Island as an end *moraine during the ice age. It is part of the barely submerged eastern continental shelf of North America and receives the waters of the Atlantic Ocean through Block Island Sound on its east. Some 145 km (90 miles) long and varying from 5 to 32 km (3 to 20 miles) wide, it contains several small islands, fisheries, and shellfish beds and is a channel for shipping. In the west the East River connects it with New York Bay.

**longitude** (mapping)    *latitude.

**longitudinal wave**, a displacement of the particles of the medium through which the wave is travelling which is backwards and forwards along the direction in which the wave is travelling. Sound waves in air are longitudinal waves.

**longshore drift**, the gradual movement of beach materials such as sand and shingle along a shore. This process is the result of waves breaking at an angle on to a beach: driven by obliquely breaking waves, a thin layer of turbulent water known as the *swash moves diagonally up the beach, carrying sand and shingle landward and depositing them when it runs out of energy. Some of this material is then carried back down into the breaker zone by the returning backwash. The net effect is that material is moved in small steps sideways along the beach, a process which may be aided by longshore currents. Longshore drift may result in extensive beach erosion, the material removed being ultimately redeposited further down the coast. In some seaside areas attempts have been made to stop such erosion by erecting groynes, man-made barriers which extend down the beach and into the sea, and behind which sand and shingle moving along the shoreline are trapped.

**Lorentz, Hendrik Antoon** (1853–1928), Dutch physicist and astronomer who is noted for his theory of the electron; but he also gave his name to the hypothesis that there is a contraction in length of any body in the direction of its motion (the *Fitzgerald–Lorentz contraction). explained the unexpected negative result of the *Michelson–Morley experiments and Albert *Einstein later made it one of the assumptions of his special theory of relativity. He won the Nobel Prize for Physics with Pieter Zeeman in 1902.

**Low Countries**, a term sometimes used, especially historically, to describe the three adjacent north-west European

**Longshore drift**, the gradual and continuous movement of sand and shingle along the coast, has been the main process in the formation of the huge shingle bank of Chesil Beach in Dorset, UK.

countries of The Netherlands, Belgium, and Luxemburg. Much of The Netherlands and small parts of Belgium are in fact below sea-level. Southern Belgium and Luxemburg are higher, rising to over 600 m (2,000 feet) in the Ardennes.

**low** (in meteorology), the region of relatively low atmospheric pressure, as measured on the ground. Lows occur either in the form of a migratory low-pressure system, such as a *depression, or as a semi-permanent centre of low pressure, such as the Aleutian subpolar low.

**lunette** (in geomorphology), either of two kinds of feature. The first kind may be a small, crescent-shaped deposit of dark, silty material, laid down by wind on the leeward side of a shallow lake, especially in south-east Australia. The other kind is a very small, crescent-shaped nick on the smoothed surface of a rock, caused by the action of glaciers. This type is formed by sharp pieces of rock frozen into the underside of the ice chipping at the surface below, as a glacier moves jerkily forward.

**Luxemburg**, a small country in north-west Europe surrounded by Belgium to the west and north, Germany to the east, and France to the south. The climate is temperate continental and there are sizeable forests, but the ground is hilly and rocky with little fertile soil. The natural wealth is mainly mineral, in the form of iron ore.

**Lyell, Sir Charles** (1797–1875), Scottish geologist whose *Principles of Geology* (three volumes published in 1830–3) was one of the most influential works on geology ever published, and profoundly affected Charles Darwin's views. Lyell demonstrated conclusively that agents still in operation—such as rivers, volcanoes, earthquakes, and the sea—could explain the history of changes on the Earth's surface. He named the *Pleistocene ('most recent') geological epoch and established the principle that the changing groups of fossil organisms were the best guides to the sequence of rock strata. His views cleared the way for Darwin's theory of evolution which Lyell, after some hesitation, accepted.

**Macau** (Macao), a narrow peninsula projecting from the Chinese mainland, with a total area of 16 km² (6 sq. mi.). The city of Macau occupies almost the entire peninsula. An overseas territory of Portugal, Macau is a free port. It has few natural resouces; water is either collected from the small granite hills during rains, or imported from China.

**Macdonnell Ranges**, a system of mountains extending for nearly 640 km (400 miles) along the Tropic of Capricorn in the centre of Australia. They are a series of parallel ridges of hard, folded Palaeozoic rocks, the highest peak being Mount Ziel at 1,510 m (4,955 feet).

**Macedonia**, a Yugoslav republic in south-east Europe, bordering Serbia in the north, Albania in the west, Greece in the south, and Bulgaria in the east. Most of the republic's territory is a plateau, from which rise forested mountain peaks. Mineral resources include iron, lead, and zinc, while the chief crops are cereals, rice, and tobacco. Sheep and cattle are reared.

**Macedonia** (Greece), an administrative region of northern Greece, covering an area of 34,177 km² (13,196 sq. mi.), and encompassing the autonomous theocracy of Mount Athos.

**Mach, Ernst** (1838–1916), German physicist whose most influential work was in the philosophy of science. He argued that science should only concern itself with the relations between observable phenomena and should not speculate on what cannot be observed, an approach that influenced many philosophers. His name is particularly remembered, however, for his experimental work in aerodynamics: the Mach number of an object is the ratio of its speed to the speed of sound in the medium through which it is travelling. When the Mach number exceeds one, the speed of the object is supersonic: if the Mach number exceeds five it is said to be hypersonic.

**Mackenzie**, a river, some 1,800 km (1,100 miles) long, in north-west Canada between the Great Slave Lake and the Arctic Ocean. With its headrivers, the Athabasca, the Peace, and the Slave, it forms the second largest river system in North America. For most of the long winter months, the whole system is ice-covered. When spring arrives, the southern head-streams thaw first and are swollen by melting snow from the Canadian Rocky Mountains. The process of 'break-up' happens extremely swiftly at each point along the river, but it is difficult for the floodwaters to force their way downstream because the lower river is still ice-covered. The result is widespread flooding. The channel becomes jammed with tangles of ice-rafts and trees which have been bulldozed into the river by great chunks of ice. This mass pushes at, gouges out, and often overflows the river bank. Even so, during summer it forms a magnificent natural route north to its vast delta, which contains large fields of natural gas.

**Mackenzie, Sir Alexander** (1764–1820), Scotsman who went to Canada and became a fur trader and explorer, opening up the Northwest Territories. In 1789 he voyaged from the Great Slave Lake to the Arctic Ocean. His route, the Mackenzie River, is named after him. In 1793, again using water routes where possible, he crossed from Lake Athabasca to the Pacific, becoming the first white man to reach the Pacific Ocean by land along a northern route.

**McKinlay, John** (1819–72), British explorer. Having emigrated to New South Wales in 1836, McKinlay was appointed by the South Australia government in 1861 to lead an expedition to search for the missing explorers Burke and Wills. Although he found only traces of part of the Burke and Wills party, he carried out valuable exploratory work in the interior.

**McKinley, Mount**, in south-central Alaska, at the centre of the Alaska Range, at 6,194 m (20,320 feet) the highest peak on the North American continent; a permanent snow-field covers more than half of the mountain. The Denali (formerly Mount McKinley) National Park is noted for its long, narrow valleys that separate parallel east–west ridges; several of the glaciers are over 42 km (30 miles) in length.

**Maclaurin, Colin** (1698–1746), Scottish mathematician who developed Isaac *Newton's work in calculus, geometry (mostly of curves), and gravitation. The Maclaurin series, a power series expansion for a function which is a special case of the *Taylor expansion series (with $a = 0$). This was named in his honour but the series ewas well known before Maclaurin published it. He also wrote papers on astronomy and did actuarial work.

**Maclure, William** (1763–1840), Scottish-born US geologist whose His *Observations on the Geology of the United States* (1809) was the first geological map of North America, and one of the earliest such maps compiled.

**macromolecule**, a very large molecule consisting of a chain of between $10^2$ to $10^6$ atoms. For example, the synthetic *polymers which have been developed in this century are all macromolecules; they are formed from monomers which are capable of reacting with themselves, building up long chains which have a small unit repeated many times. Polyalkenes, polyamides, and polyesters are of this type. Many naturally occurring substances are also formed of macromolecules, for example rubber, cellulose, starch, proteins, and nucleic acids. The solid forms are fairly soft and flexible and when the macromolecule is a long chain, it can usually be dissolved. However, if the chains are cross-linked by chemical bonds, as in vulcanized rubber or synthetic resins, they form hard, insoluble materials.

**Madagascar**, a large island country lying 450–900 km (280–560 miles) distant from the south-east African coast, to which it runs parallel. A broad plain in the west rises to the Ankaratra Mountains, which slope steeply eastward to the Indian Ocean. The eastern coast is hot, very wet, subject to cyclones, and densely clad with rain forest. The south and west are drier, and the centre mild. Here, on upland plateaux, there is fine grazing. Coffee, tobacco, cloves, and vanilla are all cultivatedfor export; rice cassava, and sweet potato are the major food crops, while the chief mineral resources are chrome, graphite, and mica. The island became sep-arated from Africa during the period of *continental drift. Many of its plant and animal species, for example lemurs (prosimians), are unique.

**Madeira**, the largest of a group of five small, volcanic islands lying in the Atlantic Ocean some 560 km (350 miles) off the north-west African coast. Only two are habitable, the other one being Porto Santo. All are in Portuguese possession but partially autonomous. Madeira itself is very mountainous, Pico Ruivo rising to 1,861 m (6,106 feet) with chestnuts and laurels on its upper slopes. The country round it is seamed and gashed by deep ravines; and long lava reefs jut out between sandy bays to the sea. The climate is subtropical.

**Madeira**, a river of north-west Brazil which rises on the Bolivian border and flows about 1,450 km (900 miles) to meet the Amazon east of Maunus. It is navigable to large ocean-going vessels for part of the way.

**made land**, (made ground), an area of dry land that has been constructed by people, generally through the reclamation of marshes, lakes, or shorelines. An artificial fill (landfill) is used, consisting of natural materials and refuse.

**Maelstrom** (Norwegian, Moskenstraumen), a marine channel and tidal whirlpool in the Lofoten Islands, north-west Norway. It is formed when a strong tidal current flows through an irregular channel south of Mosken Island. It is approximately 8 km (5 miles) wide and may at its centre reach a speed of 11.26 km/h (7 m.p.h.).

After his defection from Portugal to Spain because of an unfair hearing over a charge of theft, Ferdinand **Magellan** proposed a western route to the important Spice Islands (the Moluccas), which was embarked upon in 1519.

FERDINAND MAGELLANUS.

**Magdalena**, Colombia's longest river, flowing northward for over 1,600 km (990 miles) from its source in the Andes to the Caribbean Sea, near the seaport of Barranquilla. For much of its length it flows along a deep trench between two ridges of the northern Andes; the valley is Colombia's chief traffic artery, and contains both oil and gold.

**Magellan, Ferdinand** (c.1480–1521), Portuguese explorer and navigator. On Portuguese service in the East Indies in 1511–12 he explored the Spice Islands, but in 1517 offered his services to Spain to undertake a voyage to the same islands by the western route. Leaving Spain with five vessels in 1519, Magellan reached South America and rounded the continent through the strait which now bears his name. In 1521 he discovered the Philippines, but soon after was killed in a native war on Cebu. The survivors of this disaster escaped to the Moluccas and sailed back to Spain round Africa., with the one remaining vessel, thereby completing the first circumnavigation of the globe.

**Magellan, Strait of**, a series of channels between Tierra del Fuego, other islands, and the southern tip of mainland South America. Together they extend for 537 km (334 miles) and connect the Atlantic and Pacific oceans. Some are only 4 km (2.5 miles) wide, others 24 km (15 miles). For mariners wishing to avoid Cape Horn they offer a more sheltered, though often foggy, passage. *Westerlies predominate, sudden squalls come down from the surrounding mountains, and the currents are strong. The scenery is dramatic, with fiord-like inlets, glaciers, and snow-capped peaks. The numerous islets are rocky, presenting an additional and constant hazard to navigation.

**magic numbers** (in nuclear physics). The sequence of numbers 2, 8, 20, 50, 82 and 126 are called magic numbers, because nuclei with these numbers of either protons or neutrons are the most stable. Because the elements with these numbers are stable, they are abundant in the universe. The magic numbers indicate a shell structure of the nucleus, analogous to the shell structure in the *electronic configuration of atoms.

**magma**, molten rock, a molten silicate liquid with water and other gases dissolved in it. It originates within the *Earth's mantle, probably at depths of 70 km (45 miles) or more, but it forms only a very small proportion of the mantle. If conditions allow, as at *plate margins, magma may move towards the surface, injecting and melting its way into the rocks of the crust. If it fails to reach the surface it forms an *igneous intrusion such as a batholith, sill, or dyke. If it reaches the surface it is ejected from volcanoes or fissures as lava and solidifies. The temperature of magma reaching the surface ranges from 850 to 1,200 °C (1,550 to 2,200 °F). Magma below the crust is under greater pressure and at far higher temperatures. It tends to change its composition as it rises to the surface, as various physical and chemical processes operate; and when it reaches the surface the dissolved gases are released into the atmosphere. The composition of an igneous rock is therefore not simply related to that of the magma from which it was derived.

**magnesia**, the common name for magnesium oxide, MgO, which occurs in the mineral periclase. A white, tasteless substance, it is used in heat insulation and as an antacid. It can be made by burning magnesium in oxygen or from the ignition of the metal hydroxide, carbonate, or nitrate.

milk of magnesia, used to neutralize stomach acidity, is a suspension of magnesium hydroxide, $Mg(OH)_2$.

**magnesite** (magnesium carbonate, $MgCO_3$), an important ore of magnesium. It forms as hard, yellow-grey masses produced by the alteration of magnesium-rich rock by water containing carbon dioxide. Large deposits exist in Styria (Austria), Manchuria (China), and along the coastal range of California (USA).

**magnesium** (symbol Mg, at. no. 12, r.a.m. 24.31), a grey metallic element of low density in Group II of the periodic table, the *alkaline earth metals. Reacting readily with acids and non-metals, it forms ionic compounds in which it has charge +2. It is an abundant element: magnesium chloride is present in seawater, from which magnesium is obtained, and magnesium ores such as dolomite, talc, and asbestos are widespread. Because of its low density it is widely used for construction in the aerospace and car industries; the pure metal is soft, and has to be strengthened by alloying with aluminium, zinc, zirconium, and thorium. Important compounds of magnesium include magnesium hydroxide $(Mg(OH)_2)$, used as an antacid and laxative, magnesium sulphate (Epsom salts, $MgSO_4$), and *Grignard reagents, used in synthetic organic chemistry.

**magnetic anomalies** (in geology), local departures from the Earth's normal magnetic field owing to variations in the structure and nature of its rocks. Knowledge of such anomalies can be of value in interpreting the structure of the rocks below the surface or in detecting the presence of ore bodies. The magnetic anomalies of the ocean floors provided critical evidence for *sea-floor spreading.

**magnetic field**, the region in which a magnetic force acts. For example, the magnetic field around a permanent magnet or a wire carrying an electric current is the region in which a magnetic force can be detected. The strength and direction of this force can be represented by *lines of force. The strength of a particular magnetic field operating through a given area is given by its *magnetic flux.

**magnetic flux**, a measure of quantity of magnetism and usually defined in terms of the voltage generated when a *magnetic field is cut by a moving conductor. If 1 volt is generated between the ends of the conductor, it is cutting through 1 weber of flux per second; the weber (Wb) is the *SI unit of magnetic flux.

**magnetic polarity of the Earth**. The Earth's core contains a high concentration of ferromagnetic material which is thought to be responsible for the terrestrial magnetic field with its own magnetic poles. The phenomenon is thought to be produced in the molten part of the core, possibly by flow in the liquid. The resulting dynamo effect produces a magnetic field which appears to enter and leave the Earth at a north and south pole. The Earth's magnetic poles are not coincident with the geographic poles, and the study of their locations and movements forms part of *geomagnetism.

**magnetism**, a set of phenomena associated with magnets and with moving electric charges, both of which produce *magnetic fields in the space surrounding them. The magnetic properties of *matter are largely determined by the behaviour of the negatively charged electrons that orbit the nuclei of atoms. The magnetic field of a single electron has

In this photograph, which demonstrates **magnetism**, iron filings have been strewn over a flat surface above a horse-shoe magnet which has its poles pointing upwards. The iron filings become magnetized and align themselves along the lines of magnetic force, making the pattern of the magnetic field visible.

two components, one resulting from the spin of the electron about its own axis, and the other from its orbital motion about the nucleus. Both kinds of motion may be considered as tiny circular currents—moving charges—thus linking electronic and magnetic effects at a fundamental level.

The magnetic properties of the mineral *magnetite (loadstone) were known to the ancient Greeks and Chinese. Magnetism was first studied seriously in 1269 by Petrus Peregnius de Maricourt, who established the existence of magnetic poles and stated that like poles repel and unlike attract. In the 19th century the connection between electricity and magnetism was discovered. Charged particles are surrounded by electric fields, and when they move, or spin, magnetic fields are created. An electric current will produce a magnetic field encircling the current whose strength is proportional to the current. Conversely, if a conductor moves through a magnetic field, an electric current will flow in it. These effects are studied in *electromagnetism. The unification of electric and magnetic principles in a complete mathematical theory was achieved by James Clerk *Maxwell in 1864. The quality of some metals which enables them to become magnetized when placed in a magnetic field, developing their own internal fields, is known as ferromagnetism.

**magnetite**, naturally magnetized iron oxide ($Fe_3O_4$), a dark dense mineral, which is also the second most important ore of iron, after *haematite. It is the only strongly magnetic natural substance known, and was called loadstone by the ancients, who used it to make the first compasses.

**Majorca**    *Balearic Islands.

**Malawi**, a long, narrow, land-locked country running north to south in south-eastern Africa. Its eastern boundary includes much of Lake Malawi; Tanzania is to the north and Zambia to the west, while Mozambique is wrapped round its southern half. This is the southern end of the Great Rift Valley. The Shiré River falling from Lake Malawi is flanked by high ground until it enters swampland, with three smaller lakes. A very warm, wet summer permits the growth of rice and sugar. To the north the ground rises westward from the lake to plateaux which are cooler and wetter for most of the year. There are plantations of tea, tobacco, groundnuts, and cotton, but no minerals except *bauxite.

**Malawi, Lake**, the southernmost of the lakes in the Great Rift Valley, in south-eastern Africa. It is shared by Tanzania, Mozambique, and Malawi. Over 560 km (350 miles) long from north to south and generally some 65 km (40 miles) in width, it is fed by the Ruhuhu in the north and by the Songwe and other short streams in the west. Some 470 m (1,550 feet) above sea-level, it is drained by the Shiré River at its southern end into the Zambezi. Except in the south its surroundings are mountainous and its climate wet and reasonably mild. It was previously known as Lake Nyasa.

**Malaysia**, a country in south-east Asia, having two parts, West and East, separated by the South China Sea. East Malaysia comprises Sarawak and Sabah in the north and north-west of the island of Borneo. West, or Peninsular, Malaysia occupies the southern end of the Malay Peninsula extending south from the south-east Asian mainland, and is bounded on the north by Thailand and on the south by Singapore; it has a south-western coast on the Strait of Malacca. The climate is very warm and affected by the monsoons, which bring about 2,300 mm (90 inches) of rain in a year; and the red soil provides for paddy-fields in the lowland areas, where rice is cultivated, and high-yield rubber, oil palm, and cocoa plantations in the west of the peninsula, tin is also dredged. Inland, the Malayan highlands are forested and provide tropical hardwoods. East Malaysia and off-shore waters are rich in mineral oil.

**Maldives**, a coral island republic of the Indian Ocean, comprising some 1,800 small atolls and sandbanks built on the summits of old, submerged volcanoes. They lie 650 km (400 miles) south-west of Sri Lanka.

**Mali**, a land-locked country in north-west Africa, sharing common boundaries with Mauritania, Algeria, Niger, Burkina Faso, Côte d'Ivoire, Guinea, and Senegal. Its north is in the dry Sahara and its south is in the tropics with about 1,200 mm (nearly 50 inches) of rainfall each year. From the south-west, and through its centre flows the Niger, which provides fish. The Niger here has an inland delta which permits the seasonal growing of rice, while other areas contain sufficient pasture for cattle, sheep, and goats.

**Malta**, the largest of a group of three islands constituting a country of the same name in the central Mediterranean Sea, the others being Gozo and the tiny Comino. The main island is some 27 km (17 miles) long by 14 km (9 miles) wide and rises to hills in the south-west. The climate is very warm and rather dry, with fierce winds, and the land is barren in appearance, with few trees and no rivers or streams.

**Maluku**    *Moluccas.

**Mammoth Cave National Park**, an area in southern Kentucky, USA, incorporating a series of subterranean limestone caverns on five levels, extending in all for over 240 km (150 miles). The connecting passages are relatively small, but the caverns (including the magnificent Mammoth Dome) are high-domed with stalactites, stalagmites, and spectacular onyx 'frozen waterfalls'. There are lakes, streams and, at the lowest level, the Echo River, which contains blind crayfish.

**Manchuria** (Pinyin, Dongbei, 'Northeast'), an area of north-east China at the head of the Yellow Sea, north of Korea. The high and rugged Hinggan Mountains ring the northern part with forests of pine, elm, spruce, walnut, oak, and birch; while in the south-east, below the valley of the Sunghua River, more forested mountains thrust towards the Liaodong Peninsula, which extends into the Yellow Sea. They are for the most part volcanic, with old crater lakes, the highest being Paektu on the Korean border at 2,744 m (9,003 feet). In the centre is a rolling plain of great fertility, supporting wheat, soya beans, and other crops. An extension of the Gobi Desert lies in the west. Coal and oil are the main resources, and there are significant metal deposits.

**Mandelbrot, Benoit** (1924– ), Polish-born French mathematician who coined the term *fractal: a mathematical model for natural shapes that are irregular and do not form perfect squares, pyramids, spheres, and so on. He invented a basis for the theoretical investigation of complex dynamics. One application of this method, the so called Mandelbrot Set, is that used to explain the length of a coastline. (See also *chaos theory.)

**manganese** (symbol Mn, at. no. 25, r.a.m. 54.94), a reddish-white, hard, brittle *transition metal. It is quite reactive, and in its compounds shows *valencies from 2 to 7. Extracted mainly from the mineral pyrolusite, although also occurring naturally on the sea-bed, it is widely added to metals to improve their hardness and wear resistance. Manganese steels contain about 12 per cent manganese, and are very tough, being used in railway lines and rock-crushers.

**Manitoba**, a Canadian province on the eastern edge of the North American prairies, with a coast on Hudson Bay. More than half the province is on the *Canadian Shield, with its rich deposits of minerals. In the north its eroded plateau is covered with boulder clay; in the south, undulating country rises towards western hills. Elsewhere there is much marsh and many glacial lakes and rivers: Lakes Winnipeg and Winnipegosis occupy much of its south-eastern area. While the prairie land to the south-west of these lakes is important for grain-producing, it also has oil reserves.

**mantissa** *logarithm.

**map**, a diagrammatic representation of all or part of the Earth on a plane surface. The term map is usually confined to land areas, whereas a representation of a sea area is called a chart. The earliest maps of which we have knowledge were made by the Babylonians on clay tablets, dating from around 2300 BC. The ancient Greeks drew maps of the known world and speculated on its form: around the 3rd century BC Greek geographers agreed that the Earth was spherical; at this time the Greek astronomer and and geographer Eratosthenes estimated its circumference to be around 46,000 km (24,800 miles), not far from modern values of around 40,000 km (24,000 miles). Chinese map-making from the 3rd century BC was based on the use of a reference grid of parallel lines running N–S and E–W, and on-the-spot surveys. These maps were remarkably accurate, but Chinese world maps remained poor until the introduction of Western cartography in the 17th century. Probably the greatest figure of early geography was *Ptolemy, whose *Guide to Geography* included a world map that was revived in Europe in the early 15th century. Medieval European geographers believed that the known world of Europe, Asia, and Africa covered only one-quarter of the Earth's surface. In their *mappa mundi* (world maps) they often drew only this portion of the Earth, and the locations of features upon it were not mathematically related to their true positions on the globe. In the Arab world, however, classical astronomy and cartography continued to be studied. Islamic geographers drew world maps, based on new tables of *latitude and longitude, in which the habitable world extended well south of the equator, and the Indian Ocean was open towards the Far East. In the 13th and 14th centuries the travels of Europeans across Asia, and the introduction of sea-charts based on magnetic compass directions improved the detail of world maps. In the 15th and 16th centuries the translations of Greek and Arabic geographical works introduced European cartographers to the concept of map *projection, while the discoveries of such explorers as Christopher *Columbus led to a more accurate view of the globe. The best-known cartographer of the period was Gerardus *Mercator, whose method for projection of the globe on to a flat surface enabled navigators to plot bearings as straight lines. In the 18th century a more scientific approach to map-making began to predominate, and many European countries began systematic national topographic surveys. Others followed suit, but some parts of the world remained largely unmapped until World War II, when vast areas were mapped using information from aerial photographs.

Modern maps can be classified as either topographical, showing the physical and natural features of an area, or thematic, based on topographical maps but showing some sort of statistical data (for example, population) in map form. Navigational charts for air or sea use show selected topological features, but also such information as the location of radio navigation beacons, lights and buoys, and water depths and prevailing currents. Until the advent of aerial photography, land surveying provided most of the basic topological information for maps. However, modern map-making relies much more on aerial surveying techniques using stereo photography, and information obtained from Earth resources satellites using remote sensing techniques such as infra-red photography. Topographical information from from photographs and land surveys is now usually digitized in some way and fed into a computer. This provides a flexible database from which maps can be drawn.

**mappings** (in mathematics), in general, a term synonymous with *functions. If *A* and *B* are two sets, then a mapping of *A* into *B* is a function f with a domain *A* and a range, or co-domain, *B*; f is said to map *A* into *B*. Topologists, however, tend to use a more restricted meaning, equating mapping only with continuous functions.

**Maracaibo, Lake**, the largest in South America, lies on the east of a basin in Venezuela which is formed by two branching cordilleras of the northern Andes. It is oval in shape, more than 170 km (100 miles) long, and connected in the north by a strait to the Gulf of Venezuela and the

This German **map** drawn in the 16th century shows how Shakespeare could have arrived at his misguided belief in a 'sea-coast of Bohemia'. The map was based on information set down in Ptolemy's *Guide to Geography*, written 14 centuries before.

Caribbean Sea. Its surroundings in the north are semi-arid, in the south wet and swampy. In the lake and on its margins are some of the largest oilfields in the world, while round its southern shores there are forests of hardwood timber. The Catatumbo and other rivers feed it from the mountains.

**marble**, a common metamorphic rock formed by the recrystallization of limestone and *dolomite. It therefore consists mainly of the mineral calcite ($CaCO_3$) or dolomite (calcium magnesium carbonate) in the form of a fine- to coarse-grained mosaic. White when pure, it is often red-grey or mottled grey as a result of mineral inclusions. Its most famous occurrence is at Carrara (Liguria, Italy), where the marble was once used by Michelangelo for sculpting. It is a common facing stone in the building industry. Builders use the word 'marble' for any stone that when polished can be used decoratively.

**Marbut, Curtis Fletcher** (1863–1935), US soil scientist who first applied *Dokuchaiev's ideas about soil formation in the USA and was responsible for the translation into English of the pioneering book, *Great Soil Groups of the World and their Development* (1908) by the Russian soil-scientist, Kon-

stantin Dimitrievich Glinka (1867–1927). As chief of the Soil Survey Division of the US Department of Agriculture, Marbut created a soil classification system which greatly influenced the development of soil mapping in the USA.

**marcasite**, a common, pale yellow, lustrous mineral with the same chemical composition ($FeS_2$) as *pyrite but formed at lower temperatures. It oxidizes in air to a white powder and forms in ore veins, as a replacement deposit in limestone, and as *concretions in sedimentary rocks. Mined in large quantities at Galena, Illinois, USA, it is used for the extraction of sulphuric acid.

**Marco Polo** (1254–1324), Venetian traveller. Between 1271 and 1275 he accompanied his father and uncle on a journey east into central Asia, eventually reaching China and the court of Kublai Khan. Polo entered the Mongol diplomatic service, travelling widely in the empire for a decade and a half before returning home (1292-5) via Sumatra, India and Persia. Captured by the Genoese in 1298, he dictated the story off his travels to a fellow inmate during a year of imprisonment. His book, *Travels of Marco Polo*, became a geographical classic and was widely read in subsequent years, adding considerable impetus to the European quest to discover the riches of the East.

**marginal sea**, a semi-enclosed body of water adjacent to, and widely open to, the ocean, for example, the Gulf of Mexico, the Caribbean Sea, and the Gulf of California.

**Marianas Islands**  *Guam.

**Marianas Trench**, a trench south-west of Guam in the western Pacific Ocean, the deepest known region of the Earth's surface. At 11,033 m (36,198 feet), it is deep enough to contain Mount Everest. It is near the southern end of a submarine trench system which runs round the north and west of the Pacific *plate. Upwelling *magma is trapped beneath the advancing plate, and the adjacent ridge has very active volcanoes.

**marl**, a clay deposit particularly rich in calcium carbonate. Marls are often formed from the weathering of relatively impure chalk or limestone, as are those which occur on the lower chalk of south-east England. Others are glacial drift deposits, such as the chalky tills of Cambridgeshire, UK which were formed by the erosion and mixing together of a variety of materials. These calcareous clays used to be dug from marlpits and added to light, sandy soils in a process known as marling. This increased their cohesion and improved their fertility.

**Marquesas Islands**, a group of twelve islands in the central South Pacific Ocean, forming part of the overseas territory of French Polynesia. All volcanic, they are rugged and mountainous, Hiva Oa reaching 1,250 m (4,100 feet). Their vegetation includes pandanus trees (screw-pines), breadfruit trees, and the orchid from which vanilla is obtained.

**Marquette, Jacques** (1637–75), French Jesuit missionary and explorer who played a prominent part in the attempt to convert to Christianity indigenous American Indians. In 1673, with Louis Jolliet (1645–1700), a French Canadian map-maker, he descended the Mississippi by canoe to the mouth of the Arkansas, thereby showing that a waterway might be established from the Saint Lawrence to the Gulf of Mexico. In 1674 Marquette set out on a second expedition, but was caught by the winter. He reached the Illinois Indians at what is now Utica, Illinois in the spring. Illness forced his return, and he died at the mouth of a river now known as Pére Marquette.

An area of salt **marsh** developed at the mouth of a drowned valley in New Zealand. Deltaic sediments are building up the valley floor, allowing the new land to be progressively colonized by marsh plants.

**marsh**, a poorly drained, low-lying area alongside a pond, lake, river, or coastline which is flooded fairly regularly and supports specialized water-tolerant (and often salt-tolerant) vegetation. Geomorphologists sometimes make a distinction between marshes and fens or bogs, using the former name when their soils are largely made up of mineral particles, especially silts and clays, rather than organic, peat deposits. Different parts of a marsh are usually under water for different lengths of time—this is particularly true of coastal *salt-marshes—and so they have distinct zones of various plants, each adapted to withstand certain water conditions.

**Marshall Islands** (US Trust Territory), two widely scattered island chains in the central Pacific Ocean, north of the Equator. They comprise thirty-four atolls, all low-lying, and innumerable reefs. Coffee, copra from coconuts, and sugar-cane are the main cultivated crops.

**mass** (symbol *m*), the quantitative measure of inertia, a fundamental property of all matter. Although mass is defined in terms of inertia, it is conventionally expressed as *weight: the force exerted on matter by the gravitational attraction of the Earth. Mass is a scalar quantity, unlike weight. Two masses are equal if they have identical weight when measured in the same place in a gravitational field. The *SI unit of mass is the kilogram (kg). At speeds which are close to the speed of light, mass varies with speed. One of the startling discoveries of modern physics was the equivalence of mass and energy, a fact predicted by *relativity theory. They are often defined as a single quantity known as mass-energy. The conversion of mass to energy occurs during nuclear *fission. Huge amounts of energy are released during *fission reactions.

**mass defect**, a term in nuclear physics arising from the equivalence between mass and energy which is predicted by the *relativity theory. The mass of a particular nucleus is always less than the sum of the masses of its constituent particles, the difference between the two being the mass defect. It represents the reduction in energy of the particles when they are bound together in the nucleus.

**mass flow,** a downward slide of sediment which moves under the force of gravity. Mass flows include landslides, avalanches, rockfalls, slumping, mudflows, soil creep, and rock creep (or cambering). All result primarily from the downward force of gravity overcoming the resistance of the material forming the slope, the role of water being important in instances where it helps to lubricate the movement and where its additional weight acts as a trigger, as heavy snowfalls often do. Most occur on high, steep slopes, especially slopes with little vegetation cover, and in areas frequently shaken by earthquakes. There are three classes of mass flow, categorized according to the speed and type of motion. The fastest are the slides, falls, and slumps; these usually occur as discrete, sudden events and are often triggered by earthquakes or heavy precipitation. Flows of mud, earth, or rock debris may also move rapidly, but they tend to last for longer periods and create on the slopes definite channels which are frequently edged by levees. Creep, a much slower rate of flow which is often imperceptible except by measurements over a number of years, tends to produce bulges and shallow lobes of material.

**Massif Central**, a mountainous plateau in south-central France, all of it over 300 m (980 feet), reaching to 1,886 m

(6,188 feet) in the Monts Dore in the Auvergne Mountains. Occupying nearly a fifth of the country, it is a major watershed: the Seine, Garonne, and Rhône all have tributaries rising here, and it is the source of the Loire, Charente, and Dordogne. The core of the massif is the ancient volcanic mass of the Auvergne, whose peaks stand precipitously above a rolling terrain of fertile soil. The scenery is diverse and the climate varies almost from valley to valley. *China clay and coal are the main underground resources.

**mathematics**, the abstract science of space, number, and quantity. It was practised by the ancient Egyptians, Sumerians, Indians, and Chinese in a rudimentary form, notably for surveying and commercial purposes. Pure mathematics was developed by the Greeks and later by the Arabs, who introduced the old Hindu numerals to Europe in the 10th century. The Renaissance gave it great impetus: and in the 17th century there were advances in many fields, with the invention of *logarithms, algebraic geometry, and *calculus. The new mathematics arose in the 20th century after investigation into the logical foundations of the subject. The theory of sets was introduced, and the arrival of the computer imposed disciplines of its own, as well as freeing mathematicians from the drudgery of lengthy computation. The relationship of mathematics to *reality continues to be a philosophical problem. If mathematics is simply the teasing out of valid conclusions from arbitrary premises or *axioms (a *formalist view, widely held towards the end of the 19th century), then why is it so useful to scientists for describing the real world? Recent developments in *chaos suggest a view of mathematics as an empirical science, alongside physics, chemistry and biology.

**Mato Grosso** (Portuguese, 'big forest'), the vast plateau of central South America, descending west and south from Brazil to the flood plains of the Paraguay River. In the north it is drained by the tributaries of the Amazon, and here, it is covered with dense rain forest. Elsewhere there is pampas grassland, with much cattle-raising. Manganese is the main mineral found.

**matrices** (in mathematics), a rectangular array of elements. Matrices can be added to or multiplied by suitable similar matrices. The arrays are usually enclosed by a pair of round brackets. An $n$-by-$m$ matrix has $n$ rows and $m$ columns; an $n$-by-$n$ matrix is called square. Although possessing many of the properties of numbers, they do not in general show *commutativity with respect to multiplication. The *identity matrix, I, is a matrix such that, for any matrix $A$, $AI = IA = A$. The zero matrix, 0, is one for which $A + 0 = 0 + A = A$. The *inverse of a matrix, $A^{-1}$, where it exists, is one such that $AA^{-1} = A^{-1}A = I$; it will exist provided the *determinant of $A$ is not 0.

**matter**, that which has mass and takes up space. Sometimes the term is used in a very general sense to refer to everything, apart from radiation, present in the universe; and it is sometimes defined as a specialized form of energy. Often, however, it is applied only to atoms and molecules in bulk which are close enough together to form gases, liquids, or other states of matter such as plasmas. All forms of matter share certain fundamental properties. Every physical entity has gravitation, the property by which it attracts every other entry. Another property of matter is inertia, which causes a body to ressist any change in its condition of rest or its motion. According to Albert *Einstein's special relativity,

The **Matterhorn**, on the Swiss–Italian border, an example of the development of a glaciated peak.

matter (as *mass) and energy are equivalent. Therefore, matter can be converted into energy and energy into matter.

**Matterhorn**, a distinctively shaped mountain in the Pennine range of the Alps, on the Swiss–Italian border. It rises sharply to its peak at 4,478 m (14,691 feet) and has the appearance of a steep, horn-shaped pyramid, produced by the enlargement of several *cirques.

**Mauritania**, a coastal country in north-west Africa, bounded by Morocco and Algeria on the north and by Mali and Senegal on the east and south. Most of it lies in the Sahara. Except in the south-west corner it is arid, and everywhere it is hot. Inland from the Atlantic Ocean a region of smooth sand dunes slowly rises, over large deposits of copper and iron ore, to sandstone ridges and the granite highlands of the north-east of the country. In the east there are a few oases, where date palms grow, and in the south groundnuts and some cereals are cultivated.

**Mauritius**, the chief island (the others are Rodriguez and the Agalega Islands) of an island country in the southern Indian Ocean, about 800 km (500 miles) east of Madagascar. The main island, Mauritius itself, is volcanic in origin and nearly 2,000 km² (770 sq. mi.) in area, having steep hills and plains of lava, which have weathered into fertile soil. The slopes are forested, and the plains are green throughout the year with natural vegetation.

**Maury, Matthew Fontaine** (1806–73), US hydrographer, whose *Physical Geography of the Sea and Its Meteorology*

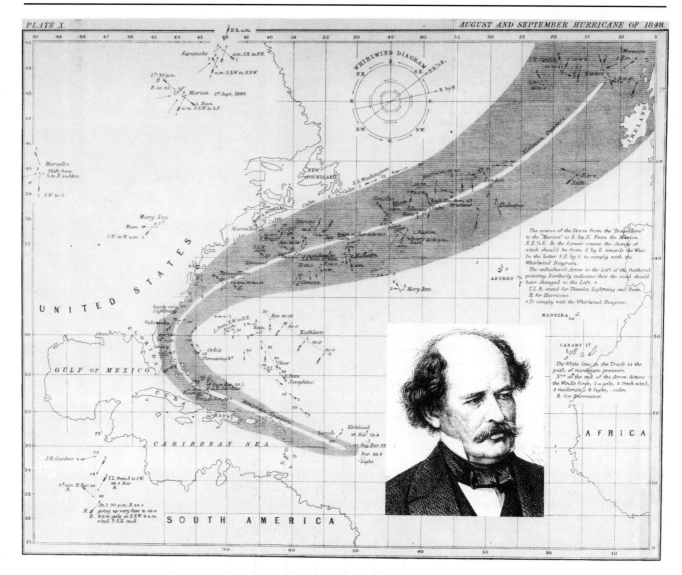

PLATE X. AUGUST AND SEPTEMBER HURRICANE OF 1848.

**Maury**,'s charts of the oceans' winds and currents, which enabled ships to shorten their voyage, had been compiled from logbooks issued by him to captains.

(1855) was the first text of modern oceanography. His guides for trade winds and ocean currents, compiled from the study of ships' logs, cut sailing times on many routes; and his system for recording such data was adopted for worldwide use in ships. He served in the Confederate navy during the Civil War, and subsequently became a respected professor of meteorology.

**Maxwell, James Clerk** (1831–79), British physicist and first director of the Cavendish Laboratory at Cambridge. He developed the theory of electromagnetism, and was the first to predict the existence of *electromagnetic radiation and to describe light as an electromagnetic wave. Underlying his theory were four equations which between them contained the laws of magnetic and electric attraction, the laws linking magnetic fields and electric currents, and a new concept—a 'displacement current' caused by an electrical strain which could exist even in a vacuum. He also made major contributions to the *kinetic theory of matter and discovered the law governing the distribution of velocities among gas molecules (the *Maxwell–Boltzmann distribution).

In 1871 he invented an imaginary creature, Maxwell's

demon, as part of a *paradox on the second law of *thermodynamics. It operates a frictionless trapdoor between two containers, one of which is evacuated, and the other filled with a mixture of two gases. By opening the trapdoor suitably, it can allow molecules of one gas only through to the evacuated container. Thus the demon can unmix two gases without expenditure of energy, which is contrary to the second law of thermodynamics. The resolution of this paradox has caused much discussion about observation and *entropy over many years.

**Maxwell–Boltzmann distribution**, a statistical equation giving the distribution of energy among the molecules of a gas in thermal equilibrium. As the temperature changes there is a shift in this energy distribution. At low temperatures, most molecules have low energies, whereas there will be more with high energies as the temperature is increased. The distribution shows how many molecules have any given energy, and how this varies with temperature. It is named after James *Maxwell and Ludwig *Boltzmann, who developed it independently of one another.

**Mazama, Mount**   *Crater Lake.

**meadow soil**, an *intrazonal soil, formed in poorly drained areas such as the *floodplains of some rivers. If the soil is waterlogged for most of the year, this slows down the decomposition of plant remains, which therefore accumulate at the soil surface. Waterlogging also causes the soil to become depleted of oxygen, resulting in *gleying. As a result, the lower horizons of the profile are grey or blue in colour. Grass grows abundantly on these damp, clay soils and they are widely used for pasture.

**mean**, an *average value of a set of numbers found by computation. There are three principal types: arithmetic mean, geometric mean and harmonic mean.

The arithmetic mean is the one usually meant by the word 'average'. It is calculated by adding up all the members of the set and dividing by the number of members. For the set $\frac{1}{2}$, 3, $2\frac{1}{2}$, 7, $-3$ it is 2, which does not appear in the set. (A mean may coincidentally be identical to a member of the set.)

The geometric mean of $n$ numbers is the $n$th root of their product. For example, the geometric mean of 16, 8 and 0.5 is $\sqrt[3]{64} = 4$. (A cube of side 4 units would have the same volume as a rectangular block with dimensions 16, 8 and 0.5 units.)

The harmonic mean is, for two numbers $a$ and $b$, defined by ($1/H = \frac{1}{2}(1/a + 1/b)$ where H represents the harmonic mean. If a boat sails downstream at speed $v_1$ and the same distance upstream at speed $v_2$, the average speed for the journey is the harmonic mean of $v_1$ and $v_2$.

**meandering**, the development of series of bends and loops in river channels which change over the centuries. Their amplitude and wavelength depend on river width, the wider the stretch of river the bigger being its meanders. Most meanders form in fine-grained material on flattish floodplains, although incised meanders cut deeply into the bedrock, probably as a result of *rejuvenation. Spectacular and regular forms—known as the Goosenecks—occur along

The Red River, which forms the boundary between North Dakota and Minnesota, USA, **meandering** over the flat bed of the now-drained glacial Lake Agassiz. The river winds to such an extent that, despite its length of 877 km (545 miles), its mouth is only 434 km (270 miles) from its sources when measured in a straight line.

the San Juan River, Utah, USA. All flowing fluids tend to develop meanders—the Gulf Stream and jet streams show them—but those of rivers produce asymmetric channels, with eroded *undercut banks opposite gentle *slip-offs. The undercutting generally occurs on the outsides of bends, where the current runs fastest; and the tendency is for a river to cut off a loop, where two curves bend towards one another, leaving an *ox-bow lake.

**mean sea-level** (or MSL), the average level of the sea surface between high and low *tides. The MSL is the elevation which is used as a fixed starting point (datum level) when expressing the height of points on land.

**mechanics** (in mathematics), the interaction between matter and the forces acting on it. Statics is the study of systems at rest (for instance, forces within structures), and dynamics is the study of systems in motion under the influence of forces (such as planetary orbits or projectiles). Much of the theory of mechanics is built upon *Newton's laws and the *equations of motion which involve the relationships between masses and forces in terms of time, lengths, and angles. Dynamics is concerned with the velocities and accelerations resulting from the action of forces. The mathematics has been developed largely to provide mathematical models of situations in the real world. The process of modelling relies on the idealization of certain physical phenomena, to give mathematical entities which can then be described geometrically and analytically. Frictionless impacts, perfectly inelastic bodies, and point particles are all such idealizations. Stressing certain properties of a physical system and ignoring others results in a mathematical model. The solution to that model has then to be reinterpreted in physical terms in order to test the appropriateness of the simplifying assumptions which were made. Approximating the Earth as a point, with its mass concentrated there, may help when dealing with planetary orbits; but it is useless when studying the tidal effect of the Moon. A different model needs to be constructed to allow investigation of that problem. *Quantum mechanics is mechanics of systems which do not follow Newton's laws.

**mechanisms of chemical reactions**, the routes along which the reactants proceed in being converted to products, that is, the precise means by which atoms are rearranged to form new molecules. If the initial rate of a chemical reaction is studied as a function of concentration, it is sometimes possible to deduce an equation (or rate law) relating the concentration and the rate. On the basis of this equation, a mechanism can be suggested. If the powers in the rate law are the same as the numbers in the *stoichiometric equation, a single step is usually proposed for the reaction. If, on the other hand, these numbers are different, a mechanism is proposed involving more than one step. Of the various steps, one is considerably slower than all the others and this is called the rate-determining step. Additional evidence is often available to support a mechanism: for example, if a multi-step reaction is slow overall, it is sometimes possible to identify an intermediate compound which has only a transitory existence during the reaction. Labelling reactant atoms with radioisotopes or heavy isotopes may be useful.

**median** (in statistics), the middle value (or average of two middle values) of a group of numbers arranged in size order. As a representative 'average' or measure of central tendency it is unaffected by irregular or freak values, unlike the mean.

The median of 1, 1, 2, 2, 3, 4, and 99 is 2, whereas the arithmetic *mean is 16.

**Mediterranean Sea**, a relatively shallow and almost land-locked sea, separating Europe from Africa and stretching for some 3,300 km (2,400 miles) from Gibraltar in the west to Israel in the east. Sicily, Sardinia, Corsica, Crete, and Cyprus are its largest islands. Its chief arms are the Adriatic and Aegean Seas, the latter connecting it indirectly with the Black Sea. Originally a vaster ocean, it shrank to its present size in the Oligocene Epoch and is still shrinking, largely because the African plate is moving into the Eurasian *plate. The *continental shelves almost meet in the Sicilian channel. Earthquakes and volcanic disturbances still occur. Its climate is mild, with moderate winter rain. From the Sahara the sirocco, and from the north the bora and mistral winds blow over it. It is virtually without tides; stillness, shallowness, and warmth together encourage much evaporation of the surface water, making the sea-water salty and relatively dense. A long tongue of this strongly saline water projects through the narrow Strait of Gibraltar into the Atlantic Ocean. In recent years some 50 per cent of the Mediterranean's grass coverage has disappeared from its sea-bed as a result of pollution from heavy metals, insecticides, oil spills, fishing, and tourism.

**meerschaum**, a hydrated magnesium silicate, occurring in river deposits and in veins. It appears as a soft pale mass, like white clay, and is easily carved before drying. Used for pipe bowls it rapidly absorbs the smoke and becomes brown. Asia Minor is the main source, but Greece, Morocco, and Spain also have supplies.

**Meitner, Lise** (1878–1968), Austrian-born physicist and mathematician, co-discoverer of nuclear fission. In 1917 she discovered in partnership with Otto *Hahn, the element protoactinium; thereafter she continued her research into the disintegration products of radium, thorium, and actinium, and into the behavioural pattern of beta rays. In the 1930s she, in cooperation with Fritz Strassmann (1902–80), investigated the products of neutron bombardment of uranium. In 1938 she participated with Hahn and Strassmann in experimenting in bombarding the uranium nucleus with slow-speed neutrons. In 1939, working with her nephew, the physicist Otto Frisch (1904–79), she elucidated the physical characteristics of neutron-bombarded uranium. They proposed the term fission for the process, and calculated that vast amounts of energy were being liberated, a conclusion which was pivotal to the development of the atomic bomb. Meitner had fled Nazi Germany in 1938, settling first in Sweden, and retiring to the UK in 1960.

**Mekong**, the major river of south-east Asia and the world's tenth longest at 4,200 km (2,600 miles). Rising in the Tanglha range of Tibet, it first tumbles through craggy gorges some 3,000 m (9,800 feet) above sea-level and then runs southward through south China into Laos. The Khone Falls in southern Laos are a series of rapids 10 km (6 miles) long, the widest in the world and a source of hydroelectricity. Below them the river enters its floodplain, which extends through Cambodia (Kampuchea). Here it becomes navigable and irrigates the land. During the dry season it receives the Tonle Sap River, whereas during the rains it reverses the flow, forcing floodwaters back into the Tonle Sap Lake. Its delta, over 320 km (200 miles) wide, thrusts into the South China Sea. The river here splits into many distributaries,

Dmitri Ivanovich **Mendeleyev**, who predicted, in 1871, the existence and properties of the elements scandium, gallium, and germanium. Their subsequent discovery within a few years provided striking support for his periodic law.

providing soil and water for one of Asia's chief rice-growing areas.

**Melanesia**   *South Seas.

**melting-point**, the temperature at which solid and liquid forms of a substance can exist together in equilibrium. It is the same as the *freezing-point, but is the term usually used in connection with substances that are solid at room temperature. The melting-point of a pure material is usually lowered by the presence of impurities. It is generally measured at atmospheric pressure. The process of melting is also called fusion.

**Mendeleyev, Dimitri Ivanovich** (1834–1907), Russian chemist who observed that when the elements are listed in order of increasing relative atomic mass, those with similar chemical and physical properties occur at regular intervals. He thus formulated the *periodic law by which he predicted the existence of several elements which were subsequently discovered, and from which he prepared the *periodic table. This periodicity indicated regularities in the structure of the atoms and was later found to be dependent on the *atomic number. The element with an atomic number of 101 is named mendelevium after him.

**Mercator, Gerardus (Gerhard Kremer)** (1512–94), Flemish geographer and cartographer who invented a sys-

Mount Connor, a large **mesa** capped by a layer of very resistant sandstone, rises more than 300 m (1,000 feet) above the surrounding plain 240 km (150 miles) south-west of Alice Springs in central Australia.

tem of map *projection. In it the lines of longitude are projected on to a cylinder touching the Earth, the parallels of latitude being at right angles to them round the cylinder. It is a projection which maintains true compass directions between points and enables accurate bearings to be taken from the map. Mercator's world map of 1569 showed a navigable north-west passage between Asia and America, and a large southern continent. This was immediately influential, whereas his more enduring projection was not adopted for many years.

**mercury** (symbol Hg, at. no. 80, r.a.m. 200.59), a silver-coloured metallic liquid, and the only pure metal which is a liquid at room temperature. It is rather unreactive but forms complexes and organomercury compounds; it forms compounds in which it shows *valency 2 and a few less stable compounds where its valency is 1. Most metals dissolve in mercury; the solutions are called *amalgams. Having a very high surface tension, it does not wet glass, and it is therefore widely used in thermometers and barometers. As an electrical conductor it is employed in switches and relays. When an electric discharge is passed through mercury vapour, it gives off a blue light, and mercury discharge lamps are widely used. Important compounds include mercury(II) chloride ($HgCl_2$), which is an antiseptic and fungicide, and mercury(II) oxide (HgO) and sulphide (HgS), which are pigments. Their use is limited, because mercury and its compounds are highly toxic.

**meridians**, the halves of the *great circles which pass through both poles and have their centres at the Earth's centre. They pass through the Equator and all the *parallels of latitude. The meridian which passes through Greenwich, UK, is the prime meridian from which longitude is defined.

**Merrimack**, a river of north-east USA. Formed by the confluence of two smaller rivers (the Pemigewasset and the Winnipesankee) in central New Hampshire, it flows south and then east into Massachusetts, where it reaches the Atlantic Ocean after a journey of 177 km (110 miles). It is both an artery and a source of power.

**Mersey**, a small river which rises on the Cheshire Plain in the north-west of England and flows westward for 40 km

(25 miles), in a gentle arc, to enter its disproportionately large *estuary. Because of its size and the depth and reverse gradient of the rock floor beneath the alluvium, it is probable that the estuary was gouged out by a tongue of ice which moved south-east from a former Irish Sea glacier.

**mesa**, a large residual hill, characteristic of desert and semi-desert areas. The name comes from the Spanish word for 'table' and refers to the hill's flat top of resistant rock. This is underlain by cliffs of softer rock whose base is surrounded by the low-angle surfaces known as *pediments. They are common in areas of horizontal layers of sedimentary rock or lava. South-west USA contains many dramatic examples of both mesas and the smaller *buttes, especially in the Colorado plateau region.

**Meseta**    *Iberian Peninsula.

**meson**, a strongly interacting elementary particle which is composed of a *quark and an antiquark. Mesons form one of the two main groups of *hadrons (the others being the *baryons) and have either zero or integral *spin.

**Mesopotamia** (Greek, 'between two rivers'), the region between the Tigris and Euphrates Rivers in west Asia, often called the 'cradle of civilization', because of the many ancient civilizations which arose there subsequent to 4000 BC. The territory today extends north-westward through Iraq into Syria and Turkey. Where the two rivers descend from the hills in lower Iraq their joint valley plain effectively constitutes a *delta roughly 800 km (500 miles) long.

**mesosphere**, the region of the atmosphere between the *stratopause, 50 km (30 miles) up, and the bottom of the *thermosphere at a height of about 80 km (50 miles). Air temperature decreases with height in the mesosphere, falling to −100 °C (−148 °F) at its upper limit, the mesopause.

**Mesozoic Era**, the third of the great eras into which geological time is divided. It consists of the *Triassic, *Jurassic, and *Cretaceous Periods and extends from 245 to 66.4 million years ago. The Mesozoic is the age of the giant reptiles and marks the start of mammalian life.

**Messina, Strait of**, a narrow strait in the Mediterranean Sea, 2.4 km (1.5 miles) to 4.8 km (3 miles) across, separating the toe of Italy from the north-east corner of Sicily. It is a geologically recent break; the area generally is greatly disturbed as it lies near the Aegean subduction zone, where the

African *plate is moving beneath its Eurasian counterpart. Evidence of continued crustal instability are the frequent and occasionally destructive earthquakes which affect the area, and the volcanoes to the north-west and south-west. The city of Messina, on the Sicilian side of the strait, was destroyed by an earthquake in 1903, while Mount Etna, 40 km (25 miles) to the south-west, frequently erupts.

**metal**, an element with characteristic properties which are a consequence of its electronic structure. Metals constitute the largest set of elements and are generally shiny, malleable and ductile, and good conductors of heat and electricity. These properties result from their structure; this consists of a regular arrangement of positively charged ions, surrounded by *electrons which are free to move throughout the metal. When metals are bombarded by ultraviolet or X-radiation, they emit electrons. Metals occur mainly on the left-hand side of the periodic table. Group I contains the *alkali metals, and Group II the *alkaline earth metals. The *transition metals, *lanthanides, and *actinides are all metallic elements. Although a few metals are found uncombined, most occur naturally as their oxides or sulphides. Many of these can be reduced to the metals by carbon, but for reactive metals *electrolysis is needed. Metals react with non-metals to form ionic compounds in which the metal becomes positively charged; and many react with dilute acids, forming salts and giving off hydrogen. Metal oxides and hydroxides are usually basic—that is, they neutralize acids; some, such as aluminium oxide, $Al_2O_3$, are amphoteric—that is, they can also neutralize alkalis. Metals can be mixed with other metals, and with some non-metals, to form alloys. These are not true chemical compounds and do not have fixed compositions; they often have properties which differ from the pure metal, however, and alloying is often used to increase the strength or some other property of the metal.

**metalloid**, an element which cannot be classified as either a *metal or a *non-metal; some common examples are boron, silicon, germanium, arsenic, and antimony. Metalloids lie in a diagonal band in the middle of the *periodic table, between the metals on the left and the non-metals on the right. They are all *semiconductors; unlike the non-metals, they do conduct electricity, although much less than metals. Unlike metals, their conductivity increases with temperature. Because of their electrical properties, metalloids have been widely used in transistors and, more recently, in micro-electronic circuitry.

**metamorphic rock**, rock that has been altered by intense heat or pressure, or both. It may originally have been *sedimentary rock or *igneous rock, or even different metamorphic rock. The changes that take place during metamorphism can affect both the structure of the rock and its composition. Very often the rock is recrystallized. Contact metamorphism is a localized form of metamorphism that is produced by the heat of an *igneous intrusion. Limestone may then be altered into marble, and clay into a hard, tough rock (a hornfels). The zone affected in this way is called a metamorphic aureole. Hydrothermal metamorphism, or metasomatism, is produced by hot aqueous fluids emanating from igneous intrusions. China clay is produced in this way from granite. In dynamic metamorphism, or cataclasis, rocks are broken down mechanically by shearing and crushing; mylonite, a fine-grained banded rock, is a typical product. Regional metamorphism takes place on a large scale. The rocks are subjected to heat, deformation, and the action of hot fluids that may affect their chemical composition. In the lowest grades of regional metamorphism, slates and *phyllites (the latter with better-developed crystals than *slate) are formed. More intense regional metamorphism results in the development of *schists, rocks with a characteristic wavy foliation. At the highest grades, *gneisses are formed: coarsely crystalline rocks with alternate light and dark bands. The normal sequence, from lower to higher metamorphic grade, is known as prograde metamorphism. The process can be reversed if, for example, rocks of a high grade are subsequently maintained for a long time at a lower temperature than was reached during the first metamorphism. Alteration from a higher to a lower grade is termed retrograde metamorphism.

**meteor**, or shooting star, a stone or metal particle, usually as small as a grain of sand, which enters the Earth's atmosphere at great speed and is heated by friction to incandescence. Many millions are received each day; most burn up, but a proportion reach the ground as meteorites or in the form of meteoric dust.

**meteoric dust**, an extra-terrestrial material of very fine grain size which has been drawn on to the Earth by gravitational forces. It has a varied chemical composition but is essentially material rich in silica, iron, nickel, carbides, and graphite.

**meteorite**, a fallen meteor, large enough to have survived disintegration. Meteorites can consist mainly of stone (aerolites), iron with nickel (siderites), or both (siderolites). Most are small particles, but some weighing several tonnes have been found. These have hurtled down at great speed, causing craters on impact and occasionally damage. One of the largest craters known is near Winslow, Arizona, USA. It measures nearly a mile across and is some 180 m (600 feet) deep, and it is over 10,000 years old.

**meteorology**, the scientific study of the atmosphere on a global scale, within regions, and at particular localities, and the formation of conclusions as to forthcoming weather. It is especially concerned with the *energy budget, *water balance, and *circulation, and involves the measurement of elements such as pressure and temperature instrumentally. Of other elements, such as cloud types and amounts of cloud, visual estimates are made. The interpretation of data and understanding atmospheric processes require a knowledge of mathematics and physics, together with an appreciation of the influence on atmospheric conditions of natural features such as oceans and mountain ranges, and of unnatural environments such as large urban areas. Dynamical meteorology is concerned with atmospheric motion of all kinds, from small-scale cloud formation to the large-scale migrations of pressure areas which form part of the pattern of global circulation; and equations in *hydrodynamics and *thermodynamics are formulated to give mathematical precision to the descriptions and explanations. Synoptic meteorology is the branch of the science which forms the basis of weather forecasting. It involves study, on a day-to-day or hour-to-hour basis, of the changing patterns of elements such as air temperature and pressure, wind speed and direction, and cloud cover that go to make up a region's weather.

**methanal** (or formaldehyde, HCHO), a pungent flammable gas, the first member of the *aldehydes. Formed by

Meteor Crater in Arizona, USA, is believed to have been formed about 50,000 years ago by the impact of a large **meteorite**. The crater is 180 m (600 feet) deep, 1,220 m (4,000 feet) across, and the circular ridge rises 46 m (150 feet) above the surrounding plain.

the oxidation of methanol, it is usually stored either as its polymer, paraformaldehyde, from which it is re-formed on heating, or as its aqueous solution, formalin. It forms a variety of resins with phenol, for example the first synthetic plastic, Bakelite, and urea; and it is also used as a disinfectant and for embalming.

**methane** (CH$_4$), a colourless, odourless gas, and the simplest *hydrocarbon, being the first member of the *alkane series. It is formed by the decomposition of organic matter in the absence of oxygen, as in swampy environments (hence the name marsh gas), and is the main constituent of the biogas produced at refuse dumps. Methane occurs widely as the main component of natural *gas, being formed during the conversion of marine organic matter to *oil and of terrestrial organic matter to *coal. It is therefore common in coalmines, where it is a constituent of firedamp. It is unreactive towards many chemical reagents but burns readily in air with a hot flame, forming carbon dioxide and water; it is widely used as a fuel for cooking and heating. Industrially it is reacted with steam at high temperatures to produce hydrogen.

**methanoic acid** (or formic acid, HCOOH), a pungent colourless liquid. It is the simplest *carboxylic acid, but differs from the others as it is a *reducing agent. It is made by heating carbon monoxide with steam under pressure and with a catalyst; when added to concentrated sulphuric acid it is dehydrated to carbon monoxide.

**methanol** (or methyl alcohol, wood naphtha, wood spirit, CH$_3$OH), a colourless liquid which has the smell of strong spirits. It is toxic and causes blindness, even in small doses. Formerly produced by carbonizing and distilling wood, it is now prepared from the reaction of hydrogen with carbon monoxide or carbon dioxide. It is a good solvent and is used in the production of methanoic acid.

**methylated spirits**, a mixture of *ethanol to which a small amount of *methanol has been added, making it unfit to drink. It sometimes also contains traces of pyridine, to give it an unpleasant taste, as well as coloured dye. It is used commercially as a fuel and a solvent.

**metre** (symbol m), the *SI base unit of length originally defined as one ten-millionth of the distance from the Equator to the North Pole, but since redefined a number of times to give a more accurate definition. The latest definition, agreed in 1983, is that a metre is the length of the path travelled by light in a vacuum in 1/299,792,458 of a second, the *speed of light being a universal constant. One metre is equal to 39.37 inches.

**Mexico**, a country lying partly on the North American continent, bordering on the USA in the north, and on Central America in the south, with extensive coastlines on the Atlantic and Pacific Oceans. The divide is the Isthmus of Tehuantepec which, together with the curving eastern coastal plain and the north-eastward-thrusting Yucatán Peninsula, constitutes the main lowland area. In the far north-west, the splinter-like peninsula of Lower California, with its high *sierras, is a southward extension of the Sierra Nevada. So also is the mountainous western Sierra Madre on the mainland, while the eastern Sierra Madre is an extension of the Rocky Mountains. The narrow coastal plain facing the Pacific Ocean in the west is largely covered by forests, yielding mahogany in southern areas, where rain is abundant. In clearings, sisal and sugar can be grown; on the mountain slopes, cotton, coffee, and tobacco. Between the mountains lie high plateaux where, in the more temperate climate, grow cacti. There are several large lakes, saline in the north but fresh in the south, from which streams run in torrents through deeply cut canyons. Mexico is very rich in minerals: silver, uranium, copper, zinc, and many others. It provides a quarter of the fluorspar in the world, and has great reserves of oil. most of the country is subject to humid trade winds from the east between May and Augusst and tropical hurricanes from August to October.

**Mexico, Gulf of**, a vast embayment of the western Atlantic, bounded by the USA on the north and east and by

Mexico on the west and south-west. With a west–east length of over 1,800 km (1,100 miles) and a width of 1300 km (800 miles), it is the largest gulf in the world. The mainland coastline (5,000 km or 3,100 miles long) is generally low and sandy, with many lagoons, and contains the great deltas of the Mississippi. Formed as a result of the *plate activity that gave rise to the Atlantic Ocean, the Gulf is a subsiding continental margin. Under great thicknesses of sediment lie some of the world's largest reserves of oil and natural gas. A branch of the Equatorial Current enters through the Yucatán Channel; the water is warmed by the constant sun and flows out as the Gulf Stream through the Straits of Florida. The tide in the Gulf is almost unique, being diurnal: it has high and low water only once every twenty-four hours.

**mica**, a group of common rock-forming minerals. Important members are *biotite and *muscovite. All micas have a good basal cleavage that makes their crystals platy in form. Chemically they are silicates of the layer type (phyllosilicates), containing aluminium and also potassium, sodium, magnesium, iron, or lithium; and they give rocks a shiny appearance.

**Michelson, Albert Abraham** (1852–1931), US physicist who with Edward Morley, an American chemist, performed a celebrated experiment to measure the effect of the motion of the Earth through the 'ether'—a medium that was believed to fill the universe—on the *speed of light. No effect was detected, however, and this unexpected result led to the proposal of the *Fitzgerald–Lorentz contraction and ultimately to the development of *relativity theory. Michelson continued to work in optics and in 1907 became the first American to win the Nobel Prize for Physics.

**Michigan, Lake** *Great Lakes.

**microclimate**, the climate of a small or very small geographical area. They are often distinct from those of neigh-

An example of muscovite **mica** studded with garnets, also of the silicate group. Muscovites are light-coloured micas in which potassium is predominant. They are widespread and abundant in igneous rocks.

bouring areas because of slight differences between the amounts of *insolation they receive and the temperature and precipitation characteristics of the neighbouring areas. Almost infinitely numerous, they are especially important because most of the living world is concentrated within them. They are associated particularly with surface *boundary layers, and are sometimes regarded as extending only to a height at which the underlying surface ceases to affect the air—a few times the height of vegetation or buildings. In hilly and mountainous areas, aspect and slope influence the amount and intensity of insolation and the resultant air and soil temperatures; this is particularly noticeable in middle and high latitudes, where cultivation in such areas is often confined to south-facing slopes. Large variations in wind speed and direction, and in quantities of precipitation, also occur in such localities. Microclimates result too from differences in soil texture and moisture content: in spring there is a more rapid rise in the temperatures of sandy soils than in those of clay soils. Differences in types of vegetation cover are also responsible: inside woodlands, insolation, wind speeds, and vertical air movements are less than outside, as are the range of daily temperatures, the mean monthly air and soil temperatures, and precipitation. People create microclimatic conditions when they make a forest clearing, construct a reservoir, or build a city. In cities temperatures are generally higher than in the countryside; this is due to the heat generated by buildings, industry, traffic, and the mass of human bodies. Moreover it results in increased convection, which leads in turn to increases in precipitation. Wind speeds are generally lower inside cities than outside, although marked local accelerations occur when air is funnelled along streets or between buildings.

**micron** (symbol $\mu$), a distance of one-millionth of a metre ($10^{-6}$ m or $3.28 \times 10^{-6}$ feet). In *SI units, the micron is now called the micrometre ($\mu$m).

**Micronesia** *South Seas.

**microwave**, a very short radio wave, reaching almost to the infra-red region in the spectrum of *electromagnetic radiation. Microwaves have wavelengths between 1 and 300 mm. Unlike radio waves with a longer wavelength, they are not reflected by the *ionosphere and therefore can only be used for direct, short-distance communication. They have application in radar, however, and in research into the *energy levels of electrons. The energy of microwave *photons is similar to that required to increase the rotational energy of atoms and molecules, and this makes them useful for cooking. Microwave ovens heat food by causing loosely bound liquid molecules throughout the food to rotate. This process is more rapid than the conduction of heat from the surface to the interior of the food. The solid plates and dishes, with their more tightly bound molecules, remain cool.

**Mid-Atlantic Ridge**, the set of submarine ridges and islands extending north–south down the middle of the North and South Atlantic Ocean, as part of a larger system of *mid-oceanic ridges. In the centre of the ridge new crust is being formed by the *upwelling of *magma. This is then dragged to the east or west of the central ridge, probably by very slow convection currents in the mantle, at the rate of a few centimetres a year. Where the ridge reaches the surface—as in Iceland—volcanic activity is forming new crust. Some 1,500 km (900 miles) wide in total, the ridge is a

A **mirage** on a dry plain in southern Kenya: what appears to be a narrow strip of water, in which the trees on the horizon are reflected, is in fact a very convincing optical illusion.

zigzag feature which rises rather gently from the deep abyssal plains on either side and has a depression running along the centre, the axial valley. This is a *rift valley, formed as the two sides move apart. The zigzags correspond roughly to the zigzag shapes of the continents on either side and are marked by *faults which run across the line of the ridge. The rocks to the east and west of the axial valley become older the nearer they are to the continents. Frequent earth tremors and, in places, volcanic activity are evidence that the ridge is an active zone of crustal spreading at the present day.

**mid-oceanic ridges** (or rises), elongated mountain ranges that extend along the approximate centre-lines of oceans. They are found in the North and South Atlantic, the Pacific, the Indian, and the Southern Oceans. The ridges rise from the sea floor to heights of 3,000 m (10,000 feet) and more. For the most part they are submerged, but their peaks and crests appear above the surface in a few places, such as Iceland and Tristan da Cunha. Oceanic ridges are sites of *sea-floor spreading. In the Atlantic, Indian, and Southern Oceans, basaltic rocks are erupted along the ridge. Creation of new crustal material thus accompanies the separation of the crustal *plates; the old material is moved away from the ridges, ultimately to slowly disappear beneath the bordering continents.

**Millikan, Robert Andrews** (1868–1953), US physicist who in 1909 made the first accurate measurement of the charge on the *electron. In his experiment he observed electrically charged oil droplets as they fell between charged metal plates, which exerted a pull upon them. The droplets, which had become charged by gaining or losing electrons, travelled at different speeds depending on the charge they carried. From speed and other measurements, he calculated charge values for many droplets, and found the values to be a multiple of a basic unit. Millikan concluded that this basic unit must be the charge on the electron. He was awarded the Nobel Prize for Physics in 1923.

**millstone grit**, the coarse-grained sedimentary rocks (sandstones, or 'grits', and shales) found in Britain between the Carboniferous Limestone series and the Coal Measures. The sand grains are bound together with a mud and mineral matrix. As the name indicates, the sandstones were formerly used for making millstones.

**mineral**, a naturally occurring substance of inorganic origin that is homogeneous and has a definite chemical composition. Nearly all the 2,500 or so minerals so far identified are crystalline; their molecular structures are regular and their chemical composition varies only within specific limits. If a mineral has no crystal form it is said to be amorphous. Minerals are generally classified by their chemical composition. The principal groups are: native elements (such as gold and silver); halides (*evaporite minerals found in salt lakes and arid environments); sulphides (such as galena—a common lead mineral); oxides (usually hard, dense minerals such as the iron ore haematite); carbonates (soft, light-coloured minerals such as calcite and dolomite); sulphates (common minerals such as gypsum); phosphates (such as apatite); and silicates (the largest mineral group, containing most rock-forming minerals: quartz, feldspar, and mica). Their uses vary: some are sources of rare or essential metals; some are used as catalysts or fluxes in chemical reactions; some are of aesthetic value as collectors' items or jewellery stones. Often the word 'mineral' is also used in a more general sense to include any material of economic value (such as oil) that is obtained from the ground.

**mineralogy**, the science of the chemical composition, physical properties, and occurrence of *minerals; and the classification of individual minerals into an overall system and their specific identification are important aspects of the subject. The earliest known book on minerals is by Theophrastus (327–287 BC); systematic study was first begun by Georgius Agricola in 1527 in Bohemia as an aid to research in the mining industry. The scientific study of minerals is still of great importance to both mining and chemical industries.

**mineral water**, water from natural springs that commonly has a high content of dissolved minerals such as calcium carbonate, magnesium sulphate, potassium, or sodium sulphate.

**Minkowski, Hermann** (1864–1909), Russian-born German mathematician, who developed the geometrical theory of numbers. He was particularly interested in the mathematical study of the special theory of *relativity, laying the mathematical foundation of Albert *Einstein's general theory of relativity. He gave his name to a unified geometric view of a four-dimensional space which combined the three dimensions of physical space with that of time. He also contributed to the theory of quadratic forms.

**Minorca** *Balearic Islands.

**Miocene Epoch**, the fourth of the five geological epochs of the *Tertiary Era, spanning the time-interval from 23.7 to 5.3 million years ago. The Miocene was a period of great earth-movements during which the Alps, the Himalayas, and the western *cordillera of America were being formed. Sediments of Miocene age are found in southern Europe.

**mirage**, an optical illusion which occurs when sharp differences in temperature and therefore in density develop between thin layers of air at and immediately above the ground. This causes light to be bent, or refracted, as it travels through one layer to the next. As a result, the relationship between objects and the horizon becomes distorted. During the day, when a warm layer occurs next to the ground, objects near the horizon often appear to be reflected in flat surfaces such as beaches, deserts, roads, and water. This produces the shimmering, floating images which are commonly observed on very hot days. If an atmospheric *inversion develops during the night and cold air collects at the surface, objects which are actually beyond the horizon may be 'projected', appearing elevated and to float above it. Alternatively, the size of objects such as telegraph poles or rocks near the horizon can be greatly exaggerated. The phenomenon known as Fata Morgana is a complex mirage often observed at the Strait of Messina. Objects such as ships or men are seen suspended in the air over the object itself or on the water.

**Mississippian Period**, the earlier of the two epochs or subsystems into which the *Carboniferous Period is subdivided in North America (the other being the *Pennsylvanian). It covers the span of time from 360 to 320 million years ago.

**Mississippi River**, the principal waterway of the USA, draining all of the country's central basin. From the source of its chief tributary, the Missouri, to its mouths is a distance of nearly 6,100 km (3,800 miles), making it the third longest river system in the world. The Mississippi itself rises from lakes in northern Minnesota and flows south for 3,780 km (2,350 miles) before emerging from enormous deltas in the Gulf of Mexico. In its upper course it falls 365 m (1,200 feet) in 2,200 km (1,370 miles)—over 18 m (60 feet) at the Falls of Saint Anthony—and navigation is also impeded by winter ice and fog. In its middle reaches it receives the waters of the Missouri and the Ohio. Then it enters its alluvial plain, winding in enormous curves and forming *ox-bow lakes. Here it has also formed *levees, great banks of sediment, which are now often raised and strengthened artificially. The river's channel here is above the height of its *floodplain, and it has to be constantly dredged in order to prevent new floods from overtopping the levees and drowning vast areas of the plain. Towards its 'bird's-foot' *delta the river becomes slower and muddier, oozing into marshes and more lakes. Over the years it has pushed the deltas some 80 km (50 miles) out to sea.

**Missouri River**, the longest tributary of the Mississippi River. From its Red Rock headstreams in the Rocky Mountains, it flows for almost 4,200 km (2,600 miles) before joining the Mississippi, of which it is the principal tributary. It runs northward first, through the mountains to Great Falls—a series of waterfalls and rapids—and then turns east across the northern Great Plains, which are largely drained by its many tributaries. It now becomes navigable for long stretches and is a source of hydroelectricity. In North

Dakota the channel swings south-east and runs for several hundred kilometres receiving water from the Cheyenne and other rivers from the western Great Plains until, near Omaha, it is joined by its largest tributary, the Platte. Below Omaha it is completely navigable, although ice in winter causes problems. The lower river carries so much sediment that it is called the Big Muddy. After joining the Mississippi its thick waters can be discerned in the main flow for many miles.

**mist**, a sparse suspension of minute water droplets in the air which forms through condensation when moist air is cooled by contact with a cold surface. Occurring near the ground it limits visibility, though not so much as *fog, which it often precedes or succeeds.

**mistral**, a strong, gusty, cold, northerly wind which blows down the Rhône valley into the Mediterranean. On average it blows on 103 days each year, most often between December and April and least in September and October; and normally it blows for three consecutive days, although it can persist for up to twelve. It occurs when pressure is low over the western Mediterranean, and particularly when a *depression forms over the Gulf of Genoa and there is a ridge of high pressure from the Azores *anticyclone to the west. In winter the cold arctic or cold continental air drawn into the rear of the Genoan depression gives temperatures down to freezing and often below: the mean minimum at Marseilles is $-5.5\,°C$ (22 °F) and the extreme $-12\,°C$ (11 °F). East-to-west hedges of cypress have been planted to protect the orchard and horticultural crops from desiccation and severe frost damage by this icy wind. In the Adriatic and eastern Mediterranean, a similar but north-westerly wind is called the maestrale.

**Mitchell, Sir Thomas Livingstone** (1792–1855), Scottish explorer of Australia who in 1828 was appointed surveyor-general of New South Wales. His first expedition was north from Sydney to the Barwon River, and his second traced the course of the Darling to within 160 km (100 miles) of its junction with the Murray. His third journey established the junction and assumed greater significance when he struck off south, entering the fertile lands around the Glenelg River. His fourth—to find a route to the Gulf of Carpentaria—was a relative failure, ending in his belief that the Barcoo ran north instead of south-west into Lake Eyre.

**mixing**, the process which results in the redistribution of temperature and water vapour in the atmosphere as two bodies of air with different characteristics are combined. Such mixing, either of different *air masses or of bodies of air from different heights within the same mass, often causes the air to become saturated, resulting in condensation and cloud formation. This happens when the relative *humidity of the mixture exceeds 100 per cent at a temperature which is midway between the temperatures of the original bodies of air.

Water masses in the ocean also mix together along their boundaries, forming water with properties (such as temperature, salinity, or nutrient content) intermediate between those of the original water masses.

**mixtures** (in chemistry), any quantity of one substance randomly distributed through another substance without any chemical reaction taking place between the components. Mixtures differ from compounds in that the latter contain two or more elements joined together in fixed proportions by chemical bonds. Mixtures retain the chemical properties of their components and can be separated by physical means into their components, whereas compounds have distinct chemical properties and can only be separated into their components by chemical means. In homogeneous mixtures the components are too small to be distinguished visually (examples include *colloids and *solutions); but in heterogeneous mixtures they can be visually distinguished (for example, a suspension such as sand in water or dust in air). Some mixtures, including alloys, can be either homogeneous or heterogeneous.

**Möbius strip**, a one-sided surface named after the German mathematician August Ferdinand Möbius (1790–1868). It may be formed from a long, rectangular band of paper. The band is twisted in the middle through 180°, and then the two ends are glued together. Such a strip has remarkable topological properties, including the fact that, unlike the original band which is two-sided, it has only one side and one edge. If one were to start painting it from any point, the entire strip could be coloured without having to lift the brush from the surface. Another unexpected property of a Möbius strip is that it is non-orientable, a technical term which means that the distinction between left- and right-handedness cannot be preserved consistently over the whole surface. When it is pierced through the middle and cut all the way round, parallel to the edge, other interesting phenomena appear; and cutting one-third of the distance from the edge produces quite a different result (see figure).

**mode** (in statistics), a form of *average. It is the value which occurs most frequently in a set, and so represents the most popular one. It is less often used than the arithmetic mean (see *mean) and the *median, but is valuable, for instance, in stock control. Consider the following shoe sales: one pair of size 3, two of size 4, five of size 5, three of size 6, three of size 7, two of size 8, and one of size 9. The arithmetic mean makes no sense here. The median is size 6, but the relevance for reordering is the most common size sold, the mode, which is 5.

**modulus**, the magnitude of a real or complex *number without regard to its sign. The modulus of any number $Z$ is denoted $|Z|$: thus $|-3| = |+3| = 3$. For a complex number, $Z = a + ib$, $|Z| = \sqrt{(a^2 + b^2)}$. A completely different meaning of modulus comes from number theory. Here arithmetic modulo $n$ refers to a system where the results of addition and multiplication are given as the remainders after all the multiples of $n$ have been removed from the numbers. Here $n$ is called the modulus of the system. For example, in arithmetic modulo 7, $4 + 5 = 2$, since $4 + 5 = 9$ has remainder 2 when divided by 7, and $4 \times 5 = 6 \pmod 7$.

**moho**, an abbreviation for *Mohorovivičić discontinuity.

**Mohorovičić discontinuity**, a world-wide zone that separates the *Earth's crust and mantle. It lies from 10 to 70 km (6 to 43 miles) below the surface of the continents and 6 km (4 miles) below the ocean floors. It is often abbreviated to moho or M discontinuity and is named after its discoverer, Andrija Mohorovivičić, a Yugoslavian seismologist, who first identified it in 1909 by studying the speeds of shock waves from earthquakes. These waves travel in the crust at velocities of 6 to 7 km/s (about 4 m.p.s.) and in the denser upper mantle at velocities of about 8 km/s (5 m.p.s.).

**molarity**, a measure of the *concentration of a solution given in *mole per litre. It is defined as the number of moles of a solute in one litre of solution—thus a 1 molar solution of sodium chloride, NaCl, contains 1 mole of NaCl (58.44 g) in 1 litre—and it can be calculated by dividing the number of moles of solute by the number of litres of solution.

**Moldova**, a country in eastern Europe bounded on the north, east, and south by Ukraine, and on the west by Romania. Wider Moldova comprises lands between the Carpathian Mountains in the west and the Dneister River in the east, including the north-east of modern Romania. The Prut river waters its western part, Bessarabia. Although land-locked, its proximity to the Black Sea gives it a mild climate. From the north into the centre runs a belt of hills with deep valleys in which vines and fruit trees flourish. Fur-

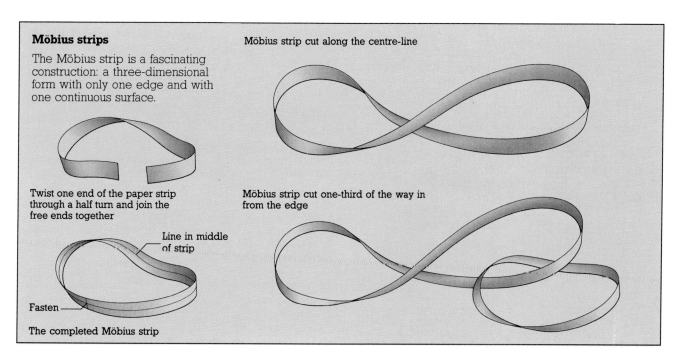

**Möbius strips**

The Möbius strip is a fascinating construction: a three-dimensional form with only one edge and with one continuous surface.

Möbius strip cut along the centre-line

Twist one end of the paper strip through a half turn and join the free ends together

Line in middle of strip

Fasten

The completed Möbius strip

Möbius strip cut one-third of the way in from the edge

ther south are low-lying steppes supporting grain, sugarbeet, and tobacco.

**mole** (symbol mol), the *SI unit of an amount of substance. This amount of substance is a set number of atoms, molecules, or ions and is defined as the number of atoms in 0.012 kg of the isotope carbon-12; it is equal to $6.022 \times 10^{23}$, and is called the *Avogadro number. This definition enables one mole of a substance to be simply identified by mass. For example, 1 mole of hydrogen molecules (relative molecular mass 2) has a mass of 2 grams, 1 mole of oxygen molecules (relative molecular mass 32) has a mass of 32 grams, and so on. The concept of the mole is particularly important in the study of gases because—in theory at least—equal numbers of molecules of any gas are described by the same mathematical relationship between pressure, volume, and temperature (see *gas laws). It also has many applications in chemistry, because substances which react with each other do so in molar proportions.

**molecular formula**, the number of atoms of each element in a molecule. Ethane has the formula $C_2H_6$, so an ethane molecule consists of two carbon atoms and six hydrogen atoms, covalently bonded together. Only molecular compounds have molecular formulae; *ionic compounds such as sodium chloride, NaCl, and giant lattices such as silica, $SiO_2$, do not contain molecules, and their formulae, called empirical formulae, give only the ratios of numbers of atoms present.

**molecular models**. These are used to show the three-dimensional shapes of molecules. There are several sorts of models; in ball-and-stick models, each atom is represented by a spherical ball, and each *covalent bond by a stick. These make geometrical relationships clear, but greatly exaggerate the distances between atoms. More realistic, though sometimes less clear, are space-filling models; in these, atoms which are chemically bonded actually touch and interpenetrate each other.

**molecular weight**   *relative molecular mass.

Space-filling **molecular models** of a polyurethane (*left*) and of polyvinylchloride, PVC (*right*). Black spheres represent carbon, white spheres hydrogen, red spheres oxygen, blue spheres nitrogen, and green spheres chlorine atoms. The models show the hexagonal carbon groups and twisting structure of the polyurethane molecule, and the relatively large size of the chlorine atoms in the PVC molecule.

**molecule**, two or more *atoms chemically bonded together. The atoms can be the same, as in oxygen, $O_2$, or different, as in water, $H_2O$. Molecules are electrically neutral, and the atoms are held together by *covalent bonds, in which the atoms share pairs of electrons. Not all substances consist of molecules: some, such as the noble gas helium, consist of free atoms, and many consist of electrically charged *ions. Gases usually consist of molecules, as do many liquids and some solids. In gases the molecules are widely separated from each other and are in constant rapid motion. In liquids the molecules are in contact with each other but can still move about. In solids the molecules are tightly packed in a regular arrangement, and can only vibrate.

**mollisol**, a *zonal soil with a thick, nearly black, highly organic surface *horizon. The mollisol layer has a loose, crumbly structure when dry and is rich in plant nutrients, particularly calcium. The lower horizons of the soil tend to be clayey. Such soils are found under grasslands in the semi-arid mid-latitudes and in sub-humid, moist continental or subtropical areas. They are among the most fertile soils in the world and tend to be widely used for commercial cereal production. They occur on the Great Plains of the USA, the pampas of Argentina and Uruguay, and the Russian steppes.

**Moluccas** (Maluku or Spice Islands), a large group of volcanic islands of Indonesia, lying on the Equator between Sulawesi and New Guinea. Very wet and fertile, the islands produce the spices nutmeg and cloves, mace, cinnamon, and pepper. Rice and sago are also grown.

**molybdenum** (symbol Mo, at. no. 42, r.a.m. 95.94), a very hard, silver *transition metal. It is often alloyed with iron and other metals to increase their strength at high temperature and their corrosion resistance. Molybdenum disulphide is a lubricant, and is used as an additive in oils.

**moment** (in physics), the turning effect produced by a *force acting at a distance on an object. It is found by multiplying the force applied by the perpendicular distance between the point of application of the force and the object on which it has an effect. In a mechanical system—for example, in the use of a spanner to tighten a nut—the moment of force is called the torque. The concept of moment is applied in many systems, including the *dipole moment of polar molecules.

**moment of inertia**, the equivalent, in a rotating system, of *mass. Symbol $I$, the moment of *inertia of a particle about any line is $I = mr^2$, where $m$ is its mass and $r$ its perpendicular distance from the line. For a system of particles, it is the sum of their separate moments of inertia. A flywheel is deliberately made with a large amount of inertia, sometimes for example by concentrating most of its bulk near the periphery. This means that when turning it is difficult to slow down or speed up, so that it can smooth out irregularities of motion; and when turning fast it stores a lot of mechanical energy.

**momentum** (or linear momentum), the quantity which measures the tendency of a moving body to continue in motion. It is calculated by multiplying the mass of the body by its velocity, and is a *vector quantity. A stationary body has no momentum. Momentum is conserved as long as no

The driver of a moving car possesses a **momentum** which will be conserved until he or she is acted upon by a force. If the car stops suddenly, for example in a crash, a seat belt may supply a restraining force to bring the driver to a rapid but safe halt. However, as this picture of a laboratory simulation of a crash indicates, the momentum of an unrestrained driver is more likely to be reduced by reaction forces as he strikes the steering column, the windscreen or even the road, with the obvious risks of injury.

outside force is acting, so the fragments of a stationary object immediately after exploding still have zero total momentum: the momentum of fragments in one direction is balanced by that of others in the opposite direction.

**Monaco**, a small country of 1.9 km² (0.73 sq. mi.) located in the hills above the Mediterranean Sea. The ancient town and fortress perch on a rocky outcrop that projects into the Mediterranean Sea. On this part of the Riviera, steep, white limestone cliffs, representing the incipient Alps, stand out along the coastline with sheltered intervening bays. The numerous caves and grottoes were long occupied by Palaeolithic peoples.

**monadnock**, a steep-sided, isolated hill, rising above a plain. The name is derived from Mount Monadnock, New Hampshire, USA, and was used to define the last remnants of former *cycles of erosion. It is now known, however, that Mount Monadnock owes its shape largely to the actions of ice, rather than of rivers. However, the term is still used, as an equivalent to *inselbergs, to describe residual hills produced by river erosion.

**Mongolia**, a large region in the heart of Asia, sandwiched between Siberia on the north and China on the south. It includes the republic of Mongolia and, in China, Inner Mongolia. Mainly a high, barren plateau, it has mountains and saline lakes in the north-west and the Gobi Desert in the south-east. In winter it is very cold, and rainfall is light. Even so, there are areas of steppe on which livestock can be sup-

ported, and some grain is grown. Coal, copper, tungsten, molybdenum, and oil have all been found.

**monochromatic light**, light of a single wavelength or frequency. Before the advent of lasers it was obtained by exciting certain atoms (for example, of sodium or mercury) in an electrical discharge. These atoms then emitted light in very narrow frequency ranges which could be further refined with special filters. Nowadays, lasers are powerful sources of monochromatic light and in some of them the frequency of the light can be varied. Such light is useful in studying the precise *energy levels of electrons in atoms and molecules.

**monocline**, a set of strata that dips more or less uniformly in one direction. It can be thought of as one half of a syncline or anticline without the other half.

**monomer**, a molecule which can react with other molecules of the same or other compound to form a new product with a higher *relative molecular mass. A simple example is ethene, which reacts with itself to form polyethene: $n\,CH_2{=}CH_2 \rightarrow (-CH_2-)_{2n}$. Here a very large number of monomer molecules react together, forming a

The **monochromatic light** beam from a laser being studied in a laboratory.

*polymer. If just two monomer molecules react, then the product is called a dimer.

**monsoon** (Arabic, 'fixed season'), a wind with seasonal change of direction and properties. It was applied originally to a wind over the Arabian Sea which blows from the north-east for six months and then from the south-west for six months. Such seasonal reversal of wind direction occurs mainly in the Indian Ocean, the western Pacific, and off the West African coast. The term is applied also to the rainy seasons of much of southern and eastern Asia and of East and West Africa. In the northern Indian Ocean and the China Seas the seasonal reversal of wind direction is very marked. It results from the latitudinal movement of the Earth's wind belts: as the *intertropical convergence zone moves north or south of the Equator, the trade winds are replaced by westerlies blowing across the Equator. Summer heating of the vast Eurasian land mass causes the normal pressure and wind systems of the mid-latitudes in the northern hemisphere to break down. The intertropical convergence zone is drawn far to the north, over Africa, the Indian subcontinent, and China: and this allows the tropical easterlies (the south-east trades) to cross the Equator. They are deflected by the *Coriolis force, acquire a westerly component, and blow from the south-west. This is the south-west monsoon of May to September. It is wet, although the rains accompanying it are not continuous, and lengthy breaks occur as the monsoon itself retreats occasionally. Winter cooling of the Eurasian land mass increases the air pressure; cold air spreads out over south and east Asia; and this causes predominantly dry weather: the north-east monsoon of October to April. The intertropical convergence zone is pushed south, and the tropical regions of the western Pacific, northern Indian Ocean, and the part of the Atlantic off West Africa are then dominated by the tropical easterlies. Where these winds cross the Equator and acquire a westerly component, they are termed the north-west monsoon. This is noticeable particularly in Indonesia and northern Australia. Only in the western part of the Arabian Sea and the northern part of the China Sea does a monsoon wind reach gale force. For the most part the winds are no more than fresh; but they pick up moisture over the sea and deposit it on land as rain. The monsoon has given its name to the type of climate found in regions where it occurs.

**Mont Blanc**, the highest mountain in the Alps and the second highest in Europe after Mount Elbrus in the Caucasus. It has several peaks, one of which rises to 4,807 m (15,771 feet). At the centre of the Savoy Alps, it straddles the French–Italian border, its Italian face in the south-east presenting a massive wall. On the north-western slopes are numerous glaciers, the best known being the Mer de Glace.

**Monte Carlo method**, a way of analysing *stochastic processes which are so difficult that a purely mathematical treatment is not practical. The procedure is to construct an artificial model of the real-world problem and then perform sampling experiments on it. The random devices which were first used in such a simulation included roulette wheels, dice, and spinning pointers, and gave the method its name. Nowadays it is possible to perform simulations on a large scale with computers, and it is a very widely used process. Although much mathematical theory has been considerably advanced recently in areas such as inventory control and queuing, the techniques developed can usually be applied only if the system obeys carefully defined probabilistic laws.

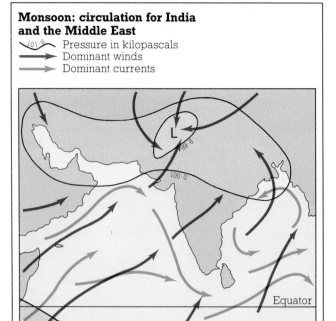

**Monsoon: circulation for India and the Middle East**
〰 Pressure in kilopascals
→ Dominant winds
→ Dominant currents

Equator

Southwest monsoon
(Northern Hemisphere summer)

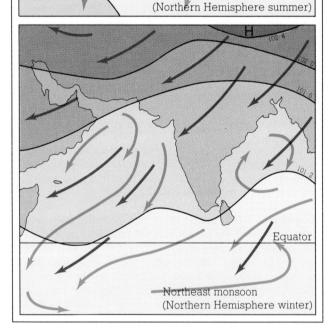

Equator

Northeast monsoon
(Northern Hemisphere winter)

If it does not, then, with the aid of a computer, the Monte Carlo method is usually the most appropriate means of analysis.

**Montenegro**, a Yugoslav republic in south-east Europe, bordering Serbia in the north-east, Albania in the south, and Bosnia-Herzegovina in the north-west. It has a long Adriatic coastline. The south-western part of the republic is *karst, while the eastern part is mainly forest and fertile highlands. Agriculture consists mainly of sheep- and goat-raising.

**montmorillonite**, a clay mineral of complex composition but essentially aluminium silicates. It is opaque, soft, and feels greasy to the touch. The minute crystals can take up or lose water or positive ions such as sodium, $Na^+$, or calcium, $Ca^{2+}$. Montmorillonite is found very extensively and is an important industrial mineral, being used as a base for paper and cosmetics and for purifying liquids. It is sometimes referred to as *fuller's earth.

**Mont Pelée**, a volcano on the island of Martinique, in the volcanic arc of the Caribbean Islands. It is famed for the appalling catastrophe of 1902, when, heralded by a great explosion, a *nuée ardente swept down the flanks of the volcano and devastated Saint Pierre, the port and capital of the island, killing 30,000 people. After the disaster Mont Pelée continued to grow and extruded a plug of consolidated lava through the crater dome. Half of it broke off along a diagonal crack to leave a spine which subsequently was elevated 275 m (900 feet) above the dome, only to disintegrate in the following year. There has been much subsequent activity, with nuée discharges, the formation of a new dome, which began in 1930, and the squeezing out of many spines of viscous lava.

**Montserrat**, a Caribbean island and British dependency, south-west of Antigua in the Leeward Islands. It is about 18 km (11 miles) long, and contains volcanic vents, hot springs, and much rugged scenery. Only a third of it is cultivable, however, and earthquakes are not uncommon.

**Mont Tremblant**, a Provincial Park in south-western Quebec, on the *Canadian Shield north of the junction of the Ottawa and Saint Lawrence Rivers. The mountain itself rises to 960 m (3,150 feet), and the Rouge River runs southward through the Park to its junction with the Ottawa. The scenery is varied, with lowland and upland views.

**moonstone**, a semiprecious fine-grained feldspar of various colours, with transparent or opalescent appearance. It is described by ancient writers as a stone that changes appearance with the waxing and waning of the moon.

**moraine**, a jumbled deposit of rocks of different sizes which have been laid down by *glaciers and ice-sheets. Lack of sorting distinguishes it from river deposits, although it can be confused with material produced by rapid mass movements on slopes. Most rocks in a moraine come from outcrops nearby; but they can also contain material brought from more remote areas, because ice-sheets can flow for long distances and transport debris both down and up hill. Distinctive, far-travelled rocks or pebbles, termed 'erratics', can provide valuable evidence of directions of ice movement. There are different classes of moraine, corresponding to different zones of glaciers or ice-sheets. Ground moraine is left as a sheet of material by ice which has melted away as stagnant, stationary blocks. Terminal moraines are curved ridges of debris, often with quite steep slopes, formed when the snout of a glacier stays and melts in the same place for some time, while being replenished by the arrival of new ice. Lateral moraines form at the sides of glaciers and are occasionally left as high, steep ramparts along valley walls. Medial forms are lines of debris within the ice which are usually made by a meeting of two lateral moraines below the junction of two ice-streams.

**Morley, Edward Williams** (1838–1923), US chemist who specialized in accurate quantitative measurements such as those of the combining weights of hydrogen and oxygen, but who is best remembered for his collaboration with Albert *Michelson in their experiment to determine the speed of light.

This terminal **moraine** marks the maximum advance of the Athabasca Glacier in the Canadian Rockies.

**Morocco**, a country in the north-west corner of Africa bounded inland by Algeria and Western Sahara and with coasts on both the Mediterranean Sea and the Atlantic Ocean. Much of it consists of the Atlas Mountains, running from the south-west to the north-east. Near the coasts it is warm and wet; in the mountains, arid. South of the mountains begins the very hot and windy *Sahara Desert. In the north is a quarter of the world's supply of phosphates, together with coal and iron. Oil and many other minerals are also found. Rivers from the mountains water the coastal plains and permit a wide variety of crops: cereals, citrus fruits, and vegetables. Vineyards, olive-gardens, and date-palm groves also thrive, especially on the inland Fez–Meknès plain.

**Moseley, Henry Gwyn Jeffreys** (1887–1915), British physicist who, while working under Ernest Rutherford, bombarded different elements with electrons and analysed the X-rays emitted. He established a precise link between the wavelengths of the X-rays and the positions of the elements in the *periodic table, and deduced that each element could be identified according to the charge on the nucleus, which he called the *atomic number. In 1913 he stated his findings mathematically in a law which now bears his name.

**motion**, the movement of a body with respect to some fixed point or origin. Motion can either be at a fixed velocity, with both the direction and the speed of the body remaining constant, or it can be accelerated, in which case either the direction or the speed, or both, will vary with time. *Newton's laws of motion are the foundation of classical mechanics.

**mottling in soils**, the occurrence of small blotches or patches that are a different colour from the rest of the soil, is caused by periodic waterlogging or uneven aeration of the material. The oxidation of iron compounds along cracks and root channels in soils subject to *gleying, for example, produces areas of red mottling in an otherwise grey soil.

**moulin** (French, 'mill'), a huge *pothole, also called a glacial mill, which has been worn through the ice of a glacier

This long-exposure photograph shows the paths of stars as they move across the sky relative to the Earth. In fact, the star tracks are due to the **motion** of the Earth with respect to the 'fixed stars'. The perceptible curvature of the tracks, indicating change in direction, shows that the motion of the Earth is rotational.

and sometimes on into the rock of its beds. It is made by streams of meltwater laden with rock particles; these are swirled round at speed, drilling the moulin.

**mountain**, a large upland mass which generally rises to distinct peaks. Although there is no absolute definition, the summits usually stand at least 700 m (2,200 feet) above surrounding valleys or plains, uplands with less elevation being accounted hills or plateaux. Mountains can be single, isolated peaks (as is Shasta, USA; Egmont, New Zealand; or Ararat, Turkey) resulting from large volcanic eruptions, block *faulting, or simply very long periods of *denudation. More often, however, they stand in lines of peaks, forming ranges or chains (as in the southern Andes or the Appalachians); these may contain extinct or active volcanoes as well as complicated sequences of folded and faulted rocks, for ranges appear to mark places where two plates of the Earth's crust have collided during the process of *continental drift. Most impressively, mountains may occur in huge and complex masses (as in the great system running from Turkey through to eastern China); these seem to be caused by major collisions between crustal plates, such as the northward drift of the Indian subcontinent against Asia. By and large, the younger the mountains are, the higher they stand above surrounding lowlands; for sooner or later mountain building

gives way to *denudation. Not only are most mountains geologically complicated, but there are also great variations in slope, elevation, and exposure to *weathering within small areas, particularly where deep gorges have been cut. Consequently, there is an extraordinary variety of local climates, producing mosaics of plant and animal communities. Although high mountains, especially tropical ones, have distinct zones of vegetation at different altitudes, the zones often vary from one side of a mountain to another, as a result of differences in wind patterns and precipitation.

**mountain building** (orogenesis), the processes within the Earth's crust which produce the uplift of mountain ranges. These processes are tectonic and appear to be linked to the movement of great chunks of crust over the Earth's surface, as described in the modern theory of *plate tectonics. Where plates collide, deep movements of molten rock, earthquakes, and volcanoes result. Strata are thrust upwards, and folding, faulting, and metamorphism occur. Over millions of years these processes build mountains. *Orogenies (periods of mountain building) seem to be rather spasmodic in geological history: the continents of Europe and North America show traces of three or four separate episodes. Owing to erosion, the oldest mountains are much lower than the youngest ones.

**mountain chain**, a belt of mountains that developed together over a long period of time as a result of tectonic processes. They are known to be related to the collision and separation of crustal *plates and are found both on the continents (the Rockies, Andes, and Himalayas) and in the oceans (the Mid-Atlantic Ridge).

**Mozambique**, a country lying along the south-east coast of Africa and bounded by Tanzania, Malawi, Zambia, Zimbabwe, South Africa, and Swaziland. The Zambezi flows across the middle of the country, generating electricity at the Cabora Bassa dam in the north-west, and the Limpopo across the south. The coastal plain is low and broad, with areas of sand between the marshy river valleys. It is wetter inland, where there are regions of fertile soil covered with tropical forest, before the ground rises northward to rocky plateaux with *savannah vegetation. Near Tete, on the Zambezi, some coal is mined.

**mud**, a semi-liquid, fine-grained sediment composed mainly of tiny clay and silt fragments. When consolidated it forms mudstone or siltstone, according to the amount of *silt it contains. Mudstones are similar to *shales in that they are not plastic, split readily, and disintegrate in water.

**mudflow**, a stream of water and mud, usually caused by intense rain falling on bare ground or by rapid melting of snow. A 'lahar' is a special kind of mudflow produced by water mixing with fresh volcanic lava; a further type is caused by bogs on hillsides overflowing their basins. Mudflows can either move very fast, causing great destruction, or travel almost imperceptibly slowly, although most move in fits and starts, as the supply of water and mud varies. These tend to be elongated, rather straight and fairly shallow, with their edges rimmed by levees of dried mud.

**muon** (in atomic physics), a particle produced by the decay of a *pion. Muons are similar to electrons: they have the same magnitude of charge and spin as electrons, but have a mass over 200 times that of the electron. There are two types of muon, the positive and negative; they are unstable, with an average lifetime of 2 microseconds, and they decay to give *neutrinos and either an electron or a positron. Muons are created in the Earth's atmosphere when cosmic rays, which are mostly high energy protons, collide with nuclei of the atoms in the atmosphere. The muons then travel to Earth at a speed very close to the speed of light. Because they are travelling so fast the muons experience the relativistic effect known as *time dilatation, and their average lifetime becomes 32 microseconds—long enough for them to reach the surface of the Earth. On average, one muon hits each square centimetre of the Earth's surface every minute. Muons belong to the group known as the strange particles, because when they were discovered they didn't seem to fit in with the accepted picture of the nature of matter.

**Murchison, Sir Roderick Impey** (1792–1871), British geologist of Scottish extraction, who first established the geological sequence of Early *Palaeozoic strata in south Wales. In 1848 he published his *The Silurian System*, an examination of Lower Palaeozoic rocks, and a year later established, with Adam *Sedgwick, the *Devonian Period based on their research of the geology of south-west England and the Rhineland. Then came *The Geology of Russia and the Ural Mountains* (1845) and the proposal, based on his explorations of Russia, of a *Permian Period of Upper Palaeozoic rocks.

**Murray River**, Australia's principal river, rising near Mount Kosciusko and flowing for 2,590 km (1,610 miles) westward to the Great Australian Bight at Encounter Bay. Mainly fed by melting snow in spring, it descends from the Australian Alps, in the south of the Great Dividing Range, to cross the vast, semi-arid Victoria Plain in a shallow *braiding stream (forming a natural boundary with New

The prolonged torrential rain—nearly 203 mm (8 inches) in 48 hours—that fell on Hong Kong in the wake of a typhoon loosened and lubricated thousands of tonnes of earth and rock on the hillsides above the industrial area of Kwun Tong. The resultant **mudflow** swept away many squatters' shacks and engulfed roads and residential buildings.

**Muskeg** swamp in the Rocky Mountain foothills of Alberta, Canada. The swamp is gradually being colonized by conifers as the waterlogged ground becomes built up by the formation of peat.

South Wales). Then it picks up its two main tributaries, the Murrumbidgee and the Darling, before entering its lower reaches in South Australia. Here it is partly navigable. It enters the sea through a lagoon, Lake Alexandrina. The significance of the Murray lies not only in its great length but also in its relative permanence when compared with other Australian rivers. In most years, seasonal precipitation on to the mountains, brought by great *depressions from the Southern Ocean supplies an adequate flow both for hydro-electricity and for irrigation.

**muscovite** (in geology), a light, silvery-coloured mineral and a member of the *mica group. It is one of the commonest minerals in igneous, sedimentary, and metamorphic rocks. It occurs as flat plates; specimens 30 to 50 m² (36 to 60 sq. yards) in size are recorded from Ontario. It is used for electrical and heat insulation either in sheets or powdered in plaster. Because of its transparency and resistance to heat it makes good furnace windows.

**muskeg**, a swampy area of peat, covered by sphagnum moss and surrounded by coniferous trees, such as spruce. It develops in former lake basins and along river channels in cold, flat areas of the Northern Hemisphere, especially in northern Canada.

**Myanmar** (Burma), a country in south-east Asia, which has a long, tropical western coast on the Indian Ocean and is cut off from the rest of Asia by mountains in the north and east. Between the mountains and down the centre of the country run the broad, cultivable valley of the Irrawaddy River and several tributary valleys. To the east is the valley of the Salween River. The country is rich in oil and precious minerals, such as silver and gemstones, and is famous for the quality of its rice and teak. Climatically it is hot and monsoonal, about 5,000 mm (nearly 200 inches) of rain falling annually along the coast, although in the eastern upland region it is drier and cooler.

**mylonite**, a *metamorphic rock produced by crushing and grinding, or cataclasis, which is followed by partial or complete recrystallization of the mineral fragments. It is dark in colour with a fine texture and is commonly banded or streaked.

# N

**Nachtigal, Gustav** (1834–85), German explorer in Africa who established the colonies of Togo and Cameroon in the Gulf of Guinea. A decade earlier, in 1869–75, he had crossed the Sahara to Lake Chad and then travelled through Chad disguised as a Muslim pilgrim, making accurate and detailed geographical notes on the way.

**Namibia** (formerly South-West Africa), a country with borders on Angola in the north, Botswana in the east, and South Africa in the south; in the north-east a long sliver of territory, the Caprivi Strip, reaches between Angola and Botswana to Zambia. In the west the Namib Desert stretches down the Atlantic Ocean coast; in the east is the Kalahari. The higher land between is also hot and arid and has no permanent rivers. Diamonds are found near the Orange River in the extreme south, and ores containing silver, cadmium, and vanadium in the north. There are also reserves of beryl, manganese, and tin.

**Nanga Parbat**, a mountain in Kashmir at the western end of the *Himalayas. It is one of the world's highest peaks, the summit being at 8,126 m (26,660 feet). A steep southern wall that rises for most of its height above the valley floor is one of its distinctive features.

**Nansen, Fridtjof** (1861–1930), Norwegian explorer, oceanographer, statesman, and humanitarian, who first became famous by crossing Greenland in 1888–9. Four years later, to test his theory of a polar current flowing towards Greenland's east coast, he set course for the North Pole in the *Fram*, specially constructed with thick-timbered sides. Caught in an ice-floe, it drifted northward for a year and then, as expected, began to drift westwards. At this point Nansen with one companion took to sledges and reached latitude 86° N., the nearest to the Pole that man had ever been. The whole journey took three years; and within that time the *Fram* drifted right round the Pole, just as Nansen had foreseen. An active member of the League of Nations, Nansen organized relief work among displaced persons, notably Russian refugees and famine victims.

**naphthalene** ($C_{10}H_8$), an *aromatic hydrocarbon which occurs in coal tar whose structure consists of two fused *benzene rings. It is a white crystalline solid which burns with a smoky flame. It undergoes reactions more readily than benzene and is employed in the manufacture of phthalic anhydride, $C_8H_4O_3$, which is utilized in the production of plasticizers, synthetic resins, and polyesters; other derivatives are used for dyes, drugs, and insecticides.

**Napier, John** (1550–1617), Scottish mathematician who, simultaneously with but independently of the German Joost Bürgi, invented *logarithms, which he described in his book *Mirifici Logarithmorum Canonis Descriptio* in 1614. His tables, modified and republished by Henry Briggs, had a lasting influence on mathematics. He also devised a simple calculating device, called Napier's bones, which provided a mechanical method for undertaking long multiplication and division, and introduced the use of the decimal point.

**nappe**, a great arch-shaped *fold in rock that has been overturned so that it is lying on its side. At the centre of the nappe there are usually deformed igneous and metamorphic rocks. Not infrequently, a nappe has been torn off at its roots by faulting. It may then be transported for some distance. Many examples of nappes can be seen in the Swiss Alps.

**Natal**, the smallest of the provinces of South Africa, facing the Indian Ocean. Its mostly narrow coastal strip is humid and subtropical, with palm trees. A broad inland belt of temperate grassland rises in places to 1,200 m (4,000 feet); here sugar cane, cotton, and tobacco can be grown. It is backed by the steep escarpment of the *Drakensberg Mountains, whose highest point in Natal is at 3,410 m (11,200 feet). The Pongola, Buffalo, *Tugela, and other rivers with their tributaries flow down from the mountains and the uplands, draining the land and providing water in all seasons. The main mineral is coal.

**national park**, an area of natural beauty protected by the government state for the preservation of landscapes, plants, and animals in their natural state for public enjoyment. It differs from the nature reserve in that the latter sets out to protect certain animals and plants (many of them endangered species) for their own sake. The first national park was established in 1872 at Yellowstone in the USA. It was followed by many others around the world, among them the Kruger National Park (1898, South Africa), one of the finest wildlife areas in the world and a refuge for the white rhinoceros; Wood Buffalo National Park (1922, Canada), a refuge for the only remaining bison herds; Angkor National Park (1925, Cambodia), with its many temple ruins and Khmer archaeological remains; Rapa Nui (1935, Chile), with its ancient burial platforms, giant statues, and stone villages; Fuji-Hakone-Izu (1936, Japan), which embraces Mount Fuji and the Izu Islands; Belovezhskaya Pushcha, Belarus, bordering on Puszcza Bialowieza, Poland (both 1939), with their primeval European forests that harbour, among much rare fauna, the tarpan horse and black stork; and Uluru (Ayers Rock–Mount Olga) (1958, Australia), which contains the largest stone monolith in the world, as well as ancient Aboriginal rock paintings. The large number of visitors that such places attract requires skilled management and funding to minimize damage to the environment.

**natural bridge**, an arch of rock across an active river or its former channels. (Similar features along coasts, produced by the sea, are called natural arches.) Natural arches form where a river which is *meandering in fairly hard rock succeeds in cutting a channel under the narrow neck of land separating the two ends of a meander loop. This is particularly likely to happen if the rock can be dissolved, as limestone can, or if there are large joints and faults. The water seeps along them and they are enlarged by floods, until the bridge is formed.

**Natural Bridges National Monument**, an area of canyons in south-east Utah, USA, so called because of its massive sandstone bridges, the largest of which is Sipapu. This is 67 m (220 feet) high with a span of 82 m (268 feet). In the Arches National Park in eastern Utah is the longest natural bridge in the world, the Landscape Arch, which stretches for 88 m (291 feet) some 30 m (100 feet) above the canyon floor.

**natural gas**    *gas, natural.

Delicate Arch, one of the many **natural** (sandstone) arches and **bridges**, all products of erosion, found in eastern Utah in The Arches National Park of Colorado.

**nature reserve**   *national park.

**Nauru**, a tiny island country just south of the Equator in the Pacific Ocean, between longitudes 166° and 167° E. Its wealth lies in phosphate deposits derived from guano, the excrement of seabirds, which is used as manure.

**neap tides**, the weak *tides that occur twice a month, during the first and third quarters of the Moon's phases, when the influences of the Sun and Moon on the movement of the oceans counteract each other. High tides are lower, and low tides higher, than at other times in the lunar month.

**Negev Desert**, or Negeb (Hebrew, 'dry'), a desert and semi-desert region in southern Israel, triangular in shape and bounded on its east flank by the northern end of the *Great Rift Valley. It occupies a mainly limestone plateau, cut by *wadis, and in the Beersheba basin at its northern end there are fertile deposits of *loess. Phosphates are the main minerals, and there is also natural gas, with some oil.

**Neogene Period**, the later of the two geological periods into which the *Tertiary Period can be divided. (The other is the Palaeogene.) The Neogene Period comprises the *Miocene and *Pliocene epochs.

**neon** (symbol Ne, at. no. 10, r.a.m. 20.18), a colourless, odourless gas; it is one of the *noble gases and forms no chemical compounds. It is obtained by fractional distillation of liquid air and is widely used in discharge lamps, giving a bright orange light.

**Nepal**, a south Asian country among the peaks and southern slopes of the Himalayas, sandwiched between China (Tibet) and India; it contains the highest mountains in the world. The peaks are in the north; below the snow-line rivers run through turfy valleys and fine forests of evergreen, oak, and chestnut before reaching the warm, wet plains of the south. Here the natural vegetation is tropical; and rice, maize, wheat, jute, and sugar cane can be grown.

**nephrite**   *jades.

The visible lines in the **neon** spectrum are all in the yellow-to-red region, accounting for the bright orange light given by neon discharge lamps like the one shown here. The sealed glass bulbs contain neon gas at low pressure and electron emitting electrodes.

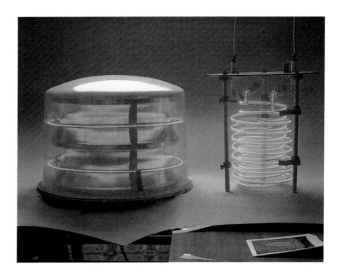

**Nernst, Walther Hermann** (1864–1941), German physical chemist who in 1906 proposed a famous 'heat theorem' embodied in the third law of thermodynamics. This states that the *entropy change of a pure crystalline solid approaches zero as the temperature approaches *absolute zero. Nernst also investigated the *specific heats of solids at low temperatures and explained the explosion between hydrogen and chlorine on exposure to light. He was awarded the Nobel Prize for Chemistry in 1920.

**Netherlands, The**, also called Holland (though this properly refers only to two western provinces), a European country on the North Sea. Bounded by Germany on the east and Belgium on the south, it is built up of sediment brought by the Rhine, Meuse, and other rivers. Everywhere, except for the extreme southern corner, is low and flat, much of the land being below sea-level. The coast, partly protected by a chain of sandbanks, has several estuaries and a large lagoon, the IJsselmeer, partly reclaimed from the Zuider Zee. The sediment is rich and supports a great variety of horticulture and livestock farming. Inland, however, there are peat bogs and patches of heath, forested to help keep the sand in place. The climate is temperate maritime, although gales and heavy fogs are not unknown. There are large reserves of oil and natural gas.

**Neumann, John von** (1903–57), Hungarian-born US mathematician and theoretical physicist who migrated to the USA in 1930. His fundamental contributions ranged over the whole of mathematics, from the purest parts of logic and *set theory to the most practical areas of application in economics, computer design, aerodynamics, meteorology, and astrophysics. His analysis of the mathematics of *quantum mechanics supplied that infant theory with the necessary environment in which to grow and founded a vigorous new area of mathematical research (algebras of operators in *Hilbert space). He founded the mathematical theory of games (see *game theory) and, with Oskar Morgenstern, exhibited its applications to economics and policy-making. But perhaps his most influential contributions were his work at Los Alamos on the harnessing of nuclear energy both for military and for peacetime uses, and his work on the design and use of high-speed electronic computing machines, the immediate forerunners of the ubiquitous computers that have so enormously changed our world.

**neutralization** (in chemistry), the reaction between an *acid and a *base or alkali, in which a salt and water are formed. The resulting solution is neutral—that is, neither acidic nor alkaline. The positive hydrogen ions of the acid are neutralized by the negative ions from the base. A neutral solution has a pH of 7 (see *hydrogen ion concentration).

**neutrino** (in nuclear physics), a weakly interacting *elementary particle which has no electric charge and apparently no effective mass. Neutrinos are difficult to detect because they interact so little with matter: neutrinos from the Sun can pass through the entire Earth with little chance of being stopped. They are classed as leptons and there are three kinds, associated respectively with the electron, muon, and tau particles.

**neutron** (in nuclear physics), a *nucleon, that is, one of the two types of particle (the other being a *proton) which form the nucleus of an atom. Neutrons are heavy, having almost the same mass as the proton, but they carry no electric charge. The mass of a neutron is 1,838 times that of the electron, and it has a *spin of $\frac{1}{2}$. While atoms of the same element always have the same number of protons in the nucleus, the number of neutrons can vary; and atoms which do have different numbers of neutrons form the *isotopes of that element. Neutrons can be emitted by a nucleus when it undergoes radioactive decay or fission. These free neutrons can be absorbed by other nuclei to cause further fission or to form different isotopes which may themselves be radioactive.

**névé** *firn.

**New Brunswick**, an Atlantic province of Canada, immediately west of the Gulf of Saint Lawrence. The north of the region, between the Saint John and the Miramichi Rivers, is occupied by a belt of resistant, intrusive rocks. This gives rise to rough, forested country, with flat-topped skylines rising in places to over 600 m (1,900 feet). A second, smaller infertile upland borders the Bay of Fundy, between Saint John and the head of Chignecto Bay. A large triangular-shaped lowland of undisturbed Carboniferous sandstone lies between the uplands, and coincides with some of the best farmland in the province.

**New England**, a region in the east of the USA, comprising Maine, New Hampshire, Vermont, Massachusetts, Connecticut, and Rhode Island. It has a natural boundary on the west in the valley of Lake Champlain and the Hudson River; its spine is the north-eastern extension of the Appalachian Mountain system; and it faces the Atlantic Ocean along a south-east coast that is often deeply indented. The main ranges are the Taconic, Green, and White Mountains, with Mount Washington at 1,917 m (6,290 feet) and the Berkshire Hills. The retreating ice-sheets of the last ice age cut the granitic uplands and left some magnificent scenery throughout: precipitous cliffs, rushing rivers, and beautiful lakes. In Vermont, New Hampshire, and Maine the changing colours of the woods in autumn are unusually spectacular; but generally the rocky soil is poor and the climate humid continental (cool summers and often severe winters). The isolated Mount Monadnock lends its name (wrongly) to *monadnocks, of which there are many. There is a wealth of granite, marble, and slate. The longest river is the Connecticut, 655 km (407 miles). Many shorter ones cut across the lake-studded coastal plain to reach a coast which is often jagged, with intermittent cliffs, but which contains fine inlets used by fishing fleets.

**Newfoundland**, the easternmost province of Canada, comprising the island of Newfoundland in the Gulf of Saint Lawrence and Labrador on the mainland. The island is triangular, with a rugged coastline over 6,400 km (4,000 miles) long, providing sheltered harbours for the fishermen of the Grand Banks. It has very cold winters, warm summers, and heavy rain. Fog is a common hazard. Inland, forests, lakes, and fertile valleys yield timber, fish, and pasture for dairy herds. Below ground are large deposits of iron, copper, and lead. Labrador is more than twice the size of the island of Newfoundland. It lies to the north and is extremely cold in winter. Glaciation has left much bare rock littered with *moraines, which interrupt drainage, and a fiord coastline.

**New Guinea**, the world's second largest island, set between the Equator and the northern tip of Australia. The western half, Irian Jaya, is part of Indonesia; the eastern half is the larger part of Papua New Guinea. With the Doberai Peninsula at its western end, its total length is some 2,400 km (1,500 miles). Mountain ranges rising to 5,030 m (16,503 feet) at Mount Jaya form its spine. Southwards they fall very sharply to a wide, well-rivered plain. Northward, where the fall is interrupted by other ranges, there are two great rivers which run through an earthquake belt to the sea. Thick, evergreen rain forest is the natural vegetation, and the soil supports a variety of tropical crops. The mineral resources are largely unexplored, but they include gold, silver, copper, and oil.

**New Hebrides** *Vanuatu.

**Newlands, John Alexander Reina** (1837–98), British chemist who, like *Mendeleyev, recognized the periodic nature of the elements. His proposal in 1864 of a 'Law of Octaves', in which similar properties tend to appear after every eighth element, was ridiculed by the Chemical Society. Later, when the significance of his work was appreciated, he was awarded the Davy Medal of the Royal Society.

**New South Wales**, a state occupying much of the south-eastern quarter of Australia, bounded by Queensland on the north, South Australia on the west, and Victoria on the south. It has a long, generally sunny coast on the Tasman Sea. The coastal lowlands, which are better watered in the north than in the south, rise sharply to the dissected plateaux and watershed of the Great Dividing Range. This comprises the New England and Liverpool ranges in the north, the

An 1829 engraving of Sir Isaac **Newton** by W. T. Fry after a portrait by Gottfried Kneller.

Blue Mountains in the centre, and much of the considerably higher Australian Alps in the south. The climate in the east is well suited to dairying and horticulture, with mild winters and very warm summers, though there are occasional storms and droughts. The western slopes of the Great Dividing Range are crossed by several rivers, notably the tributaries of the Murray, which forms the southern boundary of the state. They flow on to the great western plains, seasonally for the most part, sometimes drying to a trickle and at other times flooding. The plains form about two-thirds of the territory and are the least fertile part. While wheat and sheep are raised intensively in the Murray basin, the grasslands give way to saltbush in the north-west, where annual rainfall is less than 250 mm (10 inches). The mineral wealth includes coal, silver, copper, zinc, and lead.

**newton** (symbol N), the *SI unit of force, so named in honour of Isaac *Newton, who first established the relationship between force and motion. One newton is defined as the force which gives a mass of 1 kg an acceleration of 1 m/s². A larger unit in common use is the kilonewton (kN), this being 1,000 N.

**Newton, Sir Isaac** (1642–1727), English mathematician and physicist, the greatest single influence on theoretical physics until Albert *Einstein. He was most productive during the period 1666–7 (which he called his *annus mirabilis*), during which he laid the foundations of his future successes in mathematics, optics, dynamics (mechanics), and astronomy. He discovered the binomial theorem, and made contributions to algebra, geometry, and the theory of infinite series, all somewhat overshadowed by his most famous contribution to mathematics—the differential calculus (his 'method of fluxions') for finding rates of change of varying quantities, and his discovery of its relationship with what is now called *integration (then 'quadrature'), the problem of finding the area of a figure circumscribed by curved boundaries. A bitter quarrel with the philosopher Gottfried *Leibniz ensued, as to which of them had discovered calculus first. His optical experiments, begun in 1666, led to his discovery that white light is made up of a mixture of coloured rays. In his major treatise, *Philosophiae Naturalis Principia Mathematica* (1686–7), he gave a mathematical description of the laws of mechanics and gravitation, and applied this theory to explain planetary and lunar motion. For most purposes Newtonian mechanics has survived even the 20th-century introduction of *relativity theory and *quantum mechanics (to both of which theories it stands as a first, but very good, approximation) as a mathematical description of terrestrial and cosmological phenomena. In 1699 Newton was appointed Master of the Mint, and was responsible for an urgently needed reform of the coinage, and in 1703 was elected President of the Royal Society, whose reputation he greatly increased over the following twenty-four years. Newton interested himself also in alchemy, astrology, and theology, and attempted a biblical chronology. He was involved in several bitter controversies with fellow scientists. The newton is named in his honour.

**Newton's laws**. These laws of motion are fundamental to the understanding of classical mechanics. The first law states that every body continues in a state of rest or uniform motion in a straight line unless it is acted upon by an external force. This law is also known as the principle of inertia and provides a description of the absence of force, since any deviation from rest or straight-line motion must mean that a force is acting on the body. The second law states that the rate of change of *momentum is proportional to the applied force and in the same direction. In situations where mass is constant this law equates force $F$ with the product of mass $m$ and acceleration $a$ according to the equation $F = ma$. It thus provides a definition of force. The third law states that for every applied force, or action, there is an equal force, or reaction, which acts in the opposite direction; concisely expressed *action and reaction are equal and opposite. The crucial consideration when applying Newton's laws is that they only hold relative to inertial frames of reference—that is, ones which are at rest or moving with constant velocity. Since the Earth itself is rotating, it does not strictly provide an inertial frame, although in local problems the effect of this is negligible. When considering the flight of a space rocket, however, the Earth's rotation must be taken into account. Newton's laws, however, do not explain some of the phenomena observed in planetary motion. A more sophisticated theory is needed to explain motion at speeds close to that of light, and the behaviour of objects close in size to atoms. *Relativity theory and *quantum theory have been developed to deal with these situations respectively.

**New Zealand**, a country situated over 1,900 km (1,180 miles) south-east of Australia, comprising the North Island and the South Island together with many smaller islands in the south-west Pacific Ocean. The two main islands, separated by the fairly narrow Cook Strait, together stretch north-east to south-west over a distance of some 1,600 km (1,000 miles). The bounary between the Indian (Indo-Australian) *plate and the Pacific plate passes just south of North Island and diagonally through South Island. Movements along the boundary are responsible for many of the earthquakes of the region. Mostly the islands lie in the path of *westerlies which bring mild, wet weather across the Tasman Sea; but North Cape can be very warm while snow is falling on Stewart Island in the extreme south. Mixed arable and grazing land, with deciduous and evergreen forest, can be found throughout, and both main islands have reserves of coal. Natural gas is found near Mount Egmont on North Island, while many of the beaches are black with iron ore. The snow-capped Southern Alps, with Mount Cook in the centre, run the length of the South Island. High glaciers and narrow lakes lie among them; and their forested south-western slopes fall to the edges of still fiords, as in Fiordland National Park. From the eastern slopes rivers, harnessed for hydroelectricity, rush through stony, grey-green foothills to

Horseshoe Falls in the Canadian sector of the **Niagara** Falls complex.

the wide Canterbury Plains. Here there are great sheep runs, extending south into Otago.

**Niagara River** and **Falls**, a river forming the US–Canadian border, famous for its spectacular waterfalls. The river issues from Lake Erie and flows generally northward for 56 km (35 miles) to Lake Ontario. It is navigable on its upper course for some 32 km (20 miles), then forms a series of rapids before it splits into two above Goatland on the falls. The Canadian or Horseshoe Falls are more than twice as broad but slightly lower than the American Falls over which the cataract tumbles vertically for 50 m (167 feet).

**Nicaragua**, the largest country in Central America, bounded on the north by Honduras and on the south by Costa Rica. It has a south-western-facing coast on the Pacific Ocean and a longer, eastward-facing one on the Caribbean Sea, the Mosquito Coast. In the west are fertile plains and volcanic mountains. The climate is tropical. Cotton, coffee, and sugar are the main plantation crops, and livestock can also be raised. Gold, silver, and copper are the main mineral resources. In the north are forested hills, and in the south-west two great lakes. The country is subject to earthquakes, being near the junction of crustal *plates.

**nickel** (symbol Ni, at. no. 28, r.a.m. 58.71), a hard, grey-white, ferromagnetic metal and one of the *transition metals. It occurs naturally in pentlandite and pyrrhotite. The crude ore is roasted to give the oxide, which is then reduced to the metal with carbon. Purification is carried out by *electrolysis or the Mond process, during which it is converted to the volatile nickel carbonyl, $Ni(CO)_4$. The metal is widely used in alloys such as steel, in cast iron, and as a coinage metal. Nichrome is a nickel-chromium alloy, often containing iron also, used in the heating elements of electric fires. Other applications include nickel plating and as a catalyst for the reduction of organic compounds by hydrogen. Chemically nickel resembles iron and cobalt with valency usually 2.

**Nicolet, Jean** (1598–1642), French explorer in north America who under *Champlain's direction made a voyage of discovery of Lake Michigan and its environment. The lake was not the *North-West Passage that he was searching for, but he sailed on to explore the region of present-day Wisconsin, and the maps he made guided the early fur traders in the region.

**Nicollet, Joseph Nicolas** (1786–1843), French mathematician who emigrated to the USA in 1832 and led an expedition (1836–7) to survey the sources of the Mississippi. In 1838–41 he was government surveyor of the region between the upper waters of the Mississippi and the Missouri, producing a map which was of prime importance to American geography. His careful barometric observations of altitude were the first in the USA.

**Niger**, a large, land-locked West African country surrounded by Algeria, Libya, Chad, Nigeria, Benin, Burkina Faso, and Mali. The Niger flows through it in the extreme south-west, and the northern tip of Lake Chad lies in the extreme south-east. From these points the land rises through dry *savannah and thin, thorny scrub to sandy desert and the high plateaux of the Sahara. Some livestock-farming and cultivation is possible, though it is hot everywhere. The chief mineral resource is uranium.

**Niger River**, the great river of West Africa, flowing in a broad arc, generally eastward, for nearly 4,200 km (2,600 miles) from its source in the southern highlands of Guinea into the Atlantic Ocean. Near its most northerly point, almost in the *Sahara, it splits into a maze of channels, with marshes and shallow lakes. This provides a great region for cultivation of crops including rice. The river then turns south, in a long stretch which contains several series of rapids, a source of hydroelectricity, and so flows into Nigeria. Here it is joined by its chief tributary, the Benue, and becomes navigable in the rainy season and remains so for most of the year. It has a sluggish flow which frequently bursts the banks. On entering its great delta, the largest in Africa, it splits into a number of tributaries. Oil is found in this region, which is characterized by lagoons and mangrove swamps.

**Nigeria**, a large West African country with a southward-facing coast, bounded by Benin on the west, Niger and Chad on the north, and Cameroon on the east. The sandy coast is bordered by mangrove swamp, inland of which there is a low plain with tropical rain forest spreading up the valleys of the Niger to the north-west and the Benue to the east. Here the climate is hot and very wet; to the west and north it becomes drier as the ground rises through open woodland and *savannah to plateau land. The central Jos Plateau rises to 1,800 m (5,900 feet) with open grassland, but north of this the ground falls away to thorn-covered desert from which, in winter, blows the cool, dusty *harmattan. The main underground resource is oil, of which there are many deposits, although cassiterite, niobium, iron ore, and coal are also found.

**night**, the regular periods of darkness caused by the *rotation of the Earth, may be defined in different ways: from sunset to sunrise; half an hour after and before these (as in lighting-up time); or by absolute blackness when there is no Moon and the Sun is over 20° below the horizon. Time is sometimes reckoned by nights, the term fortnight (fourteen nights) being still in use.

**Nile**, the longest river in the world, flowing northward from Lake Victoria in East Africa for over 6,400 km (4,000 miles) to the Mediterranean Sea. The lower Nile, the centre of Egyptian civilization for thousands of years, has the longest record of annual floods of any river. The upper Nile, in contrast, was little known before the 19th century, when the search for the river's source preoccupied European explorers. The Victoria, the Albert, then the Mountain Nile flow northward from Lakes Victoria and Albert into the immense Sudd marshes of southern Sudan, where it loses enormous quantities of water through evaporation and from which it emerges calmly, with little seasonal variation in volume. At Khartoum the White Nile is joined by the Blue Nile from the Ethiopian mountains, the north-westward course of the Blue Nile being relatively short and steep—and with a strong summer peak in flow produced by monsoon rains over the mountains. Below Khartoum, the whole river shows this dramatic flood peak. Until recently, Egyptian agriculture was maintained by an annual inundation of fields in the lower valley, with floodwater, silt, and dissolved minerals. Between Khartoum and Aswan, the river flows down six cataracts in a narrow valley bordered by desert. The Aswan high dam at the First Cataract now impounds the vast Lake Nasser, which extends southward to the Second Cataract. This dam controls the Nile's flood, allowing year-round irri-

The River **Nile** near Luxor, in Egypt. The crucial importance of the river's broad, fertile flood plain can be seen clearly in this aerial photograph.

gation and electricity generation. One consequence is that the silt which used to be carried into the *delta, an intensely cultivated zone more than 180 km (110 miles) wide, no longer arrives in sufficient quantities to compensate for erosion by the sea; so the whole delta is now gradually shrinking.

**nimbus**, a cloud such as cumulonimbus and nimbostratus, as opposed to the general cumulus and stratus, from which precipitation is falling or about to fall. Nimbus clouds are the darkest, often inky in appearance. When moving fast, with a lower edge broken by vortex-like wisps, a nimbus cloud generally indicates a *squall. The term is one not used in the international cloud classification.

**niobium** (symbol Nb, at. no. 41, r.a.m. 92.91), formerly columbium, a soft, silvery white *transition metal, occurring naturally in columbite. Fairly unreactive and resistant to corrosion, it is used in special steels, high-temperature alloys, and superconductors. It is also used in nuclear reactors.

**nitrate**, a salt of nitric acid that contains the nitrate group, $NO_3$. In the soil nitrates are formed from ammonium compounds and atmospheric nitrogen and are essential to plant growth. They are found in vast quantities as Chilean saltpetre (potassium nitrate). Industrially they are produced from the neutralization of nitric acid by a base, such as ammonia. All are solid ionic compounds and nearly all are soluble in water. They are used in explosives, as a source of oxygen, and as fertilizers. However, the widespread use of synthetic fertilizers has often given cause for concern. Excess amounts of nitrates entering the *hydrological cycle may cause ecological imbalance with possible harmful consequences.

**nitre** *potassium nitrate.

**nitric acid** ($HNO_3$), a corrosive liquid which vaporizes to give red or yellow fumes owing to the presence of nitrogen dioxide. The nitrogen dioxide is formed by thermal decomposition of the nitric acid. Fuming nitric acid is a stronger *oxidizing agent than the pure acid. Nitric acid itself is a strong *acid and is widely used in many chemical reactions in the laboratory and in industry.

**nitrile**, an organic compound of the general formula R−C N, where R is an *alkyl or *aryl group. The carbon atom and the nitrogen atom of the *functional group are joined by a triple bond. Nitriles therefore undergo *addition reactions: for example, in the presence of hydrogen and a catalyst, they are converted to primary amines, $R-CH_2NH_2$. They also undergo *hydrolysis, in the presence of either acid or alkali, firstly to form the amide $RCONH_2$ and then the corresponding carboxylic acid RCOOH.

**nitrogen** (symbol N, at. no. 7, r.a.m. 14.01), a colourless, odourless gas which makes up about 78 per cent of the Earth's atmosphere by volume. In its free state it consists of diatomic molecules, $N_2$. It is produced on a large scale by the fractional distillation of liquid air, having a lower boiling point ($-196\,°C$, $-385\,°F$) than air's other main component, oxygen. It is an extremely unreactive element, forming metal nitrides only at high temperatures; even so, it forms a wide range of compounds which are of vast importance, for example in photography, and as dyestuffs, explosives, and polymers. It is used in the manufacture of ammonia and nitric acid, and also where an inert atmosphere is required. Liquid nitrogen is an important coolant. Nitrogen is an essential element for all life-forms: plants use it to build amino acids, proteins, and enzymes, and ammonium compounds and nitrates are therefore widely used as fertilizers. Some bacteria can convert nitrogen gas directly from the atmosphere into nitrogen compounds; this process is called nitrogen fixation.

**nitrogen dioxide** ($NO_2$), a poisonous brown gas with a pungent smell. It is a *free radical, having an odd number of electrons, and in consequence it is magnetic. It supports combustion and is an acidic oxide, dissolving in water to form a mixture of nitrous and nitric acids. On cooling it liquefies and pairs of molecules combine to form nitrogen tetroxide, used as an oxidant in rocketry.

**noble gases** (or inert gases, rare gases), the elements of Group 0 of the *periodic table, namely helium, neon, argon, krypton, xenon, and radon. Except for *argon, they are only present in the atmosphere at trace levels. Their inertness, or chemical unreactivity, is a result of their completely filled outer shells (see *valency); only a few compounds of the heavier elements are known—for example, xenon difluoride, $XeF_2$.

**non-electrolytes**, compounds which when molten or in solution do not conduct electricity—that is, do not undergo *electrolysis. They consist of molecules, and not ions; they are usually compounds of two or more non-metals. Simple examples are methane and ethanol.

**non-metals**, these constitute about a fifth of all known elements. They are to be found in the top right-hand portion of the *periodic table and at room temperature are all solids or gases. For instance nitrogen, oxygen, phosphorous and sulphur are all typical examples: the exception is bromine which is a liquid. They tend to form negative ions, have acidic oxides, and are generally poor conductors of heat and electricity. This last is due to the essentially covalent nature of their bonding, which means that there are no free electrons to act as conductors.

**Nordenskiöld, Baron Nils Adolf Erik** (1832–1901), Swedish geologist and explorer, and the first to navigate the *North-East Passage. He commanded a series of expeditions to Svalbard (Spitsbergen) during the course of which he mapped the area and collected extensive zoological, geological and botanical collections, His quest to discover a trade route between the Atlantic and Pacific Oceans began with several reconnoitering trips before setting out in the *Vega* in 1878. He rounded Cape Chelyuskin but was stopped by ice at the entrance to Bering Strait. In 1879 he passed East Cape and sailed into the Bering Sea completing his trip to China.

**Norfolk Island** (Australia), a small Pacific Ocean island roughly 1,450 km (900 miles) east of Australia and 800 km (500 miles) north-west of New Zealand. It is an oval some 8 km (5 miles) long and 4.8 km (3 miles) wide. In the north it rises to around 300 m (1,000 feet) above sea-level, but most of it is a low undulating plateau with grassy valleys flanked by the unique Norfolk Island pines (*Araucaria*). It was once united on the same land mass with New Zealand and the island of New Caledonia to the north, to which it remains linked by the submerged Norfolk Ridge.

**North America**, the world's third largest continent, extending from the Arctic Ocean to southern Mexico, with innumerable islands surrounding it. Included is Greenland and, sometimes, Central America. Two vast countries, Canada and the USA, stretch across it from the Pacific Ocean in the west to the Atlantic in the east. Roughly triangular in shape, it has the peninsulas of Alaska and Labrador as its two upper corners and Mexico as its elongated southern one. Its northern half was within the limit of the last ice age and is heavily glaciated; its western flank runs parallel to its junction with the Pacific *plate and is volcanic; its south is subtropical and subject to hurricanes. Structurally its western flank is composed of folded belts which rise up in the huge parallel ranges of the Western Cordillera. The centre of the continent is a basin with thick sedimentary cover. The north-east and east are mainly ancient platforms forming the great Canadian Shield. The Cordillera extends from Alaska through Canada and the USA, where the Rocky Mountains form its eastern rim, to the Sierra Madre ranges of Mexico. The central plains, drained to the north into Hudson Bay, to the east by the Great Lakes and the Saint Lawrence, and to the south by the Mississippi, form a wide corridor down which the *polar front advances to bring cold weather in winter. In the east they are bounded by the old and eroded Appalachian Mountain system of folded rocks. South of the Arctic tundra is a wide belt of coniferous forest which extends southward along the mountain slopes. East of the mountains is prairie, and to the east of that is some deciduous forest as the land rises again. The south-west is high desert plateau. Nickel and iron are the main minerals of the north, copper and zinc are dominant in the central belt, while silver is found in the south. There are deposits of many other minerals, including uranium, and large reserves of coal, natural gas, and oil.

**North Atlantic Drift**, a broad, slow-moving surface current, a continuation of the Gulf Stream, flowing across the North Atlantic Ocean and towards the Arctic Ocean. Its relatively warm waters are responsible for moderating the climate of western Europe, so that winters are less cold than would otherwise be expected at its latitude. The Drift is particularly important because it keeps many Norwegian ports free of ice throughout the year.

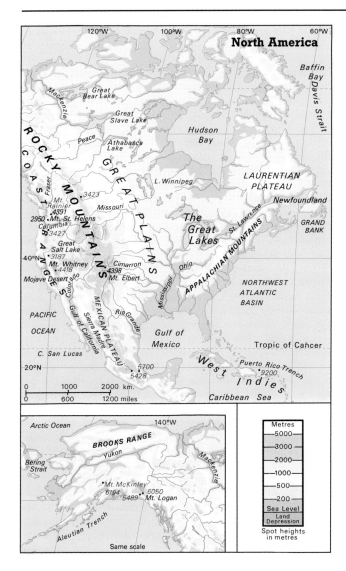

and Arafura Seas and the Gulf of Carpentaria. Here the climate is tropical, with monsoon rains of approximately 1,300 mm (50 inches) appearing in the middle of drought. Uranium is found at Rum Jungle in the north-west. Mangrove swamp and river forest give way inland to open woodland and seasonal grass. Southward annual rainfall decreases; pasture is sparse and desert tracts appear. The Barkly Tableland and the southern highlands enclose the Victoria and Newcastle River basins. Copper is mined here, and tungsten at Hatches Creek. The Macdonnell Ranges and Ayers Rock are in the south.

**North Pole**, the northern end of the Earth's axis, at 90° N., longitude 0°. Lying below the ice-covered Arctic Ocean, this geographic North Pole itself is about 4,087 m (13,410 feet) below sea-level. At the surface six months of daylight follow six months of darkness; and at the height of summer, snow on the ice melts into shallow pools and there may even be some rain. The Pole does not coincide with the north magnetic pole, which is in the Canadian Arctic, or with the geomagnetic North Pole, the northern end of the Earth's geomagnetic field (about 78° 30′ N. 69° 00′ W.). The geographic Pole was first reached by the US explorers Robert Peary and Matthew Henson by dog sleigh (1909).

**North Sea**, the sea lying between Great Britain and northern Europe. An arm of the Atlantic Ocean, it is about 1,000 km (600 miles) from north to south and 640 km (400 miles) wide, being linked to the Atlantic north of Scotland and by the Strait of Dover in the south-west. In the east it connects with the Baltic Sea. The Rhine, Elbe, Thames, Trent and many other rivers all drain into it; the courses of these rivers continue on the sea-bed, relics of the time when it was all above sea-level. It has an average depth of only 93 m (less than 300 feet), and there are several shallow areas where the water is a mere 20 m (65 feet) deep. The dissolved nutrients are good for fish, and below the sediment are the hydrocarbons that produce the UK's and Norway's reserves of oil and gas. The shallowness and shape of the North Sea has a profound effect on the tides that enter from the north, increasing their amplitude. The *North Atlantic Drift keeps the sea moderately warm.

**North-East Passage**, the Arctic sea-route between the Atlantic and Pacific Oceans. Part of the Barents Sea and all of the Kara and Laptev Seas are covered by pack-ice except during summer, and even then the route is opened from June to October only with the help of ice-breakers. First traversed by Nils *Nordenskiöld of Sweden in 1878–9, Russia now maintains a regular highway for shipping along the Passage.

**Northern Ireland**, a unit of the UK comprising the six north-eastern counties of Ireland. Structurally, it is a south-westward extension of Scotland, separated by the North Channel of the Irish Sea. Sedimentary, metamorphic, and igneous rock of various ages are covered by glacial gravels and boulder clay; it has little mineral wealth, but the soils are mainly fertile. Climatically, it is cool, with about 1,300 mm (50 inches) of rainfall annually. The wide expanse of Lough Neagh is drained to the north by the Bann River. In the south-east are the Mourne Mountains, while in the west lie Lough Erne and the mountains and rocky coasts of Donegal.

**Northern Territory**, the north and centre of the Australian continent, bounded by Western and South Australia, and on the east by Queensland. It is a large state, covering nearly 1.4 million km² (over 0.5 million sq. mi.) and its coast, with the broad peninsula of Arnhem Land, faces the Timor

**North-West Passage**, sea routes through the Arctic archipelago, north of Canada and along the northern coast of Alaska between the Atlantic and the Pacific Oceans. Martin *Frobisher was the first European to explore the eastern approaches (1576–8). In 1610 Henry *Hudson discovered Hudson Bay while seeking a northern route to the Orient. In 1616 William *Baffin discovered Baffin Bay, through which the passage was finally discovered. A transit of the passage was first accomplished (1903–6) by the Norwegian explorer, Roald *Amundsen.

**Northwest Territories**, the northernmost part of Canada, between the Yukon Territory and Hudson Bay, and including the islands of the Arctic Archipelago; the southern boundary is along latitude 60° N. The north and east is tundra on the ancient rocks of the *Canadian Shield, while to the south-west pine forest rises up to the Mackenzie Mountains. Winters are long, cold, and dark; summers short but mild. Such precipitation as there is falls mostly as snow; and the Mackenzie River running north-west into the Beaufort Sea is melt-water. The lakes are numerous: Great Bear, Great Slave, Dubawnt, Aylmer, Macdougall, and many others, the relics of glaciation. The area is rich in minerals, and

## Nuclear fission and fusion

Atomic nuclei are designated $_Z^A X$, where X is the chemical symbol for the element, $A$ is the mass number (= number of neutrons + number of protons), and $Z$ is the atomic number, giving the number of protons and hence the positive charge of the nucleus. In nuclear reactions mass number and charge are conserved.

### Nuclear fission

An atomic nucleus may be considered to be analogous to a spherical liquid droplet. When it is excited (i.e. when its internal energy is increased), it becomes distorted. If the energy is high enough to produce a large distortion, then the long-range repulsive electrostatic forces between the protons become great enough to overcome the short-range attractive nuclear forces between the nucleons, and the nucleus splits into two main fragments.

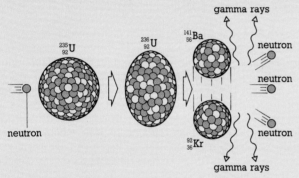

The reaction between a neutron and a nucleus of the uranium isotope $_{92}^{235}U$ is the reaction used in conventional nuclear reactors. The collision causes distortion and most of the energy of the reaction is released as kinetic energy of the fission products. Note that uranium fission can give rise to fission products other than the barium and krypton nuclei shown

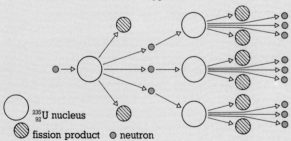

Each fission of a $_{92}^{235}U$ nucleus releases two or three neutrons. If enough uranium nuclei are present, three neutrons can cause fission in further nuclei, initiating a chain reaction.

### Nuclear fusion

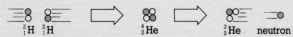

The fusion of two deuterium nuclei ($_1^2H$) to form a helium nucleus ($_2^3He$) plus a neutron. This reaction has possibilities for use in the controlled production of energy from nuclear fusion.

gas and oil are being discovered in increasing quantities both on- and off-shore.

**Norway**, a country forming the north-western part of Scandinavia in northern Europe. Its extensive coast, fringed with innumerable small islands, stretches from the Arctic Ocean to the North Sea. Inland it borders on Sweden (a long boundary), Finland, and Russia. It is mountainous, rising to 2,470 m (8,104 feet) in the Jotunheimen range. In the north, it is light all 24 hours in high summer—and equally dark in winter. Its warm climate is caused by the Gulf Stream, which usually keeps the *fiords from freezing. The south is barren moorland plateau cut by forested valleys. Norway has one of the world's largest reserves of aluminium, though the main resource is North Sea oil and natural gas; north in the Arctic the Svalbard (Spitsbergen) archipelago, contains rich deposits of coal.

**Nova Scotia**, a Canadian province comprising a hammerhead peninsula on Canada's Atlantic coast together with Cape Breton Island. No part of it is more than 56 km (35 miles) from the shoreline, which extends for 10,400 km (6,500 miles). The coast is deeply indented and provides many anchorages. On the west is the Bay of Fundy with its enormous tides; to the east, on the edge of the continental shelf, are Sable Island and the Grand Banks, with famous fishing-grounds. The sea ensures a moderate climate with heavy rainfall. The Bras d'Or Lakes in Cape Breton are the largest of the lakes, and there are many small rivers and streams. The highest point, at 532 m (1,746 feet), is in the Cape Breton Highlands. Nearly 85 per cent of the land area is forest, and coal and gypsum are plentiful.

**Novaya Zemlya** (Russia), two large arctic islands north of European Russia which effectively separate the Barents Sea from the Kara Sea. Together the islands are approximately 1,000 km (about 600 miles) long, but nowhere are they more than 145 km (90 miles) across. The narrow strait of Matochkin Shar separates the two islands. The coastlines of both islands have numerous fiord-like inlets. The northern island is extensively glaciated.

**Nubian sandstone**, a coarse-grained sedimentary rock that is found extensiely on the Arabian–Nubian Shield in Saudi Arabia and North Africa. It is *Cretaceous in age and was deposited on top of the Precambrian basement complex of *gneisses and *schists that make up the Arabian–Nubian Shield.

**nuclear fission and fusion**. Fission is the disintegration ('splitting') of the *nucleus of an atom into two roughly equal parts with the release of energy and perhaps the emission of one or more particles such as neutrons. Fission can happen spontaneously in some heavy nuclei, and in some lighter nuclei if they collide with other nuclei at sufficiently high energy. Some heavy nuclei, such as uranium, can undergo fission when they are bombarded by neutrons, and since fission produces further neutrons a chain reaction can occur. The energy released by this chain reaction is harnessed in a controlled manner in nuclear reactors, and is uncontrolled in nuclear weapons.

Fusion is the merging together of the nuclei of two light atoms to form the *nucleus of a heavier atom. If the heavier nucleus that is formed is stable, energy will be released, as it will be more tightly bound than the nuclei of its components. Fusion reactions are different from chemical reactions because in fusion reactions the nuclei as well as the electrons take part. In terms of the mass of the reactants, a fusion reaction produces about ten times as much energy as a *nuclear fission reaction. Fusion reactions occur in the Sun and other stars, and are the source of their energy. Fusion has been made to occur in an uncontrolled manner in the hydrogen bomb and research continues to harness fusion in a controlled way as a source of energy.

**nucleation**. A number of physical processes start when one region of a substance becomes different from the rest. For example, when water boils, water turns to steam in some places before others, and we see bubbles rising through the water. When a liquid crystallizes, solid crystals start to form while the rest of the material is still liquid. When a solid breaks, the molecules do not all fall apart at the same time: the break appears first in one region of the material. This is as a result of nucleation. A 'nucleus' (this is not the same as an atomic nucleus) can be anything that makes one region of the material different from its surroundings—an impurity in a liquid around which a crystal can grow, or a scratch on the surface of a saucepan where the first bubbles form. It is important to avoid nuclei if the changes they encourage are undesirable; however, nuclei are deliberately introduced in certain circumstances in order to promote and direct desirable changes.

**nucleons**, collectively, the two kinds of particle which form the *nucleus of an atom. These are the proton, which is positively charged, and the neutron, which has zero charge. Apart from the difference in charge they are very similar, and can be regarded as different states of a single particle, the nucleon.

The arrival at the sea on 16 December 1902 of the **nuée ardente** caused by the eruption of Mount Pelée.

**nucleophile**, a reagent which reacts with a centre of low electron density. The word means 'nucleus lover' and implies that a nucleophile will react with any region of positive charge. This requires that they should themselves possess a region of high electron density, or negative charge. Thus all nucleophiles have at least one *lone pair of electrons in their outer shells. They can possess an overall negative charge, an example being the hydroxide ion, $OH^-$. Alternatively, they can be neutral molecules, containing atoms of different *electronegativity. An example is ammonia, $NH_3$, in which nitrogen is the more electronegative element. There is thus a concentration of electron density on the nitrogen atom, which also possesses a lone pair, and therefore the nitrogen atom acts as a nucleophile.

**nucleus, atomic**, the central, massive part of an atom. It is made up of a certain number of *protons, which are positively charged, and usually a larger number of neutral particles, the *neutrons. The atomic nuclei of a particular element always contain the same number of protons but can have differing numbers of neutrons, nuclei containing different numbers of neutrons being called *isotopes of that element. In most naturally occurring elements the nuclear particles are tightly bound together and the nucleus is stable. However, in radioactive nuclei the binding is not so strong: particles such as electrons and *alpha particles, or radiation (*gamma rays) may be emitted, and the nucleus then decays into the nucleus of another element.

**nuée ardente**, an incandescent cloud of gas, volcanic ash, and larger particles ejected from a *volcano during an eruption. The cloud is typically emitted horizontally from the volcano and travels at great speed down its flanks. In recent times the Mount Saint Helens eruption produced a nuée ardente, but the most famous example is that of Mount Pelée in the Antilles, where in 1902 a cloud of incandescent ash accompanying a glowing avalanche overwhelmed the town of Saint Pierre in Martinique, killing 30,000 people.

**nullah** (Hindi, *nala*, brook, ravine) a dry channel of a river that flows only in wet seasons or after rainstorms. Nullahs are similar to *arroyos or wadis.

**numbers**, a value representing a particular quantity. The written forms we use today are based on the system the Arabs found in India and introduced to Europe in the 14th century. Gradually it replaced the Roman system, I, II, III, IV, . . . , which has no zero and required the abacus for computation. Cardinal or natural numbers are those used for counting: 1, 2, 3, . . . Integers include the natural and the corresponding negative numbers: 0, ± 1, ± 2, . . . Rational numbers are formed when one integer is divided by another: $\frac{1}{2}$, $\frac{7}{11}$, etc.; and they cannot be listed in numerical order, because between any two there are an infinite number of other fractions. Irrational numbers cannot be expressed as a fraction; they include $\pi$, $\sqrt{2}$, and e, the base of natural logarithms. All these together form the *real numbers. *Complex numbers are an extension of the reals, of the form $a + ib$, where $a$ and $b$ are real numbers and i is the square root of $-1$. The concept of number is always being broadened, and many differences of opinion have arisen as to whether a particular collection of numbers—for example, negative or complex—should be accepted as numbers.

# O

**oasis**, a fertile area in a desert, with a spring or well of water which normally originates as *groundwater. Oases can occur in any desert. They vary in size from small areas to vast regions of naturally watered or irrigated land. The source of the water may be more than 800 km (500 miles) away, usually falling as rain and carried to the oasis in layers of rock beneath the surface. The ice-free *dry valleys of Antarctica, for example, are also known as oases, because they support some land-based life, in contrast to the barren ice deserts which surround them. In sandy deserts they are usually found in places where *deflation has lowered the surface to a point where the water-table can be reached.

**Ob**, a great river in Siberia, flowing for some 3,500 km (2,200 miles). It is formed by the confluence of the Biya and the Katun, both of which rise in the Altai Mountains near Mongolia. Descending through lakes to the Siberian Plain, it is joined by the Tom and continues north-west through swampy forests until it receives its chief tributary, the Irtysh. Now it turns north to enter its estuary, the Gulf of Ob, which is some 65 km (40 miles) wide and 800 km (500 miles) long, the longest river estuary in the world. The Gulf opens into the Arctic Ocean. The Ob and its main tributaries are navigable for most of their length, but are ice-bound for half the year. The spring thaw in the southern, upper reaches occurs while the lower reaches are still frozen. The result is flooding among the coniferous forests of the plain, a region which is rich in oil and natural gas.

A town on the edge of an **oasis** in the Moroccan Sahara. Vegetables are being grown between the date palms.

**oblateness of the Earth**, the flattening of what would otherwise be a sphere, owing to the *centrifugal force created by its rotation, which is greatest at the Equator and zero at the poles. The result is that the polar diameter is slightly shorter than the equatorial one, there being a bulge at the Equator. Various differences between the diameters have been measured in different places. They vary because the curvature of the Earth's level surface, or *geoid, itself varies from place to place, as has been recently revealed in great detail by the observations of artificial satellites. These anomalies are due to uneven distribution of the Earth's mass in its upper layers.

**obsidian** (or pitchstone), the most common type of volcanic glass, is a shiny black igneous rock with no crystal structure. It has a characteristic conchoidal fracture and is formed by the rapid cooling of *granite magma. It was once used as the raw material for rock wool.

**occlusion** (in meteorology), the final stage in the life of a *depression. The cold front moves at a faster speed than the warm front which precedes it, and may eventually overtake it. Then it may push both the warm air and the warm front off the ground, displacing it to form a cold occlusion. On the ground warm air is replaced by cold air. Alternatively it may lift the warm air off the ground by running up the less steeply sloping warm front, leaving the warm front in contact with the ground and forming a warm occlusion. On the ground cold air is replaced by less cold air.

**ocean**, the continuous sheet of salt water that surrounds the land masses of the continents, filling the great depressions of the Earth's surface. It occupies 71 per cent of the surface of the globe and is generally considered as made up of four major areas, which in order of size are the Pacific, Atlantic, Indian, and Arctic oceans. The first three of these extend into the waters of the Antarctic, which can be regarded as a distinct Southern Ocean. Each of these great areas of open

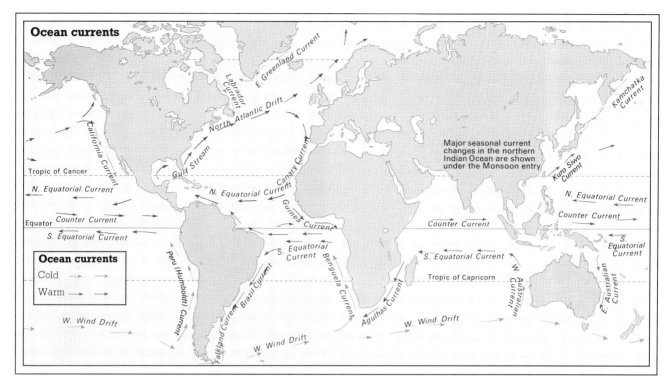

**Ocean currents**

Major seasonal current changes in the northern Indian Ocean are shown under the Monsoon entry

| Ocean currents | | |
|---|---|---|
| Cold | → | → |
| Warm | → | → |

water contains various *water masses differing in physical, chemical, or biological terms one from another. The oceans are an essential part of the natural environment, not only because they provide food and fuel and a means of communication but because they are the ultimate source of all water on the globe and supply the moisture which reaches the continents as rain; it is through the *hydrological cycle that they influence the climates of the continents. Temperature and pressure changes result in winds which are of great importance in the *circulation of the atmosphere. The continental influx of dissolved matter from rivers has resulted in its present saltiness, for when water evaporates from its surface the salts are left behind. The salinity varies in different places, the less salty water being the less dense. Temperature also affects density, colder water tending to sink to the bottom. Structurally the oceans have *continental shelves at their margins and basins and trenches in their depths. They are affected by the movement of crustal *plates more than the land is because most plate boundaries are under the ocean. Submarine ridges, mountains, volcanoes, and rift valleys all exist within the ocean depths.

**ocean basin**, a saucer-like depression of the sea-bed. It may vary in size from a relatively minor feature of the continental margin to a vast, structural division of the deep ocean. The bottom may be of solid rock, igneous or sedimentary, or of unconsolidated silt, clay, or mud, deposited over the years. On average a basin will be some 3 km (2 miles) deep in mid-ocean but many hundreds of kilometres broad—a very shallow saucer. Even so, its margins will be marked by a rocky sill dividing it from the next basin; this barrier will impede the movement of water between basins sufficiently to allow physical, chemical, and biological differences to develop between one basin and the next. The limits of individual basins are widely used to define the boundaries of seas. Where seas occur in basins almost entirely surrounded by land, these differences may be very marked. The Mediterranean, for example, is warmer and has a much higher salinity than the adjacent Atlantic Ocean.

**ocean current**, a distinct and generally horizontal flow of seawater in a given direction. Ocean currents may form permanent circulatory systems, or gyres, as in the Atlantic and Pacific oceans, or they may be relatively short-lived phenomena affecting only limited areas, particularly along coasts. They may be caused by the drag exerted on the surface by prevailing winds, which can be permanent or seasonal; or by tidal motion, which is periodic; or by the discharge of rivers. They may be affected by differences in water density, determined by temperature and *salinity (just as air temperatures affect the direction and strength of wind). The most obvious feature of the hemispheric gyres is the poleward flow on the western margins of oceans. Wind-induced currents which elsewhere seldom exceed a depth of 200 m (650 feet) here can reach 1,000 m (3,250 feet), and owing partly to the *Coriolis force they are intense; the poleward-flowing Agulhas current in the Indian Ocean can flow at 5 knots (15 m.p.h.) and is the fastest ocean current in the world. The *ocean *circulation also has a vertical component, due to different densities, which carries down oxygen to decompose organic matter and carries up inorganic nutrients to sustain surface life. Ocean currents such as the *Gulf Stream, *Kuroshio, and *Peru Current have a profound influence on climates, particularly in coastal regions. In shallow waters, *rip currents and the flows associated with flood- and ebb-tides are examples of currents having local effects.

**Oceania** *South Seas.

**oceanic ridge** *mid-oceanic ridge.

**oceanography**, the study of the seas and oceans, which is concerned not only with their structures and the water they contain but also with their climates, flora, and fauna. It embraces *hydrography but is wider in scope; in particular nowadays it involves the theory of *plate tectonics. Oceanographic research began when early observations of surface features recorded in ships' logs were supplemented by reports from survey expeditions such as those of James *Cook in the 18th century and John and James *Ross in the first half of the 19th. The American oceanographer Matthew *Maury systematized and extended this knowledge in the mid-century, when it first became possible to measure depths with precision. The world voyage of the British ship *Challenger* in 1872-6 then gave impetus to the science by providing a comprehensive view of oceanic physiography and biology. The laying of submarine cables, the sounding of depths, and inventions for extracting samples of the sea-floor, resulted in fresh studies which by their nature were international. In recent years the oceans have become increasingly important economically because of resources (notably *petroleum and *gas) found in the *continental shelves. Because the world's climate is driven by interaction between the ocean, the atmosphere and the land, oceanography is a vital element in the study, and hence prediction, of climatic change. Most nations now have institutes of oceanography, and exchange observations.

**Oder** (Polish and Czech, Odra), a major river of northern Europe, some 854 km (531 miles) long. Navigable for over two-thirds from its mouth in the Baltic Sea, it rises in the Odra Mountains of the Czech Republic. It is connected by canals with the Vistula and with western Europen waterway syssterms. Reservoirs in its higher regions and a complex system of canals control the flow of water.

**Oersted, Hans Christian** (1777-1851), Danish physicist who in 1820 discovered that an *electric current has a magnetic effect. He noticed the deflection of a compass needle placed near a wire carrying a current. The oersted, a unit for magnetic field strength, was named after him. This has been replaced in the *SI system by the *ampere per metre.

Georg **Ohm**'s work on electric currents was published in 1827, but it was not until he was awarded the Royal Society's Copley Medal in 1841 that he began to be widely recognized.

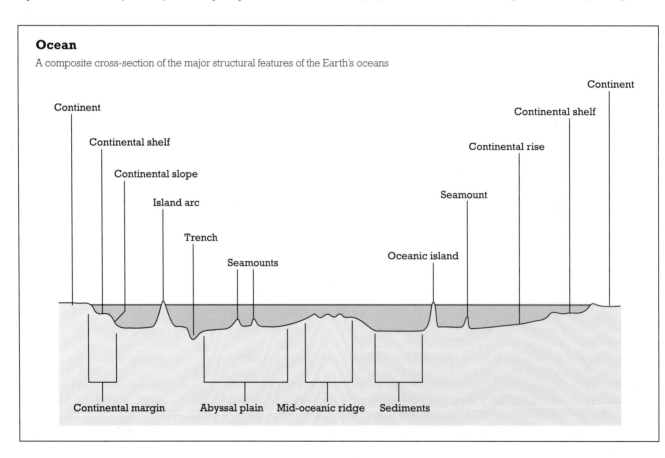

### Ocean
A composite cross-section of the major structural features of the Earth's oceans

Continent
Continental shelf
Continental slope
Island arc
Trench
Seamounts
Oceanic island
Seamount
Continental rise
Continental shelf
Continent

Continental margin
Abyssal plain
Mid-oceanic ridge
Sediments

**Ogaden**, an arid plateau lying on the horn of Africa, in the north-east of the continent. It rises northward from the Shebeli River to the foothills of the Ethiopian highlands at about 900 m (3,000 feet), from which the seasonal River Fafen flows in some years, only to dry up. There is scrub and some grazing, but frequent *drought.

**Ogden, Peter Skene** (1794–1854), Canadian fur trader and a major explorer of the American West. The first to cross the inter-mountain regions from north to south, he explored the Great Basin, Oregon, northern California, and the Snake River country. He discovered the Humboldt River in 1828 and penetrated the basin of the Great Salt Lake.

**Ohio River**, a river in the USA, in terms of volume of water, the chief tributary of the Mississippi. It developed from a stream of melt-water flowing along the edge of the ice-sheet of the last ice age. Starting at a confluence of several rivers from the Allegheny Mountains, it winds for 1,578 km (980 miles) to join the Mississippi in the south-west. After receiving the waters of its own tributaries it becomes a substantial flow, navigable for nearly all its length, although its use as a waterway is hindered by its waterfalls, a series of rapids over 3 km (2 miles) long in its middle reaches. Liable to flood with the melting of snow in spring, it is a major source of hydroelectric power.

**ohm** (symbol Ω), the *SI unit of electrical resistance, defined as the resistance between two points on a conductor when a constant potential difference of one volt, applied between these points, produces a current of one ampere in the conductor. It is named after the German physicist, Georg Simon Ohm (1787–1854). He investigated the *resistance offered by various conductors to the flow of an electric current. In 1827 he published a law which—in modern form—states that the current, $I$, in a metal conductor is proportional to the potential difference (voltage), $V$, applied across its ends if the temperature is kept constant. The law is also expressed in the form $I = V/R$, where $R$ is the resistance of the conductor.

**oil** *petroleum.

**Okavanga**, a river of south-west Africa rising in central Angola and flowing 1,600 km (1,000 miles) across north-east Namibia into Botswana, where it drains into the extensive Okavango marshes of Ngamiland.

**Okeechobe, Lake**, the southernmost and largest of the great lakes of Florida, USA. Before Florida emerged as part of the continental land mass in recent geological times, it was probably a slight depression in the sea bottom. Now it is a shallow lake some 50 km (30 miles) across and fed with fresh water mainly by the Kissimmee River in the north. It is drained through the Everglades.

**Okhotsk, Sea of**, the north-west branch of the Pacific Ocean, bordering north-east on the Kamchatka Peninsula of Siberia, the Kuril Islands, the Japanese island of Hokkaido, and Sakhalin Island. The sea, which covers an area of 1,583,000 km² (611,000 sq. mi.), has a mean depth of 777 m (2,549 feet). Strong currents flow through it; it is covered in dense fog during the summer and is ice-bound from November to June.

**Olduvai Gorge**, a ravine in northern Tanzania, East Africa. It lies at the south-east corner of the Serengeti Plain and marks the route of an ancient river that cut deep through the underlying strata to reveal a detailed slice of geological history. Archaeological research here has discovered many *fossils and artefacts linked with the evolution of humans and other mammals.

**oleum**, fuming sulphuric acid, a solution of sulphur trioxide, $SO_3$, in pure sulphuric acid, $H_2SO_4$; it is formed in the production of sulphuric acid by what is known as the contact process. When water is added to oleum, pure sulphuric acid is re-formed.

**Oligocene Epoch**, the third of the geological epochs of the *Tertiary Period, spanning the period of time from 36.6 to 23.7 million years ago. It was a time of falling temperature and general retreat of the seas. Sedimentary rocks of this age are found in the extreme south of the UK and in the Paris Basin in France.

**olivine**, a group of rock-forming minerals, particularly common in igneous rocks that are poor in silica. The olivines range in composition from magnesium silicate, $Mg_2SiO_4$, to iron silicate, $Fe_2SiO_4$; these are named forsterite and fayalite respectively. They are hard, and typically olive-green in colour. Crystals of gem quality are known as peridot.

**Olympic Mountains**, the highest part of the Coast Ranges in north-west Washington and the wettest area in the USA. Out of the virgin forest in the region, peaks rise to over 2,400 m (7,900 feet). The mountains are in Olympic

**Olduvai Gorge** was first recognized as an important fossil site by the German geologist Hans Reck, before World War I. In 1959, Mary Leakey discovered an early hominid skull there, the first of many important finds.

Oolitic limestone from the Cotswold Hills, Gloucestershire, UK. This sample is 6 cm (2.5 inches) across and shows clearly the **ooliths** that make up the rock.

National Park, which contains not only fine mountain scenery, but a spectacular stretch of the Pacific coast.

**Olympus, Mount**, the highest mountain in Greece. On the Aegean coast, it rises to 2,917 m (9,570 feet). Its snow-covered summit, at times hidden by cloud, was the legendary home of the gods in Greek mythology. It is sometimes known as Upper Olympus, Lower Olympus being an adjacent peak. The name Olympus has been used subsequently for other mountains, notably in the USA, Canada, Cyprus, Tasmania, and Turkey.

**Oman** (formerly Muscat and Oman), a country occupying the eastern corner of Arabia. It has a coast on the Arabian Sea, and inland it borders on Saudi Arabia and Yemen. Mountains rise steeply from a narrow coastal plain to a plateau which merges into the desert of the 'empty quarter' or Rub al-Khali. The plain is fertile, supporting crops of dates, coconut, and sugarcane. The climate is hot, but cattle can be bred on the mountains and camels in the oases. The main resource is oil.

**Onsager, Lars** (1903–76), Norwegian-born US chemist who extended the laws of thermodynamics to irreversible processes and derived an expression for the equivalent conductance of an electrolyte. He provided a theoretical basis for the gaseous-diffusion method of separating uranium-235 from the more common uranium-238, making possible the production of nuclear fuel. In 1968 he was awarded the Nobel Prize for Chemistry.

**Ontario**, Canada's second largest province, lying between Manitoba and Quebec and bounded by Hudson Bay in the north and the USA in the south, across the Great Lakes. It measures 1,690 km (1,050 miles) from north to south and 1,610 km (1,000 miles) from west to east. Its rocks are mainly those of the *Canadian Shield, ancient, weathered, and rich in minerals, containing half the world's nickel and much of its uranium. The highest point is no more than 610 m (2,000 feet); the north is marshy, forested, and well rivered, and there are numerous lakes. The winters are extremely cold, with much snow, and the summers are warm, although this continental climate is tempered in the south by the Great Lakes. Along their shores and inland, there are orchards, pasture, and arable land. The rivers, particularly the Niagara River at the Niagara Falls, provide abundant hydro-electric power; and the Saint Lawrence, flowing out of Lake Ontario, gives access to the Atlantic Ocean.

**onyx**, a type of *quartz used as a semi-precious stone and consisting of silica and opal. It is a variety of chalcedony composed of white and brown bands. Sardonyx has white and brownish-red bands. The chief localities of onyx are India and South America.

**oolite**, an oolitic limestone—that is, a limestone composed of *ooliths. Oolites are common rocks, of all ages. Those of Jurassic age are valuable as building stones.

**oolith**, the particles of which oolitic limestone is made. These are small, spherical concretionary bodies ranging in diameter from 0.25 mm to 2 mm (0.01 inches to 0.4 inches). They are usually composed of calcium carbonate in the form of *calcite, although present-day forms may be *aragonite. They are thought to be produced by the rolling about of grains on the sea floor so that consecutive layers of calcium carbonate are gradually built up; and they are forming at the present time in warm shallow waters such as those of the Bahamas and the Red Sea. Those over 2 mm in diameter are known as pisolites.

**ooze**, a fine-grained organic deposit which accumulates in the deep parts of the ocean floor, and contributes to the flatness of some *abyssal plains. Oozes are made up mainly of the calcareous and siliceous skeletons and shells of marine plants and animals (such as diatoms, foraminifera, and coccoliths), and they accumulate extremely slowly, usually no more than a few centimetres in a thousand years. In the Pacific Ocean the thickness of the ooze is up to 1,000 m (over 3,000 feet) thick, and probably represents 100 million years of deposition.

A collection of **opals** in their natural state with examples of cut and polished stones, one of which is mounted. Although we know that the constantly changing colours seen when polished opal is turned in the light are due to refraction and reflection, the exact nature of this optical effect is not fully understood.

**opal**, a form of silica with varying amounts of water. It is formed at low temperatures from water containing silica, and occurs in fissures in igneous rocks and in nodules in sedimentary rocks. Relatively soft and amorphous, it is easily damaged and should not be immersed in liquid. A 'play' of colours is a characteristic of opals; a white or black opal displaying blue, red, green, or orange flashes, although a yellow 'fire' opal may not flash. New South Wales and Queensland in Australia are the common sources of supply, and Hungary is the oldest, but opals are also found in Mexico, Honduras, and Nevada (USA).

## Orbitals

In the illustrations below, the shapes of the orbitals have been represented by surface boundaries enclosing regions of space within which there is a high probability (0·9–0·95) of finding an electron.

### Atomic orbitals

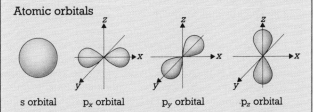

s orbital    p$_x$ orbital    p$_y$ orbital    p$_z$ orbital

The different types of orbital have different shapes: s orbitals, in which the electrons have an angular momentum quantum number $l = 0$, are spherical; the p$_x$, p$_y$, and p$_z$ orbitals ($l = 1$) are orientated at right angles to each other. Orbitals with $l = 2$ (d orbitals) and $l = 3$ (f orbitals) have more complex shapes.

### Molecular orbitals

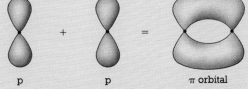

When two atoms combine to form a molecule, their atomic orbitals overlap to form molecular orbitals, which constitute chemical bonds. Two atomic s orbitals can overlap to form a sigma (σ) molecular orbital. This is the type of bonding in the hydrogen (H$_2$) molecule, where the 1s orbitals of the hydrogen atoms overlap. Atomic p orbitals can overlap to form either σ or pi (π) molecular orbitals, as shown. π molecular orbitals due to the overlap of p orbitals occur in benzene, ethene, and ethyne.

**operation** (or operator), a mathematical function that is applied to numbers, vectors, matrices, sets, and functions. Of most significance is the binary operation that acts on two objects, $x$ and $y$, to give a third, $z$, written as $x - y = z$, where – represents the operation. The most important binary operations are addition, subtraction, multiplication, and division. The operations of addition and multiplication, which are *commutative ($x - y = y - x$) and *associative ($x - (y - z) = (x - y) - z$), are essential in the development of number theory. Subtraction and division are neither commutative nor associative. The term operator can also be more loosely used as a term for symbols such as $+$, $-$, $\times$, and $\div$, which indicate the operation to be performed.

**optical activity**, a property possessed by certain crystals and solutions of rotating the plane of polarization of *polarized light as it passes through them. The activity is called dextrorotatory if the rotation is clockwise when facing the light, and laevorotatory when it is anticlockwise. It occurs when a molecule exists in two mirror-image forms that cannot be superimposed on one another. These are called *enantiomers or optical isomers; one is dextrorotatory (the D-isomer), the other laevorotatory (the L-isomer), and the optical activity of a substance depends on the proportion in which the two are present. A mixture containing both in equal proportions is called a *racemic mixture. Optical activity occurs in molecules possessing *chirality.

**Orange Free State**, a province of South Africa bounded on the north and south by the Vaal and Orange Rivers, whose tributaries drain the plateau on which it stands. Shaped like a kidney, and land-locked, it rises from its west-

Four naturally occurring **ores** of metals that are used in industry. Haematite (*top left*) is widely distributed in rocks of all ages and it forms the most important and abundant iron ore. Covellite (*top right*) is a copper ore found in veins associated with other copper minerals. Rhodochrosite (*bottom left*) is a comparatively rare manganese ore, generally associated with ores of silver and lead. Illustrated in crystalline form, it normally occurs in either granular or columnar masses. Autunite (*bottom right*) is derived from the alteration of uralite and other uranium minerals.

ern boundary with Cape Province to Lesotho and the Drakensberg Mountains in the east. The generally flat surface is broken here and there by *kopjes and low ridges. It is grass-covered—the veld—although in the wetter east wheat and maize are grown. Famous for its gold and diamonds, it also has an abundance of coal.

**Orange River**, a river of southern Africa, 2,100 km (1,300 miles) long. Rising high up in the Drakensberg Mountains, it runs south and then west through Lesotho and so into South Africa, its melt-waters and those of its tributaries irrigating the valleys. It then meanders westward, forming a natural boundary between the Orange Free State and Cape Province. Joined by its main tributary the Vaal, it continues south of the Kalahari and plunges over the Aughrabies Falls. Then, becoming the boundary between Cape Province and Namibia, the river begins to lose water by evaporation, so that in years of drought it fails to reach the sea. Navigation is in any case restricted by shoals and a sand-bar at Alexander Bay on the Atlantic coast; but the *alluvium at this mouth contains workable diamond beds.

**orbital** (in atomic physics), a pattern of electronic charge density in the space surrounding an atom. An orbital corresponds to at most two electrons, and it may be visualized as a kind of fuzzy cloud: where the cloud is dense there is a high probability of an electron being there; where it is thin the probability is small. The shape of the orbitals depends on the *quantum numbers of the electrons concerned and can be calculated from the *Schrödinger equation. When atoms form molecules, atomic orbitals on each atom overlap to form molecular orbitals. Electrons in these orbitals are labelled by a different set of quantum numbers. They are valuable to the understanding of the precise arrangement of atoms in molecules. The term is also applied to the mathematical functions that describe the orbitals.

**Ordovician Period**, the second of the periods in the *Palaeozoic Era, spanning the time interval from 505 to 438 million years ago. It follows the Cambrian and precedes the Silurian. Many Ordovician sediments are deep-water muds, clays, and limestones; and all the animals are marine. The graptolites (colonial organisms, now extinct) diversified greatly, as did the cephalopods. The period saw the first vertebrates (jawless fish) in North America and the onset of the Caledonian *orogeny with the opening of the proto-Atlantic.

**ore**, a solid, naturally occurring mineral aggregate from which one or more metallic constituents or other useful elements can be extracted. Other than gold and more rarely platinum, silver and copper, few elements are deposited in their pure state. Rather they are combined chemically with other substances, forming *minerals of various kinds. Such compounds, moreover, are normally associated with other common minerals of little or no economic value (such as quartz, feldspar, and calcite), or with earthy matter (such as sand, gravel, or clay) and may be so adulterated that the mixture cannot be called an ore, because the *grade is too low. In many clays, the grade of aluminium reaches 25 per cent, but such clay is not an ore, because the concentration of aluminium is below the *cut-off grade. Even the richest ores contain some admixture of valueless minerals, collectively called *gangue, from which the mineral of value must be separated before it can be processed and used. Often ores are found in veins, filling the faults or cracks in the rock.

Some ores have been precipitated from percolating fluids. Other ore bodies are of igneous or metamorphic origin. Weathering may erode such deposits, redepositing the ore in an alluvial form.

**organic chemistry**, the chemistry of the compounds of carbon. Carbon is unique in the very large number of compounds it can form; over 90 per cent of all known chemical compounds contain carbon. Much of the chemistry of living organisms (biochemistry) constitutes organic chemistry as the compounds involved consist largely of carbon. As there are so many organic compounds it is important that they are named systematically so that they can readily be identified. The internationally accepted rules for naming organic compounds include the following. The name of a compound consists of an optional prefix, a stem, and a suffix. The suffix denotes the *homologous series to which the compound belongs; for example -ane denotes alkane, -anol denotes alcohol, and -anal denotes aldehyde. The stem denotes the number of carbon atoms in the longest carbon chain in the molecule; thus meth- denotes one carbon atom, eth- two carbon atoms, prop- three carbon atoms and but- four carbon atoms. The optional prefix contains information about positioning and other features of the molecule. As an example consider the two *isomers with molecular formula $C_4H_{10}$. The isomer $CH_3CH_2CH_2CH_3$ is called butane. The stem but- denotes four carbon atoms and the suffix -ane shows that it is an alkane. The other isomer $(CH_3)_3CH$ is 2-methylpropane. Again the suffix indicates an alkane. The longest carbon chain has only three atoms, denoted by the syllable prop-. The fourth carbon is in a methyl $(-CH_3)$ group attached to the second carbon in the three-carbon chain; hence the prefix 2-methyl-. For a compound of any complexity the systematic name becomes too cumbersome for ordinary use. A name that is only partly systematic may be used instead, such as neohexane (systematic name 2,2-dimethylbutane). These are called trivial names. True trivial names tell nothing about the structure, and are given if the structure is unknown; their use may continue after the structure has been elucidated. Xanthophyll and furan are examples of trivial names.

**organometallic**, a compound in which a metal atom is bonded to one or more carbon atoms. The *transition metals form large numbers of organometallic compounds, which usually involve the metal in a low oxidation state or valency. There are several types of organic compounds which can act as *ligands to metal atoms. *Alkyl or *aryl groups can bond to a metal atom, as for example in the compound tetraethyl lead, $Pb(C_2H_5)_4$, which is used as an *anti-knocking compound in petrol. Alkenes, alkynes, and benzene and its derivatives can also bond: for instance, chromium dibenzene, $Cr(C_6H_6)_2$, is an example of a compound in which the metal atom is literally sandwiched between the two planar benzene molecules. As the metal is generally in a low oxidation state, organometallic compounds are usually susceptible to oxidation. Therefore they are prepared and studied in the absence of oxygen. It is found that many organometallic compounds can act as *catalysts, especially in reactions involving organic molecules. An example is the Ziegler catalyst used in the polymerization of ethane.

**Orinoco River**, a long and, in the wet season, a mighty river of northern South America. It rises in the south of the Guiana Highlands and skirts them, in a great **C**-shaped

**Orographic** clouds over the Cuillin Mountains on the Isle of Skye, Scotland, UK. Moist air is forced to rise by the physical barrier of the mountains. As it does so it moves through layers of progressively colder air until it reaches the temperature at which its water-vapour load condenses, and cloud forms. Water droplets in the descending airflow evaporate again as they leave the condensation level.

course, to enter the Atlantic Ocean after a journey of some 2,600 km (1,600 miles). Navigable for about two-thirds of that length, it is linked by the Casiquiare, a natural canal, to the Negro and the Amazon Rivers. Its middle reaches, which contain the Ature and Maipures cataracts, form part of the boundary between Venezuela and Colombia. Passing through *llanos and rain forest, it picks up numerous tributaries, the Apure and Caroní among them, and descends to its vast, swampy delta. Here it branches into several distributaries which drain into the Atlantic.

**Orkney Islands** (UK), a group of seventy islands separated from the north of Scotland by the Pentland Firth, which is less than 13 km (8 miles) wide. Only thirty or so are large enough for habitation, the biggest being Pomona (or Mainland), Hoy, and South Ronaldsay, which together shelter the bay of Scapa Flow. They are very irregular in shape and all are of red sandstone weathered and worn by the sea into undulating, treeless plateaux edged by steep cliffs; an extreme example of this *erosion is the Old Man of Hoy. The plateaux are fertile, nevertheless, and support much mixed farming. The *Shetland Islands are 80 km (50 miles) to the north-east.

**orogenesis**   *mountain-building.

**orogenies**, periods of *mountain-building that occur as a result of the movement of crustal *plates. Deformation, folding, and thrusting then take place on a large scale, accompanied by the intrusion of igneous rocks and by metamorphism. Events of this kind have taken place on many occasions during the past. Several orogenies can be identified in the *Precambrian. Important orogenies that affected Britain and north-west Europe during the *Phanerozoic include the Caledonian (*Ordovician), Variscan (*Permo-Trias), and Alpine (*Tertiary). In North America the Taconic (*Ordovician), Acadian (*Silurian), Appalachian (*Permo-Trias), Larimide (*Cretaceous), and Pasadenian (*Tertiary) orogenies are notable.

**orographic effects**, the atmospheric disturbances that are caused by, or relate to, the existence of mountains and other high land. Mountain barriers such as the Rockies can influence climates. They affect the pattern of atmospheric *circulation, in particular the location of troughs in the *waves which exist aloft at mid-latitudes in the westerly airflow. On a more local scale, mountain ranges may affect the pattern of surface airflow and induce *rain-shadows.

**Ortelius, Abraham** (1527–98), Flemish engraver, geographer, and mapmaker of Antwerp. In 1570 he published the first modern world atlas, *Theatrum orbis terrarum*, suggested by Gerardus *Mercator. Containing 70 maps, it represented the work of 87 cartographers, engraved by Ortelius in uniform style. Later he became mapmaker to Philip II of Spain.

**osmium** (symbol Os, at. no. 76, r.a.m. 190.2), a *transition metal in the platinum group and one of the densest elements known. It is found in nature in osmiridium and as a sulphide and is used for hardening alloys. When combined with oxygen at high temperature it gives osmium tetroxide, $OsO_4$, which is a commonly used biological stain and fixative.

**Ostwald, (Friedrich) Wilhelm** (1853–1932), German chemist who is regarded as one of the founders of physical chemistry, having helped to establish in 1881 the first *physical chemistry journal, *Zeitschrift für Physikalische Chemie*. He formulated the dilution law which bears his name and invented a process for making nitric acid by the oxidation of ammonia. He believed that *thermodynamics was of fundamental importance, and since at that time the effects of atomic phenomena were not measurable he refused to accept their validity. In 1909 he was awarded the Nobel Prize for Chemistry for his work on catalysis.

**outcrop** (in mining and geology), the exposed area of a stratum or vein of rock on the Earth's surface; generally, the surface area of a stratum or vein of rock whether it is exposed or not.

**outlier**, an outcrop of younger rock surrounded by older rock. It may be formed by erosion, by faulting, or by folding. The cutting of a valley through more or less horizontal strata may, for example, leave a small area of higher (and younger) rocks isolated as an outlier. *Inliers are an outcrop of older rock surrounded by younger rock.

The black horseshoe-shaped areas in this aerial view of a river in Texas, USA, are **ox-bow lakes** marking the river's previous course.

**outwash, glacial**, material washed from *glaciers and ice-sheets by streams of melt-water flowing within or under the ice and collecting shattered rock particles in the process. When ice stops advancing and melts rapidly, large numbers of melt-water streams form, and they can carry enormous loads of material. This tends to build up into sheets of rock, sand, and gravel known as outwash plains, or sandurs. *Braiding occurs, a sandur being covered by a network of channels at low flows; and floodwaters will extend across the whole surface, particularly in spring. Much of the Canterbury Plains, New Zealand, consists of outwash gravels.

**overburden** (in geology), any valueless rock or unconsolidated deposit that overlies a substance being mined (for example, shale over metal ores and coal). The term is also applied to any unconsolidated sediment that lies upon solid rock.

**overland flow** (in hydrology), water moving over the ground surface in a thin sheet, not collected into channels. Although a sheet of water cannot cause much erosion, sooner or later threads of faster flow will begin to form *rills, which can rapidly enlarge into *gullies if the overland flow continues. Good land management therefore usually aims to discourage overland flow and encourage *infiltration. Overland flow occurs in three different ways. Rain falling on any surface made impermeable by frost, which has developed a crust will run straight off. Secondly, on bare ground with little water in the soil between rainstorms, each section of a slope acts rather like a bucket: when no more water can be held in each one, overland flow occurs. This usually happens first at the top of slopes, where soil is thinnest. Thirdly, in areas of thick soil and vegetation cover, more water stays in the soil between rains and moves downhill slowly, under

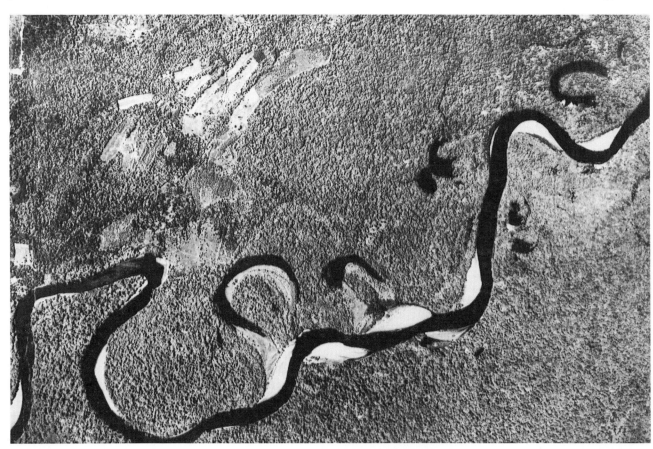

gravity, so that the ground is wetter near the foot than at the head of slopes; when it rains again, saturation and overland flow occur at the base of the slope first.

**overthrust fault**, a low-angled fault or slide in which one mass of rock rides over another, causing a large horizontal displacement of the strata. Overthrusts are common in mountain ranges such as the Alps.

**ox-bow lake**, or cut-off, a shallow, curved lake found on flat *floodplains. Ox-bows are parts of old loops which have been abandoned by *meandering rivers and which are now slowly silting up and being invaded by vegetation. They usually form one at a time, as a river cuts a new channel across the neck of land between the two ends of a meander. Really big floods, however, can sometimes cause a river to cut a completely new course on its floodplain, leaving large numbers of meanders to become ox-bows.

**oxidation** (in chemistry), the opposite of *reduction, a process where electrons are removed from the substance being oxidized. It does not necessarily involve reaction with oxygen. The process leads to an increase in *electronegativity of the substance and in its oxidation state (a measure of the electronic control that an atom has in a compound compared to the atom in its elemental state). The formation of metal ions from metal atoms is an example. It also occurs when oxygen combines with another substance and when hydrogen is removed from a substance. For example, carbon monoxide is oxidized when it burns in oxygen to form carbon dioxide and *rusting involves oxidation as iron is converted to iron(III) oxide. A useful mnemonic is OIL RIG—Oxidation Is Loss of electrons, Reduction Is Gain.

**oxide**, a compound of oxygen with another element, formed when the other element reacts with oxygen in the air, usually during heating or burning. There are several types. Acidic oxides are mostly those of non-metals and are covalent in character; when soluble in water they form acid solutions. Basic oxides are mostly those of metals and are ionic in character, consisting of the oxide ion $O^{2-}$, the peroxide ion $O_2^{2-}$, or the superoxide ion $O_2^{-}$; when soluble in water they form alkalis, and they neutralize acids to form a salt and water. Amphoteric oxides react both with strong acids and with strong bases, while neutral oxides react with neither. Mixed oxides contain metals in more than one oxidation state.

**oxidizing agent**, a substance which causes *oxidation and in the process is itself reduced. It may give oxygen to another substance (for example, when an element burns to give its oxide, it undergoes oxidation caused by oxygen which acts as the oxidizing agent), or they may remove electrons (as when iron(II) ions, $Fe^{2+}$, are oxidized to iron(III) ions, $Fe^{3+}$, when chlorine, the oxidizing agent, is bubbled through a solution of iron(II) chloride, $FeCl_2$).

**oxisol**, a clayey soil formed as a result of intense weathering in tropical or subtropical areas on land surfaces that have been stable for a long time. Oxisols are generally many metres thick and tend to lack distinct *horizons. Their bright red, yellow, or yellowish-brown colour is due to the abundance of iron in the profile. They contain little humus, because organic matter is rapidly destroyed in hot climates, and therefore crumble apart very easily, despite the presence of clay. These soils are generally not very fertile.

Oxisols occur throughout tropical South America and Africa.

**oxygen** (symbol O, at. no. 8, r.a.m. 15.9994), a colourless, odourless gas, and the most abundant element on Earth, occurring in the crust, in fresh water and sea-water, and in the atmosphere, of which it forms 21 per cent by volume. It exists both as the highly reactive molecule $O_2$ and, especially in the upper atmosphere, as the even more reactive $O_3$, or *ozone. As the element involved in respiration and a product of photosynthesis, it is essential to most forms of life. Oxygen is slightly denser than air and has a boiling-point of $-183$ °C ($-361$ °F). It is manufactured by the fractional distillation of liquid air, from which the nitrogen content is distilled first. Industrially it has many uses, such as in welding, metal-cutting, explosives, and rocket fuels. It is necessary for combustion and will relight a glowing splint, a simple laboratory test for oxygen. As an *oxidizing agent it combines with all other elements, except the *noble gases, and with many compounds.

**Ozark Plateau**, or Ozarks, an eroded tableland in central USA between the Missouri and Arkansas Rivers west of the Mississippi. Erosion of a broad, asymmetric dome has revealed a sequence of Palaeozoic strata; these dip away from the exposed core of crystalline basement rocks. The latter in the extreme north-east form the sharp, rugged hills of Saint François. These rise 240 m (800 feet) above the Salem upland, which for the most part is floored by Lower Carboniferous (Mississippian) limestone and is one of the most important sources of lead and zinc in North America. It falls away west and south to the much dissected, roughly north-west–south-east-trending Burlington scarp. This, with the succeeding Springfield Plateau, is also cut mainly in Lower Carboniferous limestone. The Springfield Plateau in turn dips towards the east–west-oriented scarp of the Boston Mountains—typical Ozark country—which reach heights of over 600 m (2,000 feet) and are developed on Upper Carboniferous (Pennsylvanian) sandstone.

**ozone**, a form of *oxygen in which each molecule is composed of three atoms instead of two (triatomic oxygen, $O_3$). It is a pale blue gas with a pungent, burning smell and is not necessarily present in seaside air. However, it does occur naturally as a result of the reaction between the oxygen (filtering up from the *troposphere) with solar ultraviolet radiation, forming a layer which spans most of the *stratosphere surrounding the Earth. Ozone is constantly being produced and constantly being destroyed within this layer. The reactions involved have been shown to be affected by the presence of certain gases, namely *nitrogen oxides and *chloro-fluorocarbons (CFCs). These gases are produced as a result of human activities and give rise to areas of ozone depletion or 'holes' in the ozone layer. The most immediate result is reduction in the protective effect of the ozone layer against harmful ultraviolet radiation from the Sun. Scientists and environmentalists have been urging that a total ban be placed on the production of CFCs to prevent irreparable damage.

# P

**Pacific Ocean**, the world's largest expanse of sea, covering one third of its surface—more than the total area occupied by land. Extending over the junctions of several of the world's crustal *plates, it contains deep trenches and volcanic *island arcs which, together with the volcanoes of the Andes, form a 'ring of fire' round much of the Pacific margin. The arcs border the trenches (such as the Marianas) which form where one ocean crustal plate goes down beneath another in a *subduction zone. The friction between the plates results in *earthquakes, and the Pacific therefore has more than its share of *tsunamis. Behind the island arcs are the relatively shallow marginal basins: the seas of Okhotsk and Japan, and the Bering, Yellow, East China, South China, Philippine, Arafura, and Tasman Seas. Only in the east do the trenches rise directly to narrow *continental shelves and thence to the mountain-bordered coasts of North and South America. It is an ancient ocean. Scat-

The smooth, flat appearance of young Antarctic **pack ice** is short-lived: within a season it can be broken up by wind and waves and piled against the coast.

tered across it are thousands of *seamounts, submerged volcanoes, and volcanic islands, many topped by coral reefs and *atolls, built upon its deep floor. It was given the name Pacific because of its general placidity, but *typhoons are relatively frequent. The North Equatorial Current flows from east to west and then splits into a counter-current and the *Kuroshio current of Japan. This crosses the northern Pacific and becomes the southward-flowing *California Current, while the South Equatorial Current, also flowing east to west, starts an anticlockwise cycle, flowing down the Australian coast and then back up the Peruvian coast as the Peru Current. The tides are generally mixed, either the two high or the two low tides each day being of unequal amplitude. On some coasts there are only single, diurnal tides—one high and one low one each day. The mean depth is 4,190 m (13,740 feet), the greatest of all oceans. There is little oxygen in the depths, but where the plates are separating there are *hot springs and vents on the ocean floor; around which submarine life thrives.

**pack ice**, a coherent mass of floes of *sea ice leaving little or no open water. Such accumulations are usually made up of masses of various ages driven together by waves or wind. When the floes are driven together they often buckle up around the margin, forming irregular ridges, so the surface of the ice is generally very uneven and hummocky.

**Pakistan**, a country in the north-west of the Indian subcontinent, bounded by Iran on the west, Afghanistan on the north-west, China on the north-east, and India on the east. The Hindu Kush, Karakoram, and Himalayas ring the north. Other ranges sweep down its western side to the Arabian Sea. Below them is the long, broad valley of the Indus. The North-West Frontier Province, containing the strategically important Khyber Pass, is very high. To the south is the plateau of the Punjab, or Panjab, meaning 'five rivers', watered by the tributaries of the Indus. Wheat is grown here; but elsewhere the climate is hot and arid, despite a summer monsoon, and the land is dependent on irrigation. To the east is the Thar Desert. Between the Sind Desert, which covers part of the Indus delta, and Baluchistan in the western hills, there are large reserves of natural gas and some oil, which is also present in the Punjab.

**Palaeocene Epoch**, the first of the geological epochs of the *Tertiary Period, spanning the time-interval from 66.4 to 57.8 million years before the present and preceding the Eocene. Great changes took place and conditions were very different from those of the preceding *Cretaceous Period. The sudden diversification of the mammals is a notable feature of the Epoch.

**Palaeogene Period**, the earlier of the two geological periods into which the *Tertiary Period can be divided. (The other is the Neogene.) It comprises the Palaeocene, Eocene, and Oligocene epochs.

**palaeomagnetism**, the field of *geophysics concerned with the measurement and interpretation of remnant magnetism or the record of the Earth's past magnetic field. Valuable information concerning *continental drift and the successive positions (or wandering) of the palaeomagnetic pole have been obtained through palaeomagnetic studies.

**palaeosol**, an ancient soil which developed on a former land surface during a longish period in the geological past.

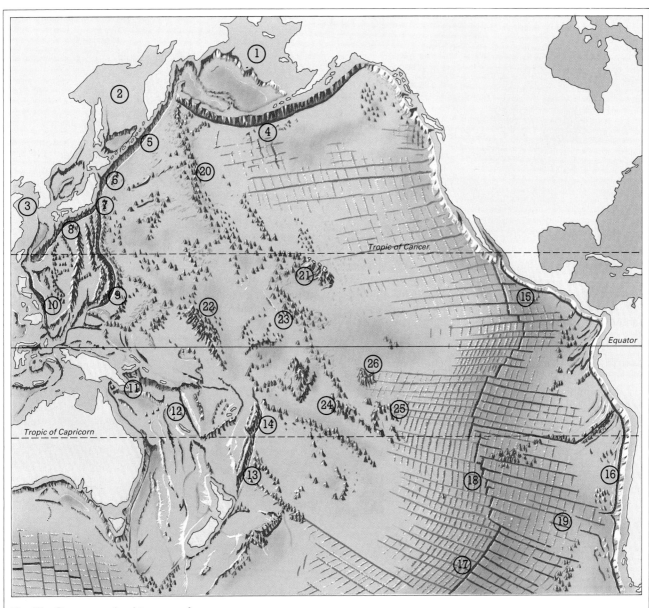

**Pacific Ocean:** seabed topography

**Shallow seas**

1 Bering Sea
2 Okhotsk Sea
3 Yellow Sea

**Trenches**

4 Aleutian Trench
5 Kuril Trench
6 Japan Trench
7 Bonin Trench
8 Ryukyu Trench
9 Marianas Trench

10 Philippines Trench
11 New Britain Trench
12 New Hebrides Trench
13 Kermadec Trench
14 Tonga Trench
15 Middle America Trench
16 Peru-Chile Trench

**Ridges**

17 Pacific–Antarctic Rise
18 East Pacific Rise
19 Chile Rise

**Island/chains and seamounts**

20 Emperor Seamounts
21 Hawaiian Ridge
22 Marshall, Gilbert & Ellice Islands
23 Line Islands
24 Society Islands
25 Tuamotu Archipelago
26 Marquesas Islands

Palaeosols are generally formed under different environmental conditions from those influencing present-day soils in the same area and therefore tend to have different characteristics from modern soils. Although some have remained at the surface, it is common to find them buried beneath more recent sediments. Sometimes the overlying sediments are removed by erosion and the palaeosol is then exposed to current soil-forming processes. Palaeosols can provide evidence about the climate at the time they were formed.

**Palaeozoic Era**, one of the four eras into which geological time is subdivided. It spans the period of time from 570 to 245 million years ago. It consists of the Cambrian, Ordovician, Silurian, Devonian, Carboniferous (in America the Mississippian and Pennsylvanian), and Permian Periods. The Cambrian to the Silurian constitute the Lower Palaeozoic; the Devonian to the Permian the Upper Palaeozoic. The Palaeozoic saw the development of many marine and terrestrial plants and animals.

**Palestine**, historically, a region of the Mediterranean comprising parts of Jordan, Egypt, and modern Israel. A land of sharp physical contrasts, it stretches from the Mediterranean Sea and the coastal Plain of Sharon in the west to the eastward-lying West Bank country known in biblical times as Judaea and Samaria. Here it slopes down to the River Jordan at the head of the *Great Rift Valley. The Negev Desert lies to the south, ending in the Gulf of Aqaba. Northward lies the hill country of Galilee, the highest and best-watered part of the region. The coastal Plain of Sharon has a Mediterranean climate with moderate winter rain, well suited to the growth of citrus fruit; it becomes drier and hotter to the south, towards Beersheba. Inland, beyond the hills, is the arid valley of the Jordan, which runs, below sea-level, from the Sea of Galilee south to the Dead Sea at 400 m (1,300 feet) below sea level. The Jordan Valley is the lowest land surface on earth.

**palladium** (symbol Pd, at. no. 46, r.a.m. 106.4), a silvery-white element, the most reactive of the platinum metals which dissolves in concentrated nitric acid and hot sulphuric acid. It absorbs hydrogen and is used as a catalyst in hydrogenation, as also in some electrical components. It forms the alloy white gold with gold.

**Pamirs**, a knot of high mountains, better described as a lofty dissected plateau, in central Asia, partly in Tajikistan and extending into China and Afghanistan. The highest point is Communism Peak, at 7,495 m (24,590 feet). Most of the valleys lie between 3,700 and 4,300 m (12,000 and 14,000 feet). The plateau is known as the 'roof of the world'; it is arid and very cold. Although there is pasture between the snowy peaks, there are few trees or streams, only great glaciers such as the Murghab, which is 230 km (140 miles) long.

An aerial view of the West Highlands Province of **Papua New Guinea**, a region of towering peaks and often impenetrable forests, shrouded in rain-cloud and mist. The country's outlying islands are fringed by low-lying coral formations.

**pampas**, large, treeless plains in South America, extending westward across central Argentina from the Atlantic coast to the Andean foothills. To the west it is dry, barren, and saline, while its south-eastern stretches are relatively cool and swampy.

**Panama**, a tropical country occupying the narrow isthmus between North and South America, bounded by Costa Rica to the west and Colombia to the east. Along its length runs a range of hills, through the centre of which was cut the pass, for the *Panama Canal, which gives access to shipping from the Caribbean in the north to the Pacific in the south. The land is fertile, supporting coffee on the higher ground and sugar cane on the coastal plains. The coastal waters yield shrimps.

**Pangaea**, the great supercontinent that is supposed to have formerly comprised *Laurasia and *Gondwana, so named by Alfred *Wegener, who proposed that Pangaea began to split up as a result of *continental drift in the *Jurassic Period, and that the fragments eventually became the continental masses we know today.

**Papua New Guinea**, a country consisting of the eastern half of the island of New Guinea north of Australia, together with the Bismarck Archipelago and other islands adjacent in the western Pacific Ocean. The mainland is divided by a central range of mountains rising to 4,509 m (14,762 feet) at Mount Wilhelm. A low-lying plain is drained by the Fly River in the south-west, and there are active volcanoes in the east. The climate is tropical and monsoonal, with heavy rainfall and temperatures ranging from 10 °C to 32 °C (50 °F to 95 °F), according to altitude. Copper and gold deposits are exploited.

**parabola**, one of the three kinds of *conic section. It is a U-shaped curve obtained by slicing a cone parallel to its slant side. A parabola can also be described as the locus of points in a plane whose distance from a fixed point, the focus, equals that from a fixed line, the directrix. The simplest alge-

braic equation of a parabola is $y = x^2$, or in polar coordinates, $r = 1/(1 - \cos\theta)$. It was *Galileo Galilei who first showed that an object moving under the influence of gravity alone describes a parabola. In the case of a very fast object, such as a bullet, the curve will be a very flattened parabola, but a parabola nevertheless. The shape is more recognizable in the line of water from a hosepipe or fountain. The property of a parabola to reflect through the focus all light travelling parallel to its axis has proved useful in reflecting telescopes, while the converse property is made use of in torches and car headlights.

**parabolic dune**    *dune.

**Paradise Cave**, a feature of the Paradise Glacier in Mount Rainier National Park, Washington, USA. As glacial caves they are formed by annual subglacial melt-water erosion and exhibit complex patterns. Individual caves measure 3 m (10 feet) high and 6 m (20 feet) wide and some are several kilometres in length.

**paradox**, a self-contradictory statement, such as 'all rules have exceptions'. In mathematics they undermine the reliability of mathematical truth. Some of the earliest were those of the Greek mathematician Zeno (see *calculus). Mathematical paradoxes were attributed to an over reliance on intuitive reasoning. During the 19th century many mathematicians sought to eliminate paradoxes by reconstructing mathematics on *axioms. However, Georg *Cantor's difficulties with infinite sets late in the 19th century not only revealed paradoxes in *set theory but also exposed problems in the reconstructed mathematics. For example, a fundamental law of mathematics is that all propositions are either true or false. But the law is also a proposition, so it can be false. Difficulties like this meant that there could still be paradoxes in classical mathematics. Several different schools (such as logicism, intuitionism, and formalism) attempted a resolution, but Kurt *Gödel's work around 1930 showed that logical principles alone could not guarantee mathematical consistency. Thus the possibility of paradoxes in mathematics remains.

**Paraguay**, an inland country in south-central South America, surrounded by Bolivia and Brazil on the north and Argentina on the south. The navigable Paraguay River, running down the middle of the country, joins the Paraná and provides access to the sea. In the west is the Gran Chaco, a region of black, fertile earth which provides rich pasture and hardwood forests. In the east, the land rises to a low range of forested hills, to the south of which there are swamps and palm-fringed, shallow lakes. Here it can be very damp, with rainfall averaging about 1,800 mm (71 inches) a year.

**parallax**, the apparent displacement of two objects relative to one another when the observer changes his point of view. It occurs when the objects are at different distances, and it can cause observational problems. In setting up optical instruments such as telescopes and microscopes, it is necessary to ensure that the cross hairs are in the same plane as the object viewed—the situation of 'no parallax', as it is called.

**parallel postulate** (in geometry), the fifth postulate in *Euclid's Elements. It is a famous postulate which has always been felt to be much less obvious than the other postulates, and many attempts were made to derive it from them. The

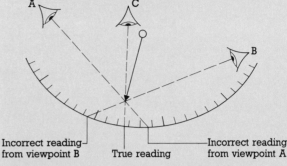

**Parallax**

Parallax is the apparent shift in the position of an object viewed against its background, when the observer's position is changed.

Incorrect reading from viewpoint B    True reading    Incorrect reading from viewpoint A

Parallax errors are a common problem in taking readings from meters. As the observer's head moves laterally, the apparent reading varies.

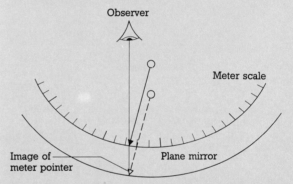

Observer

Meter scale

Image of meter pointer    Plane mirror

Parallax errors are avoided by placing a plane mirror behind the meter scale. A true reading is obtained when the meter pointer precisely covers its image in the backing mirror.

postulate states that if a straight line cuts two other straight lines and makes unequal angles with them, those other lines if extended will eventually intersect. This is equivalent to saying that only one line can be drawn through a point so as to be parallel to a given line. Many Euclidean results depend on it, such as the theorem that the angles of a triangle add up to 180°. In the 19th century, however, it was shown that by denying the parallel postulate different kinds of non-Euclidean *geometry could be devised.

**parallels of latitude**, circles of *latitude smaller than the Equator (which is a *great circle) running east–west round the earth, north and south of the Equator and parallel to it. Crossing *meridians of longitude, they are part of the grid on which the position of any point in the world can be specified. (See also *projection).

**parameter** (in mathematics), a quantity which may have various values but is constant in any particular situation or example. For instance, in the general form of a quadratic function $ax^2 + bx + c$, where $a$, $b$, and $c$ are parameters, whereas $x$ is the variable. It also means a variable in terms of which the coordinates of a point are expressed. The parametric equations of a circle with radius $r$ are $x = r\cos\theta$, $y = r\sin\theta$, and $\theta$ is the parameter. In statistics, parameter refers more specifically to a numerical characteristic of a population—for example, the mean or the variance—in

A portrait of Mungo **Park** from the *European Magazine*, London, June 1799. After returning from his first West African expedition, he wrote *Travels in the Interior of Africa*, the first reliable account of African tribal life and customs.

contrast to a statistic, which refers to a sample taken of it.

In physics, a parameter is any variable quantity which characterizes a system.

**Paraná River**, the main element in the second largest drainage system in South America. Over 3,000 km (nearly 1,900 miles) long, it is formed by the union of the Paranaíba and the Grande on the plateau of south-east Brazil; it runs south, receiving the Paraguay and other tributaries before meeting the Uruguay River to form the estuary of the River Plate. In its upper reaches it flows between high banks and over many falls, the Guaira Falls being reputed to have the greatest annual discharge of any in the world. Shoals and sand-bars hinder navigation in its lower reaches, which are liable to flood; but river craft can penetrate to its junction with the *Iguaçu at the boundary between Paraguay, Argentina, and Brazil.

**Parícutin**, a volcano in south-west Mexico which began in 1943 as an eruption in a cultivated field. Within a day there was a cinder cone 8 m (26 feet) high, and ash covered the countryside all around. Within six months it reached to 460 m (1,500 feet), and the local village was smothered. A few months later twenty villages were buried under lava. The volcano was 2,773 m (nearly 10,000 feet) high by 1952, when all activity ceased.

**Paris Basin**, a roughly circular depression in central northern France. It was formed by *Jurassic sediments covering a granitic substratum. Resembling a vast but shallow amphitheatre, it contains concentric chalk and limestone escarpments and has the Ile de France in its lowest central area. It is drained by the Seine and its tributaries.

**parity**   *symmetry.

**Park, Mungo** (1771–1806), British explorer (of Scottish extraction) of the Niger. A surgeon in the mercantile marine, Park undertook a series of explorations in West Africa in 1795–6, sailing up the River Gambia, crossing Senegal and navigating the River Niger before being captured by a local Arab chief. He escaped from captivity four months later and returned to Britain after a year and a half in the interior. Bored with his medical practice in Scotland, Park returned to the Niger in 1805 but was drowned during a fight with Africans a year later.

**Parry, Sir William Edward** and **Sir John Franklin** (grandfather and grandson), British naval hydrographers. William (1790–1855) was an Arctic explorer with several expeditions to his credit, among them a search for the *North-West Passage and a sledge journey to the North Pole which failed owing to ice conditions. John (1863–1926) ran the Royal Navy's hydrographic department during World War I, and in 1918 was largely responsible for a system of time-keeping whereby ships in the same longitudinal zone set clocks uniformly, according to Mean Time on the *Greenwich meridian.

**partial pressure of gases**   *Dalton.

**pascal** (symbol Pa), the *SI unit of pressure equal to one newton per square metre. The unit is named after the French mathematician and scientist, Blaise Pascal (1623–62). He conducted and described many experiments in hydrostatics and on the nature of a vacuum, and invented the hydraulic press.

**Patagonia**, a semi-arid plateau which forms the southern part of Argentina, beyond the Negro River. The largest desert in the Americas, it is dissected into several blocks by

Polygon wedges, many containing small meltwater pools, cover this area of **patterned ground** near the shores of the Beaufort Sea in Alaska.

river valleys that open out on to the Atlantic coastal plain. The plateau surface is generally between 500 m (1,600 feet) and 1,000 m (3,300 feet) above sea-level. While the northern zone consists primarily of scrubland, irrigated crops including peaches, grapes, and alfalfa are grown in the valleys. The region is rich in uranium and manganese, copper, iron ore, and petroleum.

**patterned ground**, land covered by small ripples, stripes, circles, or polygons produced by natural processes. Usually flat or very gently sloping, it occurs in very cold or very dry areas, although 'fossil' forms thousands of years old survive elsewhere: the stripes of chalky and sandy soils with different vegetation in the Breckland of the eastern UK are at least 10,000 years old and date from the last period of *glaciation. Patterning results from contraction cracking, which is caused by extreme heat or cold, or from the sorting of material into different sizes by the action of wind or the growth of ice. Cracking gives networks of polygons. In cold but wet areas the cracks contain wedges of ice, while in dry regions they are filled by wind-blown silt or sand. The wind produces very fine stripes or ripples in dry snow or fine sands and gravels. Larger, more durable stripes and a whole range of circles and smallish polygons result from the growth of ice lenses in extreme latitudes or at high altitudes. Materials of different sizes and colours transmit heat at different rates. Ice lenses and crystals forming in various sizes underneath particles heave them to different degrees, thus creating circular patterns on flat ground.

**Pauli, Wolfgang Ernst** (1900–58), Austrian-born US physicist who made a major contribution to the theoretical study of energies of electrons in the atom. In 1924 he enunciated the exclusion principle that no more than two electrons can occupy the same *orbital in an atom. If they do so, they must have opposite *spins and therefore different energies. In 1931 he postulated the existence of a new elementary particle, later discovered, called the *neutrino. In 1945 he won the Nobel Prize for Physics and in 1946 became a US citizen.

**Peace River**, one of Canada's great rivers, approximately 1,600 km (1,000 miles) long, descending from Williston Lake in British Columbia, and meandering eastward through Alberta. Here its old lake beds and terraces provide good farming country, while holding deposits of gypsum, coal, oil, and natural gas. In Wood Buffalo National Park it joins the Slave River, which flows into Great Slave Lake, thus making it a headstream of the Mackenzie River.

**Peano, Giuseppe** (1858–1932), Italian mathematician whose main work was in *analysis. He is also noted for providing a set of *axioms for the natural numbers. He invented a number of counter-intuitive functions, including a space-filled curve, a continuous one-to-one function from the interval [0, 1] on the line on to the unit square in the plane.

**Peary, Robert Edwin** (1856–1920), US naval officer who is recognized as the first explorer to reach the North Pole. Having surveyed the Arctic peninsula later named Peary Land, he made three attempts to reach the Pole, the last of which (in 1909) was successful. Starting from his ship *Roosevelt* off Ellesmere Island, he sent back his sledges in stages, covering the last 210 km (130 miles) with five men in two days. On arrival he made a sounding through ice, finding no bottom even at 2,740 m (1,500 fathoms).

**peat**, a dark brown deposit which is made up of the compressed, partly carbonized remains of plants. It represents an early stage in the formation of *coal. If dried out it will burn, although it produces ammonia fumes. It is common in Canada, and northern and central Europe, and forms in swampy areas. The decaying organic matter may, in marshlands, emit an inflammable gas (phosphuretted hydrogen) whose spontaneous combustion gives rise to the phosphorescent light (*ignis fatuus*) seen hovering over peaty ground.

**pebble**, a rock fragment ranging in diameter from 4 to 64 mm (about 0.15 to 2.5 inches). Pebbles are often rounded (by water or wind) but are defined by geologists only according to their size. They are larger than the fragments in gravels but smaller than cobbles.

**ped**, a natural soil aggregate or lump. Peds may be plate-like, granular, or prism-like. Plants generally grow best in a soil which has moderately sized granular peds. Soils of this sort are good because they retain sufficient moisture for plant growth without becoming waterlogged and because they provide firm support for the growing plants.

**pedalfer**, a *zonal soil formed in an area with more than 60 cm (25 inches) of rain a year, where moisture for *leaching is therefore abundant. Soluble salts are washed out of the soil, which is, therefore, characteristically abundant in iron and aluminium. Soils of this sort are widespread throughout the eastern United States. *Podzols, *alfisols, and *oxisols are examples of pedalfer soil.

**pedestal rock** (mushroom or perched rock), a pillar of relatively soft rock which usually has a capping of harder material. Some pedestals, in rocky deserts, are sculptured by the blasting action of winds laden with coarse sand, which has scoured and eroded the bases of rock buttresses. The great majority, however, were weathered and eroded by the action of running water in eating away the softer 'stem', which is partly protected by the cap-rock. Miniature forms may occur wherever soft material containing pebbles is exposed to rain. Pedestals often look strangely ornamental.

**pediment** (in geomorphology), a broad plain of eroded bedrock surrounding upland in deserts and semi-deserts. There is usually a very sharp change in slope angle between the upland and the even-surfaced pediment, which generally has a gradient of less than 11°. While some pediments show the bare rock, most have at least a thin covering of *alluvium, which gets gradually thicker away from the upland, until an alluvial plain called a 'bajada' is formed. Where small residual hills stand above wide pediments, the pediments from the air look like broad, shallow, triangular bases to them. How pediments form is not clear; probably there are different processes at work in different places. It seems likely that many are left by the slow retreat of the edge of upland blocks, as they are eroded by running water. The surface of a pediment is often scoured by streams from the upland; they shift their channels to and fro, cutting the rock and depositing the thin veneer of sediment. In other cases, *weathering or the action of water on the surface after torrential rain may help to create the pediment form.

**pedocal**, a *zonal soil formed in relatively dry climates where evaporation rates are high and rainfall is generally less than 60 cm (25 inches) a year. In these conditions soluble salts, such as calcium carbonate, are not removed by *leaching but accumulate within the profile, making the soil alkaline. Soils of this sort are widespread throughout the western United States. *Desert soils, *brown soils and *aridisols are all examples of pedocals.

**pedology** (from Greek, *pedon*, 'ground'), the scientific study of the soil. Soil is an important natural resource which supports the growth of plants for food, timber, and many other purposes. Certain types of soil can be used as building material, while others contain valuable mineral deposits. An understanding of how soil forms and why it differs from place to place is essential if man is to use this resource as widely and wisely as he can. Pedologists seek to assist by describing, classifying, and mapping soils. Although less than a century old, pedology has become important because of its practical significance.

**pegmatite**, an extremely coarse-grained igneous rock with crystals that may be up to several metres (tens of feet) in length. The composition varies, but granite pegmatites are the most common and are usually referred to simply as pegmatites. Pegmatites are usually found as *dykes and veins and are well-known sources of splendid crystals, which are usually more than 1 m in length. Some are of economic importance as sources of minerals.

**Penck, Albrecht** and **Walther** (father and son), German geologist and geomorphologist. Albrecht (1858–1945) was famous for pioneer work on the glaciations of the Alps during the Pleistocene Period, producing evidence of four ice advances named Günz (the oldest), Mindel, Riss, and Würm (the youngest). He devised the 1:1,000,000 map of the Earth and published a work on the study of the Earth's surface features for which he coined the term, geomorphology. As Professor of Geography at Berlin (1906–26) he investigated the geopolitical concept of a state's propensity to expand or contract its boundaries according to rational capabilities (*Lebensraum*). Walther (1888–1923) was noted for his theories of landform evolution which hinged on the balance between uplift and river downcutting and on the mobility of the

A specimen of **pegmatite** from Portsoy, north-east Scotland, that shows the irregular texture and different-sized crystals typical of this rock. The dominant pink rock is orthoclase, the grey, quartz, and the shiny silver crystals, muscovite mica.

Earth's crust, which challenged the basic assumptions of the erosion cycle concept.

**peneplain**, a very broad, gentle surface extending far inland from a coastline, regarded as an end-product in a *cycle of erosion. The theory has it that peneplains were produced by the downward and sideways cutting of rivers over millions of years. Although some areas of unusually hard rock remain as isolated hills, or *monadnocks, rising above a peneplain, the underlying rocks are bevelled off, regardless of their resistance. If the *base level of erosion falls—because of a drop in sea-level or uplift of the land— rivers are rejuvenated and begin to cut up the peneplain. Former peneplains that were uplifted can be recognized by the roughly level summits of mountains. Although there is evidence in the geological record that very large plains are sometimes produced by the processes the theory describes, it is extremely unusual for both climate and base level to stay the same for long enough for rivers to cut a peneplain. It is more likely that most wide plains have been fashioned by various processes, and not only by rivers.

**peninsula**, a body of land projecting into water. Peninsulas may be of any shape or size, although small ones are termed headlands and very large ones (such as India) may be called subcontinents. Peninsulas which are almost entirely surrounded by water are joined to the mainland by *isthmuses.

**Pennines**, a mountain chain forming the 'backbone' or main *watershed of England. Stretching from the Scottish border southward into the Peak District, a distance of 260 km (160 miles), the chain is made up of a series of upland blocks. These are dissected by a number of valleys or dales, and chasms which drop 90 m (300 feet) or more. The higher regions are mostly moorland and rise in the north to 893 m (2,930 feet) at Cross Fell. These areas provide rough pasture, whereas the lower, fertile slopes are generally cultivated or used for mixed agriculture.

**Pennsylvanian Period**, the later of the two epochs or subsystems into which the *Carboniferous Period is divided in North America (the other being the *Mississippian). It covers the span of time from 320 to 286 million years ago, and is named after its most famous exposures in the state of Pennsylvania, USA.

**pentlandite**, an iron nickel sulphide and an important ore mineral of nickel. It is usually found as bronze-coloured masses which are hard, opaque, and exhibit a metallic lustre. Occurring in basic igneous rocks together with other sulphide ores, it is found in many countries: Sudbury, Ontario (Canada), and the Bushveld (South Africa) are two localities. It is not common in the USA.

**perched water-table**, ground water well above a valley floor, especially after heavy rain, often giving rise to springs. Perched water-tables exist where rock, soil, or regolith becomes saturated with water even though the layers below it are not completely full. This can happen, for example, in a coarse sandstone above a heavy, impermeable clay.

**peridot**, a gem-quality crystal of *olivine, pale green in colour. Gem crystals have been found in lava on Saint John's Island (Red Sea), in Arizona (USA), and in Myanmar (Burma).

Kaikoura **Peninsula** on South Island, New Zealand, was originally an island that has been 'tied' to the mainland by the gradual accumulation of silt, sand, stones, and mud forming a narrow isthmus. The peninsula is fringed by wave-cut platforms.

**peridotite**, an intrusive *igneous rock that is rich in the dark mineral *olivine. *Pyroxene and other *ferromagnesian minerals may also be present. The rock is usually dark green with large crystals which are enriched with accessory rare metals. Peridotites are found in the Bushveld (South Africa) and at Stillwater, USA, among other places and are mined for nickel, chromium, and platinum. Peridotite is probably a major constituent of the *Earth's mantle.

**periodic groups**, sets of elements which occur in the same vertical column in the *periodic table. Elements in the same group have the same number of electrons in their outermost shell, and usually resemble each other chemically. There are also steady trends in behaviour in each group, with non-metals becoming less reactive as their atomic number increases down the column, and metals more reactive. Because the metallic nature of elements decreases from left to right across a period of the table but increases down a group, it can thus be seen from its position at the bottom left that francium is the most reactive metal and that fluorine at the top right is the most reactive non-metal. The groups are identified by roman numerals. Thus the *alkali metals are Group I and the *halogens are Group VII.

**periodic law**, a law which was first proposed by Dimitri *Mendeleyev, which now states that if the elements are arranged in order of atomic number (the number of protons in the nucleus), then elements with related properties occur at regular intervals. For elements of low atomic number, the interval is eight elements: thus lithium (at. no. 3), sodium (11) and potassium (19) resemble each other. Later the interval becomes eighteen elements: thus potassium (19), rubidium (37) and caesium (55) are similar. By placing elements with related properties in vertical columns. Mendeleyev was able to construct the *periodic table.

**periodic table**, an arrangement of the chemical elements in order of increasing atomic number—that is, the number of protons in their nuclei. The elements are arranged horizontally in seven rows called *periods; the first period consists of two elements (hydrogen and helium), the second of eight elements (lithium to neon), the third of eight elements (sodium to argon), the fourth of eighteen (potassium to krypton), and so on. Atoms which form positive *ions are represented to the left of each period, and the electronegative ones to the right. When the elements are arranged in this way, they fall into columns called groups; and it is found that elements occurring in the same group resemble each other chemically: thus all the noble gases appear in the extreme right-hand group, which is called Group 0. This pattern occurs because the properties of an element depend primarily on the number of electrons in its outermost (valence) shell. Each shell can only hold a fixed number of electrons. When the shell becomes full, a new shell is started and a new period in the table is begun. The table's arrangement therefore reveals information on the *electronic configuration of atoms. The periodic table was originally suggested by Dimitri *Mendeleyev and was used to predict undiscovered elements; the existence of germanium was predicted when it became clear that there must be an unknown element between gallium and arsenic, if subsequent elements were to fit into the appropriate groups in the table.

## The periodic table of elements

The table shows the arrangement of the chemical elements into periods and groups.

The electronic configurations are given in terms of the noble gas 'core' plus the outer electron configuration. For example, the 12 electrons of a magnesium atom have the configuration $1s^2 2s^2 2p^6 3s^2$ (two electrons in the 1s subshell, two in the 2s subshell, etc.).

Notice the trend towards increasing metallic character down the table. Thus, in Period 2, metals extend across the period only as far as beryllium in Group IIa, while in Period 6, polonium in Group VIa is a metal.

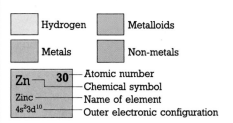

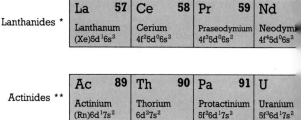

The s-, p-, d-, and f-blocks in the main table correspond to the filling of s, p, d, and f electronic subshells. As the atomic number increases, the subshells are filled in order of increasing energy, as indicated in the diagram alongside (the figures in parentheses are the maximum number of electrons permitted in each subshell). Departures from this pattern of filling occur where two subshells have similar energy levels. For instance, the irregular electronic configurations of chromium and copper are due to the closeness in energy of the 4s and 3d subshells.

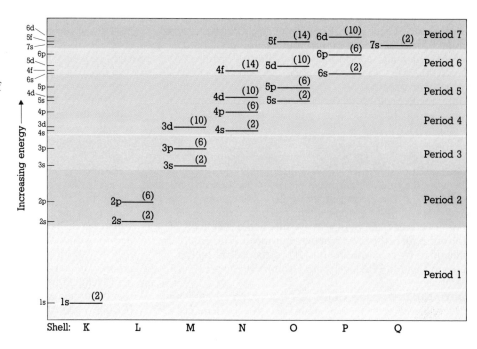

| | | | 0 |
|---|---|---|---|
| | | | **He** 2 |
| | | | Helium |
| | | | 1s² |

| | | IIIa | IVa | Va | VIa | VIIa | |
|---|---|---|---|---|---|---|---|
| | | **B** 5 | **C** 6 | **N** 7 | **O** 8 | **F** 9 | **Ne** 10 |
| | | Boron | Carbon | Nitrogen | Oxygen | Fluorine | Neon |
| | | 2s²2p¹ | 2s²2p² | 2s²2p³ | 2s²2p⁴ | 2s²2p⁵ | 2s²2p⁶ |

| | VIII | Ib | IIb | **Al** 13 | **Si** 14 | **P** 15 | **S** 16 | **Cl** 17 | **Ar** 18 |
|---|---|---|---|---|---|---|---|---|---|
| | | | | Aluminium | Silicon | Phosphorus | Sulphur | Chlorine | Argon |
| | | | | 3s²3p¹ | 3s²3p² | 3s²3p³ | 3s²3p⁴ | 3s²3p⁵ | 3s²3p⁶ |

| 26 | **Co** 27 | **Ni** 28 | **Cu** 29 | **Zn** 30 | **Ga** 31 | **Ge** 32 | **As** 33 | **Se** 34 | **Br** 35 | **Kr** 36 |
|---|---|---|---|---|---|---|---|---|---|---|
| ...s² | Cobalt | Nickel | Copper | Zinc | Gallium | Germanium | Arsenic | Selenium | Bromine | Krypton |
| | 3d⁷4s² | 3d⁸4s² | 3d¹⁰4s¹ | 3d¹⁰4s² | 3d¹⁰4s²4p¹ | 3d¹⁰4s²4p² | 3d¹⁰4s²4p³ | 3d¹⁰4s²4p⁴ | 3d¹⁰4s²4p⁵ | 3d¹⁰4s²4p⁶ |

| 44 | **Rh** 45 | **Pd** 46 | **Ag** 47 | **Cd** 48 | **In** 49 | **Sn** 50 | **Sb** 51 | **Te** 52 | **I** 53 | **Xe** 54 |
|---|---|---|---|---|---|---|---|---|---|---|
| ...henium | Rhodium | Palladium | Silver | Cadmium | Indium | Tin | Antimony | Tellurium | Iodine | Xenon |
| ...s¹ | 4d⁸5s¹ | 4d¹⁰5s⁰ | 4d¹⁰5s¹ | 4d¹⁰5s² | 4d¹⁰5s²5p¹ | 4d¹⁰5s²5p² | 4d¹⁰5s²5p³ | 4d¹⁰5s²5p⁴ | 4d¹⁰5s²5p⁵ | 4d¹⁰5s²5p⁶ |

| 76 | **Ir** 77 | **Pt** 78 | **Au** 79 | **Hg** 80 | **Tl** 81 | **Pb** 82 | **Bi** 83 | **Po** 84 | **At** 85 | **Rn** 86 |
|---|---|---|---|---|---|---|---|---|---|---|
| ...nium | Iridium | Platinum | Gold | Mercury | Thallium | Lead | Bismuth | Polonium | Astatine | Radon |
| ...d⁶6s² | 4f¹⁴5d⁷6s² | 4f¹⁴5d⁹6s¹ | 4f¹⁴5d¹⁰6s¹ | 4f¹⁴5d¹⁰6s² | 4f¹⁴5d¹⁰6s²6p¹ | 4f¹⁴5d¹⁰6s²6p² | 4f¹⁴5d¹⁰6s²6p³ | 4f¹⁴5d¹⁰6s²6p⁴ | 4f¹⁴5d¹⁰6s²6p⁵ | 4f¹⁴5d¹⁰6s²6p⁶ |

—d-block—      —p-block—

| 61 | **Sm** 62 | **Eu** 63 | **Gd** 64 | **Tb** 65 | **Dy** 66 | **Ho** 67 | **Er** 68 | **Tm** 69 | **Yb** 70 | **Lu** 71 |
|---|---|---|---|---|---|---|---|---|---|---|
| ...methium | Samarium | Europium | Gadolinium | Terbium | Dysprosium | Holmium | Erbium | Thulium | Ytterbium | Lutetium |
| ...d⁰6s² | 4f⁶5d⁰6s² | 4f⁷5d⁰6s² | 4f⁷5d¹6s² | 4f⁹5d⁰6s² | 4f¹⁰5d⁰6s² | 4f¹¹5d⁰6s² | 4f¹²5d⁰6s² | 4f¹³5d⁰6s² | 4f¹⁴5d⁰6s² | 4f¹⁴5d¹6s² |

| 93 | **Pu** 94 | **Am** 95 | **Cm** 96 | **Bk** 97 | **Cf** 98 | **Es** 99 | **Fm** 100 | **Md** 101 | **No** 102 | **Lr** 103 |
|---|---|---|---|---|---|---|---|---|---|---|
| ...tunium | Plutonium | Americium | Curium | Berkelium | Californium | Einsteinium | Fermium | Mendelevium | Nobelium | Lawrencium |
| ...d¹7s² | 5f⁶6d⁰7s² | 5f⁷6d⁰7s² | 5f⁷6d¹7s² | 5f⁹6d⁰7s² | 5f¹⁰6d⁰7s² | 5f¹¹6d⁰7s² | 5f¹²6d⁰7s² | 5f¹³6d⁰7s² | 5f¹⁴6d⁰7s² | 5f¹⁴6d¹7s² |

—f-block—

The periodicity of the properties of the elements is illustrated very clearly by a plot of atomic radius against atomic number. The elements of Groups Ia, IIa, IIb and 0 have been labelled, and show a general trend in radius down each group. Note the small radii of the noble gases (Group 0), corresponding to completion of a p subshell, and the sharp increase in radius for the alkali metals (Group Ia) as filling of a new principal electron shell begins. Plots of other properties (for example, electro-negativity) against atomic number show a similar periodicity.

**periods** (in chemistry), sets of elements which occur in the same horizontal line in the *periodic table. Across any period there is a steady change in properties ranging from metallic to non-metallic; each period ends with a noble gas. An element such as silicon, a semiconductor which has both metallic and non-metallic properties, appears in its period near the dividing line.

**periods, geological**, major divisions of geological time corresponding to geological systems, which are major divisions of the geological column (that is, of the rocks themselves). They are subdivisions of *eras. The Cambrian, Ordovician, and Silurian periods are examples. All these divisions, however, are arbitrary units of time based either on assemblages of fossils or on sedimentary strata from one location or area. They do not necessarily represent complete world-wide divisions of environmental change, of specific sedimentary processes, or of evolutionary change. They are convenient divisions of geological time which are characterized by particular events.

**permafrost**, permanently or, more accurately, perennially frozen ground whose temperature does not rise above 0 °C (32 °F) for at least twelve months. It occurs wherever temperatures are low enough, even under the shallow, cold waters of the Arctic Ocean. Usually only the sub-surface layer is permafrost and there is an *active layer at the surface which thaws in warmer weather: there can also be unfrozen pockets—termed 'taliks'—deep below the surface.

The partially melted surface layer—the active layer—of a **permafrost** region in the Yukon River valley, Alaska. The white crust covering part of the area is salt, deposited from a saline spring rising beneath the slightly domed ground.

North of 70° N. permafrost is continuous, except under rivers and lakes which do not freeze completely in winter. Between 70° and 60° N. it is discontinuous, and south of 60° N. it is sporadic in occurrence. It also occurs on high mountains in the southern hemisphere and in the Antarctic, but most is in the northern hemisphere, where it can be over 300 m (1,000 feet) thick and many thousands of years old. Any disturbance of the ground surface—particularly the removal of insulating vegetation or global warming—is likely to cause permafrost to thaw and the active layer to deepen, releasing energy. If the sub-surface contains a lot of ice which then melts, there may be sinking or collapse, which can tilt or swallow buildings and fracture roads, airstrips, and pipelines.

**permeability of rock**, the property of a rock that allows water or other fluids to pass through it. Rocks with little or no permeability are termed impermeable even though they may have high *porosity. In general, coarse sedimentary rocks such as sandstones are usually permeable; igneous rocks such as granite are neither porous nor permeable, whereas clays are commonly highly porous. The permeability of rocks is an important factor in extracting water, oil, or gas from them. Permeable water-bearing rocks or sediments are called *aquifers, impermeable rocks or sediments are called *aquiclines.

**Permian Period**, the last of the geological periods of the *Palaeozoic Era, extending in time from 286 to 245 million years ago. It follows the *Carboniferous and comes before the *Triassic. A period characterized in many parts of the world by hot deserts, it saw the extinction of many marine animals (for example, trilobites and primitive corals) and the proliferation of reptiles.

**Permo-Trias Period**, the *Permian and *Triassic Periods considered together.

**peroxide**, a chemical compound containing linked pairs of oxygen atoms $(-O-O-)$ or containing the $O_2^{2-}$ ion, the simplest example being hydrogen peroxide $(H_2O_2)$. The oxygen–oxygen link is a weak bond and can be broken by ultraviolet radiation, which starts and catalyses many reactions in the atmosphere and in nature. Peroxides are used as rocket fuels, in solution as bleaches for wool and hair, and as antiseptics. Some exist in animals and plants and are destroyed by enzymes which transfer the extra oxygen to oxidizable substances.

**Perrin, Jean-Baptiste** (1870–1942), French physicist who made detailed studies of *Brownian motion—the random motion of small particles in a liquid or a gas due to bombardment by surrounding molecules. From his observations he determined a value for the *Avogadro constant, the number of molecules in one mole of any substance. He also demonstrated that cathode rays (electron beams) carry a negative charge. He was awarded the Nobel Prize for Physics in 1926.

**Persian Gulf** *Gulf, the.

**Peru**, a country on the Pacific coast of South America, bounded by Ecuador and Colombia on the north, Brazil and Bolivia on the east, and Chile on the south. The north-east of the country is in the upper Amazon basin, and being close to the Equator it comprises tropical rain forest. In stark contrast, the south-west half is occupied by the mighty Andes, their snow-capped peaks rising to over 6,500 m (21,000 feet). Between the ranges are plateau areas of wide, rock-strewn slopes, the high mountain lake, Titicaca, in the extreme south-east, and many valleys used for cultivation and the rearing of cattle, llamas, and sheep. Here also silver, copper nitrates, and many other minerals are found in rich profusion. The coastal plain is arid and mostly desert, cooled by the *Peru Current and subject to dense mists.

**Peru Current** (Humboldt Current), a broad, shallow, slow-moving body of cool water flowing northward along the western coast of South America. In this region prevailing winds blow surface waters away from the coast, causing an *upwelling of cold sub-surface waters to replace them. Upwelling brings nutrient-rich water to the surface, and this encourages the growth of phytoplankton, the tiny floating plants that fish feed on. The region is therefore rich in marine life and an important fishing area. If the position of the Peru Current changes, as it sometimes does with an *El Niño occurrence, upwelling is inhibited, and this has serious effects on the local fishing industries.

**petrified wood**, wood which, through geological time, has quite literally turned to stone. The process of petrifaction entails the gradual, but total, replacement of the cellulose tissues of a tree by mineral forms of silica, commonly *chalcedony or *opal. The result is that the original shape, structure, and even the smallest internal details of the wood can still be seen.

**petroleum**, or crude oil, a complex mixture consisting of hydrocarbon gases and oils and occuring with natural gas, solid hydrocarbons, and salt water. It is produced by the decomposition of mainly *planktonic marine organic matter, chiefly the remains of marine plants (phytoplankton) that are trapped in sediments at the time of their deposition. It then migrates upwards and may accumulate, if conditions are favourable, in permeable rocks that can act as a reservoir. Petroleum occurs in many parts of the world: extensive deposits have been found in the Persian Gulf, the USA, Canada, Russia (the Urals and western Siberia), Libya, the Niger delta, Venezuela, the Gulf of Mexico, and the North Sea. When purified and processed it is used as the primary fuel for internal-combustion engines, and as such is of great economic importance to man. But world reserves are running out, and there are few places left for new exploration and recovery. Many pollution problems are associated with the extraction, refining, and use of petroleum, and widespread demand has led to its becoming in effect an international currency, with many associated political problems. Technological improvements are reducing the problems associated with petroleum, but if consumption continues at current rates, the known recoverable petroleum reserves will be exhausted within the next few decades, and alternative energy sources will have to be found.

**petrology**, the scientific study of rocks, their mineral composition, texture, occurrence, and origin. The study is concerned with the origin and mode of formation of all rocks, sedimentary, igneous, and metamorphic. Within the subject, petrography is concerned with the description of rocks, and petrogenesis with their origin. Much petrology entails analysis in the laboratory, particularly by microscopic examination of rock specimens and identification of the minerals present. This information is then related to field occurrences with the object of understanding how the rock originated.

**pH** *hydrogen ion concentration.

**Phanerozoic Age**, a period of geological time comprising the *Palaeozoic, *Mesozoic, and *Cainozoic (Cenozoic) Eras. It began approximately 590 million years ago at the start of the Cambrian Period and is marked by the accumulation of sediments containing the remains of animals with mineralized skeletons. Although the name is derived from the Greek *phaneros* meaning 'visible' and *zoion* meaning 'animal', the term now merely defines the base of the Cambrian.

Wind and water have stripped away the overlying layers of sandstone, shale, and volcanic ash to expose the **petrified wood** of coniferous tree trunks in Arizona, USA, which are more than 135 million years old.

**phases of matter**. A material can have different physical properties while retaining the same chemical composition. For example, water ($H_2O$) can exist as a solid (ice), a liquid (water) or a gas (steam). These different states are known as the three phases of matter. Two further states are considered to be different phases of matter: these are *plasma and *liquid crystal.

**phenocryst**, a crystal that is of larger dimensions than its surrounding matrix or groundmass within an igneous rock. Phenocrysts usually have well-formed crystal faces. They are relatively large because they crystallized earlier than the rest of the rock under slower cooling conditions. Feldspars are common as phenocrysts, although many other rock-forming minerals can appear in this form.

**phenol** (or carbolic acid, $C_6H_5OH$), a colourless crystalline solid which was first separated in its crude form from coal tar in 1834. Today it is used in the manufacture of nylon, dyes, explosives, and perfumes. It is the simplest of the *phenols, consisting of a *benzene ring in which one hydrogen atom has been replaced by a hydroxyl group. Organic compounds in which a hydroxyl group ($-OH$) is bonded to an *aryl group are collectively known as phenols. In many respects, there is only a formal resemblance between phenols and *alcohols. Usually their chemical reactions differ markedly: for example, phenols are appreciably acidic in water, while alcohols show no such acidity. Many phenols possess antiseptic properties, a well-known example being trichlorophenol, TCP.

**Philippines**, a country comprising over 7,000 islands between the Pacific Ocean and the South China Sea, covering a land area of 300,000 km² (115,830 sq. mi.). Luzon and Mindanao are the largest islands; in the central Philippines, the islands of Leyte and Samar are linked by a 2,162 m (7,095 feet) long bridge. Being at a junction of crustal *plates they contain volcanoes and are subject to earthquakes; and

as they are in the path of two *monsoons there is rain for most of the year. The climate is tropical throughout the year. Many of the islands are mountainous and heavily forested with teak, ebony, and sandalwood. Bamboo and coconut palms grow in profusion, while the soil on cleared land produces abaca (Manila hemp), rice, maize, sugar cane, and tobacco. Coal is plentiful, and there are deposits of iron, chromium, and manganese. The seas between the islands are full of tropical fish.

**phosphates**, commonly, the general term for phosphatic deposits, including guano and the phosphates of sodium, potassium, and calcium; specifically, rock phosphate (phosphorite). The deposits are sedimentary material both of marine origin (phosphate salts precipitated directly from sea water) and, more commonly, formed on land (bones or guano). Extensive deposits occur in Morocco, Algeria, and Tunisia in Africa, and Peru and Chile in South America. They are an important source of fertilizer.

**phosphorescence**, the emission of light from a substance after it has been exposed to and excited by some form of radiation. It occurs because the energy from the original radiation is absorbed by the charge cloud of electrons in the atom and this distorts the shape of the cloud. When the radiation is removed the cloud reverts to its original shape and in so doing the energy is re-emitted in the form of light. When this happens immediately the phenomenon is called *fluorescence, but in certain types of atom there is a time-lag and the material continues to glow for a time until the charge clouds of all the atoms have returned to their normal pattern. Materials which exhibit phosphorescence are called phosphors and they are used to produce the picture on a television tube: the original excitation is produced by a beam of electrons which strikes the phosphor momentarily, causing it to emit light of a particular colour. Phosphorescence is also used more widely to include any emission of light by a cold object, for example by fireflies.

**phosphorus** (symbol P, at. no. 15, r.a.m. 30.97), a non-metal in Group V of the *periodic table which exists as several *allotropes. White phosphorus is waxy, highly toxic, and catches fire spontaneously in air, and so it is normally stored under water; it is used in the making of rat poisons. When heated in an inert atmosphere it forms red phosphorus. This, the second form, is a dark red powder, non-poisonous, and generally more stable; it is used to make match heads. Black phosphorus is prepared by heating the white form under pressure; it has a layer structure and is also stable. Phosphorus occurs in nature only in a combined state, mainly as *phosphates, in limestones, bone beds, and guano. The mineral apatite, found in igneous rocks, is the major source. Extraction is by heating with coke and silica; the phosphorus is distilled off and condensed under water. Of its compounds, the oxide is a white powder used as a drying agent, and the phosphates are used as fertilizers and detergents. The element is essential to life: it is needed for the formation of bones and teeth, and for the chemistry of respiration and reproduction.

**photochemical reaction**, a chemical reaction initiated by light; which will not proceed in the absence of light. An important naturally occurring photochemical reaction is photosynthesis, in which green plants produce carbohydrates and oxygen by the action of light on carbon dioxide and water. Photography is based on a photochemical reac-

Thin sections of rock, viewed under the microscope using polarized light, form the basis of analytical **petrology**. The picture shows the characteristic colours and internal structures of olivine.

tion initiated when light-sensitive substances on the film are exposed to light.

**photoelectric effects**, the interaction of *electromagnetic radiation with matter, especially solids. Irradiation of most materials with ultraviolet light or radiation of shorter wavelength results in the emission of electrons; some substances exhibit the phenomenon with visible light also. This is called photoemission. The energy of the *photons is given up to the emitted electrons, which are called photoelectrons and can constitute a current in an electric circuit. The energy of the electrons depends on the frequency of the light; its intensity affects only the number emitted. These observations led Albert Einstein to develop further Max Planck's ideas of the *quantum theory. Photoemission has led to development of the photocell, which is used for a variety of purposes, including the capture of solar energy, in burglar and fire alarms, and for remotely operating automatic doors. Other photoelectric effects are photoconduction and the photovoltaic effect. In photoconduction the electrons which are released act as additional charge carriers within the material and so the electrical resistance decreases. This is particularly effective in *semiconductors, and the phenomenon is used in several devices for detecting not only visible light but also infra-red radiation. If light falls on certain pairs of materials, such as selenium on a metal plate, then, if they are part of a complete electrical circuit, a current will flow. This is because the light generates an electromotive force and the pair of materials becomes a cell; this is called the photovoltaic effect. As the basis of several light-sensitive devices it is one of the principles which is being used in trying to harness solar energy in order to produce electricity.

**photon**, a 'packet' or quantum of *electromagnetic radiation. Max *Planck showed that radiation can be emitted or absorbed by a system only in certain fixed amounts or quanta. These may be considered as small indivisible packets or units of energy, or as particles of zero mass. The energy of a photon depends on its frequency and is equal to $h \times$ frequency, where $h$ is Planck's constant ($6.6 \times 10^{-34}$ joule second). Photons are required to explain phenomena, such as the *photoelectric effect, that require light to have particle character. (See also *wave-particle duality.)

**phyllite**, a fine-grained *metamorphic rock intermediate between *slate and *schist. Phyllites are of sedimentary origin and are typical products of low-grade regional metamorphism. In appearance they are lustrous with light and dark minerals arranged to give a distinctive banded appearance. They are common in the eastern Alps, but occur world-wide, and occasionally are used for roofing.

**physics**, the study of the properties and interactions of matter and energy; it differs from chemistry in dealing less with particular substances and more with matter in general, although there are areas of overlap, as in physical chemistry. Physics originally was the systematic study of all nature, both animate and inanimate: in other words, what is now called science and was formerly called natural philosophy. Only in the 17th and 18th centuries did it become restricted first to the study of inanimate matter and then, with the separate development of chemistry, to the subject it is today. Isaac *Newton set the stage for classical physics, that is physics before *quantum theory and *relativity theory were developed. It includes optics, acoustics, mechanics, thermo-

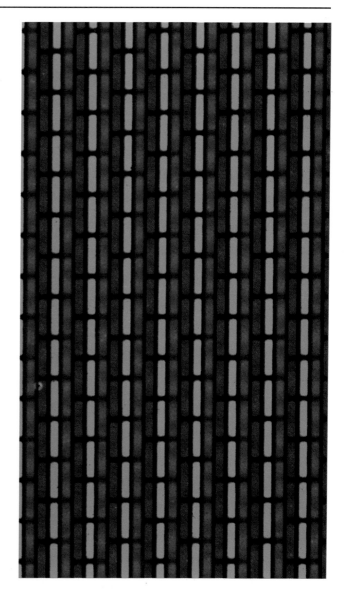

This photograph demonstrating **phosphorescence** shows a detail of the grid of phosphors on the screen of a colour television. Each phosphor is about 0.7 mm (0.028 inches) long.

dynamics, and electromagnetism. In the 20th century the most far-reaching contributions have been in the two theories just mentioned, which have led to knowledge about the universe at the smallest scale (*quarks) and the largest (cosmology and the 'big bang'). On a practical level it has given us, among many other things, nuclear energy, the transistor and the silicon chip, and the laser.

**pi** (symbol $\pi$). In geometry pi has been defined historically in two different ways, although in both cases as the numerical value of a ratio associated with the circle. The ratio of the circumference of any circle to its diameter is always the same. The ratio of the area of any circle to that of the square on its radius is also always a constant, and perhaps surprisingly it also has the same value as the previous ratio. The Sumerians, in 3000 BC, knew of this ratio and calculated it to be approximately 3. It is in fact both an *irrational number and a *transcendental number, nowadays commonly approximated by 3.142 or $\frac{22}{7}$. It has been evaluated to billions of decimal places by computer. Although the symbol $\pi$ was used during the 17th century, it was its use by *Euler in 1737 which promoted its general adoption as the symbol representing these two ratios.

**piedmonts**, areas at the foot of mountains, usually sloping gently away from the high ground. Several regions of the world are called 'Piedmont', notably the area of northern Italy at the foot of the Alps and that of the eastern USA between the Appalachian Mountains and the coastal plain.

**piezo-electric effect**, an effect shown by certain materials, which generate an electrical output when placed under mechanical sress. The phenomenon was discovered by the brothers Pierre and Jacques Curie in 1880. They found that crystals of quartz gave rise to a small voltage when compressed or stretched. Present-day applications include piezo-electric microphones, and the crystal pickups used in some record-players. In many clocks and watches the reverse effect is used—an alternating voltage causes a crystal to expand and contract rhythmically, thus providing the constant beat needed for accuracy.

**Pike, Zebulon Montgomery** (1779–1813), US army officer and explorer, born in New Jersey, who led two expeditions to survey the Louisiana Purchase of 1803. His first (1805–6) was into Minnesota, and his second (1806–7) into the south-west past Pike's Peak, which was named after him, and to the headwaters of the Arkansas River. On his return journey he was arrested by Spanish soldiers and deprived of all his records; but he wrote a book (1810) which described for the first time the region between the Great Plains and the upper Rio Grande valley.

**pion** (in atomic physics). In 1935 the Japanese physicist Hideki *Yukawa suggested that the strong nuclear *interaction could be regarded as the result of an interchange of certain particles between nucleons. These particles are now called pions. There are two types of pion: the charged pions, which can be either positively or negatively charged and have a mass 273 times that of the electron; and the neutral pions, which have a mass 264 times that of the electron. Pions have a lifetime of 30 nanoseconds. They belong to the class of particles known as *mesons.

**pitchblende**   *uraninite.

**plagioclase**, any of a series of minerals of the *feldspar group with a varied composition ranging from sodium aluminium silicate (albite) to calcium aluminium silicate (anorthite). They form a continuous series with a continuous gradation in their physical properties between albite and anorthite. Intermediate members are known as oligoclase, andesine, labradorite, and bytowntite. Plagioclase feldspars are common constituents of igneous rocks.

**plain**, an extensive area of flat or gently rolling ground where the difference in height between a valley floor and *divide is slight; it is different from a *plateau, which has much larger height differences. In many parts of the world plains are also defined as largely treeless expanses, for example the Great Plains of North America. Formed by erosion or by *deposition from rivers, glaciers, wind, or the sea, they may be underlain by rock layers whose surfaces are roughly parallel to the ground surface (in which case they are called structural plains) or they may be built or cut at an angle across the underlying strata. Small plains are formed along many coastlines and the lower reaches of rivers as the result

of erosion and deposition combined. Larger ones take millions of years to form; some of the most extensive plains in the world are found on the relatively stable blocks of extremely old rocks, such as the *Canadian Shield or in western Australia or southern Africa. Where they have fertile soils and suitable climates, they are ideal for agriculture, particularly for the cultivation of grain crops.

**Planck, Max Karl Ernst Ludwig** (1858–1947), German theoretical physicist, the originator of the *quantum theory which, with Albert *Einstein's general theory of relativity, forms the foundation of 20th-century physics. During the 1880s he published fundamental papers on thermodynamics before taking up the problem of *black-body radiation. The characteristic radiation spectra produced by such, in theory, perfect absorbers of radiant energy had confounded classical physicists. In 1900 he announced his 'radiation law', according to which this electromagnetic radiation was not emitted as a continuous flow but was made up of discrete units or 'quanta' of energy, and mathematical investigation showed that the size of these units involved a fundamental physical constant (Planck's constant). The quantum concept could now be invoked to explain atomic structure. Einstein applied it to the photoelectric effect, and Niels *Bohr to his model of the atom. For his achievement Planck received the 1918 Nobel Prize for Physics.

**plankton**, small to microscopic plants (phytoplankton) and animals (zooplankton) that drift passively in surface waters of oceans, seas and lakes, and form the base of aquatic food chains or webs.

**plasma** (in physics), a gas in which there is a large number of positively and negatively charged particles—usually positive *ions and free electrons in roughly equal numbers. This state can occur if a gas is in an intense electric field or if it is raised to extremely high temperatures. The outer regions of the Sun consist of a plasma of hydrogen. It is sometimes regarded as the fourth *state of matter.

**Plate, River**, an estuary some 270 km (170 miles) long between Uruguay and Argentina in south-east South America. A drowned river valley now forming part of the continental shelf, it is 30 km (20 miles) wide at its head, where it receives the Paraná and Uruguay Rivers and the water is fresh, and broadens to 190 km (120 miles) at its mouth at the Atlantic Ocean. Its rivers collectively drain a basin of nearly 4 million km² (1.5 million sq. mi.) and bring down huge quantities of silt which line its banks and form extensive sandbanks, especially in the south. At high tide as well as low tide this shoaling constitutes a great hazard to navigation.

**plateau**, an upstanding area of land often with a flattish surface and usually bounded by steep sides. Plateaux are normally formed by faulting, like *block mountains, but they can be the result of erosion taking place round them, or of volcanic action. Flat-topped plateaux, or tablelands, are common in limestone areas: as there are few surface rivers the strata tend to be worn down evenly. Mountainous plateaux, as in central Asia, are on the other hand normally crossed by streams. A plateau made of basaltic lava may be crossed by streams and yet be flat, because the lava flow has filled the original valleys made by the streams. Submarine plateaux may be fragments of continent which became detached from the adjacent continental land mass as a result of *plate tectonic processes. The Rochale Plateaux, for

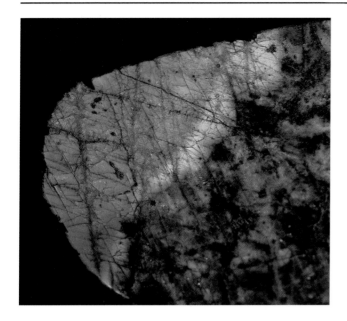

Labradorite is a **plagioclase** of the albite-anorthite series. The beautiful iridescence, known as labradorescence, is due to optical interference caused by minute inclusions in crystal.

example, may be part of the European continental mass which broke off during the opening of the Atlantic Ocean.

**plates of the Earth's crust**, large segments of the lithosphere (the *Earth's crust and upper mantle). They move slowly at rates of a few centimetres (an inch or two) a year with respect to the poles and to each other. This movement, which is probably caused by convection currents in the Earth's mantle, is one of the main topics in the study of *plate tectonics. There are eight major and many more minor plates, which together form the whole of the Earth's surface, including the ocean floors.

**plate tectonics**, a model of the Earth's crustal structure developed in the late 1960s to explain a number of observed features of both the continental surface and the sea-bed. It has its origins in theories of *continental drift, of changes in relative location and orientation of the continents (on evidence provided by study of the variations in the magnetic field of the Earth over time), and of patterns of earthquake activity. There was also increased knowledge of features of the sea-bed such as the *mid-oceanic ridges. One crucial link in the chain was the relationship between continental drift and crustal spreading on the sea floor; another was the shift from thinking in terms of continental units of crust to proposing a series of rigid *plates whose boundaries are marked by zones of intense seismic activity. Eight large plates, including the North American plate, the Eurasian plate, and the Indian plate, have been identified, as have many smaller ones. At the margins of two plates (see figure on page 262) interaction occurs, and may be of three kinds: constructive, where plates are separating and new plate material is added; destructive, where *subduction of one plate beneath another occurs; or conservative, where two plates slide past one another. The driving mechanism for plate movements is still not fully understood, but it is probably related to heat flow in the form of convection currents within the mantle. If this is so, the Earth's internal heat production will eventually become too small to sustain movement and its surface will become stable, as has already

happened with other planets (for example, Mars and the Moon) in the solar system.

**platforms, shore** *shore platforms.

**platinum** (symbol Pt, at. no. 78, r.a.m. 195.09), a silvery white, very malleable and ductile *transition metal long known in South Africa. Although sparse and therefore precious, it occurs naturally and in heavy metal sulphide ores from which it can be readily obtained by *reduction. Unaffected by simple acids and fusible only at very high temperatures, it is used in jewellery, electrical contacts, and laboratory ware; as a finely divided black powder called 'platinum black' it is employed as a catalyst in hydrogenation reactions. Platinum hexafluoride, $PtF_6$, is an extremely powerful oxidizing agent.

**Platte River**, a tributary of the Missouri River in Nebraska, USA, formed by the confluence of the North and South Platte rivers. Together with the North Platte and the South Platte which rise in the Rocky Mountains, its length is 1,480 km (920 miles). The system is important for hydroelectricity; but as the channels are generally shallow and braided, they cannot be used for navigation, and they are unsatisfactory as natural irrigators since the melt-water floods in spring and tends to evaporate in late summer.

**playa**, (Spanish, beach) an enclosed hollow in a desert or semi-desert area which contains shallow lakes from time to time, after rain. (The word is sometimes used to mean the lake and sometimes the lake bed.) The occasional floods bring not only water but fine sediment and dissolved salts into the hollow. When the water evaporates, clayey deposits are left and a layer of mineral crystals develops on their surface as the water disappears. These are often of salt or

This spectacular eruption from the Sun's surface consists mainly of hydrogen **plasma**. Although on Earth we are more familiar with solids, liquids, and gases than with plasmas, most of the mass of the universe—in stars and in interstellar space—is in fact made up of matter in the plasmatic state.

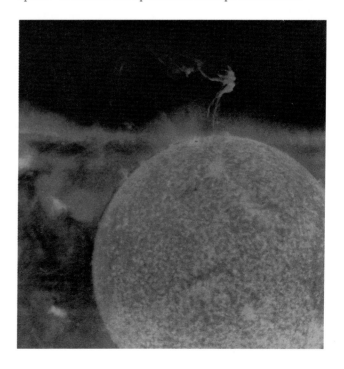

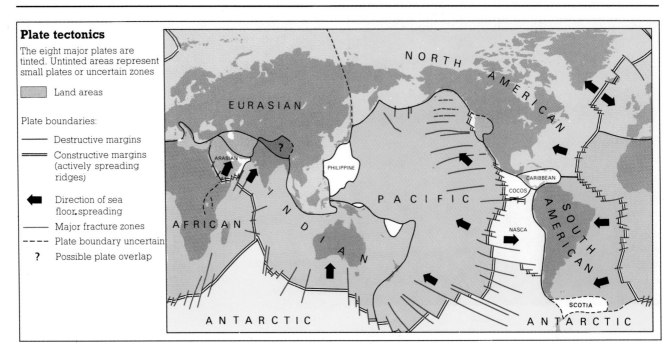

**Plate tectonics**

The eight major plates are tinted. Untinted areas represent small plates or uncertain zones

▨ Land areas

Plate boundaries:

— Destructive margins

═ Constructive margins (actively spreading ridges)

◀ Direction of sea floor spreading

— Major fracture zones

---- Plate boundary uncertain

? Possible plate overlap

gypsum, so that the surface of a playa is usually covered by a glittering white crust.

**Playfair, John** (1748–1819), British mathematician and philosopher of Scottish extraction, a friend of James *Hutton, whose ideas he clarified in *Illustrations of the Huttonian Theory of the Earth* (1802). Later work has not fundamentally altered the views presented there, particularly on the role of rivers in carving the landscape. As evidence that rivers make their own valleys, he noted that tributaries are cut to the same level as major valleys. This is Playfair's law; it can be used to distinguish the work of rivers from the *hanging valleys of glaciated areas.

**Pleistocene Epoch**, the earlier of the two epochs that constitute the *Quaternary Period and lasting approximately from 1.6 million to 10,000 years ago. It is known colloquially as the Ice Age and is characterized, especially in the northern hemisphere, by major ice advances and glaciations followed by periods of retreat, or interglacials. It was thought that there were only four or five major glacial advances during the Pleistocene, but it is now considered that there were at least eleven or twelve. The Pleistocene is also noted for the large number of mammalian species that became extinct, such as the mammoth and the mastodon. *Homo Sapiens* evolved at this time.

**Pliocene Epoch**, the last of the geological epochs of the *Tertiary Period, extending from 5.3 to 1.6 million years ago. It was a time when the temperature was falling and many of the species of mammals that had flourished earlier were becoming extinct. Both marine and freshwater Pliocene deposits are found in Europe. Those of the UK are shelly sands (the 'Crags' of East Anglia) and gravels.

**plutonic rock**, *igneous rock that has solidified at depth in the Earth's crust. Having cooled slowly, plutonic rocks are coarse-grained: *granites and *gabbros are typical plutonic rocks. A body of plutonic rock can be called a pluton, but this word has also been used in a narrower sense for a granite mass occurring at a relatively high level in the crust and more or less circular in plan.

**plutonium** (symbol Pu, at. no. 94, r.a.m. 244), one of the *transuranic elements and a member of the actinides. It was synthesized in 1940 and used in the atomic bomb dropped on Nagasaki in 1945. There are traces of the element in uranium ores, but it is produced on a larger scale from uranium-238 in nuclear reactors. There are now six known *allotropes, each with a differing density, coefficient of expansion, and resistivity. All the isotopes are radioactive, plutonium-239 having a *half-life of 24,360 years. Above a certain critical size, plutonium-239 can initiate a nuclear explosion; 1 kilogram has an energy potential of about $10^{14}$ joules. It is used as a nuclear fuel in the form of alloys. Plutonium-238, obtained from neptunium, is employed as a nuclear power source in space exploration.

**pluvials**, in climatic history, were extremely wet periods characterized by increased hydrological activity; they occurred in the low-latitude arid and semi-arid regions, while the higher latitudes were experiencing glaciation during the Pleistocene Epoch. They resulted either from a general decrease in temperature or from an absolute increase in precipitation. While they lasted, the area of the present desert regions was dramatically reduced, and features such as the North African *wadis are thought to have formed.

**Po**, Italy's longest river, rising on Monte Viso near the southern end of the Alps and traversing the north of the country to enter the Adriatic Sea after an eastward journey of nearly 670 km (416 miles). Its great valley includes the plains of Piedmont and Lombardy, which it irrigates and sometimes floods. Tributaries from the Alps and the Apennines bring it not only water but loads of sediment, which have raised its bed above the level of the surrounding country and have pushed its marshy delta well out to sea. For the last 480 km (300 miles) of its course the river is navigable by small craft.

**podzol**, a *zonal soil which occurs in the taiga or boreal forest regions of the world, where winters are cold, summers are relatively short, and the yearly rainfall between 500 and 800 mm (20 and 30 inches). The rainfall is sufficiently great to cause *leaching of even relatively insoluble minerals such as iron and aluminium from the upper part of the soil. This leaching results in the formation of a bleached, pale-coloured zone which may also be depleted of clay. The substances leached accumulate lower down the profile, where they may become cemented to form a *hardpan. Podzols are found in moorland areas of the UK, in mid-Canada, and in parts of Siberia.

**podzolic**, a *zonal soil which shows a gradual change in colour and clay content down the *profile. Podzolics are found in moist mid-latitude areas under deciduous woodlands. The upper part of the soil is usually pale and acidic because of the removal of soluble minerals by *leaching. These minerals accumulate lower down to form a brightly coloured clayey horizon. There are two main types: the grey-brown podzolics which are related to *brown earths, and the red-yellow podzolics which occur in slightly warmer climates. These soils are widely used for agriculture, together with the regular use of fertilizers.

**Poincaré, (Jules) Henri** (1854–1912), French mathematician, physicist, and astronomer who taught at the Sorbonne in Paris. One of the last of the 'universal' mathematicians, the breadth of his knowledge was vast; he chose to teach different subjects each year. His work in the qualitative theory of differential equations and in *analysis situs* (topology) laid the foundations for algebraic *topology. He published more than almost any other mathematician, both for his peers and for the general public.

**point bar**, a deposit of fine-grained sediment—usually clay and silt—left as a low, curved ridge on the inner, convex side of a meander bend. When a river is *meandering, its channel develops an asymmetrical cross-section around the bends. The deepest water is at the outer, concave side, where the bank is being undermined, and the channel shoals gradually towards the opposite, slip-off slope. In floods, the undercut banks tend to collapse, while sediment is deposited on the slip-off slopes. The effect is to shift the channel sideways and down-valley, leaving the point bars as additions to the floodplain.

**Poisson, Siméon Denis** (1781–1840), French mathematician and physicist who was a student of Joseph *Lagrange in Paris and taught at the newly formed École Polytechnique. His work in mathematical physics included celestial mechanics, particularly planetary motion, electricity, projectiles, and the theory of heat. His name is given to a statistical distribution which gives the probability of a given number of successes occurring when the number of events (successes or failures) increases indefinitely and the overall proportion of successes approaches a known value.

**Poland**, a country on the North European Plain with a Baltic Sea coast and bounded by Germany on the west, Russia, Lithuania, Belarus, and Ukraine on the east, and the Czech Republic and Slovakia on the south. The Plain is sandy in places, marshy in others and requires careful cultivation, although inland it is well drained by the Odra

---

**Plate tectonics**

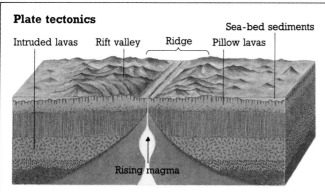

Sea-floor spreading. Slow-spreading ridges like the Atlantic have a central rift valley. More active ridges like the East Pacific Rise are more gently domed in cross-section, with thinner lava beds.

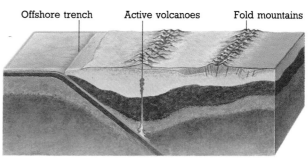

Subduction of an oceanic plate beneath a continent produces a deep offshore trench (e.g. the Peru-Chile Trench) and a parallel range of volcanically active fold mountains on land (e.g. the Andes).

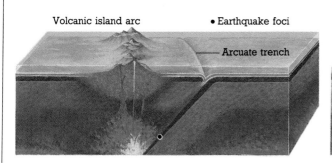

Subduction of one oceanic plate beneath another creates a deep arcuate trench, while melting of the descending plate causes volcanic activity and the formation of island arcs (e.g. the Philippines).

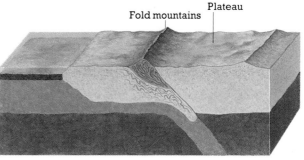

Ancient collision zones are marked by chains of intensely folded mountains (e.g. the Himalayas), often containing marine sediments that are the remains of ancient sea-beds crushed and uplifted by the collision.

## Plate margins

### Constructive plate margins

Spreading oceanic ridges allow magma to rise from the asthenosphere and form a new lithospheric layer.

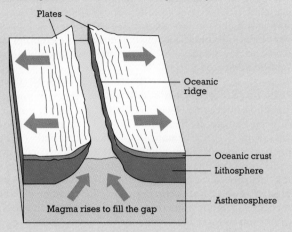

### Destructive plate margins

Either one plate is carried down into the asthenosphere beneath the other plate at a subduction zone, or one plate collides with another at a collision zone.

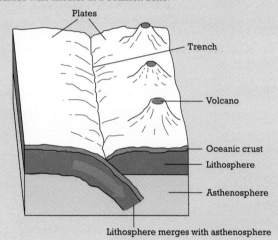

### Conservative plate margins

Sliding plates at transform faults result in an undisturbed lithosphere.

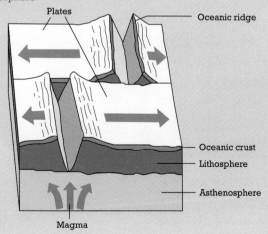

(Oder), Vistula, and other rivers. The climate is continental, with wide ranges of temperature. There are many small forests of spruce and fir, which increase in size as the land rises through rolling hills and richer land to the Carpathian Mountains in the south-east. Poland has extensive mineral resources, including sulphur, lead, and rock salt. It has substantial reserves of natural gas. Copper is found in great quantities, as is iron, while in Silesia in the south-west there is zinc as well as some of the largest bituminous and lignite coalfields in the world.

**polar coordinates** (in mathematics or geology), an alternative system to the more familiar *Cartesian coordinates for locating points in a plane. The reference line (see figure) is a rightward-pointing horizontal line with end-point O, the origin. The first coordinate of a point is its distance from the origin, and the second is the angle which the line from the point to the origin makes with the reference line, measured anticlockwise from the latter. The basis of polar coordinates is thus a distance and an angle rather than two distances. The coordinates are customarily written $(r, \theta)$, where $r \geq 0$ and is the distance from the origin, and $\theta$, with $0 \leq \theta > 360°$, is the angle. Many plane curves have a particularly simple expression in terms of this system. Circles are given by $r =$ constant, while some spirals are $r = K \theta$ ($K$ a constant). It is possible to convert from one coordinate description of a curve to the other by means of the relations $x = r \cos \theta$ and $y = r \sin \theta$. The polar system was first proposed by Isaac *Newton along with a number of alternatives which had less general application.

**polar front**, a zone approximately 160 km (100 miles) wide, separating polar and tropical *air masses in the troposphere. Generally located between latitudes 40° and 60° North and South of the Equator, these transitional zones slope polewards over the cold air and move towards the Equator in winter. The juxtaposition of cold and hot air gives rise to mid-latitude *depressions, most noticeably in the North Atlantic, where the zone can penetrate southward as far as 30° N. in winter.

**polarized light**, light in which the electric field has different amplitudes in different directions, taken at right angles to the direction of travel of the light. The amplitude of the magnetic field is similarly variable. If the electric field is always in a single direction or plane, the light is called plane-polarized, but other kinds of polarization are possible. In unpolarized light the electric field direction varies irregularly, so that overall it has the same amplitude in all transverse directions. The agents for this change are certain crystals, such as tourmaline, whose charged particles interact with the electric field. Polaroid lenses contain minute crystals which are aligned parallel to one another. Through them pass only those rays whose electric field points in a particular direction; all other light is absorbed.

**polar low**, a short-lived area of low pressure caused by a strong surface heating in unstable conditions. They commonly develop in winter above latitudes 60° N. and S. of the Equator, when polar or arctic air extends out across the ocean. They are associated with the development of cumulonimbus cloud and heavy showers of sleet and snow.

**polar molecules**, molecules which possess a *dipole moment. Polar molecules tend to attract one another, and so more energy is required to separate them; polar substances

## Polar coordinates

Polar coordinates and their trigonometric relationship to Cartesian coordinates.

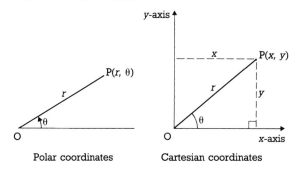

Polar coordinates          Cartesian coordinates

The point P may be defined by polar coordinates as occupying position $(r, \theta)$ or by Cartesian coordinates as occupying position $(x, y)$. By simple trigonometry, $x = r \cos \theta$ and $y = r \sin \theta$.

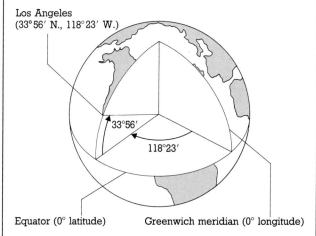

Los Angeles
(33° 56′ N., 118° 23′ W.)

Equator (0° latitude)        Greenwich meridian (0° longitude)

The idea of polar coordinates may be extended to three dimensions, with angles being measured from two axes at right-angles. Positions on the Earth's surface are thus defined by their angular distances from the Equator and the Greenwich meridian. Because the radius of the Earth is assumed to be a fixed distance, the angles alone are used. Degrees of longitude are measured east or west of Greenwich.

tend to have high boiling-points and to dissolve in polar solvents such as water.

**polder**, a piece of low-lying land reclaimed from the sea or a river, especially along the North Sea coast of The Netherlands. Procedures for ridding the soil of salt are employed before plants can grow in it. Ditches, dykes, and tide gates ensure that the land is not reflooded.

**pole** (in geometry), the point of reference, O, in a system of *polar coordinates, from which distances are measured. In addition, if any two tangents are drawn to a *conic section, the point where they meet exterior to the conic is called a pole, and the line formed by joining the two tangential points of contact is the 'corresponding polar'.

**polje**, a large, enclosed, flat-floored depression in limestone areas. Poljes are bigger than *dolines and usually have steep sides and are generally found in a *karst environment. These are sometimes breached by the channels of rivers which

then disappear underground. After very heavy rain, the rivers may back up and flood part of the flat floor. The depressions are caused by the solution of limestone by running water; and the rivers disappear underground because they have dissolved channels along the joints and faults in the rock.

**polonium** (symbol Po, at. no. 84, r.a.m. 210) was discovered by Marie *Curie in pitchblende and named after Poland, her birthplace. Polonium is a highly radioactive alpha-emitter with a *half-life of 103 years for the most stable isotope, polonium-209, and occurs in trace amounts in uranium deposits. Polonium-210 is made artificially and is used in satellites as an energy source.

**polygon**, a closed, geometric figure in the plane, all of whose sides are straight and only intersect at the corners (the vertices) in pairs. The number of edges, vertices, and angles is constant for any type of polygon. A regular polygon has equal sides and equal angles: common examples are equilateral triangles and squares. Circles can be regarded as at the limit of regular polygons, as the number of sides tends to infinity.

**polyhedron**, a closed solid figure, all of whose faces are *polygons. Regular polyhedra have faces which are congruent and there are only five possible forms: the tetrahedron, a pyramid with four equilateral triangular faces; the hexahedron, a cube with six square faces; the octahedron, with eight equilateral triangular faces; the dodecahedron, with twelve regular pentagonal faces; and the icosahedron, with twenty equilateral triangular faces.

**polymer**    *macromolecule.

**polymerization**, a chemical reaction in which a polymer is formed from two or more simple molecules, the *monomers, usually of one or two compounds. There are two principal types of polymerization. In addition polymerization, molecules with double (or triple) bonds undergo addition reactions (see *chemical reaction), with molecules of either the same compound or another compound. These molecules join together to form a long chain, the polymer. In so doing, the double bonds are replaced by single bonds. The polymer is thus an alkane, with a long carbon chain typically consisting of hundreds of carbon atoms. An example is provided by the polymerization of ethene, $CH_2{=}CH_2$. Under suitable conditions, it polymerizes to form polyethene, or polythene. In this long hydrocarbon chain, the simplest repeating unit that uniquely defines the structure is the $-CH_2-$ group, so the formula of the polymer is given by $(-CH_2-)_n$, where $n$ denotes the number of such groups joined together. Condensation polymerization involves the monomers undergoing condensation reactions (see *chemical eaction). In other words, each time a new bond is formed between the molecules, a simple molecule is eliminated from between them. The monomer molecules must possess at least two *functional groups, which can be either the same or different. Then each monomer can form a new bond in at least two different places, and thus a long chain can develop. For example, when a carboxylic acid and an alcohol react, they condense to form an ester, a molecule of water being eliminated; and if a molecule with two carboxyl groups reacts with one with two hydroxyl groups, they undergo condensation polymerization to form a polyester, such as Terylene.

**Polynesia** *South Seas.

**polynomial**, an expression in algebra which contains several terms added together (or subtracted), especially where the terms have different *powers. The following expression $7x^3 + 4x^2 + 5x - 3 = 79$ is a polynomial equation of degree 3 (the degree is determined by the $x$ term(s) with the highest power). The number in front of each x term is its coefficient (here it is 7 for the $x^3$ term). Polynomials have an important place in mathematics. Elementary shapes such as circles, ellipses, parabolas, and so on (see*conic sections), are described mathematically by polynomial equations; *power series such as the *binomial expansion are polynomials; and some families of polynomials, for example, the Hermite and the Legendre polynomials, are solutions to certain *differential equations that arise in science and engineering. The system we use for writing numbers uses the notion of polynomials. For example, 50,762 means $(5 \times 10^4) + (0 \times 10^3) + (7 \times 10^2) + (6 \times 10^1) + (2 \times 10^0)$.

**Popocatepetl**, a dormant, snow-covered volcano 72 km (45 miles) south-east of Mexico City. It is Mexico's second highest mountain at 5,452 m (17,887 feet) above sea-level. It last erupted over three hundred years ago, but still periodically emits cloud and smoke from its sulphur-filled crater. The volcanic activity is related to the Mexican subduction zone, where the Pacific *plate is moving under the North American plate.

**porosity**, the capacity of a rock to hold water. This is measured as the ratio of free space (voids between the mineral grains) to its total volume. Porosity is important in connection with water supply because it limits the rock's capacity to transmit water or to store it. Measurement is normally expressed as a percentage. The theoretical lower limit for a perfectly packed sediment with even grains is 27 per cent and the upper limit 47 per cent. In practice sediments are often cemented, and their porosities can range from 1 per cent to about 50 per cent.

**porphyry** (or porphyrite), a general term applied to any medium- to coarse-grained *igneous rock in which large, well-formed crystals are surrounded by a mass of much finer crystals: this is a porphyritic texture. The word 'porphyry' is also applied loosely to hard, white and purple rocks used by sculptors.

**Portland stone**, a light-coloured limestone of Jurassic age. The rock cuts easily and is a popular building stone. Extensively quarried in the Isle of Portland in the southof the UK, it has been used in many great buildings, notably St Paul's Cathedral in London.

**Portugal**, a west European country on the Atlantic west coast of the Iberian Peninsula, flanked by Spain on the north and east. Half of the country lies on the edge of the high and ancient Iberian plateau, in a region of rugged hills, lakes, and deep gorges. Winters are cold here, and there is moderate rain. Much of the region is covered with forests of pine and cork-oak, and from it flow three great rivers—the Douro, Tagus, and Guadiana—which water the flat and sandy coastal plain. Here it is warm, although still fairly dry; vineyards flourish, as do cereals and citrus fruits. *Pyrites form the country's main mineral resource, although there are also deposits of several other metallic ores as well as sodium and coal.

**positron**, an *antiparticle of an electron, having the same mass but a positive charge. Positrons occurring in cosmic-ray showers exist only briefly. They soon collide with electrons and are thus annihilated, producing two or three *photons. A positron can form a short-lived stable system with an electron, somewhat analogous to a hydrogen atom. This is called a positronium. Its *half-life is of the order of $10^-$ second.

**postulate** (in mathematics), a statement made at the outset of a mathematical development that is assumed for the ensuing discussion. In *Euclid's *Elements* there are five listed postulates, the fifth, the parallel postulate, being justly renowned in terms of the amount of mathematics it generated. The first three are constructions which it is assumed can always be made. Aristotle distinguished between *axioms and postulates, and Euclid's *Elements* separates postulates from common notions, but modern mathematics no longer makes these distinctions.

**potash** (potassium carbonate, $K_2CO_3$), a term misleadingly used to describe potassium, as in 'potash feldspar'. Potassium carbonate used to be obtained as an alkaline substance by leaching vegetable ashes and evaporating the solution in iron—hence the name, 'pot ash'. Caustic potash is potassium hydroxide, KOH.

**potassium** (symbol K, at. no. 19, r.a.m. 39.10), a soft, silvery element and a member of the *alkali metals. It tarnishes quickly in air and reacts violently with water, and so is stored under paraffin to avoid contact with water vapour. In the flame test it gives a lilac flame. Because it is highly reactive it is usually encountered in its compounds. Potassium is essential for living systems, especially cell processes, and its compounds are used extensively in fertilizers. When it is alloyed with sodium, the molten mixture has a high *specific heat which makes it useful as a coolant in nuclear reactors.

**potassium hydroxide** (or caustic potash, KOH), a white, crystalline *base that is readily soluble in water, giving a strong alkali. It is prepared in the laboratory by react-

Looking into the crater of **Popocatepetl**, estimated at over 0.8 km (0.5 miles) in circumference.

**Potassium chlorate** is used in fireworks because, on heating, it gives off combustion-sustaining oxygen.

ing potassium with water and industrially by the electrolysis of potassium chloride solution. Its chemical properties are similar to *sodium hydroxide, NaOH, although it is more soluble; and it is used in soap-making and as an electrolyte in batteries.

**potassium nitrate** ($KNO_3$), a white crystalline salt, also known by the older names of nitre and saltpetre. The salt is not naturally abundant and is therefore synthesized by fractional crystallization from a solution of sodium nitrate, $NaNO_3$, and potassium chloride, KCl. It is used in the manufacture of fireworks, gunpowder, and types of glass.

**potassium permanganate** ($KMnO_4$), a dark purple crystalline solid; the intense colour is due to the permanganate ion $MnO_4^-$. It is soluble in water and is a powerful *oxidizing agent. It is useful in *titrations because its colour changes when all the permanganate is reduced. This means the analysis requires no *indicator.

**potential difference** (p.d.), the difference in electric potential between two points in an electric field. It is defined by the work that must be done to move a unit charge from one to the other. In the *SI system it is measured in joules per coulomb, or *volts (V), and potential difference is commonly called voltage.

**potential energy**, the ability of an object to do work because of its position. For an object of mass $m$ that is $h$ metres above the surface of the Earth, the potential energy will be $mgh$, where $g$ is the *acceleration due to gravity. In the *SI system it is measured in joules. The concept of potential energy can be applied to a wide range of situations in which there is a potential for work to be done—for example, in a stretched spring awaiting release. Its potential energy is converted to *kinetic energy as the spring is released and returns rapidly to its original length.

**pothole**, a funnel-shaped hole in limestone where it has been dissolved by water, usually at the junction of two joint systems—that is, where cracks in the rock meet. Underground there are sometimes passages at different levels, often water-filled, connected by nearly vertical shafts. Potholes in the beds of rivers and glaciers are formed when rocks and pebbles are swirled round by eddies, because water alone can erode only soft material.

**Potomac**, the river of Washington DC, USA, 459 km (285 miles) long. Formed by a junction of streams from the Appalachian Mountains it flows south-eastward between Maryland and Virginia to Washington, DC, where it enters a 200-km (125-mile) tidal estuary before reaching Chesapeake Bay. In its upper reaches it cuts a picturesque gorge through the Blue Ridge Mountains at Harper's Ferry, where it is joined by its chief tributary, the Shenandoah. The Great Falls, a series of cascading rapids, are set in a gorge 60 m (200 feet) deep; they lie some 24 km (15 miles) above the estuary and prevented navigation inland by the early settlers.

**Powell, John Wesley** (1834–1902), US ethnologist, geologist, and administrator. His description of the Colorado canyons (1875) and his leadership of the US Geological Survey did much to encourage understanding of both geology and geomorphology. As a scientist and administrator, he spent many years advising on the best ways to develop and conserve the resources of the western USA, warning particularly against soil *erosion. As an ethnologist, he published the first comprehensive classification and distribution map of north American Indian languages (1891).

**power** (in physics), the rate of doing work, or, alternatively, the rate of transfer of energy. If one machine does the same amount of work as another, but in half the time, it has twice the power. Power is a *scalar quantity measured in *watts, a watt being one joule per second. Light bulbs are rated in terms of their wattage, as is the output from an amplifier or an electric fire. It is the rate at which the device uses energy.

This distinction between power and energy is different from everyday usage, where they are almost synonyms.

**power** (in mathematics), the product obtained when a number is multiplied by itself a certain number of times. The third power of 2, or two to the power of three, is $2 \times 2 \times 2$, written $2^3$, that is 8. The sixth power of 10, written as $10^6$, is $10 \times 10 \times 10 \times 10 \times 10$, or 1,000000.

**power series**, a mathematical *series in which each term contains a power of $x$. For example, $x - x^3/3! + x^5/5! - x^7/7! + \ldots$ is a power series which converges for all values of $x$ and gives numerical values equal to sin $x$ if $x$ is in radians (the notation 3!, or *factorial 3, $= 3 \times 2 \times 1$). A power series is an infinite *polynomial. Isaac *Newton believed his work on power series, particularly the *binomial expansion, to be among his most significant mathematical achievements.

**prairie soil**, or brunizem, a *zonal soil in sub-humid grassland areas where rainfall is between 600 and 1,000 mm (25 and 40 inches) a year. The presence of abundant organic matter causes the surface *horizons of this soil to be very dark, and there is a gradual shading into lighter-coloured lower horizons with less humus. Although some of the more soluble soil components, particularly calcium, may be washed downwards, the rainfall in sub-humid areas is insufficient to cause excessive *leaching. Like *chernozems, which they resemble, these soils are very fertile. They occur extensively in the corn-growing areas of Iowa and southern Minnesota, USA.

**Precambrian Era**, the period of time before the *Phanerozoic, hypothetically including all the Earth's history from some 4,600 million years ago to 570 million years ago. It is subdivided into the *Archaean and *Proterozoic aeons. Characteristically exposed in continental interiors (*shields), the Precambrian was once considered to be devoid of organic life but it is now known to contain a variety of organisms, including algae, microfossils, and, in the late Precambrian, traces of animals.

**precession of the equinoxes**, the movement of the *equinoxes westward round the ecliptic as the axis of the spinning Earth slowly rotates about its mean or average position. In the same way as a top wobbles or precesses about the vertical, so the earth wobbles about the perpendicular to the plane of its orbit. Its axis is inclined at an angle of $23° 27'$ to this perpendicular, and it rotates about it slowly, once every 26,000 years. The cause is the gravitational attraction of the Sun and Moon on the Earth's equatorial bulge (its *oblateness); but the precession is so slow that the movement of the celestial pole against the stars is apparent only to astronomers and is not appreciable without instruments even in a lifetime. At present the north celestial pole is about one degree from the star Alpha Ursae Minoris (Polaris). It will approach it until the year 2100 (when it will be half a degree from it), and then will begin to move further away again, describing its slow circle among the stars at a rate of about 50 seconds of arc per year. Since the equinoxes are the two points on the ecliptic where the plane of the Equator intersects it, so, as the Earth's axis moves, they precess round the ecliptic at the same rate of $50''$ a year.

**precipitation** (in meteorology), the rain, snow, sleet, or hail falling through the atmosphere to the ground. It occurs when particles which have formed in a *cloud have grown too large for upcurrents of air within the cloud to support them. The reasons why air rises, causing the water vapour in it to condense, are various; and the different mechanisms involved generally determine the nature of the precipitation. In cumulonimbus (heaped) clouds, such as arise in *tropical revolving storms, precipitation results from convection. The clouds form fairly rapidly, and the rates at which condensation occurs and precipitation falls are rarely equal. The result is showers, often short-lived and of varying intensity. Nimbostratus (layered) cloud, on the other hand, is usually formed by *advection, as, for example, when air travels over a colder land or sea surface, or by the *orographic effect of its flow up hillsides. The result may be a light but persistent drizzle, the rates of condensation and fall being equal. In *depressions, air rises because of the horizontal convergence of two air masses. The types of cloud will depend on the nature of the associated front. A warm front will have a thick layer of cloud and may give steady and continuous precipitation. A cold front may include cumulonimbus and give heavier and more intense precipitation. It is an essential part of the *hydrological cycle.

**precipitation** (in chemistry), the formation, in a solution, of solid particles that fall to the bottom as a precipitate. It may occur as a result of a chemical reaction between two solutions, or a solution and a gas, to form one or more products insoluble in the solvent. Alternatively the state of a solvent may be changed so that the solubility of the solute in it is reduced. Precipitation is frequently used to extract metal ions from solution. For example, when sodium chloride, NaCl, is added to a solution of silver nitrate, $AgNO_3$, a white precipitate of silver chloride, AgCl, is formed. The process of quantitative gravimetric analysis is based upon the production of highly pure and easily separable precipitates. A known quantity of reagent may be added to a known volume of solution of unknown concentration; the resulting precipitate is accurately weighed, and if the reaction *stoichiometry is known, the concentration of the solution can be calculated. Precipitation methods are also used in separations, using filters or centrifuges, and to show end-points in *titrations.

**Pregl, Fritz** (1869–1930), Austrian chemist who was given the Nobel Prize for Chemistry in 1923 for his work on microchemical methods of analysis. Until the early part of the 20th century, analysis in organic chemistry required large quantities of pure compounds. Pregl refined combustion analysis so that only milligrams were required, and the techniques he devised contributed greatly to subsequent progress.

**pressure**, the force per unit area experienced on a surface at any particular spot. *Atmospheric pressure is the force produced by the weight of all the air above the spot, so the greater the altitude the less is the pressure. The pressure of a solid on a solid is in proportion to the size of the area of contact. The pressure in a liquid is the product of its density and the depth multiplied by the *acceleration due to gravity.

The *SI unit of pressure is the pascal (Pa), which is defined as 1 newton per square metre. Atmospheric pressure at sea-level has the value of 101,325 Pa. In meteorology a commonly used unit is the millibar (mb), which is equal to 100 Pa. Thus atmospheric pressure can be stated, in this form, as 1013.25 mb. A unit that is used in some barometers, and in the measurement of blood pressure, is the millimetre of mercury (mmHg); atmospheric pressure is given as 760 mmHg, this being the height of a column of mercury that the atmosphere can support under standard conditions.

**Priestley, Joseph** (1733–1804), British chemist who discovered and identified most of the common gases, including oxygen, hydrogen chloride, ammonia, sulphur dioxide, and nitrogen monoxide. He supported the phlogiston theory of combustion, later proved to be false by Antoine *Lavoisier. This theory assumed that all combustible substances contained phlogiston which was given off during burning. Hence when he isolated oxygen in 1774 he called it 'dephlogisticated air'. In his *History of Electricity* (1767) he proposed the law of electric attraction and explained the formation of rings (known as Priestley's rings) when a discharge takes place on a metallic surface. He had many other interests and first trained and worked as a Presbyterian minister and wrote many books on theology. He espoused what eventu-

ally became known as Unitarianism. His support of the French revolution provoked so much hostility that he left England in 1794 and settled in America.

**prime meridian**    *Greenwich meridian.

**prime number**, a whole number other than 1 which has no divisors (factors) other than 1 and itself; the first prime numbers being 2, 3, 5, 7, and 11. All other whole numbers (called composite) can be expressed as a number of primes multiplied together, and this process is called prime decomposition. One can show that there are infinitely many prime numbers as follows. Given any prime $p$, its product with all the preceding primes, plus 1, will give a number which is not divisible by any of those primes. Therefore it is either prime itself or has a prime factor larger than $p$. So whatever prime we can find, there is always a larger one. It has been conjectured that every even number greater than 2 is a sum of two

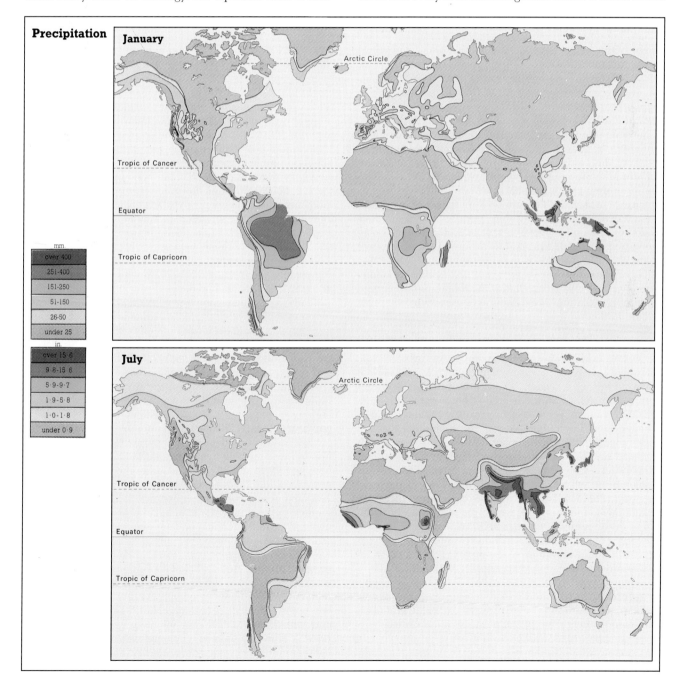

**Precipitation**

**January**

**July**

mm.
over 400
251-400
151-250
51-150
26-50
under 25

in.
over 15·8
9·8-15·6
5·9-9·7
1·9-5·8
1·0-1·8
under 0·9

primes, yet although this appears to be likely, and has never been disproved, a proof has yet to be found. The *polynomial $x^2 + x + 41$ has the interesting property that substituting whole-number values up to 39 for $x$ always produces prime numbers.

**Prince Edward Island**, the smallest province of Canada, cradled in the southern part of the Gulf of Saint Lawrence. Unlike the mainland, on the other side of the Northumberland Strait, it is almost devoid of hills and there is much farmland, the soil of which is characteristically red.

**Pripet Marshes**, in southern Belarus, the largest tract of swampland in Europe. It was a region of reeds and coarse grass through which waters from the melting ice-sheets of the last ice age made their way. The Pripet River and its tributaries, with the application of technology, have since been made to drain much of the swamp and make it cultivable. It is now mainly a region of forests with clearings, lakes, and a network of canals.

**probability**, a measure of the relative likelihood of an event. An impossibility is said to have a probability of 0, whereas a certainty has probability 1. In between are events that are more or less probable. The basis of probability theory is first to assign numerical values to some simple events, often on the basis of equal likelihood, and then to find ways to calculate more complicated probabilities from them. The probability of getting any particular face on a die is 1 in 6; and from this can be calculated the chance of a total score of 8 from the throw of two dice. If two events are independent then their relative probabilities are multiplied to give the chance of their both occurring. If on the other hand they are alternative outcomes to the same event, then their respective probabilities are added. The probability of getting two sixes is $\frac{1}{6} \times \frac{1}{6}$, or 1 in 36. The chance of a four or a five occurring in one throw is $\frac{1}{6} + \frac{1}{6}$, or 1 in 3. Probability attempts to quantify the inherent but predictable variability in many real-life situations and is the foundation of certain modern physical theories such as thermodynamics and *quantum theory.

**profile** (in geology), a vertical section through the soil from the surface down to the parent material. All the successive horizontal layers, or *horizons, which make up the soil are displayed in such a section. The depth of the profile varies from soil to soil, as do the degree of horizon development and the characteristics of the various horizons. *Chernozems, for example, have very deep profiles, each with a thick, black, highly organic upper horizon, while desert soils are relatively shallow, with poorly defined horizons and little organic matter. Many soils, then, have characteristic profiles by which they are recognizable. One of the most important characteristics of a soil is the degree of profile development, the ease with which the individual horizons can be distinguished from one another. Profile development is a record of the processes which have acted or are still acting on the soil. Description of the profile is therefore necessary in order to understand how a soil is formed.

**projection, map**, any method used to map the curved surface of the Earth on to a plane surface with the minimum of distortion. Simple graphical projections can be made by fitting a plane surface around a sphere in a variety of ways, for example, as a cylinder or cone (see figure on page 270). If the detail on the sphere is now projected on to the plane

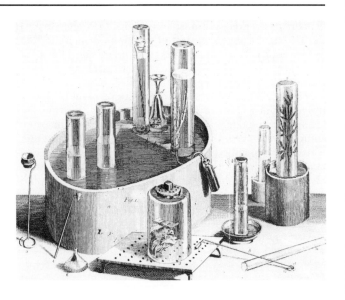

Some of the apparatus used by Joseph **Priestley** in his investigations of air, as illustrated in his *Experiments and Observations on Different Kinds of Air* published between 1774 and 1777.

surface, the points at which it touches the sphere are mapped without distortion, while elsewhere there is some distortion of scale, bearing, shape or area. Most projections used in map- and chart-making use mathematical methods based on simple graphical projections but with their formulae adjusted in some way. For example, in some projections there is no distortion of the true shape of the land (orthomorphic projections), while in others the relative areas of the different land masses remain constant (equal area projection). Orthomorphic projections are essential for surveying and navigation, because angles around any point on the map or chart are correctly represented. In navigation this is essential for the plotting of bearings, while in surveying it is necessary for accurately plotting details of triangulation.

Probably the best-known projection is that of Gerardus *Mercator, a cylindrical one, which is used for charts and navigation because on it lines of constant bearing—rhumb lines—are straight and easy to plot. But for this the meridians have to be parallel and not converge towards the poles, and so the scale increases rapidly in high latitudes, making Greenland much too large and the Antarctic impossible to show correctly, since at the poles the scale is infinitely large.

**propane** ($C_3H_8$), a colourless, flammable gas, and the third member of the *alkane series. Separated in large quantities from natural gas and light crude oil, it liquefies under pressure and can therefore be conveniently stored and transported in tanks. It is an excellent fuel and is used in the home and for internal-combustion engines. It is also used in the synthesis of ethene, which in turn is used as the starting material for the chemical synthesis of polythene and many other polymers.

**propanone** (acetone, $CH_3 \cdot CO \cdot CH_3$), a colourless, low boiling-point, highly flammable liquid with a characteristic pungent odour. It was originally made by distilling wood, but is now produced commmercially by fermentation of corn or molasses, or by controlled *oxidation of hydrocarbons. It is widely used as a solvent; as a remover of paint, varnish, and fingernail polish; and in the manufacture of drugs.

**Proterozoic Aeon**, a division of *Precambrian time: the time-interval from 2,500 million years ago to the end of the Precambrian (570 million years ago).

**proton**, a *nucleon, that is, one of the two types of particle (the other being a neutron) which forms the nucleus of an atom. A proton has a mass of $1.67 \times 10^{-27}$ kg (about 1,836 times that of the electron) and a spin of $\frac{1}{2}$. The number of protons in the nucleus determines its total positive charge and in a neutral atom this charge is exactly balanced by the negative charge of the electrons round the nucleus. The atomic number of an *element is given by the number of protons in the nucleus. Different *isotopes of an element contain the same number of protons but different numbers of neutrons. The nuclei of hydrogen atoms are isolated protons, and in nuclear and particle physics they are accelerated to very high energies to act as bombarding particles to initiate nuclear reactions.

**Ptolemy** (*c*.90–168), Greek astronomer and geographer, who worked in Alexandria. His major work, known by its Arabic title the *Almagest*, was a complete textbook of astronomy based on the geocentric system of Hipparchus. His teachings had enormous influence on medieval thought, the geocentric view of the cosmos being adopted as Church doctrine until the late Renaissance. Besides placing the Earth at the centre of the universe and explaining the motions of the planets by combining individual circular motions, the *Almagest* included detailed tables of lunar and solar motion with eclipse predictions, and a star catalogue giving the positions and magnitudes (graded from 1 to 6) of 1022 stars. Ptolemy's *Geography*, giving lists of places with their longitudes and latitudes, was also a standard work for centuries, despite its inaccuracies.

**Puerto Rico**, an island commonwealth in the Caribbean Sea, between Hispaniola and the Virgin Islands. Its west–east length is some 180 km (112 miles) and its north–south width about 60 km (37 miles) at the widest point. Its climate is tropical: hot and very wet, with occasional storms and hurricanes. The coast offers good harbours and the coastal plains are fertile, yielding sugarcane, sweet potatoes, and maize. In the interior highlands rise to 1,220 m (4,000 feet) and more; coffee and tobacco are grown on their slopes.

**pumice**, a volcanic rock formed when (usually acid) lava is expelled violently into the air during the initial gas-rich phase of an eruption. When solidified it contains many holes which make the rock very light; it can be carried long distances in the air and sea. Its main use is as an abrasive.

**Purbeck marble**, a limestone of *Jurassic Age found at Purbeck, in the south of the UK. It is completely unmetamorphosed and is therefore not a marble in the true geological sense. When cut and polished it is used as a facing stone in the building industry.

**Pyrenees**, mountains on the Franco–Spanish boundary, stretching for over 400 km (250 miles) between the Bay of Biscay and the Mediterranean Sea. The width of the ranges is about 100 km (62 miles) and the passes over them are steep, particularly on the northern side. Here they have deep, narrow valleys, forested and with cascades falling down their sides. The southern slopes are gentler and drier, with fewer trees, and there are several sizeable rivers. The

---

**Soil profiles**

The top diagram is a generalized soil profile showing the main layers, or horizons, and the physical processes by which they are defined; the lower diagrams are profiles of three particular soil types.

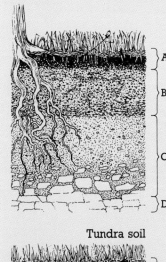

A: Leaf litter, humus, and top soil. Minerals are leached from this horizon

B: Mineral soil with humus layers and roots. Leached minerals are deposited in this layer

C: Parent rock broken down by frost, chemical processes, and root action

D: Unaltered parent rock

Tundra soil

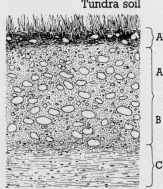

$A_o$ Peat and humus

A

Unstratified waterlogged soil

B

C Permanently frozen subsoil (permafrost)

Podzol

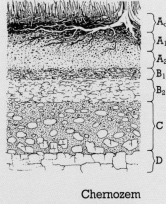

$A_o$ Litter and humus

$A_1$ Mineral and organic material mixed

$A_2$ Bleached horizon

$B_1$ Redeposited organic material from above

$B_2$ Redeposited iron and aluminium

C Broken-down parent rock

D Parent rock

Chernozem

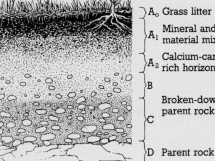

$A_o$ Grass litter

$A_1$ Mineral and organic material mixed

$A_2$ Calcium-carbonate-rich horizon

B

C Broken-down parent rock

D Parent rock

## Projection, map

The network of parallels of latitude and meridians of longitude (collectively called the graticule) from a globe may be projected on to a plane surface. There is no distortion at the standard parallel where the plane surface touches the globe.

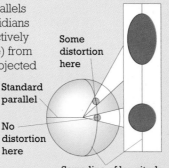

Some distortion here

Standard parallel

No distortion here

Same line of longitude

### Peters projection

Equator

A mathematically derived projection showing the relative sizes of the land masses.

### Modified conical

Standard parallels

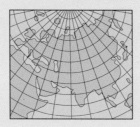

A conical projection, but with two standard parallels. Widely used in atlases for mapping small countries.

### Mercator

Equator

Standard parallel

Based on a cylindrical projection with the equator as the standard parallel. Widely used for navigational charts, but has large scale distortions at high latitudes.

### Transverse Mercator

Standard longitude

Equator

Based on a cylindrical projection at a chosen standard longitude. Widely used for sea-navigation charts. Can be used to map the poles.

western and eastern mountains are lower than the central range, which contains Andorra and rises to 3,404 m (11,168 feet) at the Pico de Aneto in Spain. Formed during the Tertiary Period, the peaks and core of the rampart are of old hard rock such as granite; but younger sandstones and folded limestones occur on the outer flanks. Iron ore, zinc, bauxite, and talc are all found below the permanent snowline, which is at 2,000 m (6,500 feet). Evidence of glacial action is best seen at Gavarnie in France, where the ice once carved out a great *cirque.

**pyrite** (iron pyrites), an iron sulphide mineral ($FeS_2$), yellow-gold in colour, and with a cubic crystal form (also known as fool's gold). It is hard and will spark if hit with a hammer. Pyrite is very common and splendid crystals exist world-wide. It is currently used in the production of sulphuric acid, but it has been mined as an ore of sulphur.

**pyroclast**, a fragment of lava that has been ejected from a volcano and blown into the atmosphere. When ejected in a molten state pyroclasts quickly cool and form *pumice, *scoria, *volcanic bombs, or hairs. If already solid when ejected they produce ashes and *ignimbrites. Rocks that are formed in this way are termed pyroclastic rocks.

**pyroxene**, a mineral group which includes some of the most common rock-forming silicates. The group contains six main members (enstatite, ferrosilite, diopside, augite, pigeonite, and jadeite) of varying chemical formulae, most of which combine magnesium and calcium with iron or aluminium (or both) in the silicate structure. Pyroxenes occur both in igneous and in metamorphic rocks.

**Pythagoras** (c.495–c.570) Greek mathematician and philosopher. His doctorine that 'all things are numbers' rejected the surface appearance of things as illusory: guenuine knowledge of the nature of things, and so appreciation of the underlying order of the world, could be had only by understanding them in arithmetical terms. Pythagoras' view was inspired by his development of the arithmetical theory of harmony in music. Other theories attributed to him (for example, the incommensurability of the side and diagonal of a square, and the Pythagorean theorem of triangles which states that square on the hypotenuse of a right-angled

A map of the world, published c.1508, over 1,300 years after the death of **Ptolemy**, still incorporates his errors in cartographic projection.

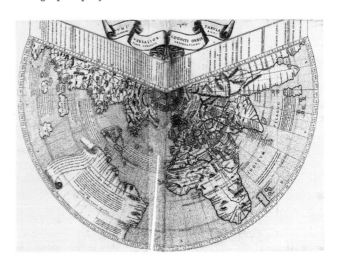

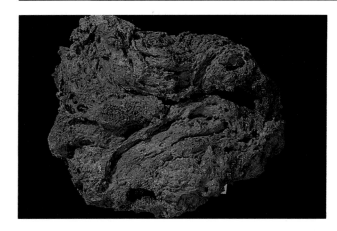

A volcanic bomb: one of the many forms of **pyroclast** ejected from volcanoes. The wrinkled skin was formed as the molten bomb cooled—a process that also preserved the dozens of small vents and cavities produced by bubbles of escaping gas. The bomb illustrated is 17 cm (6.6 in.) long and comes from Iceland.

triangle is equal to the sum of the squares on the other two sides) were probably developed only later by those at the Pythagorean school. The latter was based at Croton (now Crotona) in southern Italy. In astronomy, his analysis of the courses of the Sun, Moon, and stars into circular motions was not set aside until the 17th century.

**Pytheas** (*fl.*300 BC), Greek navigator, geographer, and astronomer; the first Greek to visit and describe the Atlantic coast of Europe and the British Isles. Born at Massalina, Gaul (Marseille, France), Pytheas sailed from the Mediterranean into the Atlantic, stopping at the Phoenecian city of Gades (Cadiz, Spain), and on to Belerium (Land's End, UK) where he visited the tin mines of Cornwall, famous in the ancient world. Claiming to have explored a large part of the British Isles on foot, he accurately estimated its circumference as 6,400 km (4,000 miles). He was one of the first to fix *latitudes by observing the Sun's altitude at a given time of day, to note that the Pole Star is not at the true pole, and to realize that *tides are connected with the Moon.

**Qatar**, a hot, arid country of Arabia, occupying a peninsula of desert on the south of the Gulf. It is bounded by Saudi Arabia inland and has a sea boundary with Bahrain to its west. Oil is present in very large quantities, both on-shore and off-shore.

**Qattara Depression**, a vast and arid basin, the lowest point on the surface of Africa, formed by *deflation, in the Libyan Desert of north-west Egypt. Some 290 km (180 miles) from south-west to north-east and 120 km (75 miles) wide, it reaches a depth of 133 m (436 feet) below sea-level. A region of soft sand, salt lakes, and marshes, it is almost impassable.

**quantum mechanics**, the general mathematical technique which is used to calculate the way atomic and subatomic particles move when they are acted on by *forces, especially those produced by electric or magnetic fields. It is particularly useful for predicting the energies of electrons in their charge clouds surrounding the nucleus of the *atom. The size and shape of the charge cloud can also be determined. The principle underlying the mathematics is that the particle is represented by a wave which can either extend over a large distance or be a short pulse which is localized at one place. The *amplitude of the wave at any point is a measure of the probability that the particle will be at that point, and the wavelength of the wave is a measure of its momentum (and hence its energy): the shorter the wavelength, the greater the momentum. Since a wave must always extend a certain distance, be it large (for an extended wave) or small (for a pulse), it follows that the position of a particle it represents cannot be fixed or known precisely; and this can be seen as one explanation of the *uncertainty principle.

**quantum number,** any of the integral or half-integral numbers which are used to express the magnitude (in terms of *Planck's constant) of physical quantities that cannot be subdivided, especially those of an electron in its charge cloud around the nucleus of an atom, but also of all the other *elementary particles. The numbers give a measure of various attributes of a particle, some of which could be envisaged in terms of the properties of macroscopic bodies. For electrons these attributes are angular momentum (denoted by $l$), magnetic moment ($m$), and spin ($s$), because in many ways they obey the same rules as those quantities do in our macroscopic world. In particle physics, however, further attributes or quantum numbers are required in order to account for all the phenomena. These cannot be associated with anything with which we are familiar. This has resulted in the coining of whimsical terms such as charm, strangeness, and colour, which bear no relation to the every-day meaning of those words.

**quantum theory,** the body of theory based on the existence of quanta of energy. It originated with the ideas of Max *Planck and Albert *Einstein. Planck suggested that electromagnetic energy can be gained or lost only in discrete quanta or packets called *photons. This enabled him to explain the spectral distribution of the radiation emitted by a body at any given temperature. Einstein took the idea a step further and proposed that all forms of energy exist as quanta, and this notion was used with success by him and by the Dutch physicist Peter Debye (1884–1966) to calculate the energy of vibrating atoms and the *heat capacity of solids. These ideas were extended by Neils *Bohr when he proposed that the electrons surrounding the nucleus of the atom could only have quantized amounts of angular momentum. His theory postulated a set of precise orbits for these electrons, each orbit having a special energy. If an electron moved from an orbit of high energy to one of lower energy its excess energy would be emitted as a single quantum of radiation with a particular frequency. The sharp spectral lines emitted by atoms were thereby explained, and for hydrogen and other simple atoms there was close correlation between the Bohr values and experimental ones. In spite of the success of the theory, however, it was not wholly satisfactory because it was unable to explain why the angular momentum of the electron should be quantized and also why the electrons orbiting the nucleus did not continuously emit radiation, which was the prediction of classical electromagnetic theory. These objections were overcome in a new theory which used *quantum mechanics and other more sophisticated mathematical techniques. These still predicted the set of fixed energies which the electrons are permitted to have; but the idea that they travel in orbits round the nucleus was replaced by a more fuzzy statistical cloud, or *orbital, which indicated the probable position of an electron at any instant of time.

**quark** (in atomic physics), the constituents of the *elementary particles known as hadrons. Five main types of quark have been established, and these are labelled by 'flavours': u (up), d (down), c (charmed), s (strange), and b (bottom or beauty). It is thought that a sixth quark also exists, or ought to exist, and this has been named the t (top) quark, although so far it has not been detected experimentally. The hypothesis is elaborate. The u, c, and t quarks have an electric charge of $+\frac{2}{3}$, and the d, s, and b quarks a charge of $-\frac{1}{3}$. Each of these types is subdivided into three further groups which are labelled with 'colours': r (red), b (blue), and g (green). (The choice of all these names is quite arbitrary, and is not related to the usual meanings of these words.) Thus there are 18 types of quark, and for each there is a corresponding antiquark, making a total of 36 types in all. All the hadrons which are known can be accounted for by a suitable combination of quarks. For example, the proton, with a charge of $+1$, is uud $(\frac{2}{3} + \frac{2}{3} - \frac{1}{3})$; the neutron, with zero charge, is udd. The quarks are held together by *interactions mediated by yet another set of particles, called gluons. All quarks have a spin of either $+\frac{1}{2}$ or $-\frac{1}{2}$, and thus a particle consisting of three quarks, a baryon, will have a half-integral spin $(\frac{1}{2}, \frac{3}{2}$, and so on). A particle composed of two quarks, a meson, will have either zero or integral spin $(+1, -1)$. Free individual quarks cannot exist; quarks can only occur in combination with other quarks to form particles.

**quartz**, one of the commonest minerals of the Earth's crust (12 per cent by volume), being pure silica or silicon dioxide $(SiO_2)$. It can occur in crystal form (single crystals weighing as much as 130 kg or 290 pounds have been recorded), as concretionary masses, or as fine-grained coloured nodules. In pure form, referred to as rock-crystal, it is transparent and colourless, but more commonly it is white or translucent. Semiprecious coloured quartz can be blue, smoky, rose, yellow, or *amethyst. Quartz occurs in both intrusive and

A cluster of **quartz** crystals, found in association with haematite and displaying a pale pink coloration due to staining by that mineral.

extrusive igneous rocks. Particularly resistant to chemical and mechanical weathering, it is a common component of sedimentary rocks (forming the bulk of sandstone) and of river and beach deposits. Its hardness is a useful diagnostic feature: it cannot be scratched by a steel penknife and will itself scratch a piece of window glass. It is an extremely important mineral for industry because of the *piezoelectric effect; it is used also as an abrasive, in paints, for carving, and as semiprecious gemstones.

**quartzite**, a metamorphosed quartz-rich sandstone, typically produced by recrystallization at fairly high temperatures. Quartzites are pale in colour, often white. Highly durable, they are used in the building industry as a construction material. They are widespread in occurrence and very common in the Scottish Highlands, UK. The term quartzite is also sometimes used for unmetamorphosed quartz sandstones, or orthoquartzites.

**Quaternary Period**, the period of geological time that follows the *Tertiary. It comprises the *Pleistocene and the Holocene Epochs and spans the interval of time from 1.6 million years ago until the present day. The earlier part of the Quaternary is notable for the widespread glaciations that affected Europe and America and for changes in sealevel. Homo sapiens evolved during this period.

**Quebec**, an eastern province of Canada, extending from south of the Saint Lawrence river north to the Hudson Strait. The southern part of the province is an extension of the Appalachian Mountains, but the major part is on the Canadian Shield, rich in minerals and largely forested. The plateau of low hills, lakes, and bogs rises to the east, though a peak in the Laurentian Mountains at 1,200 m (3,900 feet) is the highest point. Rivers drain north into Hudson Bay and south into the Saint Lawrence and its estuary, providing much hydroelectric potential. Summers are warm but winters can be extremely cold. Quebec is Canada's largest province, though smaller than the Northwest Territories.

**Queensland**, a state in north-east Australia, bounded by the Northern Territory on the west, South Australia on the south-west, and New South Wales on the south. There is a long eastern coast which faces the Pacific and is largely sheltered by the Great Barrier Reef, while the Cape York Peninsula points due north to the Torres Strait between the Arafura and Coral Seas. Here there is tropical rain forest, with the Mitchell, Flinders, and other rivers draining into the Gulf of Carpentaria. Further south, rainfall is moderate; south of the Selwyn Range the rivers dry up seasonally and there are many tracts of desert. The Great Dividing Range runs roughly parallel to the coast and contains the cooler, wet plateaux necessary for dairying, the Atherton Plateau and Darling Downs among them. The coastal hills bear eucalypts and cotton, while sugarcane and tropical fruits are grown on the alluvial coastal plains. The sandy and clayey plains of the interior are underlain by the Great Artesian Basin, whose water helps to maintain sheep and cattle. Coal is mined extensively in the centre, and there are plentiful reserves of bauxite, copper, zinc, lead, and other minerals, together with oil and natural gas.

**quicklime** *calcium oxide.

**quicksand**, an area of loose wet sand which easily yields to pressure and readily engulfs any heavy object from the surface. Quicksands are pools of water partially filled with sand, with an underlying layer of impervious clay or rock. They are found in estuaries or along flat stretches of streams or beaches. In some places they may result from the agitation of strong currents or tides, reverting to a normal and harmless part of the beach when the agitation has gone.

# R

**racemic mixture** (in chemistry), a mixture of equal proportions of the two *enantiomers of a compound showing *optical activity. One is dextrorotatory, rotating the plane of polarized light to the right as it passes through; the other is laevorotatory, rotating it to the left by a corresponding amount. The effects cancel and the mixture shows no optical activity. The name originates from racemic acid, an equal mixture of dextrorotatory (D-) and laevorotatory (L-) tartaric acid.

**radian**, the plane angle subtended at the centre of a circle by an arc which is equal in length to the radius of the circle. The whole circumference of a circle subtends at its centre an angle of $2\pi$ radians, thus $360° = 2\pi$ radians. The radian is the unit of angle used in calculations of physical quantities such as angular momentum.

**radiation, thermal**, the term used to describe the transfer of heat by electromagnetic waves, as distinct from the other two mechanisms of heat transport, *conduction and *convection. Thermal or *infra-red radiation has wavelengths longer than those of visible light and frequencies very similar to those of the vibrations of atoms in liquids and solids. It can therefore be absorbed by atoms to increase the amplitude of their vibration and hence their energy: thus they become hotter. The ability of a body to absorb radiation, however, depends very much on its surface condition. Radiation is reflected most efficiently by shiny, light-coloured surfaces, and absorbed most efficiently by matt black ones. Because the radiation is an electromagnetic wave it does not need a medium to sustain it—it can travel

Because the Moon has no atmosphere, its surface is exposed to the full intensity of the Sun's **radiation** and can reach a temperature of over 100 °C (212 °F) during the lunar 'day'. The Apollo 14 lunar module shown here is covered with a highly reflective foil to reduce absorption of the Sun's thermal radiation and thus prevent overheating.

through a vacuum with the speed of light. This is how heat travels from the Sun to the Earth.

**radioactivity**, a phenomenon discovered in 1896 by Henri *Becquerel, who noticed that uranium salts continuously emitted radiation which ionized air (made its molecules gain or lose charge) and affected a wrapped photographic plate. The radiation seemed to be a property of the uranium itself, and not to be due to energy received from any outside source. Uranium is described as a naturally radioactive material; others include radium, discovered by Marie *Curie in 1898, thorium, and radon. The radiation from a radioactive material is called nuclear radiation, because it is emitted by the *nuclei of its atoms. The nuclei are unstable; they disintegrate at random, shooting out tiny particles of matter (*alpha particles or *beta particles) sometimes accompanied by bursts of wave energy (*gamma rays). The process of disintegration is called radioactive decay, and it releases energy which ultimately ends up as heat. Some materials decay more slowly than others, the *half-life being a useful measure for comparison; and for any given material the rate of decay lessens with time because fewer and fewer unstable nuclei are left to decay. In general, radioactive decay fundamentally alters atoms, changing one element into another. This, in turn, may itself be radioactive, and so on. Uranium, after a series of such decay processes, ultimately becomes lead, which is stable. Several other decay series of this type exist in nature. Some materials become radioactive when bombarded with nuclear radiation, a phenomenon discovered by Irène Curie and Jean-Frédéric Joliot (see *Joliot-Curie) in 1934. Radioactive materials created in this way are used in industry and medicine as 'tracers', and as a source of radiation for gamma-ray photography. In a nuclear power station, neutron bombardment causes a rare type of uranium to decay and release energy at a vastly increased rate (nuclear fission).

**radiometric dating** (or isotopic dating), a method for determining the age of a rock by measuring the amount of a radioactive *isotope, either in the rock as a whole or in a mineral contained in it, and comparing it with the amount of the stable 'daughter' isotope that it decays into. It is necessary to know accurately the *half-life of the element concerned—that is, the time required for half the nuclei originally present to decay. The measured ratio of parent to daughter element can then be used in conjunction with the half-life to calculate the age of the specimen. Several isotope decay series are used for determining radiometric ages; the choice depends upon the composition of the rock and the likely age of the specimen. The uranium–lead and thorium–lead methods are used for older rocks (those more than 20 million years old); rubidium–strontium measurements for rocks more than 10 million years old; potassium–argon measurements for rocks more than 100,000 years old; and the carbon-14 method for material between 70,000 and 1,000 years old.

**radio waves**, electromagnetic radiation with the longest wavelengths in the spectrum, ranging from 30 cm to 100 km (1 foot to 60 miles). They are emitted at certain frequencies by rearrangements in molecular structure, by circular acceleration of electrons, and by certain regions in space. They are widely used for long-distance communication as they can be reflected back to earth by the *ionosphere. As radio waves cover a vast range of wavelengths and frequencies they are subdivided into various groups: for example, VHF

(very high frequency) radio waves which have a wavelength of 1 to 10 m (3.28 to 32.8 feet), and LF (low frequency) radio waves which have a wavelength of 1,000 to 10,000 m.

**radium** (symbol Ra, at. no. 88, r.a.m. 226.03), a rare, white, radioactive element discovered by Marie and Pierre *Curie in 1898 in the mineral pitchblende. The last member of the *alkaline earths, it reacts with water and tarnishes in air. It has several isotopes which are members of radioactive decay sequences, the most stable, radium-226, having a *half-life of 1,620 years before decaying to the gas radon. Its radioactivity is used in cancer treatment and luminous paints.

**radon** (symbol Rn, at. no. 86, r.a.m. 222), the heaviest *noble gas. It occurs naturally and has been noticed to increase in groundwater before seismic activity. It is highly radioactive and produced by the radioactive decay of heavy elements such as radium. The most stable isotope, radon-222, has a *half-life of 3.825 days and is used in tracer studies.

**rain**, the form of atmospheric *precipitation which consists of water droplets at least 0.5 mm (0.02 inches) in diameter (anything less being drizzle). They may reach a size of 5 mm (0.2 inches) and more by *coalescence or by the melting of large snowflakes; at some point they can no longer be supported within the cloud, and fall. *Evaporation while falling determines their size on reaching the ground; some may evaporate entirely before reaching the ground, and this happens when the air through which they fall has a low relative *humidity. The intensity and duration of rainfall are dependent on the type of cloud which harbours it. Steady and persistent rain is generally associated with nimbostratus (layered) cloud which forms at *fronts; the cloud is caused by the uplift and cooling of warm, moist air, and the resulting precipitation is called frontal rain. Cumulonimbus (heaped) cloud, which is more likely to provide an intense though short-lived downpour, is formed by *convection. Moist air, warmed at ground level, rises, expands, and is cooled adiabatically to *dew-point. The resulting precipitation is known as convectional rain.

**rainbow**, a phenomenon formed in the atmosphere through the *refraction and internal *reflection of sunlight by falling raindrops. Well-developed rainbows consist of a bright primary bow, with red on the outside, followed by orange, yellow, green, blue, indigo, and violet on the inside. A less intense secondary bow, in which the colour sequence is reversed, can form outside the primary bow and one or more faint bows inside it. All the bows have their centre on a line from the sun through the observer. Rainbows can only be seen while standing with one's back to the sun, facing the illuminated raindrops.

**Rainier, Mount**, the main, volcanic feature of a national park in south-west central Washington, USA. At 4,391 m (14,408 feet), it is the highest mountain in the Cascade Range. Its peak is crowned with snow and its upper slopes contain 26 great glaciers and many permanent ice-fields.

**rain-shadow**, an area of relatively light rainfall which occurs on the lee side of high ground. As moving air is forced to rise over a mountain range, it cools. Extensive cloud and *precipitation are generated over the windward slopes as it does so; but because the air is already drier and becomes warmed during its descent of the lee slopes, evaporation occurs and less rain reaches the ground there. This results in relatively dry surface conditions.

**raised beach**, an old beach lifted above present-day high tides by tectonic uplift or falling sea-levels. Dead cliffs are cliffs left similarly above the high-tide line.

**Raleigh**, **Sir Walter** (*c*.1552–1618), English explorer, navigator, and courtier. He organized several voyages of exploration and colonization to North America, including the first unsuccessful attempt to settle Virginia (now North Carolina); from his expeditions he brought back the potato and the tobacco plant. Raleigh was an accurate topographer and cartographer of Guyana and central Venezuela, publishing an account of his voyage up the Orinoco River in his book, *The Discourse of Guiana*, in 1596. As explorer, he contributed to the study of mathematics as an aid to navigation. During his later imprisonment (in 1603), on a charge of conspiring to dethrone King James I, he set up a laboratory where he conducted experiments in chemistry, including the condensation of fresh water from salt water.

**Raman effect**, the change in wavelength which occurs when light is scattered. In 1928 the Indian physicist Chan-drasekhara Raman (1888–1970) directed single-wavelength beams of light at various gases, analysed the scattered light, and found that longer or shorter wavelengths were also present. According to the *quantum theory, light consists of wave-energy 'particles' called photons, each with a wavelength which depends on its energy. When scattering occurs, photons strike and are deflected by gas molecules. This alters the motion of the molecules, and they may absorb or release energy. Scattered photons then have a different energy from the original photons—and therefore a different wavelength.

**Ramsay, Sir Andrew Crombie** (1814–91), British geologist of Scottish extraction who devoted himself from an early age to the study of rock strata. In 1841 he obtained employment on the British Geological Survey, becoming its director-general thirty years later. He devoted most of his attention to district stratigraphy, promoted the theory of *denudation by rivers, and developed his own theory of the glacial erosion of rock basins.

**Ramsay**, **Sir William** (1852–1916), British chemist of Scottish extraction, discoverer of the rare gases of the atmosphere, for which he was awarded the 1904 Nobel Prize for Chemistry. This work was initiated after a discussion with Lord Rayleigh (John *Strutt) in 1892 about why nitrogen prepared in the laboratory should be slightly less dense than when isolated from the air, a phenomenon already observed by Henry *Cavendish in 1785; Ramsay decided that atmospheric nitrogen must be contaminated by a heavier gas. Between 1894 and 1903 he discovered the existence of five chemically inert gases: argon, helium and, with the help of the chemist Morris Travers, neon, krypton, and xenon, and determined their atomic weights and places in the periodic

The characteristic form of **rainbows** can be seen clearly in this picture. The primary bow is caused by light rays undergoing two refractions and one internal reflection in the raindrops, while the secondary bow (barely visible here) is due to light that undergoes two refractions and two internal reflections in the drops. This explanation of the formation of rainbows was first given by the French scientist and philosopher René Descartes in his book *Météores* in 1637.

table. In 1910 with Frederick *Soddy and Robert Whytlaw-Gray he identified the last member of the rare (or noble) gases, radon, the product of radioactive decay.

**Rand** *Witwatersrand.

**random number**, a number from a sequence without any detectable bias or pattern. Random numbers are used in statistical sampling to obtain elements from a numbered population. They are chosen by means of a process which gives each number an equal chance of being picked. Roulette wheels and many-sided dice can be used, but for large populations electronic methods such as computer algorithms and tables of random numbers are available. Their use is intended to rule out bias in sampling. An example of the use of random numbers would be to select twenty people at random from a population of 1,500. The people are first listed and numbered. Then twenty numbers are chosen from a table of random numbers. To select the starting point in the tables, dice or tossed coins can be used to determine the first number to be used. Thereafter numbers can be read off consecutively. Inferences can be drawn about the population as a whole, on the basis of a random sample of the variables, provided the sample is large enough (considerably more than twenty). Random numbers form a basic tool of the *Monte Carlo method.

**Raoult, François Marie** (1830–1901), French chemist considered one of the founders of physical chemistry. He formulated the law, named after him, which relates the vapour pressure of a solution to the number of molecules of solute dissolved in it. This law explains the lowering of the *freezing-point and the raising of the *boiling-point of a solvent by the addition of a solute. Thus the freezing-point of ice is lowered by the presence of salt. It also provides a method for calculating the relative molecular masses of dissolved substances. The law is only applicable to ideal solutions since it assumes there is no interaction between the solute and solvent molecules.

**rapid** (or cataract), a low *waterfall or place along a river where the channel is partly blocked. Rapids produce chaotic, fast-flowing water. Large rocks dumped in the channel by tributaries, landslides, or glaciers are one cause. Another is the existence of hard bands of rock which the river has difficulty eroding. European explorers and fur-traders in North America learned that while some stretches could be safely 'shot', others were so dangerous that boats had to be carried overland round them.

**rare-earth element** *lanthanide.

**rare gas** *noble gas.

**Rasmussen, Knud Johan Victor** (1879–1933), Danish Arctic explorer and ethnologist, born in Greenland of part-Inuit descent. In 1921–4 he undertook a polar journey from Baffin Island to the north-east corner of Siberia by dog-sledge, making a scientific study of virtually every Inuit tribe in the region. As well as his valuable cartographic, archaeological, and ethnographic studies, he published translations of Inuit mythology and song.

**rate of a reaction** *chemical reaction.

**ravine**, a small, deep, steep-sided valley which has been caused by running water. Larger than *gullies and smaller

**Rapids** on the Nile River below Kabalega Falls, just above Lake Albert, Uganda.

than *gorges, ravines form in areas of steep slopes where there is little vegetation to protect the ground from rain. The water runs off rapidly, carrying debris which helps to cut the rock.

**Rayleigh, Lord**  *Strutt, John William and Robert John.

**reagent**, a chemical used to test for the presence of particular compounds or types of compound. Well-known examples include *lime water, used to test for carbon dioxide, *silver nitrate, which detects chlorides, and *iodine, which detects starch.

**reality**, what is real or exexistent or underlies appearances. The common-sense view that it exists independently of our perception is called realism in philosophy. Scientific theories are often thought to be realistic in character: that is, science describes actual states and structures of nature. The 20th century has seen the development of non-realistic scientific theories, notably in atomic physics. For example, most physicists think it futile to ask whether light is really particles or waves. They would say that these are convenient ideas, and that a reality beyond them is unknowable. Such a view is close to the philosophical alternative to realism called idealism. Here the external world is held to be a mental creation. Idealism does not necessarily deny objective reality. Rather it says that our ultimate interpretation of it rests on ideas or concepts. Even in non-esoteric areas of science, idealist philosophies can be detected. Frequently scientific theories are proposed as models rather than as statements of what actually exists or occurs.

**real numbers**, the numbers corresponding to the points on an infinitely long straight line. They include positive and negative whole numbers ($-1$, $7$, $416$, for example), fractions ($\frac{1}{2}$, $\frac{99}{100}$), and all the numbers in between, including *irrational numbers. Two real numbers are required to define *complex numbers.

**Recent Epoch** (in geology)  *Holocene Epoch.

**recharge**, the downward movement of water to the *water-table which replaces that lost by outflow into rivers or extraction from wells. If recharge exceeds outflow and extraction, the water-table will rise; otherwise, it falls. In natural conditions, with no extraction, there is usually a rough balance between recharge of groundwater and outflow over the course of a year. Where heavy extraction has lowered the water-table, artificial recharge can be undertaken: this involves pumping water down shafts, or leaving it to sink into the ground from shallow ponds.

**reciprocal**, (in mathematics). The reciprocal of the number $a$ is the number $\frac{1}{a}$, that is $a^{-1}$. Thus the reciprocal of $2$ is $\frac{1}{2}$.

**recrystallization**, the process of purifying or improving the quality of a crystalline substance by repeated crystallization. With each crystallization, fresh solvent is used to dissolve the substance, and some impurities are left behind as undissolved solid. The solution is then filtered and evaporated until crystallization begins; other impurities will be left in the used solvent.

**Red River**, the name of several rivers, mostly so-called for the colour of sediments carried. (1) A river of south-east Asia

A **ravine** cut through sandstone at Tamerza in western Tunisia.

which rises on the great plateau of Yunnan in southern China, and then flows south-eastward for over 800 km (550 miles) to its delta on the Gulf of Tonkin. The delta is the economic heart of northern Vietnam and produces much of the region's rice. (2) The Red River of the North flows north across the prairies of the USA into Canada, where it empties into Lake Winnipeg's southernmost point. From its source to the lake is nearly 600 km (370 miles). It acts as the boundary between North Dakota and Minnesota; its valley is an important international routeway and wheat-growing area. (3) The Red River of south-central USA, southernmost of the large tributaries of the Mississippi, is somewhat longer, at 1,640 km (1,020 miles). It rises in high plains in east New Mexico, crosses the Texas panhandle and flows eastern between Texas and Oklahoma, Texas and Arkansas, and across Louisiana to join the Mississippi near its delta.

**Red Sea**, an elongated stretch of water between Arabia and Africa. Some 2,300 km (1,400 miles) long and 350 km (220 miles) wide for much of its length, it is the sea-filled part of the *Great Rift Valley and has old volcanic mountains on both its shores. Along its axis is a deep region of newly forming, hot sea-floor: it is an embryonic *ocean (in contrast to the Pacific where there has been *sea-floor spreading for more than 160 million years). Early in its history, when the sea's only marine connection was to the Mediterranean, the evaporation of repeated influxes of seawater led to the formation of *evaporates. Seawater circulating through the hot sea floor has led to the hot brines and the thick sea-floor sediments becoming enriched in zinc and copper and other valuable metals. Coral grows well here. No rivers empty into it. Off the coasts there are numerous chains of small islands and dangerous reefs.

In the north-west are its two arms, the gulfs of Suez and Aqaba. At the opposite end it connects with the Gulf of Aden and the Indian Ocean. The currents are treacherous. A hot *khamsin wind blows off the surrounding deserts, and the saltiness of the water is increased by a high rate of evaporation in the intense heat.

**reduction** (in chemistry), the opposite of *oxidation, the name given to any process where electrons are gained by the substance being reduced. It leads to a decrease in the *electronegativity and oxidation state of the substance, and occurs in a number of ways. Firstly oxygen may be removed from a compound; for example, nickel oxide, NiO, is reduced in the presence of carbon to give nickel, Ni. Secondly, hydrogen may be added to an element or compound; thus ethene, $C_2H_4$, is reduced to ethane, $C_2H_6$. Thirdly, the charge on an atom or ion may become more negative by acquisition of further electrons; for example, copper(II) ions, $Cu^{2+}$, can be reduced to copper, Cu. Reduction may be brought about chemically or electrochemically. In *electrolysis ions gain electrons at the cathode, so also are reduced at the cathode. They lose electrons at the anode, and so are oxidized there. Reactions in which both oxidation and reduction occur are called redox reactions.

**reef**, a mass of rock which generally occurs in relatively shallow coastal waters. The top of the reef usually projects above the surface of the sea, at least during low-water periods, although it may be permanently, though shallowly, submerged. While reefs may be made of solid rock or pebbles, they are more commonly formed from organic material. Along the coast of Texas, for example, there are reefs which have been formed by the accumulation of oyster shells, and many of them are about 10 m (30 feet) thick. The most common type of reef is made of coral, the accumulated skeletons of coral polyp colonies. Coral reefs are particularly common in tropical seas, where many different forms are recognized, including *barrier reefs and *atolls. Since reefs lie at or just below the surface of the sea, they are a potential hazard to shipping. They may be marked by the formation of power-

A **reef** formed from the erosion of the headland at the entrance of Wellington harbour, North Island, New Zealand.

The apparent bending and splitting of the spoon in the glass of water is caused by the **refraction** of light. The unfilled glass also produces refraction effects, as shown by the small 'jink' in the spoon at the near rim of the glass.

ful breaking waves and are often associated with dangerous currents. The pace of coral reef-building is slowing, however. Polyps can only survive in clear, warm water, and tropical seas appear to be cooler than in the geological past.

**reflection**, the return of all or part of a beam of particles or waves when it strikes a smooth surface. All types of wave—light, sound, heat—may be reflected from a suitable surface; and provided none of the wave enters the surface, all the energy remains within the reflected wave. The surface imperfections must be smaller than the wavelength of the beam to be reflected, for otherwise the wave will be scattered and diffused. Reflection of light from a flat mirror makes the image appear laterally inverted and in a different place from the reflected object. However, it is the same way up, the same distance behind the surface as the object is in front, and the same size as the object. The two laws of reflection suppose a line, the normal, which is perpendicular to the reflecting surface and meets it where the incident ray meets the surface. Then the reflected ray lies in the plane defined by the incident ray and the normal; and the angle between the reflected ray and the normal (the angle of reflection) is the same as that between the incident ray and the normal (the angle of incidence).

**refraction**, the change in direction of a wave when it enters another medium, as for example when light passes from air to glass. If the direction of the ray is exactly at right angles to the surface no refraction occurs; but in all other cases the ray is bent towards the normal (an imaginary line perpendicular to the surface) when it enters a denser medium, and is bent away from it when it leaves. The angle between the normal and the refracted ray is called the angle of refraction, and this is related to the angle of incidence by a quantity called the *refractive index ($n$). This relation is *Snell's law. Refraction occurs because waves travel at slightly different speeds in different media and it applies to all forms of radiation. It is responsible for various strange effects in which light seems to come from somewhere other than the true direction—as in mirages and the apparent bending of the spoon at the point where it enters water (see figure).

**refractive index**, a value by which the capacity of a material to cause *refraction is measured. It is the ratio of the speeds of a wave in two different media (one of them usu-

## Reflection and refraction

### Reflection in a flat mirror

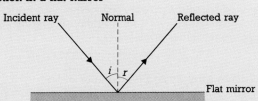

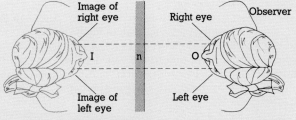

The incident ray, the normal, and the reflected ray all lie in the same plane, and the angle of incidence (*i*) equals the angle of reflection (*r*).

The observer's image in the mirror is laterally inverted, and lies as far behind the mirror as the observer is in front of it, i.e. On = nI.

### Refraction of light

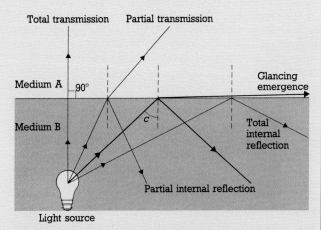

Medium A is less dense than medium B. A light ray passing from A to B is refracted towards the normal; on emerging from medium B it is refracted away from the normal. The refractive index ($_An_B$) from A to B is $\sin \theta_1/\sin \theta_2$; the index ($_Bn_A$) from B to A is $\sin \theta_2/\sin \theta_1$. A ray striking the interface at right angles is not refracted.

When a light ray passes from a dense (B) to a less dense (A) medium, some light is transmitted and some is reflected internally. When the angle of incidence is greater than the critical angle *c*, total internal reflection occurs.

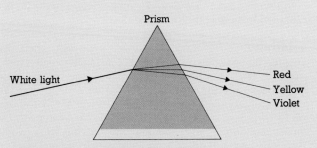

A beam of white light is split into its constituent colours by refraction in a glass prism. This is because each colour has a different wavelength and is therefore refracted by a different amount.

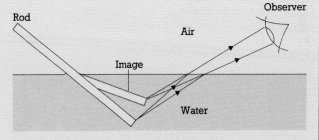

Refraction of light rays at the surface of the water results in the observer forming an image of the rod that is displaced from the rod's true position.

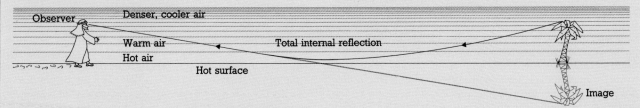

The diagram illustrates how mirages are formed. Light rays from the tree (and from the sky beyond it) are refracted away from the normal as they pass through the increasingly hot (and hence less dense) layers of air close to the desert surface. Eventually the angle of

incidence at a hot layer of air becomes great enough for total internal reflection to occur. The observer sees what appears to be a pool of water in which the tree is reflected: this — the mirage — is in fact a virtual image of the tree and the sky.

ally being air or a vacuum), and is chiefly used of light. Between air and glass the refractive index is about 1.6, and between air and water at 25 °C (77 °F) it is about 1.3: that is, light travels 1.3 times as fast in air as in water. Although the refractive index for a particular pair of media is often quoted as a single value, it does depend on the wavelength of the passing ray. Light of different wavelengths is refracted by different amounts. This is the effect known as dispersion; it is responsible for the ability of a prism to separate the lines of atomic spectra.

**reg**, a lowland desert plain whose surface is covered with stones and gravel. Regs are formed by the wind blowing away the finer particles of sand and silt, leaving the heavier material behind. The sandblasting of stones by strong winds can produce curved facets which meet at quite sharp angles; such stones are called ventifacts. In some cases, large stones may be packed into a hard, firm surface extending over a wide area. Isolated sand dunes can form and move over the pebble surface layer of a reg.

**regolith**, the mantle of loose, unconsolidated material that overlies solid rock, the bedrock on continental land surfaces. It consists of rock-waste, formed by the mechanical and chemical breakdown of the bedrock, and superficial deposits such as alluvium, till, volcanic ash, loess, and wind-blown sands. The soils which subsequently develop on this loose material are part of the regolith.

**regosols**, the immature soils developed on recently formed sediments such as dune sands, wind-blown loess deposits, and glacial tills. Although the upper part of the *profile may be modified by the presence of organic matter, these soils are too young for distinct horizons to have formed. Their characteristics, therefore, are determined by the nature of the material on which they are formed.

**regression analysis** (in mathematics), the method used to find the relationship which holds between two variables when a number of pairs of values for them are known. It corresponds to drawing the best curve through a collection of points on a graph, referred to as a scatter diagram, and finding its equation, called the regression equation. Regression equations express the mathematical relationship which best explains the pairs of values of two variables. The most usual form of equation is a 'line of best fit', where 'best' is determined by the *least squares method. Various equation curves are commonly employed, including logarithms and exponentials as well as the more familiar *polynomials. If the regression equation is non-linear in the coefficients—for example, $a_0 + b_1 \log(b_2 x)$—then a computer is almost always essential. For such non-linear regression, although the least-square principle is still valid, *iterative methods are often required actually to find the coefficients. The term 'regression' was first used in this sense by Karl Pearson (1857–1936) in the context of inherited characteristics, after the earlier use by Francis Galton (1822–1911) of the phrase 'regression towards mediocrity' (now replaced by the less emotive phrase 'regression towards the mean'). This refers to the tendency for the height, intelligence, or any other characteristic of children to be nearer the average for the population at large than is that of their parents.

**rejuvenation of rivers**. This occurs when channels are cut vertically into broad valleys or floodplains, creating a new set of steep slopes and encouraging rapid erosion. This happens either because more water becomes available or because the slope from head to mouth increases. More water can come from climatic change and produce greater volumes of *runoff, or it can come when headwater streams break through divides from neighbouring basins. Increased slope occurs either if the level of the sea or lake into which the river flows drops, or as a result of uplift.

**relative atomic mass**, the mass of one atom of an element expressed in terms of the mass of an atom of the *isotope carbon-12, defined to be exactly 12 atomic mass units (a.m.u.). On this scale hydrogen has a relative atomic mass of 1.0079, and uranium one of 238.03. The values are the *weighted means of the relative atomic masses of each naturally occurring isotope. Each isotope has its own characteristic atomic mass. Before 1960 the scale was based on a value of exactly 16 for oxygen, which gives very slightly larger values (16.000 instead of 15.9994 for oxygen, for example). Many atomic masses are close to whole numbers. This observation led William Prout in 1816 to formulate a famous hypothesis, that all atomic weights were actually integral multiples of that of hydrogen, which he thought might be considered a kind of primal matter from which all the other elements were built up. This gave a great impetus to the accurate determination of atomic weights (at that time based on hydrogen = 1), though the significance of Prout's hypothesis was not appreciated for over a hundred years.

**relative molecular mass**, the mass of one molecule of a substance divided by one-twelfth of the mass of an atom of the carbon-12 isotope. The relative molecular mass is calculated by adding up the *relative atomic masses of the atoms in the molecule, as given by the *molecular formula. Thus the relative atomic masses of hydrogen and oxygen, to the nearest whole number, are 1 and 16, so the relative molecular mass of $H_2O$ is $(1 + 1 + 16) = 18$. Strictly speaking only molecular compounds have relative molecular masses; ionic compounds have relative formula masses which are obtained from the empirical formulae.

**relativity**, the general term used in physics when discussing the behaviour of an object or a system which is moving with respect to the observer or to some other object. Whereas an observer might think that he is stationary, this is not really so: the Earth with him on it is not only rotating on its own axis, but is also orbiting the sun. Moreover, the galaxy containing the Sun may be moving as a whole through space. Thus all motion which is observed is regarded as relative either to the observer's own motion or to that of some other object. This suggests the idea that the interaction of two objects depends only on their motion relative to one another and not on the motion of each separately. Thus, if a car travelling at 16 km/h (10 m.p.h.) hits a wall, it might not be damaged very much, but if it hits another car which is approaching at 48 km/h (30 m.p.h.) their relative speed is 64 km/h (40 m.p.h.) and the collision will have much more serious consequences. What the principle of relativity in fact says is that the laws of physics are exactly the same in all systems which are moving with a constant velocity with respect to one another. If one is travelling in a jet aircraft at 965 km/h (600 m.p.h.) the laws of physics are exactly the same as they are on the Earth's surface, and any experiments done within the confines of the aircraft cabin would give the same results as if done on Earth. It would be impossible to detect that they were done while travelling at 965 km/h (600 m.p.h.). But as soon as the velocity changes, for example when the aircraft changes course or lands, this could be detected by the behaviour of objects inside it.

**relativity theory,** a theory concerning motion and developing the ideas of *relativity which were considered and extended by Albert *Einstein in his special theory of 1905. He postulated that the principle of relativity held not only for the laws of physics but also for the *speed of light. Previously it had been taken for granted that, if an observer measured the speed of light while travelling towards the source of the light, he would get a larger value than if he had remained stationary. The *Michelson–Morley experiment seemed to show that this was not so. Einstein assumed that the speed of light (in a vacuum) is the same for any observer, whatever his velocity, as long as that velocity is constant. The logical consequences of these two postulates are profound. If a person A observes another system which is moving relative to him with a constant velocity, then measurements of length and time which he makes on objects in that system will not give the same results as those obtained by observer B, who is stationary in that system. All such lengths and time intervals will appear to A to be shorter than the measurements taken by B. Not only that, but similar measurements that B makes on A will be shorter by the same amount. A further consequence is that there is an equivalence between mass ($m$) and energy ($E$), so that when an object acquires more energy its mass automatically increases, the relation being $E = mc^2$, where $c$ is the speed of light. Although these effects are extremely small for ordinary speeds they become very important when objects travel close to the speed of light. They have to be taken into account in nuclear physics and in the design of large machines used to accelerate particles to very high energies. The theory as it deals with constant velocities is called the special theory of relativity. Einstein's general theory of 1915 is concerned with motion in which the velocity changes, and treats gravitation as a consequence of the geometry of the universe. Space is 'curved' by the pressure of mass, celestial motion is controlled by this curvature, and light is bent in the gravitational fields of massive bodies. The theory has led to the concept of the *space–time continuum.

**rendzina,** a soil which forms on materials rich in calcium carbonate, such as limestone or marl. Under humid conditions, the calcium carbonate is gradually leached away and a thin surface *horizon is formed from the remaining constituents of the parent material. Typically, the surface is dark in colour because of the presence of finely divided organic matter. Major areas of these soils occur in the prairie lands of southern Oklahoma and north-east Texas, USA, and in the limestone regions round the Mediterranean.

**renewable resource** *energy resource.

**resistance** (in electricity), the ratio of the *potential difference (p.d. or voltage) across a conductor to the *electrical current which flows through it as a result. The unit of measurement is the ohm ($\Omega$), this being the resistance of a conductor requiring a potential difference of 1 volt across its ends to produce a current of 1 ampere. For a given metal conductor at constant temperature the value is the same whatever the current (*Ohm's law), but rises if the temperature rises. Any conductor possessing resistance gives off heat when a current flows through it. The effect is described by *Joule's law.

**resonance,** the oscillation of a body when it is subjected to a vibration whose *frequency is the same as its own natural frequency (or some multiple of it). By giving a swing a little push every time it reaches us, we can build up quite a large oscillation, and this is the characteristic feature of resonance. A body responds much more to a resonant frequency than to any other. Some of the power of resonance can be seen in the shattering of a glass when sympathetic vibrations of a particular pitch are set up, and in the fact that soldiers are instructed to break step when marching over certain bridges for fear of producing a resonant response which will result in collapse. In a musical instrument some part is given a natural frequency of vibration by adjusting its length or tautness. When it is played it is this frequency that predominates in the sound because most of the energy is drawn into it as a result of resonance. A similar phenomenon occurs in electric circuits, and this is employed in oscillators and radios; tuning consists in altering the resonant frequency of the receiver.

**resonance effects** (in chemistry), a system used to describe the structure of a molecule for which no single structure can be drawn, for example *benzene.

**reverse fault,** a fracture in which the rocks on opposite sides of a *fault have moved in such a way that the beds on one side overlap in the vertical plane those on the other. Horizontal distances between points on opposite sides of the fault are reduced by the fault-movement and vertical distances are increased.

**revolution of the Earth,** in its orbit round the Sun, a little more than 365.25 days. The orbit is not quite a circle but

The collapse of the Tacoma Narrows Bridge in Washington State, USA, provides a spectacular example of **resonance**. In November 1940, only four months after the bridge was opened, a gale of 68 km/h (42 m.p.h.) set up oscillations in the 860-m (2,800-foot) main span, whose design was inadequate. Resonance eventually caused the oscillations to become so large that part of the span collapsed.

an ellipse, and thus the Earth's distance from the Sun, and its orbital speed, vary slightly throughout the *year. This affects the length of the solar day, so that apparent time is up to fifteen minutes ahead of, or behind, mean time at different periods of the year. The Earth is slightly nearer to the Sun in January than in July. The difference in distance is too small to affect its climate, however, the change in *seasons being caused rather by the tilt of its axis in relation to the Sun.

**rhenium** (symbol Re, at. no. 75, r.a.m. 186.2), a rare *transition metal extracted from flue dusts. It is silvery grey and was first detected from its X-ray spectrum in 1925. It has a very high melting-point (3,180 °C, or 5,755 °F) and is chemically similar to manganese.

**Rhine**, Germany's principal waterway. It rises in the Swiss Alps and flows northward for some 1,300 km (800 miles) to The Netherlands and the North Sea. Fed by glaciers and mountain streams, it runs east through Liechtenstein into Lake Constance (Bodensee) on the borders of Switzerland, Austria, and Germany. Here it sheds its burden of mud and gravel, emerging from the lake as a clear, dark green stream. This descends in falls and a series of rapids to the head of its *rift valley, which runs between the Vosges and the Black Forest. It then meanders freely along its floodplain, separating into several channels with low islands in between. It is fully navigable here: ocean-going ships can pass through the Rhine gorge, 130 km (80 miles) long. However, Austria's dam-building programmes are causing the water level on the Vienna–Bratislava reach to fall alarmingly. Canals connect the Rhine with the Rhône river system. In 1992 the Rhine–Main–Danube canal opened, providing a through-way for shipping across Europe from Rotterdam to the Black Sea.

**Rhodes** (modern Greek, Rodi), an island in the south-east Aegean Sea off the coast of Turkey; now in Greek possession. It is the southernmost and largest of the twelve-island Dodecanese group in the southern Sporades. Most of the islands have areas of less than 300 km² (116 sq. mi.) and are relatively infertile, comprising only stony hills covered with evergreen scrub; but Rhodes, with an area of 1,400 km² (540 sq. mi.), has broad coastal plains with grazing for sheep and goats. Hills with patches of cypress, juniper, and pine forest rise in the centre, and there are terraces for fruit trees and corn. Hot summers give way to mild winters, which bring moderate rain.

**Rhodesia** *Zimbabwe.

**rhodium** (symbol Rh, at. no. 45, r.a.m. 102.91) is a *transition metal in the platinum group and is found naturally with them and in cupro-nickel deposits. Silvery white and shiny, it is used for plating jewellery, as well as in alloys of platinum and as a catalyst in ethanoic acid production.

**Rhône**, a major river of southern Europe, some 812 km (504 miles) long. It rises in the Rhône glacier of the Furka Pass in the Swiss Alps and descends westward through a long valley to Lake Geneva, in which it deposits its silt. Emerging from the lake, it enters France and is forced south by the Jura Mountains through several gorges. It meanders north-west again, is joined by the Saône, its chief tributary, and again turns south, becoming navigable. In its main valley it has the largest discharge of all French rivers, and

becomes heavy with sediment brought down from the Massif Central and the Alps by other tributaries on either side. The valley is thus extremely fertile. The river enters the Golfe du Lion on the Mediterranean through a two-armed delta, with the salt marshes and lagoons of la Camargue in the middle.

**rhyolite**, a light, fine-grained igneous rock formed by the rapid cooling of lava rich in silica; it is widespread in the south-western USA and in other volcanic regions. When heat-treated it is used as a thermal and acoustic insulator. Pumice, pitchstone, and obsidian are all forms of rhyolite.

**ria**, a long, narrow inlet or indentation of the coastline. Rias are drowned river *valleys, formed wherever a dissected area of hills and lowlands was submerged as a result of the increase in *sea-level caused by the melting of the ice-caps at the end of the last great glaciation, or by submergence of valleys caused by tectonic depression. Since they were originally eroded or carved out by rivers, they have many of the characteristics of normal valleys: moderately steep, V-shaped sides, for example, and tapering coastal ends. Sometimes, when the smaller streams which fed the main river were also drowned, complex rias with many branch-like inlets were formed. Chesapeake Bay, USA, and Milford Haven, Wales, UK, are examples of this type of ria. Rias are common along the coasts of north-west Spain, western Brittany, and south-west Ireland. The relatively sheltered waters within a ria are ideal for harbours, and are used as such by local fishing fleets in all these areas. The larger ones, offering 20 m (65 feet) depth or so of water, make ideal ports.

**Richter scale**, a logarithmic scale for representing the energy released by *earthquakes. It was devised by the US seismologist Charles Richter (1900–1985) in 1935. A figure of 2 or less means a tremor which is barely perceptible; one of 4 means a magnitude at the epicentre which is a hundred times as large and a tremor which will probably be noticeable over 32 km (20 miles). An earthquake measuring 5 on the scale may be destructive, and one measuring 8 or more will be a 'great' earthquake—one of the largest known.

**ridge** (in meteorology), a short-lived area of high surface pressure that is elongated in form. Over land or sea ridges may be accompanied by strong breezes, although the weather is fair or fine. The opposite of a ridge is a *trough.

**ridge, topographical**, an elongated area of relatively high ground, forming a junction from which opposing slopes fall away; this may range in shape from knife-edged to broad whale-back. Usually running between valleys, ridges often constitute *divides or watersheds between drainage basins, although they can run across or along valley floors. These may have been deposited, after the valleys were cut, by wind, waves, glaciers, or glacial melt water; or they may be the surface manifestations of very resistant layers of bedrock, particularly intrusions of igneous rocks.

**Riemann, (Georg Friedrich) Bernhard** (1826–66), German mathematician whose achievements are characterized by their outstandingly imaginative character. Riemann surfaces are the modifications of the complex number plane required for a proper understanding of algebraic and other many-valued functions; Riemannian geometry is the study of intrinsic properties of curved space, now fundamental to the relativistic description of our universe. His name is

Part of the complex **ria** system of Queen Charlotte Sound, at the northern end of South Island, New Zealand.

attached to several other concepts and theorems in mathematics, of which the most famous is an assertion about the complex numbers which are roots of a certain transcendental equation. This assertion, known as the Riemann hypothesis, has many deep implications, particularly about the distribution of prime numbers, but after more than 100 years it remains one of the greatest of the unsolved problems of mathematics.

**rift valley**, an elongated depression, often very extensive, with steep sides, and floors which are generally flatter than the surrounding terrain. Rift valleys are usually formed by earth movements along two parallel systems of *faults: the movements depress part of the Earth's crust between the faults to form the valley floor. They occur both on land and under the sea. Under the forces of *plate tectonics and *continental drift the crust either bulges up into huge arches, where stress along the crest causes faults, or the plates are pulling apart, causing similar faults. In some places no actual fracturing of the crust occurs and the rocks on either side are simply bent over, or 'down-warped', to form the rift. At other places the stresses result in volcanic activity both within a rift and along its sides. Often stream channels dissect the valley sides and thread on to its floor. Rift valley systems are among the largest features of the Earth's relief; but the valleys range in size from the *Great Rift Valley, which can be traced for nearly 5,000 km (3,000 miles), to those of the Rhine and mid-Scotland, to the comparatively tiny Church Stretton valley in Shropshire, UK. Most are of Tertiary age or younger; and some, as at the southern end of the Red Sea, are still opening up.

**rill**, a shallow channel cut in the surface of soil or rocks by running water. Rills usually occur on bare surfaces and are produced when thin sheets of water—resulting from heavy rain or melting snow—become concentrated into deeper, faster threads of flow which erode the surface. Many rills (especially those in soil) are very short-lived and are destroyed rapidly by rain splashes and soil creep; but those cut on harder rocks like limestone, partly by solution, can last for hundreds of years. On very steep slopes thin, almost parallel features will sometimes form; they are known as shoestring rills.

**Rio Grande** (Mexican, Río Bravo), a river over 3,000 km (1,860 miles) long, forming Mexico's boundary with Texas, USA. It rises from the *Rocky Mountains, in the San Juan Mountains of south-west Colorado, picks up various tributaries of meltwater and flows south through New Mexico to the border. Here it swings south-east, but is forced by the high ground of the Serranías del Burro to turn northward, and forms *Big Bend where there is a scenic national park. Resuming its course, it is joined from the north by its chief tributary, the Pecos. Meandering, it has always tended to change its course; and it loses much water by evaporation before reaching its delta on the Gulf of Mexico. This is the only point at which it becomes navigable.

**rip current**, a strong, well-defined flow of seawater moving away from the shore. Rip currents occur where water is piled up against a coast as a result of two longshore currents meeting head on, or of a strong *tidal stream suddenly entering shallow water, or of waves breaking obliquely across a longshore current. The rip current provides a means of returning this mass of water seaward. It is turbulent and fast-moving, carrying with it large quantities of sediment in sus-

A steep roadside bank in New Mexico, USA, with parallel **rills** caused by the run-off of seasonal rain from the pine-clad slope above.

pension. It is also unpredictable, and has been the cause of many drownings.

**river**, a copious natural stream of water flowing in a channel to the sea. Rivers are the most significant features of the Earth's land surface; more than any other agent on it they have influenced both the nature of the landscape and the location of human settlement. As the most accessible links in the *hydrological cycle, the speed and volume of their flow determine sites for irrigation and hydroelectric projects, just as their channels have determined routes for exploration, inland navigation, and trade. The drainage of land by rivers, and its enrichment by the *alluvium they carry, both encourage agriculture. A typical stream may rise near a watershed, or from a spring, or from a limestone cave or the melting end of a glacier. Seeking the steepest and shortest course downward, it cuts its way through soft rock, carrying the loosened particles with it. Joined by tributaries, its cutting power increases. Gullies become canyons or, if mass wasting erodes the sides, broad valleys are created over the years; the further it travels the more its *load increases. The stream may enter a lake, from which it emerges with its speed diminished; but joined by more tributaries it now becomes a river. The work of erosion continues, but *deposition now begins in earnest. In its lower reaches, where the gradient is less, there is more likelihood of *meandering. Melting snows or heavy rain may cause the river to flood: alluvium is deposited on the *floodplain. Finally the river enters its *delta or meets, in its estuary, the tides of the sea. A large river working on soft rock may, over the centuries, alter the whole topography of the land through which it flows. The form of a typical river depends not only on geology (especially the permeability of rock) but also on climate. In arid regions streams are ephemeral. Channels fed by melting mountain snow are generally dry in winter but swollen in spring and early summer, while in Mediterranean and some continental climates summer is the season when they are dry. In temperate regions rivers rise in winter and occasionally flood. In tropical and especially monsoon

regions, the regime is one of seasonal variations in the *discharge of rivers. River capture is the diversion of the upper headwaters of a mountain stream into the channel of a more powerful one.

**roaring forties**, the belt of strong westerly winds lying between 40° and 50 °S. of the Equator. There is no large land mass in this belt to disrupt the airflow, and the movement is continuous throughout the year. Craft sailing from the Cape of Good Hope to Australia can rely on these winds, which are often at gale force, in the southern regions of the Indian Ocean; it is known as 'running the easting down'.

**roche moutonnée** (French, 'rounded rock'), a hillock of rock partly smoothed and rounded by glacier ice. Such rocks have relatively smoothly curved backs and sides and steeper, rugged fronts. The glaciers rode easily up over the knobs, grinding and polishing their surfaces with the debris held in their basal layers, but when the sheets of ice were bent to flow downwards over the faces, they lost contact with the bedrock, forming small cavities there. In these spaces, meltwater could trickle into cracks in the rocks and freeze, so that blocks were prised away, leaving the rugged faces. They commonly occur in groups, all facing the same way.

**rock**, the various kinds of hard, solid substances in and underneath the ground. In geology the word 'rock' is used for loose, unconsolidated deposits, such as sand and gravel, as well as for hard, solid rocks like granite and slate. Rocks are classified according to the way in which they were formed. *Igneous rocks have formed from magma, or molten material; most *sedimentary rocks are made up of particles that have been transported and deposited elsewhere; *metamorphic rocks have been formed from earlier rocks, either igneous or sedimentary, that have been changed by pressure or heat, or both.

**rock-crystal**, a pure form of *quartz, is colourless and of exceptional transparency. It is much used for optical and scientific instruments and polishes well for jewellery. Occurring in *igneous rocks, it is found mainly in Brazil, although the USA, Britain, Japan, Madagascar, Switzerland, and Hungary also have sources of supply.

**rockfall**, a sudden collapse of bare rock walls. Rockfalls may seem to explode, either as the cliff face gives way, or as great chunks of rock hit the ground. Mountain slopes have many small rockfalls, particularly in spring, when ice which has frozen in cracks melts, releasing the blocks. Large falls, involving great monoliths of stone, occur more rarely because it takes a long time for rainwater and ice to loosen the block from the face. Some blocks are wedged away from the cliff from the top and gradually tilt outwards; others are undermined at the toe and topple backwards. Earthquakes often act as triggers for rockfalls.

**rock flour**, a very finely powdered debris produced by the grinding action of ice-sheets and glaciers as they drag a thick mat of rock fragments across their bed. It gives the streams which flow from ice fronts a characteristically milky colour.

**rock glacier**, a slow-moving tongue or lobe of rock fragment found in mountains and polar deserts. Rock glaciers can be as much as 3 km (2 miles) long and 0.4 km (0.25 miles) wide. They form in two ways. Some are undoubtedly the remnants of true glaciers which have become buried and choked by debris falling on to the ice from the valley sides. Others are simply great sheets of angular debris which move slowly downhill under the force of gravity, aided by the seasonal growth and melting of ice crystals within the rock mass.

**rock-salt**   *halite.

**Rocky Mountains**, or Rockies, the great system of parallel ranges forming part of the Western Cordillera of North America. From Alaska and the Canadian Arctic they extend for over 4,800 km (3,000 miles) to Mexico. Their crest forms the continental divide, rivers on one side running to the Pacific Ocean, and on the other into the Arctic and Atlantic Oceans. Most of the highest peaks of the US section are in Colorado, and they form a barrier between the Great Plains on the east and the western Great Basin. Mount Elbert in central Colorado is 4,398 m (14,431 feet) high. These are the youngest of North America's major mountain chains and

are an example of mountain-building at a constructive *plate boundary. Their great height and rugged scenery show little destruction by ice or rivers, although there has been enough *erosion to reveal their complicated geology. There is a central core of hard, dark, igneous and metamorphic rocks which rise to jagged peaks. These are flanked on either side by series of lighter, softer sedimentary rocks which were lifted and folded to their present height and have squarer, smoother shapes. The sequence of rocks and mountain-forms can be seen clearly in Canada along the railway between Edmonton, Alberta, and Kamloops, British Columbia. Numerous high peaks and plateaux are covered by snow and ice, particularly in the north. During cold periods of the *Pleistocene Epoch much more ice cover existed. It sculptured the crests and valleys into dramatic forms, as in the Wind River Mountains, Wyoming, USA. A major attraction of the Rockies today is their scenery and their national parks, both in the USA and in Canada. They are also important economically, as they contain mineral deposits, particularly of gold, silver, copper, zinc, and lead. Timber is important in both Canada and the USA, as are the snow-fed rivers which provide water for power and irrigation. The dry *chinook blows east from the Rockies.

**Rock flour** carried by a glacial stream clouds the sea off the coast of Alaska.

**Roentgen** *Röntgen.

**Romania**, an east European country with its east coast on the Black Sea, bounded by Ukraine and the republic of Moldova on the north and east, Hungary and Serbia on the west, and Bulgaria on the south. Half of it is mountainous: the Carpathians, curving from the north-west, meet the Transylvanian Alps in the centre of the country, where rainfall is heavy and there are large forests; Moldoveanu, at 2,543 m (8,343 feet) is the highest point. The rest of the country, including Transylvania to the north-west, Walachia to the south, and part of the region of Moldova to the east, is plain, much of it providing the richest soil in Europe. Here summers are very warm, and winters are very cold, with biting winds. The Danube forms the southern border as it flows east to its delta on the Black Sea. Underground the main resources are oil and natural gas, while there are also large deposits of coal and metallic ores.

**Röntgen, Wilhelm Konrad von** (1845–1923), German physicist, the discoverer of X-rays, for which he was awarded the first Nobel Prize for Physics in 1901. Röntgen was trained as a mechanical engineer before taking up an academic career in physics, and he was a skilful experimenter. He worked on a variety of topics but the two pieces of research for which he is famous were outside his normal scope. In 1888 he demonstrated the existence of a magnetic field caused by the motion of electrostatic charges, predicted by James *Maxwell's electromagnetic theory and important for future electrical theory; then in 1895 he observed by chance that a fluorescent screen began to glow brightly as soon as a current was passed through a Crookes' vacuum tube some distance away. He investigated the properties of this invisible radiation, which he called X-rays because of their unknown origin, and startled the world with the photograph of the bones of his wife's hand, taken on 22 Dec. 1895. The roentgen unit of ionizing radiation was named in his honour.

**root-mean-square** (r.m.s.), the square root of the *mean of the squares of a set of values. There are two important applications in physics. First, the pressure exerted by a gas depends on the r.m.s. of the speeds of its molecules. Secondly, an alternating current has the same heating effect as a steady current equal to its r.m.s. value. The current varies from zero to a maximum as it flows alternately backwards and forwards, and its r.m.s. value is equal to its maximum or peak value divided by $\sqrt{2}$.

**Ross, Sir John** (1777–1856), British polar explorer of Scottish extraction. After serving with distinction in the Napoleonic Wars, Ross led an expedition to Baffin Bay in 1818 and another in search of the North-West Passage between 1829 and 1833, during which he surveyed King William Land, Boothia Peninsula, and the Gulf of Boothia (the last two named in honour of the expedition's patron, the distiller and philanthropist, Felix Booth).

**Ross, James Clark** (1800–62), British polar explorer. A nephew of John *Ross, he served his apprenticeship as a polar explorer in the 1820s. In 1831 he discovered the north magnetic pole and in 1838 undertook a magnetic survey of the UK. Between 1839 and 1843 Ross commanded the *Erebus* and the *Terror* on an expedition to the Antarctic (where Ross Sea, Ross Barrier, and Ross Island all now bear his name), for which he was knighted.

**Rossby, Carl-Gustav Arvid** (1898–1957), Swedish-American meteorologist whose name is given to Rossby Waves—the huge, side-to-side swings in air and ocean currents caused by the *Coriolis force. In the atmosphere at the *polar front the sideways deviation of the current may become so great that it breaks off as an independent movement of warm and cold air: this is how depressions originate.

**Ross Ice Shelf**, the largest of many ice shelves on the coast of Antarctica. It surrounds Roosevelt Island and much of Ross Island, where the active volcano Mount Erebus and the extinct volcano Mount Terror are situated. Nearly the size of France, the ice-shelf is part of a slowly moving ice-cap which has stretched out over the sea but remains attached to the mainland. As the ice spreads seaward, thick chunks break off and float away as flat-topped icebergs, many of them several kilometres long.

**rotation of the Earth**, the revolution of the Earth round its own axis. It rotates through 360°, from west to east, in a solar day; but because its orbit round the Sun is not quite circular, the length of the solar day varies slightly from 24 hours throughout the year. Therefore Greenwich Mean Time is used for clocks instead of apparent solar time. The Earth in orbit round the Sun completes an extra revolution a year relative to the stars. For this reason another period, the sidereal day, is defined as one 365th of 24 hours (or nearly 4 minutes) shorter than a solar day. This varies by only a fraction of a second a year, although it is slowly becoming longer because the speed of the Earth's rotation is being diminished by the energy absorbed in its tides. The rotation also undergoes small and unpredictable variations due to changes in distribution of the Earth's mass, caused by such events as earthquakes.

**Rotorua**, a region of lakes, hot springs, and *geysers in the thermal belt of the North Island, New Zealand. It contains Lake Rotorua with the volcanic Mokoia Island at its centre. Sulphur and building stone are the natural products of their region, which is famed for the harnessing of steam to generate power.

**round-off errors**, the errors that arise in a calculation because some numbers are rounded off at an intermediate stage; that is, digits are dropped or replaced by zeros at the right-hand end. This may be because the quantity concerned is an *irrational number and has an infinite number of digits, or because of the limited capacity of the machine used for the calculation. The standard procedure for representing a number to $n$ decimal places is to consider the $(n + 1)$th place. For digits between 0 and 4 inclusive the $n$th place remains unchanged (rounded down); for digits between 5 and 9, one is added to the $n$th place (rounded up). For example 0.732 becomes 0.73 to two decimal places, whereas 0.738 becomes 0.74 to two decimal places. The round-off errors are 0.002 and −0.002 respectively. If $n$ is the approximation to a number $N$ and $e$ is the error, then $N = n + e$ and the signless numerical value of $e$ is called the absolute error. The numerical value of $e/N$ is called the relative error. In the above example, the absolute errors are both 0.002.

**Rowland, Henry Augustus** (1848–1901), US physicist who showed that a moving electric charge produced a magnetic field similar to that of an electric current flowing through a conductor. He demonstrated this by showing that

The **Ross Ice Shelf** forms an immense ice wall over 30 m (100 feet) high and 640 km (400 miles) long, bordering on the southern part of the Ross Sea.

the deflection of a magnetic needle produced by a charged sphere revolving about it is entirely a function of the sphere's velocity. He also conducted experiments to determine the value of the unit of electrical *resistance.

**Ruapehu, Mount**, at 2,797 m (9,175 feet), the highest point on the North Island, New Zealand, in Tongariro National Park. Its intermittently active peak rises from a volcanic plateau covered with ash, lava, and pumice-stone. There is a lake in its crater and, in winter, snow on its slopes.

**rubidium** (symbol Rb, at. no. 37, r.a.m. 85.47), a silvery white, highly reactive *alkali metal which is used in photo-electric cells. It was discovered by the German chemist Robert Bunsen and was named after the dark red colour of its flame in a flame test.

**ruby**, a gem species of *corundum ($Al_2O_3$; aluminium oxide), varying in colour from deep crimson to pale rose-red. As crystals rubies are usually six-sided prisms, the rare 'star' rubies having internal cavities which reflect light after cutting. Pigeon-blood rubies come from Myanmar (Burma), which has the best stones. Those from Sri Lanka are normally paler, and those from Thailand darker.

**runoff** (in hydrology), all the water moving out of drainage basins as surface flows, mostly as streams and rivers. It is made up of *overland flow and of water which has travelled through the soil (throughflow) or rock (*groundwater). In some basins, runoff is simply that part of precipitation over the basin surface not returned to the atmosphere by *evapotranspiration. In others, the quantity is increased or decreased by storage changes in the soil or rock; and in some basins—on limestone in particular—runoff may have little relationship to precipitation at the surface, because rivers and streams are fed by springs which may obtain their water from distant outcrops.

The amount of runoff and its variations are recorded by *hydrographs. In basins where overland flow predominates, runoff occurs rapidly after storms and a high proportion of precipitation enters channels, causing flood peaks. Where throughflow and groundwater predominate, the proportion of precipitation that runs off is less, but the variations in flow are also less, so that river discharge is more reliable. It is usually desirable to manage land use in basins so that runoff comes by sub-surface routes, rather than as overland flow.

**Rushmore, Mount**   *Black Hills.

**Russia**, a country in northern Asia and eastern Europe. Its borders touch Norway and Finland in the north, Poland in the north-west, Estonia, Latvia, Lithuania, Belarus, and Ukraine in the west, Georgia, Ajerbaijan, Kazakhstan, Mongolia, China, and Korea in the south; its maritime borders meet the Baltic Sea, Black Sea, the inland Caspian Sea, the Arctic, and the Pacific. It is separated from Alaska in the north-east by the Bering Strait. The largest country in the

A large **ruby** crystal 80 mm (3 inches) across from Aust-Agder county in southern Norway.

world, it spans eleven time zones and 160 degrees of longitude—nearly half-way around the Earth—from the shores of the Gulf of Finland in the Baltic Sea in the west to the peaks of Kamchatka in the east, from the frozen islands of Novaya Zemlya in the north to the warm Black Sea, the Caucasus Mountains, and the Pamirs and other ranges bordering China and Mongolia in the south. The north–south trending Ural Mountains divide European from Asian Russia. The plateaus and plains of Siberia make up most of the area to the east. To the west of the Urals extends the North European Plain. Great rivers include the Volga flowing south to the Caspian Sea, the Ob, Yenisei, and Lena draining north into the Arctic Ocean, and the Amur entering the Pacific Ocean to the east. East of the Lena is an area of mountains stretching from the Verkhoyanska to the Anadyr Range, which is half the size of Europe. Lake Baikal is Eurasia's largest, and the world's deepest, lake. Across the country extend belts of tundra (in the far north), forest, steppe, and fertile areas. Mineral wealth is great and includes coal, iron ore, copper, nickel, manganese, lead, zinc, uranium, diamonds, gold, silver, bauxite, tin, and platinum. The world's largest natural gas and petroleum deposits are in Siberia.

**rust**, hydrated iron oxide, reddish-brown in appearance and basically of the formula $FeO_2H$. It is a product of the *corrosion of iron and steel caused by moisture. The rate of its formation is increased by the presence of a dissolved salt such as sodium chloride and by atmospheric pollutants generally. It seldom occurs in hot, dry climates, except on coasts.

**ruthenium** (symbol Ru, at. no. 44, r.a.m. 101.07), a shiny, grey, brittle element with a high melting-point (2,310 °C, 4,890 °F). It is found in small quantities in a number of platinum ores. Industrially it is used as a hardening agent in forming alloys with platinum and other metals of the platinum group. These alloys are used in the manufacture of fine jewellery.

**Rutherford, Ernest, 1st Baron Rutherford of Nelson** (1871–1937), New Zealand-born British physicist who is widely regarded as the founder of nuclear physics, his researches in Montreal, Manchester and Cambridge having led to major discoveries concerning the nature of the *atom. While studying *radioactivity he established the nature of alpha and beta particles, and proposed the laws of radioactive decay. In 1911, he devised and supervised an experiment (now known as the Rutherford experiment) to measure the scattering of alpha particles by metal atoms. From the scattering which occurred (now known as Rutherford scattering), he concluded that the positive charge in an atom, and virtually all of its mass, is concentrated in a central nucleus, and that negatively charged electrons are in orbit round it. In essence, his view is still held today. In 1919 he bombarded nitrogen gas with alpha particles and found that the disruption of the nuclei had changed the nitrogen atoms into oxygen. This, his famous 'splitting the atom' experiment, caught the public imagination—realizing as it did the alchemist's dream of changing one substance into another. For his considerable services to science he received many honours, including the Nobel Prize for Chemistry in 1908.

**Ruwenzori**, an immense *horst of Precambrian crystalline rocks, between Lake Edward and Lake Albert in Uganda, in the western rift of the African *rift valley system. It is the

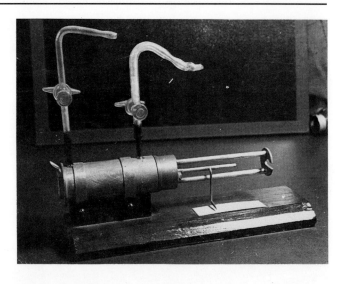

The apparatus used by Ernest **Rutherford** to bombard nitrogen with alpha particles. Alpha particles were fired into the tube from the right, and the protons produced when nitrogen nuclei were transmuted into oxygen nuclei could be detected as flashes on the fluorescent screen, visible at the left-hand end of the tube.

highest non-volcanic mountain in Africa, rising to 5,174 m (16,794 feet) in the snow-clad Mountains of the Moon. The summit stands roughly 3,600 m (12,000 feet) above the plateau. The entire mass has arisen from within a bifurcation in the rift valley. The latter marks a divergent *plate boundary.

**Rwanda**, a small country in east central Africa. It is bounded in the west by Zaïre and Lake Kivu, on the north by Uganda, on the east by Tanzania, and on the south by Burundi. The region is mountainous, and the equatorial climate is modified by the altitude. Set on the eastern edge of the Great Rift Valley, at the head of Lake Tanganyika, it is also volcanic. The soil is fertile, supporting crops of coffee and tea, and there are deposits of oil and natural gas. The mineral resources include cassiterite, wolframite, and gold.

**Rydberg, Johannes Robert** (1854–1919), Swedish physicist who established (1890) a general equation linking the various wavelengths of light emitted by hot hydrogen gas. Using wave numbers instead of wavelengths in his calculations, he was able to arrive at an expression that related the various lines in the spectra of chemical elements. The equation contains a constant now called the Rydberg constant.

# S

**Saar**, a coal-rich territory in south-west Germany bordering north-east France. Some 2,560 km² (990 sq. mi.) in area, it is crossed by the Saar River before it joins the Moselle, a tributary of the Rhine. It is underlain by a coalfield—the Saar Basin—which is about 72 km (45 miles) long and 26 km (16 miles) across. In Germany the coal deposits are exposed, but south of the Saar River they are overlain by increasingly thicker Triassic strata; they continue at depth into French Lorraine, where they have also been exploited.

**Sacramento River**, the major river of California, USA, at over 610 km (380 miles) in length. Rising on Mount Shasta in the Klamath Mountains, it runs due south to enter its lush valley. Here it is joined by the Pit, the first of its main tributaries, and reaches Red Bluff, where it becomes navigable. It irrigates the valley and is a source of hydroelectricity. On meeting the northward-flowing San Joaquin it turns west and enters San Francisco Bay on the Pacific Ocean.

**saddle** (in geomorphology)   *col.

**saddle points**, the points on the three-dimensional graph of a function of two variables, with a particular distinguishing characteristic. When such a point is approached from one direction the surface goes up and then down; approached from another direction it goes down and then up. The same point is both a local maximum and a local minimum, according to which line on the surface one considers. In the landscape a ridge between two higher summits is an analogous feature.

**Sahara**, the world's largest desert, stretching from the Atlantic Ocean across northern Africa to the Red Sea. The Sahara extends for more than 4,800 km (3,000 miles) from west to east and for nearly 2,000 km (1,250 miles) from the Mediterranean coastal plain to the Sahel. This is its present edge, but it is slowly creeping south as the desert spreads under the action of winds, and over-grazing, as agents of *erosion. Falling in the belt of *subtropical highs, it is the western part of an arid zone which extends across Arabia and into Asia. Its geology shows evidence of earlier vegetation, and satellite photographs have revealed river beds below the sand. Now, however, cultivation is confined to the *oases and to the banks of the Niger and the Nile Rivers. The surface is of three main types: shifting *dunes, denuded rock, and stones and gravel. There are intersecting *wadis, depressions, and plateaux at various levels, and great mountain ranges such as the Tibesti in the centre, which rise to 3,400 m (11,200 feet). Apart from salt from the many flats and boggy marshes, a variety of minerals, including iron, and oil and natural gas can be found. The climate is severe. Temperatures range from over 38 °C (100 °F) during the day to near freezing at night. Annual rainfall is generally less than 150 mm (6 inches), and it comes irregularly, in short but violent thunderstorms. Sometimes a drought will last for years. Air pressure drops towards the Equator, and the winds blow strongly. They are heavy with suspended dust particles and are always dry. The *sirocco and *harmattan are local winds which originate in the desert.

**Saint Christopher and Nevis**   *Saint Kitts and Nevis.

**Saint Elias Mountains**, part of the Pacific mountain system which sweeps round the Gulf of Alaska. They provide a natural barrier between the south-west corner of the Canadian Yukon and part of the coast of south-east Alaska. Effectively they are an extension of the fiord-indented Coast Range of British Columbia, which consists largely of intrusive granites. The summits of the Saint Elias range include several over 4,000 m (13,000 feet), while Mount Logan, the highest in Canada, rises to 6,050 m (19,850 feet). The high relief, latitude, and precipitation have resulted in extensive glaciation, some of the glaciers descending to sea-level.

**Saint Elmo's fire**, an electrical discharge which is sometimes seen during *thunderstorms around high projecting objects such as the mast of a ship. It occurs because an electric field, concentrating round the sharp projection, has become large enough to produce *ions in the air, which glows as a result. Saint Elmo was a patron saint of sailors and his 'fire' was believed to give protection against storms.

**Saint Helena**, an island isolated in the south Atlantic Ocean at latitude 16° S., some 1,850 km (1,150 miles) east of the Angolan coast of Africa. A British dependency, it is 16 km (10 miles) long by 10 km (6 miles) wide. It is volcanic in origin and has cliffs up to 610 m (2,000 feet) falling sheer into the sea on three sides. South-east winds keep the island cool and wet; and water-cut ravines broaden into deep valleys. There are few natural resources.

**Saint Helens, Mount**, a volcanic peak 2,950 m (9,677 feet) high in south-west Washington, USA, which erupted in 1980. It is a typical strato-volcano and is one of a chain of recent volcanoes that make up the Cascade Range. After a dormant period lasting about 130 years, Mount Saint Helens erupted in May 1980 and caused devastation in an area 32 km (20 miles) broad. Ash rose 20 km (12 miles) into the air

The eruption of Mount **Saint Helens** was one of the greatest volcanic explosions ever recorded in North America.

and drifted across the continent, settling widely. Lava flows remain a danger.

**Saint John**, a river 725 km (450 miles) long, which runs across northern Maine, USA, parallel to the Appalachian Mountains, then turns abruptly south across the central highlands of New Brunswick. Beyond these mountains it resumes its 'Appalachian' trend before turning south again to enter the Bay of Fundy at Saint John. The river is made up of alternating consequent and subsequent sections; the latter conform to the geological setting, whereas the former cut across it. At the narrow mouth of the river are the famous Reversing Falls, which result from the advance of the *Fundy tides over a rock ledge.

**Saint Kitts and Nevis** (Saint Christopher and Nevis), an island country in the Leeward Islands of the Caribbean Sea. Saint Kitts is an oval-shaped volcanic island crossed by rugged mountains and rising to Mount Misery at 1,131 m (3,711 feet). In the south-east a narrow isthmus enlarges to a knot of salt ponds. Three kilometres (2 miles) to the south-east, Nevis, which is round and smaller, rises to Nevis Peak at 1,096 m (3,596 feet). Both have an equable, tropical climate. The tiny island, Sombrero, makes up the group.

**Saint Lawrence**, a river and a gulf forming the natural components of the Saint Lawrence Seaway, in eastern North America. The river, nearly 1,200 km (750 miles) long, issues from Lake Ontario and flows north-eastward. First it passes among the Thousand Islands—in fact, over 1,500 islands, islets, and shoals—and forms part of the boundary between Canada and the USA. This section is unnavigable, owing to ice, for the four winter months. The fertile and in places heavily wooded valley continues, down-faulted, along the edge of the *Canadian Shield. Some of the world's largest deposits of asbestos are found here, while the huge volume of water that passes down from the Shield is a major source of hydroelectricity. The tidal estuary is nearly 640 km (400 miles) long and widens to over 100 km (60 miles) at its mouth. The river enters the Gulf of Saint Lawrence round Anticosti Island, north of the Gaspé Peninsula. Often fog-bound, and with drifting ice-sheets in winter, the Gulf is inhospitable. Extending for upwards of 800 km (500 miles) from north to south, it contains Prince Edward, Magdalen, and many smaller islands. The Atlantic reaches in through the Strait of Belle Isle north of Newfoundland and south through the Cabot Strait, just within the limit of the area affected by Quaternary glaciation.

**Saint Lucia**, an island country, one of the Windward Islands of the Caribbean. It is 43 km (27 miles) in length, roughly oval-shaped, and picturesquely rugged, rising to Morne Gimie at 959 m (3,145 feet). In the south-west is the dormant volcano Qualibou with its solfataras (boiling sulphur springs). The twin peaks of the Pitons have fine volcanic cones. The fertile volcanic valleys and coastal plains are well watered and the interior has virgin forests and mineral springs. There is a fine harbour. Timber, bananas, cocoa, copra, and coconuts are all grown.

**Saint Vincent and the Grenadines**, an island country in the Windward Islands of the Caribbean. It occupies a total area of 388 km² (150 sq. mi.). The main island, Saint Vincent, is 29 km (18 miles) long. Of volcanic origin, it has forested, rugged mountains rising to the active volcano of Mt Soufrière at 1,234 m (4,048 feet). There are picturesque valleys and fertile well-watered tracts. While the climate is tropical, there are hurricanes and occasional earthquakes.

**Sakhalin**, in Russian east Asia, a markedly elongated island, roughly 1,000 km (620 miles) long and oriented north–south, in the Sea of Okhotsk. It is separated from the Pacific coast of Siberia by the Tatar Strait and from the Japanese island of Hokkaido by La Perouse Strait. The northern part of the island, opposite the delta of the Amur, is relatively low-lying and includes the Manchili Plain—a veritable tundra environment. The remainder comprises subdued mountain ranges. Crab, herring, cod, and salmon are fished; other industries include petroleum extraction, coal mining, and lumbering.

**Sakharov, Andrey Dmitriyevich** (1921–89), Russian nuclear physicist and human rights activist. Born in Moscow, he worked in the early 1950s as a theoretical physicist to develop the former Soviet Union's first hydrogen bomb, devising, with others, the theoretical basis for controlled thermonuclear fusion (see *nuclear fission and fusion). During this time he was made the youngest ever member of the Soviet Academy of Sciences. Disillusioned with his work he publicly protested in 1961 against the testing of a Soviet 100-megaton hydrogen bomb, fearing the effects of widespread radioactive fallout (see *radioactivity). Thereafter, he called for nuclear arms reduction and became an active campaigner for human rights. In 1980 he was exiled to the closed city of Gorky and not released until 1986 under Soviet government reforms and policies of *perestroika* and *glasnost*. After his release he was elected to the Congress of People's Deputies, where he continued to fight for human rights in Russia. He was awarded the Nobel Prize for Peace in 1975.

**salinity** (of seawater), the proportion of dissolved salts in the ocean. Salinity is nowadays determined from measurements of electrical *conductivity, which is proportional to the concentration of dissolved salts. The average is about 35 parts per thousand (35 $^o/_{oo}$) by mass; but the salinity of subtropical and partially enclosed basins is higher as a result of evaporation (it rises to nearly 40 $^o/_{oo}$ in parts of the Mediterranean and 55 $^o/_{oo}$ in the Red Sea), while it is lower wherever fresh water from rivers or melting ice enters a sea. The principal *cations in seawater are $Na^+$, $Mg^{2+}$, $Ca^{2+}$, and $K^+$ (in that order), and the principal *anions are $Cl^-$, $SO_4^{2-}$, and $HCO_3^-$. The main salts formed by evaporation of sea water are calcium carbonate and sulphate, sodium chloride and potassium and magnesium chloride, in that sequence of precipitation; and these salts are found in *evaporite deposits. Seawater also contains trace amounts of all of the other chemical elements, though some are in concentrations so small they are barely detectable. In the ocean as a whole there is enough salt to cover the world's land mass with a layer 150 m (nearly 500 feet) thick. Extraction by evaporation is relatively simple, compared with desalination processes for the production of fresh water fit to drink.

**salinization** (of soil), the accumulation in *groundwater of soluble salts, derived from weathering or from wind- or rain-borne oceanic salts. This occurs in poorly drained areas in regions where evaporation greatly exceeds precipitation. As a result of intense evaporation these salts are carried up through the soil by capillary action and are re-deposited in distinct layers. If the *water-table is shallow—that is, less than 2 m (6.5 feet) from the surface—salt deposition occurs

Extensive **salt-flats** on Lake Grace, Western Australia. The thick crust of sodium chloride covers a mixture of mud and gypsum crystals.

at or near the soil surface; if the table is deeper than this, salt-rich layers form lower down the *profile. These salt accumulations inhibit plant growth, and soils which have undergone salinization are generally infertile.

**salt** (in chemistry), a compound generally formed by the reaction between equivalent quantities of an *acid with a *base. (See also *ionic compound).

**saltation**, the movement of sediments bouncing across a surface. It is an important component of river and wind *erosion.

**salt dome**, an underground feature formed by the upward movement, under pressure, of a low-density salt-enriched mass within layers of sedimentary rock to form a dome of salt which intrudes, rather like *magma, into the surrounding country rock. These structures are often associated with oil and gas reservoirs within the rock.

**salt-flat**, a level or very gently sloping area covered by thick deposits or crusts of salt. Salt-flats are often found around the margins of salt lakes and, in deserts, forming the flat floor of closed basins which once contained a *playa lake. When a salt lake dries up, either temporarily or permanently, the soluble salts in the water are left behind and form the crust. Salt-flat deposits are a major source of edible salt and of soda for glass-making. The flats at Bonneville in Utah, USA, and Lake Eyre in Australia are used as sites for motor speed-trials.

**salt-marshes**, flat, poorly drained areas of land subject to periodic or occasional inundation by salt water. They are commonly situated along sheltered, low-lying coasts, although they can also occur inland in salt lake basins. Coastal salt-marshes generally form in protected environments behind shingle bars and sand-pits; but they can also form in the sheltered parts of estuaries when silt and mud are deposited during times of *slack water between the tides. At or near sea-level they are rapidly colonized by salt-tolerant plants such as eel-grass, marsh samphire, and rice grass. This vegetation helps to slow down the flow of water over the surface, thus reducing *wave erosion and helping to trap more silt and mud. Gradually the surface of the marsh is built up above sea-level. Areas of high marsh, which are only flooded during *spring tides, are known as saltings.

**salt-pan**, a small, shallow basin of internal drainage found in desert areas. Salt-pans generally contain salt lakes, although sometimes the water has evaporated away leaving *salt-flats. The term is also used for very small depressions found on marshes which contain salt water. Salt is obtained from major salt-pans by evaporation.

**saltpetre**    *potassium nitrate.

**salt plug**, a particular form of *salt dome. Salt plugs are of roughly circular form, narrow in diameter, and can extend downward into the country rock for thousands of feet. They are completely intrusive, and do not crop out on the surface (they would then be termed piercement domes).

**Salween River**, one of the world's mightiest rivers, rising—along with the Mekong and Yangtze—on the slopes of Tibet's Tanglha Range. These rivers leave eastern Tibet by three famous parallel gorges. They then flow southward across the Yunnan plateau in huge trenches. The Salween is the westernmost of the three and eventually enters Myanmar (Burma), where it finally empties into the Andaman Sea. Its length is about 2,400 km (1,500 miles). Being snow-fed, the river comes down in flood in summer.

**Samoan Archipelago**, a group of mainly mountainous, volcanic islands lying 14° south of the Equator in the Pacific Ocean around longitude 170° W. Western Samoa is a country comprising nine of them; US Samoa comprises another seven to the east. All lie in a hurricane belt and suffer from tornadoes. Copra from the coconut palm is the main natural resource.

**San Andreas Fault**, a major *fault in the Earth's crust, occurring on the boundary between the North American and the Pacific crustal *plates. It is the principal fracture among a network of faults and stretches 965 km (600 miles) from north of San Francisco to the Gulf of California. The average rate of horizontal movement along the fault in north and central California is about 1 cm (half an inch) a year. Several thousand earthquakes occur along it annually, although few are of any great significance. A notable exception was the 1906 earthquake that devastated San Francisco and caused enormous loss of life.

The Carrizo Plain in southern California lies in the **San Andreas Fault**. The offset gullies clearly show the movement of the fault.

**sand**, grains of rock and mineral particles (often *quartz grains) with sizes between 2 and 0.0625 mm (about 0.08 inches to 0.0025 inches). It results from the disintegration of rocks by weathering and erosion, especially in dry climates, and may be formed by the action of the sea, by rivers, by wind action, or by the melt-waters of glaciers. It is used to make glass and, mixed with lime and gravel, cement.

**sand-bar**, a low, elongated ridge, chiefly of sand but often containing mud or shell fragments, that occurs parallel to coasts in shallow waters. Sand-bars may be formed at the mouth of a river, across a bay between two headlands, or in a zone of breaking waves off-shore from a beach. The sediment is deposited by the action of current and waves in the form of ridges which are generally, although shallowly, submerged; some may be exposed at low tide.

**sand sea**, a great sheet of *sand, found only in the hot deserts of the world. Sand seas are produced by the wholesale disintegration of large quantities of rock into highly resistant quartz particles and by the accumulation of these particles in huge deposits. When dry and bare of vegetation, their surfaces are moulded entirely by the wind, which builds and moves great ripples and dunes of sand like the waves of the sea.

**sand-spit**, a long, narrow accumulation of sand attached to the coast at one end and projecting out into the sea. Sand-spits generally form from beach material which is being carried gradually down the coast by *longshore drift. When the

**Sandstone** at Zion National Park, Utah, USA, shows a form of stratification known as cross-bedding. This type of deposition, where the layers of the bed are inclined at different angles, is a common sandstone feature.

coastline turns in abruptly, this material is not carried round the headland but is deposited seawards along the preceding line of the coast.

**sandstone**, an important class of *sedimentary rocks: consolidated deposits of material which is predominantly sand-sized. Usually rich in quartz grains, sandstones can be cemented by various materials, including silica and calcium carbonate. They form in various ways. Some, such as *arkoses, form by the accumulation of material weathered from pre-existing rocks (terrigenous sandstones). Most are formed in the sea; some are deposited in freshwater lakes; others are the products of wind action (having formed as *dunes) or have been deposited from glacial meltwaters. Some, such as *greywackes, are the products of rapid deposition. Many varieties of sandstone are quarried and used as building stone or crushed for building aggregate.

**San Marino**, a tiny, land-locked country near the Adriatic Sea in east-central Italy. It is just 61 km² (24 sq. mi.). Building stone from Mount Titano is exported.

**São Tomé and Príncipe**, a country comprising two islands in the Gulf of Guinea, off the coast of West Africa. They are situated on the Equator.

**sapphire**, a gem species of *corundum ($Al_2O_3$; aluminium oxide). Sapphires are extremely hard and are normally of a transparent blue colour (although they can be almost any other colour except red—then they are *rubies). The best deposits are found in igneous rocks in Sri Lanka, Myanmar (Burma), Australia, and Montana, USA.

**saprolite**, a deposit of silt and clay that has been formed *in situ* by deep weathering and soil-forming processes acting

upon rock. The character of a saprolite depends upon the local climate, drainage, and rock-type. It is readily formed in humid conditions on igneous or metamorphic rocks.

**Sardinia**, a large island in the western Mediterranean Sea, now part of Italy, lying just south of the smaller island of Corsica. Some 257 km (160 miles) long and 109 km (68 miles) wide, it is composed of uplifted mountainous blocks, part of an old, once-submerged, land mass. They are rugged, snow-covered in winter and parched in summer, providing only poor pasture for goats and sheep. The depressions between them are more fertile, however; and in the south-west is a region where lead and zinc are mined.

**Sargasso Sea**, an area of sea lying at the centre of circulation of the great North Atlantic currents. Its extent and position vary from summer to winter, but it remains relatively warm throughout the year and on its surface yellowish Sargasso seaweed thrives. Eels from the rivers of Europe and eastern North America come here to breed.

**Saskatchewan**, the central of Canada's three prairie provinces, bordering on Alberta on the west and Manitoba on the east. On the north it is bounded by the Northwest Territories and on the south, at the 49th parallel, by the USA. The northern third is a fairly desolate region of rivers, swamp, and lakes, including parts of Lake Athabasca (where oil shales and uranium are found) and Reindeer Lake. A belt of mixed forest between the Churchill and Saskatchewan Rivers opens southward to the prairie-plateau land, where wheat is grown and potash mined. The plateaux rise to the south-west, with a maximum height of 1,392 m (4,546 feet); here oil is found. The climate is continental, with long, very cold winters in the north and extremely warm, sunny summers. Annual precipitation is low and generally no more than 370 mm (15 inches).

**Saskatchewan River**, a river system which, for 1,930 km (1,200 miles), traverses both Alberta and Saskatchewan in Canada. The North Saskatchewan and the headstreams of the South Saskatchewan—the Bow and Oldman Rivers—all rise in the Rocky Mountains, below the divide with British Columbia. They descend eastward on winding courses to the prairies, picking up tributaries and gradually converging until both northern and southern branches are major waterways. They meet in the centre of Saskatchewan, near the head of the broad, low valley of the main river. The flow then continues to wind eastward, into Manitoba, through Cedar Lake and over the Grand Rapids into Lake Winnipeg.

**Saudi Arabia**, a country in south-west Asia occupying most of the peninsula of Arabia. Most of it is set on a plateau of deserts which rises to mountains in the south and falls away to a low plain in the east. It is dry, hot, and often windy. The ground varies between rock, gravel, and bare sand, and little grows except in the oases and along the Red Sea coast, where slight seasonal rain makes possible the cultivation of dates and a few cereals. The chief resource, oil (about a quarter of the world's reserves), is found mainly in the north-east, both on shore and in the Gulf.

**savannah**, a grassy plain in tropical and subtropical regions, with few or no trees, lying on the margin of the trade wind belts. The grasses characteristically flourish during the rainy summer period, and wither in the dry winters.

**scalars** (in mathematics), quantities having only magnitude, and no direction. A scalar quantity is one which can be measured by a scalar: examples are length and temperature. If a direction is associated with a scalar it becomes a *vector. Scalars can multiply vectors, and two vectors can be multiplied to give a scalar.

**scale, geometrical**, the relation between distances on a map or drawing and the actual distances they represent. On a graph the scale indicates the length of the interval on an axis which represents one unit. The term is also used in 'scale factor' to denote the number of times by which the size of a figure has been multiplied as a result of some transformation which it has undergone. A scaling is a transformation in which distances in a given direction are multiplied by some prescribed factor.

**Scandinavian Peninsula**, the great peninsula of northern Europe which shelters the shallow Gulf of Bothnia and the Baltic Sea. In the Swedish east and south it is Precambrian, part of the *Fennoscandian Shield which also underlies Finland. The Norwegian north and west is Palaeozoic folds with some sedimentary cover. During the Pleistocene Epoch huge and heavy ice-sheets eroded the rocks, leaving innumerable glacial valleys, *fiords, and lakes. Jostedalsbreen in western Norway is Europe's largest ice-field outside Iceland: Lake Vänern in southern Sweden is one of Europe's largest lakes. Norway's western mountains rise to the Glittertind Mountains at 2,470 m (8,104 feet), and the fiords cut deeply into them. A ridge of mountains running down the spine of the peninsula has slopes which fall abruptly westwards to the serrated and densely islanded coast of the Norwegian Sea. The southern, longer slopes are heavily glaciated and broadly terraced with a series of parallel ribbon lakes. The peninsula is rich in iron and copper. The north, which contains Lapland, lies within the Arctic Circle, but the western coastal climate is tempered by the *North Atlantic Drift. There is frequent snow in winter, when the nights are long and dark and the eastern coasts are ice-bound. The south has about 630 cm (25 inches) of precipitation in most years.

**scandium** (symbol Sc, at. no. 21, r.a.m. 44.96) is one of the Group III metals, found in many of the ores of the lanthanides in Scandinavia, from which its name originates. It is extracted from these ores by precipitation. The metal is fairly reactive; it is used to strengthen alloys but otherwise it has very few industrial uses.

**scarp** *escarpment.

**scatter diagram** *regression analysis.

**Scheele, Karl Wilhelm** (1742–86), Swedish chemist, whose wide-ranging chemical researches led to the discovery of oxygen, chlorine, manganese, and other elements and many important compounds, including a number of organic acids such as citric acid. He discovered oxygen in 1773, at least a year before Joseph *Priestley (but published his results after Priestley had announced his discovery), and made detailed studies of the role of oxygen in combustion. He was trained as an apothecary's assistant and remained a practising pharmacist all his life.

**Scheldt** (French, Escaut), an important waterway of north-west Europe, 435 km (270 miles) long. Generally aligned south-west to north-east, parallel to the North Sea coast, it rises in northern France and flows across central Belgium to join the composite Scheldt–Meuse–Rhine *delta at Antwerp. Here it turns north-west to reach the sea through the Western Scheldt, in The Netherlands. Numerous navigable tributaries and canals link it with the Somme-Seine system, the Sambre-Meuse system, and the North Sea.

**schist**, a relatively coarse-grained *metamorphic rock with dark and light minerals (especially micas) arranged in wavy bands about half a centimetre (0.25 inches) thick. Schists are typical products of regional metamorphism of intermediate grade. Schists can be derived from many sedimentary rocks (but most commonly from clays or silts). They can consequently vary in physical appearance. They are common throughout the world and predominate in older rocks.

**Schrödinger, Erwin** (1887–1961), Austrian physicist and Nobel Prize Winner who, in the 1920s, began the development of *quantum mechanics, a mathematical theory which

An example of an exposed face of **schist** at Glen Moriston, Inverness-shire, Scotland, UK. Note the bands of quartzite, injected in a molten state into the older metamorphic schist.

describes the structure and properties of atoms and the particles they contain. He started with Louis de Broglie's (1892–1987) suggestion that all particles can be regarded as matter waves, and applied conditions imposed by the *quantum theory to find the states in which these waves could exist. He spent World War II in Dublin and wrote a book, *What is Life?*, which was the inspiration of many physicists who became molecular biologists. (See also *Schrödinger equation.)

**Schrödinger equation**, the fundamental equation of *quantum mechanics. The equation treats particles as waves, and yet it enables us to 'locate' these waves—as though they were particles. The equation, named after Erwin *Schrödinger, relates the energy of the electron to the field in which it is situated. It has many possible solutions; however, since quantum theory allows electrons to have only certain specific energies, only some of the solutions are allowed. As well as enabling us to calculate the energy of electrons, the Schrödinger equation also gives us a mathematical parameter known as the *wavefunction, which is represented by the Greek letter psi ($\psi$). The wavefunction enables us to calculate the probability of an electron being at a particular place at a particular time. This means we can work out, for an electron in the field of a nucleus, where the electron is likely to be; from this we can determine the shape of the orbitals which electrons occupy in atoms.

**Scilly Isles** (UK), a cluster of about forty small islands and granite rocks lying 45 km (28 miles) from the south-west tip of England. Only five—St Mary's, Tresco, St Martin's, Bryher, and St Agnes—are large enough for habitation, and none is more than 4 km (2.5 miles) long. The climate, influenced by the Gulf Stream, is mild enough for the cultivation of subtropical plants.

**scoria** (in geology), the rough clinker-like masses formed by the cooling of the surface of molten *lava when it is exposed to the air and is distended by the expansion of the gases imprisoned in it. The same word is also used for material of this kind that has been thrown out by a volcano and has fallen to the ground as *pyroclasts. Scoria is partly crystalline and partly glassy in texture and is usually dark in colour.

**Scotia Ridge**, a mainly submerged ridge in the South Atlantic Ocean, linking Tierra del Fuego off South America with Graham Land in Antarctica. About 2,400 km (1,500 miles) in length, it contains in the east a recurved *island arc, the northern part of which is thought to border a junction of the South American and Antarctic crustal *plates.

**Scotland**, the northern part of the north-west European island of Great Britain, together with the Hebrides, Orkneys, Shetlands, and many smaller islands. The mainland, which is approximately 430 km (270 miles) from north to south, is made up of the northern Highlands (the largest part), the central Lowlands, and the southern Uplands, each running from north-east to south-west. The Highlands are separated from the Lowlands by the Grampian Mountains, divided by the Great Glen and containing Ben Nevis which, at 1,343 m (4,404 feet), is the highest peak in Great Britain. Scotland is separated from England by the River Tweed, the Cheviot Hills, the Liddell River, and the Solway Firth. It is bounded on the north and west by the Atlantic Ocean and on the east by the North Sea. It has 3,700 km (2,300 miles) of coastline, because of its deeply indented lochs and firths

(estuaries) of sea. Only about one fourth of the land is under cultivation. Sheep are grazed for meat and wool, and cattle are pastured. There are deposits of coal, iron, mica, and sand for glass. The Lowlands comprise a hilly plain which is cut into by the firths of the Tay and Forth on the east and the Firth of Clyde in the west. The eastern valleys, drier than the west, support the cultivation of cereals and vegetables. The herring catch from the North Sea provides exports, as do valuable off-shore oil fields.

**Scott, Robert Falcon** (1868–1912), British polar explorer. Entering the Royal Navy in 1881, Scott commanded the National Antarctic Expedition of 1900–4, surveying the interior of the continent, charting the Ross Sea, and discovering King Edward VII Land. On a second expedition (1910–12) Scott and four companions (E. A. Wilson, L. E. G. Oates, H. R. Bowers, and Edgar Evans) made a journey to the South Pole by sled, arriving there in January 1912 to discover that the Norwegian explorer Roald *Amundsen had beaten them to their goal by a month. On the journey back to base Scott and his companions were hampered by bad weather and illness, the last three finally dying of starvation and exposure in March. Their bodies and diaries were discovered by a search party eight months later. Scott, a national hero, was posthumously knighted.

**scree**, a mass of debris, comprising loose fragments of rock that covers a steep, bare slope or is piled up in a conical or fan-shaped mass at its foot. (Another name is talus.) The particles are detached from the rock walls by the action of rain and frost, and they fall or slide downslope until they interlock with other fragments. Active scree slopes are bare of

R. F. **Scott** working on his diary in the base-camp hut. Situated at McMurdo Sound on what became known as Hut Point, the hut was about 15 by 7.5 m (50 by 25 feet) and heated by stoves. The expedition moved in on 17 January 1911. Scott left it for the Pole on 23 October.

vegetation, since their surface is constantly disturbed by new falls of debris, bouncing downslope. They also tend to show a definite zoning of material, with the largest blocks travelling furthest and forming the lower portions of the scree.

**sea**, a geographical division of the continuous sheet of salt water that forms the *ocean. In general seas are shallower than oceans and confined by areas around the margins of continents; and although their boundaries are sometimes arbitrarily drawn, they usually reflect physical, chemical, or biological differences between one sea and another. Some virtually landlocked seas, like the Mediterranean, communicate with the open ocean only by means of narrow straits. Since the exchange of water with the open ocean is limited, such seas have very distinctive physical and chemical characteristics and relatively limited tidal action. Seas along continental margins, such as the North Sea and the China Sea, are in contrast much less enclosed and exchange water with the open ocean more easily. Extremely large inland lakes are often known as seas, particularly if they contain salt water: the Dead Sea, Caspian Sea, and Aral Sea are examples.

**sea-floor spreading**, the movement of the *plates that form the floors of the oceans away from the *mid-oceanic ridges. According to *plate tectonics it is the process by which oceans are formed and enlarged. Magma—molten igneous rock—rises through fissures at the mid-oceanic ridge to solidify (usually below the sea) and fill the gaps that are left as the plates move apart. New crust is thus formed. As a result of sea-floor spreading, the age of the rocks of the ocean floors increases as one travels away from the axis of a mid-oceanic ridge. The sea floors on each side of a mid-oceanic ridge are characterized by *magnetic anomalies that are arranged in bands parallel to the axis of the ridge and are symmetrical with respect to it. They are interpreted as representing the direction of the Earth's magnetic field at the time when the rocks crystallized.

**sea ice**, ice which has been formed by the freezing of seawater and not from ice formed on land (*icebergs). When ice crystals first grow and coalesce the salt is excluded and eventually returned to the sea and the sea-surface takes on an oily appearance; so newly forming sea ice is known as grease (or frazil) ice. As the grease ice thickens it breaks into pieces, up to a few metres across; these are known as pancake ice, because of their rounded shape and raised edges, which result from their frequent collisions one with another. Eventually, the ice thickens to form pack ice made up of individual ice floes.

In the Arctic Ocean much of the pack ice survives from year to year and there are great thicknesses of multi-year ice; the wind may tear the ice apart forming linear areas of open water (or leads) and when the floes come together again they may form pressure ridges as much as 30 m (98.5 feet) thick. By contrast in the Antarctic most of the sea ice melts each year, with the ice-cover in the Ross and Weddell Seas (see *Ross Ice Shelf) receding up as far as the edges of the ice shelves which extend from the continent. In the winter, Antarctic sea ice extends more than 1,000 m (3,283 feet) from the continent. However within the sea ice are several large areas of open water known as 'polynyas': how exactly these are maintained is not fully understood but they are thought to be important in the formation of the *water mass known as Antarctic Bottom Water.

**sea-level**, the height of the sea surface at a given time, varying continuously as a result of disturbances caused by *waves and *tides. The change in height is generally small but may be up to 20 m (65 feet). The average level of the sea through all states of the tide and wave conditions in a particular place is known as MSL, or the *mean sea-level. Sea-levels vary from place to place over the globe; and the surface of the ocean is irregular even without the effects of waves, tides, and currents. In the absence of these effects the shape of the sea-surface over the globe corresponds to that of the *geoid. The effect of major surface *ocean currents is

**Screes** at Wastwater in the Lake District, UK. Note the large rocks at the bottom of the main scree and how vegetation has colonized the less active scree.

to superimpose further small semi-permanent irregularities on the slope of the global sea-surface. Thus, there are small elevations in the subtropics, gentle depressions in the polar regions, and east–west troughs and ridges in the equatorial zone. The differences in height created by these features can be of the order of 1–2 m (3–6 feet). Along the eastern coast of North America, for example, between Nova Scotia and Florida, there is a difference in height of some 40 cm (16 inches). Sea-level south-east of Japan is about 1 m (3 feet) higher than it is off the Aleutian Islands. In addition, sea-level can be locally depressed or elevated by as much as 50 cm (20 inches), rise and fall (respectively) of atmospheric pressure. Average sea-level has varied markedly through geological time. During the last great ice age, when much of the water on the globe was locked up in vast ice-caps and continental glaciers, it was some 100 m (330 feet) lower in some places than it is today. River valleys formed at this time are now drowned to form coastal inlets known as *rias. On the other hand, during the warmest interglacial periods it was higher, to about the same degree, than it is at present. Wave-cut benches and other coastal features formed at those times are now exposed well above present high-tide levels.

**seamount**, an isolated generally conical peak rising from the ocean floor to a summit which may be a few hundred metres to a few kilometres below the sea surface. Most seamounts are *basaltic volcanoes that never grew above sea-level; but some stopped erupting at or just above sea-level, were then planed off by wave action and subsided *isostatically as the volcanic edifice cooled. Although seamounts have been identified in all three major ocean basins, they are most common in the Pacific, where it is thought there are about 10,000 of them. Some large submarine features called seamounts may in reality be small sub-marine plateaux and not of volcanic origin: the Great Meteor Seamount in the northern Atlantic, for example, rises 4,000 m (13,000 feet)

above the ocean floor and is 110 km (68 miles) across its base. Its flat summit has an area equal to 2,000 km$^2$ (770 sq. mi.).

**season**, the climatic division of the year. Seasons are caused by the movement of the Earth and its atmosphere round the Sun and the changes arising from their inclinations towards and away from it during the annual orbit. At any time of year the resulting conditions in the Southern Hemisphere, in terms of light and temperature, are generally the reverse of those in the Northern. The Poles experience only two seasons: a long winter and a short summer. In mid-latitudes there are four: winter, spring, summer, and autumn, reflecting variations in sunlight and biological response. In low latitudes there are generally two sets of two: firstly, as exemplified in the *horse latitudes, a short and cool winter followed by a long, hot summer, and secondly a wet season and a dry season. In some regions of the equatorial zone there are four seasons distinguished only by the degree of humidity and rainfall: two dry and two wet seasons. Halfway between winter and summer occur the *equinoxes, the two days in spring and autumn when day and night are equal in all places of equivalent latitude.

**sea water**, the water of the ocean, makes up about 97 per cent of all the water on the globe and initiates the *hydrological cycle. Unlike rain and the waters of streams and freshwater lakes, it contains quite a high concentration of dissolved salts, its *salinity varying from place to place. Traces of most of the naturally occurring elements are to be found, although none except sodium, chlorine, bromine, and magnesium are in concentrations sufficient to make extraction worth while.

Of great significance are the dissolved gases the sea contains, particularly its oxygen content. This is highest near the surface, where it supports marine life. The colour of sea water can be affected by additional components, for example algae can give a greenish colour to seawater while silt

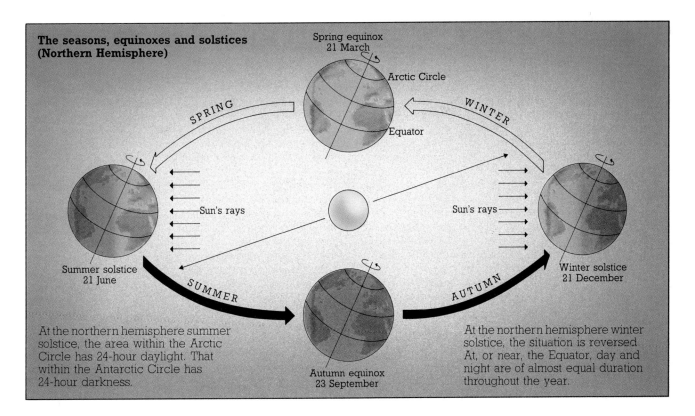

gives a yellowish colour. In the tropics, the water is an attractive clear blue because, being generally nutrient-poor, it does not support the microscopic plants and animals known, respectively, as phytoplankton and zooplankton.

**second**, the *SI base unit of time. It was first defined in terms of astronomical parameters such as the day (one revolution of the Earth on its axis). However, such parameters vary slightly, so the second had to be redefined in terms of an unvarying parameter. It is now defined as equal in duration to 9,192,631,770 periods of the radiation corresponding to the transition between two hyperfine levels of the ground state of the caesium-133 atom.

**Sedgwick, Adam** (1785–1873), British geologist who first established the order of formation of rocks in northern Wales, in the UK, and applied (in 1836) the term *Cambrian (from the Latinized derivative of Cymry, Wales) to the geological period in which they were formed. Together with Roderick *Murchison, he made a study of the shale and sandstones of Devonshire, in the UK, naming the period of its formation, the *Devonian.

**sediment** (in geology), unconsolidated material (fragments of rock) that is deposited from water on to the floor of the sea, a lake, or a river through the effects of gravity. In a more general sense 'sediment' is used to include solid materials deposited by water, wind, ice, or volcanic action, and in addition material of organic origin or material precipitated by chemical action, such as calcium carbonate. The process by which sediments become *sedimentary rocks is known as *diagenesis. It entails compaction and cementation. The weight of other sediments deposited above presses the grains of a sediment together, and water is forced out. The grains, now in close contact, are cemented together by the precipitation of secondary material, such as calcium carbonate. A consolidated sedimentary rock thus results.

**sedimentary rock**, a deposit that has been laid down by water, wind, ice, or gravity. The material of which sedimentary rocks are composed has usually been transported from its source. They have accumulated at or near the Earth's surface at normal temperatures and pressures, and are thus distinguished from igneous rocks, which have originated as *magma in a molten or semi-molten state, and from *metamorphic rocks, which have been produced by the effects of heat or pressure. Many sedimentary rocks were deposited in water in which the transported material was in a state of suspension or solution. After deposition they have been consolidated. Some, such as *loess, were deposited by the wind; some, such as boulder clay, are the result of glacial action; some have simply accumulated in place. Sediments can be divided into three groups: clastic rocks, chemical precipitates, and organic sediments. Of these, clastic sediments are the most abundant. They are made up of fragments of pre-existing rocks. Clays, sands, and gravels are in this category. Chemical precipitates include some limestones (the English Chalk, for example) and deposits formed by the evaporation of lakes or seawater. These deposited rocks include gypsum and halite (rock-salt). Organic sediments are those formed largely of the remains of once-living organisms: examples are coal, oil shale, and limestones made mainly of fossil material. By volume, sedimentary rocks make up only 5 per cent of the known crust of the Earth, compared with 95 per cent of igneous rocks. They are, however, exposed on over two-thirds of the Earth's land surface, forming thin but

Classic examples of **seif dunes** in the Namib Desert of Namibia, south-western Africa.

extensive deposits. The commonest types are shales, sandstones, and limestones. The earliest known sedimentary rocks came from the Barberton Mountain Land of South Africa; these have been dated as 3,500 million years old.

**seif dune**, an elongated dune with sharp ridges, which is formed in deserts as a result of winds blowing at right angles to one another on different occasions. A prevailing wind may spiral longitudinally along the ridge, which is built up by cross-winds often to a great height.

**Seine**, the chief river of northern France, some 770 km (480 miles) long. It rises in the east on the Plateau de Langres, and drops quickly to only 90 m (300 feet) above sea-level in the Paris Basin. Meandering in a leisurely fashion north-west across the Basin it receives among its other tributaries the Yonne on its left bank and the Marne and the Oise on its right, the system together draining the whole of the Basin. Then it loops its way westwards through Normandy, where, with dredging, it becomes navigable for sea-going craft. It enters the English Channel (la Manche) through an estuary south of the Le Havre peninsula.

**seismology**, the scientific study of *earthquakes and the resultant waves and shocks within the Earth. It is concerned with measuring the speeds at which shock waves can travel through the rocks of the *Earth's crust and mantle and how various rock bodies and interfaces deflect the shock waves. Seismologists use explosives to set off shock waves artificially. By making measurements at various points on the surface, they can then deduce the structure of the underlying rocks. This technique can be applied to other planets in the solar system.

**selenium** (symbol Se, at. no. 34, r.a.m. 78.96), a *metalloid in Group VI of the periodic table; it occurs in several different *allotropes. It occurs as an impurity in sulphide ores, from which it can be recovered. The stable, grey selenium allotrope contains chains of selenium atoms whose conductivity is increased by light; it is used as a photoconductor in photoelectric cells (see *photoelectric effects). It is also used in photocopying and as a constituent of steel. It is an essential trace element and is present in some garlic-smelling plants.

**semiconductor**, a material which conducts electricity much better than an insulator such as glass, but not nearly so well as a conductor such as metal. Unlike metals, their conductivity increases when the temperature is raised rather than when it is reduced. The increase in conductivity occurs because the extra thermal energy available at higher temperatures enables the electrons which are bound to atoms to break away. They escape, and move freely in the material. The greater the number of free electrons the more electrical charge can be transported, and so the conductivity increases. The electrical conductivity of such materials is also increased by 'doping'—that is, by the addition of small traces of certain impurities—because introduced elements may either contribute extra electrons, or reduce the number of electrons, for the conduction process. The former are called extrinsic semiconductors (or n-type, 'n' for negative) where the additional electrons act as negative current carriers; and the latter are referred to as intrinsic semiconductors (or p-type, 'p' for positive) where the current is carried by positively charged 'holes'. A hole behaves as if it were an electron with a positive charge. The elements germanium and silicon are widely used in elecronic devices and impurities such as arsenic, antimony, or phosphorous may be added to form extrinsic semiconductors; boron, aluminium, or gallium may be added to form intrinsic semiconductors.

**Senegal**, a West African country with an Atlantic coast. It surrounds the Gambia and is itself bounded inland by Mau-

Geophones being laid in the Empty Quarter, Saudi Arabia, for picking up shock waves from explosions. This use of **seismology** enables oil geologists to plot the structure of the strata below the desert's surface.

ritania, Mali, Guinea, and Guinea-Bissau. Its most westerly point (and that of continental Africa) is Cape Verde, formed by a volcano, to the north of which the coast is straight and sandy and offers a cool, dry climate. Inland there is *savannah, sparser in the north than in the south, which is wetter; the south of the country has a marshy coast. In winter the drying *harmattan wind blows from the interior. Groundnuts are grown, and there are reserves of phosphates.

**sequence** (in mathematics), an ordered list of mathematical terms. The Fibonnacci numbers, 1, 1, 2, 3, 5, 8, 13, . . . form a sequence in which each term is the sum of the two preceding terms. A linear sequence is one in which each term is obtained by adding a constant to the previous term. Triangles, quadrilaterals, pentagons, hexagons, and so on form a sequence of types of polygons.

**Sequoia National Park**, an area of outstanding natural beauty in east-central California, USA. It was established in order to conserve the giant sequoia trees it contains, among the oldest living matter on earth. (The General Sherman Tree is 9 m or 30 feet in diameter and over 83 m or 272 feet high.) The granite ridge of the Great Western Divide, scenic mountains of which Mount Whitney is the highest, deep canyons such as the Kern River Canyon, and the Marble Falls with its seven cascades are other spectacular features of the Park.

**Serbia**, a landlocked Yugoslav republic in south-east Europe, bordering Bosnia-Herzegovina in the west, Montenegro and Albania in the south-west, Macedonia in the south, Bulgaria in the east, Romania in the north-east, Hungary in the north, and Croatia in the north-west. In the south-west are the Săr Mountains and the Kapaonik Mountains, and in the east are the Balkan Mountains, while northern Serbia comprises a low-lying plain crossed by the Sava and Tisa Rivers, which flow into the Danube River. Grain and sugar beet are grown in the fertile northern plains, and coal is mined in the more mountainous south.

**series** (in mathematics), a term frequently used to mean simply a *sequence, but more precisely a sequence of terms connected by an operation. For instance, the following sequence $a$, $ar$, $ar^2$, $ar^3$, . . . combines to form the geometric series $a + ar + ar^2 + ar^3 + . . .$, where each term is a constant multiple of the previous term. In the arithmetic series $b + (b + d) + (b + 2d) + (b + 3d) . . .$, each term is formed by *adding* a constant to the previous term. *Convergent series and *divergent series have particular characteristics. *Power series have regularly increasing powers of a variable, while the *Taylor expansion is a series expanding a function.

**serpentine**, a magnesium silicate mineral that is green or greenish black in colour, and soft. There are two main varieties, antigorite and chrysotile, the latter being the major source of manufactured asbestos. Serpentine is formed by the alteration during metamorphism of *olivine and *pyroxene. It is used for ornamental purposes.

**set** (in mathematics), a collection of objects, each member of the collection being called an element. A set can be a collection of anything, but it must be precisely defined. Frequently elements of sets are abstract, for example numbers or points. A set is denoted by a capital letter and its elements by small letters. Thus a set $A$ is a collection of elements $a_1$, $a_2$, $a_3$, . . ., $a_n$ and this is written $A = \{a_1, a_2, a_3, . . ., a_n\}$, where the elements are contained within curly brackets. The symbol ∈ is used to show that a particular element belongs to the set, thus $a_2 \in A$. Every object in the universe under consideration is either in a or not. Those not in $A$ form its complement $A'$. The set containing no elements is the null or empty set ∅. That containing all elements is the universal set. Set $S$ is a subset of the larger set $A$ if all its elements are also in $A$, written as $S \subset A$. The union of two sets $A$ and $B$, written as $A \cup B$, is the set containing all elements of $A$ and all elements of $B$. The intersection of two sets $A$ and $B$, written as $A \cap B$, is the set of all elements which are both in $A$ and $B$. If $A \cap B = \emptyset$, then $A$ and $B$ are said to be disjoint.

Georg *Cantor introduced the concept of a set as an object of mathematical study, and set theory now attempts to provide a language, notation, and setting within which to do mathematics.

**Seto-Naikai**   *Inland Sea.

**Seventh Approximation**   *soil taxonomy.

**Severn**, name given to several important rivers. (1) The longest river in Britain, rising on the north-east slope of Plynlimmon in Wales and flowing in a rough arc for some 354 km (220 miles) to the Bristol Channel. It has seventeen tributaries, including the Wye, Stour, and two Avons, a great estuary, and a high *tidal bore. (2) A river in northern Ontario, Canada, flowing for 680 km (420 miles) from the Severn Lake north-east into Hudson Bay. Its valley is largely forested and swampy. (3) In southern Ontario, a stream 30 km (20 miles) long, issuing from Couchiching Lake and emptying into Georgian Bay, Lake Huron.

**Seychelles**, a country comprising an archipelago in the Indian Ocean, 4° S. of the Equator and some 1,500 km (930 miles) from the east African coast. The ninety-two islands are variously composed, the larger being of granite and volcanic rocks, sometimes surrounded by coral reefs. One group, of which Mahé at 142 km² (55 sq. mi.) is the largest, is mainly hilly; another outlying group is mostly flat. In the warm, wet climate palms and copra are the main resource.

**Shales** in Tertiary strata in sea cliffs at Tjörnes Peninsula, northern Iceland. The layers of fossil shells clearly show the marine nature of these sedimentary rocks.

**Shackleton, Sir Ernest Henry** (1874–1922), Irish-born British Antarctic explorer who, having reached latitude 82° S. with Robert *Scott in 1902, tried in 1908 to reach the South Pole. His expedition climbed Mount Erebus, reached the magnetic pole and scaled the Beardmore Glacier; but blizzards forced him back when, at latitude 88° S., he was only 160 km (100 miles) from the Pole. In 1914 he sailed again, planning this time to cross Antarctica from the Weddell to the Ross Sea; but his ship, *Endurance*, was crushed by ice in the Weddell Sea and the party was marooned. Drifting on ice-floes and using the ship's boats, they eventually made Elephant Island in the South Shetlands. Here Shackleton left his main party and sailed for rescue with five men in a small boat to South Georgia, 1,300 km (800 miles) away. In 1921 he began another expedition, but died of a heart attack on board his ship.

**shale**, a sedimentary *clay laid down in thin layers, which can easily be split apart: shales disintegrate in water. They are made up of mineral grains (quartz, feldspar, and mica) of microscopic size, together with clay particles and larger fragments of rock. Shales are very common and probably represent almost half of all sedimentary rocks. Oil shales contain so much decayed organic matter that they readily ignite, like bitumen.

**Shannon**, the chief river of Ireland and, at 390 km (240 miles) long, the longest in the British Isles. Rising on Cuilcagh Mountain it flows generally south through several lakes or loughs: Allen, Boderg, Forbes, Ree, and Derg. On its course it receives many tributaries, chief among them being the Suck, Brosna, and Deel, which together drain much of the farmland and peat bogs of the island's centre; and before entering its estuary in the south-west it becomes a source of hydroelectricity. The estuary, nearly 100 km (60 miles) long, is broad and navigable. It enters the Atlantic Ocean between the Loop Head and Kerry Head peninsulas.

**Shatt al-Arab Waterway** (Arabic, 'stream of the Arabs'), a tidal river rising in south-eastern Iraq, formed by the confluence of the Tigris and the Euphrates. It flows south-eastward for 192 km (120 miles) to the Gulf, passing Iraq's chief port of Basra and the Iranian port of Abadan. For the last half of its course the eastern bank forms the Iraq–Iran border. The river supplies fresh water to southern Iraq and Kuwait and is navigable for ocean-going vessels as far as Basra. Iran and Iraq have long disputed navigation rights, which are now in the control of Iraq.

**Shaw, Sir (William) Napier** (1854–1945), British meteorologist who introduced the millibar, a unit of measurement of air pressure, and was a pioneer of today's weather-forecasting service. His *Manual of Meteorology* (four volumes, 1926–31) was the first comprehensive treatment of the subject.

**sheet erosion**, the removal of particles of soil or soft, fine-grained sediment from broad sloping surfaces by sheets of running water. It occurs when heavy rainstorms or melting snow exceed the capacity of the surface to absorb water and it may give way, downslope, to *rills or *gullies. The effects on bare farmland—especially at the beginning of a growing season—are very serious, as it washes away seeds and seedlings as well as topsoil. Covering the surface with a mulch, or contour ploughing at right angles to the slope, are the best protection.

**sheet flood**, a thin, turbulent flow of water laden with fine sediment. Sheet floods occur on the flat surfaces of *pediments in arid areas. They are caused by torrential rains falling over upland areas, producing flash floods in their river channels. When the flows leave the uplands, they may spread into a sheet flood (and they may also build *alluvial fans). Very few reliable observations of sheet floods have ever been made, since they occur so sporadically.

**sheeting** (in geology), the jointing of rocks (usually igneous rocks) parallel to the ground surface. The joints are normally more closely spaced near the surface than at depth. It is caused by a number of factors: shrinkage on cooling, stress in the rock, and weathering among them.

**Shenandoah River**, one of the most scenic rivers of the eastern USA. Some 240 km (150 miles) long, it is formed between the Allegheny and Blue Ridge mountains by the union of its two headstreams, North Fork and South Fork. Its valley with orchards and pasture then runs north-east and the river joins the Potomac at Harper's Ferry. The Shenandoah National Park lies to the south-east in the Blue Ridge uplands.

**Shetland Islands**, a group of a hundred islands 80 km (50 miles) north-east of the Orkneys, with the isolated Fair Isle between the two groups. Only a score or so are large enough for settlement, by far the biggest being Mainland; of the others only Yell and Uist exceed 16 km (10 miles) in length. Muckle Flugga lighthouse on Uist is the most northerly point in the British Isles. The islands have deep, indented, fiord-like coasts (the sea lochs are locally called voes), and the winds are continuous and strong. Shetland sheep are renowned for their fine wool. The discovery of oil in the Brent and Ninian fields of the North Sea, north-east of Shetland, has boosted employment in the region.

**shield** (in geology), a large region on the continental *plates of the Earth's crust which has remained relatively stable over long periods of geological time. Shields are very old, usually *Precambrian, and are made up of igneous and metamorphic rocks surrounded by sedimentary platforms. Although very much worn down they are unaffected by later mountain building. Known also as cratons, they exist at or near the centres of all continental plates, away from the volcanic and earthquake zones of the plate boundaries. The Canadian and Western Australian shields are examples.

**shield volcano**, a very large volcano with gentle slopes built of *basalt which has been erupted on to the land or the sea floor. The fluidity of the lava allows it to flow considerable distances before cooling and solidifying; the resultant volcano is thus broad-based. Mauna Loa and Kilauea (Hawaii) both extend over 9,000 m (30,000 feet) from base to apex and are good examples of shield volcanoes.

**Shikoku**, the smallest of the four main islands of Japan, separated from the largest, Honshu, to the north, by the island-studded Inland Sea (Seto-Naikai). Northern Shikoku belongs to the so-called geological Inner Zone, with upstanding granitic hills. The central and southern parts, however, are included in the Outer Zone of Pacific fold mountains. This folding is associated with the destructive *plate boundary along the Ryukyu–Philippines subduction zone, where the Philippine plate is moving under its Eurasian counterpart.

**Shore platforms** at Curio Bay, South Island, New Zealand. The rock terrace here is the original floor of a Jurassic forest, dating back some 160 million years.

**shingle**, a mass of water-worn, rounded pebbles or cobbles, usually mixed with gravel and varying widely in size—from 20 to 200 mm (0.5 to 8 inches) in diameter—and occurring on the higher parts of beaches. It is carried there by powerful waves during storms; and since normal waves cannot move material of this size it tends to accumulate, forming ridges parallel to the shore. Shingle ridges sometimes form off shore as spits or *bars and are usually made of resistant materials such as flint.

**Ship Rock**, a volcanic peak in north-west New Mexico, USA, which reaches a height of 2,188 m (7,178 feet) above sea-level. Overlooking the San Juan River, it rises 430 m (1,400 feet) above the surrounding plateau, and its beauty is celebrated in Indian legend.

**Shkodër, Lake**, a vast, permanently flooded *polje on the border of Montenegro and north-west Albania. The flooding results from the fact that the floor of the polje is below sea-level. The 40-km (25-mile) long Buene (Serbo-Croat, Bojana) River connects the lake to the Adriatic Sea.

**shoestring rill**, an almost parallel *rill which occurs on very steep, bare slopes as a result of heavy rain, floods, or melting snow.

**shoreline** *coast.

**shore platform**, a horizontal or gently sloping bare rock surface on a coast, at or just above sea-level and generally backed by cliffs. Some shore platforms, particularly those that are submerged for part of the tidal cycle, appear to have been formed by long-continued water erosion. They are often called wave-cut platforms or benches. Those which are just above water-level were probably formed by subaerial weathering, aided by the destructive effects of spray and splash from storm waves.

**short-wave radiation**, *electromagnetic radiation with a wavelength in the approximate range 10 to 50 m (33 to 164 feet). Such waves can be reflected from the *ionosphere and are therefore capable of travelling large distances round the Earth. Their main application is in long-range broadcasting as *radio waves.

**shott**, a shallow lake and marshy area found in hot desert areas, particularly in North Africa. Shotts receive water from rainfall or rivers or groundwater, but tend to dry up in summer. Because of the high temperatures and the fast evaporation, the salts in the water are concentrated, producing brackish conditions and leaving a sheet of salt crystals at the surface when the shott dries out.

**shower** (in meteorology), a short, localized and often intense fall of *precipitation which is associated with heaped clouds, such as *cumulonimbus. Showers may be of rain, snow, sleet, or hail.

**sial**, a term formerly used for the material of the upper part of the *Earth's crust: the layer that makes up the bulk of the continents but is relatively thin under the oceans. It consists of rocks (granite, for example) that are rich in silica and aluminium, lying above the *sima.

**Siberia** (derived from Tatar, 'Sleeping Land'), the vast northern, central, and eastern region of northern Asia, which extends from the Ural Mountains eastward to the Pacific and from the Arctic Ocean southward to Mongolia and China. Nearly one-third is within the Arctic Circle. Here, and especially along the coastal plain, there is tundra; here also is the northern edge of the taiga or coniferous forest which stretches in a wide but irregular belt across the region. It extends over an area of about 12,800,000 km$^2$ (4,950,000 sq. mi.). There are three natural divisions. The west Siberian plain, abutting on the Ural Mountains, is low-

## SI units and equivalents in common use

| Quantity | Unit name (abbreviation) | Imperial equivalent | Definition or equivalent basic units |
|---|---|---|---|
| **Basic SI units** | | | |
| Length | metre (m) | 1 foot = 0.3048 m (exactly) | One metre equals the distance travelled by light in a vacuum in 1/299,792,458 of a second |
| Mass | kilogram (kg) | 1 pound = 0.4536 kg | One kilogram equals the weight of a substance equal to the weight of the International Prototype Kilogram, held at Sèvres in France |
| Time | second (s) | — | One second equals 9,192,631,770 periods of the radiation corresponding to the transition between the two hyperfine levels of the ground state of the caesium-133 atom |
| Electric current | ampere (A) | — | One ampere in each of two infinitely long parallel conductors of negligible cross-section 1 m apart in a vacuum will produce on each a force of $2 \times 10^{-7}$ N/m |
| Thermodynamic | kelvin (K) | — | One kelvin is 1/273.16 of the thermodynamic temperature of the triple point of water |
| Luminous intensity | candela (cd) | — | The luminous intensity of a black-body radiator at the temperature of freezing plantinum at a pressure of 1 standard atmosphere viewed normal to the surface is $6 \times 10^5$ cd/m$^2$ |
| Amount of substance | mole (mol) | — | One mole is the amount of a substance containing as many elementary units as there are carbon atoms in 0.012 kg of carbon-12. The elementary unit (atom, molecule, ion, etc.) must be specified |
| **Derived SI units** | | | |
| Acceleration | metre/second squared (m/s$^2$) | 1 foot/s$^2$ = 0.3048 m/s$^2$ (exactly) | |
| Area | square metre (m$^2$) | 1 square foot = 0.292 m$^2$ | |
| Capacitance | farad (F) | — | A s/v (C/v) (ampere-seconds per volt or coulombs per volt) |
| Charge | coulomb (C) | — | A s (ampere-seconds) |
| Density | kilogram/cubic metre (kg/m$^3$) | 1 pound/cubic foot = 16.02 kg/m$^3$ | |
| Energy (including heat) | joule (J) | 1 calorie = 4.1868 J (exactly) | N m (newton-metres) |
| Force | newton (N) | 1 pound force = 4.45 N | kg m/s$^2$ (kilogram-metres per second squared) |
| Frequency | hertz (Hz) | — | $1/s^{-1}$ (seconds $^{-1}$) |
| Inductance | henry (H) | — | V s/m$^2$ (volt-seconds per square metre) |
| Magnetic flux density | tesla (T) | — | V s (volt-seconds) |
| Power | watt (W) | 1 horsepower = 746 W<br>1 foot-pound/s = 1.36 W | J/s (joules per second) |
| Pressure | pascal (Pa)<br>bar (10$^5$ Pa) | 1 millimetre of mercury = 133.3 Pa<br>1 standard atmosphere = 101,325 Pa | N/m$^2$ (newtons per square metre) |
| Resistance | ohm (Ω) | — | V/A (volts per ampere) |
| Velocity | metre/second (m/s) | 1 kilometre/hour = 0.278 m/s<br>1 mile/hour = 0.447 m/s | |
| Voltage | volt (V) | — | J/s/A (W/A) (joules per second per ampere, or watts per ampere) |
| Volume | cubic metre (m$^3$) | 1 litre (1 dm$^3$) = 0.001 m$^3$<br>1 pint = 0.5682 dm$^3$<br>1 cubic foot = 0.0283 dm$^3$ | |

lying and very flat. It occupies the great basins of the Ob and Yenisei Rivers, which flow from the southern mountains through steppe and marshland. The climate here is continental, with warm, arid summers and extremely cold winters. The central Siberian plateau rises to over 1,000 m (3,300 feet) and is more undulating. It contains grazing land and is drained by the Lena and its tributaries. Lake Baikal, the world's deepest lake, lies in a *rift valley in the south and is frozen during winter. Eastern Siberia is mountainous, much of it volcanic, and contains enormous deposits of gold, iron, nickel, mica, bauxite, graphite, and coal.

**Siberian high**, the shallow, semi-permanent region of high pressure which develops in winter as a result of the cooling by *radiation of the Asiatic landmass. In summer it is displaced westward away from the Siberian plains by *thermals which result in areas of low pressure. Its depth is seldom more than 2,500 m (8,000 feet).

**Sibirtsev, Nikolai** (1860–99), Russian scientist who in 1895 compiled the first comprehensive system of soil classification. Based on *Dokuchaiev's theories of soil formation, it modified the existing terminology and introduced the now widely used terms zonal, intrazonal and azonal soils. Sibirtsev was also the compiler of the first map of soil zones of the northern hemisphere.

**Sichuan**, a region of south-central China surrounded by mountains. The tributaries of the Yangtze flow down from the mountains and join it in the fertile Red Basin at its centre; the river then provides the only natural outlet, through the Yangtze Gorges, to the rest of China and the sea. The Basin, nearly the size of Britain, is red sandstone into which the rivers have cut gorges. With a hot, damp climate it is very fertile. To the west the land rises towards Tibet and provides expanses of pasture for cattle and sheep. The mineral resources are varied and considerable, with important iron and copper smelting industries, coal mining, petroleum refining, and the manufacture and processing of chemicals, textiles, and food.

**Sicily**, the largest island in the Mediterranean Sea, in southern Europe. It is separated from the Calabrian mainland by the Strait of Messina, which is only 3 km (less than 2 miles) wide. Much of the island consists of mountain ranges which culminate in the snowcapped cone of Etna. The main plains are in the south, though even here the interior is hilly, with river gorges and plateaux where olive bushes, almond trees, and vineyards grow. To the north are the volcanic islands of Ustica, the Liparis, and Stromboli, the most continuously active volcano in Europe. To the south are off-shore deposits of oil.

**sidereal time**   *rotation of the Earth.

**sierozem**, a shallow, pale or grey-coloured *zonal soil which forms in cool mid-latitude desert regions. In these regions of low and irregular rainfall the vegetation of drought-resistant sage brush and bunchgrass is sparse, and soils are low in humus. Since evaporation greatly exceeds precipitation, soluble salts such as calcium carbonate are carried up through the soil by capillary action and may be deposited at or near the soil surface. These layers may become cemented to form a *hardpan. Sierozems are found in Russia, east of the Caspian Sea, and in the Great Basin region of the USA.

**sierra**, a long, jagged mountain chain, notably in Spain and Spanish America. It derives its name from the Latin *serra*, saw, since its peaks suggest the teeth of a saw.

**Sierra Leone**, a tropical West African country with a south-west-facing Atlantic coast and a fine natural harbour, surrounded inland by Guinea and Liberia. Swamps spread up river valleys, through a rain-forested coastal plain to wooded *savannah in the interior. In the sand and gravel of these valleys, diamonds are found; and there are readily exploitable deposits of bauxite, iron ore, and rutile (an ore of titanium). The climate is very wet, although in winter the drying *harmattan wind blows from the hinterland.

**Sierra Madre**, the mountain system which occupies most of Mexico. The western range runs for about 1,100 km (680 miles) parallel to the Pacific coast, while the eastern range, which is narrower and less spectacular, converges on it. Together with a jumbled mass of southern volcanoes they embrace the country's high central plateau, which is broken by block ranges and many fertile depressions. The snow-covered peaks rise to the volcanic Popocatepetl and Orizaba (Citlaltepetl) at 5,700 m (18,700 feet) and contain deep canyons, called *barrancas*, and lush, tropical valleys. There are many interior drainage basins, and rivers drain into both the Pacific Ocean and the Gulf of Mexico. The ranges contain enormous deposits of gold, silver, copper, lead, and other minerals. Many of their slopes are forested or planted for crops of cotton, coffee, and tobacco.

**Sierra Nevada**, the name given to two distinct mountain systems. (1) A greater range in eastern California, USA, which extends for some 640 km (400 miles) south-eastward between the Central Valley and the Great Basin, reaching 4,418 m (14,494 feet) at Mount *Whitney. Its eastern face rises sharply in an escarpment which is a barrier to overland travel, while its western face slopes more gradually to grassy foothills. The Donner Pass, snow-covered in winter, is the main route through. Melt-water feeds the many streams entering the Sacramento and San Joaquin valleys, and the forests yield timber. The Yosemite, Sequoia, and King's Canyon national parks offer spectacular gorges and waterfalls, granitic monoliths and glacial lakes, and giant redwood trees. (2) A range in Andalusia, southern Spain, which

A vein of native **silver** in hydrothermally altered andesite from the Bolivian Andes.

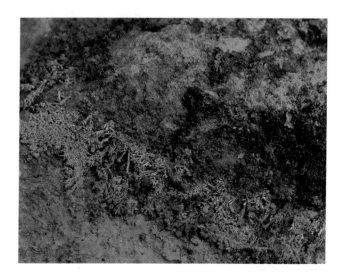

extends for nearly 100 km (60 miles) in Granada and eastward into Almería, reaching a height of 3,481 m (11,421 feet) at Mulhacén.

**significant figures**, digits giving an approximation of stated accuracy to a number. Reduction to $n$ significant figures is obtained by counting $n + 1$ digits from the left, beginning at the first non-zero digit of the number. The last figure counted is used to round off the $n$th digit, and the remaining digits are replaced by zeros where necessary. Thus 271,493, 51.73259, 0.00516001 reduced to four significant figures become 271,500, 51.73, and 0.005160 respectively. (Note that 0.00516001 itself has six significant figures.)

**Si Kiang**   *Xi Jiang.

**Sikkim**, a small Himalayan state sandwiched between Nepal and Bhutan and lying astride a strategic route between India and Tibet. Much of its north-west frontier is glaciated and dominated by the mighty mountain group of Kanchenjunga.

**Silesia**, a region of central Europe, now largely in south-west Poland. Lower Silesia is essentially a plain which is underlain by the Silesian Basin. This is oriented north-west to south-east, more or less along the line of the Oder (Odra)

The **Sinai** peninsula, other than on the northern and western fringes, is populated by nomadic Bedouin. Petroleum exploitation and the mining of many mineral ores, including manganese, are of increasing importance.

River, and is infilled with Palaeozoic, Mesozoic, and Tertiary strata. These are in turn sealed with a veneer of glacial drift, *alluvium, and *loess. To the south-east, in Upper Silesia, a corresponding anticlinal structure has brought coal-bearing Carboniferous rocks to the surface. These have given rise to an important industrial area.

**silica** (or silicon dioxide, $SiO_2$), the most abundant constituent of the Earth's crust, occurring in many types of rocks, both in its pure form and as a constituent of *silicates. There are three main crystalline forms: *quartz, tridymite, and cristobalite, the last two being rare, and found only in acidic volcanic rock. In each the silicon atom is bound tetrahedrally to four oxygen atoms, but their crystalline structures are all very different. Crypto-crystalline forms, that is forms where the crystals are too small to be seen under a conventional microscope, include chert, chalcedony, and opal. Silica is tough and has a high melting-point, which makes it useful in the manufacture of refractory materials. It is the raw material of the glass industry, and as a colloid or gel is widely used as a binder and adsorbent.

**silicates**, a very widely occurring group of compounds containing silicon, oxygen, and one or more metals. Natural silicates form the major part of most rocks and of many minerals. All silicates are based on the $SiO_4$ tetrahedron, although there is a vast range of structures adopted (according to which they are classified). They vary in composition from the relatively simple minerals, such as zircon, $ZrSiO_4$, to infinite three-dimensional arrays of $SiO_4$ units in which the oxygen atoms form bridges between the silicon atoms. Typical natural silicates include a number of gemstones, talc, clay, and mica. Portland cement contains a large proportion of calcium silicates.

**silicon** (symbol Si, at. no. 14, r.a.m. 28.09), a browny-black *metalloid which has a giant molecular structure similar to that of diamond. It is the second most abundant element after oxygen and forms nearly 28 per cent of the Earth's crust. It is found in a wide range of *silicate minerals. Industrially it is formed by the reduction of *silica, $SiO_2$, with carbon or calcium carbide, $CaC_2$, in an electric furnace. When it is purified further, it is used to manufacture silicon chips in electronics; and when very small quantities of boron or phosphorus are added (doping), it is used as a *semiconductor in transistors. Silicon forms stable compounds in which it shows a valency of 4. Silicon carbide crystals, $SiC_2$, are almost as hard as diamonds and are manufactured as abrasives. Solutions of *silicates are obtained by reacting the element with alkalis. Synthetic polymers can be formed of silicon, carbon, hydrogen, and oxygen; they are called silicones and are oily liquids, resins, or rubbery solids, widely used as waxes and water repellents.

**silicon dioxide**   *silica.

**sill**, a sheet-like body of igneous rock that has been injected concordantly (along bedding planes) into surrounding rocks while still in a molten state. The Great Whin Sill of northern England was the first to be described. The Palisades Sill of New Jersey is a well-known example in the USA. Sills are usually composed of medium-grained rock, often *dolerite.

**silt**, an aggregate of mineral grains or rock fragments with diameters ranging from 0.0625 to 0.002 mm (0.0025 to 0.00008 inches). In technical contexts, the word also refers

**Sink-holes** viewed from Takaka Hill, South Island, New Zealand. The 'marble mountain' as it is otherwise known, consists of a hard crystalline form of limestone and is very popular with potholers.

to soils made up of silt-sized particles. The silt grade is larger in grain size than *clay but smaller than *sand.

**siltstone**, a very common sedimentary rock of all geological ages, composed largely of *silt particles. Almost always laid down in water, it can comprise any mineral assemblage (although quartz is the most common constituent). It is a weakly bedded rock that often contains marine fossils.

**Silurian Period**, the third of the six geological periods of the *Palaeozoic Era. It follows the *Ordovician and precedes the *Devonian and spans the time interval from 438 to 408 million years ago. The term was coined in 1842 by *Murchison after an ancient Welsh tribe, the Silures, who occupied much of central and southern Wales where rocks of this type are well developed. The Silurian is characterized by marine sediments that vary widely, both in their lithology and in the fossils they contain. The fossils are generally similar to those of the Ordovician. They include marine invertebrates that lived in shallow water, such as graptolites (extinct colonial organisms) and trilobites (a group of arthropods long extinct). The new creatures include the first true fish and vascular land plants.

**silver** (symbol Ag, at. no. 47, r.a.m. 107.87), a brilliant white, malleable, *transition metal. It has the highest known electrical conductivity; and is one of the so-called precious metals. It occurs widely in nature—mostly in South Africa and Russia—both in sulphide ores and as the native or free metal. It normally shows a *valency of 1, although silver oxide, AgO, does exist; this is a black solid with a complex structure containing monovalent and trivalent silver ions. A dark silver sulphide forms when silver tarnishes in air because of the presence of sulphur compounds. The metal and its salts are widely used as catalysts, particularly in the production of fertilizers from ammonia. It is also used for sterling and plated silver, ornaments, and jewellery.

**silver bromide** (AgBr), a pale yellow solid, with a melting-point of 420 °C (788 °F), produced when hydrobromic acid, HBr, is added to a solution of a silver salt. It is found naturally as the mineral bromyrite. It is photosensitive and is used in photography.

**silver nitrate** ($AgNO_3$), a caustic compound important as an analytical reagent and as an antiseptic. It is used in the commercial preparation of other silver salts, particularly the silver halides, especially *silver bromide, used in photographic emulsions. In the laboratory it is used in the volumetric determination of halides, cyanides, and thiocyanates, and to indicate the presence of reducing agents. Silver nitrate is soluble in water, alcohol, and many other organic solvents. When heated to temperatures above 310 °C (590 °F), silver is produced.

**sima**, a term formerly used for the material of the layer of rocks 6–7 km (about 4 miles) thick which make up the lower portion of the *earth's crust. The sima forms most of the ocean floors, and in this context it can be thought of as representing rocks of *basaltic composition, which are relatively rich in silicon and magnesium. The sima at depth below the continents (underneath the *sial) is thought to approximate more closely to *diorite than basalt in composition.

**simple harmonic motion**, a to-and-fro motion of a special kind. In it the acceleration and deceleration of the moving body is always proportional to its distance from the centre of the oscillation: the further away it is, the more it speeds up when moving towards the centre and the more it slows down when moving away from it. The most familiar example is the motion of a spring when it is stretched and then released. Simple harmonic motion is described mathematically by the equation $d^2x/dt^2 = -\Omega x^2$, and arises whenever there is a force proportional to distance. Here $x$ is the distance from the centre of the motion, $t$ is time, and $\Omega$ is a constant. The solution of this equation is $x = A \sin(\Omega t) + B \cos(\Omega t)$, where $A$ and $B$ are constants. This shows that $\Omega$ is $2\pi$ times the frequency of the motion. Given a point moving round a circle at a constant speed, the projection of its position on to a diameter moves back and forth along that diameter with simple harmonic motion, and $\Omega$ is the angular speed of the point round the circle.

**Simpson Desert**, a desolate region of scrub and sand at the junction of the Northern Territory, Queensland, and South Australia. Also called the Arunta, it occupies the western part of the Eyre basin, extending some 320 km (200 miles) west–east and 240 km (150 miles) north–south. The average rainfall is less than 130 mm (5 inches) a year, and dunes cover most of the desert. These merge into better-watered areas near the Eyre and into salt lakes in the south.

**Sinai**, the triangular peninsula linking Asia with Africa, lying between the Gulf of Suez and the Suez Canal on the west and the Gulf of Aqaba and the Negev Desert on the east. It is bounded by the Red Sea to the south and the Mediterranean Sea to the north. Geographically within Asia, the peninsula is the north-eastern extremity of Egypt and adjoins Israel and the Gaza strip on the east. The peninsula is *fault-bounded, the eastern fault being the place where two crustal *plates slide past each other. Although it is now an arid desert with extensive *dune fields in the north, the whole region is dissected by *wadis carved in earlier, wetter periods.

**sine**, the ratio of the length of the side opposite the angle in a right-angled triangle to that of the hypotenuse. The values of the sine function vary between $+1$ and $-1$. It is one of the primary trigonometric functions and its definition can be

A **slate** quarry in North Wales, UK. Wooden wedges, placed in an opening made by a power chisel, are hammered in to split the slate along its natural cleavage plane.

extended to all numbers, including complex ones, by means of the *Taylor expansion for a sine.

The word sine comes from a mistranslation from Arabic into Latin of the ancient term meaning 'half a chord'. In the unit circle the sine of an angle is half the chord formed by continuing the opposite side.

**Singapore**, an island country at the southern end of the Malay Peninsula, only 2° N. of the Equator. The climate is hot and damp, and the land is naturally swampy. The country comprises a large, low-lying island, about 40 km (25 miles) wide by 22 km (14 miles) from north to south, and many much smaller ones. Its chief physical resource is a magnificent natural harbour.

**sink-hole**, a fairly small hollow found in the surface of limestone regions, or where limestone underlies a thin cover of other rocks. At the surface sink-holes are smaller than *dolines and larger than *potholes, and they are formed by weak carbonic acid in rainwater dissolving rock on either side of a crack (or joint) until a passage is opened underground. Often streams or rivers disappear into sink-holes, which are then known as swallow-holes. Flat limestone areas can be completely pitted by shallow sink-holes: a good example is the region round Lubbock, Texas, USA.

**Sinkiang** *Xinjiang.

**sirocco**, a warm wind which blows most frequently in the spring and autumn when *depressions in the Sahara and western Mediterranean move eastward, drawing warm, dust-laden air from the Sahara northward ahead of the cold front. It is very hot in summer, with temperatures of 35 to 40 °C (95 to 104 °F) and warm in winter. It can blow for days or weeks on end and is always dry, with relative humidities as low as 10 per cent, withering the vegetation and damaging olives and vines when these are blossoming. Its heat and aridity are increased when it descends the northern slopes of the Atlas Mountains as a *föhn wind, and it often precedes a fresh cyclonic storm in the western Mediterranean.

**SI units** (*Système International d'Unités*), a system of *units proposed in 1960 as a rational and coherent replacement for the older CGS (centimetre, gram, second) system. It has since been widely adopted throughout most of the world. The SI system defines seven basic units: the metre (m), the basic unit of length; the second (s), the unit of time; the kilogram (kg), mass; the ampere (A), electric current; the kelvin (K), temperature; the candela (cd), a measure of luminous intensity; and the mole (mol), which measures the amount of matter. All other units of measurement are defined with reference to these seven: for example, the definition of the *newton (the SI unit of force) is the force required to impart an acceleration of 1 m/s to a mass of 1 kg. (See table on page 302.)

**Skagerrak**, the strait between the southernmost projection of Norway and the north-west coast of the Jutland Peninsula of Denmark. Together with the Kattegat, it connects the North Sea with the Baltic Sea. Here the Norwegian coast is backed by hills which rise to the highlands of Telemark. In contrast, the coast of Jutland is low-lying and fringed with a belt of sand dunes and lagoons.

**sky**, the apparent dome that contains the atmosphere. Its blue colour is a consequence of the scattering of sunlight by the molecules of the atmosphere. The longer wavelengths

pass directly through, but the shorter, blue rays are scattered in all directions, giving the sky its colour. The sky is bluest on a clear day; dust and various atmospheric pollutants also scatter red and yellow light, causing a whitening of the blue sky. At sunrise and sunset the sky turns redder as much of the blue light is lost to the observer by scattering on the longer path sunlight must take through the atmosphere at these times. The scattering which gives the sky its blue colour is called Rayleigh scattering, after Lord Rayleigh (see *Strutt).

**slack water**, part of the tidal cycle of horizontal water movement near coasts caused by the rise and fall of the sea surface. It occurs between the *ebb and the flood tides, at the point when the flows are reversing direction. Slack water therefore happens twice in a tidal cycle, at low and high water, and may last for 20 minutes or more. During this time there is little or no flow.

**slaked lime**   *calcium hydroxide.

**slate**, a shiny, dark grey rock with pronounced cleavage—that is, it splits easily. Slate is the product of low-grade regional metamorphism of fine-grained sediments such as clays and shales. They cleave easily into many thin slices because of the parallel arrangement of fine-grained, flaky clay minerals in the rock as a result of lateral pressure during metamorphism. Slate is used for roofing and flooring. Classic slate areas are North Wales and the Vosges, France.

**sleet**, partially melted snow or hail, or snow and rain falling together. It commonly occurs when the air temperature at ground level is just above freezing. The Middle High German word *slōz* is phonetically descriptive.

A pall of **smog** hangs over the city of Chicago, USA, the result of a high concentration of dust and industrial pollution in the atmosphere combined with the dampness from nearby Lake Michigan.

**slip-off**, a gentle slope on the inner, convex side of the bend of a *meandering river, opposite the steep undercut face. In the straight reaches of a meandering river the cross-section of the channel is more or less symmetrical, but it becomes increasingly lop-sided and asymmetrical—a crooked, shallow V-shape—as the course of the river swings round the bend. The fastest flow is in the deep water against the undercut bank, while the slip-off slope may be covered by a *point bar, dropped in the shallows at high flows. As meanders cut across the floodplain, channels appear to 'slip off' point bars—hence the name.

**slope, ground**, an inclined area of land surface. Slopes occupy most of the land surface of the Earth. Very few areas are absolutely flat, and wherever there is some slope, however slight, the force of gravity may cause the downslope movement of material. The steeper the slope the stronger the force, which is proportional to the sine of the angle of slope. Movement will be assisted by the presence of running water. Slopes can be categorized by shape and gradient. A convex, or waxing, slope may occur at the top of a hill, and this may be followed by a free face, sloping at more than 40°. Below this there may be a constant or uniform slope, called a rectilinear facet, made of scree or some weathered material. Then, at the foot of most hills, there may be a concave, or waning, slope—perhaps a pediment—of less than 11°. Slope angles are normally measured at right angles to the contours. When land is faulted—that is, cracked or dislocated—a new slope called a fault scarp may emerge; and

A series of **snow** crystals showing some of their many forms. All consist of a central hexagonal plate with six branching rays.

when it is being bent and buckled upwards by tectonic forces then slopes are modified even as they emerge. Once new gradients have been established, streams and rivers (or glaciers) may begin to cut channels down them, creating valleys with new slopes which face and in turn drain towards their courses. Volcanic eruptions create instant slopes. *Deposition also creates slopes, although more slowly and usually on a small scale. Weathering and *mass movements on slopes modify their shapes and gradients, and significantly so if other processes of erosion and deposition are not generally active. They tend to reduce slope angles, while erosion by wind, waves, and ice on the other hand tend to increase or at least maintain them. Once a thick layer of weathered material is covered by vegetation, the form of the slope will change only slowly.

**Slovakia**, a landlocked country in central Europe, covering an area of 49,035 km² (18,927 sq. mi.) and surrounded by Poland to the north, Ukraine to the east, Hungary to the south, and Austria and the Czech Repulic to the west. The Carpathian mountains dominate the country reaching a height of 2,655 m (8,711 feet) at the Gerlach Shield in the High Tatras. Some steppe grasslands are to be found in the south-eastern lowlands; one third of the country is cultivated and two-fifths is covered in forest. The Danube briefly forms the border between Slovakia and Hungary flowing towards Bratislava and finally on to the Black Sea. Substantial deposits of iron ore, copper, magnesite, lead, and zinc are mined and some lignite is extracted. There are also numerous mineral springs.

**Slovenia**, a small country in south-east Europe, bordered by Austria to the north, Hungary to the east, Italy to the west, and Croatia to the south and east. It has an outlet to the Adriatic Sea. The country is largely mountainous and wooded, with deep and fertile valleys and coal and extensive mineral reserves.

**sludging**   *solifluction.

**Smith, William** (1769–1839), British land-surveyor and self-taught geologist, one of the founders of stratigraphical geology. Working initially in the area around Bath, he discovered that rock strata could be distinguished on the basis of their characteristic assemblages of fossils, and that the identity of strata exposed in different places could thereby be established. Smith later travelled extensively in Britain, accumulating data which enabled him to produce the first geological map of the whole of England and Wales. Many of the names he devised for particular strata are still in use.

**smithsonite**, formerly known as calamine, an ore of zinc (zinc carbonate, $ZnCO_3$). Greenish-white, brownish, or grey, it is a hard, dense mineral formed by the action of water rich in zinc sulphate on carbonate rocks. It is found mainly in Colorado, USA, and Kazakhstan. Calamine lotion is made up of zinc carbonate and ferric oxide ($Fe_2O_3$).

**smog**, fog intensified by smoke which commonly reduces visibility to around 4 m (12–15 feet). It forms in urban and industrial areas if the atmosphere contains large enough quantities of dust particles to permit condensation to occur before the air becomes saturated.

**Snake River**, the main tributary of the Columbia River in north-western USA, joining it after a journey of 1,670 km (1,040 miles). The source is in the Yellowstone National Park, from which it runs through the Grand Teton National Park and west down over the Shoshone and several other falls to the Snake River plain, notable for its cover of black Pleistocene basalt and subsequent lighter lava flows; to the north are the volcanic cones of craters of the Moon National Monument. The river turns northward to cut through the forested mountain barrier of eastern Oregon in a 200-km (125-mile) long *canyon that is one of the deepest in the world. Once clear of the Rocky Mountains, it passes through lava-levelled lowlands, before entering the Columbia. In its middle reaches it receives many tributaries and is a major source of hydroelectricity.

**Snell's law**, one of the two laws of *refraction. It states that when light passes from one medium to another, denser, medium (for example from air to glass), the sine of the angle of incidence (the angle between the incident ray and the normal) bears a constant ratio to the sine of the angle of refraction. The ratio is the *refractive index of the denser medium in relation to the lighter one (air or vacuum). Publicized by René Descartes (1596–1650) in 1638, it was formulated by Willebrord Snell (1591–1626) at least fifteen years earlier.

**snow**, the result of water vapour condensing on ice crystals in a cloud, which usually occurs when the air temperature in the lowest 300 m (825 feet) of the atmosphere is near freezing point. It falls when the aggregations so formed are too heavy to remain suspended in the cloud and do not have time to melt before reaching the ground; it rarely falls if the air temperature is above 4 °C (39 °F). The aggregation of crystals to form large, branching, hexagonal snowflakes occurs most effectively between 0 °C and −4 °C (32 °F and 25 °F) in clouds which contain large quantities of water

Where there is plenty of sunshine and wind, as here on the Mediterranean island of Gozo, **sodium chloride** can be extracted from seawater by trapping the seawater in shallow lagoons and allowing it to evaporate. On a reduced scale, the process parallels the laying down of the world's great subterranean rock-salt deposits (the main source of sodium chloride).

vapour but a relatively small number of crystals. Below −4 °C snowflake sizes generally decrease with decreasing temperature, especially when formed in clouds composed entirely of ice crystals (powder snow). With temperatures below −30 °C (−22 °F), snowflakes form when the individual crystals collide and interlock or stick together. Most heavy snowfalls are associated with the layered clouds of very active *fronts.

**Snowdonia**, a rugged, mountainous region of north-west Wales, UK, renowned for its scenic beauty. It is now a national park. Broad, glaciated valleys separate peaks and ridges. The loftiest mountain, Snowdon, has five peaks the tallest of which, at 1,085 m (3,560 feet), is the highest point in Wales and England.

**snow-line**, the altitude above which snow accumulates seasonally or perennially. On a perennial basis it is at sea-level at the poles and rises to approximately 5,500 m (18,000 feet) in equatorial regions. For seasonal snow it depends, especially at mid-latitudes, on temperature, precipitation, wind speed and direction, and the exposure and steepness of a slope.

**Snowy Mountains**, part of the Australian Alps in the extreme south-east of the Great Dividing Range. They straddle the Victoria–New South Wales boundary and include Australia's highest summit, Mount Kosciusko. The mountains comprise a series of roughly north–south-trending *fault-bounded blocks, affecting both folded Palaeozoic strata and granites.

**soapstone** *steatite.

**Society Islands** (French), a 725-km (451-mile) chain of volcanic and coral islands in the South Pacific Ocean, trending east-south-east to west-north-west. They formed as the Pacific *plate moved westward across a fixed hot-spot in the *Earth's mantle—that is, a spot where a plume of hot, mantle material and *magma is rising from greater depths. Over the hot-spot now are the doubtfully extinct twin volcanoes of Tahiti, which has the beginnings of a coral reef. Further west the volcanoes become more degraded and the reefs better developed, culminating in a near-*atoll with a volcanic stump in its lagoon.

**soda**, a general term used for *sodium carbonate. It is also used (misleadingly) as a synonym for *sodium. Caustic soda is *sodium hydroxide.

**soda ash** *sodium carbonate.

**Soddy, Fredrick** (1877–1956), British physicist who proposed the concept of *isotopes to explain the existence of atoms of an element with different masses but the same chemical properties. He outlined with Ernest *Rutherford the ways in which a radioactive element could decay into another element and with William *Ramsay established that uranium emitted helium (in the form of *alpha particles) during its decay. He was awarded the Nobel Prize for Chemistry in 1921, but in later life concentrated on propounding economic views that gained little acceptance.

**sodium** (symbol Na, at. no. 11, r.a.m. 22.99), a soft, silvery white element, a member of the *alkali metals. As *sodium chloride (NaCl), it occurs naturally in seawater and in salt deposits, and is extracted by *electrolysis of fused sodium chloride. Sodium ions are essential for sustaining life, particularly in cell processes. The chemistry of sodium is dominated by the great ease with which it forms the monovalent ion, $Na^+$; it reacts violently with water and rapidly with oxygen and the halogens, giving a wide range of important compounds. It is an excellent thermal conductor, and molten sodium, mixed with molten potassium, is used as a heat extractor in some nuclear reactors. In the qualitative analysis of organic compounds the compound is heated with sodium and plunged into water. The solution can then be tested for halogens and sulphur.

**sodium bicarbonate** *sodium hydrogencarbonate.

**sodium borate** *borax.

**sodium carbonate** (or soda ash, $Na_2CO_3$), a white, amorphous powder manufactured by the Solvay (ammonia–soda) process. In this a solution of sodium chloride, $NaCl$, in water (brine) has ammonia, $NH_3$, added to it, and then carbon dioxide, $CO_2$, is bubbled through. The sparingly soluble sodium hydrogencarbonate, $NaHCO_3$, is precipitated and is then decomposed to sodium carbonate on heating. The decahydrate, $Na_2CO_3 \cdot 10H_2O$, is known as washing soda; it effloresces to form the monohydrate on standing. Sodium carbonate reacts with water to give an alkaline solution containing sodium hydroxide, $NaOH$, and the bicarbonate ion, $HCO_3^-$. In industry it has many uses including bleaching, water-softening, and the making of soap, detergents, and glass. Some soda ash is found naturally in mines, and in the beds of dry lakes, especially in California, USA.

**sodium chloride** (common salt, $NaCl$), a white crystalline solid with a melting-point of 801 °C (1,474 °F). It has an estimated 16,000 uses and is essential for the maintenance of the chloride ion balance in the body. Occurring naturally as halite (rock-salt), it is mined and then purified by removing magnesium, iron(II), and calcium ions by precipitation with sodium carbonate, $Na_2CO_3$, and sodium hydroxide, $NaOH$. Sea water is another source. Used to produce sodium carbonate and sodium hydroxide, it is one of the most important raw materials in industrial chemistry.

**sodium hydrogencarbonate** (or sodium bicarbonate, baking soda, $NaHCO_3$), a white powder, soluble in water and stable in dry air. On heating to 270 °C (518 °F) it decomposes to sodium carbonate ($Na_2CO_3$) and carbon dioxide ($CO_2$). It is prepared by the same process used to obtain *sodium carbonate. It has numerous commercial uses, for example, in fire extinguishers and effervescent drinks.

**sodium hydroxide** (or caustic soda, $NaOH$), a white solid which deliquesces in air (dissolves moisture absorbed from the air) and is very soluble in water, forming a strongly alkaline solution. Obtained industrially by the *electrolysis of brine (a solution of sodium chloride, $NaCl$), it is used in the manufacture of other chemicals, soap, rayon, and paper.

**sodium hypochlorite** ($NaOCl$), a soluble salt formed, together with sodium chloride, $NaCl$, when chlorine, $Cl_2$, is bubbled through cold sodium hydroxide ($NaOH$) solution. Aqueous $NaOCl$ is used as an antiseptic and as a bleach.

**sodium silicates**, a range of salts, each having a different sodium : silicon ratio. The most important is the mixture

This extreme **soil erosion** on a slope in the eastern foothills of the Andes was brought about by overgrazing and clearance of trees for fuel wood. The area would normally support a dry scrub forest vegetation.

known as water-glass, which is formed by dissolving *silica in sodium hydroxide, $NaOH$, under pressure. This is a colourless viscous liquid used in various printing processes and as an adhesive, preservative, and cleaning agent.

**Sogne Fiord**, the longest fiord in Norway, extending for 180 km (110 miles) inland from the country's western coast. With a maximum depth of 1,300 m (4,200 feet), it is also Norway's deepest fiord; and in some places the mountains tower up to 900 m (3,000 feet) and more either side of it. Branches of the fiord reach north and south and almost to the Jotunheimen mountains in the east. Numerous waterfalls along its length provide power for hydroelectricity.

**soil**, the disintegrated rock with an admixture of organic matter which covers much of the Earth's surface and is capable of supporting plant growth. While the nature of the weathered rock or sediment forming the basic material determines its natural mineral content, climate is often the determinant of its texture (that is, the size of its unconsolidated particles); decayed vegetation provides its organic material in the form of humus, and topography influences the thickness of its *profile between surface and bedrock from place to place. The final factor is time: the period during which the physical, chemical, and biological processes involved in its formation have taken place. The many different types of soil (which merge into one another from one location to the next) may be classified by their profiles. In a total depth which can range from a mere 30 cm (1 foot) to 200 cm (6 feet) and more, each profile is made up of distinctive layers or *horizons. Fertility depends on the amount of air and moisture in the subsoil, the presence of water which percolates down, often causing *leaching in the process, and the work of insects and worms in mixing the mineral and organic content, both mechanically and by speeding up chemical reactions. The nature of fertility in a particular region influences the kind of vegetation that will grow. In *soil classification, mineral and organic content varies from profile to profile; and today it is the science of *pedology that helps to prescribe a soil's suitability for a food, fibre, or timber crop.

**Soil taxonomy**   Approximate concordance between Great Soil Groups and US Soil Taxonomy

| Great Soil Group | US Soil Taxonomy Order | Description |
|---|---|---|
| **Zonal soils** | | |
| Grey-brown podzols | Alfisols | Grey/brown surface horizons; subsurface horizons of clay accumulation |
| Grey desert soil (sierozem)<br>Red desert soil<br>Solonchaks | Aridisols | Low in organic matter, dry for more than six months in the year |
| Prairie soil (brunizem)<br>Chernozem<br>Chestnut soil<br>Brown soil | Mollisols | Soils with nearly black, organic-rich surface horizons; high base supply |
| Podzol | Spodosols | Soils with accumulations in subsurface horizons of amorphous materials |
| Lateritic soils | Ultisols | Moist soils with horizon of clay accumulation, and low base supply |
| **Intrazonal soils** | | |
| Bog soils<br>Peats | Histosols | Organic soils |
| Alluvial soils (meadow soils)<br>Rendzina (developed on marl) | Inceptisols | Moist soils, greatly affected by parent matter |
| **Azonal soils** | Entisols | Soils without pedogenic horizons |

**soil classification**, the grouping together of soils with similar characteristics. Soils may be classified according to some specific property, such as strength or fertility. While farmers generally distinguish soils according to their suitability for growing particular crops, soil scientists generally categorize them on the basis of their appearance or morphology. A further approach is to consider soil genesis and group together soils which are thought to have formed in the same way. There are many different soil classification systems, some of which are used world-wide while others are only employed in certain countries. One of the best known systems is the zonal classification of soils originally proposed by *Dokuchaiev. In this classification, soils are categorized by the characteristic form of their *profile, which is assumed to indicate the way in which they were formed. Modified versions of this system have been used in the UK, the USA, Australia, Canada, and many other countries. The *Soil Taxonomy is a classification system in which soils are grouped on the basis of morphological characteristics alone. It was developed in the USA, but is now widely used.

**soil creep**   *creep of soil.

**soil erosion**, the removal of soil particles, usually by running water or wind, from any part of the earth's surface. It refers particularly to hillsides and to the loss of the uppermost layers of soil, which are often the most fertile. Notwithstanding that erosion goes on very slowly all the time, as soil is dissolved by water or creeps downhill, the term is usually applied to accelerated erosion by which losses occur so rapidly or in such a concentrated area that they become very noticeable. This is a major problem in the modern world, for not only does it destroy valuable farmland but the material removed can choke rivers and irrigation channels and can bury crops under a layer of dust or mud. On land laid bare it takes a long time for natural processes to re-create the topsoil. The chief cause is removal or reduction of the protective covering of vegetation. This not only allows wind, rain, and frost to break up the surface but also reduces the ability of the ground to absorb water, so that *overland flow is encouraged, creating rills which can rapidly grow into gullies or ravines. While severe erosion also occurs naturally, particularly as a result of climatic changes, in many parts of the world today it results from unwise farming practices.

**soil taxonomy**, a system of *soil classification. The Seventh Approximation was produced by the United States Soil Conservation Service in 1960 to replace earlier schemes which grouped soils according to the way they were believed to have formed. The system was developed in several stages, or approximations, and at each stage suggestions from soil scientists world-wide were incorporated into the scheme. The final version, produced in 1975, is known as the Soil Taxonomy. It is now probably the most widely used soil classification system throughout the world. In this system, soils are described on the basis of observable *profile characteristics and the presence of diagnostic horizons. As far as possible, descriptions of the form and composition of these horizons are quantitative. The classification of soils into groups is based on these descriptions. Completely new names were coined for each type of soil in order to distinguish the system from earlier classifications. Soils are grouped first into ten major orders: the oxisols, alfisols, aridisols, entisols, histosols, inceptisols, mollisols, spodosols, ultisols, and vertisols. Each order is divided into sub-orders, which are in turn broken down into great groups, sub-groups, families and, finally, series. There are about 10,000 different kinds of soil at the series level.

**solar radiation**, all the radiation that comes from the sun. Most of it is in the form of visible and near-visible light, although the whole spectrum of *electromagnetic radiation is emitted—from radio to ultraviolet and X-rays. The quantity reaching the Earth is denoted by the solar constant, the rate at which energy passes through a unit area just beyond the atmosphere that has a value of 1,400 watts per square metre. About 80 per cent of this energy reaches the Earth's surface and the majority of it has a wavelength of 3.8 to $10 \times 10^{-7}$ m. The effective temperature of a body which would produce this distribution of radiation is about 6,000 °C (11,000 °F)—a statistic which is no indication of the temperature within the Sun (thought to reach several millions of degrees) but which does serve to indicate the energy available. In addition to electromagnetic radiation, the Sun also emits streams of energetic charged particles, such as electrons, especially from solar flares. Some of these are trapped in the *Van Allen belts and they are believed to be responsible for magnetic storms—that is, very strong disturbances in the Earth's magnetic field.

**solar power**, power derived from solar energy. The total radiation reaching the Earth from the Sun is equivalent to about 20,000 times the world's current rate of energy consumption and the intensity at the Earth's surface can reach one kilowatt per square metre. Solar energy originates in nuclear *fusion in the Sun's interior and travels through space as *electromagnetic radiation. It is the ultimate source of nearly all the world's *energy resources, and 'passive' solar heating is a major factor in maintaining temperatures in buildings. However, solar energy appears in estimates of energy consumption only when harnessed in some way, for example, in solar cells, solar furnaces, and solar-powered vehicles such as cars and aeroplanes. Research in solar power has tended to focus on the generation of electricity from solar radiation. However, new research into the direct use of the thermal energy of the Sun seems very promising. Developments in transparent insulation materials (TIMs), which transmit light but also provide good heat insulation, could be used to cut heating costs for buildings by a large amount, and also to heat water.

**solar time**   *rotation of the Earth.

**solid**, one of three most common *states of matter, the others being liquids and gases (see *plasma, *liquid crystals). Solids are characterized by having a fixed size and shape as long as the temperature does not change. This is because the forces between the atoms or molecules making up a solid are strong enough to resist the disruptive effect of their thermal vibrations. There are two main types: *crystals (such as common salt or sugar) in which the atoms are arranged in a regular pattern throughout the material, and the amorphous solids (such as glass) in which the atomic positions are irregular. Whereas crystals have definite melting-points at which they become liquids, amorphous solids tend first to become pliable on heating.

**solifluction** (or sludging), the slow downhill movement of large lobes of soil and rock containing quantities of water or ice. The masses may be covered by vegetation, or their surfaces may be bare. It happens when surface layers of material on a slope become extremely wet and they start to glide over more compact, impermeable sub-surface layers. With an *active layer it happens when ice crystals and lenses grow in the soil as it freezes in autumn and their expansion pushes the layer slightly downhill; as it thaws in spring the movement increases and the soil slithers over the frozen upper surface of the permafrost beneath. The effect of solifluction is a shallow lobe or festoon on the hillside, but if the slope is steep a landslide may result. The rather badly sorted, rubbly material moved by solifluction is known as head deposits or, in chalk coombs, as coomb rock.

**Solomon Islands**, a large archipelago in the western Pacific Ocean, between 5° and 13° S. of the Equator. The largest island, Bougainville, together with a few others in the north-west, is part of Papua New Guinea; all the rest constitute a country in which the most important island is Guadalcanal. Lying at the edge of the Pacific *plate, the region is subject to earthquakes; and there are volcanoes on the main islands. The soil is generally fertile and cocoa and tobacco are grown, although the main resource is copra—dried coconut kernels, from which oil can be squeezed.

**solonchak**, a light-coloured *alkali soil which develops in low-lying areas in semi-desert regions on parent materials which have a high salt content. Solonchaks are common, among such situations, in playa lake basins such as the Great Salt Lake, Utah, USA. They form because of intense evaporation, which leads to the accumulation of soluble salts, particularly sodium chloride and sodium sulphate, at or near the soil surface. The presence of these salt layers prevents colonization by plants, and these soils are therefore low in organic matter.

**solonetz**, a black *alkali soil which occurs in relatively poorly drained sites in semi-desert regions. It is thought to be formed from *solonchak soils by the *leaching out of the more soluble salts, particularly carbonates. This may be a result of irrigation, falling *water-table levels, or an increase in rainfall caused by local changes in climate. The lower horizons are often clayey and have columnar structures with cauliflower-shaped tops. Although some shrubs and grasses can grow on these soils, they are relatively infertile. Large areas of these unproductive soils are found in the Punjab region of India.

**solstice**, a time when the Sun appears furthest from the celestial equator. This occurs twice a year. At the summer solstice, around 21 June, the Sun at noon is directly over the Tropic of Cancer. The North Pole is inclined towards the sun, and this is the longest day in the northern hemisphere and the shortest in the Southern. At the winter solstice, around 22 December, the Sun is over the Tropic of Capricorn; the South Pole is inclined towards it, and the reverse is the case. Solstices occur because the Earth's axis is not at right angles to the plane of its orbit round the Sun—the ecliptic—but is inclined at an angle of about 66.5°.

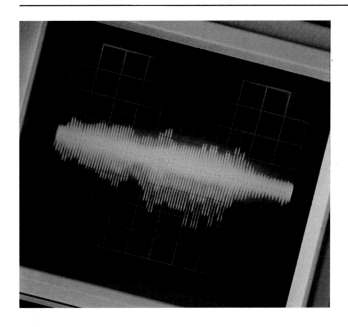

By feeding the electrical output from a microphone into an oscilloscope, it is possible to obtain a visual representation of the pressure variation in the air layers near the diaphragm of the microphone. The oscilloscope trace here was produced by a voice synthesizer saying the words 'Where are you?', and shows clearly the oscillatory character of **sound waves**.

**solum**, the part of the soil influenced by on-going soil-forming processes. It consists of the A- and B-*horizons of the profile and excludes the parent material from which soil develops. It is the zone in which plant roots grow.

**solute**, a substance (solid, liquid, or gas) which will dissolve in a solvent, forming a *solution. Whereas the solubility of solids usually increases with temperature, that of gases usually decreases with temperature but increases with pressure. Solutes differ from one another in their degree of solubility in any particular solvent.

**solution**, a liquid formed when one substance becomes completely dispersed in another substance. Solutions are homogeneous—that is, they have the same composition throughout. Sodium chloride (common salt) forms a solution in water because it is distributed evenly throughout the mixture; but a mixture of sand and water is not a solution, as parts of the mixture are pure water, and other parts pure sand. Solutions are formed by dissolving *solutes in *solvents. An aqueous solution is one in which water is the solvent. One containing only a small quantity of a solute is said to be dilute, one with a large quantity is concentrated, and one with as much as possible is *saturated. Some alloys are solutions of metals in each other, the process having taken place in the molten state; they are 'solid solutions'.

**solvent**, a liquid which can dissolve other substances, forming a *solution. Water is the most important solvent, but organic solvents, such as ethanol, chloroform, and toluene, are also commonly used. Substances may dissolve in some solvents but not others: a useful guide is 'like dissolves like'.

**Somalia**, a country on the so-called 'horn' in the north-east of Africa, with north and south-east coasts on the Gulf of Aden and the Indian Ocean and which borders Ethiopia and Kenya inland. Along its north coast, desert plains rise by steep-cliffed ridges to the red sandstone hills of a northern plateau. There it is hot and arid, the only vegetation being thin thorn-scrub. The south of the country is lower and has one permanent river, the Juba, as a source of irrigation. In this lower part there are deposits of uranium ore.

**Sonoran Desert**, arid tracts in Sonora, north-west Mexico and adjacent parts of Arizona and California, south-western USA. They lie west of outlying spurs of the Sierra Madre at the head of the Gulf of California.

**sound**, a vibratory shock to air or some other medium, which travels in the form of waves which are received by the ear and interpreted as a sensation by the brain. The ability to experience this sensation varies in the animal kingdom and deteriorates with age; but generally the frequencies of sonic waves are regarded as falling within the range 15 hertz to 20,000 hertz. Some animals can detect sound at considerably higher frequencies. Simple sounds are characterized by simple waveforms, high and low *pitch of sound corresponding to high and low frequencies, whereas in speech and music there are complex waveforms containing a number of frequencies (see *ultrasound). In a musical note these frequencies are *harmonics and bear a simple relation to one another. The ear is a sensitive organ and can detect intensities varying by a factor of $10^{12}$ from the softest to the loudest sounds. They are measured in terms of the *decibel, and the magnitude of sensation they produce is interpreted by the brain as the *loudness of sound received by the ear. It is pitch and loudness, rather than frequency and intensity, that are the sensations registered in the brain. The intensity (energy) of the lowest note on a piano must be a million times as great as that of middle C if it is to sound as loud to

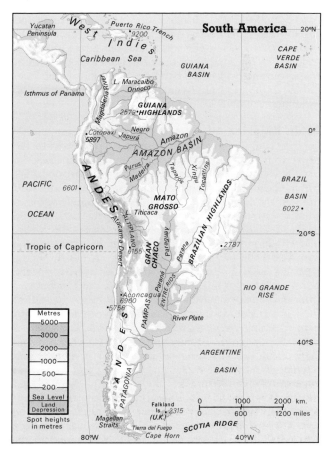

the ear. Sound waves are the alternate compressions and rarefractions (expansions) that travel through a medium such as air. Just as dropping a stone in water sets up a disturbance which becomes a series of waves travelling out from it in all directions, a sudden disturbance in the air can cause sound waves. Unlike water waves, however, which are up-and-down or transverse waves, sound waves are longitudinal waves, that is, the air moves back and forth along the direction in which the sound is travelling. To be audible, sound waves have to have a frequency between about 15 hertz (the pitch of a 10-metre (33 foot) organ pipe) and 20,000 hertz, and the hearing of most people does not extend even as far as this. Sound waves of much higher frequency, called *ultrasound, can be produced, and are useful in metal testing and medical diagnosis. The transmission of sound waves depends on the nature of the medium, which affects both the *speed of sound and the extent to which it is absorbed as it travels. The wavelength is equal to the speed divided by the frequency, so to double the frequency of a musical note (raise it an octave) the length of the string or pipe producing it must be halved. Middle C (256 Hz) has a wavelength of 3.93 m (12.9 feet) in air.

**South Africa**, a country occupying most of the southern part of the African continent. In the north-east, the Transvaal is bounded by Botswana, Zimbabwe, Mozambique, and Swaziland. Southward, the Orange Free State partly surrounds Lesotho. On the south-east coast, Natal has boundaries with Mozambique, Swaziland, and Lesotho; while the largest region of all, Cape Province, occupies the whole of the south of the country. From Cape Agulhas in the extreme south to the Limpopo River in the extreme north-east is a distance of about 1,600 km (1,000 miles). Two great rivers, the Orange and its tributary the Vaal, traverse the country from the Drakensberg Mountains in the east to the Atlantic in the west, while many shorter rivers run south and east into the Indian Ocean. There are rolling grasslands, or veld, and deserts. The climate varies widely, from warm dry summers in the south-west to hot wet ones on the eastern coast, and (according to altitude) to winter frosts on high ground in the north. The country has a wealth of minerals, including diamonds, gold, and coal.

**South America**, the world's fourth largest continent. It lies mainly in the Southern Hemisphere, is traversed by the Equator in the north and joined to Central America by the narrow Isthmus of Panama. More than two-thirds of it lies within the tropics, while the remainder tapers southward through the temperate mid-latitudes. Structurally it somewhat resembles North America, with a *plate boundary on its Pacific coast bordered by massive cordilleras, the Andes, and with more ancient highlands towards the Atlantic in the east. It has not one central basin, however, but three: the drainage basins of the Orinoco and Amazon Rivers in the north and that of the River Plate in the south, separated from each other by ancient platforms. The most extensive of these is the Mato Grosso plateau at the centre of the continent. Forming the southern basin is the vast *Gran Chaco plain. Rainfall in the equatorial regions is very heavy, especially on the coasts. Temperatures vary with latitude and altitude. South of the equatorial forest there are vast expanses of open grazing land, and wide strips of arable land on the east coast. The rain-bearing easterly winds fail to reach the west coast, however; here the main feature is the arid Atacama Desert. South of the Tropic of Capricorn the westerlies prevail, bringing rain all the year round to the

forested western slopes of the Andes, while the *rain-shadow on the east gives rise to semi-desert and steppe. The continent is poor in coal but rich in other resources: oil on the coasts and in the basins; iron on the plateaux; nitrates in the desert; and copper, tin, and other metals in the mountains. Melt-water flowing down from the snow-capped Andes provides an enormous source of energy. In many cases, however, remoteness and inaccessibility remain an obstacle to exploitation.

**South Australia**, a state in the south of the centre of the continent, lying between Western Australia and New South Wales. Contiguous also with the Northern Territory, it covers 984,400 km² (380,000 sq. mi.) and has a southern shore on the Great Australian Bight. Kangaroo Island lies 40 km (25 miles) off the Yorke Peninsula, near Adelaide. In the west is the Great Victoria Desert, from which rise the Musgrave Ranges with Mount Woodroffe at 1,515 m (4,971 feet). South-west is the arid Nullarbor Plain. In the north-east Lake Eyre receives water intermittently from a vast region of inland drainage. In the south-east faulting in the Tertiary Period has provided the great barriers to western expansion: the Mount Lofty–Flinders ranges and the Spencer Gulf. The lower reaches of the Murray River provide grass and woodland over a 640-km (400-mile) stretch. Here the climate is Mediterranean, permitting a range of crops. Iron ore, gypsum, salt, and low-grade coal are among the minerals found.

**South China Sea**    *China Sea.

**Southern Alps**, the mountainous backbone of South Island, New Zealand, with an average crest height of 2,500 m (8,200 feet). They are highest in the centre, where the snow-fields round Mount Cook feed great glaciers such as the Tasman, which is nearly 30 km (19 miles) long and very wide. The slopes in Westland are the steeper; those to the east embrace numerous U-shaped valleys, some with single fans spread out across their floors from tributary gullies, some blocked by *moraines, and some containing ribbon lakes. There are also many narrow gorges: the range is crossed at Arthur's Pass through Otira Gorge. Westland receives year-round precipitation from the westerlies, and the slopes there are densely forested. The *rain-shadow on the eastern slopes gives rise to tussocky grass for summer grazing by the highland sheep.

**Southern Ocean**, the body of water surrounding the icy continent of Antarctica, comprising the southern part of the three *oceans: the Pacific, the Atlantic and the Indian. It lies south of the *roaring forties but is nevertheless the world's stormiest ocean. Strong prevailing winds drive the surface water eastwards in the West Wind Drift or Antarctic Circumpolar Current. This is the only current to flow around the globe, unimpeded by any land mass. A cold and dense *water mass (Antarctic Bottom Water) forms around the continent, particularly over the *continental shelf of the Weddell Sea. In summer many icebergs break off from the continental ice sheet, and float north to latitude 55° S. and even further. It is believed that the *continental shelf of Antarctica may yield oil. The main resource at present is an abundant supply of krill (planktonic crustaneans), which is being increasingly harvested.

**South Georgia**, a sub-Antarctic, mountainous island under British administration, approximately 1,300 km (800 miles) east of the Falkland Islands in the South Atlantic

Ocean. It is 4,100 km² (1,600 sq. mi.) in area and rises to 2,915 m (9,564 feet) at Mount Paget. The island comprises Palaeozoic and Mesozoic sedimentary rocks and is part of the Scotia Ridge.

**South Orkney Islands**, a group of barren, mountainous islands on the Scotia Ridge of the South Atlantic Ocean, east of the Antarctic Peninsula of Graham Land and the South Shetland Islands. Like South Georgia, they are under British administration; they consist of sedimentary rocks and are isolated remnants of an *orogenic belt that once united South America and Antarctica.

**South Pole**, a geographical site at 90° S., longitude 0°, the southern end of the Earth's axis, where six months of daylight follow six months of darkness. Situated in central *Antarctica where the ice-cap is 2,722 m (8,930 feet) thick, the pole is altogether 2,922 m (9,816 feet) above sea-level. At this height no free water is to be seen. It never rains, and even in summer a thermometer stuck 15 m (50 feet) into the snow will register −50 °C (−58 °F). It does not coincide with the south magnetic pole, which occurs 1,600 km (1,000 miles) distant, near the edge of the continent in Adélie Land.

**South Sandwich Islands**, a group of small islands in the South Atlantic Ocean, under British administration, lying north of the Weddell Sea and 760 km (470 miles) south-east of South Georgia. They are part of the Scotia Ridge. As a consequence they possess some active volcanic cones, and the ocean floor descends steeply eastward to a deep trench.

**South Seas**, originally the name for the Pacific region in general but meaning later the waters round the subtropical and tropical Pacific islands, now known as Oceania. In particular Oceania includes the islands inhabited by Microne-sian, Melanesian, and Polynesian peoples. Micronesia includes islands scattered in the west Pacific Ocean, east of the Philippines: Guam, Kiribati (Gilbert Islands), Marshall Islands, Nauru, Tuvalu. Melanesia includes islands north-east of Australia: the Bismarck Archipelago (Papua New Guinea), Solomon Islands, Vanuatu (New Hebrides), New Caledonia, Fiji. Polynesia ranges north–south in the central Pacific: Hawaii, Samoa, Marquesas, Tahiti, Tonga, New Zealand. Some are volcanic and others coral; they are renowned for their beauty and climate.

**South Shetland Islands**, a group of uninhabited islands that lies about 900 km (500 miles) south-east of Cape Horn in the Drake Passage, and just north of the Antarctic Peninsula. Administered as part of the British Antarctic Territory, they are made of highly deformed sedimentary rock that may have originated further west as part of a continental strip joining Graham Land and Patagonia. They were then driven eastward as the Pacific floor migrated. Their present aspect is rocky and barren, and they are almost entirely snow-covered.

**Soutpansberge**   *Zoutpansberg.

**space**, the entire volume of the universe in which the physical world exists. Although it seems to be three-dimensional to our common sense, it is useful for scientific purposes to think of it as associated with time in a four-dimensional *space–time continuum. In that context it has been suggested that space may not be infinite, extending without

The Devil's Marbles, fine examples of heat-induced **spalling** of granite rocks. These rounded boulders, some the size of a house, lie 320 km (200 miles) north of Alice Springs, central Australia.

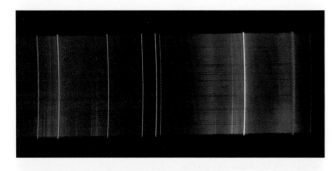

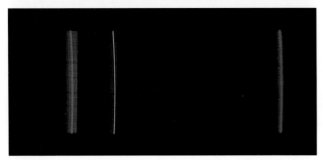

The yellow line corresponding to a wavelength of 5,876 Å in the helium emission spectrum (*top*) provides a good example of the use of **spectroscopy** to identify elements. It was first observed in the solar spectrum, and thought to be due to hydrogen. However, there is no yellow line in the emission spectrum of atomic hydrogen (*bottom*). Thus a new element—helium—was discovered in the Sun, twenty-seven years before its existence on Earth was confirmed.

limit in all directions, but may rather be closed. According to this idea space has a curvature so that if a body travels in what is believed to be a straight line it will nevertheless stay within a bounded volume. It is analogous to travelling on the curved surface of the Earth in what seems to be a straight line—you can travel as far as you please but you never leave the finite surface. All measures of the extent of space are deduced from observations made of the most distant stellar objects. If the cosmos is of some definite age then that age will determine how far our investigation of space can extend: it can be penetrated only as far as light can travel during the assumed age. Nothing further away can be detected.

**space–time continuum**, the term used in *relativity theory to denote the combination of time with the ordinary three-dimensional space in which we move about. This gives us a space or 'continuum' of four dimensions—three of space and one of time. This is a useful idea because the equations of special relativity involve time and the three space dimensions all on an equal footing with one another. Thus our passage through time as well as through space can be thought of as a compound motion through 'space–time'.

**Spain**, a country occupying most of the Iberian Peninsula in south-west Europe, bounded by France across the Pyrenees in the north-east and by Portugal on the west of the plateau, the Meseta, on which most of Spain lies. It has a rugged northern coast on the Atlantic Ocean and a gentler one on the Mediterranean Sea, where it also has an archipelago, the Balearic Islands. The plateau is very cold in winter, and very warm and arid in summer. Here and there are jagged *sierras. In the Cantabrian Mountains to the north, iron ore is mined; and from here the Ebro flows east-

ward into Catalonia. Across the centre the Tagus runs westward to Portugal, while in the south the Guadalquivir flows through the broad valley of Seville, where oranges are grown. Andalusia and the southern coastal plains are famous for their terraced vineyards, above which rises the Sierra Nevada.

**spalling**, a process of rock breakage caused either by release of pressure (as in quarry or tunnel walls) or by expansion produced by heat. Pressure release produces blocks of various sizes and shapes, whereas heat-induced spalling, common in granite rocks, causes 'onion-skin' weathering. This produces thin, curved pieces of rock which peel off from a central core.

**spar**, a general term for any pale-coloured crystalline mineral with a vitreous lustre and good *cleavage. It is also used as an abbreviation for Iceland spar, a clear crystalline form of *calcite which has the property of producing two separate images when an object is viewed through it (the property of birefringence or 'double refraction').

**special relativity**     *relativity theory.

**specific heat capacity**     *heat capacity.

**spectroscopy**, the branch of physics concerned with analysis of electromagnetic spectra. When electromagnetic radiation is reflected or scattered by a substance it is changed in a way which is characteristic of that substance. Analysing the wavelengths in the scattered or reflected light (that is, its *spectrum) can give much information about the substance. The information found from spectra depends on the radiation involved. Visible light spectra give information about the electron *energy levels in atoms, which allows us to identify the atoms. This is used in chemistry and in astronomy: spectra of the visible light from stars can be analysed to find out which atoms are present in the stars. Infra-red radiation can cause molecules to bend, rotate or vibrate, so infra-red spectra give information about their structure. Radio-wave spectra from outer space are analysed to give information about distant quasars and pulsars. Spectra can be made of parameters other than wavelength: for example the mass spectrum of a substance gives information about the mass and abundance of its components.

**spectrum**, a pattern of the amount or intensity of a parameter over a range of values: for example, the amount of particles at each value of mass over a range of values of mass; or the intensity at each wavelength of light consisting of a range of wavelengths. Thus the pattern of colours obtained when white light is passed through a prism is a spectrum of wavelengths. The same pattern of colours is produced by a diffraction grating or, in the sky, by raindrops (hence the *rainbow). The colours are conventionally described as red, orange, yellow, green, blue, indigo, and violet. The spectrum arises as a result of the different *refractive index of glass for different wavelengths present in white light. The spectrum produced by sunlight contains many dark lines. This is because certain wavelengths in the light coming from the Sun are strongly absorbed by atoms in its outer layers, so that they are missing from the spectrum. The resulting pattern of lines is called an absorption spectrum. When a substance is heated or subjected to an electrical discharge it may give out light. If this light is passed through a prism a pattern of bright lines against a dark background is produced—an emission spectrum. In both cases the particular wavelengths absorbed or emitted are those for which the *photons have an energy equal to the difference between two electron *energy levels. Each element, therefore, has its own characteristic spectrum, which can be analysed to identify it and study its energy levels. The analysis of spectra is called *spectroscopy. Certain spectral lines can be affected by external sources. Both electric and magnetic fields can change energy levels and have the effect of splitting certain lines into two or more sub-lines. The nucleus of an atom, especially if it has a magnetic moment, can also interact with the electrons and this can produce additional splittings.

**speed of light**, the speed at which *electromagnetic radiation travels through free space (in a vacuum). It has a value of 299,792,458 m (186,281 miles) per second and is a universal constant. The speed of light is slightly less in the atmosphere. It is the highest known speed in the universe and has a special significance in *relativity theory in two respects: it is regarded as absolute—that is, its value ($c$) is independent of the motion both of its source and of the observer; and it is impossible to accelerate anything to this speed, since doing so would require an infinite amount of energy. It is commonly, although incorrectly, called the velocity of light.

**speed of sound**, the speed at which *sound waves travel through a medium. For air at a temperature of 0 °C (32 °F) this is 331 metres per second (1,087 feet per second). As the temperature increases, the density of the air decreases and this enables the sound waves to travel faster; thus at 18 °C (64 °F) it is 342 m/s (1,123 feet per second). The speed of sound is much higher in liquids and solids: in water, for example, it is over four times greater than in air. It is commonly, but incorrectly, called the velocity of sound.

**Speke, John Hanning** (1827–64), British explorer of Africa and discoverer of the source of the White Nile on *Burton's expedition. Two years later, in 1860, he returned to Lake Victoria with a companion, James Grant, to confirm the discovery. Working their way up the western shore of the lake they came to its northern tip, where Speke found the Ripon Falls. Speke and Grant then followed the Nile down to Khartoum, which they reached in 1863.

**sphalerite**  *zinc sulphide.

**spheroidal weathering**, the rounding of small blocks of rock to produce core stones. Closely related to the larger-scale process of *exfoliation, it occurs principally in fine- to medium-grained rocks which have closely spaced patterns of *joints. Water enters the joints and seeps into the rock. It dissolves or alters minerals, enlarging the joints and rounding corners of the blocks. This allows them to expand slightly, developing internal hair-line cracks. Further chemical attack occurs in these cracks, and ice or salt crystals may grow, prising away thin, curved shells of weathered rock and leaving the unweathered but rounded core stones.

**Spice Islands**  *Moluccas.

**spin** (in atomic physics), an attribute of some *elementary particles which gives them intrinsic angular momentum and a magnetic moment, so that they behave like tiny bar magnets. It is impossible to say whether particles are indeed spinning in the ordinary sense of the word, but the term is a convenient label for referring to these properties of a particle. Spin (or absence of it) is one of the distinguishing characteristics of an elementary particle. It was first discovered in the electron.

**Spitsbergen**, the main group of islands within the Norwegian Svalbard Archipelago. The scenery is mountainous as a result of folding and faulting, and glaciers and snow-fields are common. The coastline shows considerable variety from the fiords of the west and north coasts of Spitsbergen (West Spitsbergen) itself to the ice front that characterizes the east coast of North East Land.

**spodosol**, a *zonal soil developed in freely-draining sandy materials in cool, moist climates where intense *leaching has removed even relatively insoluble constituents, such as iron, from the upper part of the *profile. This results in a bleached zone, known as the $A_2$-*horizon. Aluminium, iron, and organic matter accumulate as a distinct, highly coloured horizon lower down. This layer may be cemented to form a *hardpan. As such soils are low in plant nutrients, particularly calcium and magnesium, and strongly acidic, they are naturally infertile. Spodosols are widespread in the boreal forest zone of North America and northern Europe.

**Sporades**, a dispersed group of Greek islands in the Aegean Sea. The southern group, sometimes called the Dodecanese, lies along the Turkish coast. Its islands are all mountainous, and Kos is subject to earthquakes. *Rhodes is the largest; others are Karpathos and, according to some geographers, Samos and Chios. The northern group lies north of Euboea off the Greek mainland. Many of its members are noted for their greenness, a result of mantling pine forests, olive groves, and fruit orchards.

Interlocking **spurs** project into the Great Gorge of the Kali Gandak River in Nepal, creating the world's deepest valley.

**spring, natural**, a place where water emerges from underground. Natural springs occur where *water-tables intersect the ground surface or where underground rivers emerge from caves and passages in limestone or lavas. (If a flow can be traced back to a surface river it is termed a resurgence.) Caused by the positioning of permeable and impermeable rock in such a way that the latter forces the water to surface, they are known as artesian springs if it emerges under pressure, and if the flow is not distinct but in the form of many trickles it is termed a 'seep'. The water is usually very clear, although it contains large amounts of dissolved chemicals, especially in limestone areas. Except with seasonal springs, known as bourns or burns, the flow is steady, as it takes a long time for storm or drought to influence the groundwater reservoirs.

**spring tides**, the extreme *tides that occur twice a month, at the times of new and full Moon, when the Sun and Moon are pulling in the same direction (a condition known as syzygy) to influence the movement of the oceans. The water rises higher and falls lower than at other times in the lunar month; and a combination of high water and an onshore wind may cause flooding.

**spur** (in geology), a rib of land which runs out into a main valley or plain between the mouths of tributary valleys. In upland valleys cut by rivers, the main channel twists from side to side, so that the spurs are described as 'interlocking'. In valleys which have been glaciated, or where faulting and sudden uplift have occurred, *truncated spurs occur.

The Old Man of Hoy, a fine example of a **stack**, that rises 137 m (450 feet) off the western coast of Hoy in the Orkney Islands. The stack consists of red sandstone with a lava base.

Icicle-like **stalactites** hang from the roof of a cave with small, columnar **stalagmites** deposited on the cave floor; at Ogoff Dydd, near Wrexham, North Wales, UK.

**squall**, a sudden, violent, and short-lived gust of wind which occurs usually in a line parallel to and ahead of a rapidly moving cold *front. As the cold air overtakes and undercuts the warm air, at ground level, the warm air is forced to rise rapidly. This often results in the development of *cumulonimbus cloud and severe thunderstorms.

**Sri Lanka** (formerly Ceylon), a pear-shaped island country off the south-east coast of India. Some 435 km (270 miles) long and 225 km (140 miles) wide in the middle, it has very broad coastal plains which rise at the centre to highlands 2,000 m (6,560 feet) high and more. The climate is monsoonal, with very heavy rainfall; but while the plains are always hot and sticky, the hills are cooler and less humid. At high altitudes the scenery is beautiful, with mixed forests, streams, and waterfalls. On the lower slopes tea is grown; and on the well-rivered plains there are rubber-trees, coconut palms, and paddy fields. The flat stretches of coast contain many palm-fringed beaches.

**stability**, in the atmosphere, a property assessed by the effect of upward displacement on a body of air which is in equilibrium with its surroundings. If, after initial displacement, it rises further, it is considered to be unstable; it continues to rise because it remains warmer and therefore less dense than the surrounding air. It is considered to be stable if it sinks back to its original position and undisturbed state; it will do so if it is colder and denser than its new surroundings. This occurs only if its *lapse rate does not exceed the dry adiabatic lapse rate (1 °C per 100 m, or 5.4 °F per 1,000 feet). Stable air may become unstable if it becomes saturated. This may happen if it crosses a sea or lake, and water evaporates into it, or if it ascends a mountain side or frontal surface and condensation occurs. The lapse rate then falls from the dry adiabatic lapse rate to the saturated adiabatic lapse rate (0.6 °C per 100 m, or 3.5 °F per 1,000 feet). Such air is said to be conditionally unstable.

In the ocean, stability is the tendency for water at a given level to remain at that level and is greatest where density increases most sharply with depth. If the density of surface water is increased above that of underlying water (through warming, an increase in *salinity, or both) then instability results. The surface water will sink, displacing deeper water which, on rising to the surface, may itself become sufficiently dense to sink. This *convection results in the formation of sub-surface *water masses.

**stack** (in geology), a small, steep-sided pillar of rock rising from the sea near a cliffed shore. Stacks are created when a headland is attacked by waves. Initially, caves are formed in the cliffs on either side and these gradually become enlarged to produce a tunnel or archway through the headland. When the roof of this arch collapses, the detached block forms a stack. Continued erosion will gradually wear down a stack, leaving only a stump. Rocky coastlines have many stacks: round the British coast the Old Man of Hoy and the Needles are probably the most famous.

**stage-discharge**, the quantity of water which is flowing in a river when its surface is at a given height—or stage—above the bed. It is measured by a graduated rod, or stage-gauge, which is fixed firmly to the side of the channel at a place where a cross-section of it has been carefully surveyed. A series of observations of flow are made for different water depths and the results are combined to make a rating-curve for the cross-section. Then, simply noting the depth at the gauge allows the stage-discharge to be calculated.

After a long and adventurous career as a journalist and explorer Henry **Stanley** became a Member of Parliament for the Liberal Unionist Party.

**stalactites**, stony pendants formed by precipitation of calcium carbonate from slowly dripping water. They hang down like icicles from the ceilings of caves or even the arches of bridges. The word stalactite is also used, though rarely, for similar forms made of other minerals, such as gypsum or silica.

**stalagmites**, pillars of calcium carbonate deposited on the floor of a cave. Like *stalactites, they are formed by the precipitation of calcium carbonate from water dripping from the roof of the cave. They are usually found underneath stalactites but are thicker. In time a stalactite and stalagmite may meet and form a continuous column reaching from the roof of the cave to the floor. This may take many thousands of years to occur.

**standard deviation**, the most common measure of the spread, or dispersion, of a statistical sample, indicating how far the values, taken as a whole, vary from the sample *mean, $\bar{x}$. It is the square root of the *variance, which is itself the arithmetic mean of the squares of the deviation from the sample mean. The standard deviation $s = \sqrt{[1/n \Sigma(x_i - \bar{x})^2]}$. It is measured in the same units as the data. In a complete distribution (for example, the heights of all redwood trees), the standard deviation and mean, written $\sigma$ and $\mu$ respectively, refer to whole-population *parameters. It is very unlikely that the true value of $\sigma$ or $\mu$ will be known. Usually samples will be taken, each with a mean $\bar{x}$ and standard deviation $s$, and from these the actual population values can be approximated with some confidence. The normal distribution, the familiar bell-shaped curve, which arises, for example, from studying the distribution of errors of measurement, is completely determined by the mean and standard deviation. The intelligence quotient (IQ) is defined to have a normal distribution with mean 100 and standard deviation 15; from this it can be predicted that less than 3 per cent of the population will score more than 130.

---

**Standing waves**

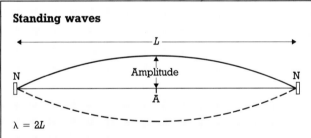

$\lambda = 2L$

When a stretched string of length $L$ with both its ends fixed is plucked at its central point, two similar transverse waves are produced. These travel outwards from the centre of the string, and after reflection at either end, interfere to produce a standing wave of wavelength $\lambda = 2L$ with nodes (N) at either end of the string and an antinode (A) in the middle.

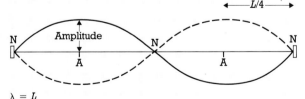

$\lambda = L$

Plucking the same string at a distance $L/4$ from one end, while holding it in the middle, and then releasing the string, produces a wave of wavelength $\lambda = L$ with nodes and antinodes as shown. This technique of plucking, known as 'playing the harmonic', is sometimes used in playing the guitar.

**standard temperature and pressure** (STP), defined as 0 °C and 1 atmosphere pressure (101,325 pascals). As the volume of a gas depends strongly on temperature and pressure, it is common to quote gas volumes at the same temperature and pressure for comparison; STP is widely used for this purpose.

**standing wave**, a wave in which the positions of the *nodes and antinodes stay in the same place. For example, when a stretched string is plucked at its central point the antinode remains at the midpoint of the string and the nodes are at the fixed ends. Standing waves (sometimes called stationary waves) are also set up when air is blown through the tube of a musical instrument. Standing waves set up in inlets or lakes are known as seiches.

**Stanley, Sir Henry Morton** (1841–1904), British-born US journalist and explorer born in Wales as John Rowlands. He travelled to America as a cabin boy, where he took the name of the cotton-broker who adopted him. He became a widely travelled newspaper correspondent, and in 1871 was sent by the *New York Herald* to Zanzibar to search for David *Livingstone, whom he greeted with the famous words, 'Dr Livingstone, I presume'. Subsequently he traced the course of the *Congo (1875–7) and opened up central Africa for Europeans. His *In Darkest Africa* (1890) had an immense sale. He resumed British citizenship in 1892.

**state of matter**, any one of the phases in which matter can exist. The three most common phases are solid, liquid and gas. A particular phase depends mainly on temperature, although pressure also plays a part. At low temperatures atoms and molecules may be bound solidly together. With the application of heat the bonds are loosened and the matter melts into liquid form. When, with more heat, the liquid vaporizes into a gas, it is because the atoms and molecules are thrown apart from one another; and they remain in this loose state for as long as the thermal agitation continues. A *plasma is sometimes regarded as a fourth state of matter, and *liquid crystal as the fifth.

**static electricity**   *electricity.

**stationary waves**   *standing waves.

**statistics**, the classification, tabulation, and study of collections of data and their interpretation in mathematical terms. Statistics are often used in order to draw an inference or calculate a measure, called a statistic. Analysis is made of a population (in the most general sense of the term) and sometimes predictions of changes are made in terms of *probability. Population may mean a collection of people, as in an experiment to discover the average height of Americans, but it may mean such things as all the lengths of time queuing at a bus stop, as in an investigation into bus time-tables. Normally a representative sample is taken, large enough for it to be generalized to the whole. In descriptive statistics the data are summarized and the population described. Inferential statistics normally proposes a null *hypothesis and then endeavours to disprove it. Because no sample can be guaranteed to be representative, statisticians need to indicate confidence limits, using calculations of mean and *variance. The quantities that differ from one member of a population to another are known as *variables. The possible relationship between different sets of data is expressed in terms of a correlation coefficient.

**staurolite**, an iron aluminium silicate, a common metamorphic mineral. Its crystals are hard and semi-opaque with a vitreous lustre, and are prized as semi-precious gems. Large crystals are found in Switzerland, Bavaria, and Georgia, USA. Staurolite is of scientific importance as an indicator of the degree of metamorphism in rocks.

**steatite** (soapstone), an alteration product of magnesium compounds, an impure massive form of *talc. It is found in compact light-grey masses, the most extensive ones being in Canada, Madras (India), and Styria (Austria). When crushed it is used in the paper, textile, rubber, cosmetics, and paint industries as a foundation.

**Stefan, Joseph** (1835–93), Austrian physicist who established the law linking the temperature of an object and the rate at which it radiates energy. According to this law, the energy radiated per unit area per unit time by a *black body (the best of all radiators) is equal to $\sigma\, T^4$, where $T$ is the absolute or kelvin temperature and $\sigma$ is a constant known as the Stefan constant.

**stereochemistry**, the study of the three-dimensional structure of molecules. Stereochemical considerations are important in both *isomerism and studies of the *mechanisms of chemical reactions. Implicit in a mechanism is the stereochemistry of the reaction; in other words, the relative three-dimensional orientation of the reacting particles at any time in the reaction.

**Stern–Gerlach experiment**, performed in 1921 by two German physicists, Otto Stern and Walther Gerlach, who found that a beam of silver atoms split into several beams when passed through a non-uniform magnetic field. The atoms, each acting as a magnet, took paths which depended on their orientation. The splitting indicated that the atoms were orientated not at random but in certain set directions only—a result predicted by the *quantum theory.

**Stewart Island**, New Zealand's third largest island, 32 km (20 miles) south of the South Island, across the Foveaux Strait. It has a rugged and deeply indented coastline and a mountainous interior, rising to Mount Anglem at 980 m (3,210 feet) in the north. It measures 63 km (39 miles) long and 32 km (20 miles) wide, and the climate is cool. Tin and feldspar are found.

**stochastic processes** (in statistics), the sequences of statistical experiments or observations (such as the throw of a die) in each of which the outcome depends on some chance factor. Stochastic processes are governed by the laws of *probability.

**stock** (in geology), a body of *igneous rock that is roughly circular in plan and smaller than a *batholith; it may be connected to underlying batholiths. Stocks can be of any coarse-grained igneous material but are most often *granites. Many of the tors on Dartmoor, in Devon, England, are exhumed stocks.

**stoichiometry**, the ratios in which the reactants in a chemical reaction combine to form the products. For example, two *moles of hydrogen react with one mole of oxygen, giving two moles of water. The stoichiometric equation summarizes this as $2H_2 + O_2 \rightarrow 2H_2O$. In stoichiometric compounds, the elements are present in simple whole number

The 1953 floods in the Netherlands, caused by a **storm surge** in the North Sea, were the worst for 400 years. The photograph shows the ruins of a restaurant on the sea front at Katwijk, a fishing town and seaside resort in the south-west of the country.

ratios: for example, the ratio is one to one in hydrogen chloride, HCl. In contrast, iron sulphide, $Fe_xS$, is a non-stoichiometric compound, $x$ taking a range of values slightly less than one.

**Stokes, Sir George Gabriel** (1819–1903), British physicist who made important advances in the studies of *fluorescence, sound, and fluid flow. He noted that most fluorescent materials emit light radiation of a longer wavelength than that received, and he established a law describing the absorption of energy as sound waves pass through a medium. He is probably best remembered, however, for his law of fluid resistance, which states that the resisting force acting on a sphere moving smoothly through a liquid or gas is in direct proportion to the velocity and to the radius of the sphere.

**stone**, the word commonly used in Britain for a small fragment of rock, is generally replaced in geological usage by more specific terms such as 'rock', 'boulder', or 'pebble'. It is, however, used as an abbreviation of 'sandstone' or 'limestone' in the names of some building stones: Portland stone, Bath stone, for example. A further use of the word in the earth sciences is as an abbreviation for a type of meteorite, the aerolites.

**storm**, a violent disturbance of the atmosphere, which may be accompanied by rain, snow, sleet or hail. Storms may blow gustily as squalls, and they may have the characteristics of *thunderstorms. Sea storms are accompanied by very high waves with long, overhanging crests, and the surface is white with foam. In a violent storm the waves may be as much as 11 m (37 feet) in height, and visibility may be greatly affected by blown spray. In the tropics they are known as cyclones or *tropical revolving storms. A storm is different from a wind of storm force on the *Beaufort scale. This is a wind with a speed between 48 and 65 knots (88–120 km/h, 55–75 m.p.h.); it is stronger than gale force but weaker than hurricane force.

**storm surge**, a short-lived local rise in sea-level which occurs when water is piled up against a coast as a result of strong onshore winds accompanied by unusually low atmospheric pressure (*lows). The increase in water-level may be as much as 5 m (16 feet) above normal high tide, resulting in widespread flooding, extensive damage, and loss of life. The effect is particularly devastating if it occurs at the time of the *spring tides. Storm surges are common in the Gulf of Mexico, along the Atlantic coast of the US, around the islands of the western Pacific, where typhoons are very common, in the Bay of Bengal and in coastal regions of the North Sea. The flood of 1970 devastated Bangladesh, and one in 1953 caused death and damage in both the UK and The Netherlands.

**strait**, a narrow stretch of water linking one sea area with another, acting as a naturally made canal. Straits provide passages not only for the water itself but also for the sediment it carries, living creatures such as fish and plankton, and for ships. Some, such as the Bosporus, are very narrow, while others such as the Bering Strait (58 km or 36 miles wide but only 55 m or 180 feet deep at its narrowest point) are surprisingly shallow. Some, such as the Strait of Magellan, are long and tortuous; others are relatively abrupt, such as the Strait of Gibraltar, which limits the tidal range of the Mediterranean Sea. Most contain strong tidal flows.

**strand line**, the vestige of an old shoreline of a lake or the sea, left high and dry by a fall in water-level or gradual uplift of the land. Strand lines usually consist of **L**-shaped nicks or notches, the steeper slope representing the old cliff-line or back of the beach, while the flattish slope in front is the remnant of the former beach or tidal platform. Sets of virtually parallel strand lines, resembling shallow flights of steps, are common in coastal areas, such as Hudson Bay, Canada, which are rising slowly after being weighed down by ice-sheets during the last ice age.

**strangeness** (in atomic physics), a term originally used in descriptions of the decay process of certain 'strange' particles which were produced in high-energy interactions; they were strange because they decayed much more slowly than expected. Strangeness is now recognized as one of the six distinct types, or *flavours, of *quarks.

**strata**, layers of *sedimentary rock. The layering, or *bedding, can result from changes in the process of deposition: pauses in deposition, for example, or changes in the type of material or the rate at which it is deposited. The thickness of a single stratum may range from a millimetre ($\frac{1}{16}$ inch) to metres (tens of feet). The word bed has the same meaning.

**Strathcona Provincial Park**, Vancouver Island, British Columbia, Canada, a mainly mountainous area of 2,145 km² (828 sq. mi.) with thick forests and many streams. Among the many peaks over 1,500 m (5,000 feet) is the Golden Hinde, which rises to 2,200 m (7,219 feet). The Park includes the southern part of Buttle Lake and is a popular retreat for ecologists, fishermen, and people searching for gold.

**stratigraphy**, or historical geology, the study of *strata, especially their character, their sequences, and the relationships between them. For the most part it deals with sedimentary rocks, but *lavas can also be treated stratigraphically. The subject has two main aspects: lithostratigraphy, which is concerned with establishing the sequences of the rocks, and chronostratigraphy, which is concerned with correlating rocks of the same age in different places, chiefly by means of the fossils they contain. A fundamental principle is that of superposition: younger rocks rest on older, provided that they have not been disturbed by earth movements. It was William *Smith who observed that certain fossils were characteristic of certain strata and that the sequence of strata was constant when traced across the country. Starting from these principles, geologists have since built up a picture of the sequence of stratified rocks and have classified into larger and smaller units—systems, series, and stages—corresponding to the units of *geological time. Stratigraphical studies also enable the geography of past times to be reconstructed. Palaeogeographical maps can be drawn to show the distribution of

Distinct **strata** in a seacliff face at Oamaru, South Island, New Zealand. The conspicuous red layer and the greenish layer above it are both sandstone of similar composition, but the red layer has been oxidized and the green layer has been reduced. Just below is soft silt-stone, above the sandstone banding is limestone, then topping this is a further stratum consisting of volcanic ash and lava.

land and sea and other geographical features that existed at some specified time in the geological past. Stratigraphy is of particular importance in exploration for oil and coal.

**stratopause**, the upper limit of the *stratosphere, with a relatively high temperature of 0 °C (32 °F) due to absorption of the Sun's ultraviolet radiation. Above it is the mesosphere, where the air temperature stops increasing and begins to decrease again. At approximately 50 km (30 miles) from Earth, it marks the beginning of the *ionosphere.

**stratosphere**, the layer of the Earth's atmosphere between the tropopause, at an average height of about 12 km (7.5 miles) above the ground in mid-latitudes during the year, and the stratopause, at about 50 km (30 miles) from the ground. It is a zone of thin, rarefied air whose temperature is almost steady at less than −50 °C (−58 °F) to a height of 20 km (12 miles) or so, above which it gradually increases with height. It is almost entirely unaffected by weather; but supersonic aircraft have introduced disturbances and it is thought that they may be changing its composition and temperature characteristics. The stratosphere contains the *ozone layer, whose interception of ultraviolet rays from the Sun permits life to exist on Earth.

**stratus cloud**, a generally shapeless, grey, layered form of cloud which forms at 500 m (1,600 feet) or below. When very low-lying, it is often the cause of fog. The layers commonly develop in stable conditions and light winds by *advection, as moist air passes over a colder surface, though dense and multi-layered stratus several hundred metres deep may accumulate in the vicinity of *fronts. Although grey stratus may look threatening, it does not necessarily presage bad weather. Only if its edges appear torn and twisted to windward, and if in its advance through the air it meets a bank of *cumulus cloud, is it likely to become *nimbus.

**stream**    *river.

**streamline**, a line that represents the natural course of air or water currents. On meteorological maps, atmospheric streamlines are drawn to show the horizontal movement of air over the earth's surface. They are continuous lines drawn parallel to the mean wind direction at a given moment or for a given period of time. They pick out areas of low pressure by spiralling anticlockwise into them in the northern hemisphere and clockwise in the southern. From centres of high pressure they spiral outwards, clockwise in the northern hemisphere and anticlockwise in the southern.

**striation** (in geology), a narrow groove or scratch in rock almost always produced by the action of a glacier. The base of a glacier often contains a great number of shattered rock fragments, which can act like a giant sanding-wheel, smoothing and polishing the solid rock beneath. But sometimes hard and jagged chunks of rock stick down below the general pad of debris and rasp and file scratches—striations—across the polished surfaces. Sets of striations sometimes run almost parallel to each other. They are good evidence of former glaciers and provide a useful clue to the direction of ice movement, but can be confused with similar scratches left by wire logging ropes!

**strike** (in geology), the general trend of the *bedding of the rocks in a region. Specifically, it is the direction of an imaginary horizontal line drawn along the plane of the bedding of an inclined bed; it is at right angles to the *dip of that bed. Strike is also a term applied to a find of a mineral or an ore.

**strike–slip fault**, or tear fault, a geological fracture produced when two blocks of rock move sideways in relation to each other along the line (or strike) of a fault plane. The movement is thus mostly in the horizontal direction. These faults are usually produced by large-scale earth movements. The San Andreas Fault in California, USA, is an example.

**string theory** (in atomic physics). The quantum physics of elementary particles assumes that the particles have no size: that is, they exist as points with no dimensions. This assumption has been very useful, but it is inappropriate in some circumstances, for example at very high energies or over very short distances. String theory claims to provide a description of particles which is appropriate for these and all other circumstances. In string theory particles are not points, but are one-dimensional objects which can be thought of as strings—though, unlike everyday string, they have no thickness, only length. There are two types of string: the open, which are curves, and the closed, which are loops. The length of the strings is defined by a relationship between the fundamental quantities Planck's constant, the speed of light and the gravitation constant, and is $1.6 \times 10^{-33}$ cm. String theories appear to avoid the difficulties which other theories

A rock on the lip of Cwm Idwal, North Wales, UK, with **striations** produced by a glacier from the last glaciation.

have with the inclusion of gravity in *grand unified theories. A further development of string theory, called superstring theory, looks promising in this regard. String theory was first proposed by Jöel Scherk and John Schwartz in 1974.

**stripped land surface**, an area where layers of relatively soft rocks have been neatly peeled away by erosion to expose the upper surfaces of much more resistant strata. The term is usually applied to plains cut on more or less horizontal rocks, but a whole landscape may be buried by soft sediments—particularly *loess, *till, or volcanic ash. When these are later stripped off, the former hills and valleys are exposed. Such occurrences are rare, requiring a major difference in resistance of the upper and lower layers of material, so that the eroding agents (which are generally rivers) find it easier to cut sideways than to carve their way downwards, as is usually the case. The phenomenon is most commonly observed in places where sequences of sedimentary rocks of very different composition lie almost horizontally, and where this has resulted in stepped sequences of alternating stripped surfaces and escarpments. The Colorado plateaux of the south-west USA are an example.

**strong force** (in atomic physics). The strong force is one of the four fundemental *forces of nature. It is carried by *pions, and is responsible for holding hadrons together to form nuclei. The strong force is by far the strongest of the fundemental forces, but it is effective only over very short distances. (See also *interactions.)

The geological **structure** of Lulworth Cove in Dorset, UK, consists of clay and limestone strata compressed into anticlinal and synclinal folds.

**strontium** (symbol Sr, at. no. 38, r.a.m. 87.62), a silvery-white malleable element, a member of the *alkaline earth metals, and a good conductor of electricity. Its principal sources are strontianite ($SrCO_3$) and celestine ($SrSO_4$). The metal is obtained by *electrolysis of fused strontium chloride, $SrCl_2$, or by high-temperature reduction of strontium oxide, SrO. Its chemical properties are similar to those of calcium and barium; it reacts vigorously with water and on heating with hydrogen, oxygen, nitrogen, and the halogens. Its compounds are used in fireworks and flares, which colour red. The isotope strontium-90 is present in nuclear fall-out and represents a danger to health. It is radioactive with a *half-life of as long as 28 years and, because it is chemically similar to calcium, becomes incorporated within bone.

**structure, geological**, the relationships between rock units; the way in which a rock is made up of individual parts. Structure includes sedimentary features such as bedding, fine laminations, or layers within the rock; folds, faults, and joints. In igneous rocks it includes the pattern and occurrence of intrusions and flow marks in lavas. In metamorphic rocks it includes the type of cleavage, foliation, and schistosity. It does not, however, in normal usage include such features as mineral structures or texture (the nature and character of individual particles which make up the rock). Geological structure thus includes at one extreme features of very large scale, measured perhaps in hundreds of kilometres or miles, and at the other features that can be studied in the space of a single exposure. Some geologists also include under the term 'structure' small-scale features that can be studied only under the microscope; others reserve for these the word 'texture'.

**Strutt, John William and Robert John** (father and son), British physicists. John, third Lord Rayleigh (1842–1919), discovered the *noble gas argon. He also made valuable contributions to physical optics and to the determination of electrical units in absolute measure, and was awarded the Nobel Prize for Physics in 1904. Robert, fourth Lord Rayleigh (1875–1947), contributed to spectroscopy. His most notable work, however, was in the investigation of minerals and rocks, determining their age by measuring their *radioactivity.

**Stuart, John McDouall** (1815–66), Scottish emigrant to Australia who crossed the continent in 1862 at his sixth attempt, from south to north and back again. Officially he was the first Australian to do so, despite John *McKinlay's effort, which had been concluded several months earlier. Stuart's Creek was named after him.

**Sturt, Charles** (1795–1869), British explorer of Australia who surveyed its largest river system and opened up the south for settlement. In 1828–9 he examined the marshes of the Macquarie and discovered the Darling and Murray Rivers. From Adelaide in 1844–5 he discovered the Sturt Desert and Cooper's Creek. He was also a good administrator, rising to the post of colonial secretary before he retired in 1851 and returned to England.

**subduction**, (in geology) the process whereby tectonic *plates of oceanic *lithosphere descend back into the Earth's mantle along margins where plates converge. The subduction zone itself is marked by a zone of deep-focus earthquakes, and its surface expression is commonly an *island arc or *ocean trench or both. The location of the deep-focus of an earthquake may be referred to as the hypocentre, and the point at the Earth's surface overlying this the epicentre. (See also *plate tectonics.)

**sublimation** (in chemistry), the process by which a solid is converted on heating directly into a gas, without going through a liquid state. Only a small number of solids sublime, carbon dioxide, $CO_2$ and *iodine, $I_2$, being examples. Ammonium chloride, $NH_4Cl$, sublimes on heating, but the vapour is a mixture of ammonia, $NH_3$, and hydrogen chloride, $HCl$; on cooling, solid ammonium chloride is re-formed. Some solids which do melt to form a liquid still evaporate quite rapidly if kept below their melting-points; iodine and sulphur are examples. This is also sublimation, and can be used as a method of purification.

**submarine canyon**, a valley or trench cut into the solid rock of a *continental shelf or slope. Submarine canyons are generally very deep, with cliff-like walls which are often as high as or higher than the Grand Canyon, Arizona, USA. The submarine canyon among the Bahamas, for example, has walls 5 km (3 miles) high. A canyon floor is often narrow and winding, like a river valley, but becomes deeper and wider towards its mouth: the Monterey Canyon off California is less than 1 kilometre (0.5 mile) wide when it starts in Monterey Bay, but is about 8 km (5 miles) across at its mouth. Many have numerous tributary valleys; and some cross the continental slope and continue into the deeper water areas of the ocean. Some begin at the mouths of major rivers. There are, for example, major canyon systems off shore from the Congo and the Hudson. This, and many similarities to valleys on land, suggests that they may have been formed by rivers when sea-level was much lower and that they were subsequently drowned. Be that as it may, they have been extensively modified by tidal scour and marine erosion, particularly by *turbidity currents. Considerable quantities of sediment, eroded from the land surface and carried into the sea by rivers, is deposited at the head of these canyons. When it moves down the floor of a canyon it causes much erosion before finally accumulating at the mouth as a huge fan on the continental slope. Submarine canyons undoubtedly act as channels by which sediment is transported from the continents into the ocean basins.

**subsidence**, the downward movement of a block of rock relative to the surrounding area. It is normally associated with faulting or with the removal or erosion of underlying beds, and can be caused by human activities (mining) or by natural agencies: solution (cave collapse) or erosion (sea cliff collapse).

In meteorology, subsidence is the widespread, slow descent of air. It is particularly associated with *anticyclones. It results from the chilling of the surface layers of air by conduction from a cold ground surface and by long-wave radiation losses, or from high-level horizontal *convergence. Air tends to become warmer and its relative *humidity decreases as it subsides.

**substitution reaction** *chemical reactions.

**subtropical high**, a region of permanently high atmospheric pressure which straddles a broad belt between latitudes 20° and 40° both north and south of the Equator. These highs control the positions and strengths of the *trade winds and of the *westerlies. In the northern hemisphere the

major *anticyclones are centres over the Azores in the Atlantic and Hawaii in the Pacific. Over continental areas, such as northern Africa, the stable and descending air gives rise to the aridity of the major deserts.

In oceanic areas, the subsiding, dry air of the subtropical highs is associated with relatively low rainfall and high evaporation; as a result, the surface waters of the anticyclonic subtropical gyres have a higher *salinity than most water in the open ocean.

**Sudan**, the name of a great belt crossing Africa south of the Sahara, and more specifically of a country at its eastern end. This has Egypt on its northern boundary, a coast on the Red Sea, and boundaries also with Ethiopia, Kenya, Uganda, Zaïre, the Central African Republic, Chad, and Libya. The largest country on the African continent, it has equatorial forest in the south and the Nubian Desert in the north; and its whole length is traversed from south to north by the River Nile. The mid-south contains the Sudd swamps with islands of vegetation scattered among the reeds and tall papyrus grass. There is a region of *savannah, and near the junction of the Blue and White Niles cotton is grown under irrigation on the wide clay plains of the Gezira. Further north are areas covered with acacia bushes, the source of gum arabic. In the extreme north years may pass without rain, and the only cultivation is on the river's banks. There are deposits of oil, copper, zinc, iron, and gold.

**Sudety** (German, Sudetengebirge), an east-west highland region of north-eastern Bohemia and northern Moravia, some some 250 km (150 miles) long, bordering on Poland. It is bounded on the west by the valley of the Nysa River, and on the east by the Moravian Gate. Its north-western section consists of a number of short overlapping mountain ranges, none greater than 48 km (30 miles) in length, which

This satellite view clearly shows how the Sinai Peninsula has split from Africa, forming the Gulf of **Suez**, the western branch of the Red Sea.

culminate in the bevelled summits of the granitic Karkonosze at 1,600 m (5,260 feet). By contrast the south-eastern section shows a gently undulating relief, although it still attains 1,492 m (4,894 feet). Mineral deposits abound; throughout the region springs of hot and mineralized water occur, resulting from widespread faulting and fracturing.

**Suez, Gulf of**, the north-west arm of the Red Sea that extends for some 290 km (180 miles) between the Sinai peninsula and Africa. It is bounded by major faults that continue the trend of those bordering the Red Sea itself. The land has subsided between the faults as Africa and Arabia pulled apart, and subsequent flooding by the sea has completed the formation of the Gulf.

**Sulawesi**, or Celebes, an island in Indonesia, lying east of Borneo. Its shape, dominated by four long peninsulas, has been described as resembling that of an octopus with four tentacles missing on the western side. It lies between the Asian and the Australian *continental shelves and is largely made up of igneous rock locally edged with coral limestone. Its mountain scenery, with some peaks rising above 3,000 m (10,000 feet), provides a fine backcloth to a number of beautiful lakes occupying structural basins, and to the waterfalls and rapids that characterize the short and steep rivers.

**sulfur** *sulphur.

**sulphates**, compounds which contain the ion $SO_4^{2-}$; they can be made by neutralizing sulphuric acid. Potassium sulphate, $K_2SO_4$, and ammonium sulphate, $(NH_4)_2SO_4$, are water-soluble; they are used in fertilizers. Calcium sulphate, $CaSO_4$, occurs naturally as gypsum, and forms plaster of Paris on heating.

**sulphides**, the compounds formed between sulphur and other elements. All the metals except gold and platinum combine with sulphur to form sulphides, many of which are insoluble in water. They frequently occur naturally and constitute many important metal ores. Sulphur also forms covalent sulphides with many non-metals such as hydrogen sulphide, $H_2S$, and carbon disulphide, $CS_2$.

**sulphites**, the series of salts containing the $SO_3^{2-}$ anion, in which sulphur has a valency of 4. They correspond to the putative sulphurous acid, $H_2SO_3$. Solutions of the alkali metal sulphites are used as reducing agents.

**sulphur** (US, sulfur) (symbol S, at. no. 16, r.a.m. 32.06), a yellow non-metallic element in Group VI of the *periodic table that exists in two different *allotropes, both of which are yellow. It occurs naturally both in the free state and in sulphides and sulphates, and is found chiefly around hot springs, and in volcanic regions. It is extracted, sometimes from considerable depths, by melting with superheated steam; the liquid sulphur collects in a pool and is then pumped to the surface almost chemically pure. This is the Frasch process. It is also found in some natural gas as hydrogen sulphide, $H_2S$, and in sedimentary rocks such as gypsum. In ancient times sulphur was known as brimstone and was employed with its blue flame and odorous smell in religious ceremonies, in witchcraft, and in sorcery. Today it is principally used in making sulphuric acid. Its compounds are many, for it is a reactive element which combines with many metals. Its compounds are employed in the manufacture of rubber, dyes, fertilizers, and insecticides, and also in the pharmaceutical industry.

**sulphur dioxide** ($SO_2$), a colourless, poisonous gas with a characteristic, choking pungency. A typical acidic oxide, dis-

**Sulphur** often occurs in areas of geothermal activity. Here it is being deposited around a fumarole near Rotorua, North Island, New Zealand.

solving in water to form sulphurous acid, $H_2SO_3$. It is used to prepare sulphur trioxide, $SO_3$, in the manufacture of sulphuric acid, $H_2SO_4$, and in bleaching and food preservation. As a by-product of the combustion of fossil fuels which contain sulphur, particularly coal, it is a major air pollutant, dissolving in water in the atmosphere and oxidizing to sulphuric acid to give *acid rain that can cause severe environmental damage.

**sulphuric acid** (or oil of vitriol, $H_2SO_4$), a colourless, corrosive, oily liquid. In its concentrated form it is a strong *oxidizing agent and is used to dehydrate many compounds. When it is diluted, a process that requires great care as it is violently exothermic, it readily dissociates and has all the properties of a strong *acid. It is manufactured by the contact process in which sulphur dioxide, $SO_2$, is passed over a catalyst to give sulphur trioxide, $SO_3$, which is then dissolved in the acid already produced to give *oleum (or fuming sulphuric acid). This is then diluted to give concentrated sulphuric acid (98 per cent $H_2SO_4$, 2 per cent $H_2O$). It is the most widely produced industrial chemical and has many uses in the manufacture of other chemicals, fertilizers, and plastics, and also in the cleaning of metals.

**Sumatra**, a very large island in the east of the Indian Ocean, a part of Indonesia but separated from the Malay Peninsula by the Strait of Malacca and from Java by the Sunda Strait. A western coastal plain 1,770 km (1,100 miles) long rises sharply to volcanic mountain ranges which contain, in the north, a great salt lake. From their eastern slopes multitudinous rivers run through otherwise impenetrable jungle to vast areas of swampland, the soil being extremely fertile. Rubber, rice, sugar-cane, camphor bushes, tea, and coffee all grow well. There are oilfields, coalfields, deposits of gold and silver and, on smaller islands off the coast, of bauxite and tin.

**Suomi**   *Finland.

**superconductivity**, a property displayed by certain metals and alloys when their temperature is lowered to within a few degrees of *absolute zero. Their electrical resistance suddenly vanishes which makes them ideal for the manufacture of coils and *cables that do not dissipate power. Very large electrical currents may be passed down such cables, making possible very efficient distribution of electrical power, for example, in a grid system. Electronic circuits using superconductors can work one hundred times faster than conventional circuits. Superconductivity also makes possible the manufacture of extremely powerful but very small electromagnets; however, the effect may be destroyed by the presence of a magnetic field, in some cases only a fraction of a *tesla. It was not until 1960 that materials were discovered which remain superconducting in fields powerful enough to allow exploitation. Among them are a niobium–titanium alloy which remains superconducting in fields of up to 10 tesla and a compound of niobium and tin, $Nb_3Sn$, which continues operating up to 20 tesla. Such substances are now widely used, particularly in the manufacture of very powerful electromagnets used in medical instrumentation and electrical traction. The transition temperature at which superconductivity occurs is different for different materials—over a range of about 25 elements and thousands of alloys and compounds it varies from 0.01 to approximately 25 kelvin. The effect is ascribed to a pairing of electrons in the bulk material. Whereas single electrons scatter,

pairs of electrons are able to move through the material without scattering: that is to say, the material offers zero resistance. The high cost of the advanced cooling systems needed for superconductivity has meant that its applications are limited. However, in 1987 several research groups discovered a class of electroceramics that exhibit superconductivity at much higher temperatures than previously known. When developed, these may make available the benefits of superconductivity on a large scale.

**Superior, Lake**   *Great Lakes.

**superoxide**, a compound that contains the $O_2^-$ ion. Superoxides are generally yellow in colour at room temperature, but as they are cooled many undergo a reversible phase transition, accompanied by a colour change to white. The *alkali metals all form ionic superoxides when they are dissolved in liquid ammonia and oxidized with oxygen gas. Chemically, superoxides are both strong oxidizing agents and strong bases, and are thus extremely corrosive.

**surface tension**, the result of forces acting on atoms and molecules at the surface of a liquid. Whereas forces within the liquid pull in all directions, the net force at the surface is inwards, pulling the molecules together so that they form a kind of tight but elastic skin. It acts at all boundaries, and has energy associated with it; thus the tendency is for a surface to be as small as possible. Drops of a liquid are spherical because, for any given volume, a sphere has the smallest surface area. Surface tension falls as temperature rises; and it differs with different liquids, those with a high degree displaying the greatest *capillary action.

**Suriname**, a country on the north coast of South America sandwiched between Guyana and French Guiana, with Brazil to the south. The climate is equatorial: hot and very wet. Thick forest covers most of the interior, which rises to highlands in the centre. Rice and sugar cane can be grown on the coast, and there are deposits of bauxite.

**Surtsey** (Icelandic), an island that appeared within a day in November 1963 as a result of volcanic activity. Its birth on

The 'skin' formed by **surface tension** can be seen clearly in this picture of a pond surface: the skin stretches elastically, but does not break, under the weight of the spider, which can thus safely walk and hunt on the water surface.

the Mid Atlantic Ridge 32 km (20 miles) south-west of Iceland was heralded by black clouds, steam, and molten lava. Within a year, while still growing, the island's cone became misshapen by weather action. After two years the island had grown to 2.4 km (1.5 miles) across and 183 m (600 feet) high, and had attracted plant and animal life.

**suspended load**, material which is completely buoyed up by the water in rivers, without being dissolved into its constituent ions. It is therefore intermediate in size and weight between the ions of the *dissolved load and the heavier particles moving as *bed load. Large rivers flowing through areas of easily eroded sediments (particularly *loess) may have so much suspended load that they look like thick soup (as does the Huang He, or Yellow River, China). Even so, material in suspension can settle out of the flow if the speed drops; and, on the other hand, large debris can move from bed to suspension in floods.

**Susquehanna**, a river of New York and Pennsylvania states, eastern USA. Some 715 km (444 miles) long, it issues from Otsego Lake in the northern Appalachian Mountains and runs swiftly southward on a twisting course, through valleys which are rich in anthracite and coal. After picking up its West Branch it enters its main valley and is liable to flood. It then crosses the coastal plain and enters Chesapeake Bay, whence its waters reach the Atlantic Ocean. It is a shallow river, and unnavigable even in its lower reaches.

**Svalbard**, a group of Norwegian islands in the Arctic Ocean, some 920 km (580 miles) north of Troms, Norway, which includes Spitsbergen. The islands are built generally of ancient rocks that were eroded down to sea-level during the *Tertiary Period and then uplifted by 600 to 900 m (2,000 to 3,000 feet). This produced a high plateau surface that was occupied by ice-sheets during the last glaciation. With the melting of the ice, the islands are slowly rising. The present scenery includes jagged peaks, fault-controlled coastlines, glaciers, and snow-fields. The climate is severe, with winter temperatures dropping to −40 °C (−40 °F), and justifies the name given to the island group (Norwegian, 'cold coast').

**swallow-hole**   *sink-hole.

**swamp**, an area of ground which, although almost permanently flooded by water, nevertheless has a thick covering of vegetation. In Europe and Africa swamps usually consist of reeds; in North America they generally contain trees, notably swamp cypresses; while the coastlines and river mouths of tropical and subtropical areas are lined by mangrove swamps. They are transitional between open water which is occupied by aquatic plants, and marshes, the surfaces of which are only flooded periodically.

**Swanland**, part of the extreme south-west of Western Australia, named after the Swan River, whose Mediterranean type of climate is suitable for agriculture. Its eastern boundary passes approximately through Southern Cross, 354 km (220 miles) east of Perth. From here to the west rainfall increases across the continuation of the semi-desert plain of the interior until, with the descent across the Darling Range fault-scarp to the coastal plain, annual precipitation rises to 760 mm (30 inches). Some sinking of the coastal region has led to the drowning of the Swan estuary. The area is noted for its flora, being rich in endemic forms.

The Everglades is an extensive **swamp** that lies in a saucer-like depression of southern Florida, USA, covering some 12,950 km² (5,000 sq. mi.). The photograph shows swamp cypresses and the large green leaves of alligator flags.

**swash** (of waves), the movement of a thin layer of turbulent, foaming water up a beach following the breaking of a wave. As this water rushes along it carries sand and shell fragments with it, depositing them when it runs out of energy. Flat waves, which have a very strong swash, often move a lot of material on to a beach in this way. Some of the swash soaks into the beach, while the rest returns to the breaker zone as *backwash; the edge of a zone of swash action is often marked by a line of seaweed and driftwood.

**Swaziland**, a small country of southern Africa, land-locked by South Africa on three sides and by Mozambique on the east. In the west are well-watered hills rich in iron ore, and from them run several rivers to the dry veld in the middle of the country. Here a variety of crops can be grown, while on the lower plains in the east there is livestock farming, together with the cultivation of sugar cane. Coal, diamonds, gold, and asbestos are mined.

**Sweden**, a country occupying the southern and largest part of the Scandinavian peninsula in northern Europe. It has a long, mountainous boundary with Norway on the north-west and a shorter one with Finland on the north-east. Its island-fringed coasts are on the Baltic Sea and the Kattegat, the channel to the North Sea. The northern part of the country is within the Arctic Circle. There are glaciers in the mountains, which everywhere are heavily forested with conifers. Parallel rivers fall to the Baltic Sea (Gulf of Bothnia) in rapids and falls, many of which have hydroelectric power stations, and forming at intervals long lakes. High-grade iron ore is found here, together with many other minerals. A region of hummocky hills and huge lakes lies to the south of the mountain range, and then the land rises again to a rocky, forested plateau. The southern coastal plain is extremely fertile; and the largest island, Gotland, has splendid beaches.

**Swiss Lakes**, lakes in Switzerland, central Europe, of which the largest are Geneva, Neuchâtel, Constance, Zurich, and Lucerne. They are glacial lakes blocked mostly by *moraines and are famous for their beauty. The deep blue Lake Geneva (shared with France) is fed and drained by the Rhône. Lake Constance (German, Bodensee), 68 km (42 miles) long (and shared with Germany and Austria), is fed and drained by the Rhine. The Lake of Neuchâtel (the largest wholly within Switzerland) nestles against the southern slopes of the Jura Mountains. Together, these magnificent lakes almost encircle the Swiss central plateau.

**Switzerland**, a country in central Europe surrounded by France, Germany, Italy, and the tiny country of Liechtenstein. It is Europe's loftiest country with the Alps stretching across the whole of its southern half. The rivers Rhône and Rhine rise here and form broad valleys. Below the forested mountain slopes, snow-covered all winter, the land is fertile and the summer temperature is warm. Northward the country stands on a hilly plateau which contains the *Swiss Lakes and rises again in the north-west to the Jura Mountains, a region important for dairying and forestry, and with vineyards on the southern slopes.

**syenite**, a coarse-grained igneous rock containing feldspar and hornblende as the essential minerals. Other ferromagnesian minerals may be present, as may small amounts of quartz. Syenites are typically found as offshoots from granites and as other minor intrusions. They are massive and pale grey or pinkish; when polished, some varieties are used as facing stones in building.

**symmetry**, the property of remaining invariant under certain changes (as of orientation in space, of the sign of the electric charge, of parity, or of the direction of time flow). Symmetrical forms have been accepted as indications of harmony and perfection by philosophers and scientist alike. It is from natural symmetries that the fundamental laws of nature arise. Examples of such laws are, the laws of conservation of momentum and energy, and the idea of mirror symmetry: that the laws of nature apply in exactly the same way in both a right-handed and left-handed world. But in 1956 the Chinese-born physicists Tsung Dao Lee (1926–    ) and Ning Chen Yang (1922–    ) suggested that this notion of 'parity' might not be conserved in weak *interactions. Their prediction was confirmed experimentally and certain elementary particles are found to behave in a right-handed way.

In geometry the study of the symmetry of figures or objects proceeds by examining which operations can be performed on them while leaving them looking the same. For example, a square can be reflected in its diagonals or in lines through the centre parallel to its sides, and the resulting configuration will be indistinguishable from the original. Similarly, rotating the square through any multiple of $90°$ about its centre preserves the original orientation. The

important aspect of the set of symmetry operations of any figure is that it always forms a group (*group theory) under the operation of composition of transformations, that is, repeating and combining them. Every shape has a symmetry group even if it only contains the identity transformation. If wallpaper patterns are suitably described in sufficiently abstract terms then it is possible to show that there are seventeen different types of wallpaper design, each classified by a particular group of rigid transformations.

**syncline**, a geological fold structure in the form of a trough or inverted arch, produced by the downfolding of stratified rocks. Each side of the fold dips in towards the centre; the younger rocks thus crop out in the centre of the syncline and the older rocks on its flanks. A syncline is the opposite of an *anticline.

**synthesis** (in chemistry), a chemical reaction in which molecules having a desired structure are made by causing atoms or smaller molecules to combine together. Certain simple molecules can be synthesized in a single reaction. The reaction of two elements A and B to form a substance AB is called direct synthesis. It is more common for the synthesis of a molecule to require a larger number of stages, or steps. A chemist wishing to synthesize a particular molecule will plan a synthesis involving the smallest number of steps, so as to minimize the occurrence of alternative substances, or by-products, which would reduce the yield of the desired substance.

**Syria**, a country of south-west Asia at the eastern end of the Mediterranean Sea. Bounded on the north by Turkey, on the east by Iraq, on the south by Jordan, and on the south-west by Israel and Lebanon, it has a narrow coastal plain with a Mediterranean climate: citrus fruit and tobacco can be grown. Behind a range of hills the Asi (Orontes) River runs northward, along a *rift valley; and beyond that the ground rises to a plateau of steppe, where cotton can be grown. This merges into hot, dry desert, relieved only by the upper Euphrates, which runs across the country. In the extreme north-east there is oil.

**Szechwan**    *Sichuan.

# T

**tablelands** *plateaux.

**Table Mountain**, a flat mountain forming the northern end of a range which terminates in the Cape of Good Hope in the extreme south-west of South Africa. Its top, viewed from a distance, is almost flat, and the dense white mist which often covers it is called the 'tablecloth'. Overlooking Table Bay, it dominates the local views from land and sea. The summit is Maclear's Beacon, at 1,087 m (3,567 feet).

**Tagus**, the longest river of the Iberian Peninsula, flowing for some 1,000 km (620 miles) across the dry, hilly interior of Spain and Portugal before draining into the Atlantic at Lisbon. It rises in the Sierra de Albarracín of eastern Spain, and its subsequent course is characterized by steep and narrow valleys and by more tranquil reaches. The river finally enters a broad estuary at Santarém.

**Tahiti**, the largest of the Society Islands, in the centre of the South Pacific, administered by France. Mountainous, with peaks rising to 2,320 m (7,612 feet), it is a tropical paradise of palms and luxuriant flora, which include the climbing orchid from which vanilla is extracted.

**Taiwan** (previously Formosa), a country comprising a large island and several much smaller ones off the south-east coast of China. The main island is almost 370 km (230 miles) long from north to south and 130 km (81 miles) wide from west to east. Climatically it is very warm and wet in summer and cooler in winter. High mountains running most of its length, richly forested with camphor, oak, cypress, and cedar, drop steeply eastward to the Pacific Ocean. Westward many rivers flow through plains bearing sugarcane, paddy, and tropical fruits. There are deposits of coal, oil, sulphur, iron, and other minerals.

**Tajikistan**, a country bounded by Xinjiang (China) on the east and Afghanistan on the south, one of the highest regions of central Asia. The Pamirs occupy a third of it while the Alai range stretches across its centre. Below the snow-line the slopes are generally great stretches of bare red and grey rocks, broken by alpine meadows, the forests near the tree-line being of firs and juniper. The valleys support vineyards, orchards, and fields of cereal and cotton, while hydroelectricity is available from river power. The mineral resources are varied and considerable.

**Taklamakan Shamo**, a vast desert in the centre of the Tarim Basin of eastern China. One of the world's largest sandy wastes, it stretches for 970 km (600 miles) from west to east and up to 420 km (260 miles) from north to south. Its borders are the high mountains of Tian Shan to the north, Kunlun Shan to the south, and the Pamirs to the west; it merges eastward into the swampy Lop Nor in the Tarim Basin. Streams from the Kunlun Shan flow northward and dry out on the sands. Small sandstone-and-clay ridges rise up above the desert floor. Blown sand covers the surface thickly in places as chains of *dunes.

**talc** (talcum), a common magnesium silicate mineral, $Mg_3Si_4O_{10}(OH)_2$, which is extremely soft and soapy to the touch. The product of the alteration of magnesium compounds, it is found most commonly in metamorphic rocks. It never occurs as distinct crystals, but always as light-grey masses. Large deposits exist in Styria (Austria) and Madras

The precipitous cliffs of **Table Mountain** overlooking Cape Town, South Africa. The sandstone strata, of which the mountain is largely made, lie almost horizontal to give it its characteristic shape: a top that is not quite flat but undulates and contains several shallow valleys.

(India). It is used in powder form in the paper, rubber, textile, paint, and cosmetic industries.

**talus**  *scree.

**Tana, Lake**, the main reservoir for the Blue Nile, occupying a depression on the north-west plateau of Ethiopia, East Africa, at 1,800 m (6,000 feet). At the southern end are the Tisisat Falls, where the river drops 42 m (138 feet) and provides hydroelectric power. The lake has sixty feeder streams and is the largest in Ethiopia, and neighbouring alluvial deposits suggest that it was once even more extensive.

**Tanganyika, Lake**, in east-central Africa between Zaïre and Tanzania, the second largest expanse of fresh water in Africa, with a length of 680 km (420 miles) and a width of up to 72 km (45 miles). With a maximum depth of 1,430 m (4,700 feet) it is also, after Lake Baikal, the world's second deepest. Set in the Great Rift Valley, it is fed mainly from the north by the Ruzizi River from Lake Kivu, the next in a chain of lakes, and is surrounded by mountains. The only outlet is the Lukuga River, which drains into the Congo basin, so that part of the overflow ultimately reaches the Atlantic; but the Lukuga often silts up, causing the lake's surface to rise.

**tangent** (in geometry), a line which touches a curve in the plane. A tangent to any of the *conic sections does not intersect the curve anywhere else, whereas a straight line may touch and later cut the graph of, for example, a cubic function. The tangent to the graph of any function at a point is the limit approached as two points of intersection of a straight line with the curve coalesce. The derivative of the function evaluated at that point gives a number which is the value of the trigonometrical tangent of the angle between the tangent line and the horizontal. A tangent plane is the equivalent notion for surfaces in three-dimensional space.

**tangent** (in trigonometry), the *sine of an angle in a right-angled triangle divided by the *cosine of that angle, or, equivalently, the length of the side opposite the angle divided by the length of the adjacent side which is not the hypotenuse. The name comes from the triangle with the radius of a unit circle as adjacent side and the circle's geometrical tangent as opposite side. Many indirect measurements can be obtained using the tangent. Knowing the distance $d$ from a tower and the angle of elevation $\theta$ of the top, the height $h$ of the tower can be calculated, since $\tan \theta = h/d$.

**tantalum** (symbol Ta, at. no. 73, r.a.m. 180.95), a heavy grey *transition metal. It occurs with niobium in the mineral tantalite, which has the formula $(Fe,Mn)(Nb,Ta)_2O_6$. The element is used to make a variety of chemically inert, high-melting-point alloys required for chemical plant and nuclear reactor construction.

**Tanzania**, a country in East Africa bounded by Kenya and Uganda on the north, Rwanda, Burundi, and Zaïre on the west, and Zambia, Malawi, and Mozambique on the south. It has a coast on the Indian Ocean and several islands, including Zanzibar. A hot, wet coastal plain rises through thick forest and areas planted with sisal to a warm plateau. Here it is drier, and the soil is poor; but to the north is Mount Kilimanjaro, below which the soil is volcanic and coffee can be grown. In the extreme north is Lake Victoria, round which cotton is cultivated, diamonds are found, and animals roam in the Serengeti National Park. Lake Tanganyika lies along the western border, and Lake Malawi in the south, both in the western arm of the Great Rift Valley. Mineral resources include iron, coal, gold, and oil.

**tarn**, a small lake in upland areas, especially an almost circular one found in the floors of *cirques. The term is usually restricted to a lake of glaciated areas.

**Tasman, Abel Janszoon** (c.1603–59), Dutch navigator and European discoverer of New Zealand. In 1642 Van Diemen, governor of the Dutch East Indies, gave him command of an expedition to ascertain whether the known part of Australia was linked to a great southern continent. Sailing round western Australia he steered due east and came to land which he named Van Diemen's Landt, the island later renamed Tasmania. A month later he sighted high land, the western coast of New Zealand, which he called Staten Landt. Exploring northwards he was attacked by Maoris, so he made for the Pacific, there discovering islands in the Tonga and Fiji groups before returning to Java. Two years later, on another voyage, he surveyed much of the north Australian coast.

**Tasmania**, Australia's largest island, 240 km (150 miles) south of Wilson's Promontory, Victoria, in the south-east of the continent. It has many smaller islands off its own shores. Roughly triangular in shape, it has coastal plains giving way inland to timbered hills, lakes, plateaux, and mountains ris-

A mountain **tarn** in the Ogwen Valley, Snowdonia National Park, North Wales, UK.

ing to over 1,500 m (5,000 feet). The climate is equable and the rainfall is moderate, at least in the west, with numerous rivers providing scope for hydroelectricity. Dairy herds and sheep can be raised, and crops ranging from apples to hops are grown. There are deposits of copper, zinc, tin, iron, silver, and lead.

**Tasman Sea**, part of the South Pacific lying between Australia and New Zealand; it merges into the Coral Sea in the north and the Southern Ocean in the south. About 1,900 km (1,200 miles) in width, it contains the Tasman Basin with the Ulladullah Trough and Thomson Deep at 5,944 m (19,502 feet) in the west. The ridge that rises to the island of Tasmania is to the south-west and the Lord Howe Ridge to the north-east. The warming East Australian Current enters from the north, while across the south cold *westerlies blow.

**Taupo**, New Zealand's largest lake, lying at the centre of the North Island. Some 40 km (25 miles) long and 27 km (17 miles) wide, it is surrounded by volcanic mountains, is fed by many streams, and is drained by the Waikato River. The district round it is known for its hot springs.

**Taylor, Brook** (1685–1731), English mathematician, and near contemporary and follower of Newton, noted for his contribution to the development of calculus. He is most renowned for *Taylor expansion, a method of expressing functions as power series (named after him, although the possibility of such an expansion was known before his time). Using the calculus of finite differences, he was the first to express the movement of a vibrating string on the basis of mechanical principles. In 1715 he published *Linear Perspective*, which contains the first general treatment of the principle of vanishing points.

**Taylor expansion**, a means, under certain circumstances and for all values of $x$, of expanding a function in one variable, $f(x)$, as a *power series. The expansion (series) for $f(x)$ is $f(a) + f^1(a)/1!\cdot(x - a) + f^2(a)/2!\cdot(x - a)^2 + f^n(a)/n!\cdot(x - a)^n + \ldots$, where $f^n(a)$ means the $n$th derivative of $f$ evaluated at $x = a$. If $a$ is zero, the expansion becomes what is known as a Maclaurin series. The notation 2!, or *factorial 2, $= 2 \times 1$.

**technetium** (symbol Tc, at. no. 43, r.a.m. 98.91), a grey *transition metal formed from the neutron bombardment of molybdenum, and discovered in waste fission products. It was the first artificially produced element, and there are still no known terrestrial sources. Technetium has sixteen radioactive isotopes, one of which is used in diagnostic tracer work.

**tectonics**, the study of the structure of the Earth's crust or of a particular region of it, is concerned with folding, faulting, and other movements that have taken place, either on a large or on a small scale. *Plate tectonics is concerned with the movement of continents, with *sea-floor spreading, and with the other processes that are entailed in the creation and destruction of crustal material.

**Tehuantepec**, the isthmus of southern Mexico, which has the southernmost part of the Gulf of Mexico on its northern side and the Pacific Ocean on the south. It is 220 km (137 miles) wide at its narrowest point. A rather flat central ridge falls northward to a very wet, forested coastal lowland; the southern shore is drier and better drained. The isthmus is the physical boundary between North and Central America.

**tellurium** (symbol Te, at. no. 52, r.a.m. 127.60), a *metalloid element in Group VI of the periodic table. It has a grey 'metallic' form composed of infinite chains of tellurium atoms. A *semiconductor, it shows greater conductivity in certain directions, according to the alignment of the atoms. Its compounds are toxic; it is used in alloys, and for colouring glass.

**temperature**, a value on a scale of numbers which indicates the degree of hotness of an object. In any material, the atoms, molecules, or ions are in a state of continuous random motion, and temperature is a measure of the average energy which the particles possess because of this motion. By definition, two objects are at different temperatures if energy in the form of heat flows from one to another when they are in contact. The direction of flow is from the higher to the lower temperature. For much of human history ideas about temperature have been subjective: it was recognized that objects could be relatively hot or cold, but absolute temperature values could not be attributed. In the 2nd century AD the Greek physician Galen attempted to quantify temperature on a scale of eight degrees, relative to the temperature of an equal mixture of ice and boiling water. *Galileo in 1592 developed a thermoscope, an air-filled bulb with an open-ended stem which was inverted over a container of water. The level of water in the stem varied with the ambient temperature, but it was also affected by air pressure. Variation due to pressure changes was eliminated in about 1644 by Ferdinand II of Tuscany, who sealed the neck of the flask. Ferdinand also established a society in Florence whose members conducted extensive thermometric experiments, and whose workmen became skilled at making accurate thermometers. In the early 18th century Gabriel Fahrenheit perfected the mercury *thermometer. His *Fahrenheit temperature scale found widespread use, but has now been largely replaced by the *Celsius (centigrade) scale devised by Anders Celsius in 1742. In Celsius's original scale, 0 °C was the boiling-point of water at a standard pressure, and 100 °C the freezing-point, the reverse of the modern Celsius scale. In 1848 the British physicist William *Thomson (Lord Kelvin) proposed a temperature scale based on thermodynamic theory, which provides a fundamental standard with which other scales can be compared. The kelvin (K) was adopted in 1960 as the international *unit of temperature. Since the 19th century other physical properties that vary with temperature, such as electrical resistance and the thermoelectric effect (see *thermocouple), have been used for temperature measurement. Many modern thermometers are designed for specific applications and temperature ranges (see figure). Cryogenic (low-temperature) thermometers include types made from doped semiconductors, used for ranges from 0.2 to 20 K (−272.8 to −253 °C). Thermistors—small beads or cylinders of semiconductors or complex metal oxides—can measure temperatures ranging from 4 to 600 K (−269 to −327 °C). For high temperatures, radiation thermometers such as the optical pyrometer are used: these need not touch the material being monitored, and can measure temperatures up to 1,800 K (1,527 °C). The most commonly used scale is the Celsius scale. All temperatures are now fixed in relation to a series of experimentally determined fixed points on the International Practical Temperature Scale. These include, for example, the freezing-point of molten gold (1064.43 °C) and the boiling-point of liquid oxygen (−182.962 °C). The lowest temperature theoretically possible is −273.15 °C, a point known as *absolute zero. In scientific work, temperatures are normally expressed using

Natural **terraces** flank the River Seti, western Nepal.

the kelvin or absolute scale. The kelvin scale uses Celsius degrees but counts them from absolute zero, so that 0 °C = 273.15 K.

**Tenerife**　*Canary Islands.

**tensor** (in mathematics), an extension of the notion of a *vector. A vector associates any direction in space with a scalar which is the component of the vector in that direction. A tensor by analogy allows the association of any direction with a vector. The state of stress at a given point in a solid object is represented by a tensor. In four-dimensional space, particularly the *space-time continuum of the special theory of relativity, tensor analysis is of considerable importance.

**tephra**, a general term for all fragments of rock that are thrown out during volcanic eruptions: *volcanic bombs, *ash, and lapilli (these being fragments of sizes intermediate between bombs and ash). Piled up in layers round a volcanic vent, tephra forms the typical cone-shaped volcano. It is composed largely of material that is freshly solidified from *magma, but it can also include fragments of earlier lava that has solidified in the vent after previous eruptions, together with pieces of the rock that have broken off the walls of the conduit as the magma ascended to the surface. The term usually applies to air-fall material, rather than deposits from laval flow.

**terminal velocity**, the constant speed obtained by an object when moving under gravity with no reactant force acting on it. For instance, when an object falls through air, the air resistance on it increases as its speed increases. Eventually, the air resistance reaches the point where it balances the object's weight. The object then continues to travel downward with a constant terminal velocity. (See also *air resistance.)

**terrace** (natural), a fairly narrow shelf of nearly horizontal ground, usually bordered on one side by a sharp drop and on another by a definite rise. The great majority of terraces are formed by rivers. (Similar features cut by the sea or lakes are *strand lines or raised beaches; while shelves caused by hard layers of rock are called structural benches.) Some terraces, however, form from chemical deposits precipitated by water saturated with dissolved minerals: these are common in limestone areas and round hot springs. River terraces are created by the *rejuvenation of rivers. Channels are rapidly cut into floodplains or broad valley floors whose remnants are left above the new course. 'Cut' features are formed of bedrock, while 'fill' ones are made of *alluvium. Either type may occur in pairs at the same height on each side of the valley, or as offset forms, at different heights on either side, suggesting that the channel cut down intermittently. Many rivers show several sets of terraces above their present channels which were produced by changes in sea-level and climate during the Pleistocene Epoch. If deposits on the surfaces can be dated, they give valuable evidence about the history of the landscape. Sometimes the *meandering of a river results in changes in its course. Then the vertical cutting is exceeded by the horizontal movement, and the shape of the relatively wide and shallow terraces indicates the former course across the floodplain.

**terra rossa**, the red-coloured soil, rich in iron oxides, found throughout the Mediterranean region. These soils are relatively shallow and contain little organic matter. The origin of terra rossa soils is uncertain; it has been suggested that they are degraded soils from which humus has been lost because of the destruction of the natural forest vegetation by man and his grazing animals over the course of many centuries. Alternatively, since they share many of the characteristics of *rendzinas and often occur in limestone areas, they may be formed by the weathering of calcareous parent materials under seasonally moist conditions.

**Tertiary Period**, the earlier of the two geological periods of the *Cainozoic Era. Lasting from 66 million years to 1.6 million years ago, it is divided into five epochs. In order of age, these are the Palaeocene, Eocene, Oligocene, Miocene, and Pliocene. The Tertiary was a period in which there were great fluctuations of climate, from the tropical temperatures of Eocene times to the great ice ages of the *Pleistocene. The fauna is particularly notable for the great diversification of the mammals, which became the dominant vertebrates.

**tesla** (symbol T), the *SI unit of magnetic flux density or magnetic induction, so named in honour of the US physicist Nikola Tesla (1856–1943). *Magnetic flux, or total quantity of magnetic field in a given area, is measured in webers (Wb). A concentration of magnetic flux of 1 weber per square metre (at right angles to the flux) gives a magnetic flux density of 1 tesla.

**Tethys Sea**, a sea that once separated *Gondwanaland and *Laurasia. Tethys existed in the geological time before the *Tertiary Period—that is, more than 66 million years ago. It was wedge-shaped, with its western extremity in the area of the Mediterranean Sea.

**Thailand** (formerly Siam), a country in south-east Asia bounded by Myanmar (Burma), Laos, and Kampuchea, and, in the south, Malaysia. It extends more than half-way down the Malay Peninsula and its north–south length is over 1,600 km (1,000 miles). The north is hilly and covered with dense forest, including teak. In the centre is a great, low-lying plain threaded with rivers which drain into the Gulf of Thailand. This is densely cultivated, with paddy fields which yield fish as well as rice; while further south, on the peninsula, rubber is grown. The climate is hot and monsoonal, and wetter in the west than in the east. Lignite is mined in various places, and there are deposits of tin, tungsten, antimony, and fluorspar.

**thallium** (symbol Tl, at. no. 81, r.a.m. 204.37), a soft, white, lead-like metal in Group III of the *periodic table, named after the intense green spectral line (Greek *thallos*, green shoot) that identifies the element. It occurs naturally in crookesite, often found with sulphur and selenium ores. It reacts readily and its compounds are extremely poisonous, and are used as pesticides.

**Thames, River**, name of three rivers. (1) England's longest river, rising in the Cotswold Hills and flowing for 340 km (210 miles) eastward, across the south of the country, to the North Sea. It becomes tidal at Teddington, and its Greater London estuary provides passage for ocean-going ships. In 1982 a moveable barrier was built across the Thames at Woolwich, to protect London from flooding. The barrier comprises curved flood gates which are rotated 90° into position from beneath the water. (2) A Canadian river, 260 km (160 miles) long, rising in the uplands between lakes Huron and Erie and flowing south-west through southern Ontario into Lake Saint Clair. It is navigable in its lower reaches. (3) A river, 25 km (15 miles) long, the lower course of the Yantic and Shentucket Rivers of Connecticut, eastern USA, emptying into Long Island Sound.

**Thar Desert**, or Great Indian Desert, a vast, arid region of western India and south-east Pakistan. Wind-blown sands of the Quaternary Period provide a *dune-strewn, undulating surface which overlies a basement of very old gneiss and sedimentary rock of varying age. Mobile dunes are separated by open sandy plains; the more stable dunes rise up to 150 m (about 500 feet). Most of the drainage, except to the perennial Indus on the north-west and the Lunai on the southeast, is internal, with short-lived seasonal *wadis.

**thermal**, a rising current of warm air which is produced when air near the ground becomes unstable as a result of daytime heating. Thermals often reach 3,000 m (10,000 feet) and are associated with the development of cumulus and cumulonimbus cloud.

**thermal conductivity**    *conduction.

**thermal radiation**    *radiation.

**thermocline**, a layer of water in which there is a greater decrease in temperature as depth increases than is found in the layers above or below it. Such layers are found both in the ocean and in large lakes. In the oceans, there is a permanent thermocline between the relatively warm waters of the *wind-mixed surface layer above and the cold deep water below. The top of the thermocline usually occurs at a depth between 200 and 300 m (600 and 985 feet), although it is at relatively shallow depths near the Equator, where there is a marked decrease in temperature over a quite moderate vertical distance. In mid-latitudes the thermocline occurs at greater depths and the change in temperature is less marked. Near the poles it develops close to the surface of the water. Temporary thermoclines may occur, either on a seasonal or on a daily basis, as a result of the heating of the surface waters both of oceans and of lakes. These features are much shallower than the permanent thermocline.

**thermodynamics**, the branch of physics concerned with the nature of *heat and its association with other forms of energy. It has its basis in three laws. The first states that energy in a system cannot be created or destroyed, it can only be changed from one form to another. Thus, when work is done compressing a gas, its molecules move about faster and it gets hotter; when it expands, it does work on its surroundings and cools. The second law states that heat always flows from a body at a high temperature to one at a low temperature, and it is impossible for heat from a cool body to flow of its own accord into a hot body, making it hotter still. The third law states that the differences in *entropy between different states of a substance approach zero as *absolute zero is approached. The practical consequence is that it is impossible to cool a body to absolute zero: it is a limit that can only be approached. An additional law, known as the zeroth law, states that if two systems are each in thermal equilibrium with a third system then they are in thermal equilibrium with each other.

**thermosphere**, the outermost part of earth's atmosphere, extending from the top of the *mesosphere at a height of about 80 km (50 miles) to outer space. It is a region in which the temperature increases with height, reaching several thousand degrees.

**Thom, René** (1923– ), French mathematician best known for his proposal of *catastrophe theory. This is one of the few serious attempts to apply mathematics to the shapes and processes of living things. Most previous attempts have tried, naturally, to be quantitative in the traditon of applied mathematics. They are defeated by the sheer complexity of nature. Thom's theory has the srength of being both qualitative and rigorous.

**Thompson, Benjamin, Count von Rumford** (1753–1814), US-born British scientist, soldier, civil servant, and founder of the Royal Institution (1799), who is remembered chiefly for his observations (1798) on the relationship between work and heat. Noting that a brass gun barrel continuously gave out heat when drilled with a blunt borer, he concluded that the heat produced by the motion of the borer, was a form of motion and was not some invisible liquid form of matter, 'caloric', released from the metal. His ideas were later developed by James *Joule, and come to form the basis of the first law of *thermodynamics.

**Thomson, Joseph** (1858–95), British explorer (of Scottish extraction) of Africa, who added greatly to geological knowledge of the continent. In 1879–80 and 1882–3 he explored East Africa, particularly the lakes of the Great Rift Valley; in 1885 northern Nigeria; in 1888 the Atlas Mountains; and in 1891 the Zambezi River, when his always frail health at last failed him.

**Thomson, Sir Joseph John** and **Sir George Paget** (father and son), English physicists who made major advances in the study of the atom. Of the many achievements of Joseph (1856–1940), the most significant was his discovery of the *electron in 1897. Investigating the nature of cathode rays, he established that they are streams of electrons, and he successfully measured their charge-to-mass ratio. In 1927, his son (1892–1975) demonstrated that electrons possess wave-like properties. Joseph Thomson won the Nobel Prize for Physics in 1906, and George Thompson shared the same prize in 1937.

**Thomson, William, Lord Kelvin** (1824–1907), British mathematician and physicist born in Belfast who made major advances in the science of *thermodynamics—the study of heat and work—which he applied to his work on the age of the Earth. In 1848 he proposed an absolute temperature scale, now called the *kelvin scale, based on energy considerations rather than the properties of any particular substance. Three years later, he put forward principles which were to form the basis of the second law of thermodynamics, a law governing the quantity of useful work which can be done using heat as an energy source.

**Thornthwaite, Charles Warren** (1889–1963), US climatologist who classified *climatic types by the moisture they make available. In any location, precipitation and solar radiation together determine the amount of water available for plant growth and *runoff. Thornthwaite named this relationship the *water balance.

**Thousand Islands**, a cluster of over 1,500 small islands and rocks in the *Saint Lawrence River, stretching from Prince Edward Peninsula at the outfall of Lake Ontario for 128 km (80 miles) to Brockville, Ontario. On the west side are the Canadian islands, which include Wolfe Island—the largest, at 127 km² (49 sq. mi.)—and Howe, Simcoe, Amherst, and Grenadier islands. They form part of the Saint Lawrence Islands National Park. To the east are

The discoverer of the electron, J. J. **Thomson** (*left*), and his son G. P. Thomson (*right*).

Grindstone, Wells, Carleton, and other islands belonging to New York State, USA.

**thunder**, the sound which accompanies the violent expansion of air when it is rapidly heated along the path of a *lightning flash. The rumbling is caused by the time difference between the sounds originating from nearer and further parts of the flash. A thunderbolt occurs when the flash occurs so close to the place of observation that the sound seems simultaneous. There is no rumble, only a crack. Thunder is rarely heard more than 15 to 25 km (10 to 15 miles) from the lightning that causes it.

**thunderstorm**, a local storm accompanied by *lightning and thunder and normally precipitation in the form of heavy rain or hail. The precondition for such storms is usually the formation of irregular, cellular groups of *cumulonimbus cloud, a fully developed cell being upwards of 1.5–8 km (1–5 miles) in diameter and 7,500 m (25,000 feet) in vertical extent. Each cell may generate thunder and lightning, together with precipitation, for 15 to 20 minutes, persistent thunderstorms resulting from the development of successive cells. Intensive squalls may be produced, and *tornadoes are also associated with thunderstorms in many parts of the world.

**Tian Shan**, a mountain system stretching for 3,000 km (1,800 miles) across central Asia in Xinjiang, China, and Kirghizia. It is bounded to the north by the plains of Dzungaria and south Kazakhstan and overlooks the great Tarim Basin to the south-east, part of the Alai range forming its south-western extremity. The massive knots and ridges are of old crystalline and sedimentary rocks, younger sediments occupying the intermontane basins. They were largely uplifted in episodes from the *Palaeozoic Era onwards; and movements still occur along fault lines, with earthquakes and massive rockfalls. Relief is extreme: the highest peaks such as Pobedy at 7,439 m (24,406 feet) contrast with deep basins such as the Turfan Depression to the east, 154 m (505 feet) below sea-level. Glaciers fall from crest lines to valleys, the largest, Inylchek, extending for 60 km (37 miles) on the western slopes of the Khan–Tengri massif.

**Tibet** (Chinese, Xizang), a mountainous country on the northern frontier of India, an autonomous region of China. It lies on the highest and largest plateau on earth, in central Asia. The plateau of Tibet has an average height of some 4,000 m (13,000 feet) and extends over about 2.6 million km² (1 million sq. mi.). It is bounded by the Kunlun Shan in the north and the Himalayas in the south. Bleak and almost treeless, it contains many other ranges, innumerable lakes, and the sources of the Brahmaputra, Huang He (Yellow), Indus, Irrawaddy, Mekong, Salween, Yangtze, and other mighty rivers. The plateau climate is arid and extremely cold in winter, a short summer bringing warm days which melt the snow so that crops can be grown. Only in the east and south are there forest-clad valleys, with semi-tropical vegetation, providing egress from the plateau. Gold, silver, iron, copper, zinc, borax, salt, and sulphur are among the largely unexploited mineral deposits.

**tidal bore**, a steep-fronted wave which occurs periodically in certain rivers and estuaries where the tidal range is particularly large. They are caused by constriction of the advancing flood or flood-tide as it enters a long, narrow, relatively shallow inlet. As water driven by this tide piles up against the flow of the river current, a large, turbulent wall-like wave of water is formed. The wave is travelling faster than waves may normally travel into such shallow water, and so is analogous to a 'sonic boon', which occurs when a pressure disturbance is forced to travel faster than the speed of sound. This solitary wave moves upstream at a speed of up to 16 km (10 miles) an hour. It gradually diminishes in height as it loses energy and eventually dies away, but this may be after many kilometres. A most impressive bore is that which rolls with a roar into the Hooghly River from the Bay of Bengal, India; another enters the Petticodiac from the Bay of Fundy, Canada, at a height of over 20 m (70 feet), while yet another occurs on the Amazon, South America, and there are many more. The most famous in the UK is that of the River Severn. At the mouth it forms a wave about 3 m (10 feet) high. This wave travels upstream at great speed and can be seen, though much reduced in size, 80 km (50 miles) or so inland. Another in the UK, on the Trent, is known as an eagre.

A **tidal bore** on the lower reaches of the River Severn, UK. The bore occurs twice daily on 130 days of the year. The highest bores, however, occur only during the twenty-five days of the spring and autumn equinoctial tides.

**tidal energy**, the energy carried by the regular tidal movement of the sea. Tidal energy could in principle supply a significant amount of the world's energy needs, but economic factors limit its use to coastlines where the tidal range is particularly great. Of the many methods proposed for extracting tidal energy, only one has been widely used, whether for ancient *tide-mills or modern *power-stations. The rising water enters an enclosed basin through *sluices in a dam or barrage; the sluices are then closed, the sea-level outside falls and the captured water flows out, driving *water-wheels or *water turbines. The tidal cycle of about twelve and a half hours and the fortnightly cycle of maximum and minimum range (springs and neaps) pose a problem in maintaining a regular power supply, and have led to ideas for more complex systems—with several basins for instance, or using *pumped storage. The *Rance barrage and two smaller schemes in the former Soviet Union and China are the only existing operational tidal power installations.

**tidal stream**, horizontal movement of seawater in a given direction, particularly in or out of an estuary or other coastal inlet, caused by the rise and fall of the sea surface. As water moves into a narrow inlet with the flood-tide it becomes constricted, and this may create fast-moving waves which can cause considerable erosion. The return or *ebb-tide may also be relatively swift because it is pushed by out-flowing river water. The term tidal stream is also used for a river which is affected by tidal conditions.

**tidal wave**   *tsunamis.

**tide**, a regular rise and fall of the surface of the sea in response to the gravitational attraction of the Moon (also the Sun, but to a much lesser degree). This attraction causes the water of the oceans to bulge out slightly on that part of the Earth facing the moon and on that part directly opposite; the daily rotation of the earth through these bulges appears to us as a rise and fall in sea-level. The attraction is strongest when the Earth, Moon, and Sun are in line (at full or new Moon), a condition known as syzygy, giving *spring tides; and weakest when they are at right angles, (during the

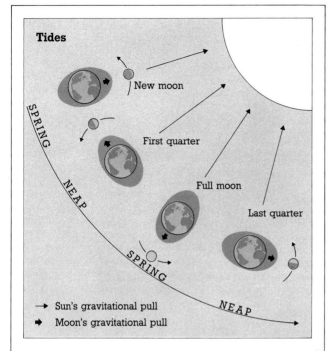

**Tides**

New moon

First quarter

Full moon

Last quarter

SPRING

NEAP

SPRING

NEAP

→ Sun's gravitational pull
➤ Moon's gravitational pull

The gravitational pull, or acceleration, of the Moon is the dominant tide-producing force. Water on the side of the Earth nearest the Moon experiences the greatest pull, and forms a bulge: that on the far side is subject to less acceleration and so 'trails behind' in a second bulge. When the Sun and Moon are in line, at new and full moon, the two gravitational forces combine to produce the high spring tides. When they are at right-angles, the lower neap tides occur.

Moon's first and last quarters), giving *neap tides. The corresponding horizontal movement of water is a current, a tidal stream, which is usually semidiurnal (two flood- and two ebb-tides in slightly more than a day) although diurnal tides occur in many places. Tidal ranges from *mean sea-level also vary around the world. In the Bay of Fundy, between New Brunswick and Nova Scotia, the difference between high and low water can be 14 m (46 feet) and more; in the English Channel it can be 10 m (33 feet), and in places as far apart as Alaska and north-west Australia differences of 6 m (20 feet) are common. The Baltic, the Mediterranean, and the Caribbean, on the other hand, are relatively tideless. If there is a world-wide average, it is probably of the order of 2–3 m (6–10 feet). Times and heights are forecast in published tide tables. Tidal streams are also affected by the deflecting influence of the earth's rotation, the lie of land, and the shape of a sea bottom—the last two in certain locations producing tide-races. The Pentland Firth, north of Scotland, experiences a tidal flow of 14 km (over 8 miles) an hour.

**Tierra del Fuego**, an archipelago at the southern tip of South America separated from the mainland by the Magellan Straits. An extension of the Andes, where they swing eastward in a hook, it points along the Scotia Ridge of the South Atlantic Ocean towards South Georgia. It comprises one large island, itself called Tierra del Fuego, and many smaller ones, the most southerly being Cape Horn. Lying in the path of the *roaring forties, it is always windy and very wet. The western coasts, broken by fiords, present sheer rock walls to the sea. Altogether the landscape is bleak, treeless, and with pasture suitable only for sheep.

**Tigris**, a great river of south-west Asia, 1,850 km (1,150 miles) long. Issuing from the mountains of eastern Turkey it runs generally south-eastward into Iraq, where it receives several large tributaries on its left bank from the Zagros Mountains of Iran. Its yellow waters, bearing huge quantities of *alluvium, create a ribbon of fertile land along with many seasonal lakes in a region which would otherwise be desert. On its right bank it is connected by natural canals across ancient Mesopotamia to its twin river, the Euphrates. This it eventually joins above Lake Hammar, to form the Shatt al-Arab Waterway, which flows through a shared delta to the Gulf. Navigable in its middle and lower reaches, the Tigris is liable to flood in spring, when its swift current is at a peak.

**till**, an unstratified deposit of silt and clay sometimes called boulder clay. It contains angular or rounded boulders which are often polished or striated as a result of glacial movement, for it was left behind after the glaciers and ice-sheets retreated. Often the boulders, which contain internal shear planes and fractures, are set in sands and clays. Till is a characteristic deposit of the *Pleistocene Epoch but is also found in more ancient sediments as *tillite. For fluvio-glacial deposits in general, the word *drift is often used.

**tillite**, a sedimentary rock formed by the consolidation of glacial drift deposits. The ancient equivalent of *till, it exhibits the same textures and structures that are associated with its younger counterpart.

**time**, the concept of the duration between events or of any process, such as the period it takes an object to travel a certain distance in space. Its measurement was originally derived from observations of the *rotation of the Earth and of its motion around the Sun. The average period between two successive times at which the Sun is exactly overhead at the Equator is a solar day of 24 hours or 86,400 seconds. Although the second was defined in terms of the solar day this was not entirely satisfactory because the Earth wobbles on its axis and so its period of rotation is not exactly regular. For this reason the second, the *SI unit of time, is now defined in terms of the frequency of a particular line in the spectrum of the caesium atom. The idea that an interval of time has a definite duration, the same for all observers, is done away with in *relativity theory; intervals have to be defined in terms of *space also. (See also *time dilation.)

**time dilation**, the principle that intervals of time are not absolute but are relative to the motion of the observers. Time, in a system which is moving, appears, to an observer who is standing still, to be passing more slowly than time in the observer's own system, which is not moving. For instance, if two identical clocks were synchronized and one placed in a spaceship travelling away from Earth, then when the spaceship returned the travelling clock would show, to an observer on Earth, that less time had elapsed than the stationary clock. This is a real effect and has been demonstrated experimentally in a number of ways: the lifetimes of fast *muons may be extended by increasing the speed of the particles. (See also *relativity theory.)

**time-scale**, a system used for measuring the passage of time. Three major systems are currently in use: rotational time, dynamic time, and atomic time. Rotational time is based on a fundamental unit of a day, the time taken for the Earth to complete one full revolution around the Sun. Current international scales of rotational time are based on the mean solar day, actually calculated from accurate astronomical observations of stars. Dynamic time is derived from mathematical descriptions of the motion of the Moon and the planets: it is independent of variations in the Earth's rotation. The first dynamic time-scale was Ephemeris Time, first proposed in 1896; in 1960, a modified version of it became the basis for the definition of the *SI second. Atomic time is based on extremely regular oscillations that occur within *atoms and form the basis of atomic clocks. In 1967 the SI second was redefined in terms of atomic time, and atomic clocks are now used as international time standards.

**time-scale, geological**   *geological time.

**time zone**, an area on the Earth's surface within which local solar time is sufficiently uniform to be regarded as the standard mean time throughout the area. For practical purposes time is determined by the *rotation of the Earth about its own axis. Because of this eastward rotation, the Sun appears four minutes later at each successive degree of longitude, so that places 15 degrees of longitude apart have times which differ from one another by one hour. When railways were first built in the UK this led to complications in timekeeping on east–west journeys, since clocks at, say, Exeter (3.5° W.) were 14 minutes behind those in London. About 1840 a system of Railway Time was introduced, by which all station clocks showed Greenwich time. This was effectively the first time zone. It was not until the 1880s that an internationally agreed set of 24 time zones was established to cover the world, each 15° (1 hour) wide. The system is applied with modifications, however, principally to allow regions which are integrated politically or economically to maintain the same time. Thus most of continental Europe keeps Central European Time, one hour ahead of Greenwich Mean Time; and North America and Russia, both with several time zones covering over 100° of longitude, apply boundaries which follow those of states or provinces. Summer time, at different dates in different zones, complicates the system but is not part of it.

**tin** (symbol Sn, at. no. 50, r.a.m. 118.69), a metal in Group IV of the *periodic table which occurs as three *allotropes. The ordinary 'white tin', $\beta$-Sn, is malleable and ductile, and when a bar of tin is bent, a distinctive 'tin cry' is heard as the crystal structure breaks. Below 13 °C (55 °F) 'grey tin', $\alpha$-Sn, is the stable form, but the change from white tin into grey tin takes place only at much lower temperatures unless some grey tin is already present. When the change does occur the tin crumbles into a powder, and this is called 'tin plague' or 'tin pest'. Above 161 °C (342 °F), it exists as the brittle $\gamma$-Sn. Tin is recovered from its ore, cassiterite, $SnO_2$, by *reduction with carbon in a furnace; it is due to the ease of this process that tin was known to ancient civilizations. In its compounds it shows valencies of 2 and 4. It resists attack by water, but is dissolved by strong acids, alkalis, and acid salts. At present the main producers of tin are Malaysia and Bolivia, although Cornwall in the UK used to be an important source. Its major use is in tin plating: tin cans are not made entirely of tin (too soft and expensive) but of steel coated with tin. Many important alloys contain tin, for example with lead to give solder, with copper to give bronze, and with niobium to give alloys that exhibit *superconductivity. Tin(II) chloride, $SnCl_2$, is its most important compound and is used as a reducing agent and as a mordant in dyeing.

A **tin** dredger working in southern Thailand. The Malay Peninsula is one of the world's major sources of cassiterite, the main ore of tin.

**titanium** (symbol Ti, at. no. 22, r.a.m. 47.90), a commonly occurring *transition metal that occurs naturally in rutile, $TiO_2$, and in ilmenite, $FeTiO_3$, as well as in much organic matter. It is present in meteorites and in the Sun, and the rock obtained by the Apollo 11 lunar mission contained up to 12 per cent of the metal. Alloys of titanium with aluminium, molybdenum, manganese, and iron are used for aircraft and missile construction, where lightweight strength is important.

**Titicaca, Lake**, South America's largest freshwater lake, with a length of 177 km (110 miles), on the boundary between Peru and Bolivia. Cradled in the Andes at an altitude of 3,810 m (12,500 feet), it is also the highest of the world's major lakes. Its great depth—270 m (900 feet)—keeps it at a moderate temperature, so that it can be used all year round for navigation and fishing (edible frogs abound). Old shorelines and terraces, which can be cultivated, indicate that it was once larger still. The lake has two basins, north and south, linked by a narrow strait. Fed with melt-water by short mountain streams, they are drained from the south by a substantial river which runs into Lake Poopó some 260 km (160 miles) away.

**titrations**, used in *analysis to measure the amount of a substance present in a solution. A *reagent is chosen which reacts with the substance under test; the reagent is made into a solution of known concentration, and the volume of this solution required to react with a known quantity of the test substance is measured. The commonest titrations are *acid–base titrations; the end-point, the point where the test substance is just used up, is then detected by an acid–base indicator. Other reactions widely used in titrations include oxidation and reduction, precipitation, and complex-formation.

**Togo**, a West African country lying between Ghana and Benin. It has a southern coastline on the Gulf of Guinea of only 56 km (35 miles) but extends inland for over 560 km (350 miles) to Burkina Faso. The tropical coast has sand-bars and lagoons, and inland there is a fertile clay plain. Northward the land rises to low mountains and a rolling sandstone plateau, where it is drier and cooler. There are reserves of calcium phosphate on the coast, and elsewhere bauxite and iron ore.

**toluene** (or methylbenzene, $C_6H_5CH_3$), an aromatic, flammable liquid hydrocarbon which consists of a methyl group bonded to a *benzene ring. It is obtained from petroleum and used as a solvent, often in preference to benzene which is more toxic. Nitrating toluene yields trinitrotoluene (TNT), which is an explosive.

**tombolo**, a narrow ridge of sand and shingle which links an island to the mainland. Tombolos are a special type of coastal spit or bar, formed by wave action (as a result of *refraction) piling material into the ridge. An example is Chesil Beach on the south coast of the UK, although most tombolos are smaller than this.

**Tonga** (the Friendly Islands), an island country bordering the Tonga Trench in the South Pacific Ocean. It comprises over a hundred and fifty islands, most of them too small for habitation and even the largest, Tongatapu, measuring a mere 40 km (25 miles) by 16 km (10 miles). Some are coral and some volcanic, with active craters. Oil has been discovered, the only other natural resource being a fertile soil for the cultivation of coconuts and bananas.

**Tongariro, Mount**, a dormant volcanic peak in central North Island, New Zealand. It is 1,968 m (6,458 feet) high and has hot springs on its slopes and a blue lake on its summit. It lies in the Tongariro National Park, in an area covered with ash, lava, and pumice-stone.

**Tonlé Sap**, a natural floodplain reservoir in central Cambodia and the largest expanse of fresh water in south-east Asia. It is fed by numerous irregular tributaries and, on its northern shore, by the perennial rivers Srêng and Sên. Dur-ing the dry season it is drained by the Tonlé Sap River, which flows for 130 km (80 miles) across the marshy Véal Pôc plain south-eastward to the Mekong River. During the monsoon season (June to November) the flow of this river is reversed by the swollen Mekong and the lake then increases in depth from 3 m to 9–14 m (10 feet to 30–45 feet) and in width from 35 km to 105 km (22 miles to 65 miles).

**topaz**, an aluminium silicate mineral much prized for its gem-quality, gold-coloured crystals. It is a very hard but fragile mineral found in a variety of colours (yellow, blue, red, green). It occurs in acid igneous rocks, in pegmatite and tin veins, and also in alluvial sands. The largest and finest crystals (up to 270 kg, or 600 pounds, in weight) come from Minas Gerais (Brazil); yellow gemstones are mined in Burma and Sri Lanka.

**topography**, the relief and surface shape of the ground, as in the sense of a topographic map, which shows relief by means of contours or shading. The term originally meant any detailed description of places, including towns, villages, stately houses, and antiquities, as well as landforms, so that a 'topography' dating from the 18th century would be very different from one compiled now.

**topology**, a branch of *geometry which studies the geometrical properties which remain invariant or unchanged under continuous transformations. It was developed when mathematicians accepted that Euclidean geometry was not the only way to describe spaces. Most of Euclid's concepts are not topological invariants. A straight line can be twisted; a circle can be squashed into an oval; an area can be

Filling the deepest part of a trough formed by a structural depression in the central Andean altiplano, Lake **Titicaca** is the highest of the world's navigable lakes.

stretched to twice its size. A ring or torus, on the other hand, can be stretched and twisted but will always possess one hole; a sheet will always have two surfaces and cannot be continuously transformed into a sphere which has only one surface, or into two sheets with four surfaces altogether. These are topologically invariant properties. This view of geometry allows much of mathematics to be simplified, in that the study of one topological space, for example the sphere, is in fact relevant to all spaces with no edges. Two spaces are said to be topologically equivalent if it is possible to change from one to the other and back again in a continuous way—that is, without cutting or tearing. Unusual objects of particular interest to topologists include the *Möbius strip, which has only one edge and one face, and the Klein bottle, which is formed by passing the neck of a bottle through the side to join a hole in the base, and has only one side. Attempts to construct it necessitate cutting a hole, so it is not equivalent to a ring. The study of topology includes the theory of *sets and has applications in the analysis of complicated electrical networks.

**topsoil**, the upper part of the soil, rich in organic matter and plant nutrients. Also called the A-*horizon of the soil profile, it is the most important part of the soil from the gardener's or farmer's viewpoint, because its quality determines how well plants will grow. *Loams are the best kind of topsoil for most purposes.

**tor**, a mass of exposed bedrock, standing abruptly above its surroundings. The block is an undisturbed, weathered piece of bedrock, not an erratic carried by a glacier. Tors are common on hard rocks with relatively widely spaced *joints—the granites of Devon and Cornwall, UK, for example, or the schists of central Otago, New Zealand—but they can occur on similarly massive sedimentary rocks, especially sandstones. The bedrock around them is usually more finely jointed than the tors themselves. Tors are clearly residual features: the material that surrounded them has been removed by mass movements, ice, or running water, or as an end-product of scarp retreat under semi-arid conditions. There are very different views about how this happens. Some geomorphologists think that the blocks are piles of core stones created by very deep weathering of the finely jointed rocks under tropical conditions: tors are then revealed by gradual removal of the weathered layer. Others, pointing to tors everywhere from the Antarctic to the trop-

Saddle **Tor**, on Dartmoor, south-west UK, shows the vertical and horizontal joints typical of exposed granite.

ics, claim that almost any weathering and erosion processes will attack poorly jointed rocks less effectively than more finely fractured ones and that tors are simply very small equivalents of *buttes or *inselbergs, with the massive jointing producing the distinctive form.

**tornado** (or twister), a violent storm with whirling winds, developed from a *thunderstorm as the air in a rapidly growing cumulonimbus cloud converges at its base and spirals upwards round a central core of very low pressure. Occasionally a twisted, funnel-shaped cloud is visible, projecting from the main cloud-base and sometimes extending to ground level. This is formed if the air is particularly moist and condensation occurs within the core. Often small in horizontal extent, ranging from 50 to 500 m (550 yards) in diameter, tornadoes move at between 20 and 55 km/h (12–35 m.p.h.) along a narrow track and can do considerable damage. Their destructive power is derived both from the high wind speeds, which are sometimes in excess of 370 km/h (230 m.p.h.), and from the steep pressure gradient within them. The noise is deafening. Most such storms have a life of only 10–15 minutes, although the most severe can persist for several hours. They may occur in most parts of the world, and are common both in West Africa, at the beginning and end of the rainy season, and in central USA. Over water a tornado can produce a *waterspout.

**Torrens, Lake**, a salt lake in South Australia lying to the north of Spencer Gulf in a *rift valley below sea-level. Fed by seasonal streams from the Flinders Range to the east, it is some 190 km (120 miles) long when full but is very shallow and shrinks in summer.

**Torricelli, Evangelista** (1608–47), Italian mathematician and physicist, a disciple of Galileo whom he succeeded as mathematician to the court of Tuscany. A law or theorem that bears his name deals with the velocity of liquids flowing

A **tornado** rips across prairie farmland in North Dakota, USA.

under the force of gravity from orifices. His most important invention was the mercury barometer in 1643, with which he demonstrated that the atmosphere exerts a pressure by showing that it could support a column of mercury in an inverted closed tube, and he was the first person to produce a sustained vacuum.

**touchstone**, black, fine-grained siliceous stone used for assaying gold and silver. The gold or silver is rubbed on the stone to produce streaks, which are compared with streaks made by metals of known purity. The comparison is made easier by treating the streaks with nitric acid, which dissolves impurities and leaves streaks of metal only. The method is not reliable for silver, but is still used today for assaying gold.

**tourmaline**, any of several silicate minerals containing sodium, calcium, iron, magnesium, and other metals. These minerals are very hard and dense, and are normally found in prismatic crystals. Found in many igneous and metamorphic rocks, they are used as semiprecious stones.

**town gas**, a flammable, manufactured gas for domestic and commercial use, made originally from coal and comprising a mixture of methane, hydrogen, and carbon. It dates from the end of the 18th century when gasworks were a common sight all over Western Europe for over 150 years, providing gas for heating and lighting. Town gas is made by the thermal decomposition of coal in a closed retort; the process also produces large quantities of residual carbon called gas coke, which can also be used as a fuel. In the 1960s this process began to be displaced by the production of gas from oil-based feedstocks, which, in turn, has been displaced in some countries by natural gas (see *gas, natural).

**trade wind**, or tropical easterly, a steady, regular wind which blows from latitudes 30° to 35° N. and S. towards the Equator. Trade winds are deflected westward by the Earth's rotation. More constant over the oceans than over the continental land masses, they are caused by the differences in atmospheric pressure between the *subtropical highs and the equatorial zone, over which sun-heated air rises and creates a low-pressure area for the winds to fill. It was the trade wind of the North Atlantic which assisted Columbus on his first voyage to the Caribbean in 1492.

**transcendental numbers**, the numbers which are not solutions of any *polynomial equation with integer coeffi-

Examples of the variety of **topaz** and **tourmalines** used as semiprecious stones. The several large, pale-coloured stones on the left are topaz, while the others are tourmalines.

cients; they are thus not algebraic and not rational because any rational number $p/q$ is a root of the linear equation $qx = p$. Since $\sqrt{2}$ is a solution of the equation $x^2 - 2 = 0$, the transcendentals are not equivalent to the *irrational numbers but form a subset of them. Georg *Cantor's countability proof of the existence of transcendentals, although not actually giving any, shocked mathematicians by revealing that far from being confined to a few numbers such as e and π, almost all real numbers are transcendental. As yet, however, there is no general criterion for constructing transcendental numbers.

**transition metals**, or d-block elements, the elements which occur in the block in the middle of the *periodic table, from scandium to zinc, from yttrium to cadmium, and from lanthanum to mercury. Their atomic structures all have partially filled d-shells, which give rise to their typical properties of variable *valency, colour, *magnetism and *complex ion formation. They are unique in using the penultimate electron shell, as well as the outermost shell, in bonding. All are hard and strong, have high melting- and boiling-points, and are good conductors of heat and electricity. The uses of the transition metals vary widely; iron is used for construction, copper for wiring and coinage, gold and silver for jewellery, and nickel and platinum as catalysts. Many of the metals are alloyed to improve their properties: for example, iron is mixed with carbon and many metals to give steels, and copper and zinc are mixed to form brass.

**Transkei**, a territory in south-east Cape Province, South Africa, consisting of three separate areas bounded by Natal on the north-east and Cape Province on the west. The land falls from the Drakensberg Mountains to the Indian Ocean and is drained by several rivers. Much of it is hilly, and the poor soil is used mainly for pasture.

**transpiration, atmospheric**, the process by which moisture escapes from vegetation into the atmosphere through the foliage after water has been taken up by a plant's roots from the soil, a process which helps to reduce the temperature of the plant. It is controlled by environmental factors such as moisture availability, atmospheric humidity, *insolation and wind speed. Transpiration rates are greatest during daylight hours. It forms part of the *hydrological cycle.

**transportation** (in geomorphology), the movement of debris across the Earth's surface by wind, running water, ice, *mass movements on slopes, waves, and currents. It is the intermediate stage between *erosion and *deposition and most material moves in fits and starts, being picked up, carried some distance, dropped for a time, and then picked up again. Moving ice has enormous transporting powers. It acts as a conveyor-belt, carrying material of all sizes on its surface as well as dragging debris along its bed. Mass movements, too, transport vast amounts of material long distances; especially if they start at the head of long slopes and are lubricated by water, or are riding on cushions of air. Water and wind have more limited powers, which depend strictly on the speed and turbulence of flow and the size, mass and shape of particles. This makes them very selective agents of transportation, and they tend to sort material into different sizes, both as they erode and as they deposit. Wind is particularly selective, only moving material of gravel size and smaller. Water, despite its limitations, operates so continuously and over so much of the Earth's surface that the overall effects outweigh those of all the other agents of transportation.

**transuranic elements**, the elements which come after uranium in the *periodic table—that is, with atomic numbers greater than 92. Sixteen have been identified so far, but research to produce more is still in progress. They are all radioactive and, as they decay to other elements in times much less than the lifetime of the universe, none occurs naturally. They are made by bombarding a heavy nucleus with a light nucleus; at first neutrons and helium nuclei were used, but recently heavier nuclei such as iron have been employed. Elements such as neptunium and plutonium have become important in producing nuclear energy, and have been manufactured in quite large quantities, but the later elements are extremely unstable; in some cases only small numbers of atoms have been produced, too small for properties like hardness or colour to have any meaning. Some theories suggest that nuclei with larger atomic numbers (such as 126) may be relatively stable, but experiments to make them have so far failed.

**Transvaal**, the northernmost province of South Africa, lying land-locked, south of the Limpopo River and north of the Vaal River. It is mainly on an ancient platform whose general height is 900 m (3,000 feet). Only the eastern boundary with Mozambique is off the plateau, which in the south rises to some 1,900 m (6,200 feet) on the Witwatersrand. It is high veld country—steppe, with low bush—and very warm with moderate rain. Its main wealth is in its minerals: diamonds, gold, uranium, copper, and coal.

**transverse waves**, waves in which displacement of the particles of the medium carrying the wave is at right angles to the direction of propagation of the wave. The simplest example is a water wave. *Electromagnetic radiation is transverse because the electric and magnetic fields that make up the wave are both perpendicular to direction of propagation.

**Transylvania** (Romanian, 'place beyond the forest'), a triangular region of tableland in central and north-west Romania, enclosed by the arc of the Carpathian Mountains on the north and east, the Bihor Mountains on the west and the Transylvanian Alps on the south. In the north the 'plains' at 400–600 m (1,300–2,000 feet) are dissected by wide swampy valleys; in the south, on the high tableland, more varied relief prevails.

**trapezium**, a particular form of quadrilateral (four-sided polygon) in which at least one pair of opposite sides is parallel. A parallelogram, having two pairs of parallel sides, is a special kind of trapezium. In general none of the lengths of the trapezium's sides need be the same. The area of a trapezium is $\frac{1}{2}(a + b)h$, where $a$ and $b$ are the lengths of the parallel sides and $h$ is the perpendicular distance between them. In the USA the figure is called a trapezoid, a trapezium being any quadrilateral having no sides parallel to one another.

**travelling waves**, waves in which the direction they can travel is unbounded—as is the case with sound waves or electromagnetic radiation in large volume, or waves on the sea where energy is transferred from one place to another by the vibrations. In travelling waves the *nodes and antinodes move along with the velocity of the wave. This is in contrast

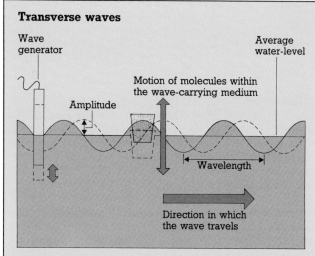

**Transverse waves**

Wave generator

Average water-level

Motion of molecules within the wave-carrying medium

Amplitude

Wavelength

Direction in which the wave travels

A cork bobbing on the surface of the water in a ripple-tank demonstrates the nature of transverse waves. As the wave travels from left to right, the cork moves vertically along with the molecules of water carrying the wave. The picture shows the situation at a particular instant (full lines) and a short time later (broken lines), illustrating the progress of the crests and troughs of the wave from left to right.

to *standing waves in which the positions of the nodes and antinodes remain fixed.

**travertine**, a light-coloured deposit rich in calcium carbonate and formed by precipitation from spring or river water. A similar deposit, spongy and porous, is known as *tufa. Travertine is denser and banded. It is a common deposit of the *Quaternary Period. Used as a building material, it is mined particularly in Italy (Tuscany and Tivoli).

**trellis drainage**, one of the *drainage patterns formed by river channels on the Earth's surface. It occurs in alternating bands of hard and soft rock, the streams wearing away the soft rock in a parallel series, with the hard rock forming escarpments on either side; or it may be caused by a regular pattern of faults or joints. They run into other channels roughly at right angles, thus forming a garden trellis pattern.

**trench, submarine**, a long, narrow, and very deep trough in the ocean floor. Steep-sided and flat-floored, trenches vary in width from a few hundred metres to several kilometres. They occur in all three major oceans (the Puerto Rican, South Sandwich, and Java trenches being among the largest), but most commonly in the Pacific, where two crustal *plates meet and one has been subducted. The Marianas Trench is the deepest, and the Tonga–Kermadec system in the Southern Hemisphere by far the longest. Generally they occur off coasts bordered closely by fold mountains or parallel to chains and areas of volcanic islands.

**Trent**, a river of central England with headwaters in the Peak District, flowing south-east then north-west for 270 km (170 miles) to enter the Humber estuary some 64 km (40 miles) from the North Sea. Its valley soon enters a floodplain; below Newark the river becomes tidal, and at the spring tides a river bore called the 'eagre' produces a wave up to 1.2 m (4 feet) high.

**triangle**, a closed figure in the plane with three straight sides which only meet at the corners (the vertices). A triangle is the simplest closed polygonal figure and forms a rigid configuration. If the lengths of the three sides are given, only one possible triangle can be formed; and three line segments arbitrarily chosen will form a triangle only if the sum of the lengths of any two always exceeds the third. In Euclidean geometry, the angle sum of any triangle is always 180°. Triangles are classified by means of the relationships, if any, among their sides and angles. An equilateral triangle has all three sides (and angles) the same. An isosceles triangle has two sides the same, and in a scalene one all the sides are different lengths. Two triangles are said to be congruent if they can be superimposed exactly on top of one another and are said to be similar if corresponding angles are the same. A right-angled triangle is one containing an angle of 90°. The area of any triangle is always 0.5 × base × height. It is possible to discuss spherical triangles where the sides are parts of great circles, that is circles on the surface of a sphere which have the same radius as the sphere. In this geometry, the angle sum of any triangle is not constant but always greater than 180° and the only similar triangles are those which are also congruent.

**Triassic Period** (or Trias), the earliest of the three geological periods that make up the *Mesozoic Era. It extends

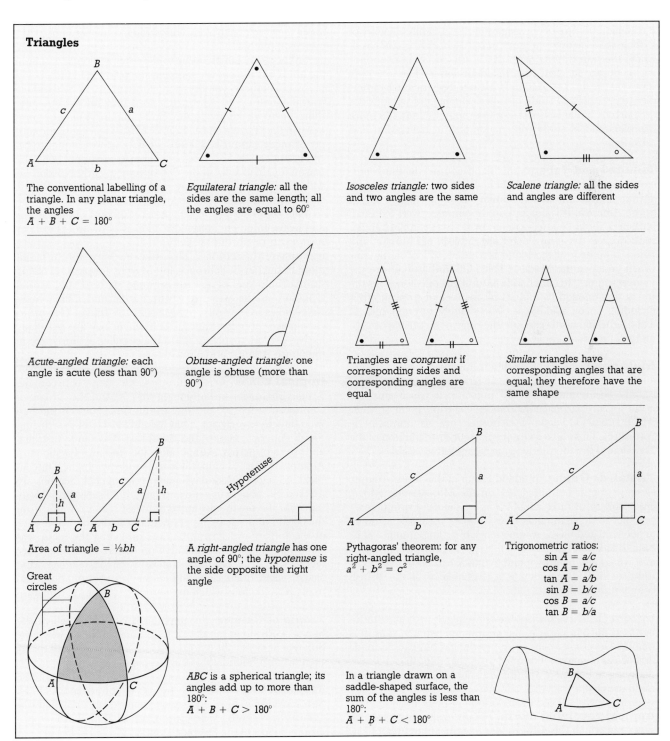

**Triangles**

The conventional labelling of a triangle. In any planar triangle, the angles $A + B + C = 180°$

*Equilateral triangle:* all the sides are the same length; all the angles are equal to 60°

*Isosceles triangle:* two sides and two angles are the same

*Scalene triangle:* all the sides and angles are different

*Acute-angled triangle:* each angle is acute (less than 90°)

*Obtuse-angled triangle:* one angle is obtuse (more than 90°)

Triangles are *congruent* if corresponding sides and corresponding angles are equal

*Similar* triangles have corresponding angles that are equal; they therefore have the same shape

Area of triangle = ½*bh*

A *right-angled triangle* has one angle of 90°; the *hypotenuse* is the side opposite the right angle

Pythagoras' theorem: for any right-angled triangle, $a^2 + b^2 = c^2$

Trigonometric ratios:
$\sin A = a/c$
$\cos A = b/c$
$\tan A = a/b$
$\sin B = b/c$
$\cos B = a/c$
$\tan B = b/a$

Great circles

*ABC* is a spherical triangle; its angles add up to more than 180°:
$A + B + C > 180°$

In a triangle drawn on a saddle-shaped surface, the sum of the angles is less than 180°:
$A + B + C < 180°$

in time from 245 to 208 million years ago. The name arises from the fact that the rocks of this period in Europe can be divided into three groups, according to age. Triassic land deposits contain few fossils (and those only of reptiles), and the rarer marine deposits of Europe yield only occasional clams and ammonites. *Evaporites of Triassic age are economically important in the UK and the USA.

**trigonometry**, the use of the trigonometric functions *sine, *cosine, and *tangent to determine the lengths of lines and size of angles, both in mathematical and real-world situations. There are a number of trigonometric identities or relations connecting the trigonometric functions, including $\sin^2 A + \cos^2 A = 1$, and $\sin (A + B) = \sin A \cos B + \cos A \sin B$. The cosine rule relates the length of the three sides of a triangle and one of the angles and is a generalization of Pythagoras's theorem; it states that $c^2 = a^2 + b^2 - 2bc \cos A$, where the convention used is that a side and its corresponding angle are labelled with the same letter. The sine rule states that $a/\sin A = b/\sin B = c/\sin C$. Spherical trigonometry, the associated study of spherical triangles whose sides are parts of *great circles rather than straight lines, is a more complex field of study with major uses in navigation and astronomy.

**Trinidad and Tobago**, an island country in the south-east corner of the Caribbean Sea, the larger island, Trinidad, lying only 11 km (7 miles) off the northern coast of South America. It is hot and, in the summer, wet. Trinidad measures about 80 km (50 miles) by 60 km (37 miles). In the south-west is the great Pitch Lake, a basin of bitumen; and across the north of the island is a range of low mountains which contains the Maracas Falls. Oil and asphalt are the main resources, together with natural gas off shore; but the soil is rich enough to support all manner of tropical crops including cocoa and sugar. The densely forested hills of Tobago, to the north-east, are the ridge of an otherwise submerged mountain range.

**triple point**, the set of conditions in which a gas, a liquid, and a solid can all exist together in equilibrium. There is only one temperature and pressure at which this can occur for any particular substance. The triple point of water ($H_2O$) is 0.01 °C (32.02 °F) at 101,325 pascals (atmospheric *pressure). This value forms the basis of the definition of the *kelvin and the thermodynamic *temperature scale.

**Tristan da Cunha**, an island group in the South Atlantic Ocean lying at latitude 37° S. on the Mid-Atlantic Ridge. They consist of three small volcanic islands: Tristan, Inaccessible, and Nightingale. Tristan rises to about 2,100 m (6,900 feet) and has a circumference of 34 km (21 miles) at its base. Bleak and barren though it is in appearance, potatoes and wheat can be grown and livestock can be reared on its tussocky turf. The group is a dependency of the British colony of Saint Helena.

**tritium** (T or $^3$H), the isotope of hydrogen with mass number 3; its nucleus consists of a proton and two neutrons. It is found in less than 1 part in $10^{17}$ of the gas but can be made in nuclear reactors. Tritium has a *half-life of 12.4 years, decaying to helium-3 with the emission of beta-particles. Its main use is as a tracer in radioactive labelling.

**tropical revolving storm**, usually called a cyclone, a system in which the wind rotates inwards to an area of low atmospheric pressure. These storms develop in all ocean regions within the *intertropical convergence zone, except in the South Atlantic, and consist of small but intense *troughs round which the wind circulates anticlockwise in the northern hemisphere and clockwise in the southern. They do not occur on the Equator itself and only rarely within eight degrees of it. Local *convergence promotes large-scale cumulus or cumulonimbus cloud with a distinctive centre of low pressure round which circulation increases in intensity and extent over a period of four or five days. The ensuing storm may cover an area of anything from 80 to 800 km (50 to 500 miles) wide and persist for two or three days. Wind at force 10 or more on the *Beaufort scale causes heavy seas; and there is torrential rain which, with driven spray, severely limits visibility. Energy is provided by the latent heat released from condensing water vapour, gathered from the warm sea, and by a rise in temperature at the eye of the storm which is due to the compression of descending air. Thus the energy source is the warm sea-surface and in practice these voltices only form above a sea-surface warmer than 27–29 °C. Such storms may advance at anything up to 25 knots (40 km/h, 25 m.p.h.); but they soon decay if they cross a coast and move inland (because the supply of water vapour is reduced) or if they move out of tropical latitudes. In the northern hemisphere generally the season for them is from the end of June to early November, with a maximum frequency in August and September. A typical speed for storms is 10 knots (16 km/h, 10 m.p.h.), and so islands in their path will have several hours of high winds and heavy rain. The initial direction is westward; they later turn north or north-east before dying out. In the southern hemisphere the season is December to May, with a maximum frequency in February and March. Tropical revolving storms have special names in some parts of the world: typhoons in the western North Pacific and China Seas; willy-willies in Australia; cyclones in the Indian Ocean. In each place there is a time of year when they are especially likely. A severe revolving storm is also called a *hurricane in the North Atlantic and elsewhere.

**tropical zones**, or the Tropics, the areas between the Tropic of Cancer at latitude 23° 27′ N. and the Tropic of Capricorn at 23° 27′ S. Only within these zones is the Sun ever directly overhead. They contain parts of North and South America, South and Southeast Asia, and Australia, and stretch across Africa and the Indian, Pacific and Atlantic oceans. Temperatures are always high. Only in highland regions does daytime air remain cool. Seasons are marked by changes in wind and rainfall. *Trade winds blowing from the north-east and south-east take up water from the oceans and release it over eastern coasts, the *monsoons of the Indian and Pacific Oceans providing the main seasonal variations. The vegetation on eastern coasts therefore tends to be lush. Large land masses remain relatively dry, except where increasing altitude causes precipitation, and many have regions which are completely arid.

**Tropic of Cancer**, the parallel of latitude at which the Sun is overhead at midday at the summer solstice, when the Sun reaches its furthest north. At latitude 23° 27′ N., it marks the northern boundary of the *tropical zones.

**Tropic of Capricorn**, the parallel of latitude at which the Sun is overhead at midday at the winter solstice, when it is at its furthest south. At latitude 23° 27′ S., it marks the southern boundary of the *tropical zones.

**tropopause**, the boundary in the Earth's atmosphere between the *troposphere and the *stratosphere. It is the point at which weather ceases and temperature ceases to fall with height. In winter it lies at an altitude of about 8 km (5 miles) above the poles and about 15 km (9 miles) above the Equator, where the air is less dense; it is higher in summer. The tropopause acts as an efficient cold-trap for water and stops it escaping into the upper atmosphere, from where it would be lost to the planet. The region is associated with cirrus cloud and lies just above the peaks of the Earth's highest mountains.

**troposphere**, the lowest layer of the Earth's atmosphere. The cold atmospheric gases that lie on top of the relatively warm surface of the planet are heated by *convection, so that the hot regions of the lower atmosphere rise up bodily through a region of higher density and the transfer their thermal energy to the cooler overlying regions. The troposphere contains about 70 per cent of the total mass of the Earth's atmosphere and much of it is dominated by stratus, cumulus, and altocumulus clouds. All weather occurs within it, so the air is in continual motion, with horizontal airflows and vertical currents. It varies in height according to season, being thinner in winter when the air is densest. In summer it extends for about 8 km (5 miles) above the poles and for about 18 km (11 miles) above the Equator, over which the air is most rarefied. Temperature decreases with altitude by about 6.5 °C per km (11.8 °F per mile), until the *tropopause is reached.

**trough** (in meteorology), an intense but short-lived area of low atmospheric pressure. On a weather map troughs are depicted by the V-shaped pattern of *isobars extending from a *depression.

**truncated spur**, a rib of land running out between a small valley towards a plain or major valley. These spurs end in abrupt, often triangular, flat slopes at the edge of the upland, rather than tapering off gradually to the level of the lowland. Their lower portions have been simply chopped off, by ice or by uplift. Glaciers enlarge existing valleys. They move slowly and cannot curve around the ends of *spurs very easily. Instead, they grind and crush their way across them, leaving a sheer, sheared valley wall with *hanging valleys. Sudden faulting and uplift of a valley side dislocates its spurs and lifts them above the valley floor.

**truth tables** (in mathematics), a means of illustrating the truth or falsity of a compound logical proposition, such as 'A and B or C and not D', in terms of the truth or falsity of each of a number of simpler propositions, such as 'A and B', 'A or C', or 'B or C'. Every possible combination of true and false classification for A, B, C, and D are tabulated and the desired combination(s) selected. Tautologies such as 'A or not A' provide a situation where every entry satisfies the proposition (is true), whereas 'A and not A' is an impossibility and every entry in the table will be false. There is a close analogy between truth tables and *Venn diagrams, which are used to illustrate relationships geometrically in terms of membership of sets.

**tsunami**, a long, high, sea wave caused by underwater earthquakes or other disturbances such as faulting or landsliding. Landslides on the sea floor are a major cause of tsunamis, and they frequently involve hundreds of cubic kilometres of sediment and rock. Because the surface of the sea floor has dropped above the slide as a result of the movement, water rushes in from the surrounding sea to restore the water level. The sea-level at the coast drops, and the flow of water towards the area of the slide is so strong that the surface of the sea bulges above the slide. Tsunami waves spread out from the area of the slide while the slide is still moving out across the foot of the continental slope. Tsunamis occur frequently on the margins of the Pacific Ocean, at the boundaries of crustal *plates. An earthquake in the Aleutian Islands in 1946, for example, caused a tsunami with waves at

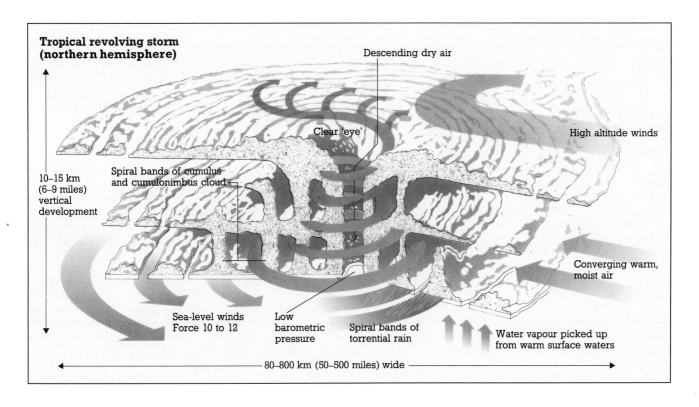

**Tropical revolving storm (northern hemisphere)**

Descending dry air

Clear 'eye'

High altitude winds

10–15 km (6–9 miles) vertical development

Spiral bands of cumulus and cumulonimbus cloud

Sea-level winds Force 10 to 12

Low barometric pressure

Spiral bands of torrential rain

Converging warm, moist air

Water vapour picked up from warm surface waters

80–800 km (50–500 miles) wide

least 30 m (100 feet) high. These waves, travelling at about 800 km (500 miles) an hour, hit the Hawaiian Islands, where they were driven ashore as a rapidly moving wall of water.

**tufa** (or calc tufa), a calcareous deposit. It is normally white, although it can be stained many colours. It occurs as spongy, porous masses deposited from springs and river waters rich in calcium carbonate. A common deposit of limestone regions, it fills cracks, fissures, and joints in rock as well as cementing gravels. Like *travertine, it is a common *Quaternary cave deposit throughout the world.

**Tugela**, a major river of Natal, South Africa, some 480 km (300 miles) long. Rising on Mont aux Sources, one of the highest points in the Drakensberg Mountains, it plunges through a wooded and dramatic gorge, dropping 856 m (2,810 feet) over a series of falls. At the foot of the escarpment it heads generally east, cutting a deep channel, until it picks up its chief tributary, the Buffalo. Then it turns south-east into its main valley and crosses the narrow coastal plain to the Indian Ocean.

**tundra soil**, a type of soil which occurs in areas such as Alaska, Canada, and Siberia, where winters are long and bitterly cold and summers are too short for trees and grasses to grow. The ground is often permanently frozen at relatively shallow depths, so soils are waterlogged for much of the year and may be subject to *gleying. The breakdown of organic material is therefore slow, and partly decomposed vegetation accumulates at the soil surface. The freezing of the soil in winter disrupts the *profile and prevents clearly defined horizons from forming. Tundra soils tend to be shallow because weathering is slow in cold regions.

Port of Seward, Alaska, damaged by **tsunamis** following an earthquake. The waves reach greater and greater height as they approach the shoreline, due to the shallowing of the sea floor.

**tungsten** (symbol W, at. no. 74, r.a.m. 183.85), a lustrous silvery white *transition metal, taking its name from the Swedish for 'heavy stone'. Also known as wolfram, it occurs naturally as wolframite, (Fe,Mn) $WO_4$, together with traces of stolzite, $PbWO_4$, and scheelite, $CaWO_4$. Important deposits occur in the USA, Russia, and China; commercially the metal is obtained by reducing tungsten oxide, $WO_3$, with hydrogen or carbon. It has the highest melting-point, 3,410 °C (6,170 °F), the lowest vapour pressure, and above 1,000 °C (1,832 °F) the highest tensile strength of any metal. Moreover, it is very resistant to corrosion, and is only slightly attacked by acids. Its main uses are in steel alloys, as filaments in light bulbs, in television and X-ray tubes, and in tungsten carbide tips for drilling and cutting tools.

**Tunisia**, a country on the North African coast, sandwiched between Algeria and Libya, which has its southern part in the Sahara. The coastal climate is Mediterranean. Grapes, olives, oranges, and several varieties of cereals all flourish on a fertile plain. There is natural gas off-shore. In the north-west of the country are hills, mostly covered in scrub though containing forests of cork-oak. Southward it becomes hotter and drier. Salt marshes cover the central belt, where there are also large phosphate deposits. The south is sandy but contains oases which yield dates.

**tunnelling** (in atomic physics), the passage of minute particles through seemingly impassable force barriers. It is also known as potential barrier penetration, and happens frequently at the subatomic level when a particle meets a barrier. Tunnelling is explained by *quantum mechanics. For example, consider an electron meeting an energy barrier—say the electron is held in position by an electric field. The electron has the characteristics of a wave, and the wave is spread out. At the point at which the particle aspect of the electron hits the barrier, the wave aspect—which is spread out—may spread into the barrier and, if the barrier is thin enough, out the other side. Since this wave is an indication

of the probability of finding the particle at a certain place (see *wavefunction), the emergence of the wave on the other side of the barrier shows that there is a probability that the particle will appear on the other side of the barrier—that is, that it will have passed through the barrier. Tunnelling has been observed experimentally, and explains a number of phenomena, including some properties of semiconductors and the escape of alpha particles from unstable nuclei.

**turbidite**, a sedimentary deposit produced when a current of water carrying a slurry of sediment flows down a slope, such as a *continental slope. These currents, known as density currents or *turbidity currents, can carry much sediment and can erode sea-floor deposits as they travel. The resulting turbidites show characteristic structures such as graded *bedding (in which the larger grains are concentrated at the base of a bed and the finer at the top). The type of sandstone known as *greywacke is typical of turbidites.

**turbidity current**, a submarine flow of sediment and sea-water which occurs when the ocean floor has been disturbed by an earthquake or when fine-grained material balanced on a *continental slope is dislodged by a storm or tsunami. This sediment is carried down and out into deeper areas at speeds of up to 80 km/h (50 m.p.h.). Over many years the force of slumps can carve *submarine canyons and greatly alter the shape of an ocean floor. As the current fans out it slows down, depositing the silt and mud as *turbidites, which have contributed to the formation of the *abyssal plains of the deep sea-bed. The Grand Bank, Newfoundland, earthquake of 1929 triggered a massive turbidity current which swept out into the abyssal plain, wrecking deep-sea telegraph cables and causing much erosion before spreading millions of tonnes of sediment, blanket-like, over the Atlantic floor. The area covered, to a depth of about 1 m (3 feet), is

**Turbidite** in red sandstone at Great Cumbrae, Firth of Clyde, Scotland, UK. Note the bedding, where part of the rock has been eroded and filled in with coarse sediment.

as large as Iceland. The sedimentary deposit laid down by a turbidity current is called a *turbidite.

**turbulence**, fluid flow (gas or liquid) which undergoes irregular fluctuations or mixing. In a turbulent flow the motion continually changes in both magnitude and direction; almost all mixing of fluids is therefore turbulent. The rate of many fast chemical reactions in solution is determined by the degree of turbulence in the mixing of the reagents, and in the combustion chambers of engines there is always turbulent mixing of the fuel with air. Streamlining is important in reducing the turbulence of the flow around an object, especially in the design of aircraft.

**Turkey**, a country of Asia and Europe, in two parts separated by the Bosporus, the Sea of Marmara, and the channel of the Dardanelles. The smaller, European part is bounded by Bulgaria and Greece. The much larger Asian part comprises the whole of Asia Minor and is known as Anatolia. It has the Black Sea on the north, Georgia, Armenia, and Iran on the east, Iraq and Syria on the south, and coasts on the Mediterranean and Aegean Seas. Here the coastal plains are fertile, as are the valleys leading to them; but the plateau above is less so. Very warm in summer and cold in winter, rugged and mountainous in the east, it is a place of forests and lakes, arid deserts, and poor grazing for goats and sheep. Its largest river, the Kizil Irmak, is saline for nearly half its course to the Black Sea. In the east rise the Tigris and Euphrates Rivers. Its mineral wealth is considerable. Chromite and iron ore are available in large quantities, and many deposits wait to be explored. The plateau is subject to devastating earthquakes, however, lying as it does at a junction of crustal *plates.

**Turkistan**, a vast and generally arid tract of central Asia, extending eastward from the Caspian Sea to the Gobi Desert and southward from Siberia to Iran, Afghanistan, and Tibet. Russian (or Western) Turkistan includes Turkmenistan, Uzbekistan, Tajikistan, Kirghizia, and Kazakhstan; Chinese (or Eastern) Turkistan forms part of Xinjiang. Between the two are the dry and lofty Pamir Mountains. The region corresponds to a belt of high winter pressure and minimal precipitation.

**Turkmenistan**, a country lying east of the Caspian Sea and north of Iran. It is an arid region containing the greater part of the Kara Kum desert with its deposits of coal and sulphur, silver, copper, and lead. Low-lying and hot, the oases produce cotton and mulberry trees (for silkworms), while livestock roam the semi-desert areas in search of sparse grass. Oil and natural gas are found in the west, on the Caspian coastal plain.

**turquoise**, a copper aluminium phosphate mineral that is found as light green-blue masses in nodules or veins. It is hard and opaque, shines with a waxy lustre, and is formed by alteration of aluminium-rich rock. Valued as a semi-precious stone, it is also used as an ornamental material. The best sources of turquoise are in Nishapur in Iran, Sinai in Egypt, and New Mexico in the USA.

**Tuvalu** (formerly Ellice Islands), a country comprising a scattered archipelago of small islands between Kiribati and Fiji in the *South Seas. Funafuti is the chief island in the group, which numbers nine, all of them coral atolls and not

An arid landscape near north Afghanistan, part of the vast region known as **Turkistan**, here traversed by horsemen of the nomadic Kirghiz tribe.

exceeding a height of approximately 6 m (20 feet) above sea level. The islands experience high temperatures and heavy rainfall and the vegetation consists mainly of coconut palms.

**Twenhofel, William Henry** (1875-1957), US geologist who made studies of *Palaeozoic sediments in North and South America. He is renowned for his work on the processes of sedimentation which he described in his book, *Treatise on Sedimentation* (1926, 1932).

**twister**   *tornado.

**typhoon**, an intense *tropical revolving storm which occurs in the western Pacific Ocean and the China Seas, chiefly during the period from July to October. It is known as a *hurricane in the Caribbean, on the noth-eastern coast of Australia, and in the Atlantic regions. In the Bay of Bengal a typhoon is often termed a *cyclone. Its speed may reach up to 60 m/s (nearly 200 feet per second).

# U

**Uganda**, an inland country in East Africa, bounded by Sudan on the north, Kenya on the east, Tanzania and Rwanda on the south, and Zaïre on the west. Its tropical climate is alleviated by its height, most of it being over 1,000 m (3,300 feet) above sea-level; and over one-sixth of its area is water. Between lakes Victoria (the source of the Nile), Kyoga, and Albert in the southern half of the country are hills with richly fertile slopes and valleys. Round the Ruwenzori Range (the 'Mountains of the Moon') in the south-west, and the old volcanic Mount Elgon in the east, coffee is grown. The*savannah country in the north supports cotton and grain. Copper is the country's chief mineral resource.

**Ukraine**, a country comprising a large region of eastern Europe stretching from the Carpathian Mountains to the Donetz River and bounded on the south by the Black Sea. To the east are Poland, Slovakia, Hungary, Romania and Moldova; to the west, Russia. Northern Ukraine is a continuation of the low plains, woods, and marshes of Belarus. To the south, and forming three-quarters of the region, is the treeless steppe: a vast plain of rich black soil with occasional low hills, deep ravines of streams, and the great Dnieper River flowing down the centre. In the extreme south is the Crimea, a peninsula with a milder climate than the steppe, which is snow-covered in winter and very warm in summer. Coal and iron ore, found in southern parts of the steppe, as well as salt, mercury, bauxite, and manganese are among the country's abundant mineral resources. The nuclear accident at Chernobyl in 1986 has rendered large tracts of the countryside uncultivable.

**ultisol**, a *zonal soil which has undergone prolonged weathering under a subtropical climate with alternating wet and dry seasons. During the wet season ultisols are subject to intense *leaching which removes even relatively insoluble constituents from the top part of the soil profile. The lower *horizons of these soils tend to be clayey, and red or yellow in colour because of the presence of iron. The upper horizons contain little organic matter and are low in plant nutrients. These soils therefore are not very fertile. They are found in the south-east United States, southern China, India, and north-east Australia.

**ultrasound**, *sound with a *frequency of 20,000 Hz or above. It is inaudible to people, but some animals—dogs, bats, and dolphins for example—can hear it. (For people, audible sound is in the range 15–20,000 Hz.) Ultrasound waves can be used to construct pictures in the same way as light waves make visible pictures, but because sound waves can pass through opaque material they can be used in places where light would be inappropriate, for example to make pictures of a person's internal organs without operating, or at sea in murky water. Ultrasound causes vibrations which can be used to clean intricate objects such as precision tools and jewellery, and also to clean surfaces during chemical reactions to make the reactions more efficient.

**ultraviolet radiation**, *electromagnetic radiation with wavelengths shorter than those of visible light and longer than those of X-rays, approximately $10^{-7}$ to $10^{-9}$ metre. The waves near the longer end of the range are called near ultraviolet and are emitted by certain atoms, such as those of mercury, when they are electrically excited. Sunlight contains much near ultraviolet. It is responsible for producing pigmentation (sun-tan) and vitamin D in the skin. Ultraviolet light can kill certain bacteria, and can cause *fluorescence in certain atoms and molecules, some of which are used in paints.

**uncertainty principle**, the statement that it is impossible to make a precise simultaneous measurement of both the position and the momentum (mass × velocity) of a body. The reason is that the mere act of, for example, measuring the position of a particle involves making contact with it in some way—if only with a ray of light—and this will alter its momentum (or velocity). Similarly, a determination of the momentum of the particle will affect its position. The more precise the measurement of one quantity the more uncertainty will there be in the other. The German physicist Werner *Heisenberg showed that the product of the uncertainties in the two quantities must be of the order of Planck's constant, $h$ ($6.6 \times 10^{-34}$ joule second). This is a very small number and it has the consequence that the uncertainties can never be detected for ordinary objects; but they become very important for atoms and smaller particles. (See also *wave-particle duality.)

**unconformity** (in geology), a relationship in which part of a sequence of *sedimentary rocks is missing. The unconformity may be apparent by a difference in the dip of the beds (their inclination to the horizontal); this results when the older rocks have been tilted and then eroded before the younger beds were deposited on them. The term 'angular unconformity' can then be applied. An unconformity may also be shown by an irregular surface between the rocks above and below it. Another type of unconformity is one in which the older and the younger beds show no difference in dip, although there is evidence of erosion at the interface between them. In such cases it can be inferred that there has been a period of non-deposition but that no movement took place during it. The terms 'non-sequence', 'diastem', or 'non-depositional unconformity' may then be applied. Unconformities are important in interpreting the relationships of sedimentary rocks. A famous example is the Great Unconformity near the base of the Grand Canyon in the

Angular **unconformity** in sedimentary rocks at Helworth Bridge, Yorkshire, UK. The older, tilted, and eroded beds have been covered by a younger deposit.

USA. A spectacular British unconformity is that at Siccar Point on the east coast of Scotland, where gently dipping *Devonian strata rest on vertical *Silurian ones.

**undercut bank**, a riverbank caused when the deepest water and fastest flow is against one bank rather than in mid-channel, particularly round the outer, concave sides of loops of *meandering rivers. Banks cut in alluvium or fine-grained sediment will tend to collapse after high flood flows have made them very wet and destroyed their internal cohesion. Undercutting is often into the actual sides of valleys, not only into deposits on the valley floor; it has the effect of widening river valleys and of reducing the *divides between them.

**Ungava Peninsula**, a broad peninsula lying on the *Canadian Shield and forming the northern part of Quebec province, bounded on the west by Hudson Bay and on the east by the mountains of Labrador. It reaches north towards Baffin Island and has a coast on the Hudson Strait which is only seasonally navigable. The base of the peninsula is the limit of coniferous forest; only cold, barren tundra lies northward. The region is studded with lakes and traversed by rivers, and has huge deposits of iron ore.

**unified field theory** *grand unified field theory.

**unit,** the name of a quantity, such as second or metre, chosen as a standard for use in measurement or comparison. Units measuring the quantities of mass, distance, area, and volume have existed since early in human history; more recently temperature, pressure, electric current, and other physical quantities have become important. Early units of linear measurement were often derived from body measurements: the Egyptian cubit, for example (derived c.3000 BC), was based on the distance from the elbow to the fingertip, and the Chinese used a unit measured from the pulse to the thumb. Later, more accurate standards were developed. The Egyptian royal cubit (524 mm, 20.62 inches) was standardized against a master cubit of black marble: from 221 BC the Chinese also had standardized measures, introduced by the first emperor, Shi Huangdi. Ancient Greek units drew from both the Egyptian and Babylonian systems of weights and measures. The Romans based their units on those of the Greeks: both the Romans and the Greeks, for example, used the foot as a length measurement. Medieval Europe inherited the Roman system, but in time many regional variations arose, and other units were borrowed from Scandinavia and elsewhere. The great European trade fairs of the 12th and 13th centuries forced merchants from different countries to adopt the same units of measurement, but many variations remained: in England, for example, there were three different sizes of gallon, one for corn, one for wine, and one for ale. In the late 18th century the metric system was introduced in France, in the aftermath of the French Revolution. The system was designed to be rational and practical, with each unit being subdivided or multiplied decimally, and a system of prefixes for multiples and submultiples covering all units (see table). The metric system spread through Europe and to many other countries during the 19th century, and in the 20th century became the basis for the modern *SI unit system, now used internationally by the scientific community. In the UK and the USA a system of units, rationalized from the European medieval system, continued to be used for most purposes except scientific work. The UK began a changeover to the metric system in 1965, but the USA still has no national legislation to introduce metric units.

The imperial units of length are the mile (1.609 km), equal to 1,760 yards, and the yard (0.9144 m), composed of 3 feet each of 12 inches (1 inch = 25.4 mm). Area of land is measured in acres, equal to 4,840 square yards (0.405 hectare). The basic unit of capacity is the gallon, defined as the volume at 62 °F of 10 pounds of pure water, and is equal to 277.42 cubic inches (4.546 litres). This is divided into 8 pints each of 20 fluid ounces. The bushel (8 gallons) is approximately 36.4 litres. The basic unit of weight is the pound, sometimes called the avoirdupois pound to distinguish it from other pounds that have been used in the past. It is divided into 16 ounces and 7,000 grains (1 grain = 65 mg and 1 pound = 0.4536 kg). The hundredweight is 112 pounds and the (long) ton is 20 hundredweight. A unit peculiar to the UK is the stone (14 pounds). The system of measurement in the USA comes from the same roots as the UK imperial measures, and many of the units are—for all practical purposes—common to both, despite minor differences in definition. Units of length are the same, and those of weight differ only in the hundredweight (100 pounds) and the ton, which is the short ton of 2,000 pounds. Unlike the imperial system there are different units of capacity for dry and liquid measure, though confusingly the names are the same. All are smaller than their imperial counterparts. For example, the gallon in liquid measure is based on a pint of 16 fluid ounces, and is 3.785 litres (against 4.546 litres for the imperial gallon). The pint in dry measure is 0.550 litre, as against 0.473 litre for liquid measure and 0.568 litre in imperial measure.

**uniqueness theorems** (in mathematics), claims together with proof that the one solution, construction, or object presented is the only one possible. Often they are paired with *existence theorems in showing that there *is* only one unique solution. A common method of proof starts from the assumption that there are two different solutions and shows this to be impossible. For example, one can prove in this way that for any whole number greater than 1 there is only one decomposition into the product of primes.

**United Arab Emirates**, seven sheikhdoms occupying the southern (Arabian) coast of the Gulf between Qatar and Oman, together with its off-shore islands. Abu Dhabi in the west is the largest and also the richest in oil and natural gas. Dubai to the east is the second largest and has oil off shore, as has ash-Shariqah. Further east, Ra's al-Khaymah and al-Fujayrah are predominantly agricultural, while Ajman and Umm al-Qaywayn are very small.

**United Kingdom** (UK), a country comprising Great Britain (*England, *Scotland, and *Wales) and (since 1922) *Northern Ireland in the north-east of Ireland.

**United States of America** (USA), the world's fourth largest country, comprising the central belt of North America together with Alaska, Hawaii, Puerto Rico, and many small Pacific Ocean islands. Mainland USA is bounded by Canada on the north, generally along latitude 49° N. and the Great Lakes, and by Mexico on the south, generally at about 32° N. and along the Rio Grande. It contains several topographically very diverse regions. The West Coast is a series of mountain ranges with attendant valleys and plateaux running roughly parallel to the climatically mild Pacific coast. In the north, the Cascade Range is cut by the valley of the Columbia River; and here, in Washington and Oregon, there are orchards and mighty softwood forests. In California, the reverse slopes of the Coast Range descend to the lush Sacramento and San Joaquin valleys, which are fringed inland by the snow-capped peaks of the Sierra Nevada. From here the Great Basin of Nevada and parts of Oregon, Idaho, Utah, and California, an arid and rugged plateau containing its own mountain ranges, extends eastward to the Rocky Mountains. The Rockies are the 'Great Divide', the main *watershed of the country. Out of their massive ranges in Montana, Wyoming, Colorado, and New Mexico (the Mountain States), emerge the westward-running Snake and Colorado Rivers, and the eastward-flowing tributaries of the Mississippi. The Great Plains, occupied by the Dakotas, Nebraska, Kansas, Oklahoma, and Texas, are cut through by the eastward flows and have become a great prairie supporting cattle ranching and wheat cultivation. The prairies extend through the Middle West (including Minnesota, Iowa, Missouri, and north-west Arkansas) to the basin of the Mississippi, which intersects the country from north to south. The *podzols of the northern states in the Middle West (Wisconsin, Michigan, Illinois, Indiana, and Ohio) are well suited to the cultivation of maize and differ greatly from the red and yellow soils of the Deep South. Here, in Louisiana, Mississippi, Tennessee, Alabama, and Georgia, the main crops are cotton, rice, tobacco, and sugarcane. In this region also there are oilfields which extend into the Gulf of Mexico. The peninsula of Florida is renowned for the warmth of its climate and for its citrus fruits. The south-eastern coastal plain, occupied by Virginia, the Carolinas, and eastern Georgia, is drained by the rivers of the Appalachian Mountains and supports much mixed farming. Mountainous New England, the north-eastern region, experiences harsh winters but contains rich pastures and many areas of great natural beauty. Inland, the Great Lakes form a great transport artery and provide hydroelectric power for the northern states. The country is rich in mineral deposits, including, in addition to oil, coal, gold, silver, lead, zinc, and phosphates.

**unloading** (in geology), the removal of the weight of overlying rock, sediment, or ice from part of the Earth's surface. *Isostatic recovery is a well-known consequence of unloading by ice. The rise in the land mass along the Baltic Coast relative to the sea-level is attributed to ice unloading; a similar rebound has taken place in the north-eastern part of North America.

**uplift**, the upward vertical movement of any area of the Earth's surface relative to any other part. Uplift can be caused by *faulting, *unloading, or, on a very large scale, by mountain-building and *plate movement.

**Upper Volta**   *Burkina Faso.

**upthrow**, the uplift of the rocks on one side of a *fault in relation to the other side of the fault (which is known as the *downthrow).

**upwelling**, the process in oceans whereby subsurface water is mixed up to the surface. It occurs as a result of winds causing a *divergence of surface water, which subsurface water rises to replace. In regions where upwelling has occurred, the surface water will be unusually cold for the latitude, particularly if it has come from below the *thermocline. It will also be rich in nutrients, which support microscopic floating algae which grow in sunlight on surface waters, and hence higher forms of marine life. Perhaps the best known upwellings are those that occur along the east-

A **uranium** mine in Gabon. The brown and dark grey colours of the earth are characteristic of the uranium ore uraninite.

ern boundaries of the tropical oceans, where surface waters move off-shore under the influence of the trade winds.

**Ural Mountains**, a long mountain chain stretching for over 2,100 km (1,300 miles) from north to south, separating European Russia in the west from Siberia in the east. Acting as a barrier to the westerly prevailing winds, it intensifies Siberia's continental climate; and it provides tributaries for the Ob River in the east and the Volga in the west. The mountains are the eroded stumps of heavily folded ranges, which date from the Palaeozoic Era, with faulting and igneous intrusions. The northern section is a single, barren, glaciated ridge which rises through tundra to a highest point of 1,894 m (6,214 feet) at Mount Narodnaya. The central section has several low passes, while in the south the system breaks up into parallel ranges which together form a barrier some 160 km (100 miles) wide. The Urals are extremely rich in mineral resources including major deposits of copper, nickel, chromite, gold, and platinum. They are thickly forested and hold huge deposits of oil, bituminous coal, and industrial metals such as iron. Heavy use of pesticides has poisoned the rivers. The Urals had been the centre of the former Soviet nuclear industry, and lakes in the region are now oozing with plutonium.

**uraninite** ($UO_2$), the chief ore of uranium, normally pitch-black in colour, hard, very dense, and radioactive. Found in high-temperature veins of igneous origin, it is associated with thorium, lead, and the rare-earth elements. Large crystals of uraninite are found in Ontario (Canada) and South

Africa. In its massive form (pitchblende) it was used in 1898 by the *Curies to identify radium, helium, and polonium, and it is still used as a source of radium.

**uranium** (symbol U, at. no. 92, r.a.m. 238.03), a dense, white, metallic element, a member of the *actinides; it is radioactive, decaying over a long period to lead. Measurement of the lead content of uranium-containing rocks can be used to date the rock. The importance of uranium stems from its use in producing nuclear energy, both in reactors and in bombs. Naturally occurring uranium consists of three *isotopes, of mass numbers 234, 235, and 238. Uranium-235 has an abundance of only 0.71 per cent, but it is the only naturally occurring isotope that is fissile—that is, can be split by a slow neutron to form smaller nuclei and release energy. The *fission process also produces more neutrons which can initiate fission in other nuclei, so starting a chain reaction. The much more abundant (99.28 per cent) uranium-238 is used in breeder reactors to produce *plutonium. Although uranium is probably about forty times as abundant in nature as silver is, it is not found uncombined. Indeed it occurs only sparingly in ores, the most notable of which are *uraninite, pitchblende, carnotite, and coffinite, a silicate. These are mined mainly in Canada, the USA, Russia, South Africa, France, Niger, Namibia, and Australia; and such is its value that ores with as little as one part of uranium in a thousand have been processed for its extraction.

**Uruguay**, a country in south-east-central South America with a coast on the Atlantic bounded by Argentina on the west and Brazil on the north-east. It has a coast on the estuary of the River Plate, and the Uruguay River flowing down its western boundary is navigable for some 320 km (200 miles). Tributaries flow westward across the country, which is mainly warm, grassy plain (*pampas) supporting cattle and sheep. In the centre and north-east the plain is broken by occasional rocky ridges and there are some deposits of iron.

**US customary measure**    *unit.

**Ushant** (French, Ile d'Ouessant), a rocky island standing 25 km (15 miles) off the coast of Finistère, the most westerly part of the peninsula of Brittany, north-west France. It marks the southern end of the Atlantic approaches to the English Channel (the northern end being marked by the Scilly Isles), and busy shipping lanes pass close by. With an area of 16 km$^2$ (6.1 sq. miles), it is composed mainly of granite, and its rugged coastline is made the more dangerous by frequent fogs and gales from Atlantic storms.

**Uzbekistan**, a country situated south of Kazakhstan in central Asia and stretching south-east from the deserts of the Aral Sea to the Alai Mountains. At the foot of these lie the fertile Fergana valley and several large oases. To the south and east are Turkmenistan, Afghanistan, Tajikistan, and Kirghizia. The Amu Darya (Oxus) flows north-west to the Aral Sea, providing a second fertile belt, between the Kara Kum sand desert and the Kyzyl Kum desert of stony clay. Oil, natural gas, coal, copper, and lead are among the natural resources. In recent decades, aluminium factories have produced uncontrolled wastes that are now affecting fruit-growing areas and livestock.

**Vaal**, the great tributary of the Orange River in South Africa, forming a natural part of the boundary between the Transvaal and the Orange Free State. Rising in the eastern Transvaal, its waters provide power for the area of the Witwatersrand. It then flows south-west through the veld and into Cape Province. Before joining the Orange it picks up the Modder, the chief of its many tributaries.

**vacuum**, theoretically a space which contains no *matter. In fact it is impossible to obtain a perfect vacuum as any material surrounding a vacuum will have a *vapour pressure and will thus release particles into the vacuum. In general use the term refers to gases at very low pressures such as exist at the limit of the earth's atmosphere. The nearest to a perfect vacuum is in space, where the concentration of particles may be as low as one per cubic centimetre, a level of vacuum that has been unable to be replicated on Earth.

**valency**, the combining capacity of an atom—that is, the number of other atoms with which it will combine when forming a compound. Using valencies, the formulae of many simple compounds can be predicted: hydrogen has valency 1, nitrogen 3, and so each nitrogen atom reacts with three hydrogen atoms; thus ammonia has the formula $NH_3$. Many elements show more than one valency in their compounds; iron has valencies 2 and 3, and forms two different chlorides, $FeCl_2$ and $FeCl_3$. The valency of an atom is equal to the number of bonds that it forms in *covalent compounds, and to the number of charges it acquires in *ionic compounds. Many valencies can be predicted from the *periodic table: for instance, elements in Groups I and VII have valency 1, those in Groups II and VI have valency 2, those in Groups III and V have valency 3, and those in Group IV have valency 4. There is no such pattern in the transition metals, however, electron shells may be regarded as spherical layers centred on the nucleus which can contain a fixed maximum number of electrons. The innermost shell, the K-shell or $n = 1$ shell, which contains a maximum of two electrons, is filled first, then the L-shell or $n = 2$ shell, which contains a maximum of eight electrons, is filled, and so on. The last shell to be occupied is usually only partly filled, and this is called the valence shell. The *noble gases are the only elements whose atoms have complete valence shells and they are very stable and unreactive. Other atoms seek the stability of a complete valence shell by gaining electrons, for example when chlorine becomes the chlorine ion, $Cl^-$, or by losing electrons, for example when sodium becomes the sodium ion, $Na^+$. Only the electrons in the valence shell are available for *chemical bonding by being either transferred (ionic bonding) or shared (covalent bonding). The electrons in inner shells rarely enter into chemical reactions (except in *transition metals).

**valley**, an elongated and usually interconnecting depression of the Earth's surface. Some valleys are formed by earth movements and faulting, others (normally U-shaped) by glaciers, and a very few by wind erosion. By far the most, however, are the work of rivers, cutting channels towards the *base level of erosion over thousands or millions of years.

The valley cut by vertical erosion is usually V-shaped in cross-section and irregular in its course, its gradient being punctuated by sudden drops (waterfalls) and long shelves (lakes). These irregularities represent local base levels which are gradually removed by *denudation, so that as the falls are worn back and lakes infilled the breaks in the profile are reduced. With lateral erosion and *mass movement, the valley broadens. *Deposition occurs as the gradient slackens, and *floodplains fill the valley floor. *Rejuvenation leaves remnants of old floodplains above the new ones in the form of terraces, the highest of which are the oldest. A lowering of the water-table may leave *dry valleys, and sudden uplift may leave *hanging valleys, while the flooding of valleys by the sea gives *rias.

**valley train**, an elongated deposit of material originally transported by a glacier which has been re-worked by rivers of melt-water, filling the floors of the glaciated valleys. Valley trains resemble *outwash plains, but are confined to valleys.

**vanadium** (symbol V, at. no. 23, r.a.m. 50.94), a brilliant white *transition metal that occurs naturally in patronite, $V_2S_5$, vanadinite, $Pb_5(VO_4)Cl$, and crude oil. It is used mainly as a constituent of steels, to give strength at high temperatures. It is also added to copper alloys to increase strength and corrosin-resistance, especially in marine environments. Vanadium-aluminium alloys are used in airframe construction, and vanadium oxide, $VO$, is a good industrial catalyst.

**Van Allen radiation belt**, a region in the atmosphere that contains high-energy charged particles—mainly electrons and protons. These regions were first detected by artificial satellites in 1958-9. The belts are at heights ranging from 2,000 to 20,000 km (1,200 to 12,000 miles) and more, and the particles, which are believed to originate from the sun, are trapped in them by the Earth's magnetic field. They were discovered by James Van Allen (1914-   ), a US physicist.

The transverse profiles of **valleys** reflect their modes of formation. The U-shaped valley below Langdale Pike in the Lake District, UK (*left*) is of glacial origin, whilst the V-shaped one in Nelson Province, South Island, New Zealand (*right*), has been cut by a river.

**Vancouver, George** (1758–98), British naval captain and explorer of North America's Pacific coast who began his expedition in 1791. Sailing by way of Australia and New Zealand he arrived at Hawaii and from there reached the California coast. Sailing northward along the coast, he then came to the island that now bears his name, sailed round it to establish its insularity (1792), and returned to winter in Hawaii. Having surveyed the same coast carefully in the following year, in 1794 he travelled north to Alaska to examine the Cook inlet. The expedition then steered south, rounded Cape Horn, and reached England after an absence of four and a half years.

**Vancouver Island** (Canada), the largest island off the western coast of North America, over 450 km (280 miles) long and 130 km (80 miles) wide at its broadest point, part of British Columbia. Its Pacific coast is deeply indented, harbouring Nootka and many smaller islands, while its eastern coast is separated from the mainland by Queen Charlotte Strait and the Strait of Georgia. An eastern coastal plain rises sharply to mountains up to 2,200 m (7,200 feet) which extend along its length, for the whole island is a partly submerged range. These rugged heights contain forests, lakes, old glaciers, and streams; while underground are coal deposits and a vast *batholith yielding copper, iron, and gold. The climate is mild, although westerlies bring very heavy rain.

**van der Waals, Johannes Diderik** (1837–1923), Dutch physicist who made a detailed study of the liquefaction of gases. In 1879 he proposed an equation, which now bears his name, linking the pressure, volume, and temperature of a gas. The equation is more accurate than Boyle's law or Charles's law (see *gas laws): it makes allowance for the forces of attraction between the molecules, and successfully describes the behaviour of a gas which is nearing a liquid state. He was awarded the Nobel Prize for Physics in 1910.

**van der Waals' forces**, a type of weak *intermolecular force that exists between all pairs of atoms and molecules that are not chemically bonded; they give rise to the existence of solids and liquids, affect the surface tension and viscosities of liquids, and cause gases to cool when they expand suddenly. Although the exact nature of van der Waals' forces varies from case to case, the most general cause is the correlation of the motions of the electrons in two adjacent molecules, producing an attractive force. The motion of the electrons in one molecule only affects the electrons in another when the molecules are very close, and van der Waals' forces operate only over short distances. The forces increase as the number of electrons in a molecule increases, so the boiling-points of the halogens increase from fluorine to iodine and those of the alkanes increase as the carbon chain lengthens. These forces are named after their discoverer Johannes *van der Waals.

**van't Hoff, Jacobus Hendricus** (1852–1911), Dutch chemist who applied the laws of *thermodynamics to chemical reactions. He derived an equation known as the van't Hoff isochore and showed that the osmotic pressure of a solution varies directly with the temperature. In organic chemistry van't Hoff studied the spatial arrangements of groups attached to a carbon atom. He won the first Nobel Prize for Chemistry in 1901.

**Vanuatu** (formerly New Hebrides), a country comprising over eighty south-west Pacific Ocean islands between latitudes 13° and 21 °S. and longitudes 167° and 170° E. Only a dozen are suitable for settlement, the largest being Espíritu Santo, Efate, Malekula, Maewo, Pentecost, Ambrim, Erromanga, and Tanna. Of volcanic origin, they are very hilly. Coffee is grown on the slopes, while the very warm, wet plains are sufficiently fertile for livestock. South-east trade winds moderate the heat from May to October. The most important mineral is manganese.

**vaporization**, the conversion of a liquid, or less commonly a solid, into a vapour. In the case of a solid the process is called *sublimation. Vaporization requires a definite amount of energy, the *latent heat, which may be provided by heating, but if vaporization is made to occur without heating, the latent heat will be taken from the surroundings. This is why the cooling of a moistened fingertip tells us when it is facing the wind; the wind evaporates the water, and the vapour takes latent heat out of the finger. The pressure exerted by a vapour of any substance is its *vapour pressure.

**vapour pressure**, the contribution to the pressure of the atmosphere or any gas by the molecules of the vaporized liquid which it contains. For example, damp air contains water vapour and this contributes to the overall pressure of the air. Normally the term refers to the saturated vapour pressure, that is, the pressure when there is an equilibrium between the liquid and the vapour in contact with it, with as many molecules passing from liquid to vapour as are passing from vapour to liquid. The vapour is said to be saturated. The saturated vapour pressure increases with temperature. The air is not usually saturated with water vapour because of the effect of air currents, but if it is, *dew can form.

**variables** (in statistics), any classifiable features of the data to be investigated. Random variables are, strictly, called variates. Data can be regarded as falling into one of four categories. When the variables have non-numerical values such as gender, colour, and place of birth, the data are called nominal. With ordinal data, such as social class and responses to attitude tests, the variables can be ordered in some way, although even the simple statistic of the mean has no application at such qualitative levels. Data with variables having intrinsic numerical properties, such as age and examination results, are quantitative and fall into two groups, those with discrete and those with continuous variables. Discrete variables take only a finite number of values; the number of children in a household is always actually a whole number, even though 'average' families are said to have 2.4 children. Continuous variables can take any value in a certain range; age is a continuous variable in spite of its being measured to the nearest month or day. Among the important characteristics of data sets are the spread of values of a particular variable, its frequency distribution, and its *mode.

**variance** (in statistics), the square of the *standard deviation—that is, the mean of the squares of variations from the *arithmetic mean. It is of little importance as a descriptive statistic, but the analysis of variance is an important tool for comparing sample groups. The variance within different groups can be compared with the variance of the group means in relation to the overall mean to show whether the groups are likely to have come from the same normally distributed population. A similar technique may be used to ascertain how many independent factors or variables are contributing to the variation within a population.

**vectors** (in mathematics), quantities which have both magnitude and direction, in contrast to *scalars, which have only magnitude. In everyday use velocity and speed are the same, but in scientific use velocity is a vector, being speed in a certain direction. Speed is a *scalar. Similarly weight, a downward force, is a vector whereas mass is a scalar. Another example of a vector quantity is momentum. In terms of pure mathematics they form an *Abelian group under addition. They can be multiplied by scalars—a force $F$ can be doubled to force $2F$—whereas addition with a scalar has no meaning. Two vectors can be added, however, $F_1 + F_2$ meaning a force equivalent to both forces acting on the object. A fixed vector is one for which the point of action is given, as well as

The medal struck by the Netherlands Numismatic Society to commemorate the award of the Nobel Prize to Johannes **van der Waals**. The reverse side of the medal (*right*) gives van der Waals' equation together with its three-dimensional graphical representation.

the direction and the size; and a point-position vector is that needed to reach a particular point from some fixed origin. In texts vectors are often denoted by symbols in bold type or by means of horizontal arrows placed over them. If line AB represents $F_1$ and line BC represents $F_2$, then $F_1 + F_2$ is represented in magnitude and direction by the line AC. They may be represented by straight lines of suitable length and orientation and used in diagrams to perform calculations. A parallelogram of vectors is used in mathematics to determine the sum of two vector quantities. The net effect of two vectors will depend on whether they are acting in the same direction, whether they oppose one another, or whether they are at some other angle to each other. The parallelogram construction states that if the two vectors are represented in magnitude and direction by two adjoining sides of a parallelogram, then their resultant is represented, also in magnitude and direction, by the diagonal of the parallelogram which is enclosed by the two sides.

**veld** (Dutch and Afrikaans, 'field'), open country in southern Africa used for farmland and pasture. The Highveld comprises land between 1,220–1,830 m (4,000–6,000 feet) high; the Middleveld regions lie between 610–1,220 m (2,000–4,000 feet); and the Lowveld lies between 150–610 m (500–2,000 feet). The soil of the Lowveld is the most fertile, yielding abundant crops of potatoes and maize, and suited to cattle grazing and industrial mining. The veld is among the world's oldest inhabited regions.

**velocity**, a measure of the movement of an object in a particular direction in a given period of time. It is a *vector quantity, as the direction of motion is specified, and in the *SI system is measured in metres per second. Speed is also a measure of the movement of the object, but the direction of this movement is not specified and so it is a *scalar quantity. The instantaneous velocity of an object can be obtained from the derivative of its displacement $x$ over time $t$: $dx/dt$.

When an object falls through the air, it undergoes *acceleration due to gravity, and speeds up. However, its downward motion is impeded by the upward force of *air resistance. Air resistance increases as the velocity of the object increases, so as the object accelerates, the upward force on it increases, slowing it down. There comes a point at which the acceleration due to gravity is matched by the slowing down due to air resistance. The object then stops accelerating but continues to fall at the velocity it had reached at the point when the forces matched. This constant velocity is known as the terminal velocity.

**velocity of light**   *speed of light.

**velocity of sound**   *speed of sound.

**Venezuela**, a country on the north coast of South America, with a coastline on the Caribbean Sea. It is bounded by Colombia on the west, Brazil on the south, and Guyana on the east. The island-fringed coast is tropical, with lagoons. Much oil is found here, notably around the shallow Lake Maracaibo. At the eastern end of the coast is the swampy delta of the Orinoco River, rich in hardwoods and with iron deposits in the south. Inland are the *Lanos and the maritime Andes, towering in from the south-west with snow-clad peaks and forests on their slopes. The Guyana Highlands lie in the south of the country and rise to nearly 2,750 m (9,000 feet), being cut by the valleys of the Orinoco's tributaries and containing the Angel Falls, the highest in the world.

**Venn diagram**, a geometric means for representing relationships between *sets. Each set is represented by a ring and all are drawn within the confines of a rectangle representing the universal set under consideration. The area common to two rings represents their intersection, and the area in the combined region, their union. Shading is often used to focus attention on the particular compound set under consideration. The complement of a set is the region outside the ring representing it. Venn diagrams provide a pictorial image of the operations described in *truth tables. They were first proposed by the English logician John Venn (1834–1923).

**vernal equinox**   *equinoxes.

**Verrazzano, Giovanni da** (1485–1528), Italian navigator and explorer, in the service of France, who was the first European to sight and visit (1524) New York and Narragansett Bays. Backed by the French government, he led three expeditions to search for a westward passage into the Pacific and thus to the East. The first (1523–4) led him to the eastern coast of North America, the second (1527) to Brazil, and the third to the Caribbean, where he was attacked and eaten by cannibals.

**vertisol**, a *zonal soil rich in a clay known as montmorillonite, which shrinks and swells dramatically with changes in water content. Vertisols are common under grassland and savannah vegetation in seasonally dry subtropical and tropical areas. During dry periods the soil shrinks and wide, deep cracks form. After rain, soil is washed into these cracks before they close. This results in the regular mixing of the soil and prevents the formation of distinct *horizons. Soils of this type are found on the coastal plains of Texas, in the Deccan region of India, and in parts of eastern Australia.

**Vespucci, Amerigo** (1451–1512), Italian merchant, navigator, and explorer. While in the service of the king of Portugal, Vespucci made several voyages to the New World and claimed, on dubious authority, to have been the first to sight

A Florentine by birth, **Vespucci** served both the Portuguese and the Spanish kings in turn at a crucial time of European expansion when his outstanding knowledge of nautical science was much in demand.

the mainland of South America (1497). The name America is said to have been derived from his own first name, but there are other suggestions of its origin.

**Vesuvius**, the only active volcano on the European mainland, overlooking the Bay of Naples on the west coast of Italy. Its main summit is about 1,277 m (4,190 feet) high, although this varies with each eruption. A second summit called Monte Summa forms a semicircular ridge round the cone and is the wall of a great prehistoric crater. The slopes are marked by lava flows, and the lower slopes are very fertile. In AD 79 Herculaneum, Pompeii, and Stabiae were destroyed by a major eruption, and there have been many others since, several of them severe.

**vibrations**, the means by which signals and information are transmitted from one place or person to another. Sound consists of vibrations of the air which are initiated, for example, by the larynx or a musical instrument. Light and radio waves are electromagnetic vibrations initiated by moving electrical charges. Mechanical or electrical vibrations are used as the basis for the measurement of time, whether a clock is controlled by a vibrating balance wheel, a pendulum, or a quartz crystal. Associated with vibrations is the phenomenon of *resonance. The geometry of structures can be so arranged that they respond more to one particular frequency than to others, enabling the selection and amplification of certain signals. Unwanted vibrations in a machine, for example, can be not only a nuisance but a cause of damage. Molecular vibrations give rise to *infra-red spectra.

**Victoria**, a state of south-east Australia, bounded by South Australia on the west and, along the *Murray River, by New South Wales on the north. It has south and east coasts extending for some 1,680 km (1,043 miles) and is separated by Bass Strait from Tasmania. The Murray basin in the north is dry, with patches of sandy desert, except seasonally along the northward-running tributary rivers. A watershed is formed by an extension of the Great Dividing Range, the Australian Alps, which traverses most of Victoria and contains Mount Bogong at 1,986 m (6,508 feet). The southward-

A view from Mount Arapiles (an outlier of the Grampian Mountains in **Victoria**, Australia, looking towards the extensive lowland plains of the agricultural district of Wimmera.

The people of the Kalolo-Logi named the **Victoria Falls** *Mosi-oa-tunya*, 'smoke-that-thunders', due to the mist created by the wide sheet of water, which cascades with increasing speed down the narrow chasm. David Livingstone was the first European to see the falls in 1855, on his descent of the Zambezi.

flowing Snowy, Tambo, and Mitchell rivers drain the Gippsland coastal plain in the south-east, while to the west the Yarra, Hopkins, and Glenelg flow across the rest of the 'Great Valley', as the lowlands are sometimes called. Oil and natural gas are found off-shore, and lignite (brown coal) mainly in the Latrobe valley in the south-east.

**Victoria, Lake** (Victoria Nyanza), Africa's largest lake, lying on the plateau between the western and eastern branches of the Great Rift Valley of east Africa. Approximately 410 km (255 miles) from north to south and 250 km (155 miles) broad, it is the world's second largest freshwater lake. Its depression—75 m (250 feet) deep—was caused by the sagging of the Earth's crust due to *plate movements and stands at an altitude of over 1,100 m (3,700 feet) above sea-level. The lake contains numerous small islands. Its shores are greatly indented with gulfs and smaller inlets. It is fed by many streams, and is drained to the north by the Victoria Nile, which spills over the Owen Falls and provides hydroelectric power before entering Lake Kyoga.

**Victoria Falls**, in southern Africa, one of the world's greatest natural wonders, on the Zambezi River where it flows between Zambia and Zimbabwe. The waterfalls are over 1.6 km (1 mile) wide and drop a maximum of 108 m (355 feet). The water plunges into a deep chasm 120 m (400 feet) wide—which itself is a fracture in the Earth's crust—and leaves it through a winding gorge 80 km (50 miles) long. The thick mist can be seen and the roar of the water can be heard as far as 40 km (25 miles) away.

**Victoria Island**, part of Canada's north-west Territories, lying wholly within the Arctic Circle and bound in the north by pack-ice. It is 515 km (320 miles) long and 274–595 km (170–370 miles) wide, with an irregular, deeply indented coastline. Hills in the north-west and south-west rise to 914 m (3,000 feet).

**Vietnam**, a country in south-east Asia, bent like an S, bordering on China on the north and Laos and Cambodia on the west, having long east and south coasts on the South China Sea. In the north the Red and Black Rivers flow from forested mountains across very warm, wet lowlands spread with paddy-fields. Rich mineral resources here include iron ore, manganese, chromite, and apatite. The south is even wetter, rice growing all down the coastal strip and in the Mekong delta. Rubber is cultivated, as are tea and coffee in areas where the ground rises to the central highlands.

**Virgin Islands**, a group of about a hundred islands in the Caribbean Sea between Puerto Rico and the Lesser Antilles, divided between British and US administration. Saint Croix, Saint Thomas, Saint John, and Tortola are the most important, ranging from 207 km$^2$ (80 sq. mi.) to 52 km$^2$ (20 sq. mi.) in area. Most are too small for settlement. They are volcanic in origin and suffer mild earthquakes. The hillsides are grassy and well suited to livestock farming.

**viscosity**, the property of a fluid which determines the ease or difficulty with which it flows. A low viscosity, for example that of a gas, means that the flow through a fine tube will be quite rapid, whereas a high viscosity (as with a thick oil) means that the motion will be sluggish. It manifests itself whenever different parts of a fluid flow at different rates (as in most actual flow), and arises from the *intermolecular forces in the fluid (its 'internal friction'). The stronger these are, the greater the viscosity. If the temperature is raised, the attraction between the molecules is reduced, and so they are able to move more independently of one another. Thus the viscosity of boiling water is only one sixth of the value at the ice point, and this is why leaks are more apparent when water is heated. Gases by contrast become more viscous at higher temperatures, due to the increasing effect of molecular collisions. The viscosity of a fluid that is turbulent (*turbulence), that is, eddying and chaotic (*chaos), is orders of magnitude greater than viscosity of fluids which are flowing in a laminar, or ordered, fashion.

**visibility** (in meteorology), a measure of range of vision. The maximum distance from which a given object can be identified in daylight depends upon the number of particles which are held in suspension in the atmosphere. On a clear day maximum visibility is approximately 240 km (150 miles), although this is usually limited by the horizon. This extreme may be reduced by the presence of smoke and dust particles, which give rise to *haze, or by water droplets which may be concentrated as mist or fog.

**Vistula** (Polish, Wista), a river rising in the northern Carpathian (Beskid) Mountains of Silesia in southern Poland and flowing first east then north for 1,068 km (664 miles) to its large delta on the Baltic Sea at Gdansk. It has few left- but many right-bank tributaries, whose powerful streams are encouraged by the north-westward tilt of this region of the North European Plain. The steep gradient of the upper course gives way at the San tributary to gentler slopes in a channel which has sandbanks and is bordered by steep cliffs.

Where the lower course enters the delta artificial cuts and embankments help to control the accumulation of two million tonnes of sediment carried annually. The river is frozen each winter and melt-water from ice and snow causes spring flooding in much of its basin.

**volcanic bomb**, a lump of liquid lava ejected from a volcanic vent; it may or may not have solidified when it lands. Usually associated with acid *igneous activity, volcanic bombs range in size from a few centimetres (inches) to two or three metres (yards) in diameter. They are of various shapes: spindle-shaped, ribbon-like, rounded, or irregular. Some develop a skin while in the air that cracks when they land; these are called breadcrust bombs.

**volcanic plug**, or neck plug of solidified *magma that blocks the channels within a volcano by which molten lava rose to the surface. Plugs are often exposed by erosion and left upstanding above the surrounding *country rock, and occasionally they are the only evidence of an ancient vent. A neck is usually vertical but those that fed side vents on the slopes of a volcano may be at an angle to the vertical. In the later stages of eruption the lava in the conduit of a volcano may solidify to form a neck. Arthur's Seat, Edinburgh, UK, and Ship Rock in New Mexico, USA, are examples. The term 'volcanic neck' is also used for the conduit that feeds a volcano.

**volcano**, a vent or fissure in the Earth's crust, either on land or under water, from which molten *lava or fragments of rock are erupted, accompanied by hot gases. As lava solidifies round the vent a volcanic cone is built up, which may be of great size. Volcanoes are of various types. What is generally thought of as the characteristic shape, with steep concave sides, is a composite cone or stratovolcano. Such volcanoes are built up of interbedded layers of *tephra and lava; Mount Fujiyama in Japan and Mount Saint Helens in the USA are examples. The rocks of which stratovolcanoes are formed are rich in silica: mainly *andesites and *rhyolites. By contrast, shield volcanoes have very gentle slopes. They are built up of successive flows of basic, fluid lava, such as *basalt, which is poor in silica. Volcanoes of this type can be of immense size; the Hawaiian Islands and Kilimanjaro in Africa are famous examples. Cinder cones have steep slopes and are built of cinder-like or slag-like material; Parícutin in Mexico, which appeared in 1943, is of this type. Volcanic activity is often associated with local earthquakes and tremors. Most of the volcanoes that are active at the present time are in a belt round the Pacific Ocean (the 'ring of fire'), where the major eruption of Mount Pinatubo in the Philippines in 1991 was a notable example. There are evident connections between the movement of crustal *plates and volcanic activity, which is concentrated in zones where plates converge, as in the circum-Pacific zone and the Mediterranean, and where plates are being pulled apart, as on the *Mid-Atlantic Ridge. Some of the largest volcanoes, however, such as those of the Hawaiian Islands, are far from plate boundaries and their location has yet to be fully explained.

**Volga**, Europe's longest river and Russia's most important waterway, being navigable for nearly its entire course of 3,700 km (2,300 miles). It rises in the Valday Hills of north-west Russia, at an altitude of only 226 m (740 feet), and winds tranquilly eastward through numerous lakes, then turns south to receive its greatest tributary, the Kama, from

Kilauea, central Hawaii, is an example of a shield **volcano**. The active vent in Kilauea's crater is Halemaumau, a vast cauldron with almost vertical walls, 396 m (1,300 feet) deep inside which the liquid lava rises and falls. At the bottom is a pool of blood-red molten slag through which come bursting fountains of lava.

the direction of the Ural Mountains. Its course is concluded by entry through a broad, many-channelled delta into the Caspian Sea. Shoals and sand-bars in summer, and ice in winter, impede navigation at various points; moreover it readily floods. Canals link it to the Baltic Sea and River Don. The Volga now carries untreated effluent from the heavy industry of southern Russia slowly killing marine life in the Caspian Sea.

**volt** (symbol V), the *SI unit of potential difference (p.d.). A p.d. of 1 volt exists between two points in an electrical conductor if 1 joule of work is done when a charge of 1 coulomb moves between them, or equivalently, if a current of 1 ampere dissipates a power of 1 watt. The volt is also a unit of electric potential (work done in bringing unit charge up to a point from an infinite distance away), and of electromotive force or e.m.f. (energy supplied per unit charge by, for example, the chemical action in a battery). The unit is named in honour of Alessandro *Volta.

**Volta**, the chief river of Ghana, West Africa. It rises in Burkina Faso in two seasonal branches: the White and the Black. Their confluence in northern Ghana results in a substantial stream which flows southward for 470 km (290 miles) through the very large Lake Volta, formed by a dam, and

the Ajena Gorge to enter the Atlantic Ocean by way of a delta on the Gulf of Guinea. It is important for irrigation and hydroelectricity, and it is navigable from its mouth for 80 km (50 miles) upstream.

**Volta**, **Alessandro Giuseppe Antonio Anastaspio**, **Count** (1745–1824), Italian physicist, the discoverer of a number of electrical instruments, including the electrophorus (for generating static electricity), the condensing electroscope, and, in particular, the voltaic pile or electrochemical battery, the first device to produce a continuous electric current, which he announced in 1800. The impetus for this invention was Galvani's contention in 1791 that he had discovered a new kind of electricity, 'animal electricity', produced in animal tissue, which Volta ascribed to normal electricity produced by the contact of two dissimilar metals. He was made a Count when he demonstrated his battery to Napoleon in 1801. The *volt is named in his honour.

**volume** (symbol $V$), the bulk of anything, the amount of three-dimensional space that it occupies. As with an area, its calculation gives rise to problems if the solid has curved sides. Archimedes showed that the volume of a sphere was $\frac{4}{3}\pi r^3$. The volume of a cylinder is $\pi r^2 h$, and in general for a solid with constant cross-sectional area, the volume is cross-sectional area $\times$ height. This provides the basis for the calculus approach to calculating volumes, whereby the actual volume can be approximated by the sum of cylindrical shells. In mensuration, volume is sometimes distinguished from capacity, the measure of what a space will hold. The litre is a unit of capacity, the cubic centimetre one of volume (1 litre equals 100 cm$^3$).

The principle of the voltaic pile—essentially a set of voltaic cells connected in series—as illustrated in a paper by Alessandro **Volta** published in 1800.

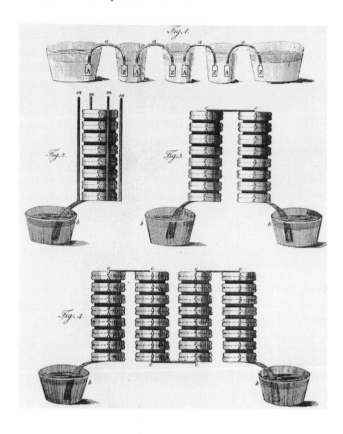

**vorticity**, the tendency for a fluid to rotate. In the atmosphere and ocean, rotatory motions occur as a result of the rotation of the Earth itself, and because of variations in frictional forces acting on and within moving air and water. Such rotatory motion occurs on all scales, from wind systems and ocean gyres, down to *cyclones and *anticyclones and the smallest swills and eddies.

**Vosges**, a mountain range 240 km (150 miles) long, west of the Rhine *rift valley in eastern France. Ancient crystalline gneiss, schist, and granite form the core of the uplands, which extend north from the Hautes-Vosges, with an average elevation of 900 m (3,000 feet), to the 'Saverne Gap' and so to the Basses (or Petites) Vosges with elevations of 400–500 m (1,300–1,600 feet). In the higher uplands the summits are weathered into fantastic crags and pinnacles. Triassic and Jurassic sandstones make up the eastern foothills, which form stepped terraces and are gashed by gorge-like valleys whose torrential streams deposit much debris when snow is melting. In the Quaternary Period small ice-caps covered the summit areas with glaciers, giving an imprint of U-shaped valleys and several *moraine-dammed ribbon lakes. Bleak summit plateaux give way to beech and spruce on the more sheltered valley sides; magnificent scenery is seen at Saverne and Ste Odile. Vittel and Contrexéville are sources of mineral waters.

**wadi**, a steep-sided valley in rocky desert areas which may contain a river. The word is Arabic (*arrogo is the term in Spanish); and it is given particularly to shallow *canyons with flat floors and nearly vertical walls, leading from uplands on to desert plains. Rain usually falls over rocky deserts in heavy thunderstorms and the bare surfaces produce massive, rapid *runoff, which creates flash floods. To be trapped in a steep-sided wadi during such a flood—which may sweep down as a wall of muddy water at head height—is generally fatal, although the waters rapidly soak into the alluvium of the valley floor and rarely reach the plains.

**Waikato**, New Zealand's longest river, in central North Island, with a length of 435 km (270 miles). Rising from Mount Ruapehu as the Tongariro River, it flows north through Lake Tampo and then north-west to the Tasman Sea. The chief source of hydroelectricity for the island, it is also navigable for its final 130 km (81 miles).

**Wakatipu, Lake**, a snake-shaped lake in the south of South Island, New Zealand. It is 77 km (48 miles) long by only 5 km (3 miles) wide and occupies a glacial trough which is dammed by a *moraine. The surface is at an altitude of 310 m (1,017 feet) and the maximum depth is 378 m (1,240 feet): this part of the floor is well below sea-level.

**Walcheren**, an island 21 km (13 miles) long in the estuary of the *Scheldt now linked by a causeway to the mainland of The Netherlands. Much of it is below sea-level, and frequent flooding has necessitated dykes for protection. Experience in reclamation here has been used in projects throughout the delta area after disastrous floods which were caused by a storm surge from the North Sea in 1953. Much of the reclaimed land, which is known as polder, provides good arable soil.

**Walden, Paul** (1863–1957), Latvian chemist who discovered the inversion reaction named after him. This is a reac-

**Wadi** Kelt, in Israel, is typical of a landform that occurs in North Africa and south-west Asia. Such valleys carry water only during times of heavy rainfall.

tion in which a compound showing *optical activity can be transformed into its optical isomer. It is of great significance in the theory of the mechanisms of certain reactions.

**Wales**, the smallest of the countries of Great Britain, measuring roughly 225 km (140 miles) from north to south and between 60 and 160 km from west to east, where it borders England. This border region, the Marches, is a stretch of pastureland much broken by hills, woods, and twisting rivers. It rises to the Cambrian Mountains, which stretch down the centre of the country. In the south-east are the Brecon Beacons and coalfields, and in the south-west the Pembroke Peninsula with its rocky coasts. Snowdonia is in the north-west. Wales enjoys an Atlantic maritime climate. Even on the higher peaks snow seldom lies long, for they face the warm westerlies which come in on the *North Atlantic Drift. The water flows into lakes, the largest of which is Bala, and into rivers such as the southward-flowing Towy and Usk. Like coal and slate, of which there are many deposits, water is an important Welsh resource.

**Washington, Mount**, the dominating feature of the Presidential Range of the White Mountains in northern New Hampshire, USA. Its massive and treeless summit at an altitude of 1,917 m (6,288 feet) offers spectacular views but experiences notoriously bad weather; a wind speed of 372 km/h (231 m.p.h.) was recorded in 1934 and it is a major centre for weather observation. The mountain is the source of three rivers, the Androscoggin, Connecticut, and Saco, and is a central attraction of the White Mountain National Forest.

**water** ($H_2O$), the normal oxide of hydrogen which covers nearly three-quarters of the Earth's surface and is present in varying degrees in the atmosphere. Pure water freezes at 0 °C (32 °F), has its maximum density at 4 °C (39.2 °F), and boils at 100 °C (212 °F), becoming a gas (steam). Water is remarkable for its heat capacity, chemical stability, and solvent action. The water molecule is a *polar molecule—the oxygen atom having a partial negative charge and the hydrogen atoms a partial positive charge. *Hydrogen bonds between molecules are the cause of some of its unusual properties. For most substances, the solid form is denser than the liquid form. However, ice is less dense than water. Hydrogen bonding is a significant factor in the internal structure of water, particularly when the water is cold. As water is cooled below 4 °C the hydrogen bonds organize the water molecules into a partially ordered structure in which they are further apart than they are in liquid water at higher temperatures. This structure is fixed once the water freezes, giving ice which is less dense than water. This is why ice floats.

Water is a neutral oxide, forming hydroxides and hydrogen with *electropositive metals and acids with non-metallic oxides. Natural water, such as *rain, is never pure but always contains dissolved substances. Limestone accounts for the *hardness of water underground. The most abundant source, *seawater, requires desalination before it can be used for drinking, irrigation, or industrial purposes. Of the estimated $1.43 \times 10^{21}$ kg of water on Earth, 97.4 per cent is in the ocean, 2.0 per cent in the ice-caps, and only 0.6 per cent as fresh water. Rivers return $3.7 \times 10^{16}$ kg/year of water to the ocean.

Heavy water is water in which one or both of the hydrogen atoms is replaced by an atom of deuterium. Deuterium is an isotope of hydrogen; its nucleus contains the same number of protons as hydrogen but also one extra neutron, so it is heavier than hydrogen. This mass difference makes the physical properties of heavy water different from those of ordinary water. Heavy water has a higher freezing-point and a higher boiling-point (3.81 °C or 38.85 °F and 101.42 °C or 214.55 °F, repectively) and is more viscous. Heavy water is capable of absorbing energy and is therefore used as a moderator in nuclear reactors.

**water balance**, a term, coined by the climatologist Charles *Thornthwaite, that refers to the relationship between the amount of water that is received over any part of the Earth's surface in the form of *precipitation, and the loss of water vapour through *evapotranspiration promoted by plant growth and evaporation from large bodies of water. On a global scale precipitation equals evapotranspiration, though amounts vary considerably between the different hemispheres and latitudes. For example, in the zones which extend between latitudes 40° North and South and the poles, precipitation exceeds evapotranspiration, whereas between 10° and 40° North and South of the Equator evapotranspiration exceeds precipitation. Thornthwaite's equation for the water balance is expressed simply in the form: inflow of water = outflow of water ± water storage. In order to evaluate the water balance for any given locality it is necessary to determine the mean air temperature and precipitation on a monthly or daily basis; the capacity which the soil in the area has to retain water; and the relationship between evapotranspiration, temperature, and length of day for the given latitude. In general, three principal sets of theoretical soil moisture conditions can be recognized: (1) conditions of moisture surplus, when precipitation exceeds potential evapotranspiration and there is ample water to sustain both *runoff and plant growth; (2) conditions of moisture utilization, where precipitation is less than potential evapotranspiration and plants are drawing water from the soil; and (3) conditions of moisture deficiency, when no moisture is available to sustain plant growth. By computing daily, monthly, and seasonal water balances, several parameters—including soil moisture and runoff, which are vital in sustaining agricultural production—may be evaluated; and in this manner it is possible to determine how much irrigation water is required, if any, to support crops.

**waterfall**, an abrupt descent of a river, usually over a rocky ledge. Some waterfalls are broad and complicated like Niagara, while others are steep and narrow chutes like Angel Falls, where water seems to fall straight down the mountainside. All are only temporary interruptions to a river's downward cutting, though it may take millions of years before they are smoothed out. They occur where a river flows from hard to soft rock or across a fault line, or where uplift of the land has caused the *rejuvenation of a river, and sometimes at the end of *hanging valleys.

**water-gap**, a place where a river cuts a narrow valley through a range of hills or mountains running its course. In some cases—as in the Himalayas—the rivers existed before the highlands were uplifted and continued to cut down as uplift took place. More often, the rivers originally flowed on rock layers well above the present land surface. As they cut downwards, they exposed the resistant rocks of today's hills, but continued to flow across them. Finally, tributaries found softer rocks either side easier to erode and carved out valleys, leaving the hills and the water-gaps.

**water mass**, a body of ocean water which is distinguishable by characteristic properties, notably its temperature

A **waterspout** over the Caribbean Sea. The dark cloud of the spout is formed from the condensation of water vapour produced when winds of different temperature meet in the upper atmosphere.

and *salinity, but also perhaps its concentrations of nutrients and certain dissolved gases. Water masses acquire their distinctive characteristics while in contact with the atmosphere, and so are said to 'form' at the surface. They eventually sink to a depth determined by their density, which in turn is determined by their temperature and salinity. An example of a water mass is the Antarctic Bottom Water, a very cold, fairly saline water mass which sinks in the vicinity of Antarctica and then flows northwards along the floors of the three oceans.

In general, water masses form in regions of *convergence of surface water, and their sinking and spreading is an integral part of the vertical, or deep thermohaline *circulation of the world's oceans.

**water of crystallization**, a quantity of water chemically incorporated in the crystals of certain *ionic compounds. For example, white anhydrous copper(II) sulphate, $CuSO_4$, will absorb moisture from the air, changing into blue hydrated copper(II) sulphate, $CuSO_4 \cdot 5H_2O$. The five water molecules are referred to collectively as the water of crystallization. Alums contain water of crystallization, an example being potash alum, $K_2SO_4 \cdot Al_2(SO_4)_3 \cdot 24H_2O$. In this case, water molecules act as *ligands, six surrounding each metal ion. The water of crystallization can be removed by heating.

**watershed** (see *divide), a line separating adjacent catchment area or *drainage basin. In popular usage the term is sometimes incorrectly used to mean a catchment area.

**waterspout**, a *tornado which occurs over open water; indeed a whirlwind which starts on land may travel over water, and vice versa. On lakes or at sea the power of water-

spouts may be considerable. Columns of water and spray gyrate in a tall column between the surface and the overhanging cloud, even sucking up shoals of small fish. These they may carry quite long distances before showering them down, so that the mythical 'rain of fishes' becomes a fact. Both the water and the accompanying wind are capable of doing considerable damage to shipping. The main occurrence of waterspouts at sea is in the tropics, although they are not unknown in other latitudes.

**water-table**, a surface below which the ground is completely saturated with water. Above a water-table, water drains downwards under gravity; below, it moves under pressure. Water-tables tend to reflect the form of the land surface: they are higher (though deeper below the surface) under hills, and in valleys are usually at about the same level as the river channels. They may rise or fall with shifts in the rock and the amount of rain received. Where they intersect the surface, *springs, seepages, and rivers occur. When rocks become saturated with water although the layers below them are not completely full, the result may be a *perched water-table. Thick layers of rock with high water-tables in which water moves long distances are termed aquifers. They are heavily exploited by wells for human use. A lowering of water-tables, especially in coastal areas, is serious if it allows salt water to flood in. In hot areas, water-tables too near the surface cause water to be drawn upwards by capillary forces and then evaporate, leaving behind salt deposits. Irrigated

areas are particularly vulnerable and soils often become too saline to be farmed. The cure is expensive: salts must be 'flushed' downwards and drainage channels dug to lower the water-table.

**Waterton–Glacier International Peace Park**, a vast tract of the Rocky Mountains with over three hundred lakes and sixty glaciers, covering the Waterton Lakes National Park of south-west Alberta, Canada, and the contiguous Glacier National Park of north-west Montana, USA. The massive peaks, with rocks dating back 600 million years, were uplifted by movements around 60 million years ago and finely shaped by ice-sheets one million years ago. The highest point of this peak-and-valley landscape is Glacier Park's Mount Cleveland at 3,185 m (10,448 feet); the lowest is Flathead River at 930 m (3,050 feet). It is often called the Land of the Shining Mountains, a name which aptly describes the panoramic and alpine scenery which it affords.

**water vapour**, water in the state of a *vapour. In the atmosphere it accounts for about 3 per cent of the mass of dry air, its distribution varying considerably in both time and space. It enters the air from sea and land through the processes of evaporation and *evapotranspiration; and its concentration, as expressed by the relative *humidity of the air, depends on temperature. Water vapour is an essential constituent of the atmosphere. It exerts a fundamental role in controlling the distribution of heat throughout the troposphere by means of its absorbent properties and through the mechanism of the *greenhouse effect. It is also fundamental to the formation of clouds and in the condensation process of *precipitation.

**watt** (symbol W), the *SI unit of power. A power of 1 watt means that work is being done, and energy is changing into some other form, at the rate of 1 joule per second. Larger units of power are the kilowatt (kW; 1,000 W), and the

The Sperry Glacier is one of sixty that have gouged out basins and created many mountain lakes in **Waterton–Glacier International Peace Park**.

megawatt (MW; $10^6$ W). The units are commonly used when quoting engine powers, or the rate of supply of electrical energy. The unit is named in honour of the British engineer James Watt (1736–1819).

**wave** (in physics), a periodic disturbance which travels through a medium, unchanged in form. For a sequence of particles ABCD in a material medium, A hands on the disturbance to B, which passes it on to C and so on. The wave transports energy, but the medium itself does not travel bodily in the direction of the wave: a cork floating in a pond bobs up and down when a ripple passes, but it does not move across the surface. All waves have three characteristic parameters: the frequency, which is the number of oscillations per unit time; the amplitude, which is the size of the oscillation, and the speed at which they travel. (See also *transverse wave, *longitudinal wave.)

**wave, atmospheric**, a periodic spatial disturbance in an airflow, which occurs both in the westerly airflow aloft, in mid-latitudes, and in the *trade winds which blow at the surface in low latitudes. Waves develop as a result of the latitudinal variation in the *Coriolis force, the existence of a horizontal temperature gradient, and the influence of *orographic effects. At the surface their form is accentuated and more cellular, since the patterns of *convergence and *divergence which are associated with their troughs assist in the development of the migratory, eastward-moving depressions and anticyclones which characterize the mid-latitudes. Waves in the low-level trade winds are generally associated with *baroclinicity, intense *thunderstorms, and *tropical revolving storms. On a more local scale, lee waves develop downwind of mountains and other high ground as a result of the disturbed airflow. They are similar in form and occurrence to the stationary ripples which develop downstream of boulders which are submerged in a shallow stream. If the air contains enough moisture for condensation to occur as it ascends from the troughs to the crests of these waves, strings of smooth, lens-shaped clouds often develop which make visible the wavelength of the waves.

**wave, electromagnetic**    *electromagnetic radiation.

**wave, wind** (in oceanography), an oscillation of the sea caused by the frictional drag of wind on its surface. Waves travel in the direction of the wind, but the water particles themselves move in roughly circular paths—they rise up on the crest, advance, descend, and retreat in the trough as the wave passes. When a wind first arises, ripples (cat's-paws) appear. They develop with the strength of the wind and the *fetch, reaching heights of 2–3 m (7–10 feet) in a moderately rough sea and speeds of 13 km/h (8 m.p.h.) before the crests break into white-caps. A storm wave can be 1 km (0.62 miles) long, 10–13 m (35–45 feet) from trough to crest, and can travel at 35 km (nearly 25 miles) an hour. Near a coast the vertical circular motion of water particles is impeded by the sloping shore. The wave, flattened to an ellipse, slows down; the crest piles up and breaks. White-caps off-shore mean that waves are breaking there, and probably eroding the sea floor. Those which break into surf on the beach remove clay and sand by *backwash. All are powerful agents in shaping the coastline.

Wind waves have *wavelengths of metres to kilometres: less well understood are much larger scale waves, with wavelengths of hundreds of kilometres, which can affect the surface currents and the structure of the upper oceans. *Rossby waves are an example of these so-called 'long-waves'.

**wave erosion**, the destruction or wearing away of the coastline and the removal of loose debris by the action of waves. The erosion can be due both to the force of the waves themselves as they pound on the shore and to the abrasion caused by the fragments of rock and sand particles carried away. The force exerted by a large wave on an exposed coast is nearly ten tonnes per square metre (one ton per square foot), and may be three times as great during storms.

This aerial view of coast and sea shows very clearly the phenomenon of **wave refraction**: on the left, the wave crests are nearly parallel to the shore; on the right, where the direction of the shoreline changes abruptly, the waves 'bend', tending to become parallel to the new direction of the shore.

Sandy and soft chalk cliffs can be torn away at a rate of 2 m (7 feet) a year, the material being deposited elsewhere along the coast. A wide beach is the best protection against such erosion, and a *shore platform is often the result of it.

**wavefunction** (in physics). A wavefunction provides a mathematical description of the behaviour of a particle which has wave properties. In physics the wavefunction for any particle is called psi, and it can be found from the *Schrodinger equation. The value of the wavefunction associated with a particle at a particular point in space and time is related to the probability of finding the particle there.

**wavelength**, the distance between equivalent points on adjoining waves in a series—between the crests on water waves for example, or the points of maximum compression in sound waves. Sound waves range in wavelength from several metres to one or two centimetres. Electromagnetic waves have the widest range of all, with wavelengths from several kilometres for some radio waves down to less than $10^{-10}$ metre for gamma radiation. They include visible light, with wavelengths between about $7 \times 10^{-7}$ metre (red light) and $4 \times 10^{-7}$ metre (violet light). Wavelength is linked to the speed of waves and their *frequency (number of waves per second) by the equation: speed = frequency × wavelength. For waves of a given speed, the higher the frequency, the shorter their length.

**wave mechanics**    *quantum mechanics.

**wave–particle duality**, one of the paradoxes of modern physics. Electromagnetic radiation such as light seems to be a wave because it exhibits the phenomena of *diffraction and *interference, and these can be explained only on the basis of a wave model. However, the *photoelectric effect suggests that light also has a particle nature and that its energy is concentrated in small packets or quanta. Conversely, electrons, which seem to be small particles, also show some wave character because they can be diffracted. Such matter waves are called *de Broglie waves. This wave–particle duality has been incorporated into the theory of *wave mechanics.

**wave power**, power extracted from the ocean waves, usually for the generation of electricity. In the open ocean, waves a few metres high carry several kilowatts of power for each metre of their width. The first proposal for extracting this power, in 1799, envisaged a huge lever pivoted on the shore and with one end on a pontoon. A century later, the first practical device used the oscillating water in a cliff-face borehole to compress air, which drove a small turbo-generator. This principle is used in the automatic buoys developed in Japan in the 1950s, generating the 100 W neded for a navigation light. In recent years other countries have also investigated systems based on osillating water columns. Some devices have reached outputs of a few kilowatts, but none is yet economically and technically proven on a large scale. Other types of system studied in the late 1970s, mainly in the UK, included hinged rafts, compressible air-bags, and a chain of cam-shaped rocking dvices. While work continues on small-scale systems, it is unlikely that wave power could make a major contribution to world energy needs until well into the 21st century.

**wave refraction** (in oceanography), the tendency of wave crests to turn from their original direction and become more parallel to the shore as they move into shallower water. It results from the fact that waves travel more slowly as the water gets shallower. Along an indented coast it tends to concentrate wave attack on the headlands and eventually leads to a straightening of the coastline.

**weak force**. The weak force is one of the four fundamental *forces of nature and is approximately $10^{10}$ times weaker than the *electromagnetic interaction. It occurs between *leptons, in the decay of *hadrons, and is also responsible for the beta decay of particles and nuclei. (See also *interactions.)

**weather**, the set of atmospheric conditions prevailing at a particular time and place (whereas *climate describes 'average' conditions over a much longer term). It is the combination, experienced locally, of heat or cold, wind or calm, clear skies or cloudiness, high or low pressure, and the electrical state of the atmosphere. In meteorology it is expressed in terms of air temperature and pressure, wind speed and direction, visibility, relative humidity, cloud cover, and precipitation. These elements add up to weather which is fine, fair, bad, or foul, whether or not it is typical or seasonable. In most parts of the world definite patterns exist. They may recur on a daily basis (as in equatorial regions), seasonally (as in the subtropics), or over a period of about a week (as in the mid-latitudes, where the movement of short-lived *depressions and of *anticyclones controls most weather conditions).

**weathering**, the process by which the physical or chemical character of materials on or just below the Earth's surface is altered while remaining stationary. It is the first stage in *denudation. Weather is not the only agent responsible, for plants and animals can also play a part; but rain, wind, and changes in temperature are the major factors. The processes are physical, chemical, and biological, often acting together or leading one to another. Physical weathering is the mechanical splitting of material by mechanical or thermal stress. It may be produced by intense heating, when rocks or minerals of different colours absorb different amounts of heat and expand to different degrees. More often it results from the growth of ice or salt crystals within fine cracks, splintering and flaking rock surfaces. Rocks also expand and crack when a layer above them is eroded, removing the former pressure, and split when penetrated by plant roots. Rainwater may enter the joints and, if frozen by frost, split them further. Little physical weathering occurs without the presence of water and some chemical effect. Chemical weathering may result from the dissolving of minerals by rain. Oxidation will involve the rusting of iron in rocks. Carbon dioxide in the atmosphere and in soil makes rainwater acidic; and carbonic acid in igneous rocks such as granite rapidly hydrolyses potash feldspar to kaolin clay, disintegrating the rock. It also breaks down the calcium carbonate in limestone into soluble calcium bicarbonate, producing *karst. Biological agents can act both physically and chemically. Moles, rabbits, badgers, and other animals burrow; earthworms and insects, especially termites, break up soil particles; tree roots split rocks. Roots draw chemicals from the soil, and falling leaves and decaying plants return more complex and organic compounds to it. Animals excrete acids; they also die and decay. Humans increasingly discharge pollutants into the air and water, the effect of acid rain on bricks and stonework in cities being much the same as that on natural rock.

**Wegener, Alfred** (1880–1931), German geologist and meteorologist who developed the theory of *continental drift. He pointed out that the coastlines each side of the Atlantic would fit roughly together and that the triangular shapes of the southern continents—including Australia (with Tasmania) and India—suggested a joining of the land mass under the Antarctic ice-sheet. He died leading an expedition to Greenland to try to prove that it was still drifting eastward from North America. Ridiculed in his lifetime, his ideas were vindicated by the theory of *plate tectonics developed in the 1960s. He also made important studies of Arctic meteorological conditions.

**weight** (symbol W), the resultant force exerted on a body by the *gravitational field in which it is situated. It is a *vector quantity since it has direction, unlike *mass, and the SI unit of weight is the newton. Weight is mass times acceleration due to gravity. It decreases with height above the Earth's surface; but nowhere in the universe is unaffected by some gravitational field, and the term 'weightless' is, strictly, a misnomer. However, the effect of weightlessness occurs with a body that falls freely, such as a parachutist before he opens his parachute or an astronaut in an orbiting spacecraft. (See also *terminal velocity.)

**well, natural**, a fissure or hole in the Earth's crust which leads to an *aquifer, a natural supply of underground water. The level of the water within a well will fluctuate according to the height of the *water-table in the region.

**Werner, Abraham Gottlob** (1750–1817), German geologist who was the first to classify minerals systematically and one of the first to attempt to establish a universal stratigraphic sequence. He was renowned internationally as a teacher and as a chronicler of rock formations. Although his theory of 'neptunism', which held that the world was once all ocean from which the rock now on dry land was successively precipitated, was invalid, the controversy that it stimulated prompted a rapid increase in geological research.

**Werner, Alfred** (1866–1919), French-born Swiss chemist, who demonstrated that stereochemistry was not just the property of carbon compounds, but was general to the whole of organic and inorganic chemistry. In 1893 he announced the theory of 'co-ordinating compounds' which had come to him in a flash of inspiration and in which he proposed two types of valency bonds. This theory, which gave fresh insight into the structure of chemical compounds, is fundamental not only to modern inorganic chemistry but also to the analytical, organic, physical, and biochemical fields, and the related ones of mineralogy and crystallography. In 1913 he became the first Swiss to be awarded the Nobel Prize for Chemistry.

**Weser**, a navigable river of the North European Plain. Formed by the confluence of the Fulda and Werra Rivers in central Germany, it flows north 440 km (273 miles) to the North Sea. Its chief tributary is the Aller. The valley floor is a flat, marshy floodplain of heavy clay over which tides once ebbed and flowed, except at the port of Bremen, in Germany, where it narrows and is bordered by higher and drier, steep bluffs of sand and gravel.

**westerlies**, winds which blow from the west towards the east. In mid-latitudes, between 35° and 60° N. and S. of the Equator, there are strong but variable planetary winds which originate on the poleward sides of the *subtropical highs and encircle the globe. Those in the northern hemisphere are disrupted by seasonal variations in pressure and by the relief of the Eurasian and North American land masses; those in the southern hemisphere are stronger (they are called the *Roaring Forties) and rather more constant. Aloft, in the *circumpolar vortex, there is also variability. In particular, between 35° and 55° N. the westerly airflow is strongest when the troposphere is dominated by the rapid eastward movement of migratory high- and low-pressure systems. In the equatorial zone, westerlies occur with the seasonal displacement of the *intertropical convergence zone, when *trade winds from the opposite hemisphere cross the Equator and are deflected by the *Coriolis force.

**Western Australia**, a state of Australia comprising all that part of the continent which is west of longitude 129° E. It measures some 1,600 km (1,000 miles) from the junction of its boundary with Northern Territory and South Australia to Shark Bay on its Indian Ocean coast. In the monsoonal north, Kimberley is a hot, rugged region of eroded uplands surrounded by grassy valleys and drained by the Drysdale and Ord Rivers into the Timor Sea; Dampier Land to its west is lower and has pasture drained by the Fitzroy River. The centre comprises three immense deserts: the Great Sandy, Gibson, and Great Victoria; these and Nullarbor Plain in the south are the only regions which offer no grazing for sheep. Elsewhere the climate is very warm to hot and the rainfall just adequate for stock-raising. The plateaux of eroded mountains in the west, such as the Hamersley Range, have seasonal rivers, and there are many seasonal lakes on the interior tableland of *granite and *gneiss in the south-west. Swanland in the extreme south-west has a Mediterranean climate: here there are forests of eucalypt, good streams, and much land for cultivation. There are large deposits of a wide range of minerals, notably gold, iron, and coal, throughout the territory.

**Western Samoa**, a country consisting of a group of nine islands in the south-west Pacific, which forms part of the Samoan archipelago. Its two major islands, Upolu and Savai'i are both volcanic and are fringed by coral reefs. The islands have tall, evergreen rain forests and swamps, with sixteen species of bird that are unique to the area.

**West Indies**   *Caribbean Islands, *Bahamas.

**Wheatstone, Sir Charles** (1802–75), British physicist and pioneer of electric telegraphy. From 1834 he was Professor of Experimental Physics at King's College, London, where his research included work on the velocity of light. In 1837 he patented an electric telegraph, and in 1843 he invented the Wheatstone bridge, a device for measuring electrical resistance. He also developed an interest in acoustics and binocular vision.

**whirlpool**, a fierce, almost circular eddy of water in rivers or the sea usually occurring when fast flows of water from different directions meet. In rivers, whirlpools can form in the plunge-pool at the foot of waterfalls, or where tributary channels meet the main flow. In the sea, they occur in narrow channels, where winds and tides are moving in different directions, or where strong currents meet each other.

**whirlwind**, a revolving column of air which arises in conditions of atmospheric instability. On land the larger whirl-

A **whirlpool** at the foot of a cliff where the tide surges out through a tunnel in the rock, at Aber Foel Fawr, Ramsey Island, Wales, UK.

winds are usually called *tornadoes and on lakes or at sea *waterspouts. When they occur in deserts, the sand and other rock particles which are lifted by the updraught can be carried many miles. Smaller eddies are also sometimes seen when the surface is very hot.

**Whitehead, Alfred North** (1861–1947), British mathematician and philosopher who wrote many popular books on a wide range of academic topics. His interests and activities included politics, the foundations of science, and the philosophies of both religion and education. In 1910 he published with his pupil Bertrand Russell (1872–1970) the first volume of *Principia Mathematica*, an attempt (inspired by developments in the late 19th century) to show how the whole of mathematics might be obtained from a few logical postulates and the concept of a set. His philosophy of nature was expounded in two later books (1919 and 1920), which put forward the doctrine that events are the ultimate components of reality.

**White Mountains**, two mountain ranges in the USA. (1) An outlier of the Sierra Nevada standing near the eastern boundary of California, with a highest peak at 4,340 m (14,242 feet). (2) The Appalachian group in eastern New Hampshire, with Mount Washington at 1,917 m (6,288 feet) in the Presidential Range. Although relatively low, this mountain is swept by fierce gales and is subject to extremely low temperatures. The whole range is heavily eroded by glaciers, as are the neighbouring Franconia Mountains. Together they contain granite gorges, *cirques, forests, and streams.

**white-out**   *blizzard.

**White Sea**, a nearly enclosed branch of the Barents Sea off the northern shore of European Russia. Generally less than 300 m (1,000 feet) deep, it lies in a depressed part of the *Baltic Shield, and was occupied by an ice-sheet during the last ice age. It is outside the reach of the warming influence of Atlantic water, and so ice tends to form by October or November, persisting until May or June; it is ice-covered for more than 200 days each year.

**Whitney, Mount**, a peak in the Sierra Nevada, California, USA. At 4,418 m (14,494 feet) it is the highest mountain in the USA outside Alaska. It consists of granite and stands at the eastern edge of the Sequoia National Park. Its rugged scenery is largely a result of glacial *erosion, which has produced deep recesses in its flanks, knife-edged ridges, and impressive valleys. Its eastern slopes are perhaps the most dramatic, rising steeply for over 3,400 m (11,000 feet) from Owen's Valley.

**Whymper, Edward** (1840–1911), British artist and pioneer of modern mountaineering. He was the first man to climb (in 1865) the Swiss Matterhorn, which he accomplished at his eighth attempt and with the loss of four of his party. In 1880 he ascended, in Ecuador, Mounts Chimborazo (6,267 m, 20,561 feet) and Cotopaxi (5,897 m, 19,347 feet), the world's highest continually active volcano. By the time of his death in 1911, mountain climbing had become a distinguished sport.

**Wilkes, Charles** (1798–1877), US naval officer and explorer who commanded an expedition which set sail in 1838 to survey the southern seas. First he visited Samoa in the Pacific and then he sailed south, passing for 2,400 km (1,500 miles) along the coast of Wilkes Land on what he named the Antarctic Continent.

Charles **Wilkes** entered the navy as a midshipman in 1818 and twenty years later led the first scientific expedition for the United States government. His surveying expeditions took him from the Antarctic Ocean through the Pacific, to sail completely around the world in four years (1838-42).

**Wilkins, Sir (George) Hubert** (1888–1958), Australian polar explorer who flew 3,400 km (over 2,100 miles) across the Arctic, from Alaska to Spitsbergen, in 1928. He returned there in 1931, this time trying to reach the North Pole by submarine. In 1933–9 he managed the *Ellsworth Antarctic expeditions, and in World War II he was Arctic adviser to the US Army. After his death his ashes were scattered at the North Pole.

**Willstatter, Richard** (1872-1942), German chemist who developed a method for separating chemicals, now called *chromatography. He succeeded in showing that green plants contain two chlorophyll pigments by passing a solution of chlorophyll through a column containing chalk. He received the 1915 Nobel Prize for Chemistry for this work. It is also recognized that the Russian botanist Mikhail Tswett worked independently on identifying the constituents of chlorophyll and developed similar analytical techniques.

**Wilson, Charles Thomson Rees** (1869–1959), British physicist of Scottish extraction who invented the cloud chamber—a device which reveals the tracks of charged particles by radioactive atoms. The particles pass through a cold vapour, leaving trails similar to those seen behind high-flying aircraft. He shared the Nobel Prize for Physics in 1927 with Arthur *Compton.

**wind**, air in natural motion. It is produced around the Earth by differences in atmospheric *pressure from one place to another, called pressure gradients. On a global scale, however, it never blows directly from an area of high pressure to one of low pressure, but is deflected by the *Coriolis force. Planetary winds change direction: winds blowing polewards from subtropical highs become *westerlies, while those blowing towards the Equator become the easterly *trade winds. Those high in the atmosphere, which are determined solely by the pressure gradient and Coriolis force, are called geostrophic winds. Nearer the ground, the airflow pattern is more complicated, being influenced not only by local heating and cooling (and therefore by changing pressure gradients) but also by the distribution of land and sea and variations in land relief. The secondary wind systems which result include those of the *monsoons, the winds of various strengths associated with anticyclones and depressions, the sea–land and land–sea *breezes, and those such as the *chinook which arise as a consequence of particular landforms. Local winds on land or sea are classified as breezes, gales, and hurricanes in the *Beaufort scale. Often they pursue a circular path, as in *tropical revolving storms. Winds may be dry or rain-bearing. They also carry dust in suspension, which makes them agents of *erosion.

**wind power**, electric power generated by wind machines. These have the advantage of being relatively safe and a pollution-free method of providing power. The number of wind machines required to produce significant power, however, makes them a noticeable feature on the landscape as they are best placed along coasts and on hilltops where the wind is strongest and most consistent. Alternative locations, such as out at sea, may provide the solution: the winds are stronger and steadier, and larger more productive machines may be constructed without fear of altering existing natural features. It is estimated that wind machines could satisfy up to one fifth of the demand for electric power in many countries, but in the 1990s the maximum was one per cent in Denmark.

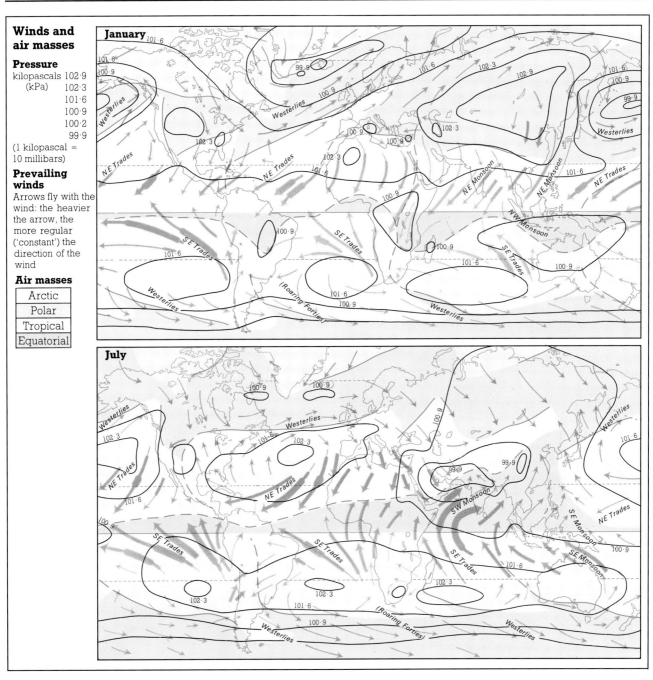

### Winds and air masses

**Pressure**

kilopascals 102·9
(kPa) 102·3
101·6
100·9
100·2
99·9

(1 kilopascal = 10 millibars)

**Prevailing winds**

Arrows fly with the wind: the heavier the arrow, the more regular ('constant') the direction of the wind

**Air masses**

| Arctic |
| Polar |
| Tropical |
| Equatorial |

**Wind Cave**, a limestone cavern in Wind Cave National Park in the Black Hills of South Dakota, USA. So named because of the strong air currents that blow alternately in and out of it, according to relative pressure. It comprises over 16 km (10 miles) of passageways which contain many curious formations of calcite. Above ground is unspoilt prairie over which deer and buffalo still roam.

**wind erosion**   *deflation.

**wind-gap**, a *dry valley cutting through ridges or through ranges of hills. Wind-gaps are *water-gaps without rivers, although they were originally cut by river channels. Their formation occurs in two stages: first the channel is cut through the ridge; then the river disappears. However, the method of formation may vary. The first process usually happens when drainage is gradually superimposed on rocks of different resistances from an overlying, uniform layer as the whole land surface is lowered. Alternatively, rivers in areas of low relief may have hills uplifted across their valleys, but continue to cut through them as antecedent drainage. Then a change in climate may reduce river flow; or, in limestone, channels may cut underground courses. Alternatively a plain may be uplifted and new, steep valleys cut into it, dismembering the drainage and leaving dry channels on the ridges. Or the tributaries of a river with a steep course may cut back through its divide and 'capture' part of the drainage of a neighbouring basin. Where the captured flow changes direction—the 'elbow of capture'—a wind-gap will be left above the new, shrunken headwaters.

**Windward Islands**   *Caribbean Islands.

**Winnipeg, Lake**, in Manitoba, Canada, a remnant of the glacial Lake Agassiz which, at the end of the *Pleistocene Epoch, covered much of southern Canada and northern

The German chemist Friedrich **Wöhler**. He was Professor of Chemistry at the University of Göttingen for over 40 years, during which time the University's School of Chemistry gained an international reputation.

USA. After the ice melted, most of the water drained across the *Canadian Shield into Hudson Bay. The present lake is 425 km (264 miles) long and 109 km (68 miles) from west to east at its widest point. It receives water from Lakes Cedar, Winnipegosis, and Manitoba and is drained north-eastward to Hudson Bay by the Nelson River. Its shores are well forested, as are its islands, and it is full of fish.

**Witwatersrand** (Afrikaans, 'ridge of white waters'), or Rand, a series of parallel ridges in southern Transvaal, South Africa, containing the *watershed that divides the tributaries of the Limpopo River from those of the Vaal River. They rise to some 1,800 m (6,000 feet) and extend west–east for over 100 km (60 miles) across the high *veld. They are famous for the gold reefs they contain at depths of up to 3,000 m (10,000 feet) underground. Coal and manganese are also found.

**Wöhler, Friedrich** (1800–82), German chemist who succeeded in preparing urea, $CO(NH_2)_2$, from ammonium cyanate. Historically this was important since it represented the first laboratory synthesis of a naturally occurring compound. His collaboration with *Liebig led to the idea of the *functional group. He also isolated aluminium and beryllium and discovered calcium carbide, from which he obtained ethyne (acetylene).

**wold**, a belt of upland country, developed on chalk or limestone. Chalk wolds extend for some 120 km (75 miles) in eastern England and are divided by the Humber estuary. To its south the Lincolnshire Wolds form a rolling upland that has

been dissected by rivers to give the impression of alternating ridges and valleys: North of the Humber the Yorkshire Wolds present a similar scenery of undulating hills and deeply incised valleys. In the west of England are the limestone Cotswolds.

**wolfram**, a tungstate mineral and the principal ore of tungsten. It has the chemical formula $(Fe, Mn)WO_4$. Correctly known as wolframite, it is found in *pegmatite and other veins as tabular crystals or in red-brown masses.

**work** (in physics), the process of a transfer of *energy. As with all forms of energy, the *SI unit of work is the joule. Work is the scalar product of the force and displacement vectors. The work done by a force is the product of that force and the distance over which it is applied in the direction in which it acts. One joule of work is done when one newton is applied over one metre.

**Wurtz, Charles–Adolphe** (1817–84), French chemist noted for his research on organic nitrogen compounds, hydrocarbons, and glycols. He developed a method for preparing aliphatic hydrocarbons by the reaction of an ethereal solution of a halocarbon with sodium. Together with Marcellin *Berthelot he succeeded in making the Sorbonne one of Europe's leading centres of tuition in chemistry.

**Wyandotte Cave**, a group of caverns and passages in southern Indiana, USA. It has been eroded in thick, horizontally bedded limestone and displays many dramatic features. These include the Grand Cathedral, a cavern nearly 0.5 km (0.25 miles) in circumference, and a giant limestone pillar nearly 20 m (70 feet) round in a cave called the Senate Chamber.

The French chemist Charles Adolphe **Wurtz**. In addition to his experimental work, Wurtz made a valuable contribution to theoretical chemistry by working out the atomic arrangements of organic compounds.

# X

**xenolith**, a piece of 'foreign' rock that is enclosed in a body of *igneous rock. Xenoliths are often fragments of country rock that have been broken off the walls of an igneous intrusion; they may also be fragments of igneous rock that solidified earlier. Once caught up in the *magma, they may be assimilated into it by melting or chemical reaction.

**xenon** (symbol Xe, at. no. 54, r.a.m. 131.30), one of the *noble gases, discovered in 1898 as a result of the fractional distillation of liquid air. It constitutes one part in twenty million of the atmosphere. Formerly xenon was thought to be totally inert, but various xenon compounds have now been prepared, particularly with fluorine, for example $XeF_2$ and $XeF_4$. Commercially xenon is obtained from liquid air; it is used in special lamps and discharge tubes and in the control of nuclear *fission chain reactions.

**Xi Jiang** (also spelt Si Kiang, English, 'West River'), the southernmost of China's three great rivers. It rises on the plateau of Yunnan and flows through the basin of the same name to its delta on the coast of the South China Sea. The plateaux of southern China separate the Xi Jiang basin from that of the Yangtze to the north.

**Xinjiang** (Sinkiang), a vast region in the west of China, bounded by Kazakhstan on the west, Kashmir and Tibet on the south, and Mongolia on the north-east. It is divided laterally by the Tian Shan range into two great basins. Dzungaria in the north is the deeper. It contains sand deserts and marshes but also considerable grazing land. The Tarim Basin in the south is like a giant saucer, rimmed by the Tian Shan, the Pamirs, and the Kunlun Shan. It is a region of internal drainage, the Tarim River looping round its northern side. The whole centre is occupied by the sandy Taklamakan desert. At the eastern end of the Tian Shan is a third major basin, the Turfan Depression, whose lowest point is 154 m (505 feet) below sea-level. Rainfall is light everywhere, and temperatures are extreme. Meltwater from the mountains permits cultivation, however, and there are numerous oases. There are oilfields and reserves of uranium and many other minerals, together with a great salt lake, Lop Nor.

**X-rays**, a form of *electromagnetic radiation with a much greater energy than light because of their shorter wavelengths ($10^{-9}$ to $10^{-11}$ m). Only extremely hot sources such as some stars emit them naturally, and any which reach the Earth's atmosphere are generally absorbed in it. They arise from electronic rearrangements in the inner *electron shells of atoms. Their powers of penetration, however, are great. Produced by allowing a beam of high-energy electrons to strike a metal target (for example, copper) inside an evacuated tube, they can penetrate some distance into most materials and have many uses. They can be directed into flesh in order to destroy diseased cells; X-ray photographs show up bones, and the relative opacity of other parts of the body. They can be used also to examine the structure of a crystal, in a process known as X-ray diffraction. This uses *Bragg reflection to investigate the structure of crystals. The wavelength of X-rays is roughly the same as the distance between the atoms in crystals. X-rays which pass through a

A plateau in the Pamir mountains of **Xinjiang**. These windswept grasslands provide pasture for the goats, horses, and camels of the Kirghiz nomads; the walled enclosure in the foreground is a goat fold.

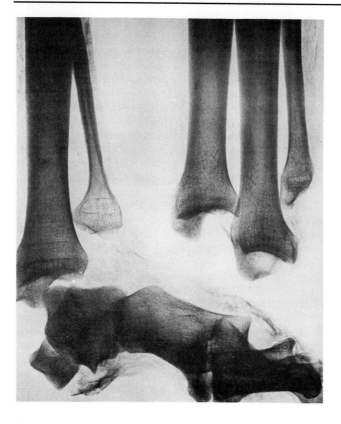

Revealing the shape and disposition of concealed bones, this **X-ray** photograph of the legs of an Egyptian mummy, taken in 1898, indicated clearly the potential of X-rays for use in medical diagnosis.

crystal at a certain angle (the Bragg angle) are diffracted by the crystal, and emerge to give a pattern which is characteristic of the crystal, and which can be analysed to give information about the arrangement of atoms within the crystal. The technique has been used to identify and determine the structure of many materials, including DNA. X-rays were discovered in Germany (1895) by Wilhelm *Röntgen.

**Yangtze Kiang** (Chang Jiang), China's longest river and at some 5,500 km (3,400 miles) the third single longest in the world, excluding tributaries. It rises on the north face of the Tanglha Range in Tibet and runs turbulently east and then south, carving gigantic gorges in the Plateau of Tibet. Known in these upper reaches as the Jinsha, it now cuts a zigzag course north-east through forested foothills to the basin of Sichuan. Here it is joined by four tributaries and becomes a major source of hydroelectric power. Hemmed in again by mountains, it has forced an eastward channel through the spectacular Yangtze Gorges and so spills into its middle basin, at last becoming navigable for ocean-going ships. This is a region of great lakes which serve as overflow reservoirs during the summer rainy season. The quantity of sediment carried here and to the lower basin is enormous: the river is muddy, shallow, and sluggish, and its banks are chequered with paddy-fields. It enters the East China Sea through two channels in a long and ever-growing delta.

**Yazoo stream**, named after the Yazoo River in the Mississippi valley, USA, which runs for a long distance almost parallel to the main river before joining it. Such cases are common on wide floodplains, where there is little obvious slope towards the main channel, and especially if the main river is flowing between raised *levees. A modified form can occur if a valley floor is slightly tilted, producing whole sets of sub-parallel tributaries which meet the main stream at acute angles; this *drainage pattern is described as 'pinnate', meaning feathered.

**Yellow River** *Huang He.

**Yellow Sea** (Chinese, Huang Hai), a north-western arm of the Pacific Ocean, so named from the colour of the silt carried into it by the Huang He (Chinese, 'yellow') River and others. Set on the East Asian continental shelf, between China and the Korean peninsula, it has a mean depth of less than 150 m (500 feet). The coastline is low, the eastern coast being fringed by innumerable small islands.

**Yellowstone National Park**, in Idaho and Montana but, mainly, in Wyoming, USA, a vast, volcanic plateau and mountain region standing some 2,400 m (8,000 feet) above sea-level among the Rocky Mountains. Established in 1872 as the nation's first *national park, it contains peaks rising to over 3,400 m (11,000 feet), evergreen and petrified forests, eroded lava flows, a black obsidian (volcanic glass) mountain, and the most scenic stretch of the Yellowstone River with its great lake, waterfalls, and 30-km (20-mile) long canyon. Volcanic activity is seen in thousands of hot springs and hundreds of *geysers, among which Old Faithful gushes every hour or so.

**Yemen**, a country in the south of the peninsula of Arabia, bordering on Saudi Arabia and Oman on the north. Behind the western, Red Sea, coast are high mountains. Here light summer rains provide for the growth of cotton and coffee; and camels, goats, and sheep graze on coarse grass high in the hills. There are reserves of oil. The lower-lying eastern part has a coast on the Gulf of Aden. Here it is very arid, mostly hot desert, though these are areas where cotton can be grown.

**Yenisei**, a great river of Siberia, about 3,860 km (2,400 miles) long. It is formed by the union of two headstreams which rise in the mountains bounding Mongolia, and flows turbulently down to the west Siberian plain over many rapids, providing much hydroelectric potential. Heading northward in its own considerable valley along the eastern edge of the plain, it is joined on its right bank by three major tributaries from the central Siberian plateau and becomes liable to flood, particularly in spring, when ice on the upper reaches melts earlier than that on the lower river. In summer it is navigable throughout its length and provides much timber from its forested banks. It enters the Arctic Ocean through an estuary some 400 km (250 miles) long.

**Yoho National Park** (Cree, *yoho*, 'wonder'), an area in south-west Canada, on the border between British Columbia and Alberta. It lies on the western slope of the Canadian Rocky Mountains, and its 1,313 km² (507 sq. mi.) occupy most of the drainage basin of Kicking Horse River. The Cree Indian name accurately describes the impression given by the Park's scenery: peaks over 3,000 m (10,000 feet) high, glaciers, lakes, valleys, and waterfalls such as the Takkakaw, which drops 380 m (1,248 feet).

**Yosemite National Park**, an area in central California, USA, in the Sierra Nevada, containing some spectacular features. The Yosemite valley, a U-shaped canyon with precipitous sides, is 11 km (7 miles) long and set at an altitude of about 1,200 m (4,000 feet). Overlooking it are pinnacles and peaks rising to another 1,460 m (4,800 feet). Elsewhere are Mounts Lyell and Dana, both with summits at over 3,900 m (13,000 feet), and the world's three largest granite buttresses or domes. The waterfalls are best seen in late spring, when gushing with melted snow. The Yosemite Falls with a total drop of 739 m (2,425 feet) are the highest in North America. The lakes too are beautiful, as are the flowering meadows and the sequoia (or redwood) groves. A road 3.3 m (11 feet) wide was driven through the Wawona or Tunnel Tree.

**Young, Thomas** (1773–1829), English physician and physicist who demonstrated that *light is a form of wave motion. His early researches were into the nature of sight and led him to propose a theory of colour vision based on the assumption that the eye can detect three basic colours (blue, green, and red) only. In essence, the theory stands today. In 1801, using two slits illuminated by sunlight, he demonstrated the *interference of light—an effect in which waves from different sources reinforce and cancel one another to form a series of bright and dark bands, called fringes, which may be seen on a screen. At the time of the experiment scientists were unsure of the nature of light. However, interference was known to be a property of waves,

Cathedral Spires, **Yosemite National Park**, one of a dozen isolated peaks in the park that rise over 900 m (3,000 feet.) above the valley floor.

and Young's demonstration that light rays interfered showed that the rays must be waves.

**yttrium** (symbol Y, at. no. 39, r.a.m. 88.91), a metallic element, the *lanthanides. Analysis of lunar rock from the Apollo 11 mission has shown an unusually high yttrium content. It is used in making europium phosphors, which give the red colour in television tubes.

**Yukawa, Hideki** (1907–81), Japanese physicist who received the 1949 Nobel Prize in Physics for predicting the existence of the *meson. He was professor of physics at Kyoto University, 1939 to 1970, where he developed his theories of forces in elementary particles.

**Yucatán**, a peninsula about 320 km (200 miles) wide that projects north-eastward from Central America for some 640 km (400 miles) between the Gulf of Mexico and the Caribbean Sea. Its northern part is a low, stony plain that shows signs of past changes in sea-level, while the land gently rises southward to about 150 m (500 feet). In places the surface is swampy and covered with jungle. The underlying limestone has been attacked by *weathering to form rounded pits called 'cenotes'.

**Yugoslavia** *Bosnia-Herzegovina, *Croatia, *Macedonia, *Montenegro, *Serbia, *Slovenia.

**Yukon**, one of the longest rivers in North America, rising in the Coast Mountains, south Yukon Territory, Canada, and draining into the Bering Sea. It passes through some striking landscapes over its course of some 2,900 km (1,800 miles). Its upper section runs through gorges and deeply incised valleys, now partly drowned by the building of a dam south of Whitehorse. It then follows a deep terraced valley through the Yukon Plateau, before winding across the swampy flats of central Alaska, USA; here it is sometimes 50 km (30 miles) wide. On the way to its swampy delta the stream swings in great *meanders, travelling perhaps 65 km (40 miles) to advance 16 km (10 miles). The river is navigable from Whitehorse, but only from June to September, owing to ice.

**Yukon Territory**, a province of north-west Canada, bounded by Alaska in the west, Northwest Territories in the east, and British Columbia in the south, and extending north to the Beaufort Sea. The northern part, much of which is within the Arctic Circle, is desolate tundra. Southward, the Mackenzie and Ogilvie mountains divide tributaries of the Mackenzie from the Yukon River, the latter flowing through the once famous region of the Klondike. Further south are numerous lakes, also ice-bound in winter, snow-covered forests, and the St Elias Mountains with Mount Logan at 6,050 m (19,850 feet). There is a wealth of minerals, notably copper, silver, zinc, lead, and some gold.

# Z

**Zagros Mountains**, a system of ranges in western Iran, extending for over 1,700 km (1,000 miles) parallel to the valley of the Euphrates and the Gulf. In the north-west they are forested and snow-capped; in the centre they rise to 4,547 m (14,918 feet) at Zardeh Kuh and contain oilfields in their western foothills; and in the south-east they become irregular plateaux of rock and sand. The whole region is unstable and liable to earthquakes owing to its proximity to a *plate boundary.

**Zaïre**, the largest country in equatorial Africa, bounded by nine other countries and with an outlet to the Atlantic Ocean at the mouth of the Congo, here called the Zaïre. Between the coast and the eastern mountains, annual rainfall varies from 1,000 mm (40 inches) to 1,800 mm (71 inches), while the temperature remains a fairly constant 25 °C (77 °F) except for cooler winters in the south. The Congo and its tributaries flow through the country. Thick forests cover the central districts and there is much swamp. In the south, however, are open highlands with extensive deposits of copper, uranium, radium, and zinc. Cobalt is also found in large quantities, while in the north-east there is gold. The eastern boundary runs down the Great Rift Valley and includes the western shore of Lake Tanganyika.

**Zambezi**, Africa's fourth longest river, flowing generally south-eastward in an immense S-curve for some 2,660 km (1,650 miles). It rises at an altitude of approximately 1,500 m (5,000 feet), within 5 km (3.11 miles) of a headstream of the westward-flowing Congo. Flowing south over the basaltic plateau of eastern Angola and western Zambia, it reaches Namibia at the Caprivi Strip and turns east to form the boundary between Zambia and Zimbabwe. Here it passes over the Victoria Falls and through the Kariba Gorge, providing hydroelectric power, and receives the Shangani, Kafue, Luangwa, and other tributaries. Its valley leaves the plateau and broadens; the flow becomes navigable for large ships; the Shiré River joins it from Lake Malawi, and it enters the Indian Ocean through a delta in Mozambique.

**Zambia**, a land-locked country lying on a plateau in central Africa, surrounded by Angola, Zaïre, Tanzania, Malawi, Mozambique, Zimbabwe, and Namibia (the Caprivi Strip). The Zambezi and its tributaries the Kafue and Luangwa run through it, while in the north the Chambeshi drains into swampy areas round Lake Bangweulu. These river valleys are very warm and wet; but the rolling plateaux surrounding them are high, drier, and less hot. Tobacco, maize, rice, and sugar cane can all be grown, and in the south-west there are forests of teak. One of the world's largest reserves of copper occurs in a region known as the Copperbelt, where lead and zinc are also found.

**Zanzibar**, one of two smallish islands (the other being Pemba) lying on a coral reef some 32 km (20 miles) off the East African coast and belonging to Tanzania. With a climate which is monsoonal, wet, and very warm, it is renowned for the variety of its lush flora and for its spices, especially cloves.

**Zeeman effect**, a discovery in 1896 by the Dutch physicist Pieter Zeeman (1865–1943). Analysing the light from hot sodium vapour, he found that the lines in its spectrum were split if the gas was in a strong magnetic field. According to the *quantum theory, light is emitted when an electron drops to a lower energy level in an atom. Identical energy changes in many atoms give light of the same wavelength and produce one spectral line. A magnetic field splits each line because electrons which previously had the same energy take on different energies depending on their orientation. For the discovery of this effect, Zeeman shared the 1902 Nobel Prize for Physics with Hendrik *Lorentz, who offered the theoretical explanation.

**zenith** (of the sky), the point in the heavens which is directly above an observer at a particular place and time, the opposite point (unseen below the observer) being known as the nadir. From an imaginary line extending between the nadir and the zenith, at 90° to the horizontal, the angular distance of a celestial body can be measured, this being the basis of astronomical navigation at sea.

**zeolite**, any one of a group of minerals that are aluminosilicates of sodium, potassium, calcium, and barium that occur chiefly in igneous rocks. They have a light, open-framework structure, with an overall negative charge, into which gases, water, and positive ions can diffuse. These characteristics enable them to be used as molecular sieves, by absorption of molecules of a specific size into the pores of the lattice. They can also act as ion exchangers, notably for softening hard water. Permutit is a synthetic zeolite containing sodium, the calcium ions in the water being replaced by the soluble sodium ions. The permutit is regenerated by treatment with concentrated sodium chloride solution.

**zero-point energy**, the residual energy possessed by a particle at *absolute zero, $-273.15$ °C ($-459.67$ °F). The properties of matter on an atomic scale are described by the laws of *quantum mechanics, which state that the energy of atoms and molecules can take only certain definite values. In other words, they can only exist in certain energy levels. The lowest energy level is called the ground state and all higher levels are called excited states. As the temperature of a substance is lowered, molecules in higher states fall to lower states and, finally, to the ground state. At the lowest possible temperature, namely absolute zero, all molecules would be in the ground state. For certain types of molecular motion, such as rotation, the ground state is one of no energy at all. On the other hand, chemical bonds vibrate, and the vibrational ground state involves the molecules retaining a small residual energy. This is the zero-point energy.

**Zimbabwe**, a land-locked country in southern Africa. It is surrounded by Zambia, Mozambique, South Africa, and Botswana. On the north-west boundary with Zambia are the Victoria Falls and Lake Kariba on the Zambezi, and on the boundary with South Africa is the Limpopo. The country stands mainly on a plateau drained by tributaries of these and other rivers. The height of the plateau modifies the heat; cattle thrive, and wheat, tobacco, and cotton can all be grown. There is coal in the west, while chromium, asbestos, gold, and other minerals are found elsewhere.

**zinc** (symbol Zn, at. no. 30, r.a.m. 65.38), one of the most widely used *transition metals. Many centuries before it was recognized as a distinct element, its ores were employed for making brass. The principal ores are zinc blende, $ZnS$, smithsonite, $ZnCO_3$, and hemimorphite, $ZnSiO_4 \cdot H_2O$; and it is extracted by roasting the ore and reducing the oxide, $ZnO$, with carbon. The metal is bluish-white, fairly hard, and brittle. It burns in air and reacts with the halogens and with sulphur. Zinc is an essential element in the growth of human beings and animals. Although it is non-toxic, inhalation of freshly prepared zinc oxide produces a disorder known as 'zinc chills'. This gives rise to flu-like symptoms but there are no known long term damaging effectss. The metal is used extensively to galvanize other metals, to prevent corrosion by coating the metal with a layer of zinc; and it forms many useful alloys such as brass and solder.

**zinc oxide** (or flowers of zinc, $ZnO$), a white powder obtained by roasting zinc or zinc blende. It is used as a pigment in paints, as a filler in plastics and rubber, and in zinc ointment and cosmetics.

**zinc sulphate** ($ZnSO_4$), once known as white vitriol, a white crystalline compound made by dissolving the metal in sulphuric acid and allowing the resulting solution to evaporate. It is used in the manufacture of agricultural sprays.

**zinc sulphide** ($ZnS$), a compound which occurs naturally as the ore zinc blende (sphalerite) from which zinc is extracted. The most important deposits occur in Belgium, New South Wales, Australia, and the USA. It is used extensively in the white pigment lithopone, a mixture of zinc sulphide and barium sulphate. It is phosphorescent and is used in making fluorescent tubes, luminous paints, and television screens.

**Zion National Park**, an area in south-west Utah, USA, famous for its deep canyons, *mesas and high, coloured cliffs. Zion Canyon itself, cut by the Virgin River, is 24 km (15 miles) long and 1 km (0.6 miles) deep. It contains rocks of many hues, and gigantic formations such as the Watchman at the south entrance rise from its floor.

**zircon** ($ZrSiO_4$, zirconium silicate), a mineral that commonly occurs in very small amounts in igneous, sedimen-

Black cubic crystals of **zinc** blende (sphalerite), one of the main ores of this metal.

The Wieringermeer Polder was the first section of the **Zuider Zee** to be reclaimed, in 1927. Today it is a rich agricultural area. The photograph shows the mosaic of fields intersected by dikes, with the Lely pumping station in the foreground.

tary, and metamorphic rock. Very hard and with a high refractive index, its transparent varieties are used as gems.

**zirconium** (symbol Zr, at. no. 40, r.a.m. 91.22), a grey, steel-like *transition metal. It is found in acid igneous rocks. When purified from hafnium, its low absorption of neutrons, its corrosion-resistance, and its retention of strength at high temperatures makes it useful for the construction of nuclear reactors. It is also used as a lining for jet engines.

**zonal soil**, a soil whose characteristics are primarily determined by such active factors of soil formation as climate and vegetation, operating over long periods of time, rather than by the passive influences of parent material and relief. Zonal soils are generally deep and well drained, and have distinctive *horizons. The distribution of different types of zonal soil parallels the global zonation of climate. From the poles to the Equator, the major zonal soils are tundra soils, podzols, chernozems, prairie soils, desert soils, and tropical latosols.

**Zoutpansberg** (Soutspansberg, Afrikaans, 'Saltpan Mountain'), a region of the northern Transvaal, South Africa. A highland zone of ancient rock, it rises above a plateau surface, from which it is separated on the north and east by fault scarps. It has been dissected by branches of the Sand River and this, together with faulting, has produced a landscape consisting of several asymmetric ridges. They extend for about 160 km (100 miles) from west to east and are crossed by deep and narrow valleys. The escarpment of one of these ridges is the Zoutpansberg proper.

**Zuiderzee**, a shallow inlet of the North Sea in The Netherlands, about 5,000 km² (2,000 sq. mi.) in extent. From about 400 AD the Fresian inhabitants built extensive dykes and *terpen* mounds to stem the high waters, creating a mixture of lowlands and freshwater lakes which lasted until the 13th century when further flooding created the Zuiderzee proper. In 1927–32 a 30-km (19-mile) long dam was built across the Zuiderzee, separating it into the outer Waddenzee, open to the North Sea, and the inner *IJsselmeer. By the 1990s much of the IJsselmeer had been reclaimed for agriculture, and its waters become fresh.

**zwitterion** (in chemistry), an electrically neutral *ion that carries both a positive and a negative charge. Zwitterions occur when a compound contains both an acidic and a basic group. Amino acids under normal conditions exist almost entirely in this state; the positive and negative groups are equally ionized. For example, the amino acid glycine exists as the zwitterion $^+H_3N \cdot CH_2 \cdot COO^-$.

# Acknowledgements

## Photographs

Abbreviations: *t* = top; *b* = bottom; *c* = centre; *l* = left; *r* = right

Aerocamera–Bart Hofmeester Rotterdam, 374.

Aerofilms, 242.

Bryan & Cherry Alexander Photography, 284.

All-Sport / Tony Duffy, 56*bl*.

Heather Angel, 66*t*, 112, 324, 327, 330.

Ardea London, 229, 234; Ardea London / Ian Beames, 371; Ardea London / John Clegg, 194*br*, 256*bl*; Ardea London / Jean-Paul Ferrero, 137, 170, 362; Ardea London / K. Fink, 213; Ardea London / P.J. Green, 11; Ardea London / Clem Haagner, 179; Ardea London / Ake Lindau, 87; Ardea London / John Mason, 93, 296; Ardea London / E. Mickleburgh, 143*t*.

Aspect Picture Library, 37.

Associated Press, 281.

BBC Hulton Picture Library, 7, 12*tr*, 74, 119, 157, 181, 189, 197, 201, 227, 236, 288, 319, 335(*both*), 355, 368(*both*).

W. A. Bentley & W. J. Humphreys, 308.

Paul Brierley, 51(*both*), 59, 61, 171, 188*bl*, 196, 203, 239, 259*tl*, 278*tr*, 313.

British Geological Survey: NERC copyright, 130, 131, 238*br*, 250, 341, 373.

Hutchison Library, 184*b*, 348; Hutchison Library / Bernard Régent, 351.

Jean-Loup Charmet, 58, 85*bl*, 233.

John Cleare / Mountain Camera, 19*tr*, 28, 32, 62, 79, 117, 141, 317, 318*bl*, 323, 331, 333, 369.

Bruce Coleman Ltd / D. Austen, 246; BCL / C. Bonnington, 356*bl*; BCL / J. Burton, 5, 47, 287*br*, 365; BCL / R. Burton, 89*l*, 149*tl*; BCL / R. P. Carr, 91; BCL / B. Coates, 26; BCL / E. Crichton, 353*tr*, BCL / G. Cubitt, 90; BCL / A. Davies, 272; BCL / A. J. Deane, 9, 66*b*; BCL / N. Devore, 192; BCL /J. Ehlers, 56*tl*; BCL / M. P. L. Fogden, 30*l*, 89*br*, 138, 293; BCL / M. Freeman, 50; BCL / C. B. Frith, 338; BCL / K. Gunnar, 48; BCL / U. Hirsch, 190; BCL / C. Hughes, 31; BCL / M. P. Kahl, 356*tr*, BCL / NASA, 273, 325; BCL / D. Overcash, 265; BCL / D. & M. Plage, 155; BCL / Dr. F. Sauer, 121; BCL / Sullivan & Rogers, 45; BCL / J. Taylor, 291; BCL / P. Ward, 96; BCL / WWF / H. Jungius, 186.

J. B. Davidson / Survival Anglia / OSF, 215.

C. M. Dixon, 241, 294, 300, 309.

Mary Evans Picture Library, 295, 366.

Explorer / Katia Krafft, 78,182, 264; Explorer / Ostman Agency, 173.

The Fotomas Index, 63, 270.

Dr Georg Gerster / The John Hillelson Agency, 292.

The Goodyear Tyre & Rubber Co Ltd, 154*tl*.

Susan Griggs Agency / Mike Andrews, 100; SGA / Paul Dix, 153; SGA / Alain le Garsmeur, 304; SGA / Anthony Howarth, 299; SGA / Dimitri Ilic, 307; SGA / Roger Werth, 289; SGA / R. Woldendorp, 76; SGA / Adam Woolfitt, 84*bl*, SGA / Ian Yeomans, 218.

Sonia Halliday Photographs / FHC Birch, 16.

Robert Harding Picture Library / Tim Megarry, 158; RHPL / Walter Rawlings, 92; RHPL / Sassoon, 13; RHPL / Tom Sheppard, 10; RHPL / A. C. Waltham, 175.

Eric and David Hosking, 111, 287*t*.

The Hulton Picture Company, 223*bl*, 321.

Institute of Oceanographic Sciences, Deacon Laboratory, 1.

N. Jackson / Physics Dept., Imperial College of Science & Technology, 316(*both*).

Eric Kay, 347.

Frank Lane Picture Agency / Steve McCutcheon, 248*br*, 254, 285, 346; FLPA / Mrs Robert Otto, 340*bl*; FLPA / W. Wisniewski, 6.

John Lundie, 102.

Colin Molyneux, 34, 128, 199, 306.

Peter Newark's American Pictures, 69, 95, 151, 188*tr*, 358*tl*.

John Noble / Mountain Camera, 150.

Oldham Claudgen Ltd, 225*br*.

OSF / M. J. Bailey, 359; OSF / Anthony Bannister, 298; OSF / Stephen Dalton, 68; OSF / M. P. L. Fogden, 46.

After A. Snider Pelligrini 1858, 73(*both*).

R. K. Pilsbury, 66*c*(*both*).

Planet Earth Pictures / Richard Chesher, 361; Planet Earth Pictures / Barry Gorman, 191; Planet Earth Pictures / Dennis Firminger, 21; Planet Earth Pictures / John Lythgoe, 328.

Popperfoto, 101, 161.

RIDA / David Bayliss, 57, 143*br*, 149*br*, 214, 238*tl*, 271, 340*tr*; RIDA / M. S. Hobbs, 318*tr*; RIDA / R. C. L. Wilson, 221.

G. R. Roberts, 39, 43*br*, 70, 86, 113, 174, 178, 187, 206, 209, 211, 223*tr*, 251, 278*bl*, 283, 301, 305, 315, 322, 326, 349, 353, 363*bl*.

Roger-Viollet, 12*tl*, 40, 53, 81, 154*br*, 205, 276.

Ann Ronan Picture Library, 12*tl*, 55(*both*), 126, 139, 208(*both*), 210, 248*tl*, 268, 354(*both*), 358*br*, 370.

F. W. Rowbotham, 336.

Science Photo Library / Lifesmith Classic Fractals, 126; SPL / Lawrence Berkeley Laboratory, 104; SPL / Dr F. Espenak, 222; SPL / Vaughan Fleming, 257; SPL / Dr R. Legeckis, 148; SPL / Hank Morgan, 219*br*, SPL / NOAA, 160; SPL / Dr E. I. Robson, 77*bl*.

Philippa Scott / NHPA, 164.

Tony Morrison / South American Pictures, 4, 19*br*, 23, 303, 310, 339.

Spectrum Colour Library, 30*br*, 207, 228, 244.

Transport & Road Research Laboratory, 219*bl*.

University of California, Berkeley, Dept. of Chemistry, courtesy of, 193.

University of Cambridge, Cavendish Laboratory, 43*tl*.

Vautier-de-Nanxe, 8, 225*l*.

ZEFA / P. Fera, 237; ZEFA / K. D. Fröhlich, 122; ZEFA / R. Halin, 17; ZEFA / Havlicek, 77*tr*, ZEFA / T. Ives, 194*t*, ZEFA / Knight & Hunt Photo, 277; ZEFA / Orion Press, 129; ZEFA / Photri, 259*br*, ZEFA / Ricatto, 75; ZEFA / H. Steenmans, 255; ZEFA / U. W. S., 22; ZEFA / Ziesler, 275.

Picture researcher: Celia Dearing

## Maps and diagrams

Eugene Fleury, 24, 168, 245.

Oxford Cartographers Limited, 4, 15, 18, 22, 27, 99, 115, 167, 220, 231, 235, 260, 267, 313, 367, end-papers.

Oxford Illustrators Limited, 2, 3, 26, 36, 52, 65, 71, 72, 80, 82, 86, 91, 94, 118, 120, 125, 128, 134–5, 140, 156, 162, 175, 178, 181, 195, 198, 217, 232, 239, 247, 263, 269, 279, 319, 342, 343, 345.

Colin Salmon, 25, 98, 103, 109, 166, 252–3, 261, 297, 337.

## Publishers' Note

The publishers are grateful to Stanley Remington for his special interest and encouragement.

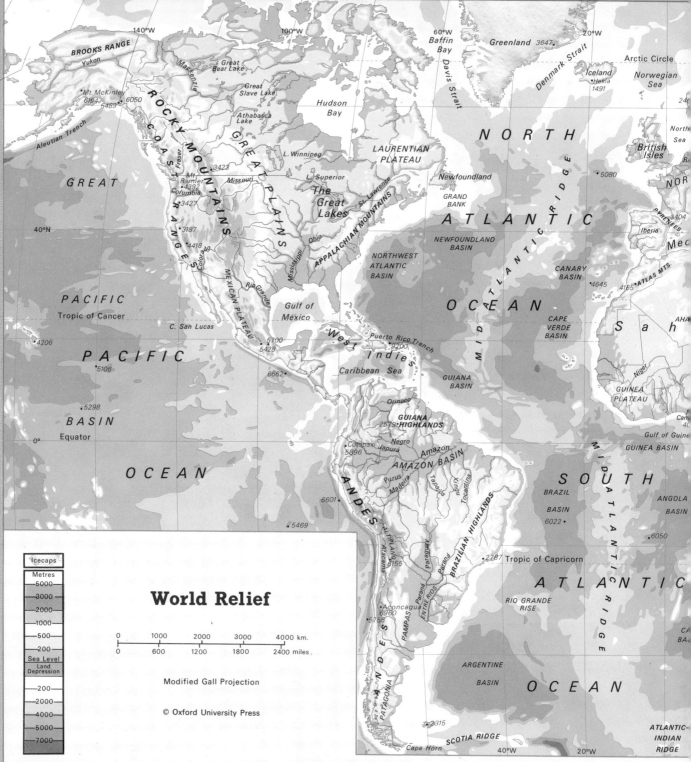

## World Relief

Modified Gall Projection

© Oxford University Press

Icecaps

Metres
5000
3000
2000
1000
500
200
Sea Level
Land Depression
200
2000
4000
5000
7000

Scale: 0 — 1000 — 2000 — 3000 — 4000 km.
0 — 600 — 1200 — 1800 — 2400 miles.

### Earth

Superficial area  510,000,000 sq. km. (197,000,000 sq. miles)
Equatorial circumference  40,076 km. (24,902 miles)
Meridional circumference  40,009 km. (24,860 miles)
Equatorial diameter  12,757 km. (7,927 miles)
Polar diameter  12,714 km. (7,900 miles)
Volume  $1.083 \times 10^{12}$ cubic km. ($2.598 \times 10^{11}$ cubic miles)
Mass  $6.5 \times 10^{21}$ tonnes ($6.4 \times 10^{21}$ tons)
Land surface area  149,000,000 sq. km. (58,000,000 sq. miles)
Highest point on land: Mt. Everest, China-Nepal border  8,848 m.(29,028 ft.)
Lowest point on land: Dead Sea, Jordan  400 m. (1,300 ft.) (below sea-level)
Average elevation of land  840 m. (2,760 ft.)
Water surface area  361,000,000 sq. km. (139,000,000 sq. miles)
Greatest ocean depth: Marianas Trench  11,033 m. (36,198 ft.)
Average depth of oceans and seas  3,808 m. (12,493 ft.)

### Continents

Asia  44,370,000 sq. km. (17,130,000 sq. miles)
Africa  30,230,000 sq. km. (11,670,000 sq. miles)
N. America  24,240,000 sq. km. (9,360,000 sq. miles)
S. America  17,810,000 sq. km. (6,880,000 sq. miles)
Antarctica  14,240,000 sq. km. (5,500,000 sq. miles)
Europe  10,350,000 sq. km. (4,000,000 sq. miles)
Australia  7,680,000 sq. km. (2,965,000 sq. miles)

### Oceans and Seas

Pacific Ocean  165,720,000 sq. km. (63,980,000 sq. miles)
Atlantic Ocean  81,660,000 sq. km. (31,530,000 sq. miles)
Indian Ocean  73,440,000 sq. km. (28,360,000 sq. miles)
Arctic Ocean  14,350,000 sq. km. (5,541,000 sq. miles)
Mediterranean Sea  2,970,000 sq. km. (1,150,000 sq. miles)
Bering Sea  2,270,000 sq. km. (876,000 sq. miles)
Caribbean Sea  1,940,000 sq. km. (749,000 sq. miles)
Gulf of Mexico  1,810,000 sq. km. (699,000 sq. miles)
Sea of Okhotsk  1,530,000 sq. km. (591,000 sq. miles)
East China Sea  1,250,000 sq. km. (483,000 sq. miles)

Hudson Bay  1,230,000 sq. km. (475,000 sq. miles)
Sea of Japan  1,050,000 sq. km. (405,000 sq. miles)
North Sea  580,000 sq. km. (224,000 sq. miles)
Black Sea  450,000 sq. km. (174,000 sq. miles)
Red Sea  440,000 sq. km. (170,000 sq. miles)
Baltic Sea  420,000 sq. km. (162,000 sq. miles)

### Ocean Deeps

Marianas Trench, Pacific Ocean  11,033 m. (36,198 ft.)
Tonga Trench, Pacific Ocean  10,822 m. (35,505 ft.)
Japan Trench, Pacific Ocean  10,554 m. (34,626 ft.)
Kuril Trench, Pacific Ocean  10,542 m. (34,587 ft.)
Mindanao Trench, Pacific Ocean  10,497 m. (34,439 ft.)
Kermadec Trench, Pacific Ocean  10,047 m. (32,963 ft.)
Puerto Rico Trench, Atlantic Ocean  9,200 m. (30,184 ft.)
Bougainville Deep, Pacific Ocean  9,140 m. (29,987 ft.)
South Sandwich Trench, Atlantic Ocean  8,428 m. (27,651 ft.)
Aleutian Trench, Pacific Ocean  7,822 m. (25,663 ft.)
Romanche Deep, Atlantic Ocean  7,758 m. (25,453 ft.)
Cayman Trough, Atlantic Ocean  7,680 m. (25,197 ft.)
Java Trench, Indian Ocean  7,450 m. (24,442 ft.)